Information Assurance and Security Technologies for Risk Assessment and Threat Management:

Advances

Te-Shun Chou
East Carolina University, USA

Managing Director:	Lindsay Johnston
Senior Editorial Director:	Heather Probst
Book Production Manager:	Sean Woznicki
Development Manager:	Joel Gamon
Development Editor:	Myla Harty
Acquisitions Editor:	Erika Gallagher
Typesetters:	Mackenzie Snader
Print Coordinator:	Jamie Snavely
Cover Design:	Nick Newcomer, Greg Snader

Published in the United States of America by
Information Science Reference (an imprint of IGI Global)
701 E. Chocolate Avenue
Hershey PA 17033
Tel: 717-533-8845
Fax: 717-533-8661
E-mail: cust@igi-global.com
Web site: http://www.igi-global.com

Library of Congress Cataloging-in-Publication Data

Information assurance and security technologies for risk assessment and threat management: advances / Te-Shun Chou, editor.
     p. cm.
  Includes bibliographical references and index.
  Summary: "This book details current trends and advances in information assurance and security, as well as explores emerging applications"--Provided by publisher.
  ISBN 978-1-61350-507-6 (hardcover) -- ISBN 978-1-61350-508-3 (ebook) -- ISBN 978-1-61350-509-0 (print & perpetual access) 1. Crisis management. 2. Computer security. 3. Computer networks--Security measures. I. Chou, Te-Shun, 1964-
  HD49.I54 2012
  658.4'72--dc23
                              2011038350

British Cataloguing in Publication Data
A Cataloguing in Publication record for this book is available from the British Library.

All work contributed to this book is new, previously-unpublished material. The views expressed in this book are those of the authors, but not necessarily of the publisher.

Table of Contents

Section 1
Attacks and Vulnerabilities

Section 2
Security Technologies

Section 4
Strategic Planning of Information Security

Detailed Table of Contents

Section 1
Attacks and Vulnerabilities

Computer attacks can be categorized based on the courses of action used to exploit vulnerabilities such as break-in, masquerading, and probe attacks. Computer attacks also can be categorized based on the result of attacks, such as corruption, leakage, and denial. In this chapter, the author categorizes the attacks in respect of attacker's motivations into ten categories, such as greed, hopelessness, and curiosity. In each category, the author uses recently occurred incidents to illustrate the motives of people who attack company IT systems.

Wireless technologies such as WiFi, Bluetooth, and cellular wireless have become instrumental in our daily life. However, attackers could possibly break into the wireless network to steal valuable information and thus cause loss of assets. Therefore, the study of wireless security is a big issue to both individuals and organizations. In this chapter the authors start with the introduction of wireless technology history. The authors then explicate the wireless security threats in wireless local area network and wireless personal area network. At last, the countermeasures of wireless attacks are presented.

Section 2
Security Technologies

Chapter 3

Gianluca Papaleo, Istituto di Elettronica e di Ingegneria dell'Informazione e delle
Telecomunicazioni, Italy & Consiglio Nazionale delle Ricerche, Italy
Davide Chiarella, Istituto di Elettronica e di Ingegneria dell'Informazione e delle
Telecomunicazioni, Italy & Consiglio Nazionale delle Ricerche, Italy
Maurizio Aiello, Istituto di Elettronica e di Ingegneria dell'Informazione e delle
Telecomunicazioni, Italy & Consiglio Nazionale delle Ricerche, Italy
Luca Caviglione, Istituto di Studi sui Sistemi Intelligenti per l'Automazione, Italy
& Consiglio Nazionale delle Ricerche, Italy

Generally, there exist two main intrusion detection techniques: anomaly detection and misuse detection. Misuse detection involves the comparison of observed traffic data with a set of well defined rules that describe signatures of intrusions. If the signature of observed network traffic is not matched with any of predefined rules, it is declared as an attack. Anomaly detection searches for intrusive activities by comparing network traffic to those established acceptable normal usage patterns learned from training data. If the pattern of observed data is different from those learned normal ones, the data is classified as an attack. In this chapter, the authors review anomaly detection and misuse detection approaches in detecting worms spreading through the Internet. The authors also investigate several aspects concerning the analysis, development and deployment of statistical anomaly detection techniques for e-mail traffic.

Chapter 4

Halim M. Khelalfa, University of Wollongong in Dubai, UAE

Mobile phone forensics is a quite new research topic in the field of digital forensics. It is associated with recovering digital evidence or data from mobile phones. Chapter Four begins with an introduction of GSM and CDMA cellular wireless technologies, followed by an investigation of forensics issues such as guidelines, procedures, tools, and threats. This chapter ends with a presentation of current researches as well as trends on mobile phone forensics.

Chapter 5

Silas Leite Albuquerque, University of Brasilia, Brazil
Paulo Roberto de Lira Gondim, University of Brasilia, Brazil

Authentication is very important in protecting computer systems. It is a process to verify an individual's identity whether s/he has enough authorization to access the computer system or not. In the beginning of this chapter, the authors explore the ideas regarding trust models in electronic transactions. The authors then research electronic transactions security using continuous authentication processes in trust in electronic communications systems, brief revision about conventional authentication models, continuous authentication concepts, and biometrics.

Chapter 6

Jenny Torres, University Pierre and Marie Curie, France
Michele Nogueira, Federal University of Parana, Brazil
Guy Pujolle, University Pierre and Marie Curie, France

Cryptography is the science that uses key to encrypt a message into ciphertext and decrypt the ciphertext back into plaintext. Identity-Based cryptography (IBC) uses a public key for encryption, which the key represents the identification of a user. The Chapter Six presents an introduction of symmetric-key cryptography and asymmetric-key cryptography technologies. An investigation of IBC attacks and its security vulnerabilities as well as the solutions against those vulnerabilities are also provided.

Chapter 7

Sue Inn Ch'ng, Nottingham University Malaysia Campus, Malaysia
Kah Phooi Seng, Sunway University, Malaysia
Li-Minn Ang, Nottingham University Malaysia Campus, Malaysia
Fong Tien Ong, Nottingham University Malaysia Campus, Malaysia
Nottingham University Malaysia, School of Engineering, Selangor, Malaysia

With respect to information technology, biometrics becomes more and more important to individual's identity and access control. Thanks to the use of more and more reliable user authentication technique, the security of information systems are therefore enhanced. In this chapter, the authors begin with an overview of audio-visual systems. Then the authors propose an audio-visual system using face and voice modality biometrics technology so that the system could handle large volume of people recognition over internet protocol.

Chapter 8

Biwu Yang, East Carolina University, USA

Firewalls protect personal computers and infrastructure networks from malicious threats. Based upon a set of rules, firewalls examine all traffic passing through and only allow legitimate messages to pass. In this chapter, the author describes various types of firewalls, security policies on firewalls, firewall architectures, and firewall implementation considerations.

Section 3
Risk Assessment and Management

Chapter 9

Laerte Peotta de Melo, University of Brasilia, Brazil
Paulo Roberto Lira Gondim, University of Brasilia, Brazil

Security risk assessment is important to the security of an organization. It is a process to ensure that the security controls for a system are fully commensurate with its risks. In this chapter, the authors raise attention to risks, attacks, threats, and vulnerabilities in a business. The main risk assessment techniques and frameworks are also discussed. Then the authors propose a pro-active framework for identifying vulnerabilities and assessing risk and demonstrate their model using a client/server approach.

Chapter 10

Cyril Onwubiko, Research Series Limited, UK

With the advance of computer technology, a large amount of personal information data could be easily and quickly retrieved without permission. As a result, how to use appropriate process to protect personal information data and corresponding privacy regulations and legislations become critical. In this chapter, the author begins with a discussion of challenges to manage privacy impact assessment of personally identifiable information. Then the issues relating to privacy impact assessment of new and in-service projects are demonstrated. Finally the author provides a model showing how to conduct privacy impact assessment on both new and in-service projects.

Chapter 11

Saeed Abu-Nimeh, Damballa Inc., USA
Nancy R. Mead, Carnegie Mellon University, USA

A lack of security and privacy requirements could lead to insecure software. Security and privacy requirements engineering focuses on identifying software security and privacy risks in early stages of a software development lifecycle. In this chapter, the authors propose a model that integrates the security risk assessment techniques with privacy risk assessment techniques. To make sure that both the existing security and the privacy risk assessment techniques follow the same methodology and require the same expertise, a classification scheme of risk assessment methods is applied. Also, the authors use pseudo-software development projects to evaluate the feasibility of their proposed model.

Section 4
Strategic Planning of Information Security

Chapter 12

Guillermo A. Francia III, Jacksonville State University, USA
Frances Shannon Hutchinson, Jacksonville State University, USA

The information data of an organization must be available when needed and well protected from unauthorized inside and outside intruders. How the information data is managed and protected must be carefully planned. This chapter discusses regulatory and policy compliance in the field of information security. The authors start with the regulatory compliance, and a variety forms of legislation that has an impact on regulatory compliance are discussed. The authors then provide guidelines on the development of policies in response to identity theft. Finally, policy compliance for achieving the policy's goals and auditing to determine whether policy compliance has actually been achieved are presented.

Foreword

Information Assurance (IA) is a combination of technologies and processes that are used to manage information-related risks. IA is not just about computer security, the protection of data in storage or while it is being processed; it is also about the protection of data in transit. IA is a composite field involving computer science, mathematics, database and network management, user training, and policy issues. A common objective of work on IA in these fields is to protect and defend information and information systems by ensuring their availability, integrity, authentication, confidentiality, and non-repudiation so that the right people can access the right information at the right time.

The Internet, social media, smart phones and tablet computers have been playing a larger role in our daily lives. The majority of computers, whether in large corporations, in small businesses, or at home, are connected together in a network that creates a global community. People have become increasingly dependent on computer networks in many aspects of their lives—from communication, entertainment and financial transactions, to education and government services. Most people understand that global economic infrastructure is becoming increasingly dependent upon information technology, and no information system is 100% secure. Information security is one of the topics that everyone knows of, but most are not really aware of the finer details. Many computer users simply think that their firewall and antivirus software provide them with all the protection they need to keep their computers secure. However, as malicious hackers become more resourceful, and users add more and more information into a growing number of databases, there exists an increased exposure to hacker attacks, information espionage, and other security breaches. Information systems—operated by governments and commercial organizations—are vulnerable to attacks and misuse through their Internet connections. Workstations connected to the Internet are currently the most common targets of malicious hackers. As a result, information assurance is a very serious concern for individuals, businesses, and governments. Not only do we need to be aware of how attacks are perpetrated, but we also need to learn how the systems can be protected against different attacks.

This book provides a valuable window on information assurance and covers the necessary components from detecting Internet worms distributed via e-mail to securing mobile communication devices. Firewalls are a critical technology to control incoming and outgoing network traffic, thereby blocking unwanted traffic and suspicious connections. They must be configured with a set of filtering rules and, like any software application, must be constantly patched to address new vulnerabilities. Authentication verifies the identity of each user or examines the validity of a device. Currently, passwords are the most commonly used authentication scheme. Because of its uniqueness, biometrics, such as fingerprint, iris or facial images, are becoming a promising means of authentication. Bill Gates predicted that biometric technologies will be one of "the most important IT innovations of the next several years" at a Gartner

Group IT/Expo event held in 1997. In order to ensure the current user is the same person that logged onto the system, research efforts have been devoted to continuously verify the user's identity using biometrics. Security and privacy are closely related. When developing an information security solution, we need to consider its impact on privacy and combine security risk assessment techniques with privacy risk assessment techniques. Risk assessment is a critical process to define both the probability and impact of undesired events. Its objective is not to eliminate the risk, but to provide the policy and methodology by which risks could be managed.

The challenges in information assurance are both difficult and interesting. People are working on them with enthusiasm, tenacity, and dedication to develop new methods of analysis and provide new solutions to keep up with the ever-changing threats. In this new age of global interconnectivity and interdependence, it is necessary to provide security practitioners, both professionals and students, with state-of-the art knowledge on the frontiers in information assurance. This book is a good step in that direction.

Qinghan Xiao
Defence R&D Canada, Canada

Qinghan Xiao *received his BSc and MSc degrees in Automation from Tsinghua University, Beijing, China, in 1982 and 1985, respectively, and his Ph.D. in Computer Science from University of Regina, Regina, Saskatchewan, Canada, in 1994. Currently, he is a Defence Scientist at Defence R&D Canada. His research interests include image processing, user authentication, biometrics, and RFID technology. Dr. Xiao serves as the Chair of the Task Force on Biometrics of the IEEE CIS Technical Committee on Intelligent Systems Applications, and is a member of the Technical Committee on Security and Privacy in Complex Information Systems of the IEEE System Council. He is the recipient of 2010 IEEE Ottawa Outstanding Engineer Award. Dr. Xiao has organized several biometrics workshops and special sessions, worked as guest editor for international journals, and given presentations at national and international conferences.*

Preface

With the rapid progression of computer technology, computer attacks become more and more sophisticated. Once these attacks successfully explore the vulnerabilities of an information system, the confidential information in the system would become accessible to those who are not authorized to access to the information. Hence, this book will be targeting on providing a source of knowledge regarding information assurance and security.

This book details current trends and advances in information assurance and security, as well as explores emerging applications. This book is divided into four sections: attacks and vulnerabilities, security technologies, risk assessment and management, and strategic planning of information security. Together, it provides the readers with a broad view of information confidentiality, protection, and management. Each section contains several chapters that are contributed by well-known researchers or recognized practitioners from different countries. At the end of each chapter, it includes a summary and bibliography for further reading.

The objective of this book is not only to introduce various network and information security technologies but also to provide solutions to meet practitioner's requirements in information assurance. Due to the rapid development in specialized areas of information assurance and security, this book will cover a broad range of topics on information assurance and security as well as provide in depth investigation of up-to-date technologies. In summary, this book will be very useful to the readers because:

- It will build up a strong, fundamental understanding of information assurance and resulting algorithms.
- It will offer balanced coverage of information security methods and their applications.
- It will address emerging methods and applications in information assurance and security.
- It will provide a strong foundation for launching new applications.
- It will include a wealth of illustrative examples and instructive results.

This book provides the readers with a unique opportunity to build a strong, fundamental understanding of theory and methods and thus to find solutions for many of today's most interesting and challenging problems regarding information assurance and security. Though this book is not focused on any information security certificate exam or personal information protection, it is designed for those scientific and technical people who want to pursue their career in the field of information assurance and security. In the mean time, we would like this book become the most utilizable one for those professionals who use it as a reference to find specific information as well as for novices who use it as a study guide to learn various information assurance and security subjects.

With the help of numerous examples, illustrations and tables summarizing the results of quantitative analysis studies, this book will serve all different kinds of reading levels. The target readers include:

- The graduate students will benefit from the broad range of topics covered by the book and therefore build a solid foundation for future investigation.
- The researchers can use it as an up-to-date reference since it offers a broad survey of the relevant literature.
- The scientists, research and development engineers, and technical managers and executives will find it useful in the design and the implementation of information security systems.

This book is organized into four sections: attacks and vulnerabilities, security technologies, risk assessment and management, and strategic planning of information security.

Section 1 provides readers with an overview of attacks and vulnerabilities, which includes two chapters. Computer attacks could be categorized based on the courses of action used to exploit vulnerabilities or on the result of attacks. In Chapter 1, the author categorizes the attacks, according to attackers' motivations, into ten categories. In each category, the author uses recent incidents to illustrate the motives of people who attack company IT systems.

An increasing number of people are using wireless technologies in their life, with a corresponding increase in the number of people who use malicious tools to abuse uprotected wireless networks, thus posing a serious threat to both indivisuals and organizations. Security becomes a highly important part of the wireless network. Chapter 2 starts with the history of wireless technology. Wireless security threats in wireless local area network and wireless personal area network are also discussed in this chapter and it ends with the presence of countermeasures of wireless attacks.

Section 2 presents the most up-to-date information assurance and security technologies available. In Chapter 3, the authors review anomaly detection and misuse detection approaches in detecting worms spreading through the Internet. The authors also produce discussions regarding the analysis, development and deployment of statistical anomaly detection techniques for e-mail traffic.

Mobile phone forensics is a quite new research topic in the field of digital forensics. Chapter 4 starts with an introduction of GSM and CDMA cellular wireless technologies, followed by investigates forensics issues such as guidelines, procedures, tools, and threats. Current researches and trends on mobile phone forensics are also discussed.

Authentication is very important in protecting computer systems. In the beginning of Chapter 5, the authors explore the ideas about trust models in electronic transactions. The authors then research electronic transactions security using continuous authentication processes in trust in electronic communications systems, brief revision about conventional authentication models, continuous authentication concepts, and biometrics.

Cryptography is the science that use ket to encrypt a message into ciphertext and decrypt the ciphertext back into plaintext. Identity-Based cryptography (IBC) uses a public key for encryption, which the key represents the identification of a user. IBC is the topic of Chapter 6. IBC attacks, its security vulnerabilities and solutions to those vulnerabilities are also covered.

As indicated in Chapter 7, biometrics gradually plays an important part on information technology in indivisual's identity and access control. With the use of more and more reliable user authentication techniques, the security of information systems are therefore enhanced. In this chapter, the authors begin with the introduction of the background of audio-visual systems. Then the authors propose an audio-visual system using face and voice modality biometrics technology and therefore the system could handle large volume of people recognition over internet protocol.

Chapter 8 is focused on Firewall. Firwalls protect personal computers and infrastructure networks from malicious threats away. Based upon a set of rules, firewalls examines traffic passing through and only allow legitimate messages to pass. In this chapter, the author introduces different types of firewalls, security policies on firewalls, firewall architecture, and firewall implementation considerations.

In Section 3, the attention is directed to the Risk Assessment and Management. Risk Assessment and Real Time Vulnerability Identification in IT Environments are discussed in Chapter 9. Security risk assessment is a process to ensure that the security controls for a system are fully commensurate with its risks. Implementing such assessment will prevent unauthorized access to saved and confidential information. For all businesses using a wireless network, security should be a priority. The authors not only examine risks, attacks, threats and vulnerabilities in a business but also explore the main risk accessment techniques and frameworks. They even present a pro-active framework for identifying vulnerabilities and assessing risk and demonstrate their model using a client/server approach.

In Chapter 10, the author describes the challenges of managing privacy impact assessment of personally identifiable information followed by a discussion on privacy impact assessment of new and in-service projects. A model showing how to conduct privacy impact assessment on both new and in-service projects is also presented.

A lack of security and privacy requirements could lead to insecure software. Security and privacy requirements engineering focuses on identifying software security and privacy risks in early stages of a software development lifecycle. Chapter 11 demonstrates a model that integrates the security risk assessment techniques with privacy risk assessment techniques. To make sure that both the existing security and the privacy risk assessment techniques follow the same methodology and require the same expertise, a classification scheme of risk assessment methods is applied. Also, the authors use pseudo-software development projects to evaluate the feasibility of thier proposed model.

The last section, Section 4, we provide strategies of security policy design and threat mitigation and response to risks. The information data of an organization must be available when needed and well protected from unauthorized inside and outside intruders. How to manage and protect the information data must be carefully planned. Regulatory and policy compliance in the field of information security and legislation's impact on regulatory compliance are explored in Chapter 12. Not only did the authors provide guidelines for the development of policies for responding to identity theft, but also they present policy compliance for achieving the policy's goals and auditing to determine whether policy compliance has actually been achieved.

Te-Shun Chou
East Carolina University, USA

Acknowledgment

Book editing is a long process. Along the way, many caring and supportive people contributed their efforts and valuable time to help complete this book. I would like to express my gratitude to all of those who supported me in any respect during the completion of this book.

To start with, I would like to thank IGI Global for giving me the opportunity to commence this book in the first place. Furthermore, I would like to thank Dr. Qinghan Xiao who helped me make this book possible and encouraged me go ahead with this book editing.

I am obliged to all chapter authors and reviewers who devoted their time and contributed in their areas of expertise by submitting their articles and by reviewing one or more chapters during the long manuscript development cycle. In the meantime, I would like to offer my regards and blessings to all of the Editorial Advisory Board members for their valuable and stimulating comments. My appreciation also goes to Ms. Myla Harty, in her role as the Editorial Assistant, who was of great help in administration needs and oversaw all aspects of editing process.

I am indebted to Ya-Fen, my wife and life partner of over twenty years. It is your belief in and support of me that gave me the strength to complete this book. Thanks also to my lovely daughters, Annie and Jun, for loving and believing in me.

Lastly, and most importantly, I wish to express my deepest gratitude to my late father, Peng-Hsiao Chou, without whom I would not be living my best life and to my mother, Hsueh-Lin Wang Chou, who always gives me one hundred percent unconditional support, encouragement, and love. This book is dedicated to my parents, especially in memoriam to my father who was always a role model in the journey of my life and will live in my heart forever.

Te-Shun Chou
East Carolina University, USA

Section 1
Attacks and Vulnerabilities

Chapter 1
Attacks on IT Systems:
Categories of Motives

Georg Disterer
University of Applied Sciences Hannover, Germany

ABSTRACT

Attacks on IT systems are deliberate acts with the determined aim of destroying, damaging or misusing a company's IT systems. This type of risk is growing significantly in the last years. Today it must be assumed that the greatest dangers for IT systems no longer emanate from individuals, but rather from mafia-like structured, organised crime. Knowing categories of motives and attributes of actors can support the discovery, investigation and persecution of attacks and malicious activities. The categories make it easier to develop preventive and reactive policies and measures to mitigate the risks of computer crime.

INTRODUCTION

For a long time now, operators of IT systems have had to reckon with their systems being attacked and, as a result, being subjected to unauthorised use, and misuse. Early cases are chronicled for 1961, for instance, when the clearing procedure at MIT's (Massachusetts Institute of Technology) mainframe computer was compromised by special programs, so that the programmers could use systems capacities without having to pay the

costs (Cross, 2008). In those days, such hackers (in the sense of burglars), with their technical skills, also switched off telephone system controls and phoned free-of-charge. And, for all intents and purposes, they triggered quite positive associations among the general public, since they out-manoeuvred big companies and monopolies, perceived as over-powerful. In films of the 70s and 80s, hackers were stylised as representatives of resistance against the establishment.

But still, financial damages have also been noted since the 60s, through manipulations of IT systems with which salary or invoice payments

DOI: 10.4018/978-1-61350-507-6.ch001

have been diverted, or the status of accounts has been altered (Dannecker, 1996). Thus, the abuse of IT systems is to be regarded as an attack, which is very difficult to prevent as long as attackers weigh up possible advantages to be gained for themselves against the effort necessary, plus the risk of being caught and the penalty, and come to the conclusion that their activity seems to be worth the risk. The definition of "attacks" covers all deliberate acts with the determined aim of destroying, damaging or misusing a company's IT systems. The concentration on attacks as deliberate and purposeful acts excludes from the discussion two categories of threatening influences on IT systems: erroneous actions (perhaps user mistakes in handling or operating, a lack of skill, or inability), or inadvertent actions (perhaps handling or operating errors through inattention or carelessness). Further threats, moreover, and the resulting damages are also excluded from the discussion: the use of IT systems can hold immense risks for companies if faults in operating processes and the shut-down of IT systems are the result. Currently, for example, so many unwanted incoming e-mails (SPAM) are received by companies that identifying and processing them at best causes costs, and at worst causes the e-mail server to grind to a halt. Information on the portion of unwanted mails vary: a mere 13 to 15% of all incoming mails are regarded as „wanted" (Messaging Anti-Abuse Working Group, 2008)—for the German Administration Offices a portion of 1.5% of wanted mails is assumed (BSI 2009). Since the majority of these mails advertise products, SPAM mails won't be spoken about here under the section "attacks", since their aim is not foremost one of the purposeful destruction (damage or misuse) of the IT systems (in this case, e-mail server) of the companies concerned.

Further essential threats of IT systems which do not fall under the category of a threat are natural incidents and catastrophies like floods, lightning and earthquakes, acts of war, technical defects and technical failure (through material fatigue, material defects, quality faults, or wear and tear and old components), function faults (e.g. through development or production faults), or organisational faults (lack of responsible staff and competencies, inconsistent deputising arrangements, insufficient controls and lack of resources for protective measures). There are classic politics and measures against these threats, like the redundant design of technical systems (e.g. CPUs and storage devices), additional dedicated devices (e.g. emergency power generators), further education/courses/training, and organisational or technical controls.

Types of Attacks

Attacks as intentional and purposeful acts to destroy, to damage or to misuse IT systems are major threats against the security objectives availability, integrity and confidentiality of information processing.

During the preparation phase of an attack, vulnerabilities of IT systems are explored by various techniques. Scanning or probing Web sites and applications attackers get information about the structure and parameters of the systems and the underlying technical infrastructure. Scanning the target systems for known vulnerabilities in applications, systems software (like web server, database, middleware, operating system), and hardware configuration. With knowledge about the IT systems attackers may try use known vulnerabilities or default settings to exploit the system.

Access systems can be attacked by programs that discover passwords and therefore enable abusing user accounts. Password-cracking programs can test a huge number of possible and even complex passwords using dictionaries; the high processing speed of their computer give attackers a chance to break into systems with these kinds of brute-force attacks.

With eavesdropping techniques attackers monitor network traffic and data transmission like wiretapping. With sniffing programs they can extract data like names of users and their passwords in order to abuse user accounts. Similarly, email server can be manipulated so that all in-/outgoing messages of a special user or a special group of users are copied to the mail address of the attackers without notice of the legitimate users.

Viruses are programs in some form of executable code that replicates itself. Viruses can spread from one IT system to another by being copied via storage devices like CDs or USB sticks or by being sent over an internal network or the Internet. To copy itself viruses need permission to execute on the infected systems, this is the reason why viruses are often attached to legitimate programs and start when the program is started. The functions of the malicious codes of viruses vary; they can alter or delete files or merely spook and frighten users by displaying odd and strange system messages. Viruses can be nested into very basic levels of technical systems so that security measures of operating systems and antivirus software cannot detect and capture them.

Worms are malicious programs typically spread by Emails. Unlike viruses, worms must be started explicitly at least once by users of an IT system. Then they unfold their harmful effects like altering files, deleting files or consuming resources like bandwidth, memory, or processing capacities. Trojan horses are programs that fulfill at first sight requested functions but additionally execute destructive functions similar to those of viruses and worms.

The most serious malfunction of viruses, worms and trojan horses is allowing the attackers to get remote access to the targeted IT systems over the Internet or other networks. Then attackers can use the systems for thieving data, altering or deleting files, down- or uploading files, keeping track input of users (keystroke logging) or outputs on screens, forcing failures of shut-downs of the IT systems, or using the systems as part of a botnet during Denial of Service attacks.

Denial of Service (DoS) attacks are a major threat to e-commerce, waves of DoS attacks against prominent Web sites gained wide publicity. Typically DoS attacks target Web sites with bogus requests for data in order to slow or block legitimate users from accessing services. With Distributed Denial of Service (DDoS) attacks the vulnerability of web sites are expanded, when attackers use hundreds or thousands of compromised systems in order to harm commercial Web sites. With the bundled resources of multiple compromised systems coordinated in networks ("botnets") DDoS attackers gain enormous destructive potential. One classical form of to harm the targeted IT systems is to "flood" them with mails or requests. Normally users of the compromised systems do not realize that their systems are infected and misused for DDoS attacks (Disterer, Alles & Hervatin, 2007).

DoS and DDoS attackers use different ways to harm the target systems. They manipulate the target systems directly to force failures and shut-downs. Or, they try to deplete resources like bandwidth, memory, or processing capacities in order to hinder or interfere with legitimate users who have honest intentions. Damages from DoS and DDoS attacks can range from inconvenience for legitimate users to a shutdown of the system and some delay until services are continued (Disterer, Alles & Hervatin, 2007).

Besides these rather technical instruments to get access to targeted IT systems, a set of social instruments is comprised with the term Social Engineering. Using these instruments attackers manipulate people to divulge sensitive information. For instance by building inappropriate trust relationships with insiders, attackers gain user names and passwords in order to abuse user accounts with unauthorized access privileges. Social Engineering contains a set of instruments to manipulate people into talking or acting contrary to their normal manner based on human behaviour like the desire to be helpful, to trust people and to avoid getting in trouble (Damle, 2002).

The most important risk induced by all of these attack types is unauthorized access to IT Systems and information. For instance attackers may gain access to payment systems, sensitive information like financial or health data of people, or commercially sensitive data like sales strategies or information from research and development.

New technical devices like smartphones and new applications like social networks pose new possibilities to attackers. Smartphones can be attacked via Bluetooth within a range of 10 meters and put sensitive information contained in address books, calendars, photos, messages at risk (Loo, 2009). Targeting social networks attackers can gain sensitive information; therefore user privacy is at risk. Identity scam and identity theft may result in reputational damage of individuals within the network community but also may influence their "offline" social life (Sood & Enbody, 2011).

Detection and Investigation of Attacks

Weaknesses in the design and implementation of company IT systems, as well as in standards and protocols (e.g. TCP/IP for Internet) on which they rely, provide the technical foundations for attacks and are the causes of problems in investigating attackers. Thus, anonymous communication is possible on the Internet through the faking or disguising of address information. In almost all cases attackers use this weakness of TCP/IP to spoof their address and sending packets of information with faked addresses in order to restrict or hinder tracing back features significantly.

The content of messages can be encoded so that those attacked, but also the surveillance or law enforcement authorities have no chance of becoming aware of dangers or of finding those causing them. Therefore the abilities to parse actors and activities are limited.

The large number of computers which are connected to the Internet creates many ways of access and of attacks on other computers which can be located very far away ("remote access"). The relatively low level of sensitivity that many users of the Web have—to be seen in their unhesi-

tating usage, in the way they download software or similar items, or the imprudent way they deal with passwords—creates additional security gaps and makes work easier for attackers.

The discovery and investigation of attacks are, moreover, made more difficult for the law enforcement authorities by the technical skills and equipment necessary for this, which are often only insufficiently at their disposal. When attackers operate beyond their own country's borders, international cooperation becomes necessary, made more difficult, too, by the differences in national legislations.

The rights to freedom demanded by society and the interests of the law enforcement authorities are often in contradiction to each other, to be found in exemplary fashion in the discussion about data retention and storage. The basic right of users to informational self-determination on the Internet can only be guaranteed effectively through the anonymity of usage—in contrast, there are law enforcement authorities, whose interests are appropriate and effective means of detection and prosecution. The corresponding law in Germany came into force on 1.1.2008 and stipulates that telecommunication providers have to store connection data for a certain period, so that investigation and law enforcement authorities can make use of them, where necessary. In contrast, there is the argument that data retention and storage is in violation not only of the users' right to informational self-determination, but also of the laws of secrecy of governing letters, post and communications.

Prosecution and Legal Evaluation

The prosecution of attackers by the state through police and law enforcement is only possible if the attacks are covered by the relevant laws. Thereby, the content of the term "computer crime" is understood in different ways. By "computer crime in the narrower sense" attacks are meant in which IT systems are part of the fundamental features of the crime, e.g. debit card (and PIN) fraud with credit cards got illegally, or with illegal access rights to IT systems, the faking of data relevant for legal proof, computer sabotage, the spying out and capturing of data, and software piracy.

One defines "computer crime in the wider sense" as that in which IT systems are implemented as a means of crime for the planning, preparation or execution of crimes which are covered by traditional legal norms, e.g. the dissemination of incriminating content, chain letters, offering stolen goods and illegal gambling, incitement to commit crimes, concluding business deals in opiates, human trafficking or arms deals, crimes of fraud in connection with online shops (like the seller receiving payment in advance, but not delivering at all, or not adequately; or the buyer accesses goods under a false identity), or infringement of intellectual property rights.

To legitimise the penalisation of some forms of attacks on IT systems, the legislative authorities had to take decisive action since there were loopholes in the system of criminal liability. Thus, in order to constitute a fraud, section 263 of the German Criminal Code presumes that a financial advantage in one's own interest, or damaging another person's assets, is achieved through causing an error. And yet, with an attack on an IT system to manipulate account details, for example, no person is being deceived, and thus there is no error; the old proverb "to err is human" can be understood here in the function of defining terminology. Accordingly, in 1986, the new section on computer fraud, § 263a, was added to the German Criminal Code, and which considers fraud in the express words of the law to be: gaining a financial advantage illegally as a result of a data-processing procedure which is influenced by incorrect program design, through the use of incorrect or incomplete data, through unauthorised use of data, or any other unauthorised effect on the procedure.

Protection Goals

Among other things, information processing in companies is subject to economic, legal and ethical demands and constraints. To guarantee their fulfilment, it is necessary to determine the relevant quality features of IT systems, and to protect these qualities from threats. To a very great extent, the demands and constraints are basically independent from the use of IT systems, and are, rather, of a general nature and (also) handed down. However, the particular potentials of IT systems require a dedicated formulation, special methods of determining and calculating risks and special protection measures.

Primarily, the following central quality features of IT systems are in danger of being attacked – and are thus the very first to be observed when establishing a company's protection needs, and developing suitable protection measures (Bursch, 2005; Mohay, Anderson, Collie, Vel, & McKemmish, 2003; Eschweiler & Psille, 2006; Eckert, 2001):

- **Availability of the system:** The system ensures unrestricted use within the constraints of the users' rights, which means that faults, waiting times or similar difficulties should not occur.
- **Integrity of the system:** The system ensures that neither the unauthorised nor the unnoticed manipulation of data can take place; the guarantee encompasses the authorisation and authenticity of the users as well as the accountability of access.
- **Confidentiality of the system:** The system ensures that no unauthorised sourcing of information is possible. In the area of e-commerce this includes, for example, safeguarding the users' anonymity so that no communication or access profiles can be created unauthorised and unnoticed.
- **Subordinate quality features,** in particular in connection with the demand for sys-

tem integrity, are the authenticity and reliability of the IT systems.

- **Authenticity of the system:** For data, for which access rights are necessary, the system ensures that users are clearly identified before access, and that the identification is verified. For verification, attributes must be used whose authenticity can be checked, or whose credibility is sufficient (e.g. password, biometric features….).
- **Reliability (accountability) of the system:** For data and functions for which this is necessary, the system ensures that every access can be clearly matched with the respective user at a later date. In this way, the user cannot deny access retrospectively. Thus, authenticity is a pre-requisite for reliability.

The protection targets are endangered in different ways through varying attacks:

- If devices of an IT system are stolen or destroyed, then the availability is jeopardised, since a legitimate user can be hindered from accessing the system. As well the availability is jeopardised when processing or transmitting capacities are so flooded with data, through targeted attacks, that sufficient capacities for legitimate users are not available.
- If the access protection of an IT system can be by-passed or overcome, then the integrity is jeopardised, because then alterations can be made to the data – perhaps to divert the flow of money or goods. The integrity is also jeopardised if information can be manipulated unnoticed while being exchanged between IT systems, e.g. bank account details or similar can be altered.
- If a third party can "eavesdrop" unauthorised on the electronic closing of deals - e.g. buying shares - then confidentiality is in jeopardy. AS well confidentiality is

jeopardised when the keying-in of authentication data by authorised users (e.g. user name, password) is observed or can be recorded by others, because misuse can be conducted with the information gained.
- If a user use a false identity or other persons' authentication data (e.g. user name, password), then the authenticity of the IT system is in jeopardy.
- If users carry out alterations on data and can later deny these alterations, then the reliability of the system is in jeopardy. As well as reliability is jeopardy if alterations to data can be done in such a way that they cannot be traced back later to those causing them.

MOTIVES FOR ATTACKS

Generally speaking, the motives of people who attack company IT systems are the same as those of classic malicious actors. In the following, possible motives and also descriptions of attributes and examples are illustrated (Eschweiler & Psille, 2006, Geschonneck, 2004).

Greed

Both the theft of material (for example equipment) and also immaterial goods (for example data), belong to this category, and are used for profit - resources, too, like processing, transmitting and storage capacities, and also software, which are used unauthorised and for the thieves' own interest. The basic course of action is similar to that of a classic theft or fraud, and is characterised by the attacker's striving for a personal advantage. Detecting such an attack is difficult, since stealing immaterial goods like data and software is possible by copying, without altering the original. Examples:

- The following incident in 2008 caused a lot of public attention (Ramelsberger, 2008; Richter, 2008; Ritzer, 2008a; Ritzer, 2008b; Nitschmann & Leyendecker 2008): A member of the IT staff at a bank in Liechtenstein illegally copies customer data in 2002 and smuggles them out of the company on disks. When he stops working there, he blackmails his former employer, threatening to pass on the data. The blackmail attempt fails, the ex-member of staff gets arrested and sentenced, but does not have to serve the sentence. So then, he approaches the German intelligence service and offers them the data, since it supply circumstantial evidence for substantial tax evasions of several bank customers. He receives approx 4 million Euros and a new identity. The US Senate carries out an investigation in order to clarify whether, and to what extent, US citizens, whose data are on the disks, are being aided by the bank for tax evasion purposes. The bank is afraid of claims for damages since it hasn't informed the customers about the theft of their data. The court responsible may have to sentence the bank, which is owned by the family presently being in power in Liechtenstein. The bank suffers a loss of customers' trust and damage to its reputation.

- An IT service provider in the U.S.A. operates transactions for several hundreds of institutions who issue credit cards, and their roughly 100 million credit card owners. During an attack, some transaction data are "eavesdropped" and make it possible for the attackers to make purchases in department stores, debiting other people's credit cards (Gold, 2009; Krebs, 2009a). The volume of sniffed data and abused cards is not published, but at end, the data breach costs the service provider more than $ 32 million on legal fees, forensic costs, reserves for potential fines and other settlement costs (Cheney, 2010).

- Several men in Thailand and India attack the IT systems of online brokers in the U.S.A., force their way into customers' accounts and then conduct transactions in their name. Sequence of events: the attackers buy stocks and shares under their own name and on their own account, and then drive their value up, using buys in the name of the "seized" customers, subsequently selling their own shares with a profit (US Department of Justice, 2007a).

- A group of hackers broke from outside the U.S.A. into a system of a bank in Atlanta (U.S.A), which processes payments of ATM cards. They got approx. 50 card numbers and personal identification numbers (PIN) from the system and raised the limits on cash that can be withdrawn from the cards. Then they distributed the cards to accomplices in over 250 cities of the world, who withdraw in total $ 9 million within 12 hours. The whole attack takes days (Gorman & Perez, 2009). In 2005 perpetrators used access to the corporate network of TJX, a retailer in the U.S.A., and stole 45,7 million debit and credit records. They used the payment card data to purchase electronics, gift coupons etc. (Owens, Dam & Lin 2009).

- A female member of staff at a service provider which draws up wages and salary statements for other companies, spies out colleagues' access data, thus getting herself unauthorised access to the IT systems. Her husband works at one of the companies for which the salary payments are calculated and transferred. Through manipulation of her husband's data, he gets over-payments (US Department of Justice, 2008a).

- An 18-year old man attacks the IT system of a (popular) online community and sends the customers 1.5 million instant messages containing finance service advertising and pornography. After this, he contacts the company, identifying himself as the author and offers to protect the IT system against such attacks. He demands, moreover, to be able to send his advertising mails - exclusively—via the system in future. Since the company doesn't react, he threatens to publish his methods of attack (US Department of Justice, 2005).

- During an attack on a system of the State of Virginia (U.S.A.), with which drugs abuse is pursued or prevented by pharmacists and hospitals, a lot of patient and prescription data fall into the hands of blackmailers, who make demands of millions. To increase the pressure, the authorities' system is attacked to such an extent that running operations can only be restored after tremendous efforts (Krebs, 2009b).

Hopelessness

Attacks are carried out to relieve acute financial trouble, felt to be of an existential nature. The problems are often caused by the addictive behaviour of the attacker or relatives, such as gambling, shopping, drugs and similar. Example:

- A member of staff at a bank, with the help of a colleague, manipulates his own account status, the aim is being to cover up his credit limits being overdrawn by his gambling losses (US Department of Justice, 2008b).

Curiosity or Obsession

Here, attackers want to try out their skills and abilities, or technical possibilities, and to satisfy their curiosity, play instinct, thirst for knowledge or similar. Mostly, there is a very low level of awareness of wrongdoing, since the attack is perceived as a game, a test or an experiment. The preparations

made for an attack can be very comprehensive. In most cases, there is no deliberate damage of the target intended. Examples:

- A student in the U.S.A. wants to try out the skills he has learnt working with computers, and sends out a worm via the Internet which penetrates other computer systems—without causing targeted damage there. However, the program replicates itself and spreads so quickly that a large number of computers break down due to overload (Casey, 2004).
- A resident of California gained control over the computers of female victims by inducing them to download malicious code from the Web disguised as audio files of popular songs. He is alleged to have used his control of victims' computer to steal personal data and to spy on them through their Web cams. Then he demanded sexually explicit photos and videos from the victims as condition not to disseminate other explicit or personal data. The accused claims that boyfriends and husbands of the victims had asked him to determine the faithfulness of their spouses. He is also accused to be engaged in payment card fraud (Claburn, 2010; Goodin, 2010).

Ambition and Need for Admiration

Attackers strive for attention, prestige and social recognition. Successful attacks are evaluated as signs of courage and competence in the attacker's social environment, and are rewarded with the corresponding recognition. Mostly a very vague perception of wrongdoing prevails—on the contrary: the attack is perceived as competition or a challenge. The trouble taken for an attack can be very comprehensive—depending on the ambition and stubbornness of the attacker.

- A hacker from Saudi Arabia manipulates Microsoft's website in such a way that a photo of Bill Gates in an awkward situation appears—an unpopular person in hacker circles, Gates is just being hit smack in the middle of his face with a cream pie, or similar. Inserted above the photo, the hacker's proud message reads "owned by Cyber Terrorist". In hacker circles, the attack on Gates or Microsoft is seen to be morally justified and overcoming Microsoft's security measures as an act of daring. The result is website defacing, the cake-thrower is glorified through the photo being published, and the hacker reaps recognition in his scene (Almeida, 2007).

- A schoolboy is fascinated by the possibility of being able to attack company websites with virus programs. He vies with other programmers of such programs—he wants to "be better", and gains recognition in his school class and peer group, where he's not well integrated, through his successes—with the virus Sasser, among others (Stillich, 2004).

Espionage

Targeted spying, the collecting and evaluating of confidential information, including in the shape of inspecting databases, or of eavesdropping on communication and data transfer—they all belong to this section. The attacks are often executed as contracts from third parties, whereby the attackers use conspirative means in order to remain incognito. The attacks are often launched over a long period of time, frequently exploiting insider knowledge, patchy controls or a lack of attention. Examples:

- Chinese hackers, who can be traced back to state offices, try to penetrate the IT systems of German authorities (including the Office of the Chancellor, the Ministries of Economy and Research and the Foreign Ministry), and Belgian authorities, to conduct industrial espionage (NN, 2007, NN, 2008). The Federal Office for the Protection of the Constitution registers an increase in attacks from China during and after current events, like the Dalai Lama's visit to Germany, or the Olympic Games in China (NN, 2009).

- A current study in North America reports about at least 1,295 computers in 103 countries worldwide, whose owners are all connected to Tibet and the Dalai Lama, and of which approximately 30 per cent are important diplomatic, political, economic or military institutions. Attackers have connected them to create a computer network, in order to spy out information stored on the computers, and to eavesdrop on communication and data transfers between them (SevDev, 2009).

- The German Federal Department of Trade and Industry warns expressly against industrial espionage through attacks on IT systems, reckoning that every fifth company has been the target of attacks once, and that there is a nationwide threat of damages in the billions (Bundeswirtschaftsministerium, 2009).

- The transmission network between the companies which are developing the F-35 Lightning II fighter plane for the US Ministry of Defence was attacked, during which a considerable amount of data was stolen. According to officials the source of the espionage appears to be in China—without having hints at relationships with state offices (Gorman, Cole & Dreazen, 2009).

- An employee of a company that develops and sells non-inflammable surface materials is accused of having gained unauthorised access to confidential production documentation via the IT system, and of subsequently founding his own company to sell such materials (US Attorney 2008a).

- Through a feigned wedding and faked documents, a Lebanese woman gains US citizenship, and, ultimately, a job at the FBI. There, she makes unauthorised use of the IT systems to conduct enquiries about relatives and friends, and to gain information about investigations of international terrorist groups (US Department of Justice, 2003).

Sabotage

The aim is to seriously damage the victim of the attack by damaging (in the worst case, destroying) important material or immaterial goods. These attacks are directed, for example, against business competitors or political opponents, and are often carried out for economic, political or terrorism-motivated clients. To recognise or notice the attacks is relatively easy, but mostly happens too late. Examples:

- A member of IT staff at police authorities gains unauthorised access to the official IT system, where he then alters criminal prosecution files regarding himself and friends by marking open cases "closed" (Casey, 2004).
- A company instructs an attacker to shut down a competing company's website (US Department of Justice, 2006a).
- In 1983, an explosives attack is carried out on the computing centre of MAN by "Red Cells", a terrorist organisation, causing damage in the millions—to protest against their participation in the manufacture of Cruise missiles and Pershings (NN, 1983).

Cyber Warfare

The discussion about offensive government activities and military attacks by means of information technologies grows recently and coined words like cyber war, cyber attacks and information warfare for offensive or deterrent actions to serve national interests (Denning & Denning 2010). For instance, the US Administration installed a "Committee on Offensive Information Warfare" which reported to policy makers and researchers the possible utility of offensive information warfare as a mode of attack and the nature and extent to which offensive information warfare may be a part of conventional military operations (Owens, Dam & Lin 2009).

Revenge and Retaliation

Here attacks often occur as a reaction to some target's actions, perceived as wrong; they aim to damage a certain company or persons by damaging or destroying important material or immaterial goods. The drive is emotional, for the most part (hate, rage, frustration and the like), and designed to cause visible damage in order to get even for the wrongdoing felt. Attacks of this kind are seldom carried out on behalf of third parties. The attacks are made mostly with a relatively short preparation time, as far as attacks go, in fact it's more of a spontaneous action. It is relatively easy to recognise or notice the attacks, but mostly happens too late. Examples:

- An IT employee is given his notice because of theft. But, what he leaves behind are programs in the company's IT systems which delete voluminous data on a pre-set date, specified by him (Casey, 2004).
- A former member of staff gains unauthorised access to his former employer's IT systems, and manipulates an important customer's data—leading to the company and the customer suffering serious financial damage (US Attorney, 2008b).
- A fired IT employee places 11,000 virus programs on his former employer's IT system (Gassner, 2009).

- An IT employee at a bank places malicious code on the IT systems he is responsible for—the malware can be activated with a time device at his command (time bomb). The employee is fired without notice because of disciplinary proceedings. Several days later the malware destroys data and adversely influences 50,000 customers' accounts (US Department of Justice, 2006b).

Envy

The impulse to commit the deed is mostly emotional here, and aims to compensate for what is perceived as an unfair or undeserved inequality in the sharing out of material or immaterial assets. Attacks are often executed by actors from inside the companies, whose envy is caused by observations at their workplace. Example:

- A man is envious of an employee of the US Navy because of his job position as system administrator. Which is why he attacks the Navy's IT system to cause damage, and thus discredit the system administrator (US Attorney, 2007).

Vandalism

Here, too, the attack is effected because of a mostly emotional drive, and is designed towards visible harm by the damaging or destroying of important goods or immaterial assets. This happens seldom as a contract from a third party. Examples:

- A former IT employee at DaimlerChrysler uses his inside information to attack the IT system of a DaimlerChrysler factory via a terminal at the reception area. The deletion of important data which he initiates forces the closure of parts of the factory for several hours (US Department of Justice, 2007b).

DISCUSSION

With the categories listed so far, motives appear which can be observed as frequent and distinctive, even if sometimes distinguishing cannot always be unequivocal, and in reality, combinations of, or faked motives may occur. Thus, in cases of blackmail for greed often sabotage is often threatened. The motives among members of groups of actors will vary, for example, in attacks which serve industrial espionage. A client who wants to get at confidential information usually looks for someone who'll carry out the job for money, because of greed, revenge or for other reasons.

Additionally, the following features are to be observed:

- The choice of examples is intended to show a few particularly striking cases, and also the wide range of behaviour modes—within the categories listed, too. Several descriptions of examples are taken from publications by public prosecutors and similar law enforcing authorities bringing charges or pursuing criminals, and are thus to be categorized as substantiated suspicions.
- Some successful attacks of hackers underline certain scepticism towards the implementation of complex and comprehensive IT systems, and actually get moral support from the general public. The connotation of the term "hacker" is seen as positive in these cases, and carries some respect and recognition for their competence and skillfulness—different then from the analogous definitions of classic crime. Moreover, the victims of attack are often large, impersonal and seemingly powerful global companies, operating without local roots, which trigger little sympathy or pity, but rather, quite often, secret glee over their mishaps.
- Among mostly younger people with an affinity for technology, attacks on IT systems are perceived as challenges which

are taken up, like a competition in sport. The publications about them in the press fan the flames even more for this impression (Kremp, 2009), and ensure that there's a certain attraction in occupying oneself with attack methods and tools.

- In the area of attacks by external offenders via electronic communication channels, it seems that the biggest danger today no longer emanates from individuals, who perpetrate attacks for reasons of personal enrichment, or to strive for social recognition, who are addicted to publicity or whose attacks are based on political views. In fact, increasingly, Mafia-type structured, organised crime can be observed, which serves only to increase personal enrichment (Kempf, 2009; LKA, 2008).

- The use of conspirative means as a cover-up, and to distract possible pursuants is increasing in all the attacks, no matter which motives they have. Most notably, the identities of attackers (through manipulation of the sender's details), the source of attacks (through so-called "zombie" computers) and the motives of attacks are covered up. On the Internet, these cover-ups benefit from the weaknesses or defects of the TCP/IP protocol family.

- Through the increased attention paid to current attacks on IT systems by the media, the vulnerability of the companies, and also details about the ways and means of attack become increasingly public. This lures potential offenders, who want to extort payments just by threatening attacks; extortion, in the meantime, counts as a serious problem (Kempf, 2009; LKA, 2008).

- Considerable danger source are attackers who do not present a clearly outlined motive, but rather are lead astray by a favourable opportunity. Thus deficits in defence and controlling measures can lead to attackers using just an opportunity (e.g. an unoccupied terminal, a laptop lying around or a note of an IT system's access data), without having planned, or prepared on purpose for such an undertaking before. The proportion of such opportunistic attacks is thought to be considerable - according to one study, it is 39 per cent of all attacks (Baker, 2008).

Basically, offenders from inside a company are to be considered for attacks on a company's IT systems, that is, staff who can obtain access, or outside offenders, that is, external persons who can obtain such an access. Exact evidence of the proportions of insiders to externals varies (PWC, 2007; D'Arcy & Hovav, 2007); it is to be assumed that more than half of all attacks are committed by inside offenders, and yet a high proportion is also carried out by the joint actions of inside and outside offenders. Since internal actors can use insider knowledge (on internal activities, habits, weak spots, social relationships …) for attacks, then higher rates of successful attacks and greater damage must be expected in their case (D'Arcy & Hovav, 2007). Furthermore, inside actors basically have all the possibilities of outside actors at their disposal, too. However, through communication networks like the Internet, which encompass the whole world, the number of potential outside actors who can break into IT systems via these networks, independently of place, is very large and heterogeneous. An appraisal of motives, skills and resources is, therefore, almost impossible—we could be dealing with "anyone" and "anything".

It must be assumed that outside offenders have certain IT knowledge and skills necessary to execute the attacks. But outside offenders increasingly use the support of programs and constructions kits accessible on WWW helping them with the design and execution of attacks. Thus, an attacker no longer has to have sound technical skills, but can help himself with readymade tools which are offered quite openly on the Web. According to estimates, there are 500 to 1,000 hackers active worldwide with sophisticated technical knowledge, who design their attacks technically and execute them independently, and in contrast there are about 100,000 so-called script kids active, whose attacks are spearheaded with pre-fabricated tools (Geschonneck, 2004). This shows that the skills necessary for an attack are less than before.

OUTLOOK

Nowadays, the possibility of attacks on company IT systems, and their misuse, has to be reckoned with, and these dangers are to be regarded as concomitants of IT increasingly permeating a company's business processes. Correspondingly, risk management has to be consequentially brought into line, and security measures set.

In general, the motives and personal characteristics of attackers of IT systems are similar to those of classic criminals. A choice of striking examples shows the broad range of the malicious activities. The categories of motives and actors described here support the development of preventive and reactive policies and measures to mitigate risks of computer crime.

Today it must be assumed that the greatest dangers for IT systems no longer emanate from the individual, but rather from mafia-like structured, organised crime, whose sole purpose is for personal enrichment. The technical faults and weaknesses of the underlying protocols support the use of conspirative means to cover up, and to distract possible offenders. Which is why the discovery, investigation and persecution of offenders is difficult.

REFERENCES

Almeida, M. (2007)., *Microsoft.com defaced.* Retrieved July, 14, 2010 from www.bit-shield. com/Link200705MS_Defaced.html.

Attorney, U. S. (2007). *Former Navy contractor sentenced for damaging Navy computer system.* Retrieved February, 20, 2011, from www.usdoj. gov/criminal/cybercrime/sylvestreSent.pdf.

Attorney, U. S. (2008a). *News release.* Retrieved February, 20, 2011, from www.usdoj.gov/criminal/cybercrime/dierkingCharge.pdf.

Attorney, U. S. (2008b). *Computer tech pleads guilty to identify theft of Calpine corporation executive.* Retrieved February, 20, 2011, from www. usdoj.gov/criminal/cybercrime/smithPlea.pdf.

Baker, W. H., & Hylender, C. D. Valentine (2008). *Data Breach Investigations Report.* Retrieved February, 20, 2011, from www.verizonbusiness.com.

BSI Bundesamt für Sicherheit in der Informationstechnik (Ed.). (2009). *Die Lage der IT-Sicherheit in Deutschland.* Bonn: BSI.

Bundeswirtschaftsministerium (2009). *Bundeswirtschaftsministerium unterstützt Unternehmen beim Schutz gegen Computerkriminalität.* Retrieved February, 20, 2011, from www.bmwi.de/BMWi/Navigation/Presse/ pressemitteilungen,did=286748.html.

Bursch, D. (2005). *IT-Security im Unternehmen - Grundlagen, Strategien.* Berlin: VDM.

Casey, E. (2004). *Digital Evidence and Computer Crime: Forensic Science, Computers and the Internet* (2nd ed.). London: Elsevier.

Cheney, J. S. (2010). *Heartland Payment Systems: Lessons Learned from a Data Breach.* Retrieved February, 18, 2011, from www.philadelphiafed. org/payment-cards-center/publications/discussion-papers/2010/D-2010-January-Heartland-Payment-Systems.pdf.

Claburn, T. (2019). *Hacker Accused of Video Extortion.* Retrieved February, 20, 2011, from www. informationweek.com/news/windows/security/ showArticle.jhtml?articleID=225701396&cid= RSSfeed_TechWeb.

Cross, M. (2008). *Scene of the Cybercrime* (2nd ed.). Burlington: Elsevier.

D'Arcy, J., & Hovav, A. (2007). Deterring Internal Information Systems Misuse. *Communications of the ACM, 50*(10), 113–117. doi:10.1145/1290958.1290971

Damle, P. (2002). *Social Engineering: A Tip of the Iceberg*. In ISACA Journal, No. 2. Retrieved February, 18, 2011, from www.isaca.org/Journal/Past-Issues/2002/Volume-2/Pages/Social-Engineering-A-Tip-of-the-Iceberg.aspx.

Dannecker, G. (1996). Neuer Entwicklungen im Bereich der Computerkriminalität. *Betriebsberater, 25*, 1285–1293.

Denning, P. J., & Denning, D. E. (2010). The Profession of IT - Discussing Cyber Attack. *Communications of the ACM, 53*(9), 29–31. doi:10.1145/1810891.1810904

Disterer, G., Alles, A., & Hervatin, A. (2007). Denial-of-Service (DoS) Attacks: Prevention, Intrusion Detection, and Mitigation. In Janczewski, J. & Colarik, A. M. (Eds.), *Cyber Warfare and Cyber Terrorism*, 262-272. Hershey Idea Group.

Eckert, C. (2001). *IT-Sicherheit: Konzepte - Verfahren – Produkte*. München: Oldenbourg.

Eschweiler, J., & Psille, D. E. A. (2006). *Security@ Work - Pragmatische Konzeption und Implementierung von IT-Sicherheit*. Berlin: Springer.

Gassner, S. (2009). *Computerkriminalität bedroht den deutschen Mittelstand*. Retrieved February, 18, 2011, from www.silicon.de/sicherheit/management/0,39039020,39171050,00/computerkriminalitaet+bedroht+den+deutschen+mittelstand.htm.

Geschonneck, A. (2004). *Computer-Forensik*. Heidelberg: DPunkt.

Gold, S. (2009). *First arrests in Heartland Payment Systems data breach*. Retrieved March, 19, 2009, from www.infosecurity-magazine.com/news/090216_HeartlandArrests.html.

Goodin, D. (2010). *PC consultant pleads not guilty to malware "sextortion" plot*. Retrieved February, 18, 2011, from www.theregister.co.uk/2010/07/21/mijangos_not_guilty_plea/.

Gorman, S., Cole, A., & Dreazen, Y. (2009). *Computer Spies Breach Fighter-Jet Project*. Retrieved February, 20, 2011, from online.wsj.com/article/SB124027491029837401.html.

Gorman, S., & Perez, E. (2009). *Hackers indicated in Widespread ATM Heist*. Retrieved February, 20, 2011, from online.wsj.com/article/SB125786711092441245.html.

Kempf, D. (2009). *ITK-Branche im Würgegriff der Hacker-Industrie?* Retrieved February, 20, 2011, from www.bitkom.org/files/documents/keynote_prof__kempf_industrialisierung_der_computerkriminalitaet.pdf

Krebs, B. (2009a). *Payment Processor Breach May Be Largest Ever*. Retrieved February, 20, 2011, from voices.washingtonpost.com/securityfix/2009/01/payment_processor_breach_may_b.html?hpid= topnews.

Krebs, B. (2009b). *Hackers Break Into Virginia Health Professions Database*. Retrieved February, 20, 2011, from voices.washingtonpost.com/securityfix/2009/05/hackers_break_into_virginia_he.html.

Kremp, M. (2009). *Last Browser Standing*. Retrieved from February, 20, 2011, from www.spiegel.de/netzwelt/tech/0,1518,614979,00.html.

Landeskriminalamt Nordrhein-Westfalen, L. K. A. (Ed.). (2008). *Computerkriminalität - Lagebild 2008*. Düsseldorf: LKA.

Loo, A. (2009). Security Threats of Smart Phones and Bluetooth. *Communications of the ACM, 52*(3), 150–152. doi:10.1145/1467247.1467282

Messaging Anti-Abuse Working Group MAAWG. (2008). *Email Metrics Program #9.* Retrieved February, 20, 2011, from http://www.maawg.org/about/MAAWG_2008-Q2_Metrics_Report9.pdf.

Mohay, G., Anderson, A., Collie, B., Vel, O. d., & McKemmish, R. (2003). *Computer and Intrusion Forensics.* Norwood: Artech.

Nitschmann, J., & Leyendecker, H. (2008). *Steuerskandal.* Retrieved February, 20, 2011, from www.sueddeutsche.de/finanzen/287/301284/text.

NN. (1983). *Anschlag auf südhessisches Rechenzentrum zeigt Schwächen bei der Security-Planung auf.* Retrieved February, 20, 2011, from www.computerwoche.de/1180467.

NN. (2007). *Chinesische Trojaner auf PCs im Kanzleramt.* Retrieved February, 20, 2011, from www.spiegel.de/netzwelt/tech/0,1518,501954,00.html.

NN. (2008). *Spionage-Angriffe auf belgische Computer.* Retrieved from February, 20, 2011, from www.heise.de/newsticker/Spionage-Angriffe-auf-belgische-Computer--/meldung/107340.

NN. (2009). *Chinesen verstärken Cyber-Attacken auf deutsche Regierung.* Retrieved February, 20, 2011, from www.spiegel.de/netzwelt/web/0,1518,617374,00.html.

Owens, W. A., Dam, K. W., & Lin, H. S. (2009). *Technology, Policy, Law, and Ethics Regarding U.S. Acquisition and Use of Cyberattack Capabilities. National Research Council.* Washington: National Academic Press.

PWC. (2007). *Wirtschaftskriminalität 2007 - Sicherheitslage der deutschen Wirtschaft.* Retrieved February, 20, 2011, from www.eulerhermes.de/de/dokumente/veruntreuung-wirtschaftskriminalitaet-2007.pdf/veruntreuung-wirtschaftskriminalitaet-2007.pdf.

Ramelsberger, A. (2008). *Steueraffäre.* Retrieved February, 20, 2011, from www.sueddeutsche.de/politik/416/434164/text.

Richter, N. (2008). *Geschäfte in der Telefonzelle.* Retrieved February, 16, 2009, from www.sueddeutsche.de/finanzen/266/448759/text.

Ritzer, U. (2008a). *Steuersünder wollen Bank verklagen.* Retrieved February, 20, 2011, from www.sueddeutsche.de/finanzen/908/302904/text.

Ritzer, U. (2008b). *Tippgeber in Todesangst.* Retrieved February, 20, 2011, from www.sueddeutsche.de/finanzen/288/301285/text.

SevDev Group. (2009). *Information Warfare Monitor.* Retrieved March, 31, 2009, from www.infowar-monitor.net/ghostnet.

Sood, A. K., & Enbody, R. (2011). Chain Exploitation - Social Networks Malware. *ISACA Journal, 1,* 31–36.

Stillich, S. (2004). *Der Wurm von der Wümme.* Retrieved March, 27, March, 2009, from www.stern.de/computer-technik/internet/:Sasser-Programmierer-Der-Wurm-W%FCmme/25454.html?id=525454&eid=501069&pr=1.

US Department of Justice. (2003). *Local FBI Employee Indicted for Public Corruption.* Retrieved February, 20, 2011, from www.usdoj.gov/criminal/cybercrime/fudgeIndict.htm.

US Department of Justice. (2005). *New York Teen Pleads Guilty.* Retrieved February, 20, 2011, from www.usdoj.gov/criminal/cybercrime/grecoPlea.htm.

US Department of Justice. (2006a). *Michigan Man Gets 30 Months for Conspiracy to Order Destructive Computer Attacks.* Retrieved February, 20, 2011, from www.usdoj.gov/criminal/cybercrime/araboSent.htm.

US Department of Justice. (2006b). *Former technology manager sentenced to a year in prison for computer hacking offense.* Retrieved February, 20, 2011, from www.usdoj.gov/criminal/cybercrime/sheaSent.htm.

US Department of Justice. (2007a). *Hackers from India Indicted for Online Brokerage Intrusion Scheme.* Retrieved February, 20, 2011, from www.usdoj.gov/criminal/cybercrime/marimuthuIndict.htm.

US Department of Justice. (2007b). *Former computer contractor pleads guilty to hacking Daimler Chrysler.* Retrieved February, 20, 2011, from www.usdoj.gov/criminal/cybercrime/johnsPlea.pdf.

US Department of Justice. (2008a). *San Jose Woman charged with fraud.* Retrieved February, 20, 2011, from www.usdoj.gov/criminal/cybercrime/leotiotaIndict.pdf.

US Department of Justice. (2008b). *Former assistant bank branch manager pleads guilty.* Retrieved February, 20, 2011, from www.usdoj.gov/criminal/cybercrime/covelliPlea.pdf.

Chapter 2
Wireless Security

Faisal Kaleem
Florida International University, USA

Kang K. Yen
Florida International University, USA

ABSTRACT

As the portability and accessibility of mobile devices have grown over the last decade, applications of wireless communication technologies have become more prevalent. Mature technologies such as Wi-Fi, Bluetooth, and GSM (Global System for Mobile Communication) cellular wireless and emerging technologies such as WiMax are becoming commonplace in both the business and consumer world. As such, it is extremely important to understand the security considerations and vulnerabilities in order to ensure that these technologies are as reliable and secure as possible.

Since the communication medium in wireless technologies, as compared to the wired medium, are "invisible airwaves", the security vulnerabilities and threats may be less obvious, resulting in individuals and organizations with no or low awareness of the associated risk of their wireless infrastructure and technology.

The purpose of this chapter is to educate individuals about the inherent security risks and vulnerabilities of common and emerging wireless technologies and to provide them with some of the best practices used in securing or minimizing these associated risks.

INTRODUCTION

The immense popularity of wireless technology has significantly changed the way we access information, browse the Internet and read our emails. Whether you are busy doing research at a college campus, enjoying latte at a coffee store while chatting with your friends, using Skype talking to your Facebook contact, while waiting to board a plane at the airport, video conferencing with your loved one during a business trip while staying at a hotel, or using Google on your Smartphone to find driving directions; you cannot ignore the importance of wireless technology,

DOI: 10.4018/978-1-61350-507-6.ch002

which is now a must-have for businesses and individuals. The degree to which different wireless technologies can be found across a broad spectrum of industries is truly astounding as they have given rise to innovative means of communication and greater convenience.

Despite their added convenience, capabilities and affordable cost, securing different types of wireless technologies is one major concern that cannot be simply ignored. In fact, to most large corporations, wireless is one of the most essential yet a very frustrating technology to secure, and manage. By offering new features and services and allowing for distributed functionality across geographically dispersed systems, threats against the nodes attached to wireless networks have increased. Relying on out-of-the box settings, the ease with which an ignorant corporate employee or a home user can plug-in an unsecure wireless device into their existing network, thus extending its signal beyond the secure perimeter, completely violates the basic principles of network security and reduces their overall security posture. This is one of the reasons why attacks to wireless networks are growing at a higher rate.

The term wireless technology encompasses many things: AM/FM radio, IEEE 802.11 and 802.16 based communications, cell phones networks, Global Positioning System (GPS), Satellite TV, Bluetooth, RFIDs, Infrared, and any other devices that are capable of establishing communication without any physical or wired connections. In this chapter we will only discuss the security issues associated with the most commonly used wireless technologies as follows:

- Wireless Local Area Network (WLAN) or Wi-Fi based on IEEE 802.11 protocol.
- Wireless Personal Area Network (WPAN) or Bluetooth based on IEEE 802.15 protocol.

The major objective behind this chapter is to assist individuals to improve their overall security awareness in the aforementioned areas of wireless technologies by exposing them to the common threats associated with these technologies and providing them with some best practices and countermeasures to use them in a more secure fashion.

For each of these wireless technologies, the chapter will provide:

- An overview of the technology and the associated terminologies,
- An overview of different types of associated threats and vulnerabilities,
- Recommendations and best practices to mitigate the associated risks.

A BRIEF HISTORY OF WIRELESS TECHNOLOGIES

Wireless communication, a branch of telecommunication, is a method to accomplish transfer of information over both short and long distances without using a guided media, like electrical wires or optical cables. Instead, different forms of electromagnetic emissions like, Radio Frequencies (RF), microwave, and infrared are used as a medium to establish communication between the sending and receiving stations.

It was around 1864 when James Clerk Maxwell theoretically conceptualized electromagnetic wave, followed by Guglielmo Marconi, who, in 1897 demonstrated their usage by transmitting Morse Code over wireless links. The year 1928 marks the beginning of the first electronic television broadcast when the visual image of "Felix the Cat" was sent on-air. Since then, wireless communications have come a long way. Satellite based communication for Radios and TVs, GPS navigation, cellular based voice and data networks, and wireless based local and personal area networks are all based on wireless technologies. The wireless technologies that will be discussed throughout the remainder of this chapter are based on RF.

RF can be defined as a rate of oscillation of an Alternating Current (AC), which with the help of an antenna can produce an electromagnetic (EM) field that is suitable for wireless broadcasting and/or communications. Any signal that is between the frequencies of 3 Hz to 300 GHz is an RF based signal.

Most of these radio frequencies are regulated by different organizations based on geographic boundary. The International Telecommunications Union (ITU) is responsible for frequency allocation at the global level, while, the Federal Communications Commission (FCC) allocates these frequency bands within the continent US.

WIRELESS THREAT ANALYSIS

The immense growth of wireless networking technology has also given rise to unique set of security risks and technical challenges. In order for a thief to steal some valuables from your home, he or she needs to be physically present there. For attackers to be able to steal information from systems connected to a wired LAN, don't need to actually walk up to those systems; they just need to be physically connected to the same network where the target system belongs. In case of wireless networks, the threat is magnified as the attacker doesn't even need to be·present in the same physical location; they can launch the attack from the parking lot or across the street. As long as an attacker is within range of the wireless transmissions, he/she can intercept or inject transmission by accessing the radio link between wireless devices. It is important to mention here that some highly sensitive directional antennas (Yagi or Helical) can be utilized by these attackers to extend the range of the wireless signal beyond the standard range to attack wireless networks.

Just like wired networks, wireless networks also need to support the three basic principles of Network Security as defined below:

- **Confidentiality:** To protect against unauthorized access to information.
- **Integrity:** To protect against unauthorized modification to information.
- **Availability:** Ensure that the requested services and the systems hosting these services are available and accessible whenever needed.

These three objectives sometimes are commonly referred as the CIA triad. Loss of Confidentiality, Integrity and Availability are common impacts as a result of successful attacks against wireless networks.

WIRELESS LOCAL AREA NETWORK (WLAN)

Wireless Local Area Network (WLAN) can be thought of as an extension to wired Local Area Network (LAN) to provide enhanced network access for mobile users. In a typical wired LAN environment, all communicating nodes are physically connected to a centralized connectivity device—the switch. In contrast, WLAN comprises of wireless nodes that are connected to an Access Point (AP) via a shared medium—airwaves. Since these wireless nodes are not physically connected to AP, they can move freely within an area such as home, office, or campus. This geographic area (or coverage area) is based on the strength of airwave signal propagated by AP.

Wi-Fi, a trade name that is given to IEEE 802.11 standard, came into existence in 1985, as a result to a decision that is made by FCC to allow unlicensed usage of several frequency bands of the wireless. These so-called garbage-bands were already in use by some commonly used consumer electronic devices such as hand-held phones and microwave-ovens that also use radio waves. To operate in these unlicensed frequency bands, wireless devices would be required to use spread spectrum technology that spreads a radio

Table 1. IEEE 802.11 Standards

IEEE Protocol	Typical Data Rate	Maximum Data Rate	Frequency Band	Comments
802.11	1 Mbps	2 Mbps	2.4 GHz	• Legacy protocol and is not commonly used.
802.11a	25 Mbps	54 Mbps	5 GHz	• Specifies 8-12 available radio channels. • Throughput is shared between all connections to the same radio channel. • Not compatible with 802.11b/g.
802.11b	6.5 Mbps	11 Mbps	2.4 GHz	• Throughput is shared between all connections to the same radio channel. • Generally combined with 802.11g to offer 802.11b/g products
802.11g	11 Mbps	54 Mbps	2.4 GHz	• Hybrid combination of 802.11a and 802.11b • Backward compatible with 802.11b • Based on Orthogonal Frequency-Division Multiplexing (OFDM)
802.11 n	200 Mbps	540 Mbps	2.4/5 GHz	• Increased data throughput using Multiple Input and Multiple Output (MIMO) antennas and receivers. • Backward compatible with 802.11a/b/g.

signal out over a wide range of frequencies making the radio signal difficult to intercept and less susceptible to interference.

The 802.11 link layer wireless protocols were developed by the IEEE for wireless LAN (WLAN) technology that specifies an over-the-air interface between a wireless client station and a base station or between two wireless client stations connecting in an ad-hoc fashion. The protocol was adopted in 1997. Table 1 provides a listing of various IEEE 802.11 standards in existence today.

It is worth to mention here that there are other 802.11 standards that were ratified by IEEE in previous years. These are either amendments or supplementary standards to the existing IEEE 802.11 family. For example, the goal of 802.11e is to provide enhancements for Quality of Service (QoS) and multimedia by improving bandwidth management.

IEEE 802.11 Topology

The IEEE 802.11 WLAN comprises of two main components:

- **Wireless Station:** This is an end user's wireless device with IEEE 802.11 capabilities. This includes laptops, desktop with an inexpensive wireless Network Interface Card (NIC), PDAs, smart phones, gaming consoles and other consumer electronic devices.
- **Access Point (AP):** A centralized wireless node that:
  ○ Logically connects all the wireless stations with each other in a WLAN.
  ○ Logically connects the wireless stations to the organization's wired infrastructure.
  ○ Logically connects separate networks in a point-to-point or multipoint fashion using the bridge functionality.

There are two network topologies defined in the IEEE 802.11 standard:

- **Ad-Hoc Mode:** Also called *peer-to-peer* mode creates a direct connection between wireless stations without using the AP. A group of two or more wireless stations configured to communicate on-the-fly (ad-hoc basis) is known as an *Independent Basic Service Set* (IBSS).

- **Infrastructure Mode:** This is the most commonly used topology where, the AP logically connects the wireless stations to each other and to the organization's wired infrastructure. In this mode, multiple Basic Service Set (BSS) that comprises of an AP and a set of wireless stations, connect to the organization's wired infrastructure to form an Extended Service Set (ESS). In ESS, wireless stations can also roam between APs and still maintain network connectivity.

IEEE 802.11 Frame

The IEEE 802 standard defines two separate layers, the Logical Link Control (LLC) and the Media Access Control (MAC), for the Data-link layer of the Open System Interconnect (OSI) reference model. The IEEE 802.11 standard provides specification for the physical layer and the MAC sub-layer of the OSI model.

At the physical (PHY) layer, the standard provides a series of encoding and transmission schemes for wireless communications. The most commonly used schemes are the Frequency Hopping Spread Spectrum (FHSS), Direct Sequence Spread Spectrum (DSSS), and Orthogonal Frequency Division Multiplexing (OFDM) transmission schemes.

The 802.11 MAC frame consists of MAC header, the frame body and the frame check sequence (FCS). The Frame body constitutes the payload or the information for both the management and data type frames. The FCS provides a way to check for erroneous packets. Cyclic Redundancy Check (CRC) is used to calculate the FCS value over all the fields of MAC header and frame body fields. The details of the fields in the MAC header are provided in Table 2.

IEEE 802.11 Security Overview

The original IEEE 802.11 specification provides security services at the link level. The standard does not provide end-to-end security as upper layer protocols like IPSec and Secure Socket Shell (SSH) can do so for network applications.

In the following paragraphs we will briefly discuss some of these protocols that provide security services for WLANs.

Wired Equivalent Privacy

The Wired Equivalent Privacy was defined as part of the IEEE 802.11 standard to provide confidentiality, integrity, and access control at the link-level.

- **Authentication:** One-way (Only AP authenticate the wireless client) open-system authentication and shared-key authentication are the two protocols that were specified as part of the standard. In an Open-system authentication the wireless client does not provide any security credentials to the AP. Instead the client attempt to associate itself with the AP by only presenting its MAC address. On the other hand shared-key authentication is based on a four-way challenge-response scheme and the knowledge of a shared secret—the WEP key.
- **Confidentiality:** Confidentiality of data is provided based on the knowledge of shared key secret and the RC4 stream cipher. The length of WEP key varies from a standard length of 40 bits to a non-standard 232 bits. A 24-bit Initialization Vector (IV) is also needed as a seed value for initializing the keys. These IVs are always sent in cleartext. It is important to mention that it is because of these IV related vulnerabilities that WEP is now known to be a vulnerable protocol.

Table 2. IEEE 802.11 MAC Header

MAC HEADER FIELDS (bits)	SUB FIELDS (bits)	DESCRIPTION
Frame Control Field (16)	Protocol Version (2)	Provides the current version of the 802.11 used
	Type (2)	Defines the function of the frame as control, data, or management.
	Subtype (4)	Determines the specific function to perform for its associated frame type.
	To DS (1)	Only used in data type frame and indicates if the frame is going to the distribution system (DS).
	From DS (1)	Only used in data type frame and indicates if the frame is exiting from the distribution system (DS).
	More Fragments (1)	Indicates if more fragments of the data or management frames are to follow.
	Retry (1)	Indicates if the data or management frame is being retransmitted.
	Power Management (1)	Indicates if the sending station is in active or power-save mode.
	More Data (1)	Indicates to station or AP that more data frames are to follow
	WEP (1)	Indicates whether or not encryption or authentication is used in the frame.
	Order (1)	Indicates that all received data must be processed in order
Duration/ID (16)		With some exceptions, this field is used for all control type frames to indicate the remaining duration needed to receive the next frame transmission.
Address-1 (48)		Depending upon the frame type, these three address fields and the fourth address field below contains a combination of the following type of addresses:
Address-2 (48)		**BSS Identifier (BSSID):** BSSID uniquely identifies each BSS. When the frame is from a station in an infrastructure BSS, the BSSID is the MAC address of the AP. When the frame is from a station in an IBSS, the BSSID is the randomly generated, locally administered MAC address of the station that initiated the IBSS.
Address-3 (48)		**Destination Address (DA):** MAC address of the destination **Source Address (SA):** MAC address of the source **Receiver Address (RA):** MAC address of the next immediate station to receive the frame **Transmitter Address (TA):** MAC address of the station that transmitted the frame on the wireless network.
Sequence Control (16)	Sequence Number (12)	Indicates the sequence number of each frame. The sequence number is the same for each frame sent for a fragmented frame; otherwise, the number is incremented by one until reaching 4095. At this time the counter is reset to 0.
	Fragment Number (4)	Indicates the fragment number of each frame sent as fragmented frame. The initial value is set to 0 and then incremented by one for each subsequent fragment of the fragmented frame.
Address-4 (16)		See above

- **Integrity:** Integrity of data is provided by creating a simple encrypted checksum based on a 32-bit CRC. The checksum for each payload is computed and both payload and checksum is encrypted using the WEP key.

WEP defines two shared keys:

- **Global Key:** This key is used to protect multicast and broadcast traffic from a wireless AP to all of its connected wireless clients.

- **Session Key:** This key is used to protect any unicast traffic between a wireless client and the AP and any multicast and broadcast traffic sent by the wireless client to the AP.

RC4 symmetric stream cipher with 40-bit or 104-bit encryption keys, in addition to 24-bit IV, is used to perform WEP encryption.

To encrypt the payload of an 802.11 frame, the following process is used:

- A 32-bit integrity check value (ICV) is calculated for the frame data and is appended at the end of the frame.
- A 24-bit IV is generated and appended to the WEP encryption key.
- The combination of IV and WEP encryption key is used as the input of a pseudo-random number generator (PRNG) to generate a bit sequence that is the same size as the combination of data and ICV.
- The PRNG bit sequence, also known as the *key stream*, is bit-wise exclusive-ORed (XORed) with the combination of data and ICV to produce the encrypted portion of the payload that is sent between the AP and the wireless client.
- To create the payload for the wireless MAC frame, the IV is added to the front of the encrypted combination of the data and ICV, along with other fields.

To decrypt the 802.11 frame data, the following process is used:

- IV is extracted from the front of the MAC payload.
- The IV is appended to the WEP encryption key and the combination is used as the input for the same PRNG to generate a bit sequence of the same size as the combination of the data and the ICV. This process

produces the same key stream as that of the sending wireless station.

- The PRNG bit sequence is XORed with the encrypted combination of the data and ICV to decrypt the combined data and ICV portion of the payload.
- The ICV calculation for the data portion of the payload is run, and its result is compared with the value included in the incoming frame to validate the incoming frame. If the values match, the data is considered to be valid. If they do not match, the frame is silently discarded.

Non Standard Protocols

Responding to several serious vulnerabilities in WEP, many nonstandard solutions were provided to secure the wireless links between the wireless clients and APs. Most vendors have implemented IV filtering to counter the freely available open source WEP cracking tools.

WEP2 was introduced with increased size of 128 bits for both keys and IV values. WEP+, which was a proprietary enhancement to the original WEP, enhances security by avoiding the usage of weak IVs. Finally Dynamic WEP was developed as a vendor specific feature that changes the WEP keys dynamically.

IEEE 802.11i

The IEEE 802.11i, which was ratified in 2004, is an amendment to the original 802.11 protocol and provides security mechanism for wireless networks. IEEE 802.11i deprecated WEP due to its inherent security vulnerabilities and introduces the Wi-Fi Protected Access 2 (WPA2) also called Robust Security Network (RSN). Before the ratification of IEEE 802.11i, WPA was introduced as an interim solution by the Wi-Fi alliance.

WPA has been designed to target both enterprise and end consumers and provides security enhancement for authentication, replay prevention, message privacy and integrity, access control, and key distribution mechanism. For enterprises, the distribution of keys to each user was done through the mandatory IEEE 802.1x that provides access control and authentication mechanism. On the other hand, the end consumer would rely on a Pre-Shared Key (PSK) mode that allows all stations to use the same key. WPA protocol works in the same manner as WEP but with 128-bit key, 48-bit IV values, and the Extensible Authentication Protocol (EAP) framework. Temporal Key Integrity Protocol (TKIP) and Message Integrity Code (MIC). TKIP is used to dynamically change the keys at a periodic interval, whereas MIC uses authentication code for each message to provide authenticity and integrity of messages.

WPA2 relies on the usage of Advanced Encryption Standard (AES) block cipher with available key sizes as 128 bits, 196 bits, and 256 bits. Both TKIP and AES are mandatory in WPA2.

IEEE 802.11w

The IEEE 802.11w-2009 was approved by the IEEE task group "w" (TGw) as an amendment to the existing IEEE 802.11 protocol to increase the security of the management frames by providing confidentiality, integrity, origin authenticity and replay protection. The IEEE 802.11i provides all these services for the data frames and all the management frames are transmitted with no encryption and/or authentication.

This standard is built on IEEE 802.11i framework to protect against attack on management frames. For example, a malicious system can cause a DoS attack by forging disassociation requests packet that appear to be sent by valid equipment. This standard will protect against this type of network disruptions.

IEEE 802.11 Threat Analysis

There are different types of security attacks against WLANs. The attacker can use various methods to facilitate these attacks against wireless networks.

The term *WarXing* is commonly used to refer to activities to detect publically accessible computer systems and wireless networks. The letter "X" represents a more specific detecting activity. Some of the examples of WarXing are:

- **WarDriving:** A technique used by attacker to locate insecure wireless networks while driving around with a device (laptop or PDAs) with 802.11 capabilities.
- **WarFlying:** This technique is the same as Wardriving, except it involves flying around in an aircraft.
- **WarBallooning:** Using a cluster of small balloons, a GPS and other wireless detection tools, an attacker let these tools float over an area to locate insecure wireless networks.
- **WarChalking:** This technique involves using chalk to place a special symbol on a sidewalk or other surface to indicate an unprotected/protected wireless network.

Some of the other examples of WarXing that relates to Wi-Fi include WarCarting, WarCycling, WarRunning, WarWalking, WarTrawling, and WarTransit.

The attacks that an attacker can perform against WLAN typically fall into two broad categories as follows:

1. **Passive Attack:**

A type of attack where an attacker, after gaining unauthorized access to wireless network, only monitors exchange of information between systems. The term passive suggests that the attacker doesn't modify the contents of collected information or cause any disruption to WLAN.

Because no modifications or disruptions are done, these types of attacks are difficult to detect and identify and the attacker can silently monitor traffic flowing in both directions. Few types of passive attacks are mentioned below:

- **Eavesdropping:** In this attack, an attacker simply monitors and listens to any communication between an AP and a wireless station. This technique is typically used to obtain network security credentials like passwords.
- **Traffic Flow Analysis:** Traffic Flow is a term commonly used in networking (wired or wireless) describing a sequence of messages exchanged between a source and a destination station.

In this type of attack, the attacker attempts to identify a pattern of communication by intelligently analyzing several messages that are exchanged between an AP and wireless station. Once again the intent is to obtain useful information without disrupting the operation of WLAN. The identification and physical location of APs and the different types of network protocols being used on WLANs can be easily obtained while analyzing the wireless traffic.

2. **Active Attack:**

These types of attacks are malicious in nature as the intent of the attacker is to modify, corrupt or inject data or to cause disruption of services provided on a wireless network. The information that is collected during passive attack is typically used to actively attack wireless networks.

These types of attacks can be detected but sometimes are difficult to prevent from. Below, we list few types of active attacks:

- **Masquerading:** Using the credentials of an authorized user (impersonating), the attacker gain access to certain network privileges, which he/she is not authorized to access.
- **Denial of Service:** DoS attack is an attack against the availability of the WLAN. The intent is to make the network unresponsive to legitimate requests thus preventing the users from accessing the network resources. Distributed DoS attacks increase the gravity of this problem by enlisting several computers (Zombies) and simultaneously launch attacks on a mass scale.
- **Replay Attack:** In this attack, the attacker captures session data (passive attack) of a user containing authentication information and then replays that information at a later time to gain unauthorized access to the system.
- **Message Alteration:** This is an attack against the integrity of the data where an attacker modifies it by making unauthorized addition, deletion, and alterations.

Threats Against WLANs

So what makes these attacks successful? The various threats that can be executed against vulnerable WLANs and the wide availability of several tools to materialize these attacks, is the answer. In the following paragraphs, we will take a look at some of the vulnerabilities and the threats against 802.11 WLANs.

1. **Default Settings:**

In most cases, vendors ship APs with default (or out of the box) settings which typically are not the recommended settings from the security perspective. The intent is to minimize possible user's frustration while making the AP works. Most of the time, the end users rely on these default settings and failed to properly configure their APs resulting in open network access to anyone.

The default password of an AP is one of those settings that most likely users forget to change.

These default passwords for APs from different vendors can be easily obtained from various websites. The preconfigured default Service Set Identifiers (SSIDs) for different brands of APs are also well documented and widely available. Finally, by default most of the APs come preconfigured with no encryption algorithm, which is a threat to the confidentiality of information.

2. Accidental Association:

Another significant challenge is to prevent *accidental association* of end user to connect to any network within range. These may be in-range networks from neighbors or they may be attacker's networks deployed specifically to exploit the connected systems to view and manipulate the wireless stations' communication.

3. Rogue APs:

These types of unauthorized and unapproved APs, when plugged into corporate networks, pose some serious threats to network security. These rogue APs are unmanaged, unknown, and unsecure in most of the cases and provide unrestricted network access to any party that locates them. They can be deployed by insiders as well as outsiders who gain physical access to the corporate facility.

Interestingly, some phishing attacks can be easily implemented using these rogue APs, where an attacker configure them with the same name as the name of a legitimate AP and waits for unsuspicious users to associate to it. As soon as the users are connected, attacker can capture sensitive data including users' authentication credentials.

4. WLAN Signal Leakage:

The wireless radio signal is not restricted by any physical medium and can extend beyond one's perimeter and leak through the physical boundaries of a home or a building. Any type of WarXing method then can be used to capture data on the wireless network including credentials.

5. Open Authentication and SSID in Clear:

By default, all APs use open authentication for client association where the AP accepts any client as long as the client provides a MAC address (legit or spoofed). Since the AP does not validate these MAC addresses, the open authentication is considered to be a weak form of authentication and is prone to unauthorized access.

Only SSID needs to be known to the wireless client in order to associate itself to the WLAN. Most APs are configured to broadcast beacon frames announcing their SSIDs. Although this beaconing can be disabled and the APs can be configured not to respond to any broadcast probe request, this does not prevent all attacks. The SSID may still be transmitted in other frames and determined using special software. Furthermore, the SSID is transmitted in clear text during the initial negotiation process between a wireless client and an AP. Attackers may be able to obtain the SSID during this process. In fact, the easiest way to obtain a particular SSID is by de-associating a wireless client from an AP. This will force the wireless client to send a re-association request packet that contains the SSID in the clear. This is possible because the management frames in IEEE 802.11 protocol are unauthenticated and unencrypted.

6. MAC Addresses in Clear:

Just like SSIDs, MAC addresses are also exchanged in clear text during the initial negotiation process and can be obtained by the attacker. At a later time, the attacker can spoof these MAC addresses to be able to access the WLAN. This can be used to defeat the MAC filter countermeasure (to be covered later).

7. Protocol Weakness:

The original IEEE 802.11 specification included the Wired Equivalent Privacy (WEP) protocol as an optional privacy algorithm to provide certain security services between the AP and wireless end station. These security services included Authentication (to verify the end station's identity), Confidentiality (to provide data encryption), and Integrity (to prevent unauthorized modification of messages in transit between the two communicating systems).

WEP is now proven to be a weak and extremely vulnerable protocol. There are several free and open source tools available on the Internet that can be used to easily discover WEP keys and crack WEP encryption. In most cases, these WEP keys remain unchanged for a longer period of time. This gives attackers ample time and opportunities to capture floating messages that are more than enough to compute these cryptographic keys. Once these WEP keys are computed, the attacker can use them to gain unauthorized access to WLAN or carry out other attacks. Furthermore, WEP does not provide any other security services including audit, non-repudiation, authorization, replay protection, and key management.

Apart from confidentiality and integrity services, WEP keys are also used as shared secret between an AP and the wireless clients during shared-key authentication, which is a challenge-response based authentication mechanism that is also provided (apart from open authentication) as part of the original 802.11 specification.

To counter the WEP vulnerabilities and to vastly improve the security of wireless networks, the much more modern, complex, and resilient Wi-Fi Protected Access (WPA/WPA2) protocols were introduced. Although these protocols were designed with security in mind, they have their own flaws that an attacker can take advantage of. Both, attacks against authentication and attacks against encryption are possible with WPA/WPA2 employed to provide security services.

8. WEP Fragmentation Attack:

This attack enables an attacker to send arbitrary data to create a legitimate connection to the AP, after capturing a single data packet from an AP. This is in contrast to replay attacks which usually require you to get an (Address Resolution Packet) ARP packet. This attack is quicker and more practical as compared to those that require capturing a significant amount of data before performing any type of attacks against the wireless networks. No WEP key is obtained in this attack rather unique IVs are captured and used till the WEP key is cracked.

Upon successful execution of this attack, the attacker can obtain 1500 bytes of RC4's (a type of stream cipher) Pseudo Random Generation Algorithm (PRGA). These bytes then can be used to generate forge packets for various types of packet injection attacks. Note that the output of PRGA is XORed with the plaintext to produce ciphertext and the ciphertext can be XORed back with PRGA to obtain plaintext.

9. Chopchop Attack:

Chopchop is an attack that targets WEP's implementation of Integrity Check Value (ICV) and XOR operation. ICV, which is based on CRC32 algorithm, is a way for WEP to include an integrity check. Upon successful execution, this attack can decrypt a WEP data packet without knowing the key. Like, the fragmentation attack, this attack doesn't reveal the key itself, but rather reveals the plaintext and it requires the capture of at least one WEP data packet.

An attacker can use this attack to interactively decrypt packets by truncating the last data byte of the captured packet while keeping it valid, guessing its cleartext, and calculating the change to the payload, which in turn yields a valid message.

10. Captive Portals:

Many public WLANs service providers use Captive Portal to authenticate users before permitting them to access the Internet. This is a technique where all client traffic is captured and redirected via a transported http proxy, to a particular web based authentication page that requires valid login credentials. Captive Portals are generally circumvented using either MAC spoofing or Domain Name Service (DNS) Tunneling.

MAC address spoofing is used by attackers to assume the identity of another system by changing their wireless client's adapter MAC address to match that of an already authenticated and connected client. Any wireless sniffer can be employed to obtain this information.

DNS tunneling is a process where the service itself is used as a transport for other protocols originally not intended to be used. One of the most valuable protocols that could be tunneled is the Secure Shell (SSH) where an attacker can gain complete unrestricted outbound access by tunneling other protocols through SSH. This attack utilizes long DNS queries and the default name server to relay the messages between the client and the attacker's computer.

11. Rainbow tables for WPA:

There is no doubt now that WPA-PSK is vulnerable to brute force attack where keys can be tested against dictionaries. This is done by observing and recording the 4-way handshake process used in establishing the connection between the wireless client and the AP. Using the de-authentication packets, an attacker can force the wireless client to disconnect from the network captures the handshake when the client reenters the network and then performs brute force to reveal the keys.

The major problem with this approach is that it requires a lot of computing power and time as the key hashing algorithm is not only complex but also depends upon the SSID of the network. This means that the passphrase "P@ssw0rd" will be hashed differently on a network with the SSID of "MyHome" than it will on a network with the SSID of "MyWirelessNetwork".

This is where the Rainbow tables for WPA come handy, which offers time-memory trade-off and provide a pre-computed lookup table containing the hashes for a range of possible passphrases, significantly improving the brute forcing process. A group of people have developed rainbow tables for the top 1000 commonly used SSIDs and a list of approximately 172,000 dictionary words resulting in 8 GB of table size.

12. MITM Attacks:

In the Man In The Middle (MITM) attack, the attacker places himself in between the victim station and the node that the victim communicates with. On the wired network, technique like ARP Cache Poisoning is utilized where the victim's traffic to the gateway is rerouted through the attacker's computer. In the wireless world, honeypot AP (just like Rogue APs), a proxy server with access to Internet, and DNS spoofing are the key elements to accomplish this type of attack.

First, the attacker lures the victim's station to associate itself to the honeypot AP. Note that the attacker's station, running a proxy server, is also connected to the same AP. Next, the wireless client sends a request to connect to a particular server on the Internet using a domain name. This domain name must be resolved to an IP address using a simple DNS lookup query. At this moment, the hacker's station performs DNS spoofing and responds to the client's DNS query by sending their own IP address. The proxy server forwards the original request over the Internet to the requested public server. Upon receiving the response from the public server, the proxy server returns it back to the victim's station. The important thing to note here is that the attacker's computer can also send fake certificate in case where victim's station attempts to connect to the public server over SSL.

Using MITM attack, sensitive information including credentials can be easily obtained, since all the packets flow through the attacker's proxy server.

13. DoS Attacks:

Since the possibility of DoS attacks exists in different layer of the network protocol stack, there is no guarantee of availability in 802.11 wireless networks. At the physical layer this could be achieved by traditional frequency jamming; at the link layer, disassociation and de-authentication packets could be utilized and at the network layer the success or failure messages of for the EAP protocol can be utilized to accomplish the DoS attack.

One of the most devastating DoS attack on wireless network is the *Queensland DoS*, where the Wireless NIC card is placed into continuous transmit mode on a specific channel. The result is that all activity in the immediate vicinity on that channel is halted. For some type of cards, this attack can disrupt all connectivity.

14. Other Threats:

Although there are some flaws in WPA/WPA2 protocols, they still remain difficult to break. That is why attackers have turned their guns to wireless clients where several attacks are possible by exploiting vulnerabilities commonly present in various layers of the protocol stack.

Furthermore, possibilities to exploit wireless stations exist even when they are not actively connected to a wireless AP. Simply leaving a wireless NIC enabled is sometimes enough for an attacker to be able to connect to the system and exploit it.

The above discussion suggests that not only the wireless networks need protection from un-

authorized users, but the innocuous users needs to be protected from inadvertently connecting to unauthorized wireless networks. And since the wireless networks in most cases are connected logically to the wired infrastructure of the organization, they must also be protected from any threats against wired networks. In the following paragraph, we will take a look at some WLAN security countermeasures.

Security Countermeasures Against WLAN Threats

In no dictionary, there exists such a word as 100% security or full security. Nevertheless, countermeasures against different threats and vulnerabilities can be applied to mitigate risks commonly associated with IEEE 802.11 wireless networks.

Some of the techniques used in securing wired networks can also be used to secure wireless networks, but techniques specific to securing WLAN must be considered as well. In the following paragraphs, we will provide some basic security guidelines to secure AP as well as the wireless clients connected to that AP.

Securing AP

Below we mention some of the guidelines to secure the wireless AP.

1. Default AP Configuration:

Most APs can be a big detriment to security and open to attack when connected to WLAN using their default configurations. These default settings should be changed before connecting these APs to a network.

2. AP-Password:

The default usernames and passwords for most APs are commonly known and available on various websites. This allows someone to have unauthorized access to the management functions of the AP. The default credentials should be changed.

3. Disable Remote Administration:

Most APs can be configured remotely using HTTP protocol. HTTP doesn't offer any confidentiality service and passes username and passwords in cleartext. Anyone eavesdropping on the network can easily obtain these credentials to access the management interface. Unless absolutely required, remote administration over HTTP must remain disabled all time. Should remote administration is absolutely required; usage of Secure Socket Layer (SSL) with HTTP is a better and a s ecure approach.

4. Default Channel:

Change the default channel to a different number. This not only improves the security but helps to avoid possible radio interference from other APs using the same or conflicting channels.

5. Default SSID:

As explained earlier, SSID can be thought of as the name of the WLAN. Most APs come preconfigured with default SSIDs that are well-known and available all over the Internet. For example, "LINKSYS". These default SSIDs should be changed to unidentifiable strings. As stated earlier, an AP and a wireless client exchange SSIDs as cleartext while performing certain management functions, so this should not be employed as the "only" technique to secure the WLAN.

6. SSID Broadcast:

APs broadcast SSIDs to announce the existence of WLANs. A wireless client upon identifying the existence of an AP can initiate the process to associate themselves with the identified WLAN. These broadcasts can be disabled to hide the existence of WLAN at the cost of manually configuring SSID on each wireless client that needs to be associated with WLAN. Once again, this countermeasure may leads to a false sense security as it can help keeping a casual attacker away but will not be effective against the determined attacker for the same reason explained in the above paragraphs.

7. Beacon Interval:

Beacon frames are management frames that contain all the configuration information (including SSIDs) about a wireless network. These frames are used by wireless clients during the association process to connect and maintain the connection to the APs.

APs, in their default configuration, periodically broadcast these frames at preset intervals to announce the existence of WLAN. APs can be configured to use the maximum allowable value for beacon interval so that these APs do not broadcast beacon frames frequently, making it difficult for the adversaries to passively locate a WLAN.

8. DHCP:

The Dynamic Host Configuration Protocol (DHCP) is a protocol that runs on APs to provide IP configuration automatically to the wireless. Since DHCP cannot perform client authentication, valid IP configuration is assigned to any wireless clients, including unauthorized devices, which can be successfully associated with an AP. There are two possibilities to mitigate the risk: First, by disabling the DHCP service and manually assigning static IP addresses on each wireless stations, which involves administrative overhead to manage and troubleshoot large WLANs. Secondly, if AP is used at a location (for example, home or small office) where the number of wireless clients can be predetermined, the number of IP configurations assigned by the DHCP service can be appropriately configured, making it difficult for an attacker to obtain a "not available" IP configuration.

9. IP/MAC Address Filters:

Most APs can be configured to allow or deny wireless client's access to WLAN based on their IP address or MAC address. Furthermore, MAC address reservations can be created and stored in AP to map MAC addresses to IP addresses. Since MAC addresses are transmitted in cleartext from wireless clients to APs, they can be easily captured and spoofed using special software defeating these filters. Nonetheless, these filters may be effective against casual eavesdropper.

10. WEP/WPA/WPA2:

Wireless data is transmitted using airwaves and anyone who wants to listen to it can do so. In order to protect wireless networks from eavesdropper, certain technologies can be employed. WEP is a deprecated security protocol that was introduced as part of original IEEE 802.11 protocol to provide confidentiality and authentication services based on a WEP key. WEP has several significant security problems and should not be used if possible, as it is proven to be a weak protocol and only marginally better than no protection at all. WEP keys can now be broken in few minutes using automated tools.

Wi-Fi Protected Access (WPA) and its upgrade WPA2 were introduced in response to several vulnerabilities that were discovered in WEP. Both protocols provide improved and more robust confidentiality and authentication services.

In a home or small business settings, WPA2-Personal should be configured if possible. On the other hand large enterprises can take advantage of WPA2-Enterprise to provide WLAN security.

In addition 802.11w can also be used to protect against certain type of DoS attacks due to the unprotected management frames.

11. Physical Security:

Most APs contain a reset button that can be pressed to configure them with their default security settings, which in most cases offers no encryption, default password and SSID. At the minimum, a DoS attack could be launched by just physically removing the AP from its current location. This suggests that APs should be physically inaccessible by unauthorized users and secured using locked enclosures.

12. AP-Placement:

An AP should be placed strategically in a way that the RF range should not extend beyond the needed boundaries. For example, an AP should not be placed near a window or in a room that is next to the sidewalk; especially if the wireless clients that will be connecting to the AP are deeper inside the house or the facility. The RF range can also be contained by configuring suitable power settings. Most APs allow configuring these power settings through the provided management interface. In some cases, directional antennas, like Yagi, can be used to concentrate the signal into the desired area making it difficult for unauthorized users to eavesdrop near the perimeter.

13. APs Using SNMP:

Simple Network Management Protocol (SNMP) is a network protocol used mainly to monitor the status of the network-attached devices by exposing management data from these systems. SNMPv1 and SNMPv2 use the concept of community strings, which are plaintext characters, to perform authentication. Once again, the default community string that is used by various devices is the word "public".

If SNMP or any other management protocol is not required, they should be disabled. At the minimum, change the default community string as often as possible, if using SNMPv1 and SNMPv2. Otherwise use SNMPv3 instead, which provides stronger security than its predecessors.

14. **Turn That Radio Off:**

Make sure to turn off the wireless APs, if not used by anyone for an extended period of time.

15. **Patch That Firmware:**

Discovered vulnerabilities in APs are corrected through vendor provided patches or firmware upgrades. Most APs provide the capability for downloading and installing these patches directly from the vendor's website. It is highly recommended that APs should remain patched and updated with the latest available firmware to avoid any security incidents.

Securing WLAN Clients

Wireless clients are systems that connect to APs and other wireless devices to access resources. It is important to apply risk mitigation techniques on these wireless clients to improve the overall security posture of WLAN. Below, there are some guidelines:

1. **Automatic Association:**

In their default state, most of the wireless clients are configured to automatically connect to any available APs, including the rogue ones. This only increases the possibility of attacks from malicious attackers operating those rogue APs.

Wireless clients should be configured to give the user an option to manually connect to available wireless networks.

2. **Turn That Radio Off:**

Nowadays most mobile devices including cell-phones are Wi-Fi enabled. As stated above,

if not configured properly, they can be automatically associated to any available APs without user's knowledge. Users who do not have any business needs to use Wi-Fi should disable their wireless interface.

3. **Ad-hoc Mode:**

If there is no business need to connect to a different wireless client in a point-to-point configuration, disable the ad-hoc mode to prevent establishing connection with malicious users in close proximity.

4. **Install a Complete Security Solution:**

Wireless clients, especially laptops should install a complete security solution including a personal firewall, antivirus, anti-spyware, and an Intrusion Detection and Prevention System (IDPS).

5. **Patch the OS and Application:**

Just like the APs, it is very important that the operating system and the installed applications remain patched to prevent attackers from exploiting any discovered vulnerabilities.

6. **Using Virtual Private Networks:**

As discussed earlier, end-to-end security cannot be provided without employing upper layer protocols. WEP/802.11i only provides link security. Users who want to connect to their organization, while using a public wireless networks (hotspots) must use VPNs as it keeps the data encrypted all the way from the wireless client to the VPN server, which acts as an entry point to the corporate private network.

WIRELESS PERSONAL AREA NETWORK (WPAN)

Commonly referred as ad-hoc or peer-to-peer network, a Wireless Personal Area Network (WPAN) is a short-range RF based wireless technology that is generally used to interconnect all the ordinary computing and communicating devices such as printers, cell-phones, personal assistant (PDA) or even home appliances. Typically, the range of WPAN is not more than 10 meters. There are several kinds of technologies used for WPANs but we will mainly focus on Bluetooth.

Bluetooth

Originally conceived as a wireless alternative to RS-232 data cables by Ericson, Bluetooth is a low-cost, low-power, short-range wireless technology that creates wireless networks on the fly, interconnecting various personal devices. These ad-hoc networks are called piconets. The interconnection between a Bluetooth enabled cell-phone and a Bluetooth enabled earpiece is a classical example of a piconet.

A piconet comprises of one master device and few other devices that act as slaves. These devices, uniquely identified by their 48-bit BD_ADDRs (Bluetooth device address) (similar to MAC addresses), can be in active or inactive state. At anytime, a piconet can include up to a maximum of 8 active devices (one master and 7 slaves) and up to 255 inactive slave devices. These devices can switch roles; meaning that a slave, with agreement with master, can adopt the role of a master anytime and vice versa. The master device assumes the responsibility for controlling and establishing the network.

Although, there is only one master within each piconet but an active slave in one piconet can act as a master of another piconet forming a dynamic topology where several Bluetooth enabled devices can be networked over an extended distance. This chain of piconets is called as scatternet.

The Bluetooth specification as standardized within IEEE 802.15, defines 79 channels across the unlicensed ISM band (Industrial, Scientific, and Medical Band) between 2.4 and 2.48 GHz (IEEE 802.11 b/g operates in the same band). All Bluetooth devices in a piconet, hop across these channels using Frequency Hopping Spread Spectrum (FHSS), which provides robustness against noisy channels by quickly changing frequencies (about 1600 times per second) throughout the available frequency spectrum. Because of this, it is rare for more than one device to be transmitting on the same frequency at the same time.

Some of the key benefits of the Bluetooth technology include:

- Replacement of variety of cables to interconnect devices in close proximity.
- Low interference because of FHSS.
- Low power consumption that is crucial for mobile devices.
- An inexpensive technology to implement.
- Automatic nature of Bluetooth to initiate communication when two Bluetooth enabled devices comes in close proximity.
- Secure communications.
- Non-Line of Sight (NLOS) communication using Omni-directional antennas.

Because of its flexibility, Bluetooth is attractive and has been used in variety of applications including:

- Mobile phones
- Low bandwidth network applications
- Wireless keyboards, mice, and printers
- GPS receivers
- Bar code scanners
- Video games consoles
- Traffic control devices
- Medical equipments

Table 3. Bluetooth Classes

Class	Power Level	Approx. Range
Class 1	100 mW	100 meters
Class 2	2.5 mW	10 meters
Class 3	1 mW	1 meter

Bluetooth Versions

Bluetooth specifications were developed in 1994 and were formalized in 1998 by the Bluetooth Special Interest Group (SIG). To date this SIG has over 13,000 members worldwide.

The first official version of Bluetooth was v1.0A with major device interconnectivity issues. This was later resolved by v1.0B. Bluetooth v1.1 was ratified in IEEE standard 802.15.1-2002 and fixes many errors that were discovered in v1.0B. This version also adds support for non-encrypted channels as well as includes Received Signal Strength Indicator (RSSI) for controlling power in Bluetooth devices. A backward compatible Bluetooth v1.2 with major improvements including higher transmission speeds was introduced in 2003.

In 2004, Bluetooth v2.0 + EDR (Enhanced Data Rate) was released. This version was also backward compatible and offered a data rate of up to 3 Mbps. In 2007, the Bluetooth SIG adopted Bluetooth v2.1 + EDR as the core technology specification. This core version radically increases the strength of security by providing the protection against both active and passive eavesdropping attacks.

Bluetooth v3.0 + HS (High Speed) introduced Alternate MAC/PHY (AMP) to utilize IEEE 802.11 as a high speed transport whereas Bluetooth was used for connection negotiation and establishment purposes. This was adopted by the Bluetooth SIG in 2009 and supports theoretical data rates of up to 24 Mbps.

In 2010, Bluetooth SIG finalized the Bluetooth core specification version 4.0 that includes "clas-sic Bluetooth" to support legacy Bluetooth protocols, "Bluetooth High Speed" based on 802.11 and "Bluetooth low energy protocols" to support devices with a battery life of up to one year.

Classes Of Bluetooth Devices

The effective range of the Bluetooth devices depends on the level of obstacle, the sensitivity level, and the class of devices at both ends. The three classes of Bluetooth devices with their respective power level and approximate range are given in Table 3.

Bluetooth Protocol

Bluetooth makes use of a protocol stack to provide different services. The following paragraphs briefly discuss some of the core protocols:

- **Service Discovery Protocol (SDP):** Bluetooth devices are deployed in an ad-hoc manner. The piconet is dynamic in nature as existing devices may go out of range and new devices become available. As the name suggests the meaning, SDP is responsible for keeping track of services provided by other devices within operating range.
- **Link Managing Protocol (LMP):** LMP is responsible for performing all the operations associated with managing link including discovery, paging, and pairing. Every Bluetooth device contains a Link Manager Unit (LMU) that keeps track of connected devices. These LMUs communicate via LMP.
- **Logical Link Control & Application Protocol (L2CAP):** L2CAP is responsible for providing connection-oriented and connectionless data services to upper layer protocols.
- **Radio Frequency Communication (RFCOMM):** RFCOMM is a cable re-

placement protocol and provides emulated serial ports. A Bluetooth device can create up to 60 simultaneous RFCOMM channels with other devices.

- **Telephony Control Protocol (TCS):** TCS provides functionality to control telephony related voice and data applications.
- **Object Exchange Protocol (OBEX):** OBEX is a session layer protocol that provides mechanism for the exchange of binary data objects. FTP commands like PUT, GET, or ABORT exists for easy file transfer.

Bluetooth Profiles

Bluetooth profiles provide definitions of possible applications and specification of general behaviors of devices. Bluetooth devices communicate via the profiles. For example, the File Transfer profile (FTP) describes how a Bluetooth enabled PDA transfers files to another Bluetooth enabled PDA, cell phone, or computer. The Hands-Free Profile (HFP) describes how a gateway device can be used to place and receive calls for a hand-free device. Bluetooth specification includes support for over two dozen profiles to support both voice and data.

Below, we list two Bluetooth profiles that are very interesting from the security perspective:

1. **OBEX Object Push Profile (OPP):** This profile provides support for exchange of binary objects. Typically, no authorization procedure is performed before the OPP transactions. An example scenario would be the exchange of a contact or an appointment between two mobile phones, or a mobile phone and a PC.
2. **Synchronization Profile (SYNCH):** This profile facilitates the exchange of Personal Information Manager (PIM) data between Bluetooth enabled devices. PIM includes private data like address book, and calendar, etc.

Bluetooth Device Pairing And Modes

Two devices need to be paired to communicate with each other. When two Bluetooth devices come into close proximity, they negotiate and agree upon a common set of communication parameters. The devices are said to be paired once connected to each other. The pairing process requires an exchange of a pre-shared passkey (password) between two communicating devices.

A Bluetooth device that is in *discoverable mode* is visible to any other Bluetooth device in close proximity. These discoverable Bluetooth devices responds to any inquiry scan by transmitting their name, class, list of provided services, and other technical information including local clock. On the other hand a device that is in *connectable mode* responds to any requests to initiate a network connection.

Bluetooth has done an excellent job interlinking devices wirelessly, but just like any other wireless technology, Bluetooth suffers from many security issues. In the following paragraphs we will discuss the security features of Bluetooth followed by the discussion of associated threats and vulnerabilities.

Bluetooth Security Overview

Being a wireless technology, Bluetooth communications are also subjected to deliberate jamming, interception and injection of signals. To provide protection, security can be established at various levels. Bluetooth provides built-in security measures at the link (device) and service level. The Bluetooth standard also provides the three basic security services listed below:

1. **Device Authentication:** Bluetooth devices perform authentication using a challenge-response based mechanism to verify their identities. This verification process is based on the knowledge of a secret key known as the Bluetooth link key. Both one-way and

mutual authentications are provided in the standard.

2. **Data Confidentiality:** A stream cipher based encryption, where the encryption key is derived from the link key, is used to encode the payload of the packets being exchanged between the two Bluetooth devices to ensure that eavesdropper cannot read the contents. Three encryption modes are defined:

   a. **Mode 1:** where no traffic is encrypted at all.

   b. **Mode 2:** Encryption is only performed on unicast (one-to-one) based traffic but not on broadcasts (one-to-many).

   c. **Mode 3:** Encryption is performed on all traffic.

3. **Service Authorization:** Service Authorization is used to ensure that a Bluetooth device has necessary permissions and privileges to access resources residing on other Bluetooth devices. For a device to be able to access services on the other device, three levels of service security and two levels of trust are defined in the Bluetooth standard as follows:

Levels of Trust:

a. **Trusted Device:** Trusted devices have established relationships with other Bluetooth devices. They have full access to all services and can exchange information without asking permission.

b. **Untrusted Device:** Untrusted devices have no fixed relationship with other Bluetooth devices. They have restricted access to services. When an untrusted Bluetooth device attempts to initiate a connection with another Bluetooth device, the user will be automatically prompted with the option of allowing or denying the connection.

Service Security Levels:

a. **Service Level 1:** Prior to accessing services, device requires both authentication and authorization. For untrusted devices, manual authorization is required.

b. **Service Level 2:** Authenticated Bluetooth devices access services without authorization.

c. **Service Level 3:** Devices access services without performing authentication and authorization.

The basic security configuration for a Bluetooth device in terms of its discoverability and connectability is done by the user, who can configure it as follows:

a. *Non-Discoverable and Non-connectable*

b. *Non-Discoverable but Connectable only if device is known to master*

c. *Discoverable and Connectable*

There are four different security modes that a Bluetooth device can implement. The first three apply to legacy versions, whereas the fourth applies to the current version. As per the Bluetooth specifications, each device must operate in of these four modes. These modes are described below:

1. **Security Mode 1:** This is the non-secure mode as none of the security measures (Authentication or Encryption) are employed and any Bluetooth device can establish communication with a device operating in this mode. This mode is only available in any Bluetooth devices prior to Bluetooth v2.1 + EDR.

2. **Security Mode 2:** This security mode is enforced at the service level only for individual services such as FTP, or synchronization. This mode, at the device level, is no different than security mode 1. Security procedure like authentication, authorization, and optional encryption are initiated after LMP link is

established but before the establishment of L2CAP channel. Applications are responsible to implement the needed procedures.

3. **Security Mode 3:** In this mode, security at the link is enforced before a Bluetooth device fully establishes a physical link. Mandatory authentication and encryption for all connections between the two devices is enforced. These security features are based on a shared link key that is required by each device. Most of the security procedures are implemented on the device independent of the applications.

4. **Security Mode 4:** This security mode is also enforced at the service level where security is setup after link establishment. Only Bluetooth devices using Secure Simple Pairing (SSP) can use this security mode.

SSP simplifies the overall pairing process by providing different association models that depends on device's I/O capabilities. Improved security is also provided through the use of public key cryptography to protect against active and passive eavesdropping. The four association models are briefly described below:

a. **Numeric Comparison:** This association model is used with Bluetooth devices that are capable of displaying a six-digit number along with a Yes/No response that a user can choose. During the pairing process, a six-digit number is displayed to the user, on both devices. Pairing is successful if the user press "yes" on both devices after matching the numbers, otherwise the pairing fails. The important distinction between these six-digit numbers and the legacy PINs is that the former is not used to generate any link and encryption keys. An eavesdropping attack on any of these devices would not be helpful in determining the link or encryption keys.

b. **PassKey Entry:** This association model was designed for scenarios where one Bluetooth device has input capability (like keyboards) while the other has only output (with display) capability. Pairing is successful when the device with display shows a six-digit number that the user enters on the device with input capability.

c. **Just Works:** This association model was designed for Bluetooth enabled devices like headset that doesn't offer any I/O capabilities. In this scenario, the user is required to accept the connection without visually verifying the authenticity of the numerical code.

d. **Out Of Band (OOB):** As the name suggests the meaning, this association model was designed to provide support for devices that use wireless technology other than Bluetooth.

Bluetooth Threat Analysis

By design Bluetooth is a peer-to-peer technology and typically lacks centralized security enforcement infrastructure. And due to its complex specifications and support for multiple voice and data profiles, Bluetooth is susceptible to a different set of security vulnerabilities and threats against those vulnerabilities. It poses great security risk especially for non-technical people who have little or no background of Bluetooth technology and its security. Some of the common weaknesses are described below:

• Because omnidirectional antennas are used in Bluetooth devices, presence of an eavesdropper is unlikely to be detected. On top of that the attacker and the attacking equipment could be very far away from the target Bluetooth devices. Additionally, if the payload of the Bluetooth packet is sent unencrypted, all contents and other relevant information can be captured using a laptop and a Bluetooth protocol analyzer. Even if encryption is used, Bluetooth packet header is always sent unencrypted that can reveal piconet address of the active slave and other useful information.

- The encryption mechanism that Bluetooth devices use has many strengths but the major issue arises when the devices are not able to use encryption key with the maximum available length. This happens during negotiation process between two Bluetooth devices, possibly running different versions, when the length of the encryption key is restricted by the device that has the shorter encryption key length. For example, if one Bluetooth device supports 128 bit key encryption and the other can support only a 32 bit, the negotiated key length would be 32 bit. It is important to mention that as per Bluetooth specification, devices are allowed to negotiate the smallest available size of encryption key—one byte. Unfortunately, many different kinds of Bluetooth devices like keyboards and headsets are manufactured often with a four digit fixed PIN code that is clearly a big security risk.

- Up until Bluetooth version 2.0 + EDR, usage of short PINs was allowed. These weak PINs, which can be easily guessed, were then used to generate link and encryption keys making the entire Bluetooth devices vulnerable.

- As, it was mentioned previously, the "Just Works" association model of Bluetooth security mode 4 has a significant weakness where the user is simply asked to accept the connection without verification. This model clearly provides no protection against the MITM attacks.

- Other vulnerabilities include lack of user authentication (as opposed to device authentication), end-to-end security, and some other security services like audit and non-repudiation.

Threats Against Bluetooth

Since Bluetooth is a wireless technology, all the threats that are associated with general wireless networking, are also applicable to it, including attacks against the confidentiality, integrity and availability of resources. Powerful directional antennas can be used to increase the range of attack of almost any kind of Bluetooth attack. For example, the Bluetooth Sniper Rifle can be used to conduct eavesdropping and attack over a mile away from the target devices.

Nowadays it is quite easy to convert a standard Bluetooth dongle, based on Cambridge Silicon Radio (CSR) based chipset, into a complete Bluetooth sniffer. Tools are readily available to write custom firmware to access raw packets exchanged between the Bluetooth devices.

In the following paragraphs we will discuss the different types of attacks on Bluetooth enabled devices. Most of these attacks fall into one of the above classes of threats.

1. **BlueSnarfing:**

   BlueSnarfing attack (also referred as BlueStumbling attack) enables attacker to covertly gain access to your Bluetooth enabled devices to access sensitive information such as phonebook, calendar notes, text messages, and even the device's International Mobile Equipment Identity (IMEI) that the attacker could use to effectively route all incoming calls from a target device to his/her mobile device. No pairing and no authentication/authorization are required to accomplish this attack.

   The attack is possible in older devices (or devices that are running with outdated firmware) due to weak implementation of the Bluetooth protocol stack, especially the implementation of OBEX that is generally used by the OPP and SYNCH profiles. Instead of using the OPP (push profile), the attacker uses a PULL profile and successfully executes GET requests against known filenames like telecom/pb.vcf (phonebook) or telecom/cal.vcs (calendar). This attack requires a device to be in discoverable mode.

BlueSnarf++ is an enhancement of the original BlueSnarf attack, where the attacker connects to OBEX FTP server.

A Google search can be used to find a list of devices that are vulnerable to BlueSnarf attack.

2. BlueBugging:

BlueBugging is the term given to the act of hacking into a Bluetooth device and using that device's command to:

- Eavesdrop on phone conversations
- Place phone calls from the user's device
- Read and write phonebook entries
- Send, receive, and delete text message from the user's device
- Connect to the Internet
- Set call forwards

BlueBugging exploits a security flaw in the firmware of some older devices to issue AT (ASCII Terminal) commands by connecting to RFCOMM channel 17 that provides an open backdoor to AT-parser service without any authentication. This attack requires the knowledge of BD_ADDR of the target device.

A Google search can reveal a list of devices that are vulnerable to BlueBugging attack.

3. BlueJacking:

BlueJacking is the act of sending unsolicited messages to a Bluetooth enabled mobile devices to entice the user of that device to respond in some fashion. These unsolicited messages that are sent via OBEX do not do any harm in terms of breaking into another device and/or stealing private information. "You are BlueJacked!" is an example of such message. Users who are not aware of this might think that their mobile phone is infected with a mobile phone virus or their phone has malfunctioned.

Current form of BlueJacking involves sending images and sounds as well.

4. HeloMoto:

HeloMoto exploits a flawed implementation of "trusted devices" is some Motorola mobile phones and carried out a combination of BlueSnarfing and BlueBugging attacks. This attack exploits the OPP to create an entry in the user's trusted device list.

5. BlueSmacking:

BlueSmacking is a DoS attack that is carried out by sending an L2CAP echo request (ping) with a large payload to a target Bluetooth device. This causes a buffer overflow and an immediate shutdown of the target device.

6. BlueSpooofing:

BlueSpooofing is an attack where a trusted device is cloned, encryption disabled and re-pairing is forced upon the target device.

7. BlueTooone:

Bluetooone method is used to enhance the range of a standard Bluetooth dongle by attaching a directional antenna (Yagi) for long distance attack.

A Google search can reveal a step by step process to perfrom BlueToooning.

8. BluePrinting:

A BluePrinting is a type of surveillance method that can be used to fingerprint a target Bluetooth device by obtaining information such as manufacturer, device model and firmware version. This attack requires the knowledge of BD_ADDR of the target device.

9. Blueper:

Blueper is a DoS attack designed to flood certain mobile devices with file transfer requests causing devices to crash or become unresponsive.

10. Blooover:

The term Blooover is derived from Bluetooth Hoover as this Java based application runs on handheld devices with Symbian OS, and sucks information. This tool is capable of causing BlueBugging attack. Blooover and Blooover II were released as a set of auditing tools to discover BlueBugging, BlueSnarfing, and HeloMoto based vulnerabilities. Once again the knowledge of the target's BD_ADDR is required.

11. Car Whisperer:

The Car Whisperer is a tool that exploits vulnerability in implementing hands-free Bluetooth enabled kits for automobiles. This tool uses default PIN codes to connect to these vulnerable car kits and injects and records audio.

12. Fuzzing Attacks:

These attacks involve observing how Bluetooth enabled devices react when some malformed or non-standard packets are sent to them. These attacks are commonly used to detect vulnerabilities in the protocol stack.

13. War-nibbling:

War-nibbling is a type of surveillance method that provides location tracking for Bluetooth enabled devices.

14. BlueFish:

BlueFish is a type of enhanced surveillance where after detecting the target device, it records its information and takes a picture in the suspected

direction of the device. This attack is used to track the location of Bluetooth devices and include times and places with associated pictures of the device presence.

15. BlueBump:

Due to the weakness in handling the Bluetooth link keys, this attack enable the devices to access services even after they become unauthorized to access them.

16. BlueChop:

This attack is a DoS attack against the piconet. This attack is possible if the master device in the piconet supports multiple connections.

17. BlueDump:

As the name suggests the meaning, this attack is used to make a Bluetooth device dumps its link key. The link key can be later used in pairing process with the attacker device.

18. Bluetooth Sniffing:

Commercial tools (e.g. FTS4BT from Frontline) are available to sniff, log, and analyze Bluetooth data.

19. Bluetooth Malware:

Certain Bluetooth enabled cell phones running Symbian operating system (OS) can be infected with worms that can propagate through Bluetooth communications. Caribe and CommWarrior are two examples of such worms that can infect these cell phones.

20. Attack Against The PIN And The Pairing Process:

This attack focuses on exploiting the Bluetooth security architecture itself rather than attacking the insecure Bluetooth protocol stack implementations. In this attack, an attempt to sniff the initialization key is made during the pairing process. This initialization key can be used to obtain the Bluetooth PIN using some brute-force techniques. BTCrack and btpincrack are two such tools that can be employed to crack the PIN.

SECURITY COUNTERMEASURES AGAINST BLUETOOTH THREATS

Bluetooth is a great technology with many useful applications. At the same time, variety of Bluetooth hacking tools and techniques are available, which makes it a little riskier to use this technology. Bluetooth is not going to go away because of a few security flaws; instead it can be secure if configured properly and used carefully with a proper understanding of this wonderful technology. In the following paragraphs we will discuss some of the best practices to mitigate threats against the Bluetooth technology.

1.   User Awareness:

The weakest link in the context of information security is the end user. No matter how big of a security arsenal anyone has, a simple mistake (clicking a phishing link) can render it completely ineffective. This is where the user awareness comes into play.

It is important that the user should have adequate level of knowledge and understanding regarding the secure use of Bluetooth. A simple rule of thumb is "If you are not sure what to do, don't do it".

2.   Disable Device When Not In Use:

In many cases, Bluetooth is typically used to interconnect devices for short duration. The best defense to minimize exposure to potential malicious activities is to keep Bluetooth devices disabled when not in use. Or enable it only when needed and disable it immediately after the completion of the intended operation.

3.   Disable Unused Services & Profiles:

Many Bluetooth devices equip their user with the capability to enable or disable profiles and associated services on-demand. Once again, this feature can be used to minimize the surface area for attack. For example, the file transfer service can be disabled if not needed.

4.   Discoverable Mode:

A Bluetooth device must be in discoverable mode for initial pairing process. Once these devices are paired, they will be able to find each other without being explicitly in discoverable mode. Bluetooth devices in non-discoverable mode are not publicly visible to other devices in range and hence are not an easy prey for attackers.

5.   Device Names:

Most Bluetooth devices by default use self-identifying names during pairing process (while the device is in discoverable mode). These names should be changed to non-default, unidentifiable names that don't identify a device type and its manufacturer.

6.   Security Mode:

If possible, use Security Mode 3 or 4. Recall that Security Mode 3 provides link-level security before the link is established between the two devices. Furthermore, avoid using the "Just Works" association model for Security Mode 4 as the devices can connect without any authentication which leads to the possibility of MITM attacks.

7. PIN Usage:

If possible, use non-guessable PIN codes comprise of at least 12 or more alphanumeric characters. Longer PIN helps prevent brute-force attack to guess password. Furthermore, it is not advisable to use any static and weak PINs ('0000' is an example of a weak PIN).

Authentication between Bluetooth devices occurs only once during the pairing process after which the authenticated device is included in the list of trusted devices. It is advisable to change the PINs on a semi-frequent basis to avoid a scenario where a previously trusted device (a friend's cellphone) tries to regain access without user notification.

8. Perform Infrequent Pairing:

Perform pairing when absolutely required using long, randomly generated passkeys. Avoid public places (such as malls or airports) to perform this procedure. Never enter passkeys when unexpectedly prompted for them.

9. Untrusted Pairing:

Unsolicited pairing request or unsolicited message requesting a PIN is possible if the Bluetooth device is in discoverable mode. In no circumstances, accept these requests from unknown or untrusted devices unless you are certain that the request is coming from a known or trusted device. Remember, once paired, the untrusted device has access to all Bluetooth services that are enabled on the local device.

Furthermore, Bluetooth users should not accept any kind of untrusted transmissions containing messages, files, and images.

10. UnPair If Device Is Missing:

It is important that physical control of devices should be maintained at all time. If a Bluetooth device is stolen or lost, immediately delete the pairing of the missing device from all other Bluetooth devices with which the missing device was previously paired.

11. Power Levels:

Bluetooth devices form WPAN. The term 'Personal' in WPAN suggests that Bluetooth devices connect to other devices in closed range. There is no need for Bluetooth devices to offer extended ranges as there are other technologies (like Wi-Fi) available to do that.

From the security perspective it is important that the Bluetooth devices create a secure range of access to authorized users only. This is done by adjusting these devices to the least possible and sufficient power level. Furthermore, try to avoid using Class 1 devices as they offer extended range of approximately 100 meters with a power level of 100mW.

12. Encryption:

In order to avoid possible eavesdropping and capture of cleartext data, enable link encryption during any kind of Bluetooth transmission. If possible, use encryption mode 3 but in no circumstance use encryption mode 1.

13. Authentication:

In order to make sure that you are talking to the legitimate device and not to a malicious one, perform mutual authentication for all type of access.

14. Install a Complete Security Solution:

This is a general security guideline and must be followed regardless of the technology. At the very least, any Bluetooth enabled device with a host operating system, must install an antivirus solution to protect from malwares that specifically target the Bluetooth devices.

15.   Patching & Upgrade:

Once again, this is a general security guideline. All Bluetooth enabled devices with a host operating system, must be patched and upgraded to the latest firmware to prevent attackers from exploiting vulnerabilities.

CONCLUSION

Wireless networking is one technology that has seen exponential growth and rapid adoption over the past few years due to many benefits it offers such as portability, mobility, and flexibility, increased user's productivity, and lower installation costs.

With this growing prevalence, both at home and the workplace, security considerations must be assessed and understood in order to manage inherent risks in wireless technology. Wireless technologies have many security issues that must be addressed. Perhaps the most significant security risk is the usage of airwaves as its underlying communication medium.

This chapter discussed the security issues in two key areas of wireless technologies and presented with some best practices and countermeasures to use these technologies safely and securely. Many institutions have published best practices and recommendations for managing risks associated with these wireless technologies. We recommended that organizations and individuals educate themselves as best possible in order to develop a risk management strategy that best suits their environment.

REFERENCES

Barken, L. (2004). *How Secure is your Wireless Network? Safeguarding Your Wi-Fi LAN*. New York: Prentice Hall.

Bicakci, K., & Tavli, B. (2009). Denial-of-Service attacks and countermeasures in IEEE 802.11 wireless networks. *Computer Standards & Interfaces*, 931–941. doi:10.1016/j.csi.2008.09.038

Bittau, A., Handley, M., & Lackey, J. (2006). The final nail in WEP's coffin. *IEEE Symposium on Security and Privacy, SP '06.*

Borisov, N., Goldberg, I., & Wagner, D. (2001). Intercepting Mobile Communications: The Insecurity of 802.11. *Proceedings Seventh Annual International Conference on Mobile Computing And Networking*, 180-189.

Cache, J., Wright, J., & Lu, V. (2010). *Hacking Exposed: Wireless Security Secrets and Solutions* (2nd ed.). New York: McGraw-Hill/Osborne.

Edney, J., & Arbaugh, W. (2004). *Real 802.11 Security: Wi-Fi Protected Access and 802.11i*. Reading, MA: Addison-Wesley.

Frankel, S.,Eydt, B., Owens, L., & Scarfone, K. (2007). *Establishing Wireless Robust Security Networks: A Guide to IEEE 802.11i*. NIST SP 800-97.

FTS4BT: Bluetooth Protocol Analyzer and Packet Sniffer. (n.d.). Retrieved from http://www.fte.com

Gehrmann, C., Persson, J., & Smeets, B. (2004). *Bluetooth Security*. Artech House.

Haataja, K., & Hypponen, K. (2008). Man-in-the-Middle Attacks on Bluetooth: A comprehensive Analysis, a Novel Attack, and Countermeasures. *Proc. 3rd Int'l Symposium, Communications, Control, and Signal Processing*, 1096-1102, IEEE Press.

Hager, S., & Midkiff, C. (2203). Demonstrating Vulnerabilities in Bluetooth Security. *Proc. IEEE Global Telecommunication Conferecne*, (3), 1420-1424. Washington, D.C: IEEE Press.

How 802.11 Wireless Works. (2003). Retrieved from Microsoft Technet website http://technet.microsoft.com/en-us/library/cc757419(WS.10).asp

Laurie, A., Holtmann, M., & Herfurt, M. (2004). Hacking Bluetooth enabled mobile phones and beyond - Full Disclosure. *21st Chaos Communication Congress*, Germany. *LeCroy—Protocol Solutions Group*. (n.d.). Retrieved from http://www.lecroy.com

L.M.S.C of the IEEE Computer Society.(2007). *Wireless LAN Medium access control (MAC) and physical layer (PHY) specifications,* technical report, IEEE Standard 802.11, 2007 revision.

Morrow, R. (2002). *Bluetooth Implementation and Use*. New York: McGraw-Hill Professional.

Potter, B. (2003). Wireless Security Future. *IEEE Security and Privacy*, 1(4), 68–72. doi:10.1109/MSECP.2003.1219074

Potter, B., & Fleck, B. (2003). *802.11 Securit.* O'Reilly.

Scarfone, K., Dicoi, D., Sexton, M., & Tibbs, C. (2008). *Guide to Securing Legacy IEEE 802.11 Wireless Networks* (revision 1). NIST SP 800-48.

Scarfone, K., & Padgette, J. (2008). *Guide to Bluetooth Security.* NIST SP 800-121.

Shaked, Y., & Wool, A. (2005). Cracking the Bluetooth Pin. *Proc. 3rd Int'l Conf. Mobile Systems, Applications, and Services*, 39-50. New York: ACM Press.

Tews, E., & Beck, M. (2009). Practical attacks against WEP and WPA. *Proceedings of the Second ACM Conference on Wireless Network Security*, 79-86.

Tews, E., Weinmann, R., & Pyshkin, A. (2007). Breaking 104 bit wep in less than 60 seconds. *WISA*, (4867) 188-202. New York: Springer.

The Bluetooth Special Interest Group (SIG). Retrieved from http://www.bluetooth.org

The trifinite group (2007). Retrieved from http://www.trifinite.org.

The Wi-Fi Alliance. (n.d.). Retrieved from http://www.wi-fi.org.

Vacca, J. (2006). *Guide to Wireless Network Security* (1st ed.). New York: Springer.

Welch, D., & Lathrop, S. (2003). Wireless Security Threat Taxonomy. *Proceedings of the 2003 IEEE workshop on information assurance*, 76-83.

WPA-PSK Rainbow tables. (n.d.). Retrieved from http://www.renderlab.net/projects/WPA-tables/.

KEY TERMS AND DEFINITIONS

Bluetooth Pairing: The negotiation process between two Bluetooth enabled devices to successfully establish communication between them.

Bluetooth Profiles: Bluetooth devices communicate via the profiles, which provide definitions of possible applications and specification of general behaviors of these devices.

Bluetooth: Bluetooth is a low-cost, low-power, short-range wireless technology that creates wireless networks on the fly, interconnecting various personal devices in close range.

CIA Triad: An Acronym that is used to denote the three basic principles of security: Confidentiality, Integrity, and Availability.

Piconet: An ad-hoc wireless network that is created using Bluetooth. The interconnection between a Bluetooth enabled cell-phone and a Bluetooth enabled earpiece is a classical example of a piconet.

Rainbow Tables: Rainbow tables for WPA offer time-memory trade-off by providing a precomputed list of hashes for a range of possible passphrases, significantly improving the brute forcing process.

WarXing: The term *WarXing* is commonly used to refer to activities to detect publically accessible computer systems and wireless networks. The letter "X" represents a more specific detecting activity. For example: WarDriving or WarStrolling.

WEP/WPA/WPA2: Wired Equivalent Privacy and Wi-Fi Protected Access are mechanisms that provide different security services for the wireless local area connection network.

Wi-Fi: A trade name that is given to IEEE 802.11 wireless local area network standard.

Section 2
Security Technologies

Chapter 3
Analysis, Development and Deployment of Statistical Anomaly Detection Techniques for Real E-Mail Traffic

Gianluca Papaleo
Istituto di Elettronica e di Ingegneria dell'Informazione e delle Telecomunicazioni, Italy
& Consiglio Nazionale delle Ricerche, Italy

Davide Chiarella
Istituto di Elettronica e di Ingegneria dell'Informazione e delle Telecomunicazioni, Italy
& Consiglio Nazionale delle Ricerche, Italy

Maurizio Aiello
Istituto di Elettronica e di Ingegneria dell'Informazione e delle Telecomunicazioni, Italy
& Consiglio Nazionale delle Ricerche, Italy

Luca Caviglione
Istituto di Studi sui Sistemi Intelligenti per l'Automazione, Italy
& Consiglio Nazionale delle Ricerche, Italy

ABSTRACT

Even if new interaction paradigms, such as the Voice over IP (VoIP), are becoming popular and widely adopted, the e-mail is still one of the most utilized ways to communicate across the Internet. However, many malicious threats are conveyed via e-mails. Usually, the authors can exploit two different approaches: i) analyzing the logs produced by e-mail servers or ii) reconstruct the e-mail flows by capturing data directly from the network by placing ad-hoc probes. In this vein, this Chapter discusses the analysis, development and deployment of statistical detection techniques aimed at the detection of Internet worms. For what concerns i), they introduce a tool called Log Mail Analyzer (LMA), which allows to overcome the complexity of inspecting multiple logs created from a heterogeneous population of mail servers. In the perspective of ii) they briefly discuss an alternative solution, based on ad-hoc network probes, to be properly placed to collect traffic and then reconstruct the e-mail flow to be monitored. Lastly, the authors introduce a threshold mechanism, based on a simple statistical framework, to automatically detect and identify different worm activities.

DOI: 10.4018/978-1-61350-507-6.ch003

INTRODUCTION

Despite new interaction paradigms, such as the Voice over IP (VoIP), are becoming popular and largely adopted, the electronic mail (e-mail) is still one of the most preferred method to communicate across the Internet. Also it is available for a variety of mobile devices, ranging from Personal Data Assistants (PDAs) to regular gaming consoles, as well as many network appliances. In addition, e-mail is constantly used also while on the road, for instance from cellular phones. As a matter of fact, ad-hoc mechanisms to handle e-mail traffic over the cellular network, such as the push e-mail, dramatically increase its usage and popularity among power users and businessmen.

Anyway, due to its ubiquitous adoption, the e-mail is one of the most used vector to spread malicious programs like viruses and *worms*. This is mainly due to the superimposition of the following reasons: *i*) e-mails can carry attachments, thus allowing malicious software to easily propagate through the Internet without the need of developing specific communication mechanisms to spread the infection. Besides, e-mail traffic, even if filtered, is commonly allowed in the majority of network deployments, or loosely regulated, as conversely happens for peer-to-peer (p2p) file-sharing applications; *ii*) e-mails can be retrieved, organized and sent through dedicated client-interfaces, which are often affected by several security breaches. Thus, they account for infecting the hosting machine and to spread the malicious entity through an automated and hidden e-mail flow; *iii*) an e-mail account is generally required to join modern social-oriented services, e.g., social networks. Therefore, it is possible to collect in a simple manner a huge amount of addresses and personal information, e.g., usernames and passwords. Such stolen accounts are often used to send malicious contents. Furthermore, the increasing diffusion of Web 2.0 applications rises the usage of malicious code within web pages composing the service itself. We cite, among the others, menaces such as the Cross-Site Scripting (XSS) and the Cross-Site Request Forgery (CSRF or XSRF) that can be injected within the Asynchronous Javascript and XML (AJAX) powered contents. Nevertheless, the e-mail infrastructure can be infected from completely different services too. As an example, malicious software can be retrieved from file-sharing networks (Caviglione, 2009). Then, if executed it can attach to the client-interface devoted to manage e-mails as to "hijack" the network infrastructure running the e-mail delivery service. Yet, file-sharing client-interfaces can have built-in malware code in order to spawn *botnets*. Even if they are usually adopted for cycle-stealing software, botnets can also use the e-mail traffic of hosted machines to spread the infection or to produce unsolicited e-mails, e.g., spam messages. Lastly, e-mails are also plagued by other hazards, such as phishing. Even if they are relevant problems, both in terms of traffic and waste of resources, investigations devoted to recognize and prevent such issues are out of the scope of this Chapter. Conversely, it focuses on a statistical framework for the detection of *worms*.

The Literature shows two main approaches to perform worm detection: *misuse* based and *anomaly* based. The first one employs the signature concept, while the second one tries to create a model to characterize users' normal behaviors. Misuse detection lacks the ability of identifying the presence of worms not fitting a pre-defined signature. Conversely, in anomaly detection the system defines an expected network performance and, if there are significant deviations from the given profile, spawns an alarm. Despite the particular techniques, the needed conceptual steps to effectively recognize and take subsequent actions to detect anomalies within e-mail traffic are: *i*) performing monitoring actions by gathering information about the observed e-mail flow and *ii*) investigating the collected data by using some criteria to reveal anomalies (possibly in an automatic way).

In this perspective, in this Chapter we present new techniques to detect worms spreading through the Internet. For what concerns i), we introduce two different approaches. Firstly, we showcase a tool called Log Mail Analyzer (LMA), which allows to overcome the complexity of analyzing multiple logs created from a heterogeneous population of mail servers. Additionally, we briefly discuss an alternative solution, based on ad-hoc network probes, to be properly placed to collect traffic and then reconstruct the e-mail transactions to be monitored. As it will be explained in the rest of the Chapter, the two approaches enable the data collection phase to be done *off-line* and *on-line*, respectively. Nevertheless, as of today, there are many studies and proposals of Anomaly Detection Techniques (ADT), especially in the field of worms and virus detection. Then, owing to the availability of collected data, we showcase a novel statistical *threshold method*, to identify various worm activities. The latter uses a statistical evaluation of ISO/OSI L7 parameters (e.g., the number of sent e-mails in a well-defined time period, or specific patterns observable from a small set of protocol messages). The approach is based on the assumption that an *indirect worm* (i.e., a worm traveling within e-mails) needs to spread quickly. To do so, it sends a relevant amount of e-mails in a short timeframe, thus resulting in many concurrent anomalous behaviors.

We point out that, this Chapter summarizes the experience of the Authors in analyzing e-mail traffic in *real* deployments, rather than developing heuristics tested on *synthetic* data. Some concepts and numerical results have been partially borrowed from (Aiello, Avanzini, Chiarella, Papaleo, 2006a), (Aiello, Avanzini, Chiarella, Papaleo, 2006b), (Aiello, Avanzini, Chiarella, Papaleo, 2007), (Aiello, Chiarella, Papaleo, 2008) and (Aiello, Chiarella, Papaleo, 2009). Interested readers can also investigate such papers (and, the references therein) to gain more knowledge on desired aspects. Summing up, the contribution of the Chapter is twofold. On one hand it is in the field of e-mails data processing and acquisition. On the other hand it introduces a novel and simple statistical framework to perform anomaly detection.

The remainder of the Chapter is structured as follows: Section II presents the related work in the field of the analysis of e-mail traffic, as well as the state-of-the-art in worm detection. Section III showcases a novel tool specifically developed to process and collect information about e-mail traffic, and briefly investigates a probe-based mechanism. Then, Section IV discusses the threshold-based mechanism to detect worm activities within the overall e-mail load, and, lastly, Section V concludes the Chapter.

RELATED WORK

The server-centric nature of the e-mail infrastructure enables to easily gather and retrieve information about its status. In fact, servers can be configured to maintain a detailed trace of the performed operations on one or more files; such file(s) is called *log(s)*. By collecting and inspecting logs is then practical to evaluate the "health" of the e-mail service infrastructure, according to a variety of performance metrics. For instance, it is possible to control if a given portion of the service is up and running or what is the degree of Quality of Service (QoS) guaranteed to users or customers. It is important to stress that a plethora of different events can be logged. Among the others we recall here: system calls, transactions of any kind, network usage, erratic behaviors, CPU workload, and users' accesses to resources. As consequence, the operation of understanding logs to reveal interesting patterns is called Log File Analysis (LFA), and it has been extensively investigated both in theory and practice, for instance in reference (Andrews & Zhang, 2000). Also, in reference (Andrews, 1998) a discussion on how LFA could be used for generic testing purposes of particular applications is available. Moreover this approach can be also performed to clarify requirements when designing the software itself.

Owing to the rich set of information that can be logged, LFA is also proficiently used for security purposes. The framework developed in reference (Tongshen, Qingzhang & Kezhen, 2004) enables the analysis of logs produced by a firewall appliance. Put briefly, each record is classified, parsed in detail, and stored in a database for subsequent data mining operations. An interesting characteristic of the proposed system is the capacity of generating a "response", e.g., to enable filtering operations on hosts responsible of attacks. For what concerns LFA for web-services, which are both very promising and popular paradigms to access remote resources (even the classical e-mail), reference (Stearley, 2004) portraits some preliminary ideas, while references (Takada & Koide, 2002) and (Koch, Ard & Golub, 2004) showcase solutions to properly investigate and visualize the amount of collected data. All the presented tools are intended as "general purpose", i.e., aimed at digging into several heterogeneous sets of data. In this perspective, the Log Mail Analyzer (LMA), which will be discussed in a deep detail later, represents an ad hoc solution developed and tweaked for investigating logs produced by e-mail related traffic.

Notwithstanding, it is also feasible to monitor the e-mail flow (and, as a consequence, to detect anomalies or specific issues affecting the overall service) by using classical network analysis tools. Rather than inspecting the logs of mail servers, is then possible to directly collect network traffic as already happens for many other monitoring purposes (e.g., to recognize remote attacks like port scanning or early detection of Denial of Services). But, such approach has some limits, e.g., it has scalability issues. Anyway, this can still be useful for the scopes of our work, since it allows to easily perform monitoring, and consequently, statistical anomaly detection in an *on-line* flavor. Providing a detailed analysis of tools for network monitoring is out of the scope of this work. However, since

we will present a solution for the monitoring of e-mails by collecting the related Protocol Data Unit (PDUs) from the network by deploying probes in critical points, reference (Caviglione, Aiello & Papaleo, 2010) (and references therein) extensively discusses the pros and cons of such frameworks.

For what concerns *worm detection*, as briefly introduced, the literature proposes two main approaches (Axelsson, 1998) and (Verwoerd & Hunt, 2002): misuse intrusion detection and anomaly intrusion detection. The first is based upon the signature concept, which is an accurate mechanism, but it lacks the ability of identifying the presence of intrusions that do not fit a pre-defined signature, resulting not adaptive (Ilgun, Kemmer & Porras, 1995) and (Kumar & Spafford, 1995). The second tries to create a model to characterize what is considered as a normal behavior. Basically, an expected network behavior is defined, and, if there are significant deviations in the short-term usage from the profile, an alarm is produced. This mechanism is adaptive, allowing to react to new threats, but it has a high rate of false positives (Denning, 1987), (Estevez-Tapiador, Garcia-Teodoro & Diaz-Verdejo, 2004), (Du, Wang & Pang, 2004) and (Wang & Abdel-Wahab, 2006).

For the sake of completeness, we give a quick description of the main intrusion detection methods used nowadays. A more exhaustive and complete survey is available in references (Chiarella, 2010) and (Garcia-Teodoro, Daz-Verdejo, Maci-Fernandez & Vazquez, 2009) while (Lauf, Peters & Robinson, 2010) offers a detailed analysis of such mechanisms in ad hoc environments.

In misuse detection, the intrusion detection decision relies on the knowledge of a model of the intrusive process, both in terms of specific attacks and system vulnerabilities. Then, we can define what constitutes legal or illegal behaviors, by performing a comparison. This technique tries to detect evidences of intrusive activities irrespective of the background traffic, i.e., any action that is not explicitly recognized as an attack is considered acceptable. As a consequence, a Misuse Intrusion Detection System (MIDS) has to operate no matter what is the normal behavior of the system. This places very strict demands on the model of the nature of the intrusion. The main advantages of this approach are: very low false alarm rates, and preventive or corrective actions can be performed easily. Conversely, the drawbacks include: the difficulty of gathering the required information on the known attacks, and updating the system to face new vulnerabilities and environments is non-negligible and time consuming. Moreover, the profile describing an attack is heavily influenced by a given technology (e.g., the operating system, software versions and platforms), resulting in a tool closely tied to a specific environment. In a more detailed fashion, MIDS can be divided into several categories and the most important are: *state-modeling*, *expert system*, *string matching* and *signature analysis*.

In *state-modeling* MIDS, the intrusion is encoded as a number of different states, representing time series models. According to the amount of states detected in the observation space, the system decided if the intrusion has taken place. In *expert system* MIDS, a set of rules describing attacks are employed. Audited events are then translated into "facts" carrying their semantic signification in the expert system, and the inference engine draws conclusions using both rules and "facts". *String matching* MIDS are based on a simple, often case sensitive, sub-string matching procedure of the characters in text that is transmitted between systems (or, arising from the use of the system itself). *Signature analysis* MIDS follows exactly the same knowledge-acquisition approach as expert systems, but the knowledge acquired is exploited in a different way. The semantic description of the attacks is transformed into information that can be found in the audit trail in a straightforward way, decreasing the semantic level required to describe an attack. This technique allows a very efficient implementation; therefore it is applied in many commercial intrusion detection products. All the

showcased techniques have the issue of needing frequent updates to keep up with the stream of new vulnerabilities discovered.

In *anomaly detection*, there is the hypothesis that *something that is abnormal is probably suspicious*. The construction of an anomaly detection system starts by forming an opinion on what constitutes normal for the observed subject, and then deciding the percentage of the activity to flag as abnormal, and how to make this particular decision. More precisely, behavior based intrusion detection techniques assume that an intrusion can be detected by observing a deviation from normal or expected behavior of the system or the users. The model of normal or valid behavior is extracted from reference information collected by various means. The intrusion-detection system later compares this model with the current activity. If a deviation is observed, an alarm is generated. Roughly, anything that does not correspond to a previously learned behavior is considered intrusive. The primary advantage of anomaly-based detection is the ability to detect novel attacks for which signatures have not been defined yet. Moreover, they are less dependent on operating system specific mechanisms. On the other hand, if the system is not well calibrated, high false positives rates may occur. In addition, a behavior can change over time, introducing the need for periodic on-line retraining of the reference profile, resulting either in the unavailability of the service or in additional false alarms. Anomaly Detection Systems (ADS) can be divided into two main classes: *self-learning* and *programmed*.

Self-learning systems learn by examples what constitutes the "normal status" for the installation. Typically, this is achieved by observing the traffic for an extended period of time, and then by building some models of the underlying process. Self-learning systems can be further classified into sub-classes. To name the most important, we mention: rule modelling, statistical-based and machine learning-based. The *rule modelling* ADS studies the traffic and formulates a set of rules describing the normal operations performed by a system. In *statistical-based* ADS the network traffic activity is captured and a profile, representing its stochastic behavior, is created. The earliest statistical approaches corresponded to univariate models, which modelled the parameters as independent Gaussian random variables, thus defining an acceptable range of values for every variable. Later, multivariate models considering the correlations between two or more metrics were proposed. Lastly, *machine learning* ADS are based on establishing an explicit or implicit model that enables the patterns analysed to be categorized. A well-defined characteristic of these schemes is the need for labelled data to train the behavioral model, which is a procedure that places severe demands on resources.

Before introducing some popular worm detection techniques, it is interesting to investigate which kind of threats spread via e-mail. Obviously, worms are the primary one, but also spam and viruses are relevant issues. Nowadays Internet users are flooded by a huge amount of infected e-mails. The majority of mass-mailing worms do employ a Simple Mail Transfer Protocol (SMTP) engine as the infection delivery mechanism (see, e.g., the *I Love You* worm). To give the idea of the magnitude of the problem, in January 2003 the infected population of the Slammer worm doubled in size every 8.5 seconds (Moore et al, 2003) with 90% of vulnerable hosts infected in just 10 minutes. In August 2003 the SoBig worm caused an estimated five billion dollars in damages, and at the peak of its infection, it was responsible for approximately the 73% of all Internet email traffic (Gaudin, 2003). In the same year Sober (known as, W32.Sober@mm) appeared and remained present with many variants until 2005 (among the others, the W32.Sober.L@mm). In late January 2004, the MyDoom worm became the fastest-spreading e-mail worm (Roberts, 2004). As regards recent years, we just mention the most famous: Nyxem (known as, W32.Blackmal.E@mm), Stration in

2006, and Storm Worm (also known as Trojan. Peacomm) in 2007.

Due to such variety of threats, nowadays worm detection has become a very active branch of research. Nevertheless, this highly impacts over big and small business company both in terms of costs and manpower. Researchers from the industrial and the academic worlds have proposed many ideas and solutions. To this aim, EMT (Li, Herkshop & Stolfo, 2004) is a data mining system, based on the clique theory (Bron & Kerbosh, 1973) that computes behavior models of user e-mail accounts. A misuse system is Honeycomb (Kreibich & Crowcroft, 2003), where attack signatures are automatically generated on a per-port basis. Roughly, it relies upon pattern matching techniques and honeypots (Dagon et al, 2004). Reference (Zou, Gao, Gong & Towsley, 2003) proposes to search for worm epidemic patterns by using Kalman filtering applied to illegitimate traffic (e.g., network scanning). They calculate the trend of traffic growth in order to compare it with an exponential epidemic model. As a drawback, this approach needs a relevant amount of hosts to be effective (in the order of magnitude of 2^{20}). Besides, it detects only direct worms, which are those not spreading by e-mails. Yet, if the worm diffusion is based on hit lists (i.e., lists of real hosts to attack) it is not detected by this approach. To cope with such issues, in Section IV a novel statistical anomaly detection technique for worms, which has been named *base-line* method, will be presented.

MONITORING OF E-MAIL TRAFFIC

In this Section we introduce two solutions developed to monitor the e-mail traffic, also in order to have enough data to be investigated via statistical methods to reveal worm activities. The first one deals with analyzing the logs produced by e-mail servers, while the second one relies on sniffing e-mail traffic directly from the network.

However, the core of this Section discusses the first approach, which is novel, while the second method has been introduced as a simple way to perform e-mail traffic analysis "live". In addition, we can use this approach as a possible benchmark.

The Log Mail Analyzer

As said, the most popular e-mail servers allow to log a rich set of events in a very simple manner. A log can be produced with the single-mail granularity, thus being very precise. At this level of detail, it is possible, for instance to recognize whether a single e-mail has been properly transmitted. However, the problem with this approach is that a log file is of difficult comprehension for at least two reasons. Firstly, a server under heavy loads can produce very burdened logs, and secondly a single transaction is commonly split across several entries. In addition typical mail servers use different modules for dispatching e-mail to users, and each one writes its own information to a separate log file.

As a typical example, Figure 1 depicts the architecture of Postfix, which is a *de-facto* standard for delivering e-mail services. Put briefly, Postfix is an e-mail server composed by a set of independent software modules. Specifically, the e-mail flow enters the Postfix via the *smtpd* mod-

ule. Upon receiving e-mail, it removes the SMTP protocol encapsulation, enforces some integrity checks (also in order to not endanger the overall software framework), and dispatches the sender, recipients and message contents to the *cleanup* module. Similar actions are performed for *local* e-mail submissions. Messages received through the *sendmail* compatibility command are queued in the *maildrop* queue by the privileged postdrop command. Conversely, e-mails from internal sources are sent directly to the *cleanup* server. Such sources have not shown in Figure 1, for the sake of clarity, but can include: e-mails forwarded by the local delivery agent, messages returned to the sender by the *bounce* module, and postmaster notifications. The *cleanup* module implements the final processing stage before the e-mail is queued, for instance by completing the message header. The module places the final result into a single file within the *incoming* queue, and notifies to its manager the arrival of a new message. The *rewrite* module actually arranges addresses in the standard "user@fully-qualified-domain" form.

A given module has its own identifier within the log file. The format of each entry is quite "steady", i.e., it always resembles the format presented in (1).

<date-time> <host> postfix/<module>[pid]: <qid>: (1)

Figure 1. The block diagram of the Postfix architecture

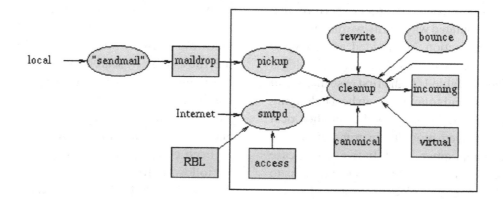

Where, among the others, the *pid* is the process id of the module responsible of producing the specific entry, while the *queue id* (qid) is a unique message identifier for a given transaction. We will exploit later the qid to properly parse the needed information in order to manipulate log with the discussed solution.

By inspecting in more details a log file, we can notice that an e-mail has different lines of information about a given transaction. Reconstructing a transaction is quite impossible for a human, so as a first step, we decided to develop a tool to transform a log in a cleaner format. We call such operation as *normalization*. As a consequence, we say that the resulting log is *normalized*. Thus, a normalized log contains all the needed information properly merged within a unique file. Through this tool we can access different and important information about e-mail traffic in a non time-consuming way. We named such system Log Mail Analyzer (LMA), and it has been coded in Perl to improve portability. It is freely available at http://sourceforge.net/projects/lma/. Interested readers can test the tool, as well as utilize it in production environments. Also, being released under the GNU General Public License (GPL) it is also possible to investigate its internals gaining more comprehension or reuse interesting features.

Summing up, LMA has two main purposes: to facilitate system and network managers in answering users' requests and to work as an intrusion detection tool. In this way, the system administrator can gain in a quick way a clear picture of all the e-mails sent/received in order to perform in a simple (or automated way) virus/worm detection. A sample transaction, subdivided according to specific locations, which can be observed in a log is summarized in Table 1. In the first case the e-mail comes from a local source (i.e., an host belonging the same LAN) and it is directed to another local one. The involved modules in transaction are: pickup, cleanup, qmgr, local. In the second case the mail comes from a local source and it has to be routed to a remote place (e.g., a mail server

accessible through the Internet). In this case, the used modules are: pickup, cleanup, qmgr, smtp. In the third case the e-mail comes from an external "domain" and it is directed to another remote one (e.g., open relay SMPT servers, or a SMTP server with Simple Authentication and Security Layer). In this scenario, the modules engaged are: smtpd, cleanup, qmgr, smtp. In the last use-case, the e-mail arrives from an external resource to an internal one, thus, needing the intervention of the smtpd, cleanup, qmgr and local modules. We highlight, as an example, that *193B2005* is the qid of a transaction allowing to trace it across the logs.

To handle in an efficient flavor such complexity, the LMA is composed by *three* different modules: *the log-translator*, the *DB-generator* and the *DB-query*. We point out that the LMA can be used both in a standalone fashion, or integrated with a complex data-mining and analysis system for detection. Let us briefly analyze all the core components of LMA. The main task performed by the log-translator is to parse a set of log files in a fast and effective way, also by taking into account a rich set of configurations and filters set by the user. At the time of writing, the current implementation of the log-translator only supports log generated by Postfix and Sendmail. Also, it can be highly configured via a proper configuration file. We omit here, for the sake of clarity how such file is organized: interested readers can refer to the documentation bundled with the software.

As already hinted at, the log-translator gathers all the desired information about a transaction by analyzing the qid. Put briefly, it automates the following steps: i) find out the qid related to a specific e-mail, ii) search for the other instances of a given qid (which can also be split over several files by the log-rotate function) and iii) reconstruct the whole transaction. The produced output is a plain text in a human-readable form.

Each entry identifies a single transaction in the following format: date and hour, DNS name, the IP address of the host, mail server IP address,

Table 1. Simple transactions and the related locations for a given entry

From local to local	From local to remote
postfix/pickup[31859]: 193B2005: uid=6666 from=<user> postfix/cleanup[31986]: 193B2005: message-id=<000001c6017b$1 3d5ed30$cd32a8c0@familiarityl> postfix/qmgr[45890]: 193B2005: from=<user@lma.it>, size=1997 (queue active) postfix/local[48931]: 193B2005: to=<receiver@lma.it>, relay=local, delay=0, status=sent	postfix/pickup[81586]: 14GH342H: uid=6666 from=<user> postfix/cleanup[81683]: 14GH342H: message-id=<000001c6017b $13d5ed30$cd32a8c0@familiarity> postfix/qmgr[13460]: 14GH342H: from=<user@lma.it>, size=989 (queue active) postfix/smtp[81685]: 14GH342H: to=<receiver@external.it>, relay=smtp. external.it[xxx.xxx.1.11], delay=4, status=sent
From remote to remote	**From remote to local**
postfix/smtpd[55666]: connect from host. external.it [xxx.xxx.1.11] postfix/smtpd[58567]: 14GH364H: client=host. external.it[xxx.xxx.1.11] postfix/cleanup[58570]: 14GH364H: message-id=<000001c6017b$ 13d5ed30$cd32a8c0@familiarity> postfix/qmgr[236]: 14GH364H: from=<user@ external.it>, size=989 (queue active) postfix/smtpd[58567]: disconnect from host. external.it[xxx.xxx.1.11] postfix/smtp[58574]: 14GH364H: to=<receiver@ external.it>, relay=relay external.it[yyy.yyy.1.12], delay=4, status=sent	postfix/smtpd[82056]: 14RT666H: client=host. external.it[xxx.xxx.1.11] postfix/cleanup[82057]: 14RT666H: message-id=<000001c6017b $13d5ed30$cd32a8c0@familiarity> postfix/qmgr[13460]: 14RT666H: from=<user@ external.it>, size=8569 (queue active) postfix/local[82059]: 14RT666H: to=<receiver@lma.it>, relay=local, delay=1, status=sent

e-mail address of the sender, e-mail address of the recipient and the e-mail status (e.g., sent or rejected). The e-mail status is a numeric value representing the SMTP reply codes. We recall that the most relevant codes for IDS purposes are: 250 (sent), 450 and 550 (mailbox unavailable). We underline that such format has been designed to avoid the most common mistakes happening in log analysis, as documented in reference (Chuvakin, 2009). A possible example of an entry created by LMA upon inspecting logs is as follows:

23/03/2006 192.168.1.49 hugo@stiglitz.com aldo@raine.com250

In a nutshell, it means that on March 23rd 2006, the host with the assigned IP address 192.168.1.49 produced a successful transaction between hugo@stiglitz.com and aldo@raine.com. We point out that the timestamp can be in different formats (e.g., also including the time with different degrees of precision) and that we used a private IP address for the sake of privacy. Table 2 resumes the entries of a LMA-generated record.

Once we have gathered all the useful information from log files we need a way to manipulate them efficiently. To this aim, the module DB-generator can store data according to two different flavors. The first one relies on the Berkeley DB, while the second uses My-SQL. Berkeley DB is a *database library*, which offers low-level and raw operations to store/retrieve data over simple files. Besides, it enables the creation of embedded applications since it can be directly linked against the main LMA executable. As a consequence, there is not the need of installing third party software and it is more portable. Moreover Berkeley DB is very fast in information retrieval due to the lack of inter-process communication accounting for additional latencies.

The retrieval is done via a simple Application Program Interface (API) wrapped to perform high level operations. For our scopes we have chosen DB-HASH and DB-BTREE implementations where a single value *key* is linked to a *data* value. Due to the limit of the single-key paradigm, it is difficult to easily perform a rich set of queries. To cope with such drawback, we created five different tables, implementing a tiny database search

Table 2. Summary of the entries generated by the LMA

Parameter	Description
Timestamp	the moment when the e-mail has been sent. It is possible to have this information in different formats. For instance in Unix timestamp format or in the Julian standard date.
Client Name	the hostname of e-mail sender (specifically the one observable within the HELO identifier)
Client IP	the IP address of the sender host
From	the e-mail address of the sender
To	the e-mail address of the receiver
Status	the server response in the form of SMTP codes

engine. The first one is the *main table*, containing all information about the e-mail traffic: every e-mail is indexed by an integer number, and the value is a *pipe-delimited string* containing five different entries (date, sender IP, sender e-mail address, receiver e-mail address and e-mail status). The other four tables are *secondary* tables, whose keys are as follows: *data*, *IP*, *sender* and *receiver*. Obviously, each key points to different lines of the main table.

Let us clarify how to access the DB architecture with an example. Imagine we want to perform a search for all the e-mails sent from a given IP address. The database architecture of LMA acts as follows:

1. search for the required IP address in the *sender IP* table (e.g., xxx.xxx.xxx.0);
2. obtain a list of mail identifiers, which are keys in the *e-mail* table (e.g., xxx.xxx.xxx.0 →2 | 45| 78| 3456| 8960, …);
3. each entry in the list is used to retrieve all the data about that specific e-mail (e.g.,

2 → date|host|xxx.xxx.xxx.0|mailserver| from|to|250).

Another option concerns the usage of a Data Base Management System (DBMS) equipped with the Structured Query Language (SQL), like MySQL already offering a very powerful query engine. Lastly, to enhance the process, we developed a minimal query interface for the DB. The available queries are reported in Table 3.

A final remark is about possible issues arising when using the LMA in production-quality environments. In fact, real network topologies can make difficult to identify the real amount of e-mail traffic related to a particular portion of the network or a host. For example, let us consider when an antivirus server is in place. In this case, each e-mail received is sent to an antivirus server, before being dispatched. Once checked, is then sent back to the e-mail server again: this flow is commonly managed via the SMTP (see, for example the Amavisd configuration available at the URL: http://www.amavis.org/howto). Finally, the e-mail can be delivered to the recipient address. How-

Table 3. The minimal query interface implemented by the LMA framework

Query Mnemonic	Description
IP-STORY	lists all the e-mails sent by the selected IP address
FROM-STORY	lists all the e-mails with the given from field
DAILY-EMAIL	lists all the e-mails traffic in a given day
DAILY-REJECT	same as DAILY-EMAIL, but only displays rejected e-mails (e.g., due to non-existing users)

ever, upon inspecting logs, we found the given e-mail logged twice: the first time when it reaches the e-mail server and the second one when it is sent back from the antivirus server.

This behavior interferes with the global statistical analysis of e-mail traffic. In this case is very useful to exclude some parts, i.e., the one produced by the antivirus server. The same problem arises if we want to analyze only a well-defined sub-network (for instance, to isolate a group of hosts in the case of *early infection*). Anyway, we can develop a quite simple workaround against such issues by using a configuration file. The latter allows to select the part of the network, or a single host, we want to monitor in terms of IP addresses. As an example, we can monitor e-mail traffic from xxx.xxx.xxx.0 and yyy.yyy.0.0 networks. In addition, we can introduce filtering disciplines by applying a white-list to the DB or the mail server type (see, http://sourceforge.net/ projects/lma/ for a complete description). We point out that a white-list consists in ignoring e-mail traffic produced by an host belonging to the list itself. Therefore, we can "ignore" e-mails sent by the antivirus or anti-spam servers.

Lastly, to prove the effectiveness of the proposed system, in Section IV we will present some practical utilizations of the data processed through the LMA for statistical anomaly detection purposes of e-mail traffic produced in a real environment.

A Probe-Based Architecture

In the previous section we showcased LMA, which is based on processing logs to have a "knowledge base" on the e-mail traffic to be used for monitoring purposes. However, log-based techniques can be also suboptimal. Thus, we must develop other solutions for the efficient monitoring of e-mails. The approach we propose here is highly experimental. In fact we developed a probe-based framework deployed in a real network used by hundreds of users daily. Besides the contribution in the experimental field, we underline that at

the best of the authors' knowledge, other works on indirect worm detection are usually based on *synthetic* or *pre-made* set of data. Consequently, the contribution of this section is twofold. On one hand, it concerns the methodological viewpoint, while on the other hand, it is on testing the system against traffic collected in a *real production-quality* environment. Nevertheless, the experience acquired by testing our probing deployment can be used only to collect data about e-mails in order to test innovative and "self-developed" heuristics. Section IV will present some numerical results about our monitoring campaign. As a reference scenario to develop the framework, we used the network of the Genoa Research Area (http://ge.cnr. it) of the Italian National Research Council (CNR). The network is composed by 11 interconnected LANs; roughly, each LAN corresponds to a given Institute. The overall population is of more than 800 hosts and appliances. Each LAN has a class C of public IPv4 addresses. Therefore, we do not take into account the presence of Network Address Translation (NAT) devices or issues related to mixed public/private addressing schemes. As regards the single LAN, it is connected to a switch via a 100 Mbit/s Ethernet link. The access to the Internet is granted by a router (with firewall capabilities) through a fiber link of 100 Mbit/s provided by GARR, i.e., the Italian Academic & Research Network. Figure 2 depicts the physical structure of the testbed. Another challenging characteristic, which has not been depicted, is that in our network we have five different mail-servers, varying from Postfix to Sendmail.

For what concerns standard security systems, our network exploits an antivirus server running Sophos. Additionally, to prevent spam we also adopt both SpamAssassin and Greylisting (Harris, 2010). The joint usage of such countermeasures guarantees to rely upon a variety of different techniques to protect the e-mail service against spam and malware. Among the others we recall: header and text analysis, bayesian filtering, DNS block-lists, and collaborative filtering databases

Figure 2. The physical testbed adopted to test the probing architecture under investigation

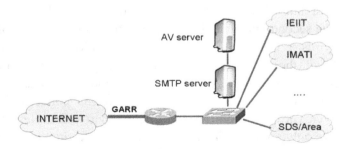

to detect spam. Furthermore, traffic produced through the TCP port 25 is monitored and filtered. This dramatically decreases the impact of at least two threats: *i*) infected hosts becoming spam-zombie machines and *ii*) issues related to the SMTP relaying misuse. This is particularly true for the specific nature of hosts belonging to our Institution. In fact, being a Research Center, almost all the hosts are configured with users having root privileges, increasing the risks arising by the installation of malicious SMTP servers.

Even if we can still investigate logs as discussed in the previous Section, we do employ a probe to directly evaluate the produced traffic. The reasons are: to have a benchmark to compare the effectiveness of the LMA, and to have a fallback solution if log analysis is impeded for some reason.

Let us investigate in a general manner the adopted framework. We have deployed a probe based on Ntop (Deri, Carbone & Suin, 2001), (Deri, 2010) and (Caviglione et al, 2010). It is an open-source Web-based traffic measurement and monitoring application, which enables to track relevant network activities including traffic characterization, network utilization and protocol usage, as well as congestion detection. In more details, we employed Ntop as a "protocol analyzer", i.e., as the tool to capture SMTP messages and to collect them. Then, we write some Perl modules in order to track the single SMTP transactions starting from the collected PDUs. Figure 3 depicts the placement of the monitoring facilities within

our network deployment, which has been utilized as the testbed.

Since we have the main objective of monitoring e-mail traffic, and to have a visual feedback, we also adopted Mailgraph, which is a very simple mail statistics front-end for Postfix and Sendmail. With this quite basic, yet effective, configuration, we are able to monitor the SMTP traffic flow, and detect all the most relevant events (e.g., e-mails storm) and statistics. Summing up, this approach differs from the one implemented by the LMA since SMTP actions are reconstructed "live" by resembling PDUs rather then "off-line" upon inspecting logs. To have a "benchmark", we employed also an host with Snort properly installed. We decided to adopt Snort since it is a well-known IDS also implementing a good logging and reporting system. In the next Section will present some numerical result collected when adopting the aforementioned method for detecting worm-related activities.

THE BASELINE ANALYSIS METHOD

In this Section we present the statistical framework employed to detect worm and anomalies. We will also show a performance evaluation of the method by using e-mail traffic collected in a real-environment, as explained in Section III. This is one of the major contributions of the work if compared to previous ones. In fact, as the best of the authors knowledge, other works suffer of scar-

Figure 3. Deployment of the monitoring facilities among the overall network architecture

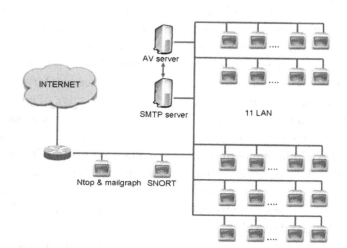

city of real data due to lack of network resources or privacy problem: almost every work in this field uses synthetic or pre-made set of data. The statistical level of confidence has been omitted. On one hand, this has been done to maintain as simple and possible the Section. On the other hand, collected results remained "steady" through the measurement campaign, as well as we still employ in a production-quality environment the proposed approach without any noticeable deviations on the presented performance evaluation.

To develop our framework, we adopted two different level of granularity. The main goal is to extract a simple, yet effective, feature to detect anomalies "nested" within the overall e-mail load. Specifically, as the first step of our analysis, we analyzed the global e-mail flow in a given time interval. For example we isolated the activity performed over a month and we subdivide it in five-minutes slices. Then, we check that the volume of e-mails sent in a day does not exceed a given threshold. Put briefly, the rationale under this approach is to study the temporal correlation between the observable behavior (which can be modified by the presence of a worm) of a given entity (ranging from the single host to the entire network) and its "clean" behavior (which is sup-

posed to be representative of a normal activity, i.e., there are not any virus or worms). We define this kind of investigation as *base-line* analysis.

What we called the base-line is presented in (2):

$$\mu + k\sigma \qquad (2)$$

Where, μ and σ are the mean and the variance, respectively. Besides, k is a parameter allowing to weight the variance. In the following, we will investigate how-to empirically choose k in order to maximize the detection accuracy. Such values are commonly calculated for each month and for the overall amount of observed e-mails. In this way, we can model the network behavior for a month-wide time interval. Before continuing, we also *preprocess* the data by subtracting the mean to the values and by removing all the intervals with a negative number of e-mails. This is done since we want to not investigate no-activity periods, or more general, poor activity ones. In a similar way we do the same for the e-mail traffic produced by the single host, which means all the e-mails with the same IP observed in a selected period. Moreover, for this particular kind of e-mail flow, we analyze how many different e-mail addresses every host uses. The same is then done by counting the e-mails rejected by the mail server, and so on. Consequently, we call such different statistical analysis, based on computing different base-lines as: *global flow, single IP flow, from, rejected e-mail flow*, and *single IP rejected e-mail flow*. For what concerns performances, employing an unique base-line for detecting worms (or, if needed, other misbehaviors) could not suffice. Nevertheless, worms have a very broad range of characteristics, thus it could be impossible to detect different worms with the same, or a unique, base-line. However, it is possible to mix different base-lines in order to detect peculiar behaviors and to avoid false positives triggered by other base-lines not suitable for a given worms. Then, we can use a simple threshold to reveal the menace. Figure 4 depicts the conceptual block-diagram for mixing different information provided by different base-lines. Notice that every kind of detection has its own weight coefficient.

From our preliminary analyses, we found that weights proposed in Figure 4 are the most suitable for the purpose of detecting worms in our setting. Specifically, we employed: Global Email Flow (GEF) = 1, Global Email Flow-Reject (GEF:Reject) = 0,33, Global Email Flow-From (GEF:From) = 0,33, Single IP Email Flow (SIPEF) = 0,5, From = 1 and Reject Email Flow (REF) = 1. We point

out that relying on a threshold is not completely novel. Rather, it is novel to use simple computations (i.e., the statistical parameters composing the base-line). However, we selected the threshold for the following reasons: *i*) it is simple to compute, and do not account for additional complexity, also in the perspective of embedding our approach in cost-effective network appliances and *ii*) also the aforementioned Snort implements a threshold method, so it is possible to have a benchmark for a vis-à-vis comparison. We point out that, as it happens for each base-line, also the threshold is calculated in a statistical way.

Dataset Description And Selection of the K Parameter

To test the effectiveness of our approaches (i.e., the efficiency of the LMA and the performances of the base-line method), we employed a dataset composed by all the e-mails delivered through ten C-class networks in a period of 900 days. Specifically the period of observation started from January 2004 to November 2006. As said, we performed some pre-processing of data. This has been done to avoid average values also depending on non-interesting time periods, such as nighttime, weekends or holidays. As an example

Figure 4. Block diagram for mixing different base-lines for detecting worms

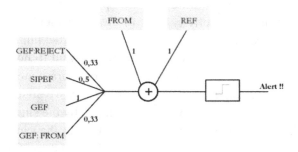

of the impact of pre-processing over the dataset we present the following case. The average number of daily sent e-mails in the year 2004 was equal to 524. If "pruned" from weekends and holidays (where, anyway some legitimate activity can be present), the average number of daily sent e-mails become 773 for 179 days of activity. Obviously this heavily impacts over the thresholds to be employed both for base-lines calculation and for the decision thresholds, as well as for the weight coefficients for each base-line.

Before introducing the performance evaluation, let us briefly discuss the impact of the parameter k on the effectiveness of the detection of the worms. Computing the optimal value for k can be done through different approaches, for instance both off-line or on-line. It can be optimized by using proper techniques (see, e.g., (Caviglione & Cervellera, 2008) and references therein for details about the role of optimization applied to networking-oriented applications).

Also, it can be computed dynamically, thus being updated in real-time. However, to maintain the solution simple and not time consuming, we employed an off-line and statically computed value of k. We found that with $k = 3$ we had the 100% of detection accuracy with the base-line. Figure 5 depicts the various performances in term of

"accuracy" achieved by varying k. We defined as the accuracy the number of worms detected from a well-defined set by the resulting base-lines. We highlight that values > 14 and < 3 have not been depicted since they had a totally unsatisfactory performances. As presented in Figure 5, we can observe that the value of $k=3$ guarantees an accuracy of 100%. Therefore, the "optimal" base-line is given by (3):

$$\mu + 3\sigma \tag{3}$$

Lastly, a final remark concerns the selection of the time-slice adopted for calculating all the involved statistical quantities. In fact, there is not a "universal" time-slice guaranteeing the detection of infected hosts or worms within the e-mail volume. Alas, it varies according to many parameters, such as, the population of the network. As a paradigmatic example, let us take into account the month of February 2004. Firstly, we subdivided the entire month in slices of 5 minutes. For each slice we computed the average number of sent e-mails. Then we made the overall average of such values in order the have "global" value. However, this approach still needs some tweaking. In fact, using a slice of five minutes resulted in too many alerts. Besides, many of them exceeded

Figure 5. Different degrees of accuracy (defined as the percentage of detected worms from a given set) versus different values of k. Values > 14 and < 3 have not been depicted since they had a totally unsatisfactory performance

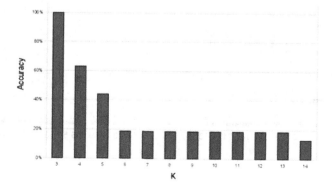

the threshold only for few e-mails. A possible palliative is to correlate all the five minutes slices composing an hour period. This is done under the hypothesis that a host infected by a worm has a duplex behavior: it sends many e-mails both in a short and longer periods. To clarify the concept let us consider the analysis for the month of April 2004. The five minutes base-line resulted in 63 e-mails, while the one hour base-line resulted in 463. In five-minutes analysis we found 16 alerts, while in one-hour analysis only 3: this is a very huge gap. By making further investigations, we discovered the presence of a relevant number of e-mails sent/received through an highly populated mailing list. Therefore, they account for "sudden peaks" if happening in a five minutes time-frame, while they are highly mitigated when "absorbed" in the overall load produced within an hour.

Performance Evaluation

In this Section we discuss the effectiveness of our approach by investigating some performances when conducting different type of base-lines detections.

Let us analyze an off-line analysis performed in a seamless way by using the LMA. To extract the interesting features, we adopted the minimal query interface presented in Table 3. Even if minimal, it reveals to be very effective both for intrusion and indirect-worm detection purposes. In fact, as an example, let us consider the mail activity graph of one of the monitored networks, depicted in Figure 6. Then, we calculated the average amount of e-mails produced during the working time, and we found it equal to 80. By inspecting the figure, we clearly notice a 180 e-mails peak.

Then this peak catch our attention and we decided to make a deeper analysis of the mail log to understand if it is due to normal activities or

Figure 6. Number of e-mails sent over the network per hour

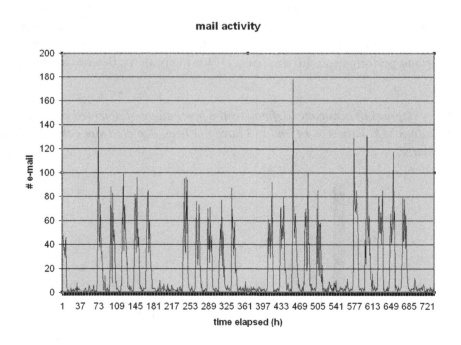

an intrusion. Roughly, we have to discriminate between the traffic produced by a mailing-list or a worm. By making a simple query through the LMA we analyzed the mail server log and we found that an host, owned by a single person, used many different e-mail addresses in a short time, which is a suspicious behavior, as reported in Figure 7. Then, we quarantined all the e-mail traffic generated by the "suspicious" IP address, and after the lag time between virus generation and virus protection, we found that an indirect worm infected the host. Obviously, this procedure must be automated, for instance by using also the base-line method, but it gives the idea of the simplicity of making detection if a tool to correctly parse and manipulate the logs is available. Additionally, this approach can be also exploited to detect what we define as stealthy worms, which are worms spreading very slow or by exhibiting a very small activity.

As a consequence, they are hard to detect within a huge load of e-mails. In fact the activity of this kind of worms results hidden in the global flow analysis, since their behaviors allow the camouflage within the normal activity. Thus, the "noise" produced by legitimate e-mails exceeds signal produced by worms. To detect also stealthy worms, we have to perform an analysis on the traffic flow of the single host, which means all the e-mails with the same IP-Client sent in a selected period. In this way, we are able to find also this kind of worm activities "on-the-fly", i.e., when no deeper investigations are needed. This is the case of users reporting some misbehaviors on their hosts, or upon receiving alerts from a remote security center.

Let us now discuss a typical base-line analysis. For the sake of brevity, we will not present all the possible base-lines. Rather we will showcase how we detected threats by adopting only three different statistical markers; all the base-lines have been

Figure 7. Graph of different e-mail addresses used by a single host in a month

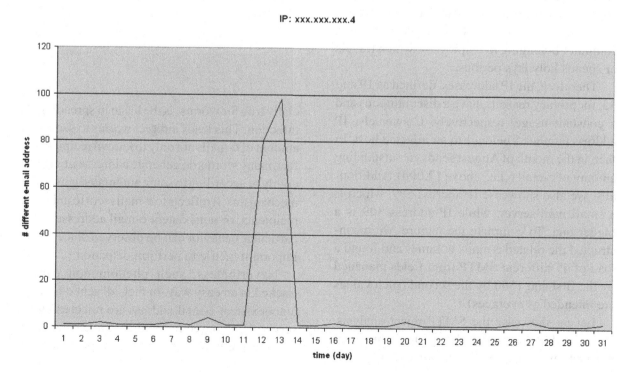

chosen with $k=3$ and the weights used to merge them to reveal threats are the same proposed in Figure 4. We recall that we used the same dataset previously adopted for testing the LMA, which has also used here to pre-process data, as well as to extract the needed features.

Firstly, we do present the performances of what we defined as sender analysis (labeled as FROM in Figure 4). As said, peaks revealed by the flow analysis (both in the flavor of single and global) are not always hoaxes. In fact, mailing list activities account for using a variety of different addresses. This fact can be "automatically" handled by using the from base-line analysis, which is equal to inspecting the SMTP from field of each host. As said, a single-user host is not likely to use different e-mail accounts in a short time-frame (moreover, in a concurrent manner). At the same time it is not true that usually a worm continuously changes the SMTP from field when sending infected e-mails. By inspecting Figures 8 and 9, we can identify various kind of activities. Notice that we have not any data for the month of May 2005, and we have only few activity days for the month of April 2005. In fact, the IP addresses under investigations are permanently assigned to "normal" hosts, i.e., computer belonging to employees, which travels or spends holydays periods.

Therefore, the IP addresses, defined as 19 and 35, for privacy reasons, have a discontinuous and a constant usage, respectively. Conversely, IP address number 5 belongs to an infected host. In fact, in the month of August sends an outstanding amount of e-mails (i.e., above 12,000). Additionally, we also showcase IP address 599, which is a small mail-server, while IP address 309 is a bigger one. To complete the picture, we reconstructed the related e-mails volumes and found a load of 45 different SMTP from fields managed by the first and 1500 by the second (such values are intended as averages).

Let us showcase the SMTP reject analysis, which has been named as GEF:REJECT in Figure 4. One typical feature of malware, and it is espe-

Figure 8. Numerical results of the "from base-line" analysis performed over the year 2005 of our dataset. Details of IP addresses number 5, 309 and 599

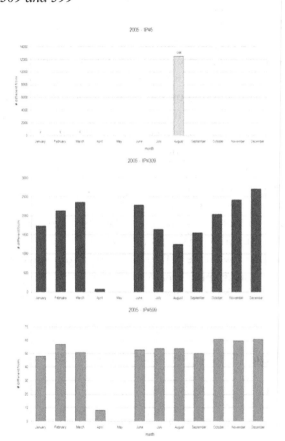

cially true for worms, is the haste in spreading the infection. This leads indirect worms to send a big amount of e-mails not only to known recipients. In fact, many worms do generate addresses, both randomly or according to some automated generation mechanisms. It reflects to e-mails sent to unknown recipients, or nonexistent e-mail addresses. This particular behavior can be observed since it is an important metric to perform detection.

Nevertheless, such phenomenon can be tracked in an easy way. In fact, all sent e-mails to a nonexistent e-mail address are rejected by the server. As a consequence, this erratic behavior is also tracked in the log. As an example to support

Figure 9. Numerical results of the "from base-line" analysis performed over the year 2005 of our dataset. Details of IP addresses number 35 and 19.

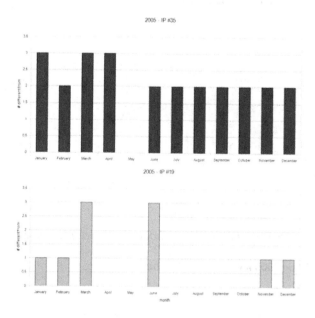

our ideas, let us discuss what we observed with our tools in August 2005. Figures 10, 11, 12 and 13 summarize the collected values with different degrees of temporal resolution.

Data has been preprocessed by excluding the months of April and May since they presented only a very small amount of activity. Then, on the average, we can observe that the normal amount of rejected e-mails is about 14,195. By using the proposed base-line approach, we can automate the procedure of detecting worms. In fact, if we further "zoom" within data, we can detect that the anomaly begin on August the 22nd at 12 a.m. and reaches its peaks at 5 p.m.. The base-line automatically reveals that the hourly average was of 13 e-mails and from 12 a.m. to 2 p.m. the loads dramatically increases to 12,820 rejected e-mails.

Figure 10. Overall number of rejected e-mails per month

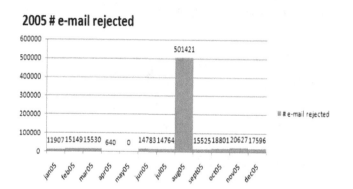

Figure 11. Overall number of rejected e-mails in the month of August

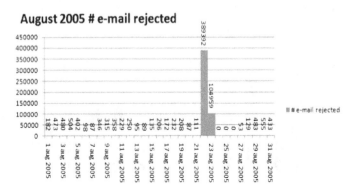

Figure 12. Overall number of rejected e-mails per hour during a day containing a possible anomaly

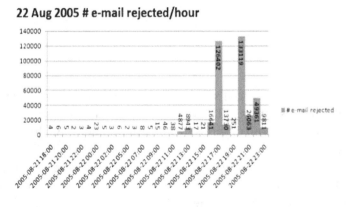

Figure 13. Overall number of rejected e-mails calculated in a 5 minute slice to compute base-line and detect anomaly

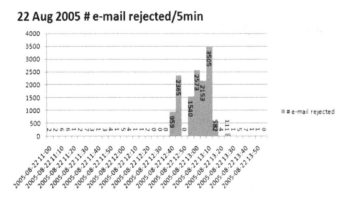

Additionally, we do present a "resumed" performance evaluation of all the worms detected by employing the proposed approach. Table 4 portraits such results. Specifically, we showcase how we employed our base-line method to detect 14 worms during the year 2004. We point out that we present this data, since in 2005 we changed completely our network policies and we added several firewalls and other sophisticated security countermeasures (e.g., we added an additional antivirus engine in out Mail Transfer Agent). Thus, starting from year 2005 the number of threats dramatically decreases.

Obviously, also our mechanisms allowed to precisely quantify the need of additional countermeasures, as well as, testing them on-line by using our experimental probing architecture. Besides, we noticed that all worms found with single flow analysis can be also detected by jointly using the from and reject analyses.

Lastly, we also tested the effectiveness of the proposed solutions by performing additional investigations by using our probe-based architecture, proposed in Section III.2. Put briefly, we collected

the same results. Then, the two methods allow to guarantee same results and can be selected according to the specific needs. For instance, in presence of large data set containing the past history of the e-mail infrastructure, using the LMA is the best choice. Rather, if a prompt on-line monitoring is needed, and when logs are not available, deploying the probe-based mechanism can allow to deploy a quick monitoring infrastructure (especially, since we based it on the widespread and open source NTop). Anyway, we can use both to feed the proposed base-line approach, which turns out to be simple yet effective. As a final notice, the proposed approach is able to detect, at least, the same threats revealed by Snort, thus demonstrating characteristics needed to adopt our methods in *carrier-grade* deployments.

CONCLUSION AND FUTURE WORK

In this Chapter we investigated several aspects concerning the analysis, development and deployment of statistical anomaly detection techniques

Table 4. Threats revealed with the base-line method. Baseline is the base-line computed on the global e-mail flow, while from and rejects are base-lines computed for local e-mail flows

Date	Infected Host	Analysis
28/01/04 18:00	X.X.6.24	Baseline, from, reject
29/01/04 10:30	X.X.4.24	From, reject
28/04/2004 14:58-15:03	X.X.7.20	Baseline, from, reject
28/04/2004 15:53-15:58	X.X.5.216	Baseline, from, reject
29/04/2004 09:08-10:03	X.X.6.36 and X.X.7.20	Baseline, from, reject
04/05/2004 12:05-12:10	X.X.5.158	Baseline, from, reject
04/05/2004 13:15-13:25	X.X.5.158	Baseline, from, reject
31/08/04 14:51	X.X.3.234	Baseline, reject
31/08/04 17:46	X.X.3.234	Baseline, reject
23/11/04 11:38	X.X.3.101 X.X.3.200 X.X.3.234 X.X.5.123	Baseline, reject
22/08/05 17:13	X.X.10.10	Baseline, from, reject
22/08/05 17:43	X.X.10.10	Baseline, from, reject
22/08/05 20:18	X.X.10.10	Baseline, from, reject
22/08/05 22:08-22:13	X.X.10.10	Baseline, from, reject

for e-mail traffic. Firstly, we introduced two approaches to investigate the traffic flow produced by e-mails. The first one is the LMA, which is a tool to manipulate the information available within the logs produced by e-mail servers. It allows to cope with the complexity and the "obscure" nature of how logs are organized. LMA can be used both to provide a support to humans, being aimed at producing an human-readable output. Besides, it also uses two databases to store information, which can be used to feed an automated IDS. Then, we also presented an alternative framework based on Ntop-equipped probes, as a way to gather the same information available from logs but from another perspective. In fact, in this case, the behavior of the e-mail traffic is observed by "sniffing" the PDUs and resembling them via *ad hoc* Perl scripts.

The second contribution of the paper is then what we defined as base-line analysis, which is a simple statistical technique to detect anomalies. Put briefly, it relies upon a metric allowing to detect anomalies by using a threshold. We then presented a brief performance evaluation by using data collected with the proposed methodologies. In this way we tested both the effectiveness of the approaches employed for data collection and for detection. Another contribution is on the availability of real e-mail traffic, as well as performing tests in a production environment, rather than using simulations and synthetic models. We point out that LMA is daily employed in our institution and the base-line method daily protects our network.

Future work aims at making our collected data freely available for research purposes. This will allow other people to test their ideas against a real traffic source, rather than relying upon synthetic patterns. Moreover, being LMA publicly available and released under GPL, we aim at refining and testing it in other deployments. Besides, we hope to make LMA able to support other mail servers. For what concern the base-line method, which is highly empirical, as a part of our ongoing research, we plan to make it self-adjusting in an automated

and dynamical way. Obviously, this work need a huge amount of data to have enough "past history" to tune all the involved parameters. This reason offers additional support to our vision: monitoring tools and IDS are both important to react against threats conveyed though e-mails. In other words, they both are fundamental building blocks, thus the research to be made must be heavily focused on such aspects.

REFERENCES

Aiello, M., Avanzini, D., Chiarella, D., & Papaleo, G. (2006). *A Tool for Complete Log Mail Analysis: LMA*. Paper presented at the Terena Networking Conference 2006 (TNC2006), Security on the Backbone: Detecting and Responding to Attacks, Catania, Italy.

Aiello, M., Avanzini, D., Chiarella, D., & Papaleo, G. (2006b). *Worm Detection Using E-mail Data Mining. Paper* presented at the Primo Workshop Italiano su PRIvacy e Security (PRISE2006), Roma, Italy.

Aiello, M., Avanzini, D., Chiarella, D., & Papaleo, G. (2007). *SMTP sniffing for intrusion detection purposes*. In Proceedings of Secondo Workshop Italiano su PRIvacy e Security (PRISE2007), Roma, Italy, (pp. 53 – 58).

Aiello, M., Chiarella, D., & Papaleo, G. (2008). *Statistical anomaly detection on real e-mail traffic*. In Proceedings of the International Workshop on Computational Intelligence in Security for Information Systems (CISIS2008), Genova, Italy, (pp. 170 – 175).

Aiello, M., Chiarella, D., & Papaleo, G. (2009). Statistical anomaly detection on real e-mail traffic. *Journal of Information Assurance and Security (JIAS)*, *6*(4), 604–609.

Andrews, J. H. (1998). *Testing Using Logfile Analysis: Tools, Methods and Issues*. In Proceedings of the 13th International Conference on Automated Software Engineering (ASE 98), (pp. 157 – 166).

Andrews, J. H., & Zhang, Y. (2000). *Broad Spectrum Studies of log File Analysis*. In Proceedings of the 22nd International Conference on Software Engineering, Limerick, Ireland, (pp. 105 – 114).

Axelsson, S. (1998). *Intrusion detection systems: A survey and taxonomy*. Technical Report 99 - 15, Chalmers University of Technology, Goteborg, Sweden Department of Computer Engineering.

Bron, C., & Kerbosch, J. (1973). Finding all Cliques of an Undirected Graph. *Communications of the ACM, 16*(9), 575–577. doi:10.1145/362342.362367

Caviglione, L. (2009). Understanding and Exploiting the Reverse Patterns of Peer-to-Peer File-Sharing Applications. *Network Security, 1*(7), 8–12. doi:10.1016/S1353-4858(09)70087-X

Caviglione, L., Aiello, M., & Papaleo, G. (2010). *A Scalable and Cost-Effective Framework for Traffic Monitoring in Virtual LANs*. Paper presented at the 21st International Tyrrhenian Workshop on Digital Communications (ITWDC): Trustworthy Internet, Isola di Ponza, Italy.

Caviglione, L., & Cervellera, C. (2008). A Peer-to-Peer System for Optimized Content Replication. *European Journal of Operational Research, 196*(2), 423–433.

Chiarella, D. (2010). Worm *detection: a monitoring behavior based system for Anomaly Detection*. Ph.D. Thesis INF/01 DISI-TH-2010-1, DISI - University of Genoa.

Chuvakin, A. (2009). *Five Mistakes of Security Log Analysis*. netForensics Inc., Retrieved March 2011, http://www.computerworld.com/s/article/print/96587/Five_mistakes_of_log_analysis

Dagon, D., Qin, X., Gu, G., Lee, W., Grizzard, J., Levine, J., & Owen, H. (2004). *HoneyStat: Local Worm Detection Using Honeypots*. In Proceedings of the 7th International Symposium on Recent Advances in Intrusion Detection (RAID), Sophia Antipolis, France.

Denning, D. E. (1987). An intrusion detection model. *IEEE Transactions on Software Engineering, 3*(2), 222–232. doi:10.1109/TSE.1987.232894

Deri, L. (2010). *The nTop Project Homepage*. Retrieved March 2011, http://www.ntop.org/

Deri, L., Carbone, R., & Suin, S. (2001). *Monitoring Networks Using Ntop*. In proceedings of 2001 IEEE/IFIP International Symposium on Integrated Network Management, Seattle, WA, USA, (pp. 199 – 212).

Du, Y., Wang, W.-Q., & Pang, Y.-G. (2004). *An intrusion detection method using average hamming distance*. In Proceedings of the Third International Conference on Machine Learning and Cybernetics, Shanghai, (pp. 2914 – 2918).

Estvez-Tapiador, J. M., Garcia-Teodoro, P., & Diaz-Verdejo, J. E. (2004). Anomaly detection methods in wired networks: A survey and taxonomy. *Computer Communications, 27*(16), 1569–1584. doi:10.1016/S0140-3664(04)00238-5

Garca-Teodoro, P., Daz-Verdejo, J., Maci-Fernandez, G., & Vazquez, E. (2009). Anomaly-based network intrusion detection: Techniques, systems and challenges. *Computers & Security, 28*(1), 18–28. doi:10.1016/j.cose.2008.08.003

Gaudin, S. (2003). *August was Worst Month Ever for Viruses, Worms*. Technet News.

Harris, E. (2010). *The Next Step in the Spam Control War: Greylisting*. Retrieved March 2011, http://projects.puremagic.com/greylisting/

Ilgun, K., Kemmerer, R. A., & Porras, P. A. (1995). State transition analysis: A rule-based intrusion detection approach. *IEEE Transactions on Software Engineering, 21*(3), 181–199. doi:10.1109/32.372146

Koch, T., Ard, A., & Golub, K. (2004). *Log Analysis of User Behavior in the Renardus Web Service.* In Proceedings of the 2004 Joint ACM/IEEE Conference on Digital Libraries, Tuscon, AZ, USA, (pp. 378 – 382).

Kreibich, C., & Crowcroft, J. (2003). *Honeycomb: Creating Intrusion Detection Signatures Using Honeypots.* In Proceedings of the Second Workshop on Hot Topics in Networks (HotNetsII).

Kumar, S., & Spafford, E. H. (1995). *A software architecture to support misuse intrusion detection.* In Proceedings of the 18th National Information Security Conference, Baltimore, USA, (pp. 194 – 204).

Lauf, A. P., Peters, R. A., & Robinson, W. H. (2010). A distributed intrusion detection system for resource-constrained devices in ad-hoc networks. *Ad Hoc Networks, 8*(3), 253–266. doi:10.1016/j.adhoc.2009.08.002

Li, W.-J., Hershkop, S., & Stolfo, S. J. (2004). *Email Archive Analysis Through Graphical Visualization.* In Proceedings of the 2004 ACM Workshop on Visualization and data Mining for Computer Security, Washington, USA, (pp. 4 – 9).

Moore, D., Paxson, V., Savage, S., Shannon, C., Staniford, S., & Weaver, N. (2003). *Inside the slammer worm* (pp. 33–39). IEEE Magazine of Security and Privacy.

Roberts, P. (2004). *Mydoom Sets Speed Records.* IDG News, January 2004, Retrieved March 2011, http://www.pcworld.com/article/id,114461-page,1/article.html

Stearley, J. (2004). *Towards Informatics Analysis of Syslogs.* In Proceedings of the 2004 IEEE International Conference on Cluster Computing, San Diego, USA, (pp 309 – 318).

Takada, T., & Koide, H. (2002). *Tudumi: Information Visualization System for Monitoring and Auditing Computer logs.* In Proceedings of the Sixth International Conference on Information Visualization, London, UK, (pp. 570 – 576).

Tongshen, H., Qingzhang, X. C., & Kezhen, Y. (2004). *Design and Implementation of Firewall-log-based Online Attack Detection System.* In Proceedings of the 3rd International Conference on Information Security, Shanghai, China, (pp. 146 – 149).

Verwoerd, T., & Hunt, R. (2002). Intrusion detection techniques and approaches. *Computer Communications, 25*(15), 1356–1365. doi:10.1016/S0140-3664(02)00037-3

Wang, Y., & Abdel-Wahab, H. (2006). *A Multilayer Approach of Anomaly Detection for Email Systems.* In Proceedings of the 11th IEEE Symposium on Computers and Communications (ISCC2006), Cagliari, Italy, (pp 48-53).

Zou, C. C., Gao, L., Gong, W., & Towsley, D. (2003). *Monitoring and Early Warning for Internet Worms.* In Proceedings of the 10th ACM Symposium on Computer and Communication Security, Washington DC, USA, (pp. 39 – 58).

ADDITIONAL READING

Information Sciences Institute University of Southern California. (1982). Simple *Mail Transfer Protocol.* RFC 821, http://www.ietf.org/rfc/rfc0821.txt, Aug. 1982, IETF.

Liljenstam, M., & Nicol, D. M. (2004). *Comparing Passive and Active Worm Defenses.* In Proceedings of the 1st Conference on Quantitative Evaluation of Systems, Twente, Netherlands, (pp. 18 – 27).

MITRE Corporation for the Office of Information Services. (2002). Federal Aviation Administration Information System Security Technology Version 2.0 30 September 2002.

KEY TERMS AND DEFINITIONS

Base-Line Analysis: A simple statistical analysis method based on the formula $\mu + k\sigma$, where μ is the average, σ is the variance and k a weight coefficient.

Indirect Worm: A worm spreading through e-mails rather than ad-hoc mechanisms.

Log Mail Analyzer (LMA): An open source tool, written in Perl, to manipulate logs produced by e-mail servers.

Chapter 4
Forensics Challenges for Mobile Phone Security

Halim M. Khelalfa
University of Wollongong in Dubai, UAE

ABSTRACT

This chapter provides a complete reference on mobile phone forensics to students, researchers, lawyers, forensics examiners, information security officers, as well as organizational security personnel.

First, the author reviews the currently used guidelines and procedures in digital forensic investigations, and then presents their current adaptations to mobile phone forensics, including criteria for the selection of forensics tool for mobile phone. Due to the world popularity of GSM phones, a detailed description of the SIM file system is presented. The forensic strength and weaknesses of the classes of physical and logical forensic tools are discussed .Current approaches to overcome the impediments of both classes are reviewed in terms of usability and forensic soundness. Then, the newest challenge to the digital forensic community, anti-forensics (AF) is raised, including the risks faced by mobile phone forensics investigation. Finally, the author addresses the issue of current research as well as trends on mobile phone forensics.

INTRODUCTION

This information age is witnessing a revolution within the information revolution: the mobile information age. According to GSM association, (GSM-1, 2011) the total number of phone connections has reached well over 4.94 billion connections in March 2011. The three billion mark was reached just a year ago on April 16, 2009. One needs to consider that this landmark has been reached, only 17 years after the first GSM network was launched in 1991. Four years later, GSM users reached one billion in 2004; two years later, GSM users passed the two billion mark in the first quarter of 2006, and one year and half

DOI: 10.4018/978-1-61350-507-6.ch004

later, GSM users reached 3.5 billion in January 2009. According to the same source, the world counts more than seven hundred mobile operators in more than two hundred and eighteen countries and territories. We witness on average fifteen new connections per second or one million three hundred thousand new connections daily. The mobile phone market is no longer restricted to the seven most industrialized countries. It spans the entire world. Today, the GSM has about 85% of the global mobile services market. Each year, more than one billion new mobile handsets are sold. They make more than 7 trillion minutes of calls and send about 2.5 trillion text messages (Mullins, 2007).

The current advances of mobile broadband services with higher speed and larger bandwidth will offer more Internet based services with richer multimedia to an ever wider fringe of the world population. GSM is just one of the cell network technologies used for mobile telephony. The ever increasing growth and popularity of using mobile phones has led to having mobile phones being involved in criminal incidents. Law enforcement officials, information security officers, lawyers, and researchers are faced with a series of new challenges: mobile phone forensics (Zhihong, 2008).

This challenge is particularly crucial for the newly emerging offspring of e-commerce, the mobile commerce where transactions are made using mobile devices such as PDA and cell phones (Dai-Yon Cho, 2007). Several facts back up the importance of digital forensics in mobile commerce. First, it is predicted that by the end of 2013, revenues from mobile services will reach well over one trillion of US dollars; an ideal target for cybercriminals. Second, mobile commerce involves three main actors: *the mobile customer, the mobile vendor, and the cellular network provider* (Tindale, 2005). A major factor in the adoption by consumers of mobile commerce is trust in the other two actors; that is trust in mobile technology and in mobile vendors.

The purpose of this chapter is to provide a wide spectrum of end users with a complete reference on mobile phone forensics. End users include students, researchers, incident response team members from private and governmental institutions, lawyers, forensics examiners, information security officers, as well as organizational security personnel.

A particular effort aims at enhancing organization capabilities for elaborating appropriate security policies for mobile phones, and providing forensic specialists and incident response team members with recommendations and guidance on how to address security incidents involving digital information residing on mobile phones and other related medias.

Several challenges face the investigator of mobile phone forensics. The forensic professional should keep up with:

- an ever evolving technology and changes,
- a widespread use of mobile phones,
- a wide variety of mobile phones,
- an increased sophistication of criminals who use the technology gap to enhance their stealth.

First, there exist different types of cellular networks with different characteristics. They include: GSM, 3GSM, CDMA, CDMA 1x, CDMA 1X EV-D0, TDMA, PDC, iDEN, and analogy.

Second, mobile phones can be divided into three main types: basic, intermediate, and smart. Each type has specific hardware and software characteristics. Some of the hardware characteristics include processor speed, memory capacity, display features, card slots, interfaces, battery type, battery location, interfaces, text input, camera options, and wireless capabilities. Some of the software characteristics include: operating systems and application software. Both types of software can be proprietary, open source or commercial like windows mobile.

Third, the forensic community should take into account the fact that manufacturers of cell phones use short product-release cycles to keep up with the competitions. One side effect of such a strategy is that useful documentation for new modes often lack. In addition, forensic tools for mobile phones include commercial tools, device management tools, open source tools, in-house tools, flasher boxes (Jonkers, 2010) and even hacker tools. Moreover, for economic reasons, commercial providers of mobile phone forensic software tend to focus on most commonly used types of handsets. As a result, a significant proportion of mobile phone handsets cannot be analyzed with commercial tools. This creates an additional challenge for the law enforcement community as well as the digital forensic professional: a criminal can choose to use a type of handset that is not amongst the most commonly used. As an example, a criminal can import a handset from another country or continent as to enhance his of her stealth.

Hence, the investigating team should be very careful in selecting the proper set of tools to use as to be able to acquire the need evidence without modifying or deleting crucial device content. Yet, current literature yields that law enforcement and jurisprudence has been taking into account the fact that some alteration may be necessary during the process of gathering digital evidence. Digital forensics researchers saw the need to develop a formal modelling of digital investigation if one were to guarantee reproducibility (Casey, 2007) of the investigation process.

The rest of this chapter is divided into several sections. The background section provides the reader with the necessary background needed to understand the current challenges in mobile phone forensics.

It introduces the basic concepts of cellular telephony with an emphasis on the most widespread cellular network technologies GSM and CDMA. It also provides the reader with an introduction to digital forensics, computer forensics, mobile device forensics and their differences. The next section focuses on the mobile phone forensic process. It presents the most currently used guidelines and procedures for digital forensics. It is followed by a review or adaptations of the computer forensics guidelines to mobile phone forensics. The next section reviews the main criteria for the selection of forensics tool for mobile phone. This followed by an in-depth analysis of the different approaches to acquire data from the different types of storage media available on a mobile phone memory. At that point, we present the classes of physical and logical forensic tools, emphasizing their forensic strength and weaknesses. This is followed by a review of the classes of physical and logical forensic tools, presenting their forensic strength and weaknesses. This is followed by a recent analysis of forensics tools by NIST that describes the capabilities of the different tools as well as their coverage of content recovery. Current approaches to overcome the impediments of both classes of forensic tools are then reviewed. These approaches include the use of filtering protocols and the use of the ad-hoc method of flasher boxes. The forensic soundness of the flasher box method is reviewed via a reproducibility model. Then we present a summary highlighting the advantages and disadvantages of the different approaches. Due to the importance of the storage media, a thorough description of the forensic investigation of the two major cellular networks GSM and CDMA phones is presented. At this point, the chapter analyzes the forensics of mobile phone from the operating system point of view. The four most popular operating systems are considered: Windows Mobile, Symbian, Iphone, and Androids. More challenges to the forensic investigators are reviewed; they include: Anti-forensics, data hiding in SIM cards, the threat of clone mobile phones commonly known as Chinese mobile phones, the problem of hashing techniques in evidence integrity, and view of mobile phone forensics from the network provider side. The next section reviews the current trends of research in mobile phone forensics. Four main actions are reviewed: the effort of academia to use formal methods to model the forensics of mobile phone, the design of academic degree specializing in mobile forensics, efforts to entice mobile phone manufacturers to agree on minimal set of components common to all smart phones, and last but not least, current effort by the mobile phone forensics community to solve the increasingly crucial challenge of the challenges of on-scene triage of cell phones. Finally, the conclusion summarizes the issues covered in this chapter.

BACKGROUND

Definitions and Concepts

Cellular Wireless Technology

Cellular wireless technology is the foundation of mobile wireless communications, including cellular telephony. The latter provides (Forouzan, 2007) communications between mobile unites called mobile stations, or between mobile units and fixed or land units. Cellular networks use multiple low-power transmitters of at most 100 watts, and use radio transmission and allow user's mobility. Coverage is provided by dividing a geographical area into small coverage areas called cells. An area is divided into cells. A cell has a hexagonal shape and is served by a base station. Each cell is assigned a band of frequencies. Crosstalk and interference are avoided by assigning adjacent cells different frequencies. However, frequencies can be reused in distant enough cells. In order to minimize interference, the size of a cell varies as a function of the area population. Densely populated areas are divided into small cells whereas sparsely populated areas are divides in relatively larger cells. The two most dominant cellular network technologies are CDMA (Code Division Multiple Access), and GSM (Global System for Mobile Communications). CDMA is used in the US while

GSM is used in the rest or the world. Other cellular network technologies include: Time Division Multiple Access (TDMA) and Integrated Digital Enhanced Network (iDEN). Digital Advanced Mobile Phone Service (D-AMPS). TDMA use standardized open protocols. IDEN uses a Motorola proprietary protocol. D-AMPS, is a digital version of the original analog standard for cellular telephone phone service AMPS. (Stallings, 2002)

Cellular technology can be divided into generations. The first generation was based on providing voice communications using analogy signals. The second generation provided mainly higher quality voice communications using digital signals. The third generation and beyond are designed to provide a variety of services including multimedia and internet based applications. CDMA and GSM are the mostly used cellular technologies in the 2nd generation and beyond, with GSM as the market leader occupying an increasing large part of the cell phone market in the world. (Forouzan, 2007)

All cellular network technologies are based on the same concept.

At the center of the cell, there is a base station (BS). It includes an antenna, a controller, and a series of transceivers. The transceivers are used to communicate on the channels assigned to the cell. The base station Antenna is called the BTS or Base Transceiver Station. The control unit is called the Base Station Controller.

Each Base station is connected to the Mobile telecommunication switching office or (MTS0). This latter controls several BSC and manages calls between mobile units. It is connected to the Public switched telecommunication network (PSTN). The MTSO is responsible for connections between mobile units as well as between mobile units and fixed lines (Figure 1).

The GSM Cellular Network

At the heart of the system, there is a BSS or base station subsystem. It consists of base station controller and base transceiver stations (BTS).

Figure 1. Wireless cellular network organization

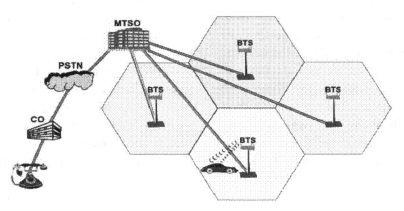

(NIST800-101) A BTS is associated with single cell. It allows communications with mobile stations. It consists of a radio antenna, a radio transceiver, and a link to a base station controller (BSC). The latter can assign radio frequencies, manages the transceivers, and the hand off operations for mobile users moving from one cell to an adjacent one. A BSC can be collocated with a single BTS, or it can control multiple cells by controlling multiple BTSs. The cellular network is linked to the Public switched telecommunication network (PSTN) via the MSC or mobile switching centre. The MSC uses several databases to perform its tasks. One of the most important one is the HLR or Home Location Register; it is the central database for user service information (Stallings, 2002). This database maintains information relative to the subscriber, the services subscribed to, and the location where the subscriber last registered with the network. It is used to generate billing records; they are called the call data records. Both the database and the billing records (often called data records) are used by investigators as a source of evidence. The following diagram (Figure 2) gives an overview of a GSM cellular network organization.

Under GSM standards, a mobile phone is known as a mobile station. It is divided into: mobile equipment (ME) and a SIM or subscriber identity module. The ME is the physical part of the phone. It consists of a radio transceiver, digital signal processors, and internal memory. The SIM module is a portable smart card. Except in special emergency situations, a GSM phone is useless unless a SIM card is inserted into it.

The CDMA Cellular Network

CDMA (Sharma, 2009) cellular networks have the same wireless network organization as GSM networks. The CDMA cellular system is known under its standard name IS-95 from Telecommunications Industry Association (TIA) in the US. GSM and CDMA are the two mostly deployed cellular systems in the world. Yet, there are eight time more users of GSM than users of CDMA phone. GSM covers most of the world while CDMA is mostly used in the US, and part of Asia. In the US, Verizon and Sprint use CDMA technology.

GSM mobile phones cannot operate without a SIM card. However, a GSM user needs only change SIM card to switch network operators. Regular CDMA phone do not use SIM cards. A user can also acquire a new phone, insert his or her old SIM card and use the services provided by the network operator. In the US, AT&T and T-Mobile use GSM technology CDMA phones are not card enabled, in that they don't need the

Figure 2. GSM wireless network organization

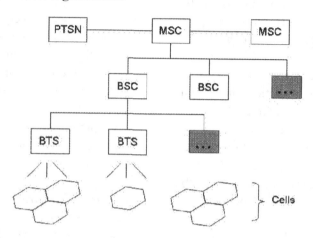

equivalent of a SIM card to operate. User of a CDMA phone cannot use a new CDMA phone without contacting their career network, having their old phone deactivated, and subsequently the new phone activated. New CDMA phones provide for the use of a SIM equivalent the Removable User Identity Module for users who travel to countries where GSM is used. We will see that this is a fundamental factor when it comes to the forensic investigation of both types of phones. While in a GSM phone the SIM card holds all of the user account information, that information is stored in the internal memory (flash) of a CDMA phone.

Basic Concepts of Digital Forensics

The International organization of computer evidence (IOCE) produced a report that suggested a series of definitions and principles to be adopted by all the member states. (IHCF, George Mohay)

- **Digital evidence:** Information stored or transmitted in binary form that may be relied upon in court. (11) distinguishes three forms of digital evidence:
  - Data that is stored on a computer or digital device which plays the role of a passive data repository.
  - Information or meta information present on a digital device which played an active role in a criminal offense
  - Information or meta information present on a digital device which was the target of a criminal offense
- **Original Digital Evidence:** Physical items and those data objects, which are associated with those items at the time of seizure.
- **Duplicate Digital Evidence:** A duplicate is an accurate digital reproduction of all data objects contained on the original physical item.
- **Copy:** A copy is an accurate reproduction of information contained in the data objects independent of the original physical item.
- **Forensic Computing:** The Preservation, Recovery and Examination of Seized Computer Evidence.
- **Law Enforcement Officer:** Any officer who may seize or preserve electronic evidence.
- **(Civilian) Support Staff/Contractor and/or Vendor:** Provision of directed technical services, for example, recovery of data, media analysis, encryption and steganography.

- **Forensic Examiner/Analyst:** Responsible for the recovery, analysis, and subsequent presentation of electronic evidence to a court of law.
- **Investigator:** Responsible for the Investigation and/or direction of specialists involved with computer evidence examination. Ultimately responsible for the presentation of the case to the Prosecutor.
- **Prosecutor:** A member of the legal profession who is responsible for presenting the case against the suspect in a Court of Law.

If a mobile phone is found in a crime scene, a series of guidelines must be followed to ensure the consistency and forensic soundness of the results of the investigation. A digital forensic investigation is a process consisting of the following steps (Wayne, 2006), (Murphy, 2010):

- Crime scene identification/control
- Evidence identification
- Evidence preservation & collection
- Evidence transportation
- Examination and Analysis
- Report and Presentation

Ultimately, the results of such a process are digital evidence that must be presented to a court of law. Similarly to traditional forensic investigation, the entire digital investigation process as well as the resulting digital evidence must be admissible in a court of law. In the next section, we present a series of guidelines, principles and procedural models, currently used in the elaboration of digital forensics policies and procedures as well as in training of digital forensic investigators.

Guidelines and Principles of the Mobile Phone Forensic Process

Generally speaking, when forensics investigators examine digital evidence, they are confronted with two main issues: the medium that contain

or hold the data, and the evidential data itself. There have been several efforts to develop standard principles aiming at preserving the integrity, availability and accountability of the evidence as to making the latter admissible in a court of law. The United Kingdom association of police officers (ACPO) and the international organization of computer evidence (IOCE) developed each a similar set of important principles on how to handle digital evidence.

The ACPO Principles: Good Practice Guide for Computer Based Electronic Evidence

The ACPO developed a good practice guide for computer based electronic evidence. A major concern of the ACPO principles is to allow the prosecution to prove to a court of law, that the evidence being presented to the court is the same evidence as the one first collected by the police investigators. When dealing with digital evidence one has to take into account the fact that the content of computing devices may be altered automatically without the user initiating or being aware of the changes. The operating systems, software applications, may periodically change the content of the data. The changes can also be initiated through malicious actions by criminals as to delete, hide, alter, the evidence. A careful capture of an image of the involved digital devices is warranted. Investigators should make sure that all relevant data is captured. The ACPO guidelines are:

1. *No actions performed by investigators should change data contained on digital devices or storage media that may subsequently be relied upon in court.*
2. *Individuals accessing original data must be competent to do so and have the ability to explain their actions.*
3. *An audit trail or other record of applied processes, suitable for replication of the results by an independent third-party, must*

be created and preserved, accurately documenting each investigative step.

4. *The person in charge of the investigation has overall responsibility for ensuring the above-mentioned procedures are followed and in compliance with governing laws.*

The IOCE Principles

The IOCE developed a set of principles, known as The Proposed Standards for the Exchange of Digital Evidence:

1. *When dealing with digital evidence, all of the general forensic and procedural principles must be applied.*

2. *Upon seizing digital evidence, actions taken should not change that evidence.*

3. *When it is necessary for a person to access original digital evidence, that person should be trained for the purpose.*

4. *All activity relating to the seizure, access, storage or transfer of digital evidence must be fully documented, preserved and available for review.*

5. *An Individual is responsible for all actions taken with respect to digital evidence whilst the digital evidence is in their possession.*

6. *Any agency, which is responsible for seizing, accessing, storing or transferring digital evidence is responsible for compliance with these principles.*

Brian (2009) distinguishes between a digital investigation and a forensic digital investigation. The former can be perceived as a process

Figure 3. The Daubert Method

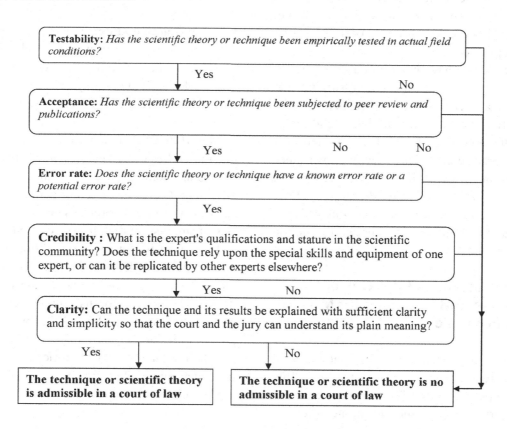

that attempts to explain a series of digital states and events. The latter is a special type of digital investigation, where a set of rules must be satisfied so that the results of the investigation can be accepted by a court of law. In addition to the above principles, the Daubert method is applied to a digital forensic investigation. The Daubert method (Wayne, 2006) is commonly used in court to admit or refute evidence produce via a new scientific technique tool. It is based on 5 principles: testability, acceptance, error rate, credibility, and clarity (Figure 3).

In addition to the above evidential principles, a series of procedural models have been developed to assist the investigator in applying the above principles. The US department of justice developed a set of guidelines called The Electronic Crime Scene Investigation – A Guide for First Responders, (Ashcroft, 2001). The guide is divided into four parts: securing and evaluating the scene, documenting the scene, collecting evidence, and packaging, transporting, and storing evidence. The following checklist (Table 1) details the different steps of each part.

Other models have been proposed in the literature. They all emphasize the most important phases of a digital forensic investigation: the preservation, acquisition, examination and analysis, and the reporting phases. These models provide the forensic investigators with proper guidance when dealing with digital evidence; yet most focus on computer forensics (Figure 2). Obviously, the flowchart depicted in (Figure 4) is too general and ambiguous to be applied for mobile phone forensics.

A Critical Review of the Current Guidelines and Practices for Mobile Phone Forensics

The reader may have witnessed that the term "digital forensics" may be used interchangeably with "computer forensics"; yet, computer forensics investigation and mobile phone forensics

investigation are different. A major difference between computers and mobile phones is that computers are devices that either "ON" or "OFF" while mobile phone can be in up to four states of operations (Wayne, 2006). A mobile device can be in several states (Wayne, 2004):

- **Nascent state (Figure 5):** a brand new device fresh from the assembly line, with no data is said to be in the nascent state. This state can be reached by a utilized phone by performing a hardware reset or allowing the battery to discharge.
- **Active state:** A phone is said to be in active state when the device in powered on, its file systems contain data, and the user can perform task on the phone.
- **Quiescent state:** This state is a dormant state that conserves battery energy. The device does not appear active, but it is actually maintaining user data, as well as the date and time.
- **Semi-active state:** This state is between active and quiescent. It is reached when a timer goes off after a period of inactivity that reduce the display light and other functions in order to conserve battery energy.

Reith (2002) computer forensics is a discipline that researches who, what, when, where and how crimes are committed using computers... Actually, digital forensics is more general ontologically than computer forensics because the forensics of small scale digital devices (SSD) is quite different from the forensics of traditional computers. SSDD include cell phones, PDA's, audio/video devices, gaming devices, and embedded devices. The current forensic guidelines for computer systems do not address all the forensic issues related to SSDD.

The US Department of Justice (DOJ) model had been augmented by (Wayne, 2006) to be applicable to mobile phone forensics (Table 2).

Table 1. Steps of a digital forensics process

Part 1: Securing and Evaluating the Scene
a. Ensure the safety of all individuals at the scene. **b.** Protect the integrity of traditional and electronic evidence. **c.** Evaluate the scene and formulate a search plan. **d.** Identify potential evidence. **e.** All potential evidence should be secured, documented, and/or photographed. **f.** Conduct interviews.
Part 2: Documenting the Scene
a. Create a permanent historical record of the scene. **b.** Accurately record the location and condition of computers, storage media, other digital devices, and conventional evidence. **c.** Document the condition and location of the computer system, including power status of the computer (on, off, or in sleep mode). **d.** Identify and document related electronic components that will not be collected. **e.** Photograph the entire scene to create a visual record as noted by the first responder.
Part 3: Collecting Evidence
a. Handle computer evidence, whether physical or digital, in a manner that preserves its evidentiary value. **b.** Recover non-electronic evidence (e.g., written passwords, handwritten notes, blank pads of paper with indented writing, hardware and software manuals, calendars, literature, text or graphical computer printouts, and photographs).
Part 4: Packaging, Transporting, and Storing Evidence
a. Take no actions to add, modify, or destroy data stored on a computer or other media. **b.** Avoid high temperatures and humidity, physical shock, static electricity, and magnetic sources. **c.** Maintain chain of custody of electronic evidence, documenting its packaging, transportation and storage.
Packaging Procedure **a.** Properly document, label, and inventory evidence before packaging. **b.** Pack magnetic media in antistatic packaging (paper or antistatic plastic bags). **c.** Avoid folding, bending, or scratching computer media such as diskettes, CD-ROMs, removable media, etc. **d.** Properly label evidence containers.
Transportation Procedure **a.** Avoid magnetic sources (e.g., radio transmitters, speaker magnets). **b.** Avoid conditions of excessive heat, cold, or humidity while in transit. **c.** Avoid shock and excessive vibrations.
Storage Procedures **a.** Ensure evidence is inventoried in accordance with authoritative policies. **b.** Store evidence material in a secure area away from temperature and humidity extremes. **c.** Protect evidence material from magnetic sources, moisture, dust, and other harmful particles or contaminants.

The Good Practice Guide for Computer Based Electronic Evidence (ACPO) has also suggested the following procedures when handling cell phones:

- Before handling a suspect phone, consider what other types of evidence, such as DNA or fingerprints, are needed from the phone and follow the appropriate handling procedures.
- Switching the phone off is advisable, because of the potential for loss of data if either the battery expires or network activity occurs, causing call logs or other recoverable data to be overwritten.
- If the phone remains on for some purpose, it should be kept charged and not tampered with, then switched off before transport.
- To prevent accidental operation in transit, the phone should be packaged in a rigid container, secured with support ties.
- The container should be placed into an evidence bag, sealed to restrict access, and the labelling procedures completed for the exhibit.

Figure 4. Collecting digital evidence (Source: US DOJ)

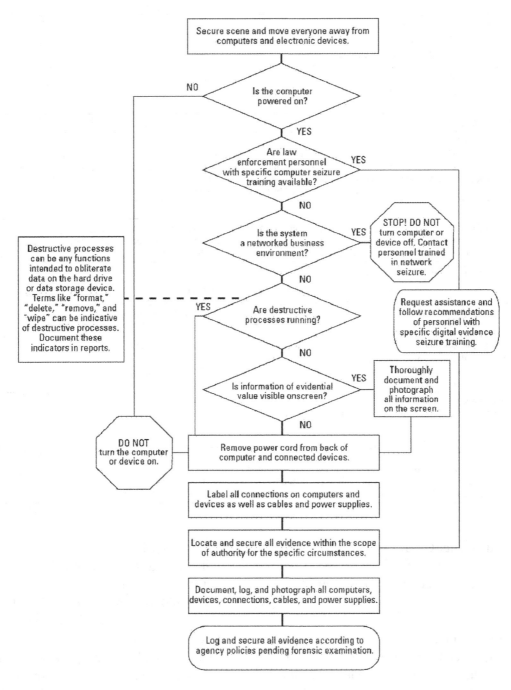

Figure 5. Operating states of a mobile device

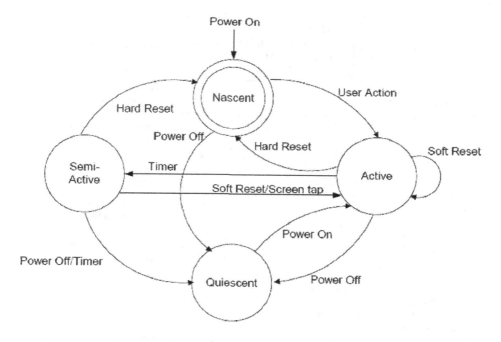

Table 2. Securing and evaluating the scene

Securing and Evaluating the Scene
• Proper authorization must have been obtained prior to the start of the investigation • Digital evidence is fragile. The mobile device may need to be tested for DNA or fingerprint. Cautiousness is warranted. • Investigator should be familiar with characteristics of mobile devices and its associated accessories. • The area where the mobile device was found must be thoroughly searched • During interviews, ask the potential owner of the phone for relevant code and password such as PIN. • Phone may need special attention (presence of explosives, immersion in liquids, damaged phones), specialist should be called for • All evidence must be accounted for • All evidence must be identified
Documenting the Scene
• Photograph all the digital devices present on the crime scene. • Photograph also the cables, peripherals cables, cradles, power connectors, removable media, and connections. • Photograph the content of the phone screen if viewable; alternatively write down the screen content. • The chain of custody procedure should be maintained to ensure the integrity of evidence as well as protect against allegations of tampering.
Collecting Evidence (ACPO guidelines for mobile phones)
• If the phone is found connected with a computer, pull the plug from the computer to stop any data transfer of synchronization activities that may tamper with evidence present on the phone or its associated storage volumes. • Such a computer should be seized along the connecting hardware. • Do not remove any hardware from inside the phone (SIM cards, removable cards) • Isolate the phone from the radio network. (Look at Figure 6) to avoid evidence alteration.
Packaging, Transporting, and Storing Evidence
• A seized device must be sealed and tagged properly • The tag must be signed and dated by the forensics investigator who seized the device. This action starts a chain of custody. • Selecting the proper method for sealing the seized mobile phone is critical. Using an inappropriate method may lead to loss of valuable evidence. (see Figure 7)

Figure 6. Radio isolation of a mobile phone

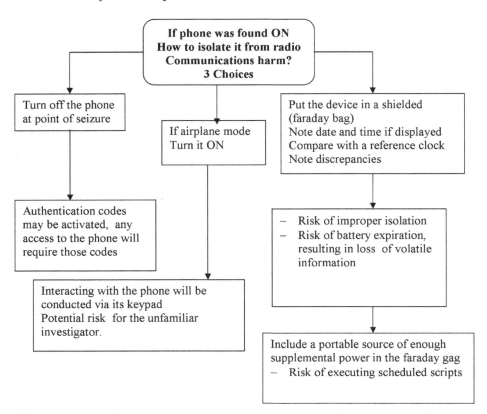

CRITERIA FOR THE SELECTION OF FORENSIC TOOLS

We can conclude that the evidence acquisition and analysis are the most crucial processes in a digital forensic investigation. They correspond respectively to:

- Obtaining an image of the digital device, its peripherals, and associated media
- Searching and finding digital evidence from the obtained image.

The acquisition process starts with an identification phase that determines the cell phone manufacturer, its model, and the service provider. This information is used by mobile phone forensics investigators not only to select the appropriate set of acquisition tools needed by the investigation, but also to be able to unlock the phone if need be as well as asks for relevant information stored in the service provider databases.

The main criteria used in the selection of acquisition tools include:

- **Usability:** the conviviality and user friendliness of the tool can increase the productivity and reliability of an investigator.
- **Comprehensiveness:** the more comprehensive a tool is the more impartial it is in terms or reporting both inculpatory and exculpatory evidence.
- **Determinism:** a deterministic tool will produce the same expected results for the same set of instructions and the same set of input values.

Figure 7. Seizing a seized mobile device

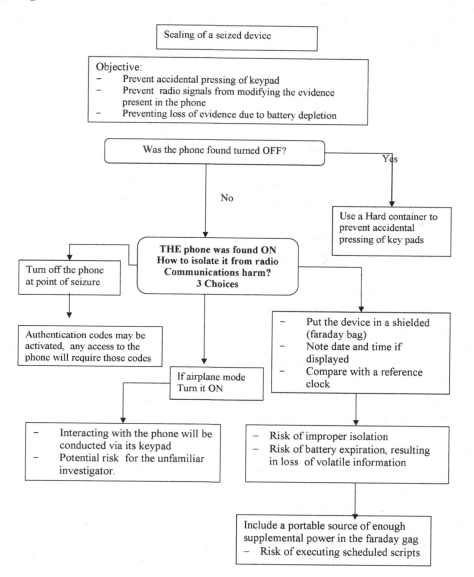

- **Accuracy:** the output of the tool has been tested and its error rate estimated.
- **Verifiability:** the accuracy of the output can be verified and explained using original data, their intermediate translations, as well as the results presented by the tool interface. translated from the tool
- **Admissibility:** by the Daubert method.

- **Quality:** the level of technical support provided by the tool manufacturer, and the frequency of upgrades available.
- **Capability:** the type of evidence the tool can retrieve the flexibility of the tool, its interaction with office applications.
- **Affordability:** the cost versus performance ratio of the tool.

Forensic tools are typically designed to acquire data from the internal memory of a handset and any removable identity modules such as SIMs found in GSM and other types of phones. Both forensic and non-forensic software tools often use the same protocols to communicate with the device. However, non-forensic tools allow a two-way flow of information to enhance or customize one's cellular device (e.g., to add customized phone rings, wallpaper, themes, etc.), while forensic tools are designed specifically to acquire data from the device without altering device content and to calculate integrity hashes over the acquired data. Most practitioners use a collection of both forensic and non-forensic tools along with other accessories to form their "toolbox." Tools not designed specifically for forensic purposes are questionable, however (New07). Before considering their use, they should be thoroughly evaluated and the implications of any associated forensic issues should be fully understood. In some situations, non-forensic tools might be the only means to retrieve data that could be relevant as evidence and may be appropriate to use when the proper precautions are taken.

The software based forensics tools, whether commercial or open source are designed for a safe acquisition of data present in the internal memory chips of the phone set itself or in its removable storage modules such as memory cards (SIM card for GSM phones). The main objective is to avoid any data modification as well as to preserve the integrity of the data by calculating integrity hashes of the data collected. Investigators should be aware that even if using non-forensic tools may be necessary under particular circumstances, there is a risk for evidence alteration or loss. The mean reason is such tools were not initially designed for forensic investigation, but rather they were designed for a friendly user interaction of the device at hand. Usually such tools were not design as to block any write operations on the investigated device, nor do they restrict the flow of information in either direction. Yet, in the real world, often investigators may combine the different software acquisition methods.

How do you Select a Forensics Tool for Cell Phones?

The selection of a forensic tool is based on the the functionalities it offers 1. Ideally, a forensic tool should provide for the automated acquisition, examination, and reporting of evidence. In addition, the interfaces used by the tool to interact with the cell phone are important. Generally speaking there are three types of interfaces that a tool can use to collect evidence from a cell phone:

- Infra red
- Bluetooth
- Serial cables

Priority should be given to acquisition with a serial interface as there is less risk of device modification than when using the wireless interface approaches. The capabilities of some popular cell phone forensics tools are presented in (Table 3). The reader can find further information about the information items that can be recovered by the different tools (Table 4).

The above selection criteria can be enhanced further by looking at the level of abstraction at which the tool can operate. Forensics tools can operate at different levels of abstractions. (Wayne, 2009) distinguishes four levels of abstraction (Figure 8). In reverse hierarchical order they are:

- The raw data level: this is the lowest level and the closest to the raw machine. The data is recovered at the level of a record or of fields of a record.
- The decoded data level: the raw data collected at the previous level is interpreted and decoded into a format readable by humans.
- The assembled data level
- The translated data level

Table 3. Capabilities of cell phone forensics tools

Capabilities of Cell phones forensics Tools		Device Seizure	GSM. XRY	Mo-bile-edit	TULP2G	Pi-lot-link	Oxy-genPM	Bit-PIM	Secure-View	Phone-Base2	Cell-DEK
Software	Commercial software	★★	★	★	★		★		★	★	★
	Open Source Software					★		★			
Functions	Acquisition	★	★	★	★	★	★	★	★	★	★
	Examination	★	★	★			★	★	★	★	★
	Reporting	★	★	★	★		★		★		★
Targets	Palm OS Phones	★			★						
	Pocket PC	★									
	RIM OS phones	★									
	certain GSM devices	★	★	★	★		★		★	★	★
	Certain TDMA devices	★							★		
	Certain CDMA devices	★	★		★			★	★	★	★
Interfaces	Cable	★	★	★	★	★	★	★	★	★	★
	Bluetooth		★		★		★		★	★	★
	Infra-Red		★	★	★				★	★	★
Recovery	internal SIM	★		★	★		★		★		★
	External SIM	★		★	★				★	★	★
PC/SC-compat-ible smart card reader for external SIM card	PC/SC- compatible smart card reader for external SIM card		★		★				★	★	★
Radio-isolation SIM card	Radio-isolation SIM card		★		★				★		

The lower the level, the more accurate the data one can gather but at the same time the more difficult it is to decode and interpret the data. Conversely, the higher the level a tool operates at, the more error prone it is but also the easier is is to interpret and decode.

Challenges of using Mobile Phone Forensics Tools

The previous section provided a through overview of the two main methods of evidence acquisition from mobile phone: the physical and the logical methods.

The digital evidence present on a cell phone is recovered using mostly forensics tools rather than non-forensics tools. This recovery can be physical or logical; however as surprising as it

Table 4. Content recovery coverage of some forensics tools

Content Recovery Coverage	Device Sei-zure	GSM. XRY	Mobile-edit	TULP2G	FCR	Foren-sicSIM	SIM-Con	SI-NIS2	Se-cure-View	Phone-Base2	Cell-DEK	USIM-detec-tive
International Mobile Subscriber Identity -IMSI	★	★	★	★	★	★	★	★		★	★	★
Integrated Circuit card Identifier- ICCID	★	★	★	★	★	★	★	★		★	★	★
Mobile Subscriber iSDN- MISDN	★	★	★	★	★	★	★	★		★	★	★
Service provider name SPN	★			★		★	★	★		★		★
Phase Identification phase	★	★	★			★	★	★		★		★
SIM service Table SST	★			★		★	★	★				★
Language Preference LP	★			★		★	★	★				★
Abbreviated Dialling Numbers- ADN	★	★	★	★	★	★	★	★		★	★	★
Last Number Dialled- LND	★	★	★	★	★	★	★	★		★	★	★
Short Message Service SMS	★	★	★	★	★	★	★	★		★	★	★
– Read/Unread	★	★		★		★	★	★		★	★	★
– Deleted												
PLMN Selector- PLMN-Sel	★			★		★	★	★		★	★	★
Forbidden PLMN -FPLMNs	★			★		★	★	★		★	★	★
Location Information LOCI	★	★	★	★	★	★	★	★		★	★	★
GPRS location Information- GPRSLOCI	★					★	★	★				★

Figure 8. Levels of abstractions of SIM forensic tools (Source: NISTR 7617)

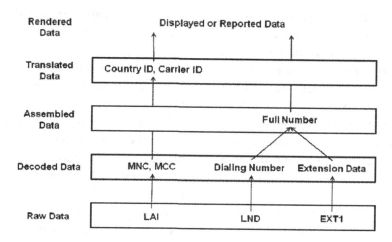

may seem, logical tools are more commonly used than physical recovery tools. This is due to the fact that the manufacturers of forensic tools for cell phones have to take into consideration the following factors before creating a new forensic tool or upgrading an existing one:

- First, the cell phones differ from traditional computers (PC's and laptops), in that, cell phones very often have proprietary operating systems, and the storage structure for data varies from one manufacturer to another.
- Second, new cell phone models appear continuously throughout the year. In addition, there are frequently new comers into the cell phone manufacturing industry, while some manufacturers do quit definitively the industry and leave the market.
- When a new cell phone hits the market, obviously, it has new features not present in the previous models. A forensic tool manufacturer must decide whether to upgrade its tools to adapt to the new phone or not. If so, the manufacturer would have to buy several units of the new phone, test them and eventually update its tool accordingly.

One further constraint concerns the carrier which may demand the phone manufacturer for specific modifications of the phone, such as the storage location assignments.

- Last but not least, 80% of the market is controlled by six manufacturers, out of which two control 50% of the market. There is has a direct impact on the decision of the manufacturers of forensic tools for cell phone. If the choice of the tool manufacturer can be justified in terms of economics, this can only make the task of the investigator harder.

Using Filtered Phone Managers to Acquire Evidence

The above constraints may cause delays to the upgrade of the forensic tool, thereby forcing the forensic investigator to using other means in order to acquire evidence from a newly released phone. Such means include forensic tools and non forensic tools. Sometimes manufacturers of forensic tools in their rush to provide an upgraded tool, shorten the testing and validation procedures thereby increasing the risk of a court of law rejecting results obtaining with such tools.

In such cases, investigators often may have to resort to using phone managers to recover data from a cell phone since phone managers are always readily available from the manufacturers and are generally up-to-date. This seems to be an attractive solution to the problem faced by the investigators. However, investigators should be very careful when using phone managers. They must bear in mind that a phone manager is not a forensic tool; thus its usage can be questionable for several reasons:

- It does not protect data from accidental read/write operations.
- It allows both READ/WRITE operations, and does not prevent accidental alteration of data during these operations.
- Its operation have not been tested and validated as forensic tool operations are.
- It does not provide the investigator with means of calculating a cryptographic hash of the data collected.

Yet, there is a positive note about phone managers. They usually use the same protocols as forensic tools. (Wayne, 2008). Recent research efforts have overcome the risk of data alteration when using phone managers through the use of a filter that extends the idea of the write block restriction to the protocols used by phone managers. The filter blocks any undesired command from altering the data on the phone. The implementation of the phone manager filter is based on the way system call hooks are implemented in modern operating systems such as UNIX, and Windows. (Wayne, 2008) Applied the concept of filters to windows 32 based phone manager. For such phones, the filter is based on hooking API of some questionable commands that would block their execution. For example, the NOKIA PC suite uses a proprietary protocol called FBUS. Its filter operates at the FBUS frame level (Table 5), and blocks any command frame that is not included in a predefined white list.

What one should retain from the NOKIA PC suite case is that filters can be very effective at blocking unwanted commands if API interception occurs at the lowest possible. The authors argue that another advantage of using low level API interception is the possibility of extending the idea the filtering to phones from other makes. One last but not least aspect about the use of phone manager filters in a forensic investigation is to validate such a tool.

Using Flasher Boxes: An Alternative to Traditional Forensics Tools

Flasher devices are used as an alternative method of acquisition of evidences for mobile devices forensics. (Al Zarouni, 2006; Al Zarouni, 2007, Expert) They complement the two traditional forensics acquisition methods, i.e.- the logical and physical acquisition methods. Advocates of flasher devices emphasize the limitations of the traditional methods. For instance, logical or software based acquisition methods rely mainly on the operating system of the devices to gather data. In addition such methods use standardized communication protocols while interacting with the device. We have seen that logical devices can be extended with filters. Yet, some cell phone models don't respond to current command-based forensics methods, Physical methods allow a direct access

Table 5. FBUS frame format

Bytes	0	1	2	3	4-5	6-n	N+1	N+2
Content	Frame ID	destination	source	Command	Length	Data	checksum	

to the phone memory without interference from the phone operating system. But such methods are complex since they require from the investigators an intimate knowledge of the hardware involved; particularly the flash memory chips. In addition, investigators would need to conduct reference tests for every new phone on the market. A direct memory access method would eliminate most of those problems

Mobile phone flasher devices are small devices meant to be used to servicing mobile phones. The legality of such services vary from nation to nation. Legal usage of flashers includes (Al Zarouni, 2006; 2007):

- Removing locks installed by network providers that bar users from using their cell phone with another network provider,
- Removing restrictions on SIM cards.
- Upgrading or modifying a cell phone firmware. This would enable a user who bought a cell phone in one part of the world two of the world to customize it and use it in another part of the word; be it by changing the language used or by resetting for use with another network provider.

In addition, flashers can be used for illegal purposes such as modifying a mobile phone International Mobile Equipment Identity (IMEI) of stolen or lost mobiles that have been locked by the network providers upon requests from the original owner.

Flashers can be divided into 2 classes:

- The first class consists of branded devices that are devices available from well known brands. Branded devices are more expensive than their unbranded counterparts. Each branded device comes with a serial number. Manufacturers of such devices post a list of approved suppliers on their website. Most manufacturers provide up-

dates of the firmware. Several forums are available for help and guidance on new phones. Last but not least, these flashers cover both GSM and CDMA cell phones
- The second class consists of unbranded devices which provide less functionalities and help to the end user. Very often, users get a bare device and have to search the Internet on their own for the appropriate software.

The following is a list of the most popular brands of branded devices (Harrington, 2007):

- UFS3 tornado
- Furious Gold
- Smart Clip
- GTS
- Unibox
- JAF
- N-Box
- Vygis

The Forensic use of Mobile Phone Flasher Boxes

(Harrington, 2007) mobile phone flashing is the process of obtaining a dump of the memory of a cell phone. However, several drawbacks exist and need be raised. Breeuwsma et al., found that using a flashing box to acquire low-level copies of the cell phone flash memory is not risk free. Most flasher boxes work by: first entering the bootstrap mode of the phone, uploading the flasher software to RAM, and executing that software for a low access of the flash memory. It is not unlikely that data may be written or even erased during the operations. Amongst the possible underlying causes of such integrity threats, we may cite the following::

- For some phone models, a full acquisition of the entire memory chip is not always possible
- There is no guarantee that the usage of flasher box does not alter the integrity of the unreachable areas of the memory chip.
- There is a possibility of an erroneous manipulation. Indeed, it is not uncommon that a flash box interface presents write and read buttons close enough to each other; henceforth increasing significantly of accidental violation of integrity.
- If there is a need to remove the battery to connect the flasher device to service ports, there is a very high likelihood of loosing volatile data.
- Some phones may require that a fully charged 9volt battery be connected to the cable so that the phone can be operated reliably and consistently by the flasher boxes.
- Care must be taken to avoid a possible loss of volatile data when using a flash box. A flash box uses cables to connect to mobile phone with an RJ 45 interface on the box end, and a set of pins on the phone ends. It is this end of the connection that may lead to a loss of volatile data. The location of the service ports may call for special measures from the investigators if the service ports are located under the phone battery, or under the SIM card. SIM removal may cause permanent loss of SIM-related data.
- In case a suspect cell phone does not contain a SIM card, investigators should privilege using a flash box on that phone as to recover data related to the removed SIM card.

Given the multitude of flasher devices on the market, there is no standard validation method for the flasher method. Current literature yields that law enforcement and jurisprudence has been taking into account the fact that some alteration may be necessary during the process of gathering digital evidence. Solutions used by practitioners are based on methods that can be verified to behave in an acceptable way (Jonkers, 2010).

Digital forensics researchers saw the need to develop a formal modelling of digital investigation if one were to guarantee a reproducibility of the investigation process. (Lei Pan, 2005)

The quality of reproducibility of a digital forensic investigation should take into account two fundamental requirements:

- The ability to reproduce the experimental conditions every time the process is repeated.
- The variety of digital devices and forensics tools the forensic team may need during their investigation.

Pan and Batten (Lei Pan, 2005) developed a model for digital investigation that would maximize the reproducibility of an investigation results. Their model enhances the previous read-only models by integrating:

- the possibility data alteration through write operations,
- A time-stamping mechanism of the different read and writes operations.

In their model, reproducibility is affected by four possible events (Jonkers, 2010):

- Two consecutive read operations that retrieve the same data value twice. This event is called RAR for Read-after-Read. It is a forensically safe event.
- The result of a write operation is retrieved by a subsequent read operation. This event is called RAW for Read-after-Write. It is also a forensically safe event.
- A write operation modifies the value of a previously read data. This event is called WAR for Write-after-Read. It is forensically dangerous.

- After the second write the value written by the first write is lost. This event is called WAW for Write-after-Write. It is forensically unsound.

(Jonkers, 2010) introduces the concept of forensic soundness as an alternative to the previous requirement of forensically acceptable. The authors suggest a sequence integrity tests related to the use of mobile phone falser boxes. The main objective is to prove or disprove:

- reproducibility
- possibility of counter-expertise
- the influence of power cycle on a phone internal memory

The binary images resulting from a memory acquisition is modeled by a vector whose element are the successive bytes of the image, and whose size is the size of the binary image in bytes.

The *mth* memory acquisition of phone memory is represented by a vector A_m of dimension s. Each element of A_m is one-byte long.

Potential differences between two memory acquisitions of the image of the same phone can be evaluated by comparing the respective bytes of the two acquisitions. Given two acquisitions m and n, the indices where the corresponding values of A_m and A_n differ describe the set of memory locations where the two acquisitions differ. Two measures are derived: The image difference, $D_{m,n} =$ number of pairs $(A_m(i), A_n(i))$ such that $(A_m(i)$ is different $A_n(i))$.

The location Difference, $L_{m,n} =$ Set of indices I such that $(A_m(i)$ is different $A_n(i))$

Example:

We assume:

Figure 9. Predicability of the acquisition of phone memory binary Image

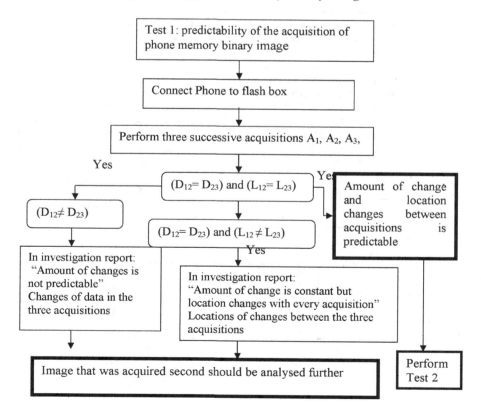

- A binary image is 5-byte long.
- Two acquisitions that resulted in the following binary images A_1, and A_2
- $A_1 = (07,DE,11,F0,CC)$ and $A_2 = (FF, 11, F0,52)$

Hence, $D_{1,2} = 3$ and $L_{1,2} = \{1,2,5\}$

(Jonkers, 2010) uses the above measures to build four tests to prove or disprove the alteration of source evidence and also reproducibility:

- Test 1 tests whether a single acquisition modifies the content of a phone memory (Figure 9).
- Test 2 tests whether keeping a phone connected or disconnecting it between acquisitions has an impact on the phone memory (Figure 10).

- Test 3 tests whether only empty spaces are overwritten by an acquisition (Figure 11).
- Test 4 tests whether full power cycle has an impact on a phone memory Figure 12).

The tests are described in the following flowcharts.

Keonwoo (Keonwoo, 2008) investigated the different methods of data acquisition for cell phone forensics; their advantages and disadvantages are summarized in (Table 6).

Forensic Tools

In section, we present a series criteria that most current digital forensic guidelines recommend when selection a forensic tools.

Tools for digital forensics can be divided in two main groups according to the way data ac-

Figure 10. Connections and disconnections of the phone between acquisition

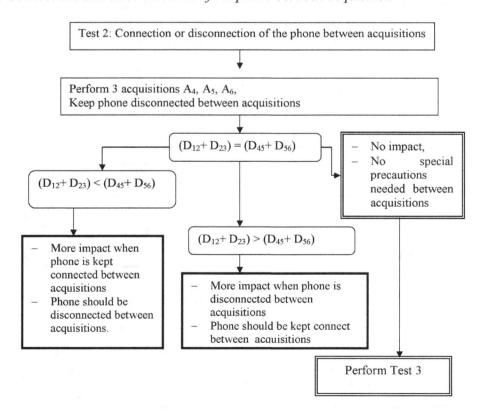

Figure 11. What data is overwritten by an acquisition

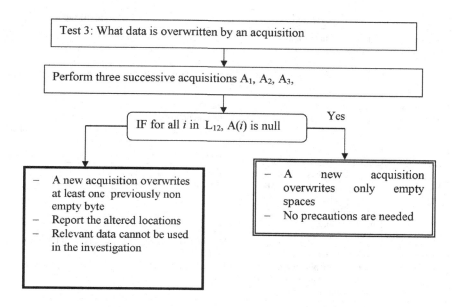

Figure 12. Influence of full power cycle on the acquisition process

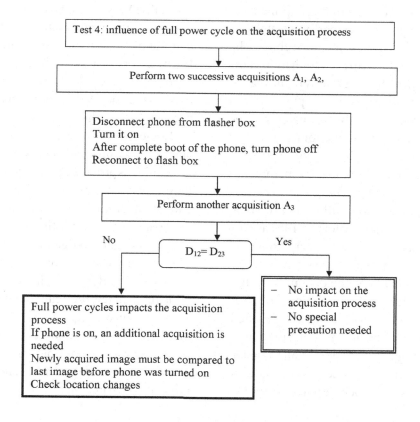

Table 6. Method of acquistion of memory data from a cell phone

Method		Advantages	Disadvantages
Logical Methods	Software-based forensic tools	• Easiest data extraction method	• Support may not be available for all types of mobile phones due to a lack of specific data cables and data drivers • Keeping the cell phone "ON" may increase the risk of compromising the integrity of the evidential data through radio communications.
	Flash box based tools	• Can be the only available method	• Legality of the device • Documentation does not exist or is unreliable • Forensic soundness not guaranteed since the tool can install a client application of the cell phone (dedicated dll) • Image extracted may be just a partial image of the phone memory
Physical methods	JTAG Methods	• Access to physical memory without de-soldering of the memory chip • Complete acquisition of memory image	• Processor must be JTAG enabled • Difficulty to locate JTAG ports due to proprietary concerns
	Physical extraction methods	• Full physical acquisition of the all available data • Only applicable method if the phone is damaged or not functioning	• Difficulty in extracting a memory chip form the printed circuit board (PCB). • Problem of socket compatibility to the foot print of the memory chip.
	Boot Loader	• May help bypass PIN or password control	• Modifying the boot loader may erase data

quisition is performed. The first group includes physical acquisition tools that perform a physical bit-by-bit copy of the phone memory chips. The second group includes logical acquisition tools that perform a logical bit-by-bit copy of the logical store of the phone (file system). A physical tool acquires data through a hardware analysis of the phone memory chips, while the logical tool can acquire data only through the help of the operating system (API for example). Each method has its advantages and disadvantages.

Physical acquisition tools allow an investigator to search for and analyse deleted files as well as remnant of data present or hidden in the logically reachable file system space or in the areas of memory unreachable by the operating system (unseen by the file system). The data collected using a physical tool must be parsed, decoded, translated, sometimes enciphered, and ultimately translated in a language or representation understandable by humans. The process is very tedious, and demands skills and expertise when performed manually. Very often the collected data has to be imported into an automated tool for examination and reporting of potential forensic evidence. Investigators who select this approach should be aware that there exist very few automated tools exist on the market that permit making a complete image of a cell phone memory.

Logical acquisition tools allow a much simpler and easier acquisition process since they are based on primitives provided by the operating system and they access data structures (files) whose structure and organization are more familiar and easier to understand by an investigator. However, logical tools allow an investigator to view only what the file system views and manages. Files hidden in the unused part of the phone memory, as well logically deleted files cannot be recovered.

The logical acquisition of digital forensic evidence from cell phone uses standard information synchronization protocols such as AT, Sync ML to acquire data from the phone itself. Other protocols used include FBUS, MBUS, and OBEX.

Given that some phone sets support several synchronization protocols, some logical acquisition tools can use more than one such protocol. Data present on smart card is retrieved using the APDU (Application Protocol Data Unit) interface. The format of the retrieved data varies according to the coding scheme used by the phone manufacturer. Most tools try to overcome this problem by translating the encoded data into ASCII. Table 7 illustrates how three tools acquire and present the data to the user.

Software based forensic tools for cell phones do not include only commercial and open source tools; they also include tools originally built for device management, device diagnosis, in house built tools, and even hacking tools. This is due to the wide variety of phones that exit and may be seized by an investigator. (Shivanka, 2009) There exits generally three categories of phones:

- general phones such as the ones manufactured by well known manufacturers such as Nokia, Samsung, LG, Motorola, Blackberry digital devices, And Chinese phones which may clone part of general category cell phone without following known standards (Shivankar, 2009).

Importance of the Memory of a Mobile Phone in a Digital Forensic Investigation

The memory of a mobile phone plays a prominent role in acquisition of digital evidence because all forensic tools acquire evidence from the mobile phone diverse types of memory.

A cell phone uses both volatile and non volatile storage technologies. (Wayne 2006) They include volatile RAM, non volatile flash ROM, EEPROM, and memory cards. Generally, the non volatile memory holds the operating systems, application software installed by the network provider or by the user, in addition to user's files holding text, data, images and video. The volatile memory is used for dynamic storage by the operating system. Data held in the volatile memory is lost when the phone is either powered off, or if the power goes below a given threshold. The next section describes the file systems on SIM card by the GSM cellular networking technology.

GSM: Forensic Investigation of The SIM File System

For GSM phones, the most commonly used cell phone technology in the world, the subscriber identity module or SIM contains user specific information; include the user's identification, the user's phone number, as well as the algorithms used to identify the user to the network. The SIM holds also user's personal information such as phone book entries and text messages. A GSM phone requires a SIM to operate. A SIM is special type of smart card. It has a processor, 16 to 128KB of EEPROM, RAM for dynamic execution of programs and applications, and ROM for the operating system, the user authentication algorithms, and encryption algorithms. SIM access is protected by two secret codes called PIN. This section describes the following aspects of the SIM file systems: its structure, its types of files, its access modes as well as access control polices.

On a SIM card, the file system is stored in the EEPROM memory. It is logically organized as a hierarchy of n-ary files. The file system holds three types of files: master files, dedicated files, and elementary files. A master file called MF which corresponds to the root of the tree. Dedicated files (DF) play the same role as traditional directories or repertories. A DF is actually a sub tree of the file system that groups the DF as the root of the sub-tree, and a set of elementary files (EF) which correspond to regular files.

A file consists of a header and an optional body. The header contains information about the structure and attributes of the file, while the body contains the data the file holds. The MF and DF

Table 7. Acquistion and ASCII decoding of IMEI related information by three logical tools

Tool Request/	Response (Hex)	Request/Response (ASCII)
GSM .XRY	41 54 2B 43 47 53 4E 0D	A T + C G S N .
	0D 0A **33 35 36 36 36 31 30 30 35 37 30 34 30 39 32** 0D 0A 0D 0A 4F 4B 0D 0A	. . **3 5 6 6 6 1 0 0 5 7 0 4 0 9 2** . . . . O K . .
PhoneBase	1E 00 0C 7F 00 02 D2 01 C0 7C 1E 00 10 1B 00 07 00 01 00 00 41 01 41 00 0E 1C	. . . . . Ò. À ¦. . . . . A. A. . .
	1E 10 00 7F 00 02 1B 01 05 6C 1E 10 00 1B 00 1C 01 39 00 01 00 01 41 14 00 10 **33 35 36 36 36 31 30 30 35 37 30 34 30 39 32** 00 01 42 5B 50	. . . . I. . . . . . 9. . . . A. . . **3 5 6 6 6 1 0 0 5 7 0 4 0 9 2** . . B (P
Secure View	55 55 55 55 55 55 55 55 55 55 55 55 55 55 55 55 55 55 55 55 55 55 55 55 55 55 55 55 55 55 ... (6 more rows) 1E 00 10 1B 00 07 00 04 00 00 41 01 60 00 2F 19	U U U U U U U U U U U U U U U U U U U U U U U U U U U U U U . . . . A. `. / .
	1E 10 00 7F 00 02 1B 00 05 6D 1E 10 00 1B 00 1C 04 39 00 01 00 01 41 14 00 10 **33 35 36 36 36 31 30 30 35 37 30 34 30 39 32** 00 01 45 5E 57	. . . . m. . . . . . 9. . . . A. . . **3 5 6 6 6 1 0 0 5 7 0 4 0 9 2** . . E ^ W

files do not have a body, while an EF has a header and a body.

A thorough understanding of the SIM file system calls for an analysis of the header attributes and structure. Each file has a file two-byte long identifier. It is used to address the file as well as identify the type of the file. The first byte of the header determines the type of the file. For GSM, the following standard values are adopted for the first byte of the file (Figure 13):

- **'3F'**: Master File;
- **'7F'**: 1st level Dedicated File;
- **'5F'**: 2nd level Dedicated File;
- **'2F'**: Elementary File under the Master File;

Figure 13. Hierarchical structure of the GSM file system

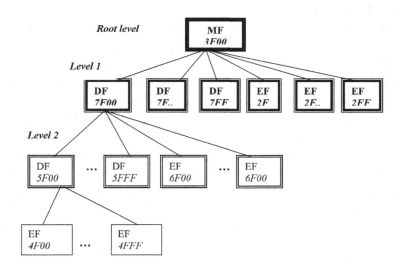

- **'6F'**: Elementary File under a 1st level Dedicated File;
- **'4F'**: Elementary File under 2nd level Dedicated File.

In addition, GSM ensures the uniqueness of a file identifier by imposing a set of conditions on file naming:

- The file ID is assigned at the time of creation of the file concerned;
- A parent cannot have two children files with the same ID
- A child cannot have the same ID as any of its ancestors.

Master File

The master file is the root of the file system. There is only one Master File (MF). It has a two-byte identifier whose value is 3F00. Only the master file has 3F00 as an ID.

Dedicated Files

A dedicated file consists only of a header. The current SIM specification defines four first level dedicated files. These files are immediate children of the master file (MF). They can co-exist on a multi-application card. They are described in Table 1.

The 2nd-level DF is defined under DF_{GSM}, and they all are located under DF_{GSM} (Figure 14).

Elementary Files

An EF consists of a header and a body. GSM uses three types of elementary files:

- *Transparent elementary files*
- *Linear fixed elementary files*
- *Cyclic elementary files*

A *transparent elementary* file is a sequence of bytes. The content of this data structure is accessed via a relative address consisting of the address of the first byte plus an offset. The address of the first byte is '0000' (Table 8).

A *linear fixed elementary file* consists of a sequence of equal-length records. The first record is labeled record no. 1. The header of a linear fixed EF includes fields that indicate the length of a record as well the total length of all bytes in records. A linear fixed file can have at most 254

Figure 14. GSM dedicated files

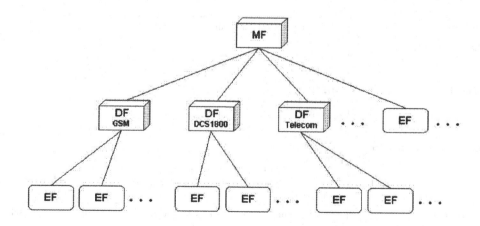

Table 8. Format of a trasparent elementary file

Header
Sequence of bytes

Table 9. Format of a linear fixed elementary file

Header
Record #1
Record #2
... ...
... ...
Record #n

records, and the maximum size of a record is 255 bytes. (Table 9)

There exists several ways of accessing a record in a linear fixed EF (Table 10).

A *Cyclic EF* consists of a fixed number of equal-size records. Cyclic EF files are used to store chronological records. This data structure is cyclic in that there the first and last record are linked so that NEXT (last record) = first record, and PREVIOUS (first record) =last record (Table 11).

A linear fixed file can have at most 255 records, and the maximum size of a record is 255 bytes.

As a convention, the last updated record becomes record 1, and the record holding the oldest data is record n. The operations on a cyclic EF file are summarized in (Table 12).

Currently GSM includes only two DF levels under the Master File (MF). Figure 15 illustrates

an instance of the logical tree structure of a GSM file system.

Using the set rules of Table 12, the possible valid selection scenarios for this file particular file system, are derived in Table 13.

The above description of the SIM file system would not be complete without a look at the intricacies proper to elementary files. They include the range of characters set used, the encoding schemes, as well the data structures that support the elementary files.

An often overlooked aspect of a SIM card or other types of identity modules is the type of character sets and encoding schemes used. A single byte can be convoluted to hold more than one relevant type of information. This can be seen (Wayne, 2009) in the case of the EF_{PUCT} (Price per unit and currency table). In (3GPP07), EF_{PUCT}

Table 10. Access rule for a linear fixed elementary file

Methods of accessing a record of a linear fixed EF	
1. Absolute addressing	Record can be accessed via the record number
2. IF record pointer is not set	**THEN** • *Actions can be performed on either the first or last records* • *Use the NEXT or PREVIOUS Command, to reach the sought record.*
3. IF record pointer is set	**THEN** *Actions can be performed on either:* • *the current record* • *or accessing a Different record via the NEXT or PREVIOUS operations*

4. A record can be identified using Pattern Seek	You can start:
	• Forward:
	    o either from the beginning of the file
	    o or from the record just after the record being pointed to by the record pointer
	• Backwards:

5. IF selection action is aborted	The record pointer will point the same record it was pointing to before the selection took place.

Table 11. Cyclic elementary file

Header
Record #1
Record #2
... ...
Record #n

(identifier 6f41) has a size of bytes. Bytes 1 to 3 hold the currency code, while bytes 4 and 5 hold the price per unit. Bytes 1, 2 and 3 are the respective first, second and third character of the alpha identifier. The coding of the elementary price per unit is not as straightforward.

Indeed, (3GPP07), states that:

- Byte 4 and bits b1 to b4 of byte 5 represent the Elementary Price per Unit (EPPU) in the currency coded by bytes 1-3.
- Bits b5 to b8 of byte 5 are the decimal logarithm of the multiplicative factor represented by the absolute value of its decimal logarithm (EX) and the sign of EX, which is coded 0 for a positive sign and 1 for a negative sign.

A major reason for such convolution is that GSM designers were faced with the limits of memory size.

Along the same way, GSM supports three types of character encoding: a 7-bit GSM character set, an 8-bit character set, and a 16-bit UCS2 character set. In the case of the 7-charcater set, whose support is mandatory, characters are packed into 8bit bytes to make use of the 8th bit of each byte. (Wayne, 2009)

The data structures supporting EFs allow for resolving potential overflow of information due to the size of large numbers. An EF can be extended via the use of linked extension. A special type of EF file is used for that purpose (Figure 16). An EF file can have up to four extension elementary files EXT1 through EXT4. A record can span more than of EF (the original EF and its linked extension). If the value to be stored on the linked extension overflows, it will be fragmented on a series of linked record with the same extension file (Figure 17).

SMS Messages and SIM Files

The EF_{SMS} holds the text messages exchanged by the subscriber. Each entry in the EFSMS holds a SMS message segment. A segment can hold up to 140 bytes of textual content. Longer message are fragmented into up to 255 concatenated message segments (Figure 18). Each message segment include at least:

Table 12. Valid operations on a cyclic elementary file

Operations on a cyclic EF file	
Update	• Only Previous Record can be used • An UPDATE operation references only previous records
Read	In a READ operation, the accessed record can be accessed via: • the NEXT operation • the PREVIOUS operation • the CURRENT operation • Or the record number itself.
Rules for both types of operations on an EF file	
Rule 1	*IF* accessing a Cyclic EF succeeds, *THEN* the record pointer will initially indicate the most recently updated record in that file.
Rule 2	*IF* accessing a Cyclic EF fails, *THEN* The record pointer will point the same record it was pointing to before the selection took place

Table 13. Valid selection operations

Most Recently Selected File	Valid Selection Possible										
	MF	DF1	DF2	EF1	DF3	DF4	EF3	EF4	EF5	EF6	EF7
MF		yes	yes	yes							
DF1	yes		yes			yes			yes		
DF2	yes	yes					yes	yes			
EF1	yes	yes	yes								
DF3		yes				yes			yes		
DF4		yes			yes					yes	yes
EF3	yes		yes			yes					
EF4	yes		yes	yes		yes					
EF5	yes	yes			yes	yes					
EF6	yes	yes			yes	yes					
EF7	yes	yes			yes	yes					

Figure 15. Istance of a logical GSM file system struture

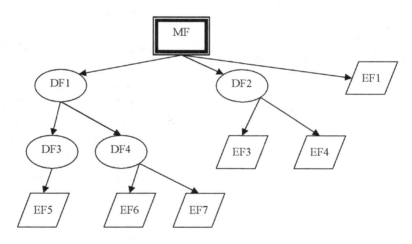

Figure 16. Example of overflow of thefield of the ADN number (Source: NISTR7617)

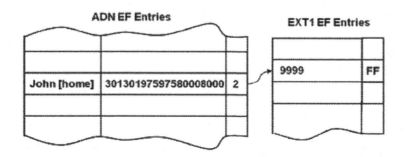

Figure 17. Overflow of the EXT1 file (Source: NISTR7617)

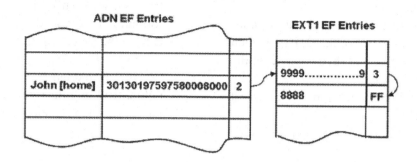

- A message reference number common to all the segments of a message
- The body of the message or part of the body of the message
- A segment index specifying the position of the segment within the message
- And a segment count specifying the number of segment forming the message

The reader should be aware that concatenation does not imply necessarily contiguity of the concatenated segments of an SMS message. When a user deletes SMS messages, the EF will experience fragmentation like a hard disk fragmentation on a PC. Some deleted segments may be reclaimed for reuse; thus they may get overwritten and therefore unrecoverable forensically. Other segments would remain unmodified and thus their content can be recovered by the investigator.

EMS messages are also stored in the EF_{SMS}. Because such messages involve more than just plain text, they are usually longer than an SMS text message and use more than one segment.

Amongst the EF files of interest to forensics investigator (Savoldi, 2007; GSM11.11) there is:

- The EF_{IMSI}, defines a unique number associated with every GSM cell phone subscriber.

- EF_{ELP}, contains information about the preferred language of the users with their order of importance.
- $EF_{MISDN:}$ defines uniquely the international telephone number assigned to a cellular subscriber. Can be used to determine to trace (at the service provider level) the phone calls the user made.
- EF_{ADN}, contains abbreviated dialing numbers used by the user, giving indication to a forensic investigators about whom the user calls frequently or whom the user is receiving frequent calls from
- EF_{FDN}, contains Fixed dialing numbers
- EF_{BDN}, contains Barred dialing numbers
- EF_{SMS}, contains all the SMS sent and received by the phone

Figure 18. Concatenation of message segments (Source: NISTR7617)

SMS EF Entries

65	First part of the message...}	1	3
65	{continues onto second part...}	2	3
65	{and the last.	3	3

- EF$_{MMs}$, contains all the MMS sent and received by the phone
- EF$_{LOCI}$: the phone's current location, continuously maintained on the (U)SIM when the phone is active and saved whenever the phone is turned off.
- EF$_{LND}$, Contains information about the last dialed numbers.
- EF$_{FSPN}$, Holds the service provider name

- EF$_{PLMNsel}$, This EF contains the coding for n PLMNs, where n is at least eight. This information determined by the user/operator defines the preferred PLMNs of the user in priority order. (GSM11-11)
- EF$_{FPLMN}$, forbidden PLMNs, contains a list public land mobile networks (PLMN) that the phone cannot contact directly

Figure 19. File identifiers and directory structures of GSM

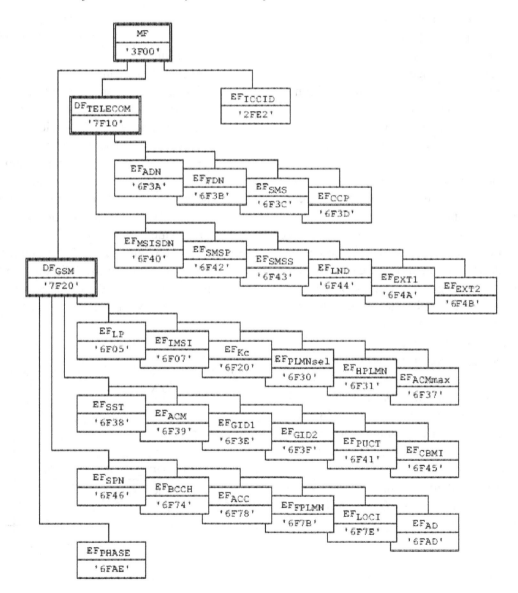

- EF$_{PUCT}$, holds information about the cost of calls in the currency chosen by the user, giving financial information to a forensic investigator.
- EF$_{ICCID}$, defines uniquely the SIM card with the integrated circuit card ID imprinted on the card.
- EF$_{SST}$, indicates which services are allocated on the SIM card and whether they are activate or not.

Reserved File ID's

The current GSM file system standard (Figure 19) has reserved a set of file for administrative and operational use. Tables 14 and 15, depict the reserved ID for dedicated and elementary files respectively.

Security and File Access Conditions for the GSM File System

Under GSM, the access conditions of a SIM file depend on the file itself and the command that is using the file. Before any action on a file is performed, the access conditions on the selected file must satisfied.

Some commands have similar access conditions on any file.

- READ and SEEK have the same access conditions regardless of the file.
- SELECT and STATUS have the access condition ALWAYS regardless of the file.
- GSM does not provide access conditions for the MF and DF files.

GSM provides sixteen different access condition levels for SIM files (Table 16).

Table 14. Reserved dedicated files

Level	Administrative use					
1	7F40 to 7F4F					
2	5F10 to 5F1F	5F20 to 5F2X				
Level	Operational Use					
1	'7F 10' (DFTELE-COM),	'7F 20' (DFGSM)	'7F 21' (DFDCS1800)	'7F 22' (DFIS-41),	'7F 23' (DFFP-CTS)	'7F 24' (DFTIA/EIA-136)
	'7F 25' (DFTIA/EIA-95),	'7F 26' to '7F2F	'7F 80' (DF-PDC) *	'7F 90' (DFTETRA) **	'7F 31' (DFiDEN)	
2- under 7F10	5F50					
2- under 7F20	'5F30' (DFIRID-IUM),	'5F31' (DFGlobal-star),	'5F32' (DFICO),	'5F33' (DFACeS),	'5F3C' (DF-MExE),	'5F34' to '5F3B' '5F3D'to '5F3F
	'5F40'' (DFEIA/TIA-553')	'5F41' to '5F4F				
	'5F50' to '5F5F					
	'5F60'to '5F6F'					
	'5F70' –'5F7F' (DFSoLSA),					

(*) is used in the Japanese PDC specification

(**) is used in the ETSI TETRA specification

Table 15. Reserved elementary files

Administrative usage				
Root Level	Elementary files in MF			
	2F01	2FE0 to 2FEF		
Level 1	Elementary files in DF 7F4X	Elementary files in the DF '7F 10',	Elementary files in the DF ' 7F 20',	Elementary files in the DF '7F 21';
	6F00-6FFF	'6F 10'-'6F1F'	'6F 10'-'6F1F'	'6F 10'-'6F1F'
Level 2				
	Elementary files in all 2nd level DF	Elementary files in 5F10 to 5F1F	Elementary files in 5F20 to 5F2F	
	4F10 to 4F1F	4F00-4FFF	4F00-4FFF	
Operational use				
Root Level	Elementary files in MF			
	2F10 to 2F1F			
Level1	Elementary files in the DF '7F10"	Elementary files in the DF '7F2x"		
	6F20 to 6F2F 6F30 to 6F3F 6F40 to 6F4F	6F20 to 6F2F 6F30 to 6F3F 6F40 to 6F4F		
Level 2	Elementary files in all 2nd level DF			
	4FYX Y= 2, F X=0,F			

Table 16. Access condition levels for the GSM file system

Level	Access Condition	Details
0	Always	The action can be always performed without any constraints
1	CHV1 card holder verification 1	Action is possible if: • a correct CHV1 value has already been presented to the SIM during the current session; • OR the CHV1 enabled/disabled indicator is set to "disabled"; • OR an UNBLOCK CHV1 has been successfully performed during the current session;
2	CHV2 card holder verification 2	The action shall only be possible if: • a correct CHV2 value has already been presented to the SIM during the current session; • OR an UNBLOCK CHV2 has been successfully performed during the current session;
3	Reserved for GSM Future Use	
4 to 14	ADM	Levels 4 to 14, along with their respective requirements are under the responsibility of the relevant administrative authority
15	Never	The action cannot be performed over the SIM/ME interface. The action can be performed within the SIM itself.

Here, one should note that there is no hierarchy in the access condition levels. In other words, if an access condition of level H2 has been satisfied, that does not imply that actions requiring that an access condition of level H1 (H1<H2) will be possible.

Description of the Operations on GSM Files

Table 17 specifies which file, each command can act upon.

The most important security related functions include: Verify CHV, Change CHV, Disable CHV, Enable CHV, and Unblock CHV. They are described in Tables 18, 19, 20, 21.

Content of Some Relevant Elementary Files (EFs)

Wayne, 2009 distinguishes four main categories of EF files that are relevant to a forensic investigation involving GSM cell phones. They store

Table 17. GSM command sepcifications

Function	Action	File type				
		MF	**DF**	**EF transparent**	**EF linear fixed**	**EF cyclic**
SELECT	Selects a file. After a successful selection the record pointer in a linear fixed file is undefined. The record pointer in a cyclic file shall address the last record which has been updated or increased	*yes*	*yes*	*yes*	*yes*	*yes*
STATUS	Returns information concerning the current directory. A current EF is not affected by the STATUS function.	*yes*	*yes*	*yes*	*yes*	*yes*
READ BINARY	Reads a string of bytes from the current transparent EF. Shall only be performed If the READ access condition for this EF is satisfied.			*yes*		
UPDATE BINARY	Updates the current transparent EF with a string of bytes. Shall only be Performed if the UPDATE access condition for this EF is satisfied. An update can be considered as a Replacement of the string already present in the EF by the string given in the update command.			*yes*		
READ RECORD	Reads one complete record in the current linear fixed or cyclic EF. This function shall only be performed if the READ access condition for this EF is satisfied. The record pointer shall not be changed by an unsuccessful READ RECORD function.				*yes*	*yes*

continued on following page

Table 17. Continued

		File type				
UPDATE RECORD	Updates one complete record in the current linear fixed or cyclic EF. Shall only Be performed if the UPDATE access condition for this EF is satisfied. The UPDATE can be considered as A replacement of the relevant record data of the EF by the record data given in the command. The record pointer shall not be changed by an unsuccessful UP-DATE RECORD function.				yes	yes
SEEK	Searches through the current linear fixed EF to find a record starting with the given pattern. Shall only be performed if the READ access condition for this EF is satisfied.				yes	
INCREASE	Adds the value given by the ME to the value of the last increased/up-dated record of the current cyclic EF, and stores the result into the oldest record. The record pointer is set to this record and This record becomes record number 1. This function shall be used only if this EF has an INCREASE access condition assigned and this condition is fulfilled					yes
INVALIDATE	The current EF. After an INVALIDATE function the respective flag in the file status Shall be changed accordingly. shall only be performed if the IN-VALIDATE access condition for The current EF is satisfied. An invalidated file shall no longer be available within the application for any function except for the SELECT And the REHABILITATE functions.		yes		yes	yes
REHABILITATE	This function rehabilitates the invali-dated current EF. After a REHA-BILITATE function the respective flag in The file status shall be changed accordingly. This function shall only be performed if the REHABILI-TATE access condition for the current EF is satisfied		yes		yes	yes

Table 18. Verify CHV

Verify CHV	IF CHV not disabled AND CHV not Blocked THEN IF CHV presented to SIM is correct (successful verification) THEN Number of CHV remaining attempts is reset to 3 ELSE Number of CHV remaining attempts decreased by 1 IF Number of CHV remaining attempts = 0 THEN CHV Blocked NO access allowed until a successful UNBLOCK action ELSE Continue ELSE verification is not possible
Change CHV	IF CHV not disabled AND CHV not Blocked THEN Present OLD CHV and NEW CHV IF OLD CHV presented is correct THEN Number of CHV remaining attempts Reset to 3 NEW CHV value becomes valid ELSE (OLD CHV presented false) Number of CHV remaining attempts decreased by 1 IF Number of CHV remaining attempts = 0 THEN CHV Blocked NO access allowed until a successful UNBLOCK action ELSE Continue ELSE Change of CHV is not possible

the following type of information respectively (Tables 22, 23, 24).

- Service-related Information
- Phonebook and Call Information
- Messaging Information
- Location Information

In Table 25, it describes the access conditions for each of the four relevant EF categories.

CDMA Forensics: Case of CDMA Phones (Murphy, 2010), (R-UIM)

An ESN or electronic serial number uniquely identifies a CDMA phone number in the USA. It is located under the battery of the cellular phone.

Table 19. Disable CHV

DISABLE CHV	APPLICABLE ONLY FOR CHV1 IF CHV not disabled AND CHV not Blocked THEN IF CHV 1 presented is correct THEN Number of CHV remaining attempts Reset to 3 CHV1 is disabled Files protected by CHV1 have ALWAYS as access conditions ELSE (OLD CHV presented false) Number of CHV remaining attempts decreased by 1 IF Number of CHV remaining attempts = 0 THEN CHV Blocked NO access allowed until a successful UNBLOCK action ELSE Continue ELSE DISABLE of CHV is not possible

Table 20. Enable CHV

ENABLE CHV	APPLICABLE ONLY FOR CHV1 IF CHV not disabled AND IF CHV not Blocked THEN IF CHV 1 presented is correct THEN Number of CHV remaining attempts Reset to 3 CHV1 is ENABLED Files protected by CHV1 have ALWAYS as access conditions ELSE (OLD CHV presented false) Number of CHV remaining attempts decreased by 1 IF Number of CHV remaining attempts = 0 THEN CHV1 is BLOCKED CHV1 is ENABLED NO access allowed until a successful UNBLOCK action ELSE Continue ELSE ENABLE of CHV is not possible

Table 21. Unlock CHV

UNBLOCK CHV	UNBLOCKS a CHV Present UNBLOCK CHV and New value for CHV IF UNBLOCK CHV presented is correct THEN CHV= new value for CHV Number of UNBLOCK CHV remaining attempts Reset to 10 Number of CHV remaining attempts Reset to 3 ELSE (UNBLOCK CVH is false) Number of UNBLOCK CHV remaining attempts decreased by 1 IF Number of UNBLOCK CHV remaining attempts = 0 THEN CHV is BLOCKED ELSE Continue

The ESN is generally written in decimal (11 digits) and/or hexadecimal (8 hex digits). When a user switches from one phone to another, she/he must provide the ESN of the new phone top the network carrier before it can be activated. This is a unique 32 bit number assigned to each mobile phone on the network. The examiner should be aware that the hex version of the ESN is not a direct numeric conversion of the decimal value. An ESN converter can be found at http://www.elfqrin.com/esndhconv.html. The ESN is being replaced by the MEID or Mobile equipment ID for reasons of compatibility with the IMEI (International Mobile Equipment Identity) used by GSM and UMTS. Another reason for the change is due to the fact that phone manufacturers are running out of ESN identifiers.

The Mobile Equipment ID (MEID), also found under the battery cover, is a 56 bit number. The MEID is listed in hex, where the first byte is a regional code, next three bytes are a manufacturer code, and remaining three bytes are a manufacturer-assigned serial number. Usually, CDMA phones do not have a Subscriber Identity Module (SIM) card. Recently, we have seen newer hybrid phones that contain dual CDMA and GSM technology and can be used on either CDMA or GSM networks. Qualcomm has developed a RUIM or Removable User Identity Module Smart Card. As a dual-mode smart card the R-UIM allows users to roam across

Table 22. EF containing service related information

EF	Description
ICCID	The Integrated Circuit Card Identifier (ICCID); Unique numeric identifier for the SIM Up to 20 digits long. It consists of: • an identifier prefix (89 for telecommunications), • a country code, • an issuer identifier number, • and an individual account identification number (ITU06). Except the prefix, the components of an ICCID are variable. Mandatory EF
IMSI	The International Mobile Subscriber Identity (IMSI) Unique 15-digit numeric identifier assigned to the subscriber. It consists of: • a Mobile Country Code (MCC), 3-digit long • a Mobile Network Code (MNC), 2 or 3-digit long • and a Mobile Subscriber Identity Number (MSIN), assigned by the carrier takes up the remainder of the 15 digits. The fourth byte of another EF, Administrative Data (AD), gives the length of the MNC Mandatory EF
MSISDN	The Mobile Station International Subscriber Directory Number (MSISDN) intended to convey the telephone number assigned to the subscriber for receiving calls on the phone, but is updatable by the subscriber. Optional EF.
SPN	The Service Provider Name contains the name of the service provider. Optional EF, If present, it can be updated only by the administrator (i.e., Administrator access).
SDN	The Service Dialing Numbers contains numbers for special services such as customer care optional EF
EXT3	The Extension3 (EXT3) EF contains additional data for SDN entries.

CDMA and GSM networks. It is standardized as IS-820. R-UIM is built on GSM 11.11 by adding CDMA Directory Files (DF) populated with Elementary Files (EF) and functions.

Inside these dual technology phones is located a slot for a SIM card. The identifying information under the battery of these phones may list an IMEI number in addition to the ESN/MEID number.

CDMA phones also have two other identifying numbers, namely, the Mobile Identification Number (MIN) and Mobile Directory Number (MDN). The MIN is a carrier-assigned, carrier-unique 24-bit (10-digit) telephone number. When a call is placed, the phone sends the ESN and MIN to the local tower. The MDN is the globally-unique telephone number of the phone. Prior to Wireless Number Portability, the MIN and MDN were the same but in today's environment, the customer can keep their phone number (MDN) even if they change carriers.

Let us look at the various forensics methods for CDMA phone. They include software tools, flashing, JTAG dump, physical extraction of memory chips, and a cloning method.

The software toolkits for CDMA phones use BREW commands. BREW or Binary Run time Environment for Wireless developed by Qualcomm for CDMA mobile phones is the interface between the applications and the phone operating system. As stated before, such tools may not acquire the complete content of a phone memory, especially deleted files or remnants of files. A look at the

Table 23. EF containing phone-book and call information

EF	Description
ADN	The Abbreviated Dialling Numbers Retains a list of names and phone numbers entered by the subscriber. The type of number (TON) and numbering plan identification (NPI) are also maintained in this EF. It also holds an index to an EXT1 EF record for overflow data (i.e., an unusually long sequence of digits).
LND	The Last Numbers Dialled Contains a list of the most recent phone numbers called by the device. A name may also be associated with an entry (e.g., a called phonebook entry) and stored with the number. It also holds an index to anEXT1 EF record for overflow data.
EXT1	The Extension1 (EXT1) EF record is used to maintain overflow digits for ADN, LND, And other EF entries.
FDN	The Fixed Dialling Numbers Same functionality as ADN ; it also contains a list of names and phone numbers However, this EF restricts dialling to just the numbers prescribed by a card manager. If the FDN storage capacity cannot hold all of the information for an entry, an index to an Extension2 (EXT2) EF record is used to indicate where the additional data is maintained.
EXT2	The Extension2 (EXT2) EF record is used to maintain overflow digits for FDN and other EF entries.
	EF containing messaging information
EF	**Description**

SMS	The Short Message Service EF
	Contains text and associated parameters for messages:
	• received from or sent to the network,
	• Or are to be sent out as an MS-originated message.
	SMS entries contain text and header information such as:
	• the time an incoming message was sent as recorded by the mobile phone network,
	• the sender's phone number,
	• the SMS Center address,
	• And the status of the entry.
	The status of an entry can be designated as:
	• unoccupied free space
	• or as occupied by one of the following:
	    o a received message to be read,
	    o a received message that has been read,
	    o an outgoing message to be sent,
	    o Or an outgoing message that has been sent.
	Deleted messages are usually flagged as free space and the content left unchanged on the SIM until overwritten.

Table 24. EF containing location related information

EF	Description
LOCI	The Location Information EF Contains the Location Area Information (LAI) for voice communications. The LAI is composed of the MCC and MNC of the location area and the Location Area Code (LAC), an identifier for a collection of cells (3GPP09b).
LOCI GPRS	The GPRS Location Information EF Contains the Routing Area Information (RAI) for data communications over the General Packet Radio Service (GPRS). The RAI is composed of the MCC and MNC of the routing area and the LAC, as well as a Routing Area Code (RAC), an identifier of the routing area within the LAC.

Table 25. Access conditions for the four EF categories

CHV1	CHV2	ADM	NEVER
AND	FDN	IMSI	ICCID
EXT1	EXT2	EXT3	
SMS		SPN	
LOCI		AD	
LOCIGPRS		PHASE	
MSISDN			

Table 26 (Kessler, 2010) shows that Bitpim, an open source tool can be very valuable since it allows a logical dump of the phone memory. Once connected to the phone, the investigator will be able to dump file system data, interpret phonebook, wallpapers, ringers, calendar entries, and memos, call log, and, text messages. One advantage of using a tool like Bitpim is the simplicity of the acquisition method as compared to the use of JTAGS of the extraction of the memory chips. The down side of the software tool method is the unavailability of proper cables and proper driver for each type of phone since they do not support all the cell phones in the market (Table 26).

Flashing (hacking and development tools) is usually the last resort method for a phone that is not damaged. First specific cables are needed. Second the "hacker" nature as well as the lack of documentation of the tool makes it forensically unsound.

The main problem of the JTAG approach is finding information about the appropriate connection ports. We have already seen that this information can be very hard if impossible to get. But if the ports can be determined, this method has two advantages over the other methods. The JTAG approach provides a forensically sound access to flash memory without de-soldering of the memory chip and it also provides a complete forensic image

The physical extraction method is the riskiest and the most difficult one since it calls for de-

Table 26. Software frensics tools for cell phones

Software forensics tools for Cell Phones	CDMA	GSM	iDen	SIM	Logical Dump	PhysicalDump
BitPim	X				X	
Data Pilot Secure View 2	X	X				
Paraben Device Seizure	X	X		X	X	
SIMCon				X		
iDen Media Manager			X			
Manufacturer / Other	X	X	X	X		
Cellebrite	X	X	X	X	X	X
CellDEK	X	X	X	X	X	X
Oxygen Forensic Suite	X	X		X		
XRY / XACT	X	X	X	X	X	X

soldering of memory chips; a delicate operation that may damage the chip permanently. It is advised that this method be used in desperate cases where the phone itself has been damaged to the point where the other methods cannot be applied.

An alternative method, called cloning (Murphy, 2009) can be used when one or more the following conditions hold:

- The phone LCD screen is broken
- The full file system was extracted successfully but there is no available tool to decrypt the proprietary EFS, EFS2 formats.
- The investigator seeks to minimize the physical manipulation of the original evidence
- The investigator applied various software tools on the broken reports and received conflicting reports

The objective of the cloning method is to transfer the user setting and user created data in their original settings from the original phone to an identical phone in make, model, and firmware version.

The cloning process is divided into four steps;

1. Preparing the forensic machine and the target phone
2. Creating a complete copy of the file system residing on the original phone
3. Transferring the data to the target phone-creating the clone phone
4. Verifying that the data transferred from original phone to the clone phone has not been tampered with.

At that point evidential data can be viewed on the clone phone in their native format. In the next session, the forensics of the most common operating systems for cell phones are presented (Murphy, 2010), (R-UIM).

Forensics of Mobile Phones Operating Systems

Now that we covered the two most important cellular networks, lets us look at how the forensics challenges raised by the most commonly used operating systems in today's cell phones: Windows Mobile Devices, Symbian (9.x) devices, and Androids.

Windows Mobile Forensics

Current Windows mobile devices (WMD) use the Windows mobile platform which is based on the Window CE operating system (Savoldi, 2009). Most commercial forensics tools for WMD use Remote API, and thus can retrieve only active data; deleted data cannot be retrieved. Physical acquisition tools include commercial tools such as XCAT and Cellebrite, and open source tools such as XDA. This section starts with a brief overview of the forensically relevant components (software and hardware) of mobile devices, and then the different acquisition methods for windows mobile devices are discussed (Klaver, 2010; Breeusma, 2007; Casey, 2010; Pooters, 2010). A WMD includes several hardware elements; three of them are forensically relevant: the processor, the flash memory, and the RAM memory.

1. Processor
   ◦ Most of the processors used in Windows mobile devices are systems on chip (SOC) processors. They integrate most of the peripheral devices of a smart phone into a single chip.
   ◦ A major challenge facing the investigators of WMD phones is the access to the chip data sheets that provide the necessary information for a physical data extraction. Very often chip manufacturers restrict the access to the datasheets to manufacturers of phone handsets; thus forcing foren-

sics professionals to resort to reverse engineering.

2. Flash memory: this type of non-volatile memory is often used to store data on a mobile phone. Data cannot be updated directly on flash memory. It needs be copied to RAM, updated then written back into a different location on the flash memory. We distinguish two types; NOR flash and NAND flash.

    ○ NOR flash: processor code can be executed directly from NOR flash memory. This type of memory is forensically relevant because it cannot only store code, but it can also store user's data. Such data may remain present in memory even after user's data is deleted even after a full reset of the device.

    ○ NAND flash: code cannot be executed directly from a NAND flash memory it has to be copied to RAM first.

Flash memory can be reused if two rules are satisfied:

*   Rule1: flash memory must be overwritten (erasing) to all "1s" before it can be reused

*   Rule2: this operation is performed by erasing on a large number of blocks, (128 to 512 kilobytes).

*   A block becomes candidate for erasing if the majority f its pages are not active. It's still active pages will be copied to another location on the flash, and then the whole block will be erased

*   Because erasing operations wears out flash memory, manufacturers of flash memory use policies that spread such operation uniform ally over the entire flash memory. Pages and blocks are

    3. RAM: Active processes reside in RAM. A process addressing space is divided into: the dlls needed by the process,

Table 27. Addressing space of RAM based dlls

RAM based dlls
Free Space
Stack:
Heap
Code

the stack, the heap, and the code. In-between the stack and the dells there is a free space for the stack to grow. Between the code and the stack, the heap is located (Table 27).

The forensically relevant software components of a Windows Mobile device (WMD) include the boot loader, the heap area, the file systems, the registry hives, and the databases.

1. Boot loader:
    ○ On some mobile devices, the boot loader can be used to obtain physical image of a WMD memory, especially when the investigator is blocked by an access code. Sometimes the boot loader has to be modified before a physical image can be obtained.

    ○ Manufacturers often hide from the common users a boot loader feature that allows for the copying of various types of memory from the phone to an external device. If the investigator can access this functionality, physical images of the phone memory can be obtained reliably and fast even when a phone is locked.

    ○ If such functionality is not readily available, several solutions exist: replacing the boot loader, patching it, or getting the phone password. While all the alternatives are time consuming and labor intensive, the first two are also risky since modifying the boot loader may lead to a reorganization of the flash memory with a subsequent erasing of evidential.

2. The Heap

It is the portion of memory allocated dynamically by the operating system to a process that uses it as a working memory. The heap area is reclaimed by the operating system once the process terminates. However, the data stored in that heap will not be deleted automatically. Permanent erasing of heap block happens if the heap manager has to rearrange the memory blocks to satisfy requests from processes of heap allocation.

3. File systems

The flash memory of WMD has TFAT partitions as well as binary partitions. The former are used for user data and firmware extensions while the latter are used for firmware and the boot loader program. The TFAT partition holds a Transcation Safe variant of Windows FAT file system. It is called safe because loss sudden loss of power will not affect the integrity of the file system. Usually, most of the user created files reside under the traditional "My Documents" folder. However traces of the user's activities can be found in several locations. In addition to registry entries, usage artifacts include index. dat files and embedded database files (.vol files) (Casey, 2010). Investigators can face additional challenges because some of the files that hold information about user's activities are locked by the operating system and cannot be copied by the acquisition tools. These files include: cemail.vol, pim. *.vol and the registry hives. Moreover, this can be exacerbated by the difference in interpretation of the same data by different tools.

4. The registry hives;

The information contained in the registry hives of a windows mobile device has the same structure as on other windows OS. Similarly, the information can be accessed using the Microsoft remote registry editor. Information of interest includes;

- *HKCU\ControlPanel\Owner* which holds the contact details entered by the user
- *HKCU\System\State\Shell* which holds the most recently used items
- *HKCU\Software\Microsoft\pM SM\ SavedUsers* which holds Windows Live ID
- *HKCU\ControlPanel\Home\ CurBgImageName* which holds the Home screen background image.
- *HKCU\Comm\EAPOL\Config* which holds the WIFI access point information

5. Databases

In the versions of WCE greater than 4.0, the file system stores the various databases and the registry. Several forensic tools support TFAT making the extraction of the file system image. The Windows Mobile OS saves artifacts about the creation, reception, opening, composition and sending of emails and MMS, and even their deletion.

The most relevant databases are: cemail.vol, pim.vol. The cemail.vol file includes the following attributes of an email: the header information (To, From, Subject, attachment file names). The pim.vol includes information about call history, contact information, and contact database.

Once an email message is opened on Windows mobile device, at least one file is created: an .mpb file which holds the message content is created under *\Windows\Messaging*. If needed .att files are also created to store the email attachments in the *\Windows\Messaging\Attachements* folder.

Investigators should look under the \Windows\ Messaging folder for .mpb files, because it may include remnamts of SMS and MMS that were deleted from the cemail.vol file.

In some devices, even the remnants of sent messages may be recovered. Investigators are urged to look for *.dat files under the *\Mydocuments*

UAcontents folder; such files contain copies of images sent via SMS.

Another issue of interest to investigators of windows mobile devices, is the search for possible spyware applications that could control have been controlling the device remotely with or without the knowledge of the owner. Investigators are advised to look for a "*smartphone.log*" file under the following folder: *Program_files\Applications\ Smartphone folder.*

We have seen in that primary objective of an investigator who finds a mobile phone in a crime scene is to avoid any modifications to the status of the phone as much as possible. The recommended solution is radio isolation of the phone. However, a phone is always active whether the phone is in an active state or a quiescent state. Periodically, the OS performs memory management actions such as reorganizing flash pages, erasing blocks with expired pages, reorganizing the heap through compaction and relocation. Turning off the phone has also its inconvenient:

- Activation of a security code that may bar any logical acquisition of data
- Activation of the garbage collector.

For most tools, evidential data is not acquired through a direct access to the phone flash memory but through an abstraction layer; thus they do not allow a complete physical acquisition of the flash memory. Most often, such content can be found in the cemail.vol database. Due to its proprietary format, only few tools exist that perform a direct parsing of the format. Hex viewers can be used to acquire data directly from the flash memory. In addition, most tools require that a software agent must be installed on the mobile device itself; hence accepting the execution of unsigned programs and raising the risk of malicious activities. Both XACT and ITutils (RAPI) are considered as pseudo physical acquisition tools for Windows mobile devices. The former is a commercial tool while the second is an open source one. In both cases, ActiveSynch

must be installed on the acquisition device. XACT can interpret cemail.vol data automatically; but this tool is too expensive for investigators with small budget. XACT stores the agent software on a removable media like a memory card which is then inserted in the mobile phone; thus avoiding modifications to the phone memories will be avoided. If Itutils is used instead, investigators can mount a copy of the acquired cemail.vol file into a Windows Mobile Emulator, and use a free software tool to analyze it. Itutils extracts more data than commercial forensics tools. However, Itutils will two create files, itsutils.dll and itsutils.log on the target device; thus resulting in data overwriting.

In the following, we will focus on how to analyze data extracted from the flash memory of WMD. NAND flash is divided into pages of size 0x210 or 0x840. The last 0x10 byte of a page hold metadata that include: (Klaver, 2010), (Breeusma, 2007)

- the logical block number of the page in bytes 0,1,2, and 3
- the page state in byte 6. A page can be active (0xF9), expired (0xF8), or free(0xFF).

(Klaver, 2010), proposes the following method to reconstruct a file system acquired from a NAND flash memory:

Step1 While (pages available)

- *get the page offset*
- *read 0x210 bytes*
- *read byte (0x206) to check the state of the current page*
- *read byte(0x200, 0x201, 0x202, 0x203) to get the LBN*
- *case (state of the page is:*
  - *0XF9: add (file offset, LBN) to active pages list*
  - *0XF8: add (file offset, LBN) to expired pages list*

○ *0XFF: add (file offset, LBN) to free pages list*

Step2 Sort the list of active pages according to their LBN

Step3 While the active page list is not empty

- *go to offset of the page*
- *read 0X200 bytes*
- *compare the NBL of the current active page with the previous LBN by evaluating*
  ○ *gap= LBN – previous LBN*
- *if gap > 1*
  ○ *while gap>1*
    - *write empty page to output*
    - *decrease gap by 1*
- *write 0X200 bytes to output*

Step4 While the expired page list is not empty

- goto offset of the page
- read 0X200 bytes
- write 0X200 bytes to output

According to (Klaver, 2010), once the file system has been reconstructed, it can be investigated for forensic evidence. Artifacts of applications on windows mobile devices are disseminated in several locations. The most important artifacts of user activities include; the file system, registry, and volume files.

Both cemail.vol and pim.vol are in Microsoft proprietary format CEDB and EDB. Practitioners found a way to decode both volumes by:

1. using Encase to extract the Cemail.vol from the image of the file system
2. using the cedb400.dll, open cemail.vol,
3. reading the relevant data.
4. Using a WCE emulator, to store the EDB volume, then read the pim.vol using an EDB API (Klaver, 2010)

In the case of Cemail.vol, forensics investigator can make use of the platform builder (PB) a developer environment, provided by Windows CE. The cedb400.dll, located under *WINCE520\\ PUBLIC\COMMON\OAK\BIN\I386\,* provides the necessary functions to read a CEDB database. Klaver developed xpdumpcedb.exe, an API based tool that reads any CEDB formatted volume (in our case a cemail.vol) and outputs the active data of the volume in an XML file. The algorithm used by the tool is based on the following pseudo-code:

1. *CeMountDBVol(filename)*
2. *CeFindfisrtDatabaseEx*
3. *While database= CeFindfisrtDatabaseEx*
   ○ *CeOidGetInfoEx(database)*
   ○ *CeOpenDatabaseEx(database)*

While record=CeRecordPropsEx(database)

- *While property in record*
  ○ *Print property*
  ○ *Update MD5*
- *Print MD5 of record*

Forensics of Symbian -Operated Cell Phones

Let us consider the issues facing the forensic investigator of a Symbian phone. Savoldi, 2009 analysed the security requirements of Symbian 9.x, derived the forensics methods available for that operating system family, then compared it to the methods available for Windows Mobile.

The current version of Symbian (9.x) operating system is based on the concept of a trusted computing base (TCB). Symbian distinguishes three levels of trust:

- The TCB: the highest level of trust requiring the most stringent conditions for access. At this level we find only the kernel, the file server, the software installer, and its registry. In addition, any component

Table 28. Windows mobile vs. Symbian forensics

Method of acquisition	Windows mobile	Symbian smart phone
Logical	Yes	Yes but only if based on connectivity services
Flash boxes	Yes	No open source tools only because of the Symbian operating system constraints that only properly signed applications can be used
Boot loader	Yes	The boot loader cannot be modified or replaced with a boot-loader with more memory dumping capabilities for the same reasons as for the flash boxes.
JTAG	Yes	Yes
Chip extraction	Yes	Yes

requires to be certified, and also must be formally verified to be secure before being granted complete and unrestricted access to the system resources.

- The TCE or the trusted computing environment: this level includes system components that need to access only certain sensitive capabilities of the system to perform their duties.
- The third level includes the rest of the applications whose access is ruled by the capability list associated with the application.

Along the same philosophy, some of the API's on Symbian are capability protected. This trust requirement has a direct implication of the acquisition methods available to forensic investigators

In the literature, there is a focus on the user volume image because it contains most of the user artifact activities. It resides on flash memory. Other relevant volumes reside in either ROM or RAM. Table 28, summarizes the currently available acquisition methods to a forensic investigator of a Symbian 9.x phone (Pooters, 2010; Savoldi, 2008).

The FAT16 file system (Pooters, 2010) holds the currently installed applications as well previously installed ones. They both can be crucial evidence to forensic investigators. Some of the locations known to contain information about installed applications are summarized in Table 29.

iPhone Forensics

The iPhone Operating system is based on OS X (Punja, 2008), it can be updated using the iTunes facility. It can be used when syncing an iPhone with a computer to set the following attributes:

- Contacts, Calendars, Email account settings, Web pages
- Ringtones, Music and audio books
- Photos, podcasts, and videos

Andrew Hoog and and Katie Strzempka (Andrew, 2010) conducted an analysis of several forensics tools for the IPhone focusing on four criteria: installation, acquisition, reporting, and accuracy (Figure 20).

An overall average was taken from all of the tools combined, which came out to be 3.3. Anything below, meeting, or above this average was listed as "Below", "Meet", or "Exceed.

In addition to the above methods, there is an approach that uses the capabilities of iTunes to extract evidential data not obtainable by the current commercial methods; the process involves a copy or backup of the data files.

The backup data can be imported to either a Windows or MAC computer before it can be parsed. The author provides the location of the most sought out databases such as SMS, Calendar, and Call history.

Table 29. Locations known to contain information about installed applications

C:\Private\100012a5\DBS_10207216_SWInstLog.db.	Keeps a log of all application installations. It keeps track of; • The application name • The application SID, • Date and time of installation • Version, name of the application vendor
C:\Private\101F4CD2\	Keeps tab of the layout of the menu application. When an application is uninstalled, some version of the OS may remove parts of the menu.
C:\sys\install\sisregistry\	Contains the registries for the (pre-) installed applications. \Backup.lst. add new entries whenever an application is installed. When an application is installed an entry is added. It contains the application name, vendor name and some other unknown binary data. Every time an application is installed, a directory is created. The directory name is equal to the SID of the application. C:\sys\install\sisregistry\(SID)\. It contains a registry file 00000000.reg, which contains the location of all the files that are extracted from the application installation (SIS) file.
C:\sys\uninstall.	Holds log files for uninstalled applications. For every uninstalled application, a subdirectory (SID)_00000000 is created.
(xxx).log added.	This file may include log entries for each file that was deleted or changed during the uninstallation process.
C:\sys\hash\.	Holds files with SHA-1 hashes for each installed application. The file name of the hash files is equal to the corresponding binary file name in C:\sys\bin\.
C:\sys\bin\.	Holds the binary files of the installed applications: library files (.dll) and executable files (.exe).

Androids Forensics

Android is an open software platform for mobile handheld devices. It has been developed by the Open Handset Alliance, whose mission is to accelerate innovations in mobile and to offer consumers a richer less expensive experience. This platform includes an Operating system, middleware, and core mobile applications for mobile devices. It is built on top of the open Linux kernel. It can run on a variety of processors like, Intel, ARM, and MIPS. The android platform allows the development of applications that can take advantage of all the functionality offered by the phone. It uses a virtual machine, the Dalvik virtual machine that allows each application to run concurrently in a separate virtual machine. Each installed application has its own user ID and group ID. Data created by a given applications cannot be accessed automatically by other applications unless explicit permission has been granted. The permissions are defined statically, verified during installation, and cannot be altered afterwards. If the android security architecture allows for a safe

Figure 20. Comparison of iPhone forensics tools

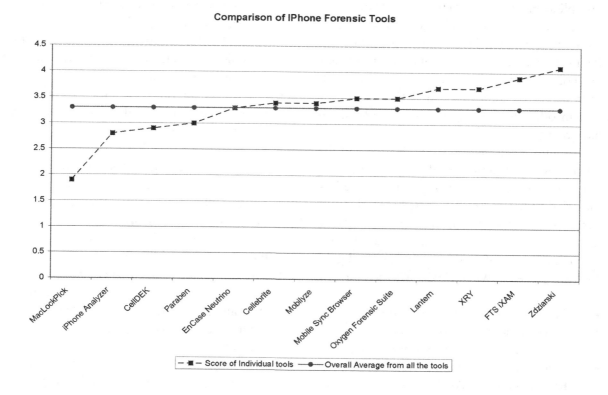

runtime environment, it can be major challenge to a forensic examiner. (Lessard, 2010)

Android can store data in both microSD card and flash memory. SD cards are based on FAT32 and can be examined using known forensic tools. Examining an Android flash memory is not as easy. Currently Androids use the YAFFS2 file system. YAFFS stands for yet another family of file systems; it is a file system developed specifically for NAND flash memory. YAFFS2 uses pages of 2096 bytes, while the older YAFFS uses pages of 512 bytes.

Android forensics is still nascent. Traditional techniques are used to image the SD memory card. Imaging the flash memory is more difficult. If the examiner has access to root password, the examiner can run the UNIX dd command to acquire a bit-by-bit image of the physical memory. In case /root password is unavailable, it is worth

trying the Android debugging tool. If this service is enabled, an image of the phone flash memory can be extracted. Asides from theses legal methods, there is also the possibility to obtain root access using hacking tools such as the Nandroid set of tools (Brent, 2010). It requires the use of a new SD card and the execution of a NANDmod tool. Once root privileges are acquired, a program called SPRecovery must be installed on your machine. Once installed, you will be able to use the dd command and backup your flash memory on the empty SD card. Since a this last method is based on the installation of a third party software on the device it is not forensically sound.

Anti-Forensics

Anti-forensics (Alessandro 2010) is a recent off-spring of the still relatively new field of digital forensics. Digital forensics is a newly created discipline, based on the traditional field of forensics. It uses science and technology to investigate crimes where digital devices have been involved. It aims at establishing facts that can be presented in a court of law. Several definitions of AF have been suggested, some relate AF to breaking into a system, others to avoiding detection, while others have related it to intrusion.

An intuitive definition would be that anti forensics aims at affecting negatively evidence that may be relevant to a particular crime as well as making the entire forensic investigation difficult at best and impossible at worst for the investigating team. In a digital context, the target of digital anti forensics consists of the different steps of a digital forensic process: (Wayne 2006; Wayne 2007)

- Crime scene identification/control
- Evidence identification
- Evidence preservation & collection
- Evidence transportation
- Examination and Analysis
- Report and Presentation

Marcus (2005), AF aims at attacking the existence, amount, and quality of evidence present on a crime scene, as well as hindering the ability of the investigator to examine and analyse such evidence.

In a standardization effort, the following definition has been proposed (Harris, 2006); "any attempts to compromise the availability or usefulness of evidence to the forensics process". Several actions can be taken to attack the availability of evidence; they include: preventing the evidence itself to be created, hiding it from the investigator, manipulating evidence as to make unavailable.

The most commonly used anti-forensic techniques include four major categories (Marcus 2005):

- **Data hiding:** this category includes root kits, steganography, and encryption.

- **Artifact wiping:** this category includes disk cleaners, free space and memory cleaners, and prophylactics
- **Trail obfuscation:** log cleaners, spoofing, misinformation, zombian accounts, and Trojan commands
- **Attacks on the computer forensic process**: file signature altering, hash fooling, and nested directories.

A criminal may use root kits (Bluden, 2009) to prevent the creation of evidence by turning off some system logging features. Another alternative is to hamper system binaries to attack the credibility of the logged data. Encryption is used in anti forensics, but its objective is not data hiding. Rather it is meant to make to complicate the acquisition and analysis phases for the investigator.

Steganography attacks do not make information unintelligible, but hide its content as well as the fact that such information exist. Data can also be hidden in storage areas not reachable by the operating system. Artifact wiping aims at destroying evidence, making it unrecoverable. Trail obfuscation aims at misdirecting the investigator by hiding or deleting evidence about the source and the nature of an attack. (Marcus, 2005) Attackers can use log cleansers to modify metadata of log files, delete compromising entries, and modify time stamps. They can also use spoofing techniques and economizers to hide the origin of the attack. Zombie accounts and Trojan can also be used to ensure untraceable back door unauthorized accesses. The forensic tools themselves can be the target of attacks. We should keep in mind that software forensic tools are as much prone to bugs that any system or application software (MAFIA). Attackers can also install rootkits in target systems that would act as malicious system hooks and hide compromising processes or evidence. The hashing algorithms of the forensic tool can be attacked as to create collisions. Altered evidence files can be modified so that their hash value looks the same at safe copies of the original files.

Last but not least the investigator can be the target of anti-forensics attacks. This type of attack may include overwhelming the investigator by creating a huge amount of evidence that cannot be searched, analyzed and reported within the time and budgetary constraints of the investigating team.

The availability of evidence is violated if evidence becomes unavailable if it is destroyed or altered. Evidence loses its usefulness if it is altered, compromising the availability of evidence is related to hostile actions or attacks that threaten the existence of an evidence, that may threatened.

Data Hiding in a SIM Card

Savoldi et al, (Savoldi, 2007) researched the SIM/USIM file system beyond the specifications provided by the GSM standard reference literature (gsm11.11). (Savoldi, 2007a) developed an open source tool, SIM brush, that explores the entire SIM file system structure. SIMbrush has been based on the SELECT command of the GSM protocol, so that there is no risk of alteration of the data present on the SIM card. The tool was used to explore not only the "traditional" or standard files of interest from a forensic point of view, but it helped discover that on 128 K SIM card, there exist 16549 bytes of non standard space made of non standard files that can be accessed either in ALW mode or CHV1. Hence any malicious user, can hide incriminating information in the non standard files in addition to the potential use of steganogarphy to hide information in a standard file. Compared to removable storage volumes such as SIM cards or memory cards, a phone internal memory is more vulnerable to anti-forensics activities

Anti- Forensics Using Androids

According to Gartner, the mobile phone market will be dominated by two major operating systems in 2014: Symbian and Android. It is predicted that RIM and Windows mobile will see their share of the market decline significantly (Hachman, 2010).

A major objective of the android OS is to guarantee that by default, any android application runs in a securely isolated environment. Android uses the concept of sandboxes in order to inhibit any running application from communicating or accessing other applications without a set of explicitly declared required permissions. Applications are granted static permissions that cannot be modified during their lifetime. When the application is installed, the operating system verifies that an application has the proper permissions. An application may access the capabilities of another application if the user has signed it with the appropriate certificate. A significant feature of the android OS is the possibility for an application or a user to create a private directory. Such directory can be created in any type of storage volume selected by the application. In addition a private directory is accessible only by its parent application. No other application can see it. If such a feature may be welcome by information security practitioners, it may become a nightmare for forensics investigators. Indeed, private directory are deleted when the application is uninstalled.. The use an android-based mobile phone can hide or compromising information in this private directory. The use will select the compromise information present in his/her applications; export it to the private folder. In addition, it is trivial that any user eager to hide compromising digital evidence would create the private folder in the phone internal memory rather than in a removable memory volume such a memory cards. (Distefano, 2010)

Metasploit: Anti-Forensics Project

This project, was created by Vinnie Liu, and maintained by a community of members. Its objective is the development of tools and techniques for removing forensic evidence from computer systems. The Metasploit website of the group specifies the objectives of the group as:

Metasploit Pro is enterprise-grade software for security professionals who specialize in penetration testing and require an advanced solution for multi-level attacks that enables them to get deeper into networks more efficiently." However, (Hilley, 2007) this group has been unveiling holes in forensic programs and tools making them publically available, therefore giving more weaponry and power to Anti-forensics.

Challenge of Chinese Phones

Chinese mobile phones are clones of existing cell phones of well known cell phone manufacturers. They create very serious problems for a digital forensic investigator, especially during the preservation and acquisition phases of a forensic investigation. Commonly used guidelines about seizure and identification of regular mobile phones call for the application of specific rules about when, how, a found phone should be turned on or off. Similar recommendations exist on measures to take about the identification of a phone and its subsequent radio isolation. such recommendations may not necessarily apply in case the incriminated cell phone is a Chinese phone. The removal of the battery of Chinese phone does not result in the loss of temporary data such as the date, time, and call logs (Shivankar, 2009). Actually it was discovered that if a Chinese phone was kept off for an extended period of time, such temporary data would be permanently erased. Chinese phone can complicate or make impossible the identification of a phone. Normally, when a phone is found on as crime scene, an investigator can identify the phone via the display the manufacturer of the phone, the service provider or the Operating system used. Manufacturer logo, serial number, type of cradle or power adaptor can help the investigator identify the phone type and manufacturer.

How can an investigator recognize a Chinese phone?

The authors (Shivankar, 2009) offer some clues to the investigators:

- The absence of a manufacturer name or logo
- Potential differences in weight and thickness with an genuine device.
- The potential absence of an International Mobile Equipment Identity (IMEI) umber, which is normally located in the cavity where the cell phone battery resides.

If the investigator determines that the incriminated phone is a potential clone of a regular phone, the following steps should be taken:

- Search the web for clones for that particular brand or brand and type. Example, "search clone Nokia E72".
- Remove the battery and check if an IMEI number is found the battery cavity, its validity can be checked by accessing the following site: www.numberinplans.com
- The battery should be placed immediately to avoid any side effects.

In the event the phone is found locked or if the phone locks due to some inadvertent manipulation, the investigator is advised to get help from the forums on the internet such as:

http://forum.gsmhosting.com/vbb/f457/china-mobile-phones-secret-codes-508805/ , http://forums.techarena.in/tips-tweaks/1167057.htm.

On the Hashing Techniques used for Mobile Device Forensics

Cryptographic hashing techniques are used by digital forensic investigators to be able to verify the integrity of the digital evidence collected on the digital device. A hashing function, sometimes called a message digest, takes as input an arbitral long string of bytes and produces a fixed size output string. It's typical output size varies between 128 to 512 bits. It is a one way functions, in that given an input it produces an input. But given an output string, it is impossible to derive the corresponding input string. In addition a good hash function is collision resistant; that is two different inputs cannot produce the same output string. Commonly used hash functions include MD5, SHA-256, SHA-384 and SHA-512 (Bruce Steiner, 2003)

Preliminary research (Ayers, 2007) showed that for the majority of the tool tested, were consistent when individual files were hashed; however that did not hold anymore when the over files are hashed together. (Sobieraj,2007) researched images created by mobile phone cameras, and found out that the time and data stamp that are part of an image metadata (Exif or exchangeable image file format are not dependable. A further investigation at Purdue University, has conducted a series of tests on different forensic tools; the results had shown consistency except for MMS messages.

A Provider's Side View of Mobile Forensics Investigations

Mobile phone forensics investigator often has to search for clues about the location of events,

persons, or devices related to a given crime. Such information is obtained via subpoena from the network provider. Investigators ask for the call record details of incriminated cell phones. Usually this information is obtained from the data logged by the antennas of the base stations of the cell phone network. One often overlooked issue is the quality of information obtained from the base stations. Normally, a base station has three antennas: a north bound antenna, a south east bound antenna, and a south west bound antenna. Each antenna has a 120° coverage of the base station cell (Figure 21).

A mobile phone within a given cell will be serviced by the antenna that is receiving the strongest signal from the phone. If an antenna is overloaded it may hand off a phone to a less loaded antenna. (O'Connor, 2009) found that there is a crossover area of at least 40° at the borderline between the areas covered by two adjacent antennas (Figure 22).

The authors stresses out that in rural areas, cell towers cover a much wider area than in urban areas. It varies widely making the location and

Figure 21. Cell tower with its three antennas

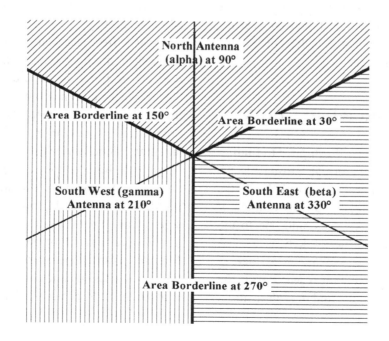

Figure 22. Cell tower with cross over areas

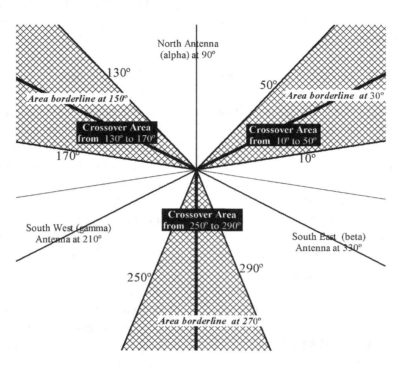

time of a phone call imprecise. Very often, for load balancing reasons, the antennas of a cell tower are rotated as to be located in the middle of populated areas. While analyzing CDR evidence, a mobile phone forensic investigator must check the potential impact of the cross over interference, the size of a cell as well as the potential rotation of the antennas.

FUTURE RESEARCH DIRECTIONS

Today's forensic tools are ill equipped to finding information in unordinary format, unusual places, or obfuscated information (Garfinkel, 2010). Given the ever increasing complexity of the task faced by forensic investigators, and due to the frequency of phones on the markets as well as their make and origin (Shivankar, 2009), there is an increasing trend of academic researchers in the field to focus on abstraction and modularization.

Purdue University has introduced laboratories for undergraduate courses in mobile phone forensics (Mislan, 2010). Anti-forensic attacks on digital investigation has led researchers to investigate the formal modeling of a digital investigation (Rekhis, 2010).

Asides from the run of the mill academic research in digital forensics, there is a need for research in digital forensic education. In today' society we have been witnessing an ever increasing availability of connectivity options as well as processing power. Our society is becoming more and more ubiquitous. Mobile devices, especially small scale digital devices such as mobile phones are competing with traditional mobile computing devices such as laptops. (Nance, 2010) the significant increase of digital crimes has forced law enforcement authorities to incorporate digital forensics as an official part of criminal investigation procedures, opening the door for expertise and skills in digital forensics. At, The Digital Forensics

Minitrack of the Hawaii International Conference for Systems Science in January 2009, a Digital Forensics Research in Education Working Group was formed, and a research agenda was set. The objective of the group is to develop educational material, methodologies and educational environments that can help the teachers and trainers. The group has set three main goals:

- Involving academic researchers in solving problems related to digital forensic education.
- Developing networking relations amongst the interested researchers.
- Develop a education agenda in tune with the need of the law enforcement agencies and forensic tool manufacturers.

Standardization of Forensic Models for Mobile Phones

Last but not least is the issue a standard forensic model for mobile phones. Ericsson President and CEO Hans Vestberg has predicted that by 2020, 50 billion devices will be connected to the web up from five billions now (Higginbotham 2010). This declaration confirms an earlier prediction that by 2020 mobile phones will be the primary means of digital communication (Brodkin, 2008). We have already seen that there is tree types of mobiles phones: basic, intermediary and smart phone. Sales in the latter type grew by 75% from 2009 (Choney, 2010). Forensics investigators would be solving more and more cases involving smart phones in the near future. Unlike computer forensics, there is no standard process for the forensic examination of smart phones. Smart phones raise several challenges to the forensic practitioner: (Chevonne, 2010):

- The type of memory used may include: flash memory, removable memory, SIM/R-UIM card

- The different states a smart phone can be in: nascent, active, active, quiescent, or semi-active.
- Smart phones are prone to modification due to radio communications
- Most smart phones use one or more proprietary technologies such as file system structure, database encoding, *memory chip circuitry*
- New models from different manufacturers are put on the market several times a year.
- Obsolete models are still in operation
- Practically each model from each manufacturer may require specific cables and drivers
- Existing forensic tools may not support all phones, sometimes a forensic tool supporting a model from a given manufacturer may not support a new model from the same manufacturer
- Physical extraction of evidence from flash memory calls from connection through specific ports whose location requires access to proprietary documentation.

(Chevonne, 2010) introduces the idea of a platform independent forensic process model based on the property of invariance. The author suggests the use of a Smart phone Components List (SCL) in order to develop a functionality-independent forensic process model. The SCL is based on the fact that the core components of a smart phone will remain the same independently of the manufacturer, the make, of the technological advances. For example, a smart phone will always include the following components:

- A GSM or CDMA connection, a PIM, a SIM or USIM card
- An LCD screen, Internet capabilities,
- A processor, an operating system, file systems
- Storage capabilities, RAM or ROM
- Radio capabilities

On-Scene Triage of Mobile Devices

Currently, law enforcement agencies use digital forensic laboratories (DFLs) to process mobile devices soundly, effectively and efficiently. Yet, the proliferation of mobile phones is overloading DFLs. The resulting backlog of cases is an increasing impediment to investigations involving mobile phones. There are increasing situations that call for an immediate extraction of data from the mobile phone for several reasons. So far, the reader has been familiar with reasons due to avoiding any alteration of the phone data by remote communications, or due to periodic operating system memory management operations. There are also emergency reasons relevant to life and death situations such as kidnapping cases, bomb threats, and even military or intelligence cases. In such situations, it is unfeasible to send the involved phones to a DFL and wait for the forensic analyst report. There exist three types of makeshift solutions to the problem: thumb/scroll through, federal kiosk, lab in a kit. (Mislan, 2010a). All three methods are vulnerable to a threat of data alteration or data wiping. Current efforts aim at developing a set of methods and tools that can be used by non-technical personnel timely, effectively, and soundly in case of where the gravity of the case warrants it.

CONCLUSION

Mobile phone forensics is the youngest off spring of the relatively new field of digital forensics. We have seen that digital forensic investigation is a process consisting of a series of steps that ultimately produces digital evidence that must be admissible in a court of law. After an overview of cellular network technologies, the chapter presents the currently used guidelines and procedures in digital forensic investigations. Given that by their nature mobile phone technology differs drastically from computers, the author reviews the current adaptations of the commonly forensics guidelines used to mobile phone. The forensic strength and weaknesses of the different forensic acquisition methods are discussed, along with commonly accepted criteria used when selecting a forensic tool for cell phones. At this point, the two most important cellular networks, GSM and CDMA are investigated in terms of forensics. This is followed by a review of the four mostly used operating systems in mobile phones: Windows Mobile, Symbian, iPhone, and Androids. The chapter raises also issues related to some of the most important challenges faced today by forensic investigators: anti-forensics, data hiding in SIM cards, the threat of clone mobile phones, the problem of evidence integrity, and view of mobile phone forensics from the network provider side. Finally, four main research actions are reviewed: the effort of academia to use formal methods to model the forensics of mobile phone, the design of academic degree specializing in mobile forensics, efforts to entice mobile phone manufacturers to agree on minimal set of components common to all smart phones, and last but not least, current effort by the mobile phone forensics community to solve the increasingly crucial challenge of the challenges of on-scene triage of cell phones

REFERENCES

Al-Zarouni, M. (2006). *Mobile Handset Forensic Evidence: a challenge for Law Enforcement.* Proceedings of the 4th Australian Digital Forensics Conference, Edith.

Al-Zarouni, M. (2007). *Introduction to Mobile Phone Flasher Devices and Considerations for their Use in Mobile Phone Forensics.* Proceedings of the 5th Australian Digital Forensics Conference.

Ashcroft, J. (2001). *Technical Working Group for Electronic Crime Scene Investigation.* US Dpt of Justice, 2001. Retrieved from ww.ncjrs.gov/pdffiles1/nij/187736.pdf

Ayers, R., Jansen, W., Moenner, L., & Delaitre, A. (2007). *Cell phone forensic tools: An overview and analysis update.* Retrieved from http://csrc.nist.gov/publications/nistir/nistir-7387.pdf

Bluden, B. (2009). *Anti forensics: the rootkit connections.* Black Hat USA, 2009

Breeuwsma, M., de Jongh, M., Klaver, C., Van Der Knijff, R., & Roeloffs, M., (2007) Forensic Data Recovery from Flash Memory. *Small Scale Digital Device Forensics Journal, 1*(1), June 2007

Brent. (2010). *Android Rooted: What is Nandroid Backup?* march 2010, http://www.simplemobilereview.com/android-rooted-what-is-nandroid-backup/

Brian, D., (2009). Digital forensics works. *IEEE security and Privacy, march/April 2009, 7*(2).

Brodkin, J. (2008). *Mobile phones to be primary Internet device by 2020, experts predict.* NetworkWorld, Retrieved from http://www.networkworld.com/news/2008/121508-pew-report.html

Casey, E. (2007, June). What does "forensically sound" really mean? *Digital Investigation, 4*(2), 49–50. doi:10.1016/j.diin.2007.05.001

Casey, E. (2010). Introduction to Windows Mobile Forensics. *Digital Investigation, 6*(3-4), 136–146. doi:10.1016/j.diin.2010.01.004

Chevonne, T. D. & Dampier, D. A., (2010). A platform Independent Process Model for

Christian, S. J. Peron &. Michael Legary. (2006) Digital Anti-Forensics: Emerging trends in data transformation techniques. Seccuris Labs. Retrieved from www.seccuris.com/documents/papers/Seccuris-Antiforensics.pdf, Cowan University, Perth Western Australia, December 4th 2006

Dai-Yon, C., Hyun Jung, K., & Hyoung-Yong, L. (2007) *Analysis of Trust in Internet and Mobile Commerce Adoption, System Sciences, 2007.* HICSS 2007. 40th Annual Hawaii International Conference on Jan. 2007 Page(s):50 – 50.

Distefano, A., Gianluigi, M., & Francesco, P. (2010). Android ant-forensic through a local paradigm. *Digital Investigation, 7,* 2010. doi:10.1016/j.diin.2010.05.011

Emmanuel, S. (2010). P., (2010), Network forensic frameworks: survey and research challenges. *Digital Investigation, 7.*

Expert: 'Flasher' technology digs deeper for digital evidence. (n.d.). Retrieved from http://www.physorg.com/news95611284.html

Forouzan, B. (2007). *Data communications and Networking.* New York: McGraw-Hill.

General characteristics of the subscriber identity module file system. (n.d.). Retrieved from http://mobileforensics.files.wordpress.com/2007/02/sim-file-system.pdf

George, M. (2005). *Technical Challenges and Directions for Digital Forensics.* SADFE'05 Proceedings of the first international workshop on systematic approaches to digital; forensic engineering, 2005.

3GPP07 Specification of the Subscriber Identity Module - Mobile Equipment (SIM - ME) interface, 3rd Generation Partnership Project, TS 11.11 V8.14.0 (Release 1999). *Technical Specification,* June 2007.<URL: http://www.3gpp.org/ftp/Specs/archive/11_series/11.11/1111-8e0.zip>.

Grafinkel, S. L. (2010). Digital Forensic research: the next 10 years. *Digital Investigation, 7,* 2010. Smartphones Based on Invariants, Fifth International Workshop on Systematic Approaches to Digital Forensic Engineering.

GSM-1. (2011). *Global GSM and 3GSM Mobile Connections*. GSM world. Retrieved from www. gsmworld.com (accessed March 11th, 2011).

GSM-11-11 (n.d.). *Digital cellular telecommunications system (Phase 2+); Specification of the Subscriber Identity Module - Mobile Equipment (SIM-ME) interface (GSM 11.11)*. ETSI, European Telecommunications Standards Institute, http://www.ttfn.net/techno/smartcards/gsm11-11.pdf

GSM-2. (n.d.). Retrieved from http://gsmworld.com/newsroom/press-releases/2070.htm#nav-6

Hachman, M. (2010). Gartner: Android, Symbian will win Mobile OS wars. Retrieved from http://www.pcmag.com/article2/0,2817,2368992,00.asp

Harrington, M. (2007). *Hex Dumping Primer Part 1*. Retrieved from.

Harris, R. (2006). Arriving at an anti-forensic consensus: Examining how to define and control the anti-forensic problem. *Digital Investigation, 3S*, 2006.

Higginbotham, S. (2010). Ericsson CEO Predicts 50 Billion Internet Connected Devices by 2020. Retrieved from http://gigaom.com/2010/04/14/ericsson-sees-the-internet-of-things-by-2020

Hilley, S. (2007). Anti-forensics with a small army of exploits. *Digital Investigation*, 4.

Hoog, A., & Strzempka, K. (2010). *iPhone Forensics White Paper, Independent Research and Reviews of iPhone Forensic Tools*. Retrieved from http://www.viaforensics.com/education/white-papers/iphone-forensics.

http://digitalforensicsmagazine.com/blogs/wp-content/uploads/2010/07/Cell-Phone-Evidence-Extraction-Process-Development-1.8.pdf

http://www.mobileforensicscentral.com/mfc/include/Hex_Primer_Pt_1.pdf

IHCFC Workshop - Guide to Forensic Computing Training Courses. (n.d.). http://www.ioce.org/core.php?ID=17

IOCE-1999. Retrieved from http://www.ioce.org/fileadmin/user_upload/1999/1999%20training%20workshop.doc

IOCE-2002. Retrieved from http://www.ioce.org/fileadmin/user_upload/2002/G8%20Proposed%20principles%20for%20forensic%20evidence.pdf

Keonwoo, K., Dowon, H., & Jea-Cheol, R. (2008). Forensic Data Acquisition from Cell Phones using JTAG Interface. *Security and Management, 2008*, 410–414.

Kessler, G. (2010). *Cell Phone Analysis: Technology, Tools, and Processes. Mobile Forensics World*. Chicago: Purdue University.

Kevin, J. (2010, May). The forensic use of mobile phones boxes. *Digital Investigation, 6*(3-4), 168–178. doi:10.1016/j.diin.2010.01.006

Klaver, C. (2010). Windows Mobile advanced forensics. *Investigation, 6*(1-2), 147–16.

Lei, P., & Lynn, M. B. (2005). *Reproducibility of Digital Evidence in Forensic Investigations*. DFRWS, Digital Forensic research Workshop, 2005, New Orleans, LA, USA

Lessard J., & Kessler G.C. (2010), Android Forensics: Simplifying Cell Phone Examinations. *Small Scale Digital Forensics Journal, 4*(1), September 2010,

Marcus, K. R. (2005). *Lockheed presentation, Anti-forensics*. Retrieved from www.cyberforensics.purdue.edu

Marcus Rogers Anti-Forensics. (2005). *Lockheed martin*. Retrieved from www.cyberforensics.purdue.edu

Mislan, R. (2010). *Creating laboratories for Undergraduate Courses in Mobile Forensics*.

Mislan, R. (2010a). The growing need for on-scene triage of mobile devices. *Digital Investigation, 6,* 112–124. doi:10.1016/j.diin.2010.03.001

Mullins, K. J. (2007). The Mobilr Phone Network (GSM) Turns Twenty. Digital Journal, Retrieved March 11, 2001, http://www.digitaljournal.com/article/225547

Murphy, C. (2010). *Celullar Phone Evidence Data Extraction and Documentation.* Digital Forensics Magazine, 2010.

Murphy, C. (2010). The fraternal clone method for CDMA cell phones. *Small Scale Digital Forensics Journal, 3*(1), June 2009.

Nance, K., & Armstrong, H. (2010). *Digital Forensics: Defining an Education Agenda.* Proceedings of the 43rd Hawaii International Conference on System Sciences – 2010.

O'Connor, T.P., (2009). Provider Side Cell Phone Forensics. *Small Scale Digital Device Forensics Journal, 3*(1), June 2009.

Owen, P., Thomas, P., et al. (2010). *An Analysis of the Digital Forensic Examination of Mobile Phones.* 2010 fourth International conference on Next Generation mobile applications, services, and technologies.

Pooters, I. (2010). Full user data acquisition from Symbian smart phones. *Digital Investigation 6*(3-4), 125-135 (2010). Proceeding SIGITE'10, ACM Conference on Information Technology Education.

Punja, S., & Mislan, R. (2008). Mobile device analysis. *Small Scale Digital Device Forensics Journal, 2*(1), 2008.

Qualcomm CDMA technologies. (n.d.). *R-UIM: QUALCOMM'S System Solutions to Support Removable User Identity Module Smart Cards.* Retrieved from www.laneros.com/attachment.php?attachmentid=17476&d=1117732896

Apup Ramabhardran, Forensic investigation process model for windows mobile devices, Security Group, TaTa ELxi

Reith, M., C. Carr & G. Gunsch. (2002). An examination of Digital Forensics Models. *International Journal of Digital Evidence, 1*(3), Fall 2002.

Rekhis, S., & Boudriga, N. (2010). *Formal Investigation of Anti-forensic Attacks.* 2010 International Workshop on Systematic Approaches to Digital Forensic Engineering.

Savold, i A. & Gubian, P., (2008). *Symbian Forensics: an overview.* International Conference on Intelligent Information Hiding and Multimedia Signal Processing., 2008.

Savoldi, A., & Gubian, P. (2007). *SIM and USIM File system: a forensic perspective.* ACM Symposium on applied Computing 07.

Savoldi, A., & Gubian, P. (2007a). *Data Hiding in SIM/USIM Cards: A Steganographic Approach.* Second International Workshop on Systematic Approaches to Digital Forensic Engineering (SADFE'07).

Savoldi, A., & Gubian, P. (2009). *A comparison between windows mobile and symbian s60 embedded forensics.* Fifth International Conference on International Conference on Intelligent Information Hiding and Multimedia Signal Processing., 2009

Scheiner, B. (2003). *Practical Cryptography.* New York: John Wiley.

Shaoyen, C. (2009). *Research on mobile forensic software system based on windows mobile.* 2009 international conference on wireless networks and information systems.

Sharma, L. K., et al. (2010). Taxonomy of cell planning. *International Journal of Reviews in Computing, 3,* June 2010, http://www.ijric.org/volumes/Vol3/9Vol3.pdf

Shivankar, R., & Ashish, K. S. (2009), *Mobile Forensics: guidelines and challenges in data preservation and acquisition, 2009.* IEEE Student Conference on Research and Development, SCOReD 2009.

Shoniregun, C. A., Tindale, I., Logvynovskiy, A., & Fanning, T. (2005). Securing mobile product ecology for mobile commerce (mC). *Services Computing, 2005 IEEE International Conference on, 2*, 11-15 July 2005, 211 – 216.

Sobieraj, S., & Mislan, R. (2007). *Mobile phones: Digital photo metadata*. Retrieved from http://www.cerias.purdue.edu/symposium/2007/materials/pdfs/E26-CF9.pdf

Suzanne, C. (2010). Smart phone growth explodes, dumb phones not so much. http://technolog.msnbc.msn.com/_news/2011/02/07/6005519-smart-phone-growth-explodes-dumb-phones-not-so-much

Wayne, J., & Aurelian, D. (2008). *Overcoming Impediments to Cell Phone Forensics.* HICSS '08 Proceedings of the Proceedings of the 41st Annual Hawaii.

Wayne, J. & Aurelian, D. (2009). *Mobile Forensic Reference Materials.* A methodology and reification, NIST IR-7617, National Institute of standards.

Wayne, J. & Aurelian, D. (2010). *Guide to Simfill use and development.* NIST IR-7658, National Institute of standards.

Wayne, J. & Ayers, R. (2006). *Guidelines on Cell Phone forensics: Recommendations of the National Institute of Standards and Technology.* Draft, Special publication 800-101.

Wayne, J. & Ayers, R. (2006), *Guidelines on PDA forensics.* NIST Special publication 800-72.

Wayne, J., & Scarfone, K. (2008). *Guidelines on cell phones and PDA security.* NIST Special Publication 800-124

William, S. (2002). *Wireless communications and networking.* New York: Prentice hall.

Yinghua, G., & Slay, J. (2010). *A function oriented methodology to validate and verify forensic copy function of digital forensic tools.* 2010 International conference on availability, reliability and security.

Zareen, A. (2010). *Mobile phone forensics: Challenges, analysis, and tool classifications.* Fifth International workshop on systematic approaches to digital forensic engineering, SADFE '10.

Zhihong, L., & Minxia, L. (2008). Research on Influencing Factors of Consumer Initial Trust Based on Mobile Commerce. *Electronic Commerce and Security, 2008 International Symposium on, 3-5 Aug. 2008 pp. 263 – 267.*

KEY TERMS AND DEFINITIONS

Android: Android is an open software platform for mobile handheld devices. It has been developed by the Open Handset Alliance, whose mission is to accelerate innovations in mobile and to offer consumers a richer less expensive experience.

Anti-Forensics: Methods used by criminals to hinder a digital forensic investigation process.

CDMA: Code Division Multiple Access describes a communication channel access method that employs spread-spectrum technology and a special coding scheme.

Cell Phone: A device whose major function is primarily handling incoming/outgoing phone calls over a wireless network (e.g., GSM, CDMA) with limited task management applications.

Digital Evidence: Information stored or transmitted in binary form that may be relied upon in a court of law.

Flash Memory: It is a non-volatile computer storage chip that can be electrically erased and reprogrammed. It retains data after the power is removed.

Digital Forensics: A digital forensic investigation is a process consisting of crime scene identification/control, evidence identification, evidence preservation and collection, evidence transportation, examination and analysis, report and presentation. The results of such a process are digital evidence that must be presented to a court of law.

GSM: Global System for Mobile communications is an open digital cellular technology for transmitting mobile voice and data services.

JTAG: Joint Test Action Group, also called boundary-scan.

Logical Forensic Rools: A bit-by-bit copy of logical storage objects (e.g., Address book, Personal Information Management data, Call logs, text messages, stand-alone data files) that reside on a logical store (e.g., a file system partition).

Memory Image: File containing the complete and exact data and structures of a media storage device.

SIM Card: Subscriber identification module. A smart card that contains essential subscriber information and additional data providing network connectivity to mobile equipment operating over a GSM network.

Small Sale Digital Devices: Embedded Chip devices, Personal Digital Assistants, Cellular Telephones, Audio /Video Devices, Gaming Devices.

Smart Phone: A full-featured mobile phone that provides users with personal computer like functionality by incorporating PIM applications, enhanced Internet connectivity and email operating over an Operating System supported by accelerated processing and larger storage capacity compared with present cellular phones.

Symbian: Operating systems and software platform for smart phones.

Chapter 5
Applying Continuous Authentication to Protect Electronic Transactions

Silas Leite Albuquerque
University of Brasilia, Brazil

Paulo Roberto de Lira Gondim
University of Brasilia, Brazil

ABSTRACT

Perform a commercial transaction using the Internet or a mobile device (e.g., smart-phone) is quite common in today's world. Every moment increases the number of companies that offer their products and services through this virtual world. Thus, the security issues become evident and shown to be essentials for the parties involved in an electronic transaction feel safe when performing their actions. A fundamental security aspect to build trust among the parties is that they must be permanently authenticated to one another during the entire transaction. Then, conventional methods of authentication (username and password, digital certificates, etc.) do not provide the desired security level. At this moment, come into play continuous authentication processes that aim to maintain the parties' authenticity throughout the transactions period (ideally using methods transparent to users). Considering these requirements, one can realizes that some biometric recognition methods are well suited for providing this type of authentication.

In this sense, this chapter explores some possibilities for continuous authentication use to increase electronic transactions security and addresses issues such: Trust in electronic communications systems, conventional authentication models, continuous authentication concepts and biometrics.

DOI: 10.4018/978-1-61350-507-6.ch005

INTRODUCTION

In a globalized world which is connected through the many communication networks in existence, the ability to do online commercial transactions is essential. More importantly, people who are in constant movement -between home, office, meetings and in traffic, wish to be able to perform these commercial transactions wherever they are and whenever they want. Therefore, electronic commerce and its variants (m-commerce, t-commerce, u-commerce) are more than mere possibilities; they are imposed by our daily needs. However, in order for this commerce to be considered reliable, it is necessary that some information security services be provided through these platforms. It is assumed that one potential executor of an electronic transaction demands, in terms of security, that the data used is accessed only by authorized people or entities (confidentiality), and that such data cannot be modified by intruders (integrity) and that the parties of the transaction recognize and trust the identity of their peers (authenticity). Only then a transaction can be considered reliable.

Specifically concerning authenticity, a very usual way to guarantee this is to use authentication processes of the involved parties. There are several authentication protocols globally recognized and created by several authors and standardized by various regulatory bodies, but almost all of such are concerned only with parties' authentication at a time immediately prior to the transaction completion. This is justifiable for situations in which the transaction has a small duration, but in cases of long sessions execution, where time interval is considerably larger, vulnerability to intruder attacks increase and it is no longer possible to guarantee that an earlier authentication (at the beginning of a transaction) is sufficient to ensure the authenticity of the parties. This lack of long-term guarantee can be found in the analysis of mechanisms used to protect such transactions, because they often use time intervals as limiting factors for the sessions validity, and once these ranges are exceeded, new authentication processes (usually explicit) should be triggered.

At this moment one must think of continuous authentication, which basically consists of constant repetition, throughout the transaction execution, regardless of duration, of procedures to verify the participants' identity.

After deeper analysis, other requirements present themselves alongside that of authentication continuity: transparency to users, so that the action of those users in the main process (buying, selling, banking, etc.) is not interrupted by an explicit re-authentication process, and the use of multiple and complementary authentication mechanisms (multimodal authentication) which enables greater process flexibility and allows the use of mobile equipment of reduced computational possibilities.

Biometric techniques have proven to be interesting alternatives for meeting the mentioned requirements. Whether in physiological or in behavioral aspects, biometrics constitutes more than identifying peers based on "something they have" or "something they know", it is identifying users (rather than pieces of equipment) by "what they are", i.e., based on something that is inherent to them and that uniquely identifies them.

All of these issues have been discussed in the academic community and various papers have been individually published which explore the many aspects addressed herein. It is therefore with the main objective of being a joint bibliographic reference that contemplates these several aspects that this chapter aims to:

Describe and analyze authentication processes that can be used continuously and transparently to increase the authenticity guarantee of the parties involved in an electronic transaction.

Furthermore, we intend to:

- Analyze trust aspects related to creating environments in which electronic transactions may happen and where application of continuous authentication appears somewhat promising;

- Examine authenticity problems within environments involved in electronic transactions
- Check special features of such transactions to justify the continued use of authentication;
- Analyze the biometric techniques (physiological and behavioral) and verify their relevance to the achievement of continuous, transparent and multimodal authentication;
- Examine some authentication techniques based on continuous information exchange generated from the use of applications used in generic transactions.

To achieve the aforementioned goals, the rest of this chapter is divided into the following sections:

Trust in electronic communications systems, in which ideas about trust models that support electronic transactions are explored (trust and reputation; trust in computational environments; entities and relations of trust models; trust and authentication);

Brief revision about conventional authentication models, in which some of the main authentication models currently used to provide authenticity to the parties involved in general electronic transactions are shown and some deficiencies in terms of continuity are evaluated (user/password and PIN based authentication schemes; token and digital certificate approach; EAP types);

Continuous authentication concepts, item where the main concepts related to continuous authentication processes are expressed and analyzed (continuous, static, intrusive and non-intrusive authentications, continuous authentication levels; multimodal authentication);

Biometrics, where the biometric techniques are considered in detail, ways and mechanisms to enable continuous authentication of users are described, both with regard to their physiological characteristics, and in relation to their behavior (physiological biometry and behavioral biometry);

Other forms of continuous authentication, which explores some techniques that are not directly related to biometry but can also enable continuous authentication;

Conclusion, which considers the results of the research related to the subject.

TRUST IN ELECTRONIC COMMUNICATIONS SYSTEMS

As said before, in this section some ideas about trust models in which electronic transactions should be based are explored.

Trust and Reputation

In order to be able to speak about trust models to be used in environments where electronic transactions occur, it is important first to explore some definitions that allow a better general understanding of their meaning.

The first and most important definition is that of the word trust. Some classical definitions bind trust to belief or faith in the moral aspects of entities in which we trust (trusted party), which makes any kind of betrayal unimaginable by those entities that trust (trusting party). Although this concept is consistent with everyday life, it refers to situations related to human relationships ("moral aspects"); such concept does not suit what is being explored in this work because the entities involved in electronic transactions are not always people, but they are also complex systems consisting of hardware, software and people. Thus, other more comprehensive definitions should be considered.

In Josang ET AL (2007), trust is approached from two distinct and complementary aspects: hope (an entity hopes that another entity will act in favor of the first) and dependency (an entity is willing to depend on another to achieve a given goal).

Wang & Vassileva (2007) consider that trust is somewhat subjective and is linked to people's views. Therefore, one can say that it is transferred from one entity to another (transitivity) - "I trust you, you trust them, so I trust them" - which then configures a web of trust (Datta et al., 2003).

In general, the concept of trust that matters for this work should consider: the belief created by direct agreements or by transitivity (web of trust) with entities with which one wants to make a transaction; the hope that there will not be any kind of betrayal by the trusted party; and the level of dependency that the trusting party accepts.

Another concept as important as trust is that of reputation, which can be understood as what is usually said within a community about an entity (derived from their behavior towards others) (Josang et al., 2007) or the public opinion about the character and honest conduct of an entity in a given environment (Wang & Vassileva, 2007).

Trust and reputation are complementary concepts and one can say that a valid way to measure trust is to analyze an entity's reputation. In the same way, the good reputation of an entity can be constructed from the trust that many have in this entity. Contrary to appearances, trust and reputation are not always proportional. It is possible, for example, to trust someone or something, despite its bad reputation, as it is possible not to trust one entity despite its good reputation. In both cases, what creates trust (or distrust) is beyond the reputation of the entity.

A third important concept in the as regards electronic transactions is the one of a trust model. This can be understood as a structure formed by three components: entities, their behaviors and their relationships. Entities represent the various parties involved in the processes and are mainly characterized by two roles: trustee (trusted party) and trustor (trusting party). However, depending on the type of relationship between the parties, some intermediate entities with specific roles can emerge to enable, for example, security mechanisms. Entities are linked to their behaviors, which can generate good (or bad) reputation and give rise to more or less trust. Finally, relationships represent the various links between the entities and afford behavioral assessment, information provision and service delivery in general.

Each component must be adequate for achieving consistent levels of reliability for the transactions that occur within one such structure. Adjustments should arise from answers to questions like (Koien & Haslestad, 2003): Which entities are reliable? How can you trust these entities? Which security aspects should be observed so that trust is justified? The answers to these questions usually determine the fundamentals that should be considered by a trust model that affords a security transaction.

Trust in Computational Environments

As may be perceived about the above definitions, relationships between entities (humans or not) are generally based on trust and reputation systems. This paper focuses on the relationships between complex systems involved in electronic transactions, and it appears to be necessary to have computer systems to facilitate the connections between the various parties (trustee, trustor and intermediate elements). For those connections to be considered reliable there must be, among all mechanisms, parties responsible for ensuring safety against ill-intentioned elements. One of the most usual ways to avoid problems caused by these elements is to use tools that enable access control through reliable authentication and authorization processes. These tools are generally provided by services providers and have a single purpose: to protect them against access made by unauthorized users. However, users' protection against faulty access to non-trusted providers generally remains an unresolved problem.

Hence grows the importance of trust and reputation systems that focus not only on the protection of service providers, but also, and in a proportional way, on the protection of the users of these services. This protection is usually feasible, at first, through a legal agreement between the concerned parties which defines the scope of each one's work, their obligations and rights. After that, physical and logical links are created between the various stakeholders considering the computing environments. These links must include the provision and use of mechanisms to guarantee security to transactions. Only from this warranty can those involved computer systems be trusted (Abrams & Joyce, 1995).

This guarantee, however, is not general. You can divide it into levels based on greater or lesser resistance capacity against attacks made by malicious users. Thus, although other parameters linked to the reputation of the involved parties may be used in order to qualify the level of reliability (system more or less reliable), one can say that the more secure a system, the more reliable it will be. It is then possible (even presumable) that the level of reliability of a system is one of the aspects considered in the decision about execution of critical applications.

The security mechanisms referred above, which are applied to the physical and logical connections, often use cryptographic processes to enable the guarantee of confidentiality and integrity of the information transmission, along with the very authenticity of the involved entities. It should be noted that these information security services generate different types of trust. This can be understood by the fact that an authenticity guarantee provides more or less trust in entities (identity trust). Conversely ensuring confidentiality and integrity indicates more or less trust in links between involved entities (connections trust). There is a third type of trust, the one related to the provision of the service itself (trust in providing the service). This is derived from the previous two types and from the reputation of those involved in terms of the services, i.e., entities may trust the identities of their peers, the connections between the parties may be deemed reliable and yet there is no reliability in the service provision because of involved parties' reputation aspects.

Entities and Relations of Trust Models

The various parties and entities involved in the processes that are based on trust models, as previously mentioned, are basically characterized by two roles: trustee (trusted party) and trustor (trusting party). However it is possible that other intermediary entities exist in order to facilitate the transactions between the two main roles. These roles can be played by several real entities, depending on the purpose of the trust model and especially on the kind of business that is being handled through the transactions between the parties.

In ETSI TS 133 234 (2010), for example, it is proposed a trust model that considers the existence of three basic entities: a cellular network, a wireless network (WLAN – Wireless Local Area Network) and the user. The problem to be addressed in this example is related to the possibility of interconnections between heterogeneous wireless networks. In this particular situation, the cellular network (elements of a communications network that provides mobile telephone services, and considers one or more carriers, one or more domains and one or more access technologies) and the WLAN (entity that provides public access to the IEEE 802.11 network and is composed of access points and other network elements that lie behind these) provide data communication services to the user (element that moves between networks and is formed by the WLAN and cellular network subscriber, by the processing and communication capable equipment and by the connected security devices - modules for user identification, for example).

In this case, it is possible to consider that the cellular network and the WLAN are the trusted parties and the user is the trusting party. Note that in this particular example the trusted parties are complex entities formed by several different functional components (base stations, switching and control centers, authentication centers, etc.).

There should also be trust models between the various functional components, so that the networks might be believed to be reliable by the trusting party. Despite these internal complexities, and probably because of them, intermediate elements that stand between trusted parties and the trusting party are not perceived.

Another example of trust model (this one more appropriate to the topic of this chapter - electronic transactions) is reviewed in Pourshahid & Tran (2007). In this case it is suggested that a structure that allows book commerce by a Virtual Book Store (VBS) through the Internet be used. In this case, the two main entities are the VBS and the Buyer. An appropriate trust model to this situation should consider, unlike the previous example, some intermediate elements that allow the execution of transactions, namely:

- The Internet access provider used by the books buyer (ISP–Internet Service Provider);
- The similar provider that enables the existence of the site from which electronic transactions are conducted (also an ISP);
- The payment service provider responsible for transferring money from the buyer's bank account (or credit card) to VBS;
- The transport service provider (in this case, to carry books)
- Different data communications networks that connect the entities described above.

It is observed that the existence of intermediate entities generates a considerable increase in the complexity of the trust model suitable for solving the problem. In the first example, the relations are restricted to links between the user and the cellular network (controlled by a legal contract for cellular network access), user and WLAN (also dependent on a service contract for communications network access) and the cellular network and WLAN (in this particular case, depending on the level of coupling between these entities, they can have their links controlled by a contract between organizations and, with a high degree of engagement, an entity could belong to another - typically the WLAN could belong to the cellular network operator). The number of connections is small and trust of the entities in their peers, as can be seen, is basically governed by legal contracts.

In the second example, because of the amount of intermediate entities, relations become considerably more complex. Figure 1 shows the various entities and their connections. In this case only the connections between the VBS and the Buyer are considered and those with intermediate elements (links that involve data communication networks and those between intermediate elements are neglected for simplicity). Note that the most important relationship of this model is the one that has a direct relation with the kind of business considered (buying and selling books), i.e., the one between the Buyer and VBS (named B-V). Nevertheless, all other relationships interfere in B-V and are important for the business to be conducted thoroughly and satisfy all parties. Thus, the relation B-A should be trusted, because if they are not, the Buyer can not trust the content he receives from their ISP, and consequently may not feel safe to make a transaction that involves his money through this provider. Similarly, in B-P and V-P, both the Buyer and the VBS must trust the Payment provider (bank or credit card operator), and vice versa, because it is through this that an entity pays and another receives the money. The ISP that is accessed by VBS and hosts its website must also be trusted by the VBS (relation V-H) because it stores critical information and makes the virtual business possible. In addition, this ISP must also be trusted by the Buyer (B-H) because this is the ISP that will provide the data that will come from the VBS with which the business will be conducted. The freight company must also be trusted by both the Buyer (B-F) and VBS (V-F),

Figure 1. Electronic Transaction Trust Model

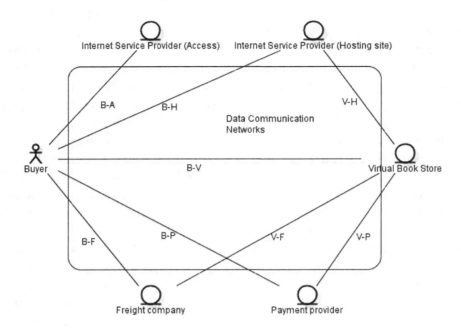

because these entities expect that the delivery of the product sold be done satisfactorily.

Considering the computing and communications environment used in the second example for transactions, one can notice the following types of trust:

- **Identity trust:** each entity must trust the identity of their peers (main and intermediate entities) and this can be done by means of authentication mechanisms that will be discussed later;
- **Connections trust:** the entities do not want their data to be modified (integrity) or seen by unauthorized parties (secrecy), which can be made possible through techniques and processes based on encryption (not the focus of this chapter);
- **Trust in providing of the service:** each entity has a specific role in the model and each is responsible for providing a particular service (book sales, goods transporta-

tion, payment management, etc.). These services must be reliable so that the entire transaction can be completed successfully. As examples, it is considered that it is not interesting to use a freight company that has the reputation of damaging products being delivered and it is not advisable for the VBS have their site hosted by an ISP that does not have a structure that affords satisfactory implementation of electronic transactions (similar examples can be seen by considering each entity). It is noticed that, especially for this type of trust, reputation of the entities is fundamental.

The two examples discussed above represent trust models that are possible solutions for specific problems. For other issues, the cases should be analyzed separately and require the generation of appropriate trust models.

Trust and Authentication

A major goal of authentication mechanisms is to verify the identity of those requesting the authentication and then authorizing the execution of services for those entities. Hence the existence of trust is an extremely important aspect so that transactions can occur, because the various parties involved in a transaction need to authenticate to each other so that their identities can receive credit and there will be trust between the parties.

These aspects were discussed in previous items, where the concept of peer identity trust, which is closely related to authentication processes used by the various stakeholders, was addressed. In general, one can say that the authentication that takes place between two or more entities wishing to conduct electronic transactions creates levels of identity trust of the parties involved (Thompson et al., 2002). From the moment that an authentication process is triggered, it creates a secure connection between those involved (authenticated entities) which provides reliable information transit (at least in the scope of the parties' authenticity) without any need for new endorsements, in principle. Validity periods of the authentication processes should also be considered, because problems might occur during the interval when parties are exchanging information (spoofing attacks, for example) which will void the initial authentication process. Thus, an authentication process executed at a given time ensures trust in the identity of peers in an electronic transaction for a limited period. This point creates the need for a re-authentication process to be triggered and subsequently to validate previous authentications. It should be noted, at this moment, that the application of continuous authentication will minimize the need for re-authentication. This happens because, as will be discussed later in this chapter, continuous authentication induces, in a constant manner, the execution of the authentication process of the involved parties. This allows the parties to remain reliable throughout the operation period (session).

BRIEF REVISION ABOUT CONVENTIONAL AUTHENTICATION MODELS

In this section some of the main authentication models currently used to provide authenticity to the parties involved in general electronic transactions will be shown and will some deficiencies in terms of continuity be evaluated. Subjects like user/password and PIN based authentication schemes, token and digital certificate approach and EAP types will be explored.

The authentication between parties involved in electronic transaction, as seen earlier, is the action that enables peers' identity reliability and allows the process continuation in general. Usually the model used to allow this authentication to occur is static (Calderon et al., 2006). This model is based on a binary decision process ("authorized" or "unauthorized") whose result is valid for a specified time (session). This decision process is based on three steps:

- Application, in which the supplicant user (who wants to authenticate themselves later) firms some kind of contract with the authenticating entity (for which the supplicant will want to authenticate); this contract is based on supply and storage of identifying parameters that will be used later to validate the authentication;
- Presentation, in which the supplicant will request access to resources provided by the other entity which, in turn, prompts the supplicant's credentials to be used to authenticate it; it is stressed that these credentials can be of three categories - something the user knows (a password, for example), something the user has (a token, for example) or something that is inherent to the user and is part of his identity (a biometric characteristic, for example);
- Validation, step where a comparison is made between the parameters presented in

the previous phase (password, token, biometric characteristic, etc.) and those that are stored in appropriate databases and which were obtained and agreed on at the registration stage.

The decision process is based, then, on the result of the comparison performed in this validation. If the result is positive (presented data refers to stored data), the supplicant gains access to the resources requested, if not, access will not be granted.

It should be noted that, if one wants that mutual authentication occurs between the parties, it will also be necessary that a process analogous to that described above be performed in the opposite direction (authenticating entity to supplicant).

User/Password and PIN Based Authentication Schemes

As previously noted, one of the ways used to perform the authentication process is that based on the use of the username (ostensible data) and password (given secret known only by authorized parties) parameters, which are credentials of the first category (something the user know). These parameters must be agreed upon at registration and used during the presentation so that the user is authenticated to the entity (and vice versa, where applicable).

Although widely used, the username and password based authentication mechanism has several weaknesses (Furnell et al., 2000), (Sauver, 2009). Some of the most important are briefly commented herein:

- **problems in creating passwords** - in situations where the user is given the opportunity to choose his own password, it is common that words be chosen (numeric or alphanumeric) that have some particular significance to the user (birthdays, names of people known, etc.) or that exist in the

language of the individual; in both cases, these passwords are subject to brute force attacks (search all possibilities) based on known dictionaries (linked or not to the individual) (Schneier, 1996) which considerably diminishes chosen password security. One way to minimize this problem is to require the individual to use a mixture of letters, numbers and special characters for creating passwords that are not part of any dictionaries (existing or created by the attacker from knowledge about the individual);, the other solution to this problem is based on providing a password created randomly (or pseudo randomly) for the user by the very system responsible for the registration of user identification parameters. With both indicated solutions, one can perceive the inconvenience of the hard memorization of the password, which is solved with the annotation of the password in some protected site, which in turn may also be a problem since that location may not be well protected and the password may be found by a malicious user, which will certainly generate a false authentication;

- **problems in storing user parameters** - that is specifically observed when the user's password is stored in clear text in the authenticating entity database; in this case, an attacker who can access this database can capture the clear authentication data and will be able to login as if he was the very user, a way to minimize this problem is to store parameters associated with the password (typically hash values) instead of the password itself, so if the attacker has access to database, user password will not be obtained in clear;

- **problems with transmission of information between the user and authenticating entity** - for the user to perform their authentication, they need to send their information to the authenticator, and if the communications channel between the user and the entity is unprotected (physically and logically), there is the possibility of an intruder capturing the user data (typically the sensitive parameter - the password) and use them later to perform a false authentication; a solution to this problem is to send, instead of clear password, dynamic parameters (synchronized with authenticator) calculated from the password that does not allow, when caught by an intruder, the deduction of that password; in this case, it should also be possible to calculate those parameters in the authenticator's environment so he can validate the user authentication.

Another form of authentication, similar to that based on username and password, is based on the use of a PIN (Personal Identification Number) linked to secret parameters stored by the user (usually on a removable storage device) and by the authenticating entity. This method mixes credentials of first (something the user knows) and second (something the user has) categories and is typically used for device authentication to access network communication servers (authentication of mobile phones on their networks, for example) and, despite a few differences from the method based on username and password, it is equivalent to this in the scope of this work.

The PIN, particularly as regards mobile phones (please note that this device has evolved significantly and many are used, nowadays, to conduct electronic commerce transactions that make up what is known as m-commerce), may be used to authenticate both the device and the cellular network user (SIM - Subscriber Identity Module) [Furnell et al., 2008]. Specifically in this case, the user shares the secret parameters with the mobile communication network. These parameters are on a removable device (SIM-card) that the user carries with them (usually inserted in the device) and in an element of the cellular

network (typically the authentication center). The authentication process may occur similarly to the previously treated case, and therefore, many problems in the process based on username and password also occur in the authentication that is based on the use of PIN.

Considering the aspect of continuous authentication, it is clear that the forms mentioned are flawed in view of the fact that they are executed, in most cases, only for the opening of the session. If someone wants those methods to be used continuously (or at least several times during a session), the regular holder of the parameters (password, PIN, etc.) will need to reintroduce them, which will probably generate interruptions in the transaction that is being conducted.

Token and Digital Certificate Approach

An authentication token is a device that stores information that can be used by a user to prove his identity to an authenticating entity and is usually small enough to be held without problems (in the user's pocket, for example). It falls into the latter category of credentials (something the user has) and is used most often for creating dynamic keys or passwords synchronized between the token and mechanisms (hardware or software) linked to the authenticating entity (Gorman, 2003). Every time the user needs a password to perform authentication, the token creates this parameter considering data and algorithms that are also aware of the authenticating entity, so the same password will be created on both sides of the authentication process and will validate the identity of the holder of the token. The main problem of this process is that tokens are bound to be lost. Subsequently, the person who finds or obtains this item will be able to authenticate themselves and the authenticating entity will think that the intruder is the authentic user (the owner of the token). For this reason, it is usual to mix dynamic passwords created by this process and static passwords known by the user and the authenticating entity, which gives more reliability and security to the process as a whole from the moment that the two types of credentials for authentication should be used: something the user has (a token) and something the user knows (a static password).

Tokens can also be used for storing digital certificates. They become similar to smart cards that store digital certificates and perform cryptographic processing (symmetric and asymmetric) that provide security to transactions.

A digital certificate is a data structure that contains values of a public key (asymmetric cryptography) and a set of identification information of the entity to which this key is bound (RFC 5280, 2008). This link is typically made and signed by certification authorities that are part of a PKI (Public Key Infrastructure). The reliability of the certificate comes from the signature made by the certification authority (also contained in the certificate). One can thus observe the principle of trust transitivity, because the certificate is trusted as long as the certificate authority that signed it is a trusted entity ("I trust in the authority, so I trust the certificate signed by her too"). This idea can be extended to other certification authorities and PKI members who sign the certificates of lower level authorities (who sign certificates of entities that are not authorities, for example), and so on until the PKI root certification authority be reached. Hence, if there is a trusted certification authority in the certificate chain of a certificate, the certificate will be trusted.

Another model that can be used to provide digital certificate reliability is the web of trust. In this case the certificate is self-signed (signed by the holder) or signed by users who attest the validity of the certificate they are signing. In both cases (PKI and web of trust), the certificate reliability is made possible by Trusted Third Parties (TTP) who sign and / or distribute the certificate validating its authenticity.

Digital certificates can be used in various ways, to lend authenticity to users (people) and equipment (web servers, mail servers, etc.). It is common to use it, for example, to create digital signatures that guarantee the authenticity of documents and instead of password parameters in case of login processes. Regarding electronic transactions, in most cases digital certificates have a key role in providing authenticity to the parties involved (or at least one party) and to enable cryptographic keys that allow one to guarantee the confidentiality and integrity of information exchanged among stakeholders (TLS (RFC 5246, 2008) and HTTPS (RFC 2818, 2000), for example).

Because they are logical data structures, certificates can be stored in various places: in the computer memory (hard drive), removable media (floppy disks, CD-ROMs, pen drives, etc.), into tokens and smart cards. The certificate has ostensible data only, and can therefore be transmitted freely for his integrity and authenticity remain secured through the signature of the entity that created it. Linked to the digital certificate, the holder also has a private key (related to the public key contained in the certificate) that is usually protected physically and logically (or at least logically) from unauthorized access. Thus, to use a private key, it is necessary that the user possesses it (2nd category of credentials—something the user has) and know the password (usually a passphrase) used for logic protection (1st category of credentials—something the user knows).

Considering the aspects of continuous authentication, the methods listed in this section have shortcomings similar to those observed in the methods of the previous section.

EAP Types

EAP (Extensible Authentication Protocol) is a framework that supports multiple authentication methods and typically runs directly in the link layer. It is designed for authentication to access network resources and data communications. While providing functions that are the basis for several methods of authentication, it cannot be

Figure 2. EAP—generic messaging [adapted from Albuquerque et al., 2010]

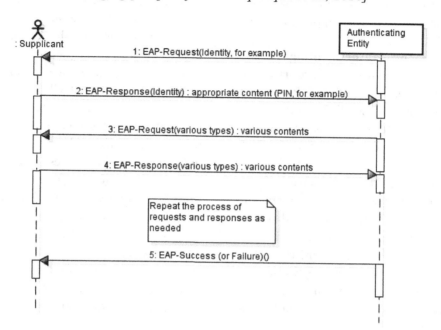

considered a specific authentication method (Albuquerque et al., 2010).

This protocol is based on challenge and response mechanisms and, unlike several other protocols of the same genus, its authentication processes are always initiated by the authenticating entity, rather than the entity being authenticated (the supplicant). The framework enables the use of remote authentication servers that can assist the work of the authenticating entity by receiving tasks for implementation of specific EAP methods. In such cases, the authenticating entity may delegate to the remote authentication server the method execution and serve only as a passage for the flow of information between the remote server and the supplicant.

Linked to the conventional models of authentication discussed above, and working in conjunction with more sophisticated methods based on biometrics, EAP permits the use, as parameters of messages exchanged in its methods, of values derived from different authentication mechanisms (passwords, PIN, digital certificates, biometric

information, etc..), so it can be used to facilitate the exchange of messages based on these mechanisms. This exchange of authentication messages occurs following these steps (Figure 2):

1. The authenticating entity calls for the supplicant log in sending them a message of a specific type (identity, MD5-challenge, etc.).
2. The supplicant sends back an appropriate response to the authentication type requested;
3. The authenticating entity makes additional requests and the supplicant responds with appropriate messages as often as necessary;
4. After exchanging the appropriate number of messages, the authenticator ends the process signaling the result to the supplicant (authentication success or failure).

The EAP works according to a model consisting of the following layers (RFC 3748, 2004):

*   **EAP Method:** responsible for executing the authentication algorithms and the

fragmentation of the data (this is necessary because this task is not supported by the framework);

- **Supplicant or authenticating entity (depending on where you're running the considered step of the Protocol):** layer that enables the differentiation between authenticating entities and supplicants regarding execution of specific EAP methods;

- **EAP layer:** receives and transmits EAP packets via the lower layer, implements the detection of duplicate packets and packet retransmission process, and demultiplexes the EAP packets to upper layer (the supplicant or the authenticator, as appropriate);

- **Bottom layer:** receives and transmits EAP frames between the supplicant and the authenticating authority.

Some specific EAP methods that use some of the static authentication parameters mentioned above will be described below, in summary.

- EAP-TLS (EAP-Transport Layer Security) (RFC 5216, 2008)

This method considers the use of TLS [RFC 5246, 2008] bound to the operation of the EAP framework and represents a very safe solution, although it is difficult to implement. The TLS can be used, for example, to promote mutual authentication of the elements that participate in an exchange of EAP messages based on the use of digital certificates that contain asymmetric cryptographic keys. The protocol provides an encrypted end-to-end tunnel for data transfer between the environments of the supplicant and the authenticating entity.

- EAP-TTLS (EAP-Tunneled Transport Layer Security) (RFC 5281, 2008)

It is an EAP method that encapsulates a TLS session (also uses digital certificates) that enables, during the handshake, the authentication of a server to a client (or mutual authentication) and the generation of material for the creation of cryptographic keys that will be used subsequently, during data exchange, for the creation of a tunnel that will provide cryptographic security to the information in transit between the parties. Once the secure tunnel is created, a new authentication is done (client to server or mutual authentication) in a secret way using EAP mechanism (or other authentication methods). An especially interesting feature of this method is that it is possible to resume a session already closed, which significantly decreases the time required for the authentication process as a whole (renders new complete authentication processes unnecessary).

- EAP-SIM (EAP Method for Global System for Mobile Communications Subscriber Identity Module) (RFC 4186, 2006) and EAP-AKA (EAP Method for 3rd Generation Authentication and Key Agreement) (RFC 4187, 2006)

They are EAP methods developed by 3GPP (3rd Generation Mobile System) and used for authentication and session key distribution in mobile cellular networks using the features of the GSM Subscriber Identity Module (SIM) and the mechanism for Authentication and Key Agreement (AKA) found in 3rd generation mobile networks (UMTS and CDMA2000). The authentication in both cases is based on Challenge and Response mechanisms and uses specifics sets of cryptographic algorithms from cellular networks. It should be noted that these methods use parameters derived from PINs linked to users in networks communication. These parameters (ostensive and secret) are previously shared between users and authenticating entities, as seen before.

- ERP (EAP Re-authentication Protocol) (RFC 5296, 2008)

It is an EAP method used to minimize the supplicants re-authentication problems that exist when they pass between authenticating entities (motivated by the spatial movement of mobile equipment, for example) or when they need to extend the authentication between them and a specific authenticating entity (need of session time increasing, for example). Note that this is the first mechanism, among the ones discussed so far, which shows concern for maintaining the continuity of a secure session, which is a major focus of ongoing authentication processes that will be seen later. In this sense, a promising idea is to use the ERP steadily, taking advantage of vacant spaces in the transmissions, using parameters obtained from continuous authentication processes that run locally (close to the involved parties). The ERP has relative independence of the lower layers responsible for the transmission of messages and of other EAP methods. ERP can thus be used in aggregation with these methods and share their security parameters.

CONTINUOUS AUTHENTICATION (CA) CONCEPTS

In this section, the main concepts related to continuous authentication processes will be described and analyzed. Subjects related to continuous and static, non-intrusive and intrusive authentications, continuous authentication levels and multimodal authentications will be treated.

Continuous, Static, Intrusive and Non-Intrusive Authentications

From reading of the previous section, one sees clearly that the majority of conventional authentication methods are static, i.e., they run only to open a secure session (authenticated parties) and have no intention of running constantly to maintain the authentication originally done (Calderon et al., 2006). A major drawback to this approach is linked to the implementation of relatively large sessions. In these periods, it is possible that the authenticated user get away from the equipment used for their authentication (a personal computer, a smart-phone, etc.), creating an opening for a malicious individual. In the absence of the legitimate user, the attacker can then operate the equipment posing as the user who performed the initial authentication. The damages from this action are of various kinds and affect the legitimate user and the organization by which the user was originally authenticated.

The continuous authentication processes show interesting and viable alternatives to replace the static processes. The continuous focus implies the execution of authentication tasks distributed throughout the duration of the secure session created between authenticated parties. After running the initial authentication process, the mechanism responsible for continuous authentication shall constantly check whether the user that is conducting the transactions is the one that performed the initial authentication and opened that session (Klosterman & Ganger, 2000).

Authentication tasks are usually performed at determined instants of pre-defined time periods or imposed by certain types and quantities of actions taken during the session.

It is common for example, to execute authentication tasks every 30 seconds (or period appropriate to the situation considered). Note that the definition of the appropriate period is critical to maintaining the usability of the system. If the period is too short (a second, for example) processing time dedicated to the authentication activity could derail the execution of other activities. Conversely, if the period is too large (an hour, for example), the security of the authentication process may be compromised.

Otherwise, it is possible that authentication tasks be driven from the moment the user has performed any ten steps (or any other amount of steps appropriate to the case examined) after the last authentication task.

Alternatively, tasks can be triggered when certain types of actions are performed (usually critical actions that require a higher level of security than usual).

Despite the fact that continuous authentication may be observed in all of the previous cases, we find that in these specific cases, the authentication procedures are carried out discreetly and at specific times determined by previously defined rules. For these situations it is even possible to use classical authentication processes (username and password, digital certificates, etc.) that are fired frequently during the session.

This last approach is considered intrusive and somewhat uncomfortable for the user, since they must periodically interrupt their normal activities to perform, explicitly, an authentication process.

An interesting option to minimize this problem is to use non-intrusive authentication procedures not requiring the interruption of normal activities (biometrics, for example) and operating transparently to the user.

A more sophisticated and interesting approach is to mix the two types of mechanisms discussed (classical processes and biometrics) applied non-intrusively to the user most of the time and intrusively (which demands the cessation of normal activity of the user) at moments when the previous form is not capable of providing the desired authentication.

Continuous Authentication Levels

Analyzing the problems of "when" and "why" to activate the authentication tasks mentioned earlier, (Calderon et al., 2006) propose four different levels of continuous authentication, as seen below:

Level 1: User Authentication

Level at which the user has verified his identity early in the session and, thereafter, periodical authentication tasks are held to maintain "authenticated" user status for the duration of the session. In order for normal user activities not to be disrupted non-intrusive authentication methods that are transparent to the user are preferable. However, when these methods are not sufficient to prove the authenticity of the user, another method may be used, one that generates an intrusive interruption in the normal use of the system at hand.

A simple example of this level of authentication can be observed when a user authenticates to a system explicitly and starts using it normally but needs to be away for a while at one point. When the user returns, after a certain interval of inactivity in the operation of the system, it calls for an explicit re-authentication to validate his identity again. In this case, the mere use of the normal system, although not a conventional method of authentication, represents the non-intrusive procedure indicated above. One inconvenient aspect seen in this example is that the system will only require a process of explicit re-authentication if it remains inactive for a specified time interval. That being the case, if a malicious user gains access to the system as soon as the authentic user is absent, the system will not be able to stop this security breech.

A more sophisticated example of a process of this level considers the use of a more reliable non-intrusive authentication (maintaining a token permanently attached to a system or some kind of facial recognition scheme, for example) during the normal operation of the system. In this particular case, the deficiency observed in the previous example does not exist.

Level 2: User-Resource Authentication

In this situation, the generic user authentication treated at level 1 is being kept and, furthermore, if someone wishes to access certain more sensitive features of the system, it prompts an explicit re-authentication. Note that this re-authentication occurs even though the user is continually being authenticated by the non intrusive authentication process previously mentioned.

This level of authentication is designed to prevent a wrong access of an authentic user to resources disallowed for his profile (set of privileges), i.e., even if recognized as lawful by the system, the user must have appropriate privileges and perform specific authentications to be able to access the resources that are better protected.

Level 3: User-Resource-System Authentication

In the two previous levels, the user accesses the system by devices that are part of the communications network of the very organization that owns the system. However this is not always possible. To that end, level 3 enables, besides the aspects considered in the previous levels, user authentication via remote devices, positioned in places outside the organization which are therefore not controlled by it.

Level 4: User-Resource-System-Transaction Authentication

There are situations where not only are certain resources sensitive, but some kinds of transactions are critical too. Operations that manipulate financial data of an organization, for example, do not represent access to resources, but rather to the execution of critical transactions. For these cases, level 4 authentication also requires the continued execution of an explicit authentication process, as seen at level 2 for the case of access to restricted resources.

Thus, at level 4 the authentications dealt with in previous levels will be imposed, as will specific authentications to control access to critical

transactions that can be made possible through the system operation.

As can be seen, this level of authentication provides the highest degree of protection by continually checking the authenticity of the user's identity, whether he is operating the system from the organization environment or outside it, besides considering specific needs of authentication for access to sensitive resources and critical transactions.

Multimodal Authentication

Most security systems involved with the problem of access control (systems, facilities, specific resources, etc.) utilizes one or more techniques to validate the authenticity of the user's identity, allowing his access or not (Ikeh & Crosby, 2010). Accordingly, the greater the amount of reliable authentication procedures used to verify the authenticity, the more reliable the access control system.

It is common or organizations concerned with those issues to carry facilities and resources that can only be accessed from the moment the individual proves his identity through more than one authentication method (card access and password, password and fingerprint recognition, etc.). This kind of process that involves the combined use of various authentication methods is known as multimodal and usually works in connection with the concept of continuous authentication.

Duly, after the initial authentication process (typically based on classical methods of authentication and/or physiological biometrics), not just one but several methods are working in parallel and constantly to enable the continuous authentication required. Though clearly requiring greater processing resources of the environment where the authentication system works, this form has the great advantage of allowing the authentication process not to be interrupted even if one of the methods do not produce the expected results.

In extreme cases, if all the methods involved in continuous and multimodal authentication fail -which is unlikely, a static intrusive method can also be imposed to the user as the basis for a new authentication.

Multimodal authentication systems generally utilize non-intrusive processes. This is necessary because one such process must operate in a parallel and constant manner, and if they depend on user intervention, there will not be time to perform even the normal operation of the system to which access is being controlled. Ergo, the importance of biometrics (explored in the next section) arises. Many of the procedures based on biometrics, being non-intrusive, can be used in parallel without user awareness, allowing for the existence of multimodal biometric systems that recognize physiological and/or behavioral features enabling or disabling user access to specific resources (Azzini et al., 2008), (Anand et al., 2010).

BIOMETRICS

In this section, the biometrics techniques will be considered in detail, ways and mechanisms to enable continuous authentication of users being described, both with regard to their physiological characteristics, and in relation to their behavior. The main subjects addressed will be the physiological biometry and behavioral biometry.

General Aspects

The term biometrics can be understood in a broad sense, as the study or measurement of characteristics inherent to living beings. However, this definition is too broad and deserves further refinement to be fully adequate to the subject that will be explored in this section.

In Riera ET AL (2009) a more relevant definition is quoted that can be understood as follows: Biometrics is a science based on mechanisms for automatic analysis of human aspects that aims to recognize or differentiate an individual from their peers based on physiological and behavioral characteristics.

Linked to the definition of biometrics, there is also the concept of biometric feature, which can be understood as a unique and measurable aspect of an individual that can be used for recognition or to verify his identity, both automatically.

This latter concept considers some key requirements that deserve more detail. The first concerns the fact that biometrics exploits the unique features. This aspect indicates that a given characteristic, when operated in more than one individual, should include differences in appropriate levels to the sense of the considered analysis. To that effect, this feature can be used as a means of differentiating between similar individuals.

Another requirement linked to the explored concept indicates that the biometric characteristics must be measurable, i.e., there must be practical ways of measuring these characteristics so that they can be quantified and represented by means of objective parameters.

Automatic recognition capabilities and identity verification must also be aspects enabled by biometrics. In the first case, measurements taken of the unique characteristics should be sufficient for the individual to be recognized without the need for further analysis. Alternatively, those same measurements should allow an individual to have their identity verified by comparing measured parameters to those stored in identification databases.

It should be noted that these unique features that are provided by individuals and which can be measured and quantified aiming to differentiate between similar individuals are exactly what sets the 3rd class of credentials previously mentioned (something that is inherent to the user and is part of their identity).

Properly, it is clear that the methods of biometrics can be used both as identification (recognition of the individual) and authentication process (validation of the alleged identity).

For biometrics to generate objective results, comparisons are often made between the parameters measured at the time of authentication and those previously stored in databases created from the registration of the characteristics of individuals (Clarke et al., 2002a). These comparisons are not always perfect (in fact, there is almost never total similarity between measured and stored characteristics) and to create a binary response (authentic or inauthentic) the system must use precision levels considered sufficient for the proper authentication of the individual. Under the circumstances, if a high level of accuracy is chosen (a higher level implies more equality cases between measured and stored values) and the individual is recognized, the certainty that the process generated a correct result will be great. However, the increase of such level also raises a problem: the increased likelihood that the individual is not recognized. It is necessary, then, that intermediate levels (neither high nor low) be chosen, consistent with the desired recognition process. Typically these levels are chosen in proportion to levels of criticality of resources whose access controls are being made possible through the biometric process.

Suitably, the concepts of False Acceptance Rate (FAR), False Rejection Rate (FRR) and Equal Error Rate (EER) arise (Anand et al., 2010), (Clarke et al., 2002a). The FAR represents the rate of erroneous acceptances of the system, i.e., the relative number of individuals who do not have corresponding data in the identification database but who are recognized by the system. The FRR indicates the opposite situation, i.e., the rejection rate (no recognition) of individuals whose data are in database. The EER represents the percentage linked to the level of accuracy in which the FAR and FRR have the same value.

These figures are represented graphically in Figure 3. It demonstrates that, in situations where the level of accuracy for the recognition process is low (small values of "x") high rates of incorrect acceptance (FAR) and low rates of mistaken rejection (FRR) are observed. Conversely, if the chosen level of accuracy is high, higher FRR and low FAR will be perceived.

Biometry Types

In general, biometrics can be divided into two categories or types (Clarke et al., 2002b), (Rahal

Figure 3. FAR X FRR (adapted of (Clarke et al., 2002a))

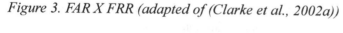
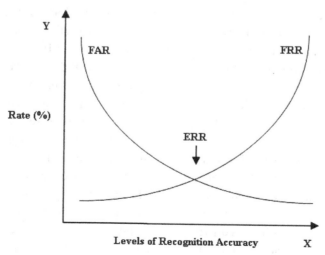

Figure 4. Fingerprints

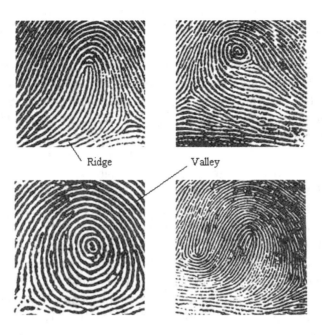

et al., 2006): behavioral and physiological bio-metrics. These categories are explored in detail in the next items.

Physiological Biometry

This category of biometrics is based on measurement of physiological aspects perceived in the human body. It should be noted that, as stated, for these aspects to be considered biometric, they must meet the requirements above.

Some examples of physiological Biometry will be described below.

Fingerprint Recognition (Clarke et al., 2002a), (Jain et al., 2004), (Rahal et al., 2006), (Anand et al., 2010)

This is one of the most widely used forms of biometrics. It enables access control to numerous resources (facilities, computers, telephones, etc.) and is at a consolidated stage of development.

This type of recognition is based on verification of standards related to the placement of lines

created by the alternation of ridges and valleys (or furrows) of individuals digitals (Figure 4). These patterns show apparent differences when different individuals are compared.

It is not common to apply this method to achieve continuous authentication, however it is possible to use specific devices adapted to allow this kind of authentication.

Facial or Face Recognition (Clarke et al., 2002a), (Jain et al., 2004), (Rahal et al., 2006), (Anand et al., 2010)

This method of biometric recognition is based on various measurements and characteristics that can be found in a human face. The parameters usually chosen to represent a face are those that do not change (or change little) over time. Examples of these parameters are measurements taken from areas around the cheekbones, eyes, nose and mouth. The recognition process is divided in phases: image capture (usually done through a photo or video camera), processing (measurement of parameters chosen previously), comparison (measured data

Figure 5. Measurement of face's parameters

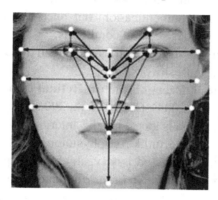

X stored data) and decision (if there are sufficient coincidences considering captured and stored data, the individual is regarded as authentic).

An important advantage of this method over other mechanisms of physiological biometrics is the fact that it cannot be intrusive. This is possible because all stages can be performed without the explicit intervention on the user. Therefore, this method is seen as quite adequate to enable continuous authentication.

Figure 5 shows some possible measures that can be captured and used in the process of facial recognition.

Hand Geometry Recognition (Jain et al., 2004), (Rahal et al., 2006)

This method of physiological biometrics is based on measuring distances and shapes observed in people's hands. These measurements are often made from the view of the palm and focus on features such as length and width of the fingers and the distances between their joints.

Similarly to the previous case, the recognition by hand geometry is also made from the capture of the desired parameters carried out by suitable equipment. Figure 6 shows some examples of equipment used to capture the images and the results of the scanned format of the hand.

Note that the equipment depicted, may capture the parameters related specifically to the individual's hand, as well as allow data entry by typing on a keyboard. These devices can therefore be used to perform multimodal authentication processes based on biometrics (recognition of the shape of the hand) and insertion of secret parameters (e.g., passwords).

Similar to fingerprint recognition, the application of this method to achieve continuous authentication is not common, but it is also possible for specific devices to measure, in a constant

Figure 6. Hand geometry recognition procedure

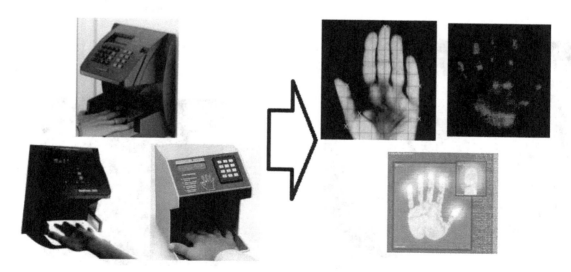

manner, features of hand geometry and allow continuous authentication.

Iris Recognition or Scanning (Clarke et al., 2002a), (Jain et al., 2004), (Rahal et al., 2006), (Anand et al., 2010)

This form of biometric recognition enables the identification and authentication of a person from specific features found in the iris of the human eye. It is believed that these features remain unchanged throughout the life of the individual, which is a very interesting aspect when dealing with physiological characteristics of human beings.

An aspect that makes this process one of the most accurate of its kind is that the probability that two equal Irises be found is extremely reduced (around 10^{-78}).

Among some specific features that are subject to the measurement procedures applied to the iris, the main parameter to be analyzed is the trabecular meshwork, which is a complex mesh like a spider web and that is formed by crumpled tissues.

Given the great accuracy of this physiological characteristic, it is necessary to use equipment that enables high resolution so as to capture a detailed image of the iris.

Because of the accuracy demands for the measurements that support this type of recognition,

it is not common to use this method to provide continuous authentication, but once again it is feasible under specific conditions.

Figure 7 shows the iris of a human eye and its trabecular meshwork.

Retina Recognition or Retinal Scanning (Jain et al., 2004), (Rahal et al., 2006)

The retina is located in the anterior part of the human eye and, unlike the physiological elements previously discussed, is not visible without specific equipment. This area of the human eye has a lot of blood vessels that form a complex web that can be seen if the back of an eye is observed. Given the fact that it is a difficult area to record (capture its image), special equipment use and complete immobility of the eye are required for error-free capture. As with the on iris-based process, recognition of the retina is considered one of the most accurate of its kind, and not commonly used to provide continuous authentication.

Figure 8 shows a retina with its web of blood vessels that form a quite specific pattern.

Behavioral Biometry

This category is based on the measurement of perceived behavioral patterns in the actions of human beings. Just like the physiological biometry, for these aspects to be considered biometrics, they must meet the requirements listed above (unique

Figure 7. Iris

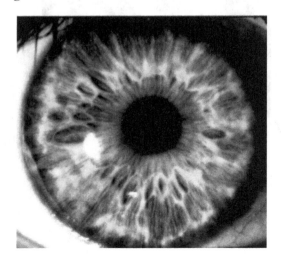

Figure 8. Retina

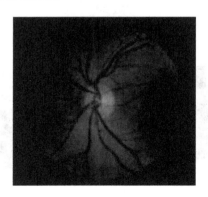

and measurable features, capabilities of automatic recognition and identity verification).

Some examples of behavioral Biometry will be described below.

Keystroke Analysis or Dynamics (Clarke et al., 2002a), (Jain et al., 2004), (Clarke & Furnell, 2007), (Rahal et al., 2006)

This biometric recognition technique is based on the way people perform typing using keyboards. This method is not as accurate as the processes related to physiological characteristics and it is unlikely for a pattern of typing to be considered unique, however, this technique provides a sufficient amount of information to enable probable identification of an individual.

The typical measurement performed in this case focuses on the different ranges observed between successive keystrokes. These measurements can be performed in an intrusive way at times immediately prior to the authentication of the individual (typically the user must enter a predefined text pattern which is stored in identification databases) or in a non-intrusive way during a normal process of individual typing (in this case there are no predefined texts and measurements are made transparent to the user). Although comparative analysis between measured patterns and stored ones is simpler in the first case, the second form is usually not discarded and the two ways can be executed sequentially.

Two very positive aspects of this method that promote its use to provide continuous authentication are: no specific equipment is required for the measurement of biometric features (just use the keyboard in which the individual is accustomed to typing) and it is possible to implement this method in a non-intrusive and transparent way to the user. As a result, despite the reduced accuracy if compared to other biometric methods, the possibility of capture and analysis of extensive samples of keystrokes can accomplish, without the user even noticing, appropriate rates of correct authentication.

Mouse Dynamics or Movement Analysis (Pusara & Brodley, 2004), (GOUDELIS ET AL, 2005)

This method is based on the detection of individual patterns of mouse movement to perform specific tasks. Some implementations of this type of biometric recognition techniques use artificial intelligence (AI) to learn the particular pattern of an individual and to compare it with the movements captured in a given space of time for analysis. These AI techniques perform their learning from, for example, speed measurements of movements and frequencies of mouse clicks.

This process is not very accurate and is generally used in conjunction with other similar methods (keystroke analysis, for example) so that the error rates (false acceptance and false rejection) are reduced. Just as with the previous one, this method can also easily be used to provide continuous authentication.

Voice or Voiceprint Recognition (Clarke et al., 2002a), (Jain et al., 2004), (Rahal et al., 2006)

This method is based on individual voice aspects that span both physical characteristics (tone of voice) and behavioral ones (way to speak). Hence, in some situations this process can be regarded as a physiological biometric technique and at other times it can be viewed as a behavioral biometrics method, and at other instances, both.

This biometric mode is one of the most widespread, being used not only as a means of authentication, but also (and perhaps mainly) in speech recognition applications for remote commands execution and for speech conversion into written text.

For authentication situations, sound wave patterns (frequency, amplitude, etc.) emitted by the individual are captured by special equipment (microphones) and compared to the elements stored in identification databases. It should be noted that these bases of identification are created from previous capture of relevant sound patterns samples made by users to be authenticated in the future.

About the possibility of using this method to provide continuous authentication, note that this is an appropriate subject since normal system operation demands the constant use of the user's voice (operation via voice commands, for example).

Handwritten Signature Recognition (Clarke et al., 2002a), (Jain et al., 2004), (Rahal et al., 2006), (Anand et al., 2010)

This biometric process promotes recognition of handwritten signature created by an individual. For this standard of writing be captured, resources such as touch screens, scanners and special tableaux created specifically for this purpose can be used. The signature recognition is based on measurable aspects usually obtained from the analysis of the signature image. Sometimes the form of image acquisition is not relevant, but only the digitized signature itself. However, there are more sophisticated implementations of this method that also consider other aspects -time an individual takes to sign, the instrument pressure used to sign and the instrument inclination to the surface of capture, for example, and require the mandatory use of specific capture mechanisms that provide the signature image along with the other considered parameters.

As in previous methods, the acquired patterns should also be compared to ones existing in bases for identification of the individual to be authenticated.

Given their specificity, this method is not suited to providing continuous authentication.

OTHER FORMS OF CONTINUOUS AUTHENTICATION

As could be noticed in the last section, some biometric recognition methods are great tools for performing continuous authentication processes (face recognition, keystroke analysis, mouse dynamics and voiceprint recognition, for example). One of the most important aspects that lead to this conclusion is the fact that these processes may be non-intrusive and allow normal operation of the systems without any unwanted interruptions. Another important point is that most methods can be implemented consistently and continuously throughout the period of systems use.

In addition to the methods described, there are others which propose to enable continuous authentication. This section will explore some techniques that are not related directly to biometry but that can also enable continuous authentication.

Some conventional methods that focus on static authentication performed at the beginning of transaction sessions can be adapted to permit continuous authentication. From conventional methods mentioned in a previous section of this work, one can consider that the most suitable are those based on 2nd category of authentication credentials (something the user has).

A typical example of this category of methods and their respective adaptation is the use of tokens to perform the authentication process. In the classical approach, the token is used to provide passwords that will be used in conjunction with secret parameters known by the user (and by the server). However it is possible that the token stores a secret parameter that identifies the user and that can be constantly consulted by the system to which the user performed the initial authentication. This can provide continuity in the authentication that opened the current session. The system's consultation may happen constantly at configurable time intervals, without interference from the user (Damous et al., 2008) (this represents basic features of continuous authentication).

The more suitable tokens for use in this type of architecture are those that can perform wireless communications with systems that require authentication. Bluetooth or RFID tokens, for instance, may be used, which remain in possession of their users (in their pockets, for example) and that enable continuous authentication to the used system. If the user left the vicinity of the equipment that is performing wireless communication with the token (usually his individual workstation), the system will stop functioning until a new authentication process is explicitly conducted. To that regard it is interesting that one uses wireless communication technologies that enable only small areas of coverage (in the order of meters) to prevent the continued operation of wireless communication even after the user has left the vicinity of their workstation.

In addition to wireless tokens, one can also use tokens directly connected to the workstation ports (USB, for example). In this circumstance, the layout of continuous authentication operation is similar, however there is one inconvenience: token may be unwillingly left attached to port upon user withdrawal from the workstation area. Another method that aims to provide continuous authentication without the use of biometric recognition suggests that information extracted continuously from the use of web applications hosted on remote servers may be used to enable continuity of authentication performed at the beginning of the session (Veras & Ruggiero, 2005). This authentication process is based on the continuous maintenance of trust between the parties (user and web server) created from the initial authentication occurred between the parties. A security policy is needed, one related to the use of the web application that can be constantly checked. The process enables the analysis of the actions taken by the user using the application and, if such actions stray from what the policy advocates for system use, it may ask the user to perform a new explicit authentication process.

It should be noted that this process does not exactly achieve the continuous authentication of a specific user, but continued authentication of users whose behaviors are appropriate to the considered policy. Thus, in the absence of a legitimate user, if a malicious user is granted access to the system in the same way that the originally authenticated user, the method will not be able to determine the intrusion and will not request a new explicit authentication process.

Similarly to the previous example, Brosso (2006) proposed an authentication method based on continuous user behavior. This process links the use of environment contextual information and user behavior to the use of physiological biometrics techniques. The system establishes levels of trust created to authenticate the user by analyzing its behavior in the target environment of the security process. To be able to detect an intruder user trying to impersonate the user at a time of genuine absence, the system makes comparisons between the current user behavior (mapped through certain types of predefined actions) and past behaviors stored in a behavioral basis linked to the user in question. If the system notices changes in standard user behavior (this change must exceed a threshold set in the system to allow small variations to conventional behavior), it triggers a mechanism for identification based on facial recognition that can validate the authenticity of the lawful user or prove the intrusion.

Note that the continuous authentication method employed by the system described above, although not considered a method of behavioral biometrics, uses the same basic ideas of it, i.e., the analysis of current behavior compared to behaviors stored on historical basis.

CONCLUSION

This chapter had the main objective of describing and analyzing authentication processes that can be used continuously and transparently to increase the authenticity guarantee of the parties involved in an electronic transaction.

According to the analysis herein, trust aspects related to creating environments in which electronic transactions may happen and where application of continuous authentication appear somewhat promising.

Problems of authenticity in environments involved in electronic transactions were also examined and special features of such transactions were verified to justify the continued use of authentication.

Given their importance in the context of continuous authentication, various biometric techniques (physiological and behavioral) were studied and considered interesting solutions to enable user authentication processes, and the relevance of some of these in the context of continuous, transparent and multimodal authentication was proven.

Finally some authentication techniques based on continuous information exchange generated from the use of applications used in generic transactions were examined.

Electronic transactions were clearly found to require security requirements that can never be disregarded for their implementation. Guarantee of authenticity between the parties and guaranteed confidentiality and integrity of information that travels between the parties are crucial for confidence in any electronic transaction to exist.

The chapter focused on the specific problem of authentication of the parties and indicated that it is not advisable to use systems that do not enable this kind of service for the implementation of an electronic transaction.

Not only was the importance of authentications during the beginning of the transaction perceived, but also the need for ongoing security process maintenance throughout the entire session. It was seen that, if there is no maintenance of authentication made at the beginning of the process, problems may arise related to the misuse of the transaction session by malicious users, particularly when the user is removed from the location used for transaction completion.

On that ground it was suggested that continuous authentication processes be used to guarantee the authenticity of the parties (particularly the client user) for the duration of the electronic transaction session considered. These procedures, which can be executed in a non-intrusive (transparent to those involved) and constant way throughout the duration of the transaction, may provide a more lasting kind of authenticity that the one initially treated.

It stressed however, that the ideal authentication form must consider both types discussed: the traditional authentication, static and intrusive, held to launch the electronic transaction, and the continuous authentication, dynamic and non-intrusive, to maintain the authenticity of the parties throughout the transaction period.

It is also said that such complementarity is, in certain occasions, even necessary, as in the case of possible continued use of the ERP that may carry information created from continuous authentication processes performed close to the parties involved.

At another point, several methods of biometric recognition based on physiological characteristics or behavioral aspects of humans were described whose importance is evident in order to achieve the overall process of authentication. It has also been signaled, more specifically, that the most appropriate biometric methods (among those mentioned) to provide continuous authentication of people are: face recognition, keystroke analysis, mouse dynamics and voice recognition. Nevertheless, other methods were shown to be useful in providing continuous authentication if applied under specific conditions.

The presentation of proposals for continuous authentication methods that are not based on biometrics lead to the conclusion that, although not considered to be behavioral biometrics per se, these methods are generally based on behavior analysis of user that is authenticated to the system being used to conduct the electronic transaction.

We find that the study of the field in question is very promising and timely. The chapter now closed did not aim to exhaust all existing information on the subject, but rather to indicate and comment on the main themes that are currently being discussed in the academic community regarding implementation of continuous authentication to provide generic electronic transactions security.

REFERENCES

Aboba, B., Blunk, L., Vollbrecht, J., Carlson, J., & Levkowetz, H. (Eds.). (2004). *Extensible Authentication Protocol (EAP)*. RFC 3748, 2004.

Abrams, M. D. & Joyce M. V. (1995). *Trusted System Concepts. Computers & Security, 14*(1). Elsevier Advanced Technology.

Albuquerque, S. L., Gondim, P. R. L., & Monteiro, C. C. (2010). *Aspectos de Segurança na Interconexão de Redes Celulares e WLANs*. Paper presented at 10th Brazilian Security Symposium (SBSeg2010).

Alireza Pourshahid, A., & Tran, T. (2007). *Modeling Trust in E-Commerce: An Approach Based on User Requirements*. Paper presented at IEEE International Conference on Electronic E-commerce (ICEC 2007).

Anand, R., Bajpai, G., Bhaskar, V. (2010). *3D Signature for Efficient Authentication in Multimodal Biometric Security Systems*. IACSIT International Journal of Engineering and Technology, 2 (2)

Arkko, J., & Haverinen, H. (2006). Extensible Authentication Protocol Method for 3rd Generation Authentication and Key Agreement (EAP-AKA). *RFC, 4187*, 2006.

Azzini, A., Marrara, S., Sassi, R., & Scotti, F. (2008). A fuzzy approach to multimodal biometric continuous authentication. *Fuzzy Optimization and Decision Making, 7*(3). doi:10.1007/s10700-008-9034-1

Brosso, M. I. L. (2006). *Autenticação Contínua de Usuários em Redes de Computadores. Unpublished doctoral theses*. Brazil: University of São Paulo.

Calderon, T. G., Chandra, A., & Cheh, J. J. (2006). Modeling an intelligent continuous authentication system to protect financial information resources. *International Journal of Accounting Information Systems*, 7.

Clarke, N., & Furnell, S. (2007). Advanced user authentication for mobile devices. *Computers & Security*, 26.

Clarke, N., Furnell, S., Rodwell, P., & Reynolds, P. (2002a). Acceptance of Subscriber Authentication for Mobile Telephony Devices. *Computers & Security, 21*(3). doi:10.1016/S0167-4048(02)00304-8

Clarke, N., Furnell, S., Rodwell, P., & Reynolds, P. (2002b). *Biometric Authentication for Mobile Devices*. Paper present at 3rd Australian Information Warfare and Security Conference 2002.

Cooper, D., Santesson, S., Farrell, S., Boeyen, S., Housley, R., Polk, W. (2008). *Internet X.509 Public Key Infrastructure Certificate and Certificate Revocation List (CRL) Profile*. RFC 5280.

Damousis, I. G., Tzovaras, D., Bekiaris, E. (2008). *Unobtrusive Multimodal Biometric Authentication: The HUMABIO Project Concept*. EURASIP Journal on Advances in Signal Processing archive, 2008.

Datta, A., & Hauswirth, M. (2003). *Beyond "web of trust": Enabling P2P E-commerce*. Paper presented at IEEE International Conference on Electronic E-commerce (ICEC 2003).

Dierks, T., & Rescorla, E. (2008). The Transport Layer Security (TLS) Protocol Version 1.2. *RFC, 5246*, 2008.

ETSI TS 133 234 (2010). Universal Mobile Telecommunications System (UMTS); LTE; 3G security; *Wireless Local Area Network (WLAN) interworking security*, 9.2.0, Release 9.

Funk, P., & Blake-Wilson, S. (2008). Extensible Authentication Protocol Tunneled Transport Layer Security Authenticated Protocol Version 0 (EAP-TTLSv0). *RFC, 5281*, 2008.

Furnell, S. M., Clarke, N., & Karatzouni, S. (2008). Beyond the PIN: Enhancing user authentication for mobile devices. *Computer Fraud & Security, 2008*(8). doi:10.1016/S1361-3723(08)70127-1

Furnell, S. M., Dowland, P. S., Illingworth, H. M., & Reynolds, P. L. (2000). Authentication and Supervision: A Survey of User Attitudes. *Computers & Security*, 19.

Gorman, L. O. (2003). Comparing Passwords, Tokens, and Biometrics for User Authentication. Contributed paper. *Proceedings of the IEEE, 91*(12).

Goudelis, G., Tefas, A., & Pitas, I. (2005). *On Emerging Biometric Technologies.* Paper presented at 3rd COST 275 Workshop - Biometrics on the Internet.

Haverinen, H., Ed., & J. Salowey, Ed.(2006). *Extensible Authentication Protocol Method for Global System for Mobile Communications (GSM) Subscriber Identity Modules (EAP-SIM).* RFC 4186, 2006.

Ikehara, C. S., & Crosby, M. E. (2010). *Physiological Measures Used for Identification of Cognitive States and Continuous Authentication.* Paper presented at 28th ACM Conference on Human Factors in Computing Systems (CHI2010).

Jain, A. K., Ross, A., & Prabhakar, S. (2004). An Introduction to Biometric Recognition. *IEEE Transactions on Circuits and Systems for Video Technology, 14*(1). doi:10.1109/TCSVT.2003.818349

Josang, A., Ismail, R., Boyd, C. (2007). A survey of trust and reputation systems for online service provision. *Decision Support Systems, 43* (2). Elsevier Science Publishers B. V.

Klosterman, A. J., & Ganger, G. R. (2000). *Secure Continuous Biometric-Enhanced Authentication.* CMU SCS Technical Report CMU-CS-00-134, 2000.

Koien, G. M., & Haslestad, T. (2003). Security Aspects of 3G-WLAN Interworking. *IEEE Communications Magazine, 41*(11). doi:10.1109/MCOM.2003.1244927

Narayanan, V., & Dondeti, L. (2008). EAP Extensions for EAP Re-authentication Protocol (ERP). *RFC, 5296*, 2008.

Pusara, M., & Brodley, C. E. (2004). *User ReAuthentication via Mouse Movements.* Paper present at 2004 ACM workshop on Visualization and data mining for computer security.

Rahal, S. M., Aboalsamah, H. A., & Muteb, K. N. (2006). *Multimodal Biometric Authentication System – MBAS.* Paper presented at 2nd Information and Communication Technologies (ICTTA '06).

Rescorla, E. (2000). HTTP Over TLS. *RFC, 2818*, 2000.

Riera, A., Soriafrisch, A., Caparrini, M., Cester, I., & Ruffini, G. (2009). Multimodal Physiological Biometrics Authentication. In *Biometrics.* Theory, Methods, and Applications. IEEE. doi:10.1002/9780470522356.ch18

Sauver, J. S. (2009). *Passwords.* Paper presented at Northwest Academic Computing Consortium (NWACC) Security Meeting.

Schneier, B. (1996). *Applied Cryptography: Protocols, Algorithms, and Source Code in C* (2nd ed.). John Wiley & Sons.

Simon, D., Aboba, B., & Hurst, R. (2008). The EAP-TLS Authentication Protocol. *RFC, 5216*, 2008.

Thompson, M. R., Olson, D., Cowles, R., Mullen, S., & Helm, M. (2002). *CA-based Trust Model for Grid Authentication and Identity Delegation.* Memo published by Grid Certificate Policy WG. Retrieved July 17, 2010, from http://www.gridcp.es.net/Documents/GGF6/TrustModel-final.pdf.

Véras, A. L. M., & Ruggiero, W. V. (2005). *Autenticação Contínua de Usuários em Aplicações Seguras na Web*. Paper present at V Brazilian Symposium on Information and Computer Systems Security.

Wang, Y., & Vassileva, J. (2007). *A Review on Trust and Reputation for Web Service Selection*. Paper presented at 27th International Conference on Distributed Computing Systems Workshops (ICDCSW'07).

KEY TERMS AND DEFINITIONS

Behavioral Biometry: Biometrics based on the measurement of perceived behavioral patterns in the actions of individuals that are unique and measurable features and that enable automatic recognition and identity verification, e.g., keystroke dynamics, mouse dynamics, handwritten signature.

Biometrics: Techniques used to identify and / or authenticate individuals based on particular characteristics of these individuals that uniquely identifies and are inherent to them, i.e., "what they are".

Continuous Authentication: Authentication process that aims to maintain the parties' authenticity throughout all the transactions period, not only at the transactions begins, using authentication mechanisms that run throughout the considered period.

E-Commerce: Kind of business transaction that uses, as its main means, electronic equipment, e.g., computers, smart-phones, digital televisions, and that is based on an extensive communications infrastructure like the Internet. There are variations on this type of business based on specific media, e.g., m-commerce (based on mobile phones) and t-commerce (based on television).

Multimodal Authentication: Combined use of multiple and complementary authentication mechanisms (based on ownership factors, knowledge factors and / or inherence factors) which enables greater process flexibility and allows a more reliable access control process if compared to an authentication process based only on an isolated mechanism.

Physiological Biometry: Biometrics based on physiological characteristics (which are part of the human body) of the individual, e.g., hand geometry, fingerprints, face's parameters, retina image.

Trust Systems: Systems based on trust between the various parties (trusted parties and trusting parties) and that enables greater security for the execution of transactions between the parties. The concept of trust that matters for this work should consider: the belief created by direct agreements or by transitivity (web of trust) with entities with which one wants to make a transaction; the hope that there will not be any kind of betrayal by the trusted party; and the level of dependency that the trusting party accepts.

162

Chapter 6
Identity–Based Cryptography:
Applications, Vulnerabilities and Future Directions

Jenny Torres
University Pierre and Marie Curie, France

Michele Nogueira
Federal University of Parana, Brazil

Guy Pujolle
University Pierre and Marie Curie, France

ABSTRACT

Since computer systems and communication become each time more pervasive, information security takes attention, requiring guarantees for data authentication, integrity and confidentiality. Pervasive communication and computer systems intend to provide access to information and services anytime and anywhere, demanding cryptographic systems more practical and that consider the characteristics of emerging network paradigms, such as wireless communication, device constraints and mobility. Identity-Based Cryptography (IBC) is an asymmetric key cryptographic technology that employs as user's public key any unique information related to the identity of the user. IBC efficiently manages keying material and provides an easy way to issue a pair of keys applying user information. However, it assumes the existence of a Trusted Third Party (TTP), called Private Key Generator (PKG), which is responsible for generating the corresponding user private key. Relying on a TTP and using an identity as the base of the scheme result in different weaknesses on the system, as the inherent key escrow problem. This chapter investigates those weaknesses, and it points out the stat-of-the-art of proposed solutions to avoid them. This chapter also provides an overview of Identity-Based Encryption (IBE), Identity-Based Signature (IBS) and Identity-Based Key Agreement (IBKA), emphasizing IBE due to being an open problem for many years. This chapter concludes highlighting IBC applications and future trends.

DOI: 10.4018/978-1-61350-507-6.ch006

INTRODUCTION: CONTEXT AND GOALS

Conventional and emerging applications, such as *m-government, m-commerce and m-health*, require more and more information protection for supporting the development of the Information Society (Underwood, 2010). Such applications consider *information* as their main resource, presenting security requirements challenges in order to ensure an adequate protection to network elements and data communication. Further, the fast development of communication technology has resulted in changes on the way that people perform daily activities, allowing them to access information anywhere and anytime, and producing new requirements for security information (Perry, 2001).

Since information systems and sophisticated communication infrastructures become extensive, the number of threats in the network increases every day. These threats can be classified in two specific types, called attacks and intrusions. An attack is any action that explores a weakness of the system in order to compromise the integrity, confidentiality, availability and non-repudiation of the information. An intrusion also exploits weaknesses of the system, but it results from a successful attack. Nevertheless, the main goal is to disrupt services to access or alter confidential information and, then, use it in a malicious way. Attacks can occur in different levels of the network protocol stack, such as attacks that compromise servers on the application level, or denial of services (DoS) and sniffing on the communication level (Avizienis, 2004).

Nowadays, there are an unlimited number of security technologies, being cryptography the most used for achieving information security in the emerging information society. Cryptography has emerged in the last 20 years as an important discipline that provides the base for information security in many applications. Cryptographic techniques are now in widespread use, especially in financial services, in public sector and in personal privacy, such as in e-mail (Menezes, 1996). The main goal of cryptography is to guarantee *confidentiality, integrity, authenticity* and *non-repudiation*. These characteristics can be achieved trough the cryptographic primitives: Encryption, Digital Signature and Key Agreement. *Encryption* supports *confidentiality*. *Digital Signature* provides *authentication, integrity* and *non-repudiation*. And *Key Agreement* defines an easier way to distribute secret keys in order to establish a secure communication (Gorantla, 2005).

Due to the cryptography importance and the changes in information security caused by emerging networks, this chapter proceeds as follows. First of all it presents a general view about the background on cryptography. Next, it reviews IBC concepts, emphasizing the main primitives: signature, encryption and key agreement. Then, the chapter presents the main vulnerabilities and attacks on IBC. Further, it analyzes the main solutions applied to mitigate IBC weaknesses. Finally, this chapter provides future trends for this subject considering Internet context and emerging applications, such as cloud computing, mobile computing applications and nanocomputing. The chapter concludes with our point of view in relation to IBC based on this theoretical study.

BACKGROUND

The protection of sensitive information against unauthorized access or fraudulent changes has been a primary concern throughout centuries. The ability to protect the confidentiality of information, to prevent unauthorized access to data or services and to prevent the unauthorized modification of data is a fundamental requirement of security, as well as the ability to know whom you are talking to. Modern communication techniques, using computers connected through networks, make all

Figure 1. Cryptosystems Classification

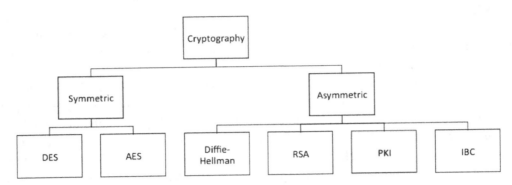

Cryptography

Cryptography is the art of "secret writing" (Coppersmith, 2010). It intends to provide secure communication over insecure channels. In cryptography, a sender transforms plaintext into ciphertext (encryption). A receiver uses cryptography to transform the ciphertext back into plaintext (decryption), to verify the sender's identity or to verify data's integrity. As we move into an information society, cryptography has become one of the main tools for guaranteeing privacy and access control on electronic payments, corporate security and countless other fields. There are two kinds of cryptosystems: symmetric and asymmetric, as presented in Figure 1.

data even more vulnerable for threats that can easily compromise its confidentiality, privacy and integrity. Also, new issues have come up, being most of them irrelevant before. Cryptology, the study of cryptosystems, can be subdivided into two disciplines: cryptography and cryptanalysis. Cryptography concerns itself with the design of cryptosystems, while cryptanalysis studies the breaking of cryptosystems. These two aspects are closely related since setting up a cryptosystem claims the analysis of its security (Van Tilborg, 1999).

Symmetric-Key Cryptography

In symmetric-key cryptography, know also as *Secret-key Cryptography*, the transmission of secret messages has been achieved by transforming the message using some common mechanism known only to the sender and receiver, but unknown to everybody else. Although the methods have changed, the basic paradigm of relying on a common secret to encrypt and decrypt messages remains in widespread use even today. Nowadays, this technique is called *Symmetric-key Encryption* or *Secret-key Encryption*. The history of symmetric-key cryptography dates back to the development of public key cryptosystems in the 1970s (Jao, 2008). Some examples of symmetric key cryptosystems include:

- **Caesar Shift Cipher:** Shifts all letters in the alphabet forward or backward by a certain number of letters. The key consists of the amount of the shift.
- **Substitution Cipher:** Replaces each letter in the alphabet with a different symbol. The key consists of the bijection between the letters and the replacement symbols.
- **Enigma Cipher:** An electro-mechanical device, used by Germany in World War II. The key is determined by the initial configuration of the wheels and the wiring.

- **Data Encryption Standard (DES):** Adopted by the United States government in 1976 as a Federal Information Processing Standard (FIPS). The key is an integer between 1 and 256 bits.

- **Advanced Encryption Standard (AES):** Adopted as a U.S. government standard in 2001. There are three different versions, with key sizes of 128, 192, and 256 bits.

Not all of the cryptosystems mentioned before are considered as secure. The first three ones have been already broken, and DES is vulnerable to brute force attack where the attacker checks every possible key. AES is believed to be secure if used properly under modern notions of cryptographic security (Jao, 2008).

One of the conventional encryption benefits is the fastness for encrypting data. However, for transmitting secure data can be quite expensive due to the difficulty of secure key distribution. For a sender and recipient to communicate securely using symmetric encryption, they must agree upon a key and keep it secret between themselves. If they are in different physical locations, they must trust some secure communication medium to prevent the revelation of the secret key during transmission. Anyone who overhears or intercepts the key in transit can later read, modify, and forge all information encrypted or authenticated with that key. As seen before, the persistent problem with symmetric encryption is key distribution, and the way to send the key to the recipient, without someone intercepting it, becomes more difficult.

Asymmetric-Key Cryptography

As a solution to the key distribution problem in symmetric-key cryptography, asymmetric-key cryptography, also known as *Public-key Cryptography*, was invented. In secret-key cryptography, the two parties need to agree on a common secret key before they can communicate, while in public-key cryptography defines two different keys. One of them is called the public key e, open to the public. Anyone can view the public key but no one should be able to alter it. The other key is the private key d or decryption key. It must be known only by the person who wants to receive secret messages encrypted with the corresponding public key. Such cryptosystem relies on the fact that it is impossible to guess the private key d, knowing only the public key e (Penev, 2005).

The first development in this area was in 1976 with the Diffie-Hellman key exchange protocol. The protocol provides a way for two parties, being a party a user (agent, human or software that uses a computer or network service) or an entity (a component, a being or existence considered as distinct, independent, or self-contained), to derive a common secret key using nothing else other than the transmission of public messages (Jao, 2008). Given users A and B, they agree on a prime p and an integer g. The user A chooses a random integer x, and it transmits g^x (mod p) to B. B chooses a random integer y and transmits g^y (mod p) to A. The user A raises g^y to the x power to obtain $g^{xy} = (g^y)^x$ (mod p). Similarly, B computes $g^{xy} = (g^x)^y$ (mod p). Finally, A and B use the value of g^{xy} (mod p), as their shared secret. The only values transmitted in public were p, g, g^x (mod p), and g^y (mod p). In general, it is believed to be computationally infeasible to determine the value of g^{xy} (mod p), given only the values transmitted in public, and the security of the system derives from this assumption (Jao, 2008).

After Diffie and Hellman proposed their ideas, Ron Rivest, Adi Shamir and Len Adleman laid the foundations of today's Public Key Infrastructures (PKI) proposing the RSA algorithm. The RSA algorithm resides on the fact that factoring relatively big numbers in their prime factors is very difficult and takes an enormous amount of time and computational resources to accomplish (Penev, 2005). Chosen two primes numbers p and q having equal length, *n is equal to pq*. A random integer e is chosen such that $1 < e < \varphi(n) = (p-1)(q-1)$. The public key is *(n, e)*, and the private key is $d = e^{-1} \pmod{\varphi(n)}$. For encryption, given a message m, output c is equal to $m^e \pmod{n}$. And for decryption, given a ciphertext c, output *m is given by $c^d \pmod{n}$* (Jao, 2008).

In order to achieve a better security, A and B will need to use several cryptographic security mechanisms (Paterson, 2003). In particular, to achieve confidentiality they will need to use public key based key management with a TTP. If a TTP binds the public key to a user or system, which means to attest to the identity of the party holding the corresponding private key, the complete range of security services may be obtained. The user may obtain integrity, authentication and non-repudiation through digital signatures. To accomplish security services across organizational boundaries, many inter-linked TTPs will be required. This set of interlinked TTPs forms a security infrastructure that users can rely upon to obtain security services. When this security infrastructure is designed to distribute public keys, it is known as a public key infrastructure. Traditional PKIs are the primary means of deploying asymmetric cryptography. Because of the inherent public nature of the encryption or verification keys, the integrity of the public keys is usually protected with a certificate. The PKI is the infrastructure that supports the management of keys and certificates (Paterson, 2003). The components of a PKI are:

- **Certificate Authority (CA):** The CA is the entity, being an entity a component in the system, which generates the certificates. It is responsible for ensuring that the correct key is bound to the certificate, as well as ensuring the certificate content.
- **Registration Authority (RA):** The RA is responsible for ensuring that the user who receives the certificate is a legitimate user within the system. The functionality of the CA and RA is sometimes carried out by a single entity.

- **Certificate Storage:** In most systems, certificates as well as update information such as certificate revocation lists are stored in a CA-managed database. The main business of the repository is to provide data that allows users to confirm the status of digital certificates.
- **Software:** The software that is going to use the certificates needs to be aware of what the certificate content represents within the scope of the system security policy.
- **Policies and Procedures:** Although the core of a PKI is mainly technical, there is a strong requirement for ensuring that the mechanisms are used correctly. The Certificate Policy (CP) and Certification Practice Statements (CPS) define how the certificates are generated and managed.
- **Public Key Certificate:** The CA issues a public key certificate for each identity, confirming that the identity has the appropriate credentials. A digital certificate typically includes the public key, information about the identity of the party holding the corresponding private key, the operational period for the certificate, and the CA's own digital signature.
- **Certificate Revocation List (CRL):** CAs must also issue and process CRLs, which are lists of certificates that have been revoked. The list is signed by the same entity that issued certificates.
- **PKI Users:** They are organizations or individuals that use the PKI, but do not issue certificates. They rely on the other components of the PKI to obtain certificates, and to verify the certificates of other entities that they do business with.

In a PKI system, the CA first authenticates the user by checking whether the user owns the identity and whether he/she knows the value of the corresponding private key. If the authentication succeeds, the CA issues a certificate, which includes a signature on the public key and identity, signed under the CA's private signing key. Anyone, who would like to have an authenticated copy of the public key of the user, must verify the certificate by using the CA's public key (Chen, 2007). In a traditional PKI, the CA generates the keys for the client, or the client can generate the keys for itself and provide a copy of the public key to the CA certifies it. The choice of mechanism will be dictated by the security policy of the system or will be influenced by the key usage. If a signature key must be used to support non-repudiation, then the client generates the key. On the other hand, if it must be used to keep company information confidential, then it will be better the CA to generate the key.

Identity-Based Cryptography (IBC) is a specific type of asymmetric cryptographic technology. Compared with a traditional asymmetric cryptographic system based on a PKI, in this technology a public key can be derived from an arbitrary data string, and the corresponding private key is created binding this string with a system master secret owned by a trusted authority. The purpose of identity-based cryptosystems is to simplify the key management process, which is a heavy load in the traditional certificate based cryptosystems (Gorantla, 2005; Chen, 2007).

Cryptanalysis

Cryptanalysis is the art of deciphering encrypted data in order to break into secure communications. The goal of cryptanalysis is to find some weakness or insecurity in a cryptographic scheme, permitting its subversion or evasion. There are a wide variety of cryptanalytic attacks. Cryptanalytic attacks are designed to subvert the security of cryptographic algorithms, and they are used to attempt to decrypt data without prior access to a key. They lay on what an attacker knows and what capabilities are available and can be classified in:

- **Ciphertext-Only Attack:** The cryptanalyst has access only to the ciphertext but does not have access to corresponding plaintext. The cryptanalyst tries to determine the plaintext or the decryption function from the knowledge of a piece of ciphertext.
- **Known-Plaintext Attack:** The cryptanalyst has access to a ciphertext and its corresponding plaintext and tries to determine the decryption function.
- **Chosen-Plaintext Attack:** The cryptanalyst may choose a plaintext and learn its corresponding ciphertext. This is most common against asymmetric cryptography, where a cryptanalyst has access to a public key, he can encrypt a plaintext and study the resulting ciphertext.
- **Chosen-Ciphertext Attack:** The cryptanalyst may be able to choose ciphertexts and attempts to find their corresponding plaintexts.
- **Adaptive Chosen-Plaintext and Adaptive Chosen-Ciphertext Attacks:** In both adaptive attacks, a cryptanalyst chooses further plaintexts or ciphertexts based on prior results.
- **Man-in-the-Middle Attack:** This attack is relevant for cryptographic communication and key exchange protocols. The idea is that when two parties are exchanging keys for secure communications, an adversary puts himself between the parties on the communication line. The adversary then performs a separate key exchange with each party. The parties will end up using a different key, each of which is known to the adversary. The adversary will then decrypt any communications with the proper key, and encrypt them with the other key for sending to the other party.
- **Timing Attack:** This attack is based on repeatedly measuring the exact execution times of modular exponentiation opera-

Figure 2. Identity-Based Cryptographic Primitives

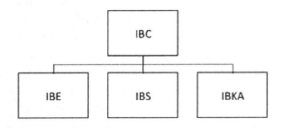

tions. It is relevant to at least RSA, Diffie-Hellman, and Elliptic Curve methods.

Public-key algorithms are based on the computational difficulty of various problems. The most common are the integer factorization, and the discrete logarithm. Public-key cryptanalysis concerns numerical algorithms for solving these computational problems. For instance, the best-known algorithms for solving the elliptic curve-based version of discrete logarithm are much more time-consuming than the best-known algorithms for factoring, at least for problems of more or less equivalent size.

While cryptanalysis investigates weaknesses in the algorithms, other attacks on cryptosystems are based on actual use of the algorithms in real devices, and are called side-channel attacks. If a cryptanalyst has access to know the amount of time the device took to encrypt a number of plaintexts or report an error in a password or PIN character, he may be able to use a timing attack to break a cipher that is otherwise resistant to analysis. An attacker might also study the pattern and length of messages to derive valuable information; this is known as traffic analysis. Poor administration of a cryptosystem, such as short keys, will make any system vulnerable. On the other hand, social engineering and attacks against the personnel who work with cryptosystems may be the most productive attacks of all (Conrad, 2007).

IDENTITY-BASED CRYTOGRAPHY (IBC)

In 1984, Shamir proposed the concept of Identity-Based Cryptography (Shamir, 1985). IBC is a specific type of asymmetric cryptographic technology. This scheme allows any pair of user to communicate securely and to verify each other's signatures without exchanging private or public keys. In the scheme the user chooses any information as his public key, such as e-mail, name or IP addresses. Hence, IBC reduces system complexity and cost for establishing and managing PKI (Baek, 2004), since it eliminates the need of a public key infrastructure. The system assumes the existence of a TTP, called the PKG. This trusted authority owns the private master key, which implies that the protection is provided by the PKG. In the next subsections, we introduce the main IBC mechanisms based in the three fundamental identity-based cryptographic primitives: Encryption (IBE), Signature (IBS) and Key Agreement (IBKA). Figure 2 illustrates these three IBC primitives.

Identity-Based Encryption (IBE)

IBE is a primitive of IBC. This cryptographic primitive is based on Public Key Encryption (PKE) that enables any pair of users to communicate without exchanging private or public keys, but assuming the existence of a trusted authority (Shamir, 1985). In IBE, user's public key is derived from any user identity value, and the trusted authority generates its corresponding private key. This identity value can be any arbitrary ASCII string, for instance, any combination of name, social security number, phone number, e-mail, IP address and others.

IBE comprises parties and a trusted authority. Parties are users or entities interchanging secure messages in a communication. The trusted authority generates and stores a pair of master keys for the system: public master key and private master key. This pair of keys is used to create the respective

Figure 3. Identity-Based Encryption

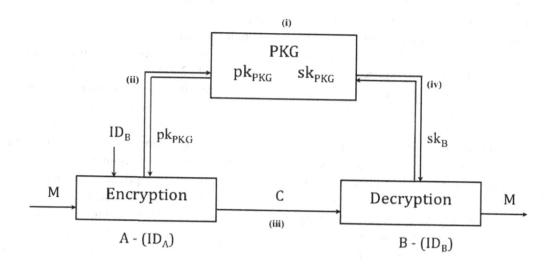

public and private keys for the parties. The public key presents a user's identifier, and the private key is created binding the identifier with the private master key. The sender A can use the receiver's identifier information, which is represented by any string to encrypt a message. The receiver B, having obtained a private key associated with his identifier information from the PKG, can decrypt the ciphertext. As illustrated in the figure, a general IBE scheme operates as follows:

1. The PKG first generates a pair of keys for the system, called public and private master keys (pk_{PKG}, sk_{PKG}). The public master key is published and remains as a constant system parameter for a long period, while the private master key is retained by the PKG in order to generate the corresponding user's private key.

2. The sender A contacts the PKG to obtain the public master key, previously published.

3. This public master key (pk_{PKG}), combined with the recipient's identity value (ID_B) corresponds to the recipient's public key. With that key, the sender A encrypts the plaintext message M and obtains a ciphertext C.

4. When the recipient B receives the message encrypted (C), it authenticates himself to the PKG and this last one verifies if the user owns the identity and binds the identity with the PKG's private key. A private key (sk_B) associated with his identity (ID_B) is delivered to the recipient B to decrypt the message. A secure channel between the user and the PKG is required for transmitting the private key. In general, a SSL connection is a common solution for a large-scale system. However, for the user authenticates itself to the PKG, some mechanisms like username and password or smart cards can be used.

Private keys need to be generated only once. All successive communications corresponding to the same public key can be decrypted using the same private key.

The process mentioned above can be summarized in four procedures: *Setup, Extract, Encrypt* and *Decrypt* (Boneh, 2001; Gagné, 2003). *Setup* generates the system parameters and master keys. System parameters are published, whereas only the trusted authority will know master keys. The PKG runs *extract* when the user wants to retrieve his private key. This procedure uses system parameters and the master key to generate the private key corresponding to the identity value string. Finally, users execute *Encrypt* and *Decrypt* procedures to encode and decode ciphertexts, respectively.

The original motivation for IBE is to help the deployment of a public key infrastructure in order to simplify systems in the management of a large number of public keys (Boneh, 2001). This simplifies keying material management, eliminating the need for directories and certificates. IBE also improves the process of public key revocation, keys delegation, user credentials management and forward-secure encryption (Gagné, 2003). In the case of public key revocation, IBE provides with the public key an expiration time, thus implementing short-lived public keys. This expiration time can be a day, week, month or year depending on the frequency at which the user must renew the private key. The user can employ the private key only during the current date. Once it expires, the user needs to obtain a new private key from the PKG.

IBE also can be used in order to delegate decryption keys. In this case, the user plays the role of the PKG and gives to subordinates the private keys corresponding to their responsibilities. Subordinates can decrypt messages according to their responsibilities, and cannot decrypt messages of others. Another IBE's applications are the management of user credentials and the forward-secure encryption. For managing user credentials, it includes a permission level in the public key, which means that the recipient will be able to decrypt the message only if he has the permission required. In a forward-secure scheme, secret keys are updated at regular periods of time. The exposure of the secret key corresponding to a given time period does not enable an adversary to break the scheme for any prior time period (Canetti,

2003). With the use of IBE in this scheme, if the private key of a time period is compromised, all the messages encrypted in previous time periods remains secure.

IBE remained an open problem for many years (Baek, 2004). In 2001, Boneh and Franklin solved Shamir's open problem proposing the first functional IBE scheme based on weil-pairing and elliptic curves techniques. In this scheme, as in the others IBE schemes, the security of the PKG's private master key is fundamental because the security of all other private keys depends on it. One way to increase its security is to distribute the private master key among various sites using techniques of threshold cryptography (Gagné, 2003). In the same year Cocks (2001) used a variant of Boneh and Franklin scheme to construct his scheme. It is the only practical IBE scheme that does not use pairings; instead it uses quadratic residues. If there exists an integer x such that $x^2 \equiv q \pmod{n}$; q is called a quadratic residue modulo n if it is congruent to that perfect square. The security of this scheme is based on the hardness of the integer factorization problem, which consists in finding a value x satisfying $x = y^2 \bmod n$, where $n = pq$, being p and q two large primes and y a given value. The scheme encrypts data string bit by bit, requiring $(\log n)$ bits of ciphertext per bit of plaintext; then, the length of the ciphertext becomes long, making it an inefficient scheme (Baek, 2004; Chen, 2007).

After those schemes, many other schemes, derived from the IBE scheme of Boneh and Franklin, were created, including Hierarchical Identity-Based Encryption (HIBE), Authenticated IBE, Fuzzy IBE, Public Key Encryption with Keyword Search (PEKS) and others (Gorantla, 2005). In 2002, Horwitz and Lynn introduced the concept of hierarchical IBE (Horwitz, 2002). However, Gentry and Silverberg (2002) presented the first secure and practical HIBE scheme. They argue that with a single PKG a heavy workload can be generated on it, becoming a bottleneck (Gagné, 2003). A root PKG issues private keys for PKGs below it, which issues private keys for users in their domains in the next level (Gorantla, 2005). An advantage of HIBE is that if a domain-level PKGs private key is compromised, the private keys of higher-level PKGs do not. In the same year, Lynn proposed the authenticated IBE scheme, which allows communication with integrity (Lynn, 2002). This scheme provides message authentication at no additional computational cost. The receiver can verify the identity of the sender, and whether or not the message has been tampered, eliminating the need for digital signatures when authentication is required. The session key is hashed with a random value to obtain a different mask each time the encryption function is executed (Gagné, 2003).

In 2004, Boneh, Di Crescenzo, Ostrovsky and Persiano proposed the PEKS scheme (Boneh, 2004) constructed in order to protect the privacy of the contents in a computer network communication. The message is encrypted with some keyword, and this scheme allows a gateway to verify if the message contains the keyword or not, in order to route the message to a correct destination. In the same year, Sahai and Waters proposed a Fuzzy IBE scheme (Sahai, 2005). This scheme allows the encryption of data using biometric input as public key. There has been recent interest about the challenge of generating cryptographic keys from biometric inputs. The primary difficulty in generating a strong key is that the measured value can change vaguely in each sampling. This effect can be explained by differences in sampling devices, environmental noise or small changes in the human attribute itself.

Nowadays, new schemes are proposed using the techniques mentioned above (*quadratic residues, bilinear pairings, hierarchical IBE, authenticated IBE, PEKS, fuzzy IBE*) with the purpose of achieving better efficiency compared to existing schemes. The algorithms presented in each scheme are based in the general scheme of IBE: setup, extract, encrypt and decrypt.

Identity-Based Signature (IBS)

Digital signature is the most basic primitive in cryptography. It provides means to an entity binds its identity to a piece of information, and to achieve authenticity, integrity and non-repudiation. The process of signing permits an entity to transform the message and some secret information into a tag called *digital signature* (Gorantla, 2005). In 1984, Shamir (1985) proposed Identity-Based Signature (IBS), where the user public key is his identity. The corresponding private key is issued by a trusted authority, PKG, and it derives from a private master key that only the PKG knows. This eliminates some of the costs associated with PKI and certificates, providing more efficient schemes.

In an IBS scheme, the signer A obtains a signing key associated with his identifier information from the PKG. Then, he signs a message using the signing key. The verifier B uses A's identifier information to verify B's signature and he don't need to get A's certificate. As illustrated in the figure, a general IBS scheme operates as follows (Baek, 2004):

1. The PKG creates its public and private keys pair (pk_{PKG}, sk_{PKG}).
2. The signer A authenticates himself to the PKG and obtains a private key sk_A associated with his identity ID_A.
3. Using his private key sk_A, A creates a signature σ on his message M.
4. Once obtained the signature σ and the message M from A, the verifier B checks whether σ is a genuine signature on M using A's identity ID_A and the PKG's public key pk_{PKG}. If it is the same, he returns *Accept*, otherwise, he returns *Reject*.

An identity-based signature process consists of four phases: *Setup, Extract, Sign* and *Verify*. The PKG initializes the system in the *setup* phase by indicating the system parameters, and chooses and keeps a private key. The private key is used

Figure 4. Identity-Based Signature

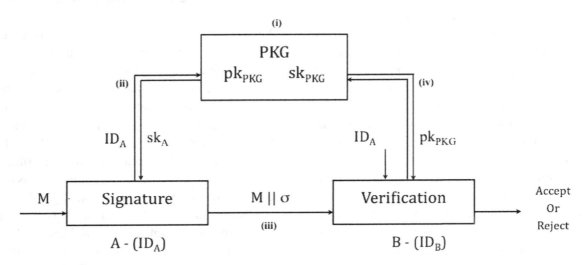

in the *extract* phase to calculate private keys for the participating users in the system. In the *sign* phase, a signer with an identity ID signs a message using the private key given by the PKG corresponding to his identity ID. To verify a signature of an entity with identity ID, in the *verify* phase, a verifier in an IBS scheme just uses the identity ID (Gorantla, 2005).

A number of IBS schemes have been published since 2000 (Chen, 2007). Shamir proposed an IBS scheme based on integer factorization problem. Later, satisfactory and practical solutions for IBS schemes were proposed. Guillou and Quisquater proposed a "paradoxical" IBS using their interactive zero-knowledge protocol. An IBS scheme using pairings was first proposed by Sakai, Ohgishi and Kasahara, however they did not present the security analysis in their scheme. Paterson proposed an IBS scheme based on pairings with brief security arguments but without rigorous proof. Hess proposed a provably secure IBS, which is secure against existential forgery under adaptively chosen message and fixed ID attacks. In 2003, Cha-Cheon proposed an IBS scheme based Gap Diffie-Hellman groups. They provided a definition of security for IBS schemes called security

against existential forgery under adaptively chosen message and ID attacks and proved their scheme secure. Cheon, Kim and Yoon later proposed an IBS scheme that enables secure batch verification. Yi independently proposed an IBS scheme, based weil-pairing and quadratic residues. Chen, Zhang and Kim proposed an IBS scheme without trusted PKG (Gorantla, 2005).

Identity-Based Key Agreement (IBKA)

Key agreement is a cryptographic primitive that is used to share a common secret key between entities for establishing a secure communication. This secret key is used as a session key to construct a secure channel between entities concerned, hence no single entity can predetermine the resulting value. It can be subdivided into key transport protocol and key agreement protocol. In key transport protocol, one entity creates the shared key and distributes it to others securely, whereas in key agreement protocol, each entity computes the common secret key using the information contributed by all involved entities (Lee, 2005). In 2001, an IBKA protocol based on weil-pairing was proposed by Smart (2002) combining the key agreement protocol with digital signatures.

A key agreement protocol is said to provide implicit key authentication, of entity B to entity A. If A is assured that no other entity besides B can possibly ascertain the value of the secret key. A key agreement protocol that provides mutual implicit key authentication is called an authenticated key agreement protocol. The desired properties for an authenticated key agreement scheme are described below:

- **Known-Key Security:** Each run of the protocol should result in a unique secret session key. The compromise of one session key should not compromise other session keys.

- **Forward Secrecy:** If long-term private keys of one or more entities are compromised, the secrecy of previously established session keys should not be affected. We say that a system has partial forward secrecy if some but not all of the entities long-term keys can be corrupted without compromising previously established session keys, and we say that a system has perfect forward secrecy if the long-term keys of all the entities may be corrupted without compromising any session key previously established by these entities.

- **Key-Compromise Impersonation Resilience:** Compromising an entity A's long-term private key will allow an adversary to impersonate A, but it should not enable the adversary to impersonate other entities to A.

- **Unknown Key-Share Resilience:** An entity A should not be able to be forced into sharing a key with any entity C if A thinks that she is sharing the key with another entity B.

- **Key Control:** No entity should be able to force the session key to be a preselected value.

An IBKA scheme can be specified by three procedures: *Setup, Extract, and Key Agreement.* The *setup* algorithm is executed by the PKG. This part of the key agreement protocol is only performed once and creates a system public and private master keys pair as well as the public parameters. The *extract* algorithm creates the identity key for a given identity. This algorithm is executed by the PKG. If all IDs are known and the range is not too big it is possible to execute this step for all IDs offline, and the master secrets can then be destroyed, if required. Finally, the devices taking part in the key agreement compute the session key. Only if both endpoint addresses match their identity keys, a valid session key is created (Schridde, 2008).

A large number of IBKA protocols have been published in the past several years. Chen, Cheng and Smart gave an overview of these IBKA schemes. In 2002, Smart proposed an IBKA protocol based on weil-pairing. After that, Chen and Kudla modified the Smart scheme in order to make it more efficient and, more interestingly, to let it hold the new property of PKG forward security, which they defined to mean that the compromise of the PKG's private key will not compromise previously established session keys. They also are the first to suggest the concept of authenticated key agreement between members of separate domains (Chen, 2007). Scott proposed another IBKA protocol based on Tate pairing. Shim discussed a weakness in Smart's scheme and proposed an IBKA protocol, which he claimed efficient and secure. However, Sun and Hsieh showed that Shim's scheme is insecure against man-in-the-middle attacks. Later, McCullagh and Barreto proposed an efficient key agreement protocol with security proof in Bellare and Rogaway model, which can be instantiated in escrow and escrowless mode without imposing extra computational effort. But, Xie pointed out a flaw and showed that an adversary can launch key compromise attack on this scheme. Choo also demonstrated that McCullagh and Barreto's scheme and its 'fix' variant are not secure. Xie proposed an IBKA scheme, secure in Bellare-Rogaway model (Gorantla, 2005).

IBC Vulnerabilities and Attacks

Due to its characteristics, IBC presents different security issues. The main security vulnerability lies in the inherent key escrow problem, due to the dependence on the PKG (Oh, 2005). Further, IBC is prone to other different vulnerabilities such key revocation and distribution problems, resulted from the use of insecure channels to deliver secret keys. The PKG must be delegated a considerable amount of trust because it can generate any user private key and thus decrypt any message. As consequence, IBC cannot offer non-repudiation which is a considerable drawback that prevent IBC from being practically applied in the real world.

Due to key escrow problem founded in IBC, if the PKG is compromised or the private master key is lost, then anyone can compute user private keys. As the PKG always knows user's private key, a malicious PKG can impersonate the user, decrypting any ciphertext or falsifying a signature. This means that the user privacy or authenticity in the system is compromised. This problem seems to be inevitable because the IBC depends on the PKG, which uses a single private master key to generate user's private keys. The PKG is involved in issuing private keys to users whose identity is assumed to be unique in the system (Gangishetti, 2007). On the other hand, if we suppose that we can trust the PKG, the user first must authenticates it and prove that he is the person who deserves the keys. The way the recipient retrieves the private key is also considered a problem because a secure channel between the user and the PKG is required. This is another drawback of IBE, where a user's secret key may be exposed to an adversary in an insecure channel, which means that the security is completely lost.

Identity revocation is another weakness in the IBC schemes. Those schemes assume that once keys are issued, they are always valid. However, if an e-mail address used as public key is compromised, the user needs to get a new e-mail address or a new public key. In order to avoid that problem, an expiration time is included into the public key. Therefore, only the private key corresponding to that period of time can be compromised. Nevertheless, if the e-mail was not really compromised, but it was misspelled, as any string can be considered as public key, also typos are considered keys. Thus, the recipient is not going to be able to decrypt the message ignoring the reason, but even if recipient knows about the mistake, it's going to be impossible to prove the server he owns the message.

Nowadays, no solutions exist to solve all these issues at the same time (Oh, 2005). Schemes that solve a problem still face another. That is why some variant systems were proposed to avoid vulnerabilities mentioned before, such as Certificate-Based Encryption (CBE), Certificateless Public Key Encryption (CL-PKE) and Secure Key Issuing. In general, most of cryptographic schemes are vulnerable to attacks based on semantics and human factors, which requires additional infrastructure. In IBC, there are some common attacks related with the variant systems proposed. First of all, we can distinguish two types of attacks, the attack of an uncertified client and the attack of the certifier. In the first one, the adversary assumes the role of an uncertified client. After proving knowledge of the secret key corresponding to its public key, the attacker can make decryption and update queries. In the second one, the certifier attack, the adversary assumes the role of the certifier modeling an eavesdropping trusted authority. After proving knowledge of the master secret it can make decryption queries.

When a third party is involved, two main kinds of attacks can happen, key replacement attack or a malicious PKG attack (Au, 2007). In the key replacement attack, a third party tries to impersonate a user after compromising the user private key and/or replacing the user public key with some value chosen by the third party. However, it does not know the user partial key, which depends of the IBC scheme. In the malicious PKG attack, the PKG, who knows the partial key of a user, tries to impersonate the user, even if it does not know the user private key, or it is not able to replace the user public key.

EXISTING SOLUTIONS FOR IBC SECURITY VULNERABILITIES

IBC security issues motivated the development of different variant schemes. This section describes some solutions already proposed in order to eliminate issues found in IBC.

Certificate-Based Encryption (CBE)

If a certificate is revocable, then third parties cannot rely on that certificate unless the CA distributes certificate status information indicating whether the certificate is currently valid. This certificate status information must be widely distributed for all relying parties, requiring a heavy infrastructure. The certificate revocation problem is the reason against extensive implementation of public key cryptography. CBE mitigates this problem by making certificate revocation implicit. Certificates have an expiry date in order to obtain a new certificate from the trusted authority to decrypt, eliminating third-party queries on certificate status (Galindo, 2008; Gentry, 2003).

Gentry (2003) introduced the notion of CBE to overcome the drawbacks of the conventional PKE and IBE. Gentry's scheme combines PKE and IBE preserving most of the advantages of each one. With PKE, each client generates its own public/private key pair and requests a certificate from the CA, while a CA uses an IBE scheme to generate the certificate. This certificate has all the functionality of the conventional PKI certificate and can also be used as a decryption key. This functionality provides an implicit certification so

that the user is required to decrypt the ciphertext using his private key along with a certificate from his CA (Lu, 2008; Gentry, 2003). This scheme is considered as escrow-free, due to the CA doesn't know B's private key (Gentry, 2003).

CBE was proposed as an intermediate paradigm between IBE and PKE, because it is not key escrowed and simplifies the certificate management. An additional property of CBE is that the up-to-date certificate can be sent over an insecure channel, in contrast to IBE, which means that distributing keys is not an issue anymore. The most important advantages of CBE, if we compare with other cryptosystems, are: the removal of the third party certification, the simple key distribution and the absence of key escrow. As main disadvantages, we mention the continuous communication between users and the CA, which makes the CA to be more vulnerable to electronic attacks as denial-of-service. This feature can be partially reduced by having a hierarchy of multiple CAs. Another disadvantage with respect to IBE is that public keys are not identity-based (Galindo, 2008).

Certificateless Public Key Encryption (CL-PKE)

In 2003, Al-Riyami and Paterson (Al-Riyami, 2003) proposed a new PKE scheme called Certificateless Public Key Encryption. Their idea was to combine the functionality of a public key scheme with that of an identity-based scheme in order to avoid the drawbacks present in both of them. In contrast to traditional public key cryptographic systems, the CL-PKE doesn't require to use certificates to guarantee the authenticity of public keys. It does rely on the use of a TTP called Key Generation Center (KGC), who owns the master key and doesn't have access to user private keys. This scheme is certificate-free like IBE, and unlike IBE but similar to CBE, is key-escrow-free.

The KGC supplies an entity A, in a secure way, with a partial private key D_A that is previously computed from the identifier ID_A (user identity and master key). Then, A combines its partial private key D_A with some secret information in order to generate its private key S_A that remains not available to the KGC. On the other hand, A's public key is computed by combining A's secret information with the KGC's public parameters. In order to generate private and public key, identity A must chose the same secret information. This scheme is not identity-based, because the public key is not computed from the identity. Also, there is no certificate for A's key, which means that no security is applied to the protection of the key. A's public key might be made available to other entities by transmitting it along with messages or by placing it in a public directory (Al-Riyami, 2003). Now, if an entity B wants to encrypt a message to A or verify a signature from A, it requires the recipient's identifier ID_A and the public key P_A. Likewise, to decrypt a ciphertext, a receiver requires the partial private key corresponding to their identity (which is given to them by a key generation center) and the private key corresponding to the distributed public key (Dent, 2008).

Certificateless public key cryptography was designed to overcome the key-escrow limitation of IBC without introducing certificates and the management involved on it. Nevertheless, the level of trust placed in the third party is as high as that placed in CAs, which means that the key escrow problem remains an open problem. In the scheme, the third party can break the system generating false public keys. However, it is not going to be able to decrypt the messages that were encrypted using a properly generated public key. This scheme is intermediate between the IBE and the traditional PKI approaches (Al-Riyami, 2005).

Secure Key Issuing

In most of the identity-based cryptosystems (Cocks, 2001; Underwood, 2010), secure key issuing in identity-based public key cryptosystems is a challenging task due to the inherent drawback of key escrow and the requirement for secure channel between the PKG and users (Wang, 2008) in order to the PKG to deliver private keys. There are two main approaches of secure key issuing, the multiple key issuing authorities and the embedding user chosen secret information in the private key issued by the key issuing authorities.

In 2001, Boneh and Franklin presented the first key issuing protocol (Boneh, 2001). They used distributed PKGs instead of one PKG. In this scheme, user obtains partial private keys from each PKG and combines them to get the private key. In 2004, Lee et al. proposed a key issuing protocol, addressing the key escrow problem and secure channel requirement (Lee, 2004). In this protocol, a user private key is issued by a KGC, and multiple Key Privacy Authorities (KPAs) protect its privacy. The KGC checks user's identity and issues a user's partial private key through a blinded technique, while other KPAs performs key generation in a sequential way. This blinding factor between the user and the KGC or KPAs ensures a secure channel. The scheme assigns the role of user identification to the KGC and key securing to KPAs. In 2005, Gangishetti et al. proposed a new key issuing protocol, which involves one PKG and nKPAs (Gangishetti, 2007). The PKG gives a registration identity to the user during the registration; user uses this registration identity as blinding factor while collecting the partial private keys from KPAs.

Since the private key of a user is computed by the PKG and the nKPAs, the privacy of user's private key is kept if at least one authority remains honest. Only the legitimate user who knows the blinding parameter can unblind the message to retrieve the private key. Nevertheless, if all of the KPAs cooperate, which means that all of the third parties are unreliable, they can recover the private key and therefore the key escrow problem come up. This kind of "attack" is known as a cascade. If every member of the cascade, in this case the KPAs, is independent then the system could be considered trusty. The scheme requires a lot of computation due to multiple KPAs. The scheme is also vulnerable to DoS since KPAs can't distinguish entity's legitimate key securing request from an adversary's malicious request.

Below there is a theoretical comparative table about the solutions proposed before. In the literature, these variant systems have been proposed in order to avoid the main disadvantage presented in IBC, the key escrow. As it shows, all the presented schemes remove key escrow, however in some cases they lose the identity-based property since public keys are not longer determined from an identity.

IBC APPLICATIONS AND FUTURE TRENDS

The goal of cryptography is to assure aspects like confidentiality, authentication and integrity for protecting information, preventing spoofing and preventing forgery, respectively. Nowadays, encryption technology is considered a field of research related to information security that has been introduced in our daily lives becoming increasingly important due to its relation with emerging technologies like wireless, cloud computing, cognitive radio and quantum computation among others.

As various applications of wireless networks have been proposed, security is one of the major issues becoming one of the most important challenges. Wireless communication is open to interference and interception, and malicious nodes might create, alter, or replay routing information to interrupt network operation. These nodes may also launch a Sybil attack, in which a single node presents multiple identities to others, or an identity replication attack, in which clones of a compromised node are put into multiple network places. Moreover, malicious nodes may inject bogus data into the network to consume its limited resources, and selfish nodes can drop data packets of other nodes. It is widely known that cryptographic mechanisms can provide some of the strongest techniques against most vulnerabilities. Several key management schemes for wireless communications can be found in the literature, among them identity-based key management schemes. These schemes have a simple key management process and reduced memory storage cost compared to other methods (Da Silva, 2008). The IBC mechanism has been already applied not only to provide end-to-end authenticity and confidentiality, but also to save network bandwidth and computational power of wireless nodes (Deng, 2004). Nevertheless, adversaries with adequate equipment can eavesdrop on communications,

Table 1. Solutions for IBC security vulnerabilities

	Identity-Based Encryption (IBE)	**Certificate-Based Encryption (CBE)**	**Certificateless Public Key Encryption (CL-PKE)**	**Secure key Issuing**
Cryptographic Approach	Identity-based cryptography	Identity-based encryption + public key encryption	Identity-based encryption + public key encryption	Identity-based encryption
Advantage	Certificate-free Identity-based	Key-escrow-free	Certificate-free Key-escrow-free	Certificate-free Key-escrow-free Identity-based
Disadvantage	Key escrow	Certificates No user identity	No identity-based	Multiple PKGs
Trusted Third Party	PKG	CA	KGC	KGC

making the network susceptible to external attacks even when using cryptography (Da Silva, 2008).

Recent developments of wireless communication lead to the problem of growing spectrum shortage. Cognitive radio, as a novel technology, tends to solve this problem by dynamically utilizing the spectrum. Security in cognitive radio network becomes also a challenging issue, since attackers have more chances compared to wireless network. These weaknesses are introduced by the nature of cognitive radio, and may cause serious impact to the network quality of service. Nevertheless, since cognitive radios can be adapted to any environment, it is important to select a secure means of communications. Generally, security mechanisms can be divided into two categories: protection based and detection based. Protection based technology can be viewed as the first line of the security system, using cryptography to prevent malicious attackers outside the networks from both passive and active attacks. Detection based technology is used to detect the intrusion attack inside the network, preventing the situation when cryptographic system has been broken through. Cryptography is already implemented in this kind of communications satisfying multiple security requirements (Clancy, 2008; Zhang, 2009).

On the other hand, cloud computing is a new paradigm of computing in which virtualized resources are provided as a service over the Internet. Hence, authentication of users and services becomes important for the trust and security of the cloud. Nowadays, an identity-based hierarchical model for cloud computing was already proposed (Li, 2009). With this model, an identity-based authentication scheme for cloud computing (IBACC) is used. IBACC is more efficient and lightweight than other authentication schemes, which contributes good scalability to larger cloud systems. Finally, quantum computing is in advanced stage of development due to recent nanotechnology advances in this area. Quantum computers promise to be so fast and powerful computers with a capacity for processing data able to crack even the most advanced encryption methods through brute force. Quantum cryptography has arrived as a reality in advance of quantum computers, and the way it works relies upon a twist of quantum physics known as the Heisenberg Principle. This principle is based on the idea that by simply looking at a tiny particle like a photon, it changes permanently. It means that if the state of a photon is used to generate a cryptography key, then that key is altered and the data rendered unreadable. This makes breaking the encryption impossible (Calixto, 2008).

In most of emergent technologies the initial research doesn't focus on security aspects. Nevertheless, what became a common factor between them is the use of different cryptographic techniques in order to secure the communication. Even if IBC is becoming a field of research vastly developed, it needs to be adapted to the technology used. Nowadays, almost everybody uses encryption in cellular phones, mobile PCs, credit cards, train tickets, transport cards, without even realizing it. These kinds of devices own constraints in terms of resources, requiring an optimization of cryptography technologies to efficiently be applied in areas like smartcards, SIM cards, quantum computers and others.

CONCLUSION

IBE is a primitive of IBC which original motivation was to simplify certificate management. Adi Shamir was the first scientist that proposed a cryptographic scheme based on public key cryptosystems with a different way of generating key pairs. Nowadays, IBE is a research area that had became increasingly widespread, despite of the disadvantages founded in IBC technology.

Since public keys are the user's identities, IBC makes certificates obsolete. This is the main improvement of the scheme because certificates are the main reason for heavy infrastructures of today's PKI. However, IBC suffers the inherent key escrow problem. Many schemes have been proposed to eliminate this weakness. CBE, PKE and secure key issuing are some of the proposed schemes, which are consider as key escrow-free schemes, nevertheless they presents some other disadvantages against IBE.

The key escrow problem is the main drawback founded which unfortunately all IBC schemes have. Once the PKG knows the user's private key, it can impersonate a user, decrypting or signing messages. However, in an ordinary PKI system, there is a similar problem because a certification authority can generate a key pair, and certify that the public key belongs to a specific user impersonating the user as in IBC. Consequently, it is necessary to mention that schemes involving a trusted authority will always be affected in this sense.

This book chapter surveyed the state of the art of the main weaknesses founded in IBC and the solutions proposed in order to avoid these vulnerabilities. The presented schemes are still considered as insecure and even if they eliminate this drawback, in some cases they lose the identity-based property. Also, there are no schemes that eliminate all IBC vulnerabilities together, however the main features to consider the moment of applying a cryptographic scheme bounded to new technologies is particularly the means of communication and the devices implied. This means that it is imperative to consider wireless technologies and capacity devices for an adequate performance of cryptographic algorithms, which involves processing speed.

REFERENCES

Al-Riyami, S. S., & Paterson, K. (2003). Certificateless Public Key Cryptography. In C.-S. Laih (Ed.), *ASIACRYPT 2003: Vol. 2894. Lecture Notes in Computer Science* (pp. 452-473). Springer, Heidelberg.

Al-Riyami, S. S., & Paterson, K. (2005). CBE from CL-PKE: A generic construction and efficient schemes. In S. Vaudenay (Ed.) *PKC 2005: Vol. 3386. Lecture Notes in Computer Science* (pp. 398-415). Springer, Heidelberg.

Au, M. H., Mu, Y., Chen, J., Wong, D. S., Liu, J. K., & Yang, G. (2007). Malicious KGC attacks in certificateless cryptography. In R. Deng & P. Samarati (Eds.), *Proceedings of the 2nd ACM Symposium on information, Computer and Communications Security* (pp. 302-311). Singapore, ASIACCS '07. New York, NY: ACM.

Avizienis, A., Laprie, J. -C., Randell, B., & Landwehr, C. (2004). Basic Concepts and Taxonomy of Dependable and Secure Computing. *IEEE Transactions on Dependable and Secure Computing, 1*(1), 11-33.

Baek, J., Newmarch, J., Safavi-Naini, R., & Susilo, W. (2004). A Survey of Identity-Based Cryptography. In *Proceedings of the 10th Annual Conference for Australian Unix User's Group, (AUUG '04)* (pp. 95-102). Springer-Verlag.

Baek, J., Susilo, W., & Zhou, J. (2007) New Constructions of Fuzzy Identity-Based Encryption. In R. Deng and P. Samarati (Eds.), *Proceedings of the 2nd ACM symposium on Information, computer and communications security, ASIACCS '07 (Singapore, March 20 - 22, 2007)* (pp. 368-370). New York, NY: ACM.

Boneh, D., Di Crescenzo, G., Ostrovsky, R., & Persiano, G. (2004). Public key encryption with keyword search. In *Advances in Cryptology, Eurocrypt '04: Vol. 3027. Lecture Notes In Computer Science* (pp. 506-522). Springer-Verlag.

Boneh, D., & Franklin, M. (2001). Identity-Based Encryption from the Weil Pairing. In J. Kilian (Ed.), *CRYPTO 2001: Vol. 2139. Lecture Notes In Computer Science* (pp. 213-229). Springer, Heidelberg.

Calixto, M. (2008). Quantum computation and cryptography: an overview. *Natural Computing, 8*(4), 663–679. doi:10.1007/s11047-008-9094-8

Canetti, R., Halevi, S., & Katz, J. (2003). A Forward-Secure Public-Key Encryption Scheme. In *Proceedings of the 22nd international Conference on theory and Applications of Cryptographic Techniques - EUROCRYPT 2003: Vol. 2656. Lecture Notes in Computer Science* (pp. 255-271). Springer-Verlag, Berlin, Heidelberg.

Chen, L. (2007). An Interpretation of Identity-Based Cryptography. In A. Aldini and R. Gorrieri (Eds.), *Foundations of Security Analysis and Design IV: Vol. 4677. Lecture Notes in Computer Science* (pp. 183-208). Springer-Verlag, Berlin, Heidelberg.

Clancy, T. C., & Goergen, N. (2008). Security in Cognitive Radio Networks: Threats and Mitigation. In *3rd International Conference on Cognitive Radio Oriented Wireless Networks and Communications. CrownCom 2008* (pp. 1-8). Singapore.

Cocks, C. (2001). An Identity-Based Encryption Scheme Based on Quadratic Residues. In *Proceedings of IMA 2001: Vol. 2260. Lecture Notes in Computer Science* (pp. 360-363). Springer-Verlag.

Conrad, E. (2007). *Types of Cryptographic Attacks*. GIAC Research in the Common Body of Knowledge.

Coppersmith, D. (2010). Cryptography. *IBM Journal of Research and Development, 31*(2), 244–248. doi:10.1147/JRD.1987.5390134

Da Silva, E., Nogueira, M., dos Santos, A., & Albini, L. (2008). Identity-Based Key Management in Mobile Ad Hoc Networks. *IEEE Wireless Communications Magazine, Techniques and Applications, Special issue on ". Dependability Issues with Ubiquitous Wireless Access, 15*(5), 46–52.

Deng, H., Mukherjee, A., & Agrawal, D. P. (2004). Threshold and Identity-based Key Management and Authentication for Wireless Ad Hoc Networks. In *Proceedings of the international Conference on information Technology: Coding and Computing (Itcc '04): Vol. 2. ITCC. IEEE Computer Society*. Washington, DC.

Dent, A. W. (2008). A survey of certificateless encryption schemes and security models. *International Journal of Information Security, 7*(5), 349–377. doi:10.1007/s10207-008-0055-0

Gagné, M. (2003). Identity-Based Encryption: a Survey. *CryptoBytes, 6*(1), 10–19.

Galindo, D., Morillo, P., & Rafols, C. (2008). Improved certificate-based encryption in the standard model. *Journal of Systems and Software, 81*(7), 1218–1226. doi:10.1016/j.jss.2007.09.009

Gangishetti, R., Gorantla, M. C., Lal Das, M., & Saxena, A. (2007). Threshold key issuing in identity-based cryptosystems. *Computer Standards & Interfaces, 29*(2), 260–264. doi:10.1016/j.csi.2006.05.001

Gentry, C. (2003). Certificate-based encryption and the certificate-revocation problem. In *Proceedings of the 22nd international Conference on theory and Applications of Cryptographic Techniques EUROCRYPT 2003: Vol. 2656. Lecture Notes in Computer Science* (pp. 272-291). Springer-Verlag, Berlin, Heidelberg.

Gentry, C., & Silverberg, A. (2002). Hierarchical ID-Based Cryptography, In Y. Zheng (Ed.), *Proceedings of the 8th international Conference on the theory and Application of Cryptology and information Security: Advances in Cryptology, Asiacrypt '02: Vol. 2501. Lecture Notes In Computer Science* (pp.548-566). Springer-Verlag.

Gorantla, M., Gangishetti, R., & Saxena, A. (2005). A Survey on ID-Based Cryptographic Primitives, *Cryptology ePrint Archive*, Report2005/094. Retrieved from http://eprint.iacr.org/2005/094.

Horwitz, J., & Lynn, B. (2002). Toward Hierarchical Identity-Based Encryption. In L. R. Knudsen (Ed.), In *Proceedings of the international Conference on the theory and Applications of Cryptographic Techniques: Advances in Cryptology, Eurocrypt '02: Vol. 2332. Lecture Notes In Computer Science* (pp. 466-481). Springer-Verlag.

Jao, D. (2008). *Public Key Cryptography. Contents 2007*. ON, Canada: University of Waterloo.

Kumar, K. P., Shailaja, G., & Saxena, A. (2006). Secure and Efficient Threshold Key Issuing Protocol for ID-Based Cryptosystems. *Cryptology ePrint Archive*, Report 2006/245. Retrieved from http://eprint.iacr.org/2006/245.pdf.

Kwon, S., & Lee, S. (2006). Identity-based key issuing without secure channel in a broad area. In *Proceedings of the 7th international conference on Information security applications: Part I: Vol. 4298. Lecture Notes In Computer Science* (pp. 30-44). Jeju Island, Korea, Springer-Verlag, Berlin, Heidelberg.

Lee, B., Boyd, C., Dawson, E., Kim, K., Yang, J., & Yoo, S. (2004). Secure key issuing in ID-based cryptography. In *Proceedings of the Second Workshop on Australasian information Security, Data Mining and Web intelligence, and Software internationalisation – Vol. 32* (pp. 69 -74). Dunedin, New Zealand, ACM International Conference Proceeding Series, vol. 54. Australian Computer Society, Darlinghurst, Australia.

Lee, H., Kim, D., Kim, S., & Oh, H. (2005). Identity-Based Key Agreement Protocols in a Multiple PKG Environment. In *Computational Science and its applications - ICCSA 2005: Vol. 3483. Lecture Notes in Computer Science* (pp. 877-886).

Li, H., Dai, Y., Tian, L., & Yang, H. (2009). Identity-Based Authentication for Cloud Computing. In M. G. Jaatun, G. Zhao, and C. Rong (Eds.), *Proceedings of the 1st international Conference on Cloud Computing: Vol. 5931. Lecture Notes in Computer Science* (pp. 157-166). Beijing, China, Springer-Verlag, Berlin, Heidelberg.

Lu, Y., Li, J., & Xiao, J. (2008). Generic Construction of Certificate-Based Encryption. In *Proceedings of 2008 The 9th International Conference for Young Computer Scientists* (pp. 1589-1594).

Lynn, B. (2002). Authenticated ID-based Encryption. *Cryptology ePrint Archive*, Report 2002/072. Retrieved from http://eprint.iacr.org/2002/072.

Menezes, A., Van Oorschot, P., & Vanstone, S. (1996). *Handbook of Applied Cryptography*. United States, December 16, CRC Press.

Oh, J., Lee, K., & Moon, S. (2005). Lecture Notes. In *Computer Science* (*Vol. 3803*, pp. 290–303). How to Solve Key Escrow and Identity Revocation in Identity-Based Encryption Schemes, In *Information Systems Security* Berlin, Heidelberg: Springer-Verlag.

Paterson, K. G., & Price, G. (2003, July 9). A comparison between traditional public key infrastructures and identity-based cryptography. *Information Security Technical Report, 8*(3), 57–72. doi:10.1016/S1363-4127(03)00308-X

Penev, T. (2005). *Identity Based Public Key Infrastructures, Darmstadt University of Technology*, Department of Informatics, Bachelor Thesis.

Perry, M., O'hara, K., Sellen, A., Brown, B., & Harper, R. (2001). Dealing with Mobility: Understanding Access Anytime, Anywhere. *ACM Transactions on Computer-Human Interaction, 8*(4), 323–347. doi:10.1145/504704.504707

Sahai, A., & Waters, B. (2005). Fuzzy Identity-Based Encryption. In *Advances in Cryptology, Eurocrypt '05: Vol. 3494. Lecture Notes In Computer Science* (pp. 457-473), Springer-Verlag.

Schridde, C., Smith, M., & Freisleben, B. (2008). An Identity-Based Key Agreement Protocol for the Network Layer. In *Proceedings of the 6th international conference on Security and Cryptography for Networks, Amalfi, Italy. Lecture Notes in Computer Science*. (pp. 409–422) Springer, Heidelberg.

Shamir, A. (1985). Identity-based cryptosystems and signature schemes. In G. R. Blakley and D. Chaum (Eds.), *Proceedings of CRYPTO 84 on Advances in Cryptology, Santa Barbara, California, United States* (pp. 47-53). Springer-Verlag New York, New York.

Underwood, S. (2010). Visions of the future. *Communications of the ACM, 53*(7), 25–25. doi:10.1145/1785414.1785426

Van Tilborg, H. C. A. (1999). *Fundamentals of Cryptology: A Professional Reference and Interactive Tutorial* (1st ed.). Norwell, MA, USA: Kluwer Academic Publishers.

Wang, C., & Liu, J. (2008). A Practical Key Issuing Scheme in Identity-Based Cryptosystem. In *Proceedings of the 2008 ISECS International Colloquium on Computing, Communication, Control, and Management - Volume 01* (pp. 454-457). CCCM. IEEE Computer Society, Washington, DC.

Zhang, X., & Li, C. (2009). The security in cognitive radio networks: a survey. In *Proceedings of the 2009 international Conference on Wireless Communications and Mobile Computing: Connecting the World Wirelessly* (pp. 309-313). IWCMC '09. ACM, New York, NY.

KEY TERMS AND DEFINITIONS

Approach: Ideas intended to deal with a problem.

Attack: Penetrate in another computer or network for the purposes of causing damage or disruption.

CBE: Certificate-Based Encryption, a system in which a certificate authority uses ID-based cryptography to produce a certificate.

Ciphertext: Coded text.

Cryptography: Study of hiding information.

Encryption: Transform information (plaintext) using an algorithm to make it unreadable (cipher).

Entity: Is a component. A being or existence considered as distinct, independent, or self-contained.

Identity-Based Cryptography: A type of public key encryption in which the public key of a user is some unique information about the identity of the user.

Identity-Based Encryption: Is an important primitive of identity-based cryptography.

Keying Material: Initial set of parameters necessary to establish and maintain cryptographic keying relationships.

Master Key: Is the PKG's private master key used to generate user's private key.

Party: User or entity interchanging secure messages in a communication.

PKE: Public Key Encryption, a type of encryption system where there are two keys.

PKG: Public Key Generator, a trusted authority responsible to manage private keys.

Plaintext: unprotected information.

Security: Protection against danger, loss, and criminals.

User: Is an agent, human or software that uses a computer or network service.

Vulnerability: Weakness that allows an attacker to reduce a system's information assurance.

Chapter 7
Audio Visual System for Large Scale People Authentication and Recognition over Internet Protocol (IP)

Sue Inn Ch'ng
Nottingham University Malaysia Campus, Malaysia

Kah Phooi Seng
Sunway University, Malaysia

Li-Minn Ang
Nottingham University Malaysia Campus, Malaysia

Fong Tien Ong
Nottingham University Malaysia Campus, Malaysia

ABSTRACT

Biometrics is a promising and viable solution to enhance information security systems compared to passwords. However, there are still several issues regarding large-scale deployment of biometrics in real-world situations that need to be resolved before biometrics can be incorporated together. One of these issues is the occurrence of high training time while enrolling a large amount of people into the system. Hence, in this chapter, the authors present the training architecture for an audio visual system for large scale people recognition over internet protocol. In the proposed architecture, a selection criteria divider unit is used to decompose the large scale people or population into smaller groups whereby each group is trained subsequently. As the input dimensions of each group is reduced compared to the original data size, the proposed structure greatly reduces the overall training time required. To combine the scores from all groups, a two-level fusion based on weighted sum rule and max rule is also proposed in this chapter. The implementation results of the proposed system show a great reduction in training time compared to a similar system trained by conventional means without any compromise on the performance of the system. In addition to the proposal of a scalable training architecture for large-scale people recognition based on audio visual data, a literature review of available audio visual speaker recognition systems and large-scale population training architectures are also presented in this chapter.

DOI: 10.4018/978-1-61350-507-6.ch007

INTRODUCTION

Information security means protecting information and information systems from unauthorized access, usage, disclosure, disruption, modification or destruction. In the area of networked and distributed information sharing environments where prevention of unauthorized access is crucial, information security has become an important research issue. This is because finding effective ways to protect information systems, networks and sensitive data within the critical information infrastructure itself is a challenging topic. One way to protect information or information system is by ensuring that only authorized people or users are able to access it. In a generic information security system, the user authentication method used is a possession-based cryptographic method whereby the authentic user is required to "possess" the knowledge of the cryptographic key (password) in order to establish the authenticity of the user. However, the possession-based cryptographic method is insecure when too short a password is used whereas expensive to maintain when too complex passwords are used. Furthermore, in a multiuser account scenario, passwords are unable to provide non-repudiation in which case, it is difficult to ascertain the actual user when the password is divulged to a friend (Jain, Ross, & Pankanti, 2006). The limitations associated with the use of passwords can be mitigated by the incorporation of an alternative and more reliable method. A promising alternative is that of biometrics in which the biological traits of a person is used as the authentication factor.

Biometrics are automated methods of identifying a person or verifying the identity of a person based on their physiological or behavioural characteristics. Behavioural characteristics are traits that are learned or acquired whereas physiological characteristics refer to physical traits of a person (Bolle, 2004). As these characteristics are unique and differ between individuals, thus, it can be used as a form of identity access management and access control. Dynamic signature verification, speaker verification, and keystroke dynamics are examples of commonly used behavioural characteristics. Examples of physiological characteristics used include hand or finger images, facial characteristics, and iris recognition. There are two types of functionalities of biometrics namely authentication and identification. Authentication (also called verification) is the act of verifying a claim of identity. In short, if you stand in front of an authentication system and claim to be a certain user, the system will only check if you are who you claim to be. On the other hand, identification (or recognition) is an assertion of who someone is. In this case, the decision of the recognition system will be made so as to identify the identity of the user. Hence, this makes biometrics an important emerging technology to counter security threats in the growing electronically connected world especially in applications for information systems, e-commerce, tele-health and internet applications. Nonetheless, biometric technology that relies only on a single biometric trait may not be able to meet market requirements. Multi-biometric systems (biometric systems that integrate two or more biometric traits for identity verification) have several advantages over single-biometric systems. First, multi-biometric systems can address the problem of non-universality, since multiple traits would ensure sufficient coverage even for a large-scale population (Ross & Poh, Multibiometric Systems: Overview, Case Studies and Open Issues, 2009). Secondly, multi-biometric systems provide anti-spoofing measures by making it difficult for an intruder to simultaneously spoof the multiple traits of a legitimate user (Hong, Jain, & Pankanti, October 1999). However, simple integration of two or more biometric traits is insufficient. The development of cutting-edge technology that can produce new discoveries and intellectual properties for biometrics security is highly desirable.

A rapidly developing area with high potential for biometric technology is in the banking and financial sector where biometric technology can be used to detect and prevent electronic fraud. Over the years, applications such as online banking, e-commerce and web-based applications have followed a global commercial trend to migrate from standalone or small-scale services to remote and large-scale internet services. In large-scale internet, the use of password and Personal Identification Number (PIN) does not provide adequate protection against electronic fraud. An alternative is biometrics or multi-biometric systems which can provide promising solutions to augment existing password security systems especially for large-scale people authentication over the internet. Due to remote and large-scale internet services or applications, cost-effective biometrics or multi-biometrics are highly demanded. For example, it is expensive for banks to provide every customer a fingerprint, palm or iris scanner. However, the increasing availability and the low cost of audio and video sensors such as low cost web camera with built-in microphone and smartphones, makes audio visual (voice and face) multi-modal biometric the most suitable alternative to be considered for remote and large-scale internet applications. Another advantage of audio visual recognition is that it can be done continuously, without the need for significant effort and active co-operation by the users. This makes them ideal for online applications or applications where continuous monitoring may be required. Besides that, the least intrusive and most socially acceptable biometrics is voice and face as after all this is the basis of recognition by fellow humans.

In this chapter, we present the design and development of an audio visual system for large scale people recognition over internet protocol (IP). The proposed audio visual system over internet protocol uses multi-biometrics technology particularly, face and voice modality and communication over internet protocol to enable large-scale authentication for remote and large-scale internet applications. The organization of the chapter is structured as follows. Section 2 provides a detailed literature review on previ-

ously developed audio visual authentication and recognition systems. Section 3 discusses the audio and visual processing techniques employed in the front-end processing of the audio visual recognition system with focus on the feature extraction method that will be used in the presented audio visual system. Section 4 presents a brief review on available training architectures designed for large-scale audio visual recognition. This is followed by the proposed training architecture for large-scale people recognition, the split-train structure, and the proposed fusion algorithm to combine the results from the classifiers. Section 5 presents the integration of the proposed audio visual system and method of communication over internet protocol to enable long distance access. In Section 6, simulation results showcasing the effectiveness of the proposed training architecture is presented. Section 7 summarizes the contributions of this chapter.

BACKGROUND

The earliest development of audio visual systems uses static facial images in combination with audio data to overcome the limitations of uni-biometric system. An example of such systems is the audio visual system developed by (Chibelushi, Deravi, & Mason, Voice and facial image integration for speaker recognition, 1993) and (Brunelli & Falavigna, 1995). The work by (Chibelushi, Deravi, & Mason, Voice and facial image integration for speaker recognition, 1993) uses acoustic and static visual information taken from face images at different head orientations, image scales and varying subject positions. To combine the audio and visual information a simple weighted summation fusion is utilized. The proposed system was implemented on an audio visual database that consists of audio recordings and face images from only ten speakers. Implementation results show that the use of both voice and facial information can not only strengthen the security of the system but also improve the identification accuracy of the overall system compared to voice-only or visual-only recognition. The work by (Brunelli & Falavigna, 1995) uses a text-independent speaker identification system that combines audio-only speaker identification and visual information. The system uses five classifiers; two classifiers corresponding to the acoustic features and three classifiers corresponding to the visual features. The acoustic features (static and dynamic) were derived from the short-time spectral analysis of the speech signal whereas the visual features were extracted from three regions of the face, i.e. eyes, nose and mouth. The individually obtained classification scores are then combined using a simple weighted product approach. However, as only static facial images are used during the extraction of the facial features, such systems are more susceptible to spoofing attacks compared to systems which use dynamic audio and visual features. This because it will be much more difficult for an imposter to impersonate both audio and dynamical visual information simultaneously compared to individual data. Moreover, the audio speaker recognition system uses text-independent technology. Investigative studies by (Lüttin, 1999) on text-independent and text-dependent speaker systems yields a better performance record for text-dependent systems compared to text-independent systems. Note that the difference between both text-dependent and text-independent speaker recognition systems lies in the speech content constraint used to identify the speaker. In brief, text-dependent systems require the same phrase or utterance used during enrolment to recognize the speaker whereas text-independent systems are not limited by the type of phrase or utterance used during enrolment. Apart from the experimental results obtained in (Lüttin, 1999) to support this fact, this fact is also noticeable in daily life when people can sometimes rapidly recognize a speaker solely by hearing a familiar word e.g. "hello" (Aronowitz, Burshtein, & Amir, 2004).

The work by (Jourlin, Luettin, Genoud, & Wassner, 1997) uses a text-dependent audio visual speaker verification system that utilizes both acoustic and visual dynamic information. The developed system was tested on the M2VTS database (Pigeon & Vandendorpe, 1997). 14 lip shape parameters, ten intensity parameters and its scale were used as the visual features whereas Hidden Markov Models (HMMs) (Gales & Young, 2008) were used to perform audio-only, visual-only, and audio visual experiments. The audio visual score was computed as a simple weighted sum of the audio and visual scores. The simulation results obtained demonstrated a reduction of false acceptance ratio (FAR) (Ross & Jain, Information fusion in biometrics, 2003) from 2.3% when the audio-only system was used compared to 0.5% when the multimodal system was used. (Dieckmann, Plankensteiner, & Wagner, 1997) developed a system which uses a combination of dynamic and static data for three different modalities; face (static), voice and lip motion (dynamic) to identify a person. The three modalities are analyzed independently and classified using three different classifiers. A fusion scheme which utilizes majority voting and opinion fusion were then used to combine the outputs of the three classifiers. In the scheme, two out of the three experts had to agree on the opinion and the combined opinion had to exceed the predefined threshold. The identification error decreased to 7% when all three modalities were used compared to 10.4%, 11% and 18.7%, when voice, lip movements and face visual features were used individually. However, the simulations only considered different brightness. It is observed that non-ideal conditions and other factors such as pose and expression variations were not considered. (Ben-Yacoub, Abdeljaoued, & Mayoraz, 1999) later developed both text-dependent and text-independent audio visual speaker verification systems by utilizing the acoustic and frontal face visual information from the XM2VTS database (Messer, Matas, Kittler, Luettin, & Maitre, 1999). The developed system uses a combination of experts to increase the performance and robustness of the systems. Since multiple experts were employed in the system, the authors also investigated the use of different binary classification schemes for post-classifier opinion fusion namely, Support Vector Machines (SVM) (Bishop, 1995), Bayesian classifier (Jensen & Nielsen, 2007), Fisher's linear discriminant (Belhumeur, Hespanha, & Kriegman., 1997), decision trees and multilayer perceptron (Bishop, 1995) to obtain the final decision of different experts. Nonetheless, as the authors primary focus in the above systems lie in the back-end processing of the audio visual system (fusion scheme), non-ideal or non-controlled conditions of the audio and visual data were not considered in the simulations of the developed systems.

The work by (Fox & Reilly, 2003) presents a text-dependent speaker identification system that uses dynamical features for both audio and visual modes. The developed system was implemented on the XM2VTS database using left to right HMMs as the classifier. The non-ideal conditions of the audio data were simulated during the experiments by adding additive white Gaussian noise to the clean audio at different signal-to-noise ratio (SNR). Based on the simulation results obtained, the authors reported that the use of dynamic visual mode does not only improve the performance of the system in the presence of noise (low SNR values) but also improves the performance of the system when tested with clean audio. Hence, proving that the use of dynamic features for both audio and visual information is more advantageous compared to the sole use of dynamic audio information. The later work by the same authors in (Fox, O'Mullane, & Reilly, 2005) presents an adaptive approach to fuse the resultant scores for the audio and visual modalities by taking into consideration the reliability of the audio visual data present. (Nefian, Liang, Fu, & Liu, 2003) developed an audio visual speaker identification system based on the temporal sequence of audio and visual observations (face and lips) of the sub-

jects. A hierarchical decision fusion approach is employed to obtain the final output. In the lower level fusion, acoustic and visual features of speech are integrated using a coupled hidden Markov model (CHMM) (Brand, Oliver, & Pentland, 1997) and embedded hidden Markov model (EHMM) (Nefian & Hayes, 1999). This is followed by a late integration scheme which combines the likelihood of the face and audio visual speech to obtain the final identity of the speaker in the upper level fusion. The audio visual speaker recognition system developed by (Kar, Bhatia, & Dutta, 2007) uses both speech and lip motion to recognize a person's identity. 18 Mel frequency cepstrum coefficients (MFCCs) and 20 principal component analysis (PCA) (Turk & Pentland, 1991) coefficients were used as the audio and visual features respectively. The developed system was simulated with white Gaussian noise to observe the performance of the system in the face of non-ideal conditions. In addition to the simulation of non-ideal conditions for audio data, the superiority of Gaussian mixture model and Hidden Markov Models for the task of speaker recognition and lips tracking were also investigated.

The more recent work by (Dean & Sridharan, 2010) utilizes the state-of-the-art cascading appearance-based feature extraction system (CAB) proposed in (Potamianos, Verma, Neti, Iyengar, & Basu, 2000) to extract static and dynamic features from the visual frames. These visual features are then used in conjunction with traditional perceptual linear predictive (PLP) acoustic features to identify the identity of the speaker. Factorial HMM-adapted SHMM (FHMM-adapted SHMM) is used as the classifier. The authors also provided a comparison study on the performance of feature level fusion using FHMM-adapted SHMMs and the usage of two independent unimodal classifiers with the latter method using normalization and weighted output score fusion to as the fusion technique. Results of the experimental studies show that the output fusion approach gives a better performance compared to the feature-fusion

Figure 1. Overview of front-end processing for audio and visual information

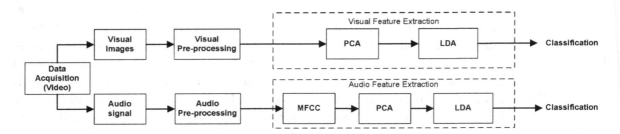

system. Furthermore, the output fusion approach has a significantly much simpler implementation compared to the feature-fusion system. The poor performance of the feature-fusion system is consistent with research studies done by (Chibelushi, Deravi, & Mason, A review of speech-based bimodal recognition, 2002) which relates the poor performance due to the extra complexity and synchronicity issues involved in training feature-fusion models.

FRONT-END PROCESSING FOR AUDIO VISUAL RECOGNITION

Figure 1 illustrates the overview of the front-end processing for audio and visual information in a typical audio visual recognition system. The front-end processing consists of three main components namely data acquisition, pre-processing and feature extraction. To obtain audio visual data, web-cameras with built-in microphones can be used as the data acquisition device. Then, the visual images and audio signal are split from the video and applied to its respective pre-processing unit to condition the raw data e.g. segmentation of region of interest. Depending on the type of biometric measure that is being used, different algorithms can be employed during the feature extraction to extract the most discriminant features from the pre-processed audio and visual data.

Front-End Visual Processing

During the visual pre-processing, face segmentation and resizing of images are done to obtain the region of interest (face) and reduce the dimensionality of data to be processed. The processed images are then applied to the visual feature extractor to extract the most discriminating features from the original data. In this chapter, principal component analysis (PCA) (Turk & Pentland, 1991) and Linear Discriminant Analysis are used as the visual feature extractors. Principal component analysis is first applied onto the original data to reduce the dimensionality of data and generate a set of compact and optimal description of the data set. However, as PCA does not provide any indication of discrimination between data in different classes, linear discriminant analysis (LDA) (Belhumeur, Hespanha, & Kriegman., 1997), otherwise known as Fisher Linear Discrimination (FLD), is subsequently applied so that different classes of training data can be separated as far as possible and the same classes of patterns are as compact as possible. The mathematical approach to implement PCA and LDA is explained as follows.

Principal Component Analysis (PCA)

Let a face image Z_i be a two-dimensional $M \times M$ array, the training set of n face images by $Z_i = (Z_1, Z_2 ..., Z_N) \in R(M^2 \times N)$ and assuming that each image belongs to one of C classes.

First, the image is normalized by subtracting the mean of the image from each of the data dimensions. This produces a normalized data set, $\overline{Z_l}$, defined in (1), whose mean is zero. The resultant normalized data set is multiplied by its transpose to obtain its covariance (2).

$$\overline{Z_i} = Z_i - \frac{1}{N}\sum_{i=1}^{N} Z_i \qquad (1)$$

$$\Omega = \overline{Z_l}\overline{Z_l^T} \qquad (2)$$

From the covariance matrix obtained, the eigenvalues and eigenvectors are calculated and the eigenvectors are sorted in a descending manner according to the eigenvalues; e.g. eigenvector corresponding to the largest eigenvalue to eigenvector corresponding to the smallest eigenvalue. This sorted eigenvalues are also termed as eigenfaces, V, (Turk & Pentland, 1991). Finally, by projecting Z_i the original face images onto the transposed of the obtained eigenfaces, the corresponding eigenface-based features, U_n, can be obtained, refer to (3).

$$U_n = V^\tau Z_i \qquad (3)$$

Linear Discriminant Analysis (LDA)

As the eigenface-based features does not provide any information for class discrimination and only reduces the dimension of the original data, Z_i, LDA is performed onto the obtained eigenface-based features so that different classes of training data for each group is separated as far as possible and patterns for the same class are as compact as possible. This is done by projecting the data onto a lower-dimensional vector space such that the between-class distance to the within-class distance is maximized (Belhumeur, Hespanha, & Kriegman., 1997). The within-class scatter matrix

and between-class scatter matrix can be calculated according to (4) and (5) respectively.

$$S_W = \sum_{i=1}^{C}\left(U_{n,i} - \overline{U_{n,i}}\right)\left(U_{n,i} - \overline{U_{n,i}}\right)^T \qquad (4)$$

$$S_B = \sum_{i=1}^{C} n^i \left(\overline{U_{n,i}} - \overline{U_n}\right)\left(\overline{U_{n,i}} - \overline{U_n}\right)^T \qquad (5)$$

where $\overline{U_{n,i}}$ is the mean image of the i-th class in the n-th group, $\overline{U_n}$ is the mean image of the n-th group and c is the number of classes in n-th group. Then, the optimal projection in which the between-class distance to the within-class distance is optimized is obtained by (Belhumeur, Hespanha, & Kriegman., 1997) (6):

$$W_{opt} = \arg\max \frac{\left|W^T S_B W\right|}{\left|W^T S_w W\right|} = [w_1 \quad w_2...w_{c-1}] \qquad (6)$$

where $W^T S_B W$ and $W^T S_W W$ is the scatter of the transformed feature vectors of S_B and S_W respectively and $[w_1 w_2 \dots w_{C-1}]$ is the set of generalized eigenvectors for S_B and S_W corresponding to the $(C\text{-}1)$ largest generalized eigenvalues e.g.,

$$S_W W_i = \lambda_i S_b W_i \ i=1,2,\dots, C\text{--}1 \qquad (7)$$

Finally, the most discriminating features of the n-th group, P_n, are obtained by projecting the eigenfaces onto the optimal projection, W_{opt}.

$$P_n = W_{OPT}^{\ \ T} U_n \qquad (8)$$

Front-End Audio Processing

Prior to applying Mel-frequency cepstrum coefficient (MFCC) (Campbell, 1997) to extract the audio features, a simple voice activity detector is first applied to determine the voiced and unvoiced sections from the audio file. The voice activity detector employed in this chapter is based on short-time analyses namely; short-time energy and short-time zero-crossing rate. Once the voiced segment of the speech signal is determined, MFCC is applied on the voice signals to extract the audio features. PCA and LDA is subsequently applied onto the extracted MFCC features to reduce the dimensionality of the data and as the feature selection technique respectively. The projected LDA features obtained are then applied to the radial basis function neural network for classification. The mathematical implementation of the voice activity detection algorithm used and the MFCC feature extraction technique is as follows. The implementation of PCA and LDA is similar to that as discussed in section 3.1.

Voice Activity Detection

Speech is a one-dimensional non-stationary signal that varies in the time-domain. In short segments, a speech signal will appear to be nearly stationary. Hence, by dividing the time series of an input speech into several frames and applying mathematical operations to the signal, the attributes of the signal e.g. voice activity, audio content, can be determined. In this chapter, a simple voice activity detector using short-time energy and short-time zero-crossing rate is used in the system.

Short-time energy is an indication of the amplitude of the signal at an interval. The concept of using short-term energy to determine the voiced sections from the unvoiced sections is based on the motivation that when voice signals exist in the speech signal, there will be a burst of energy somewhere along the time axis of the speech signal. Thus, by determining the short-time energy of the signal, the voiced segment of the signal can easily be differentiated from the unvoiced segment of the entire signal as voiced signals will possess higher energy compared to the unvoiced signal. Short-time energy, E_i, can be computed according to (9)

where $f_w(n)$ represents the windowed frame, $w_R(n)$ the window function defined in (10) and $f_i(iL + n)$ refers to the i–th frame with L length (Enqing, Guizhong, Yatong, & Yu, 2002); ($0 \leq n \leq L-1$),

$$E_i = \sum_{n=0}^{L-1} f_w^2 = \sum_{n=0}^{L-1} \left(f_i \left(iL + n \right) \bullet w_R(n) \right)^2 \qquad (9)$$

$$W_R(n) = \begin{cases} 1 & 0 \leq n \leq L-1 \\ 0 & otherwise \end{cases} \qquad (10)$$

The function of zero-crossing rate (ZCR) is similar to that of short-time energy but instead of calculating the amplitude of the speech signals within the frame, it calculates the weighted average of the number of times the speech signal changes sign within a particular time window. Zero-crossing rate is combined with short-time energy in this case to aid in determining the starting and ending points at which the voice signals begins and end. The short-time zero-crossing rate can be mathematically represented as follows:

$$ZCR_n = \sum_{m=-\infty}^{\infty} 0.5 \, | \, \text{sgn}\{x[m]\} - \text{sgn}\{x[m-1]\} \, | \, w[n-m]$$

$$(11)$$

where

$$\text{sgn}\{x\} = \begin{cases} 1 & if \quad x(n) \geq 0 \\ -1 & if \quad x(n) < 0 \end{cases},$$

$$w\{n\} = \begin{cases} \dfrac{1}{2N} & if \quad 0 \leq n \leq N-1 \\ -1 & if \quad otherwise \end{cases}$$

and N refers to the total number of samples and n refers to the current sample.

Mel Frequency Cepstral Coefficients (MFCC)

Before speaker recognition can be performed, it is necessary to extract distinctive features from the audio signal that can discriminate between different speakers. Most of the features used for speaker recognition are usually obtained from the speech spectrum. This is because anatomical variations (e.g. shape and dimension of vocal tract system) that naturally occur among different people and the difference in speaking habits will be portrayed as differences in acoustic properties of the speech signals produced (Campbell, 1997). Hence, by analyzing the acoustic properties in the speech spectrum, it is possible to extract speaker-dependent features from the speech spectrum to aid in the task of speaker identification. The feature vectors that represent the speaker-dependent information can be extracted from the speech spectrum by deriving the spectral information contained within the short time-windowed segment of the speech. A common approach widely used is the extraction of features using filter-banks, since evaluation results by (Reynolds D.A., 1994) found these features to be more robust to noise. In this chapter, the cepstral coefficients derived from a mel-scale frequency filter-bank, also known as mel-frequency cepstral coefficients (MFCC), will be used to represent the speech spectrum.

To calculate MFCC, first the speech signal is divided into time frames consisting of an arbitrary number of samples. Then, each time frame is windowed with a Hamming window to prevent spectral leakages. The filter coefficients of a Hamming window can be computed using (12),

$$w(n) = \begin{cases} 0.54 - 0.46 \cos\left(\dfrac{2\pi n}{N-1}\right) & 0 \le n \le N-1 \\ 0 & otherwise \end{cases}$$

$$(12)$$

where $w(n)$ is the filter coefficients, N is the total number of samples and n refers to the current sample. Subsequently, Fast Fourier Transform (FFT) (Lathi, 2009) is applied to each windowed frame to convert the speech signal from the time-domain to the frequency-domain. Then, the magnitude of the signal, $|X(n)|$, which is now in

the frequency domain, is applied to a collection of triangular filters, also known as filter banks, H_i, to compute the log energy output of each filter, X_i. The filter bank parameters used in our implementation is based on the Slaney's Auditory Toolbox in (Slaney, 1998) which consists of a total of 40 equal area filters whereby the first 13 filters are linearly spaced in the range of 200-1000 Hz at a step of 66.67Hz whereas the next 27 filters are logarithmically spaced in the range of 1071-6400 Hz with a step of approximately 1.071. The step spacing, sp, of the logarithmic filters can be computed by (13):

$$sp = \exp(\ln(f_c / 1000) / k) \qquad (13)$$

where f_c is the centre frequency of the last of the logarithmically spaced filters and k is the number of logarithmically spaced filters. Each of the equal area filters can be defined as (Ganchev, Fakotakis, & Kokkinakis, 2005):

$$H_i(n) = \begin{cases} 0 \\ \dfrac{2(n - f_{bi-1})}{(f_{bi} - f_{bi-1})(f_{bi+1} - f_{bi-1})} & n < f_{bi-1} \\ & f_{bi-1} \le n \le f_{bi} \\ \dfrac{2(f_{bi+1} - k)}{(f_{bi+1} - f_{bi})(f_{bi+1} - f_{bi-1})} & f_{bi} \le n \le f_{bi+1} \\ 0 & n > f_{bi+1} \end{cases}$$

$$(14)$$

where $i = 1,2,...M$ refers to the i-th filter for a total of M filters, n to the n-th coefficient of the N-point DFT and f_{bi} to the $M+2$ boundary points that specify the M filters.

$$X_i = \log_{10}\left(\sum_{k=1}^{N-1} |X(n)| \bullet H_i(n)\right) \qquad (15)$$

Finally, the MFCCs are obtained by computing the Discrete Cosine Transform (DCT) (Lathi, 2009) of the filter bank coefficients.

$$C_j = \sum_{i=1}^{M} X_i \bullet \cos\left[j\left(i - \frac{1}{2}\right)\frac{\pi}{M}\right] \qquad (16)$$

where j is the number of cepstral coefficients and M is the number of filters in the filter bank. Although different MFCC implementations use different filter-bank parameters in their implementation, investigative studies (Ganchev, Fakotakis, & Kokkinakis, 2005) have shown that the speaker verification or recognition performance does not differ much between different implementations. This is due to the fact that the first 15 coefficients, which are mostly used in most applications, are closely correlated to each other for different MFCC implementations (Sigurdsson, Petersen, & Lehn-Schiøler, 2006).

TRAINING ARCHITECTURE FOR LARGE-SCALE PEOPLE RECOGNITION

In this sub-section, we will first provide a literature review on the available large-scale people training architectures for people recognition. This is followed by the proposed training architecture, split-train structure, which is adapted to train both the facial and audio data for a large amount of people.

Review on Large-Scale People Training Architectures

The most common problem faced by large-scale population architectures is the high-dimensionality of data that needs to be processed at a given time. This will inevitably result in an increase in computational costs especially during the classification process as the amount of data that a subject needs to be compared to will be significantly increased compared to a small-medium size population system. In addition to the increase in computational costs, the performance of clas-sification algorithms may deteriorate rapidly or fail to function completely when applied to large databases (Guo, Zhang, & Li, 2001). This is because as the data sets get larger, the sample distribution of different classes becomes more complicated and tends to overlap between classes. Hence, classification learning algorithms which are geared towards small-sample, low dimensional and limited-class problems becomes ineffective for solving large-scale classification problems. Apart from the problem of scalability, the problem of additions in the future to the present large-scale population architectures is another dire issue. For small-moderate population architecture, the retraining of the entire architecture, although not commendable, with the latest addition is still possible considering the amount of data that needs to be considered. However, with large-scale population architectures, alternatives need to be found since the retraining of the entire system with the latest addition is not a feasible step. This is because, in addition to performing extra work on the same set e.g. training previously available set again, there will also be an evident increase in training time for a large-scale population system compared to a small-moderate system. For example, the training of an architecture which consists of ten people may take only a mere second but the training time of the same architecture will increase by several folds if a million people are applied to the system. This is not recommended especially for online large-scale systems which require fast processing time regardless of how many additions there are to the present system.

Considering the main concern in large-scale population systems is the handling of the high-dimensionality of data, this problem can be solved by modifying the training structure of present systems to account for this aspect. A common approach is the divide and conquer strategy. Based on the principle of divide and conquer, by decomposing the large set of data into small subsets, the high-dimensionality of data can be reduced to manageable chunks. Subsequently, the distribution of data will become simple enough so that conventional methods can be successfully applied. The decomposition of the large population into smaller subsets can be done using clustering methods or by feature ranking. Feature ranking-based methods will choose a set of the most discriminatory features of the face and the population is sorted based on these features as done in works proposed in (Guo, Zhang, & Li, 2001), (Zhou, Chindaro, & Deravi, 2009) and (Tse & Lam, 2008). The work in (Zhou, Chindaro, & Deravi, 2009) uses a data sampling strategy. In addition to significantly reducing the size of training data, the proposed data sampling strategy is also aimed at tackling the problem of imbalance within the large amount of training data when image pairs are sampled during feature extraction. For classification, the authors proposed a modified Kernel Fisher Discriminant (MKFD). The problem with classic KFD (Mika, Ratsch, Weston, Scholkopf, & Mullers, 1999) is that as the size of the total number of samples for training increases, the gram matrix that is used to solve the optimization problem in the kernel will increase proportionally. Since keeping such a large matrix does not only require a large amount of memory but makes the optimization problem computationally very expensive and infeasible for practical implementations, the authors proposed the MKFD to tackle classification of large datasets. The proposed method uses a subset of the training samples (obtained by sampling strategy) to construct the linear combination of the ratio of the intra-class variations of the mapped feature points over the extra-class variations. Thus, requiring only one variable to be optimized during classification and subsequently reducing the amount of computation required.

The work by (Liu, Su, Chiang, & Hung, 2004) decomposes the large number of training images into a number of clusters based on the owner-specific cluster dependent LDA subspace (OSCD-LDA). To obtain the OSCD-LDA sub-space, Liu et.al first performs global PCA to reduce the dimen-

sion of the original data. Then, k-means clustering is applied on the global-PCA subspace obtained to group the most similar cluster that is closest to the owner together. Subsequently, LDA is performed on each cluster to finally obtain the OSCD-LDA. On the other (Lu & Plataniotis, 2002) partitions the large data set into small subsets using a separability criterion then a hierarchical classification framework based on nearest neighbour classifier is used to classify the faces in the system. Contrary to the conventional similarity criterion where similar data are clustered together, the concept of separability criterion is to partition the data based on the maximized difference or separability between classes. The separability criterion is chosen by Lu instead of similarity criterion as it is reasoned that the similarity criterion may be optimal for approximating the real face distribution for object reconstruction but may not be efficient for classification tasks. To ensure that the classes are maximally separated in the proposed clustering algorithm, the total between-class scatter is used. Although the proposed classification framework was demonstrated to be able to effectively classify the maximally separated groups, the hierarchical classification framework may not be effective if an ever-growing amount of people is applied to the system. This is due to the application of nearest neighbour classifier as the classifier. The disadvantage of nearest neighbour classifier is that it requires a large amount of storage space and takes a relatively longer classification time compared to other classifiers. Moreover with two levels of nearest neighbour classifiers, an even longer classification time would be required and this time would be amplified when the amount of people to be classified increases.

Compared to the aforementioned clustering methods, the works in (Lu, Yuan, & Yahagi, 2006) uses fuzzy c-means clustering to partition the original group into small clusters. In fuzzy c-means clustering, the membership of a given data point may belong to several groups instead of just one. As a set of features may belong to several groups, the classification framework uses an exclusion algorithm to remove unlikely face patterns in the clusters during classification. To reduce the computational complexity of the framework, sub-networks which contain the same elements are then merged into a single sub-network. The advantage of this framework is that a parallel neural network is used and the shortcomings of the nearest neighbour classifier are overcome. However, if new people are added into the system, the entire framework from the distribution of the clusters to the training of the neural network has to be redone to take into account the addition as it is impossible to know which clusters the newest addition will fit into without reapplying the entire framework.

The aforesaid literature review on large-scale recognition systems focus solely on the face. On the topic of large-scale speaker recognition, there had been previous investigative studies (Reynolds D., 1995) on the effect of the performance of speaker recognition systems to that of large populations and the proposal of framework models for large population speaker recognition purposes (Chaudhari, Navrratil, Ramaswamy, & Maes, 2001). However, to our knowledge, there has been little research focus on large-scale people recognition systems based on both audio visual data (not including audio visual speech recognition systems). Hence, in the following sub-section, we present the concept of applying the previously proposed split-train structure (Ch'ng, Seng, & Ang, 2010) to both audio and visual data sets to reduce the overall amount of training time required to train a large-scale population audio visual people recognition system. To combine the scores of the modular RBF neural network classifiers and the different modalities, we propose an identification algorithm that uses max fuse strategy and sum rule to combine the output scores from the modular neural networks and the two different modalities.

Proposed Split-Train Structure

Figure 2(a) shows the architecture of the split-train structure adapted to include the training of the audio data in addition to the visual data. The proposed split-train structure basically consists of a selection criteria divider and multiple processing units. Prior to training, the large set of audio visual training data is decomposed into smaller subsets by the selection criteria divider. The visual data, $Y = Y_1..Y_N$, refers to the feature vectors that represent the training images whereas audio data, $X = X_1.. X_N$, refers to the extracted MFCC features. The purpose of dividing the original data into smaller groups is to reduce the amount of data that is processed by each processing unit at a given time. The criteria for division can be of any arbitrary criteria and not necessary the similarity of facial features between subjects as normally done by clustering methods. For example, the data may be divided based on the individuals' placing in the database, state of residency, ethnicity or gender. The advantages of using a selection criteria that is statistically independent of actual facial features composition is that the large population of people can be quickly sorted into groups based on the pre-existing knowledge of the individuals' at hand and without any additional complex computations when new data are added. Thus, a new group can be formed or the latest addition can be arbitrarily absorbed into any of the present groups. Subsequently, only that particular processing unit which contains the new data needs to be retrained to take into account the newest addition.

The number of processing units used in the system is dependent on the number of groups, N, the large population is divided into. For example, if the initial population consists of 100 people, the said population may be divided into two groups of 50 people each and only two processing units will be required to train the system. Each processing unit in the visual and audio training contains the basic components found in a typical audio visual recognition system, feature extractor and

Figure 2. Split-train structure for (a) training phase and (b) testing phase for audio visual data

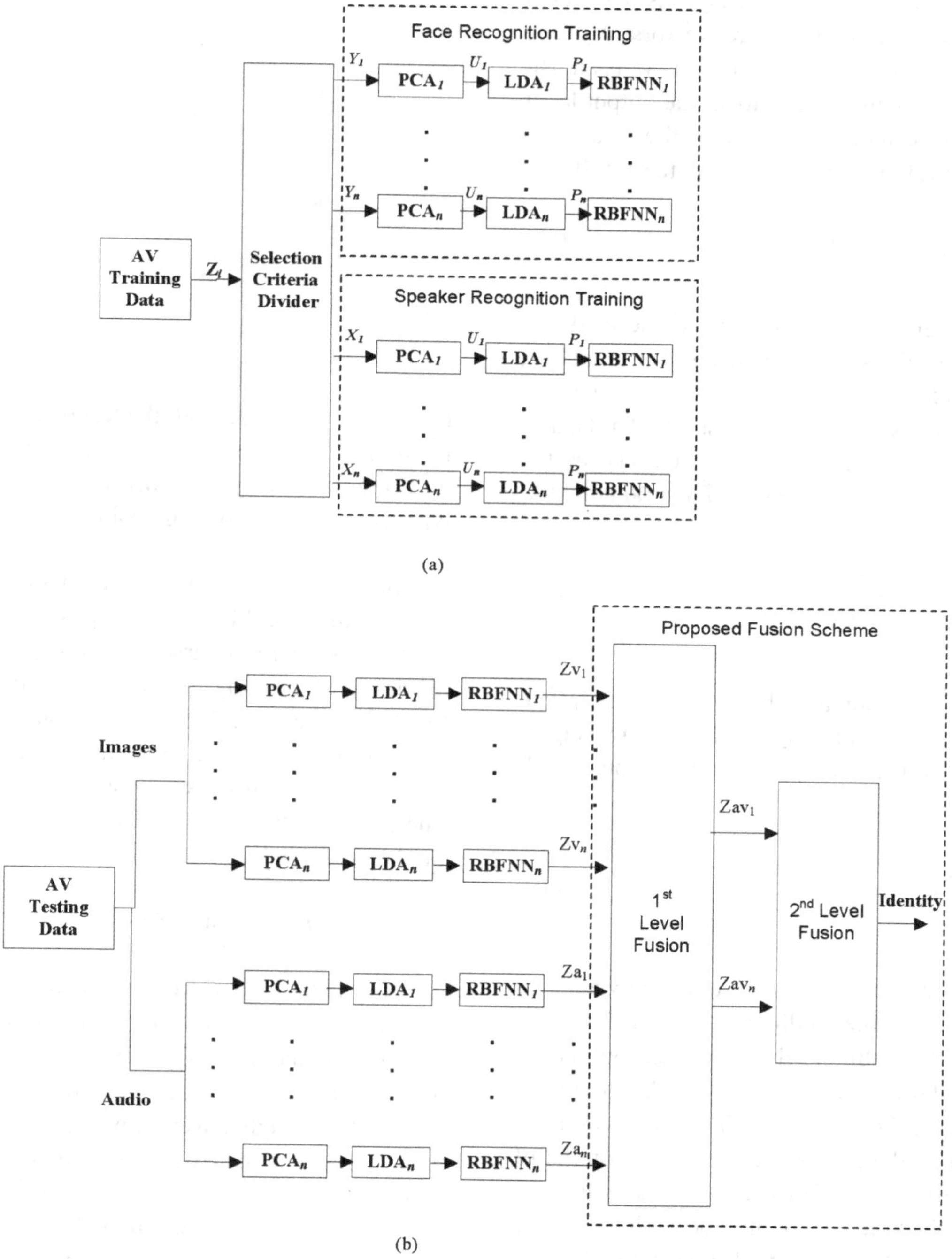

(a)

(b)

classifier. In this case, PCA and LDA are utilized as the feature extractor/reduction and feature selector method for both the visual and audio modalities. A three-layer radial basis function (RBF) neural network (Chen, Cowan, & Grant, 1991) is used as the classifier. The structure of the RBF neural network is shown in Figure 3. The number of units in the input layer is dependent on the dimension of feature vectors, P_n. The number of units in the hidden layer, M, is adjustable and the number of units in the output layer is equal to the number of classes in the group. The output of the hidden layer is calculated as follows:

$$h = \theta w_n \left(\| P - P_C \| \right) \tag{17}$$

where Q refers to the inputs to the network, Q_c are the centers associated with the basic functions, θ is the radial basis function, w_n is layer weights and $\|.\|$ denotes the Euclidean distance. The Gaussian function, defined below, is adopted as the radial basis function in our RBF neural network:

$$\theta = \exp \left(-\frac{\| P - P_C \|^2}{2\delta^2} \right) \tag{18}$$

where δ is the spread. The output of the system is determined by linearly combining the weights of the receptive field to that of the output as follows:

$$x_n = \sum_{n=1}^{M} \theta \times w_n \tag{19}$$

Since the split-train structure is now adapted to train both the audio and visual data, the method of combining the individual outputs of the modular RBF neural network classifiers and the fusion scheme to combine the scores from different modalities to obtain the final output of the system is vital. For the case of an audio visual verification system, it is possible to reduce computational complexity during testing by first determining which group the claimed identity is trained under and applying the test data of the probe directly onto that particular group only. However, for audio visual recognition systems,

Figure 3. Structure of RBF neural network used in the proposed system

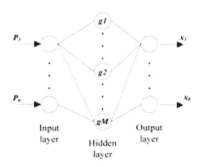

to thoroughly compare all the test data to that of the trained data, the test data is applied to all the units simultaneously as shown in Figure 2(b). This will lead to the following problems: (1) Which group will yield the correct identity? (2) How to fuse the scores from the two different modalities? To solve these problems, we propose a two level fusion scheme. In the first level, a weighted sum rule is used to combine the audio and visual scores for all the groups. Let's denote the resultant audio scores from n groups as $Za = Za_1, Za_2 \ldots Za_n$ and the resultant visual scores as $Zv = Zv_1, Zv_2 \ldots Zv_n$. The output of the first level decision fusion, Zav, can be computed as:

$$Zav_n = w \cdot Za_n + (1 - w) \cdot Zv_n \tag{20}$$

where w is the fusion weights. A weighted sum rule is used instead of a simple sum rule to take into account the reliability of the modalities. For instance, if the audio data has a high signal-to-noise ratio, a higher weight will be assigned to the visual scores, to take into account the low reliability of the audio data. However, if the quality of both modalities is approximately the same, the weighted sum rule can easily be modified to an equal-weight fusion, by assigning $w = 0.5$.

In the second level fusion, a max fuse strategy is used to determine the output from which group that will yield the final identity. For example, to determine the identity of test data x, after obtaining the summed audio visual scores from (20), the identity of test data x when compared to all the training samples in each group is first obtained by determining the identity to which the maximum score belongs to for that particular group. This is repeated for all groups.

The resultant output from this step would yield N identities as each group would output an identity. To reduce N identities down to one identity, the score associated to each of these N identities is compared against one another and the identity which has the highest value is finally output as the identity of the test data. The identification algorithm used in the second level fusion is summarized as follows:

1. Obtain combinative audio visual scores, Zav_N, for all groups.
2. **For each** test data, j
   2.1. Determine maximum score, $Zmax_N(j) = \max| (Zav_N(:,j)) |$.
   2.2. Find index of maximum score, $Id(j)$
   2.3. **For each** group, N
      2.3.1. Compare $Zmax_N(j)$ and find highest value, $Y = \arg\max |(Zmax_N(j))|$
      2.3.2. Final Identity = index of Y

INTEGRATION OF PROPOSED AUDIO VISUAL SYSTEM AND COMMUNICATION OVER INTERNET PROTOCOL

Figure 4 shows the integrated architecture of the proposed audio visual system and method of communication over internet protocol. The integrated system generally consists of a server and client. The video and audio samples of the subject is first obtained at the client and subsequently transmitted over internet protocol to the server where the recognition process is done. The communication over internet protocol consists of three aspects:

(1) Encoding/decoding, (2) packetization, and (3) transport protocols. Encoding is vital before streaming to ensure transmission efficiency. This is because raw video consumes a large amount of bandwidth. In our integrated system, MPEG2 and MPGA encoder (Watkinson, 1999) are used to encode the video and audio signals respectively. The encoded data is then converted into packets of data during packetization. There are two types of packetization done. The first is done within the encoder itself to format the data to allow transmission over a standard IP circuit. Once this is done, the packets are sent to the stream wrapper where the second packetization is done. The purpose of the second packetization is to wrap control data around the data packets so that the streaming server can control the real-time streaming of the media data (D., 2004). The type of stream wrapper that is used during the second packetization depends on the type of transport protocol that is used to stream the data over IP.

There are three different streams formed during the first packetization by the MPEG2/MPGA encoder and they are elementary stream (ES), packetized elementary stream (PES) and transport stream (TS). Each of these stream are formed at different points of the packetization stage, refer to Figure 4. The elementary streams refers to the raw output from the MPEG video and MPGA audio encoders and the standardized input for MPEG decoders. These streams contain only one type of content. Thus, to produce an output at least two elementary streams are required. Then, the elementary streams are formed into packetized elementary stream. The packetized elementary streams are easier-to-handle versions of elementary stream and contain timing information that allows video and audio streams to be synchronized (Wes, 2008). These PESs are then multiplexed and encoded by the system bit stream into system packets by adding packet headers and optional adaptation fields. There are two types of system bit streams; transport stream and program stream. The difference between transport stream and

Figure 4. Integrated architecture of the proposed audio visual system and method of communication over internet protocol

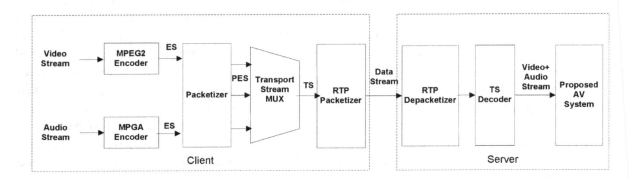

program stream lies in their clock source. The latter uses a common clock source whereas the former does not. Hence, transport stream packets also carry clock information that is needed for real-time signals to synchronize. Since there is no guarantee that the network in which the proposed audio visual system over internet protocol is implemented on is error free, transport stream is a better option compared to program streams as it is specifically designed for transmitting and storing compressed audio, video and other data in lossy or noisy environments.

For the second packetization, real-time transport protocol (RTP) is used. During RTP packetization, RTP headers are added to the transport stream packets which contain information on the content of the packet and the source of the packet. The RTP-header called payload type identifier stores information on the type of payload that is contained within a particular packet whereas the Synchronization SouRCe (SSRC) stores the source of the packet. In addition to the aforementioned information, the RTP packets also contain timing, synchronization information and sequence numbers. In the event that the packets arrive at the server out of sequence, the sequence numbers can be used to place the incoming packets back in sequence. The sequence number can also be used

for packet loss detection (Wu, Hou, Zhu, Zhang, & Peha, 2001). The RTP packets are then sent over internet protocol using user datagram protocol (UDP) as the lower-layer transport protocol. The lower-layer transport protocol is directly in contact with the network and functions to provide basic transport functions such as multiplexing, error control, congestion control or flow control (Wu, Hou, Zhu, Zhang, & Peha, 2001). Packets which are received successfully at the server are depacketized and decoded before it is applied to the proposed audio visual system.

SIMULATION RESULTS AND DISCUSSION

In this section, the proposed audio visual system was implemented on three databases; CUAVE database (Patterson, Gurbuz, Tufekci, & Gowdy, 2002), UNMC-VIER database (Wong, et al., 2010) and XM2VTS database (Messer, Matas, Kittler, Luettin, & Maitre, 1999). The aim of the simulation is to evaluate the performance of the proposed audio visual system to that of a similar audio visual recognition system in which the inputs are applied to the system as it is without the application of decomposition methods to divide the inputs into smaller groups. In addition to the absence of a divider, the difference between the reference system and the proposed system also lies is in the number of feature extractors and neural networks used. Note that the former only uses *a* feature extractor and neural network for each modality whereas the latter uses *multiple* feature extractors and neural networks as each decomposed groups contain its own feature extractor and neural network. The same feature extractors (PCA and LDA for visual, MFCC, PCA and LDA for audio) and RBF neural networks (Chen, Cowan, & Grant, 1991) are used for both the reference system and the proposed system. In the following text, we will refer to this reference system as the conventional system. For a fair comparison, the same training and testing data set were used for the implementation of both systems and simulations were conducted on the same workstation. The workstation has the following specifications; Intel Xeon CPU W3505 2.53GHz and 3.48 GB of RAM.

The CUAVE database contains video and audio data of 36 subjects with each subject speaking a ten-digit utterance, ("zero one two…nine") seven times. Thirty-five subjects were selected and used for the training and testing phase of both systems. For the visual part of the implementation, five frames per subject were used for training and one frame per subject for testing. The frames were randomly selected from the video. For the audio part of the implementation, five training samples per subject were used for training and one sample per subject for testing. To obtain the audio training and testing samples, for each speaker, the digit "zero" was manually segmented from the ten-digit utterance.

The UNMC-VIER database contains video and audio data for 123 subjects with each subject speaking thirteen different utterances, refer to (Wong, et al., 2010) for further details of the database specifications. However, for our implementation, only 115 subjects were used during the training and testing phase. For the audio and visual part of

the implementation on the VIER database, similar to the CUAVE database, the same number of frames and audio samples were used for training and testing respectively. Note that only the first shot from the controlled room was used to obtain the visual training and testing data. Since the test frame was obtained at random from the sequence of frames demultiplexed from the video, some of the test data used during the testing phase may possess facial expression variation as the first shot from the controlled environment also contains facial expression variation. To obtain the audio training and testing samples, the digit "zero" was manually segmented from the first three shots of the database for each subject.

The XM2VTS database contains images and speech of 295 subjects captured over four sessions. In each session, the subject was asked to speak three utterances. In our simulation on the XM2VTS database, only 200 subjects were used; particularly only the data from DVD003a was used. The settings for the training and testing phase of both the visual and audio parts are similar to that used for both CUAVE and VIER database. Note that only the video from session one was used to obtain the visual frames for training and testing but the audio samples "zero" for training and testing were segmented from both session one and session two.

All training and testing images were scaled to 32×32 resolution. To calculate the MFCC coefficients, a window size of 400 samples and window step of 100 samples was used. The fusion weight *w* used for the implementation of both the conventional and the proposed system implementation systems were set to 0.5 as it was assumed that the reliability of both modalities were the same. For the implementation of the proposed audio visual system, the number of groups the split-train structure is decomposed into is five, $N = 5$. The training time and audio visual recognition rate obtained for the conventional system and proposed audio visual system is tabulated in Table 1. Training time here refers to the time taken in seconds to

Table 1. Training time and recognition rate of a conventional system and the proposed training system

Database	Conventional		Proposed System	
	Time (unit)	Recognition rate (%)	Time (unit)	Recognition rate (%)
Cuave	5.38	100.0	3.74	100
VIER	1743.87	96.5	11.76	96.5
XM2VTS	9511.16	98.5	73.71	99.0

train the RBF neural network only. Based on the results obtained in Table 1, it can be observed that as the number of subjects to be trained increases, the training time needed to train the same system has drastically increased. However, by using the proposed training structure, there was a significant reduction in the training time recorded. In addition to the reduction in training time needed, the proposed system also displayed comparatively similar performance compared to that the same system trained using conventional means.

CONCLUSION

The use of audio visual based authentication or recognition systems together with passwords can further enhance the security of present information systems. In this chapter, we have presented the available research works on audio visual systems and previously proposed training architectures to tackle the problem of large-scale population recognition. We have also presented a novel training architecture called split-train structure, for large-scale people recognition based on audio visual data. In addition to the proposal of a novel training architecture, a two-level fusion scheme was also proposed for the testing phase of the proposed audio visual system to combine the scores of different modalities and the scores from the different groups. Weighted sum rule was used to combine the scores of different modalities whereas the max rule was used to determine the final output of the system.

The main advantage of the proposed audio visual system is the much lowered training time needed to achieve equivalent performance to that of a similar audio visual system trained by conventional means. This fact can be observed in our simulation results whereby the training time was significantly reduced when the system was trained using our proposed training structure.

REFERENCES

Aronowitz, H., Burshtein, D., & Amir, A. (2004). Text independent speaker recognition using speaker dependent word spotting. *Proc. ICSLP*, (pp. 1789-1792).

Belhumeur, P., Hespanha, J., & Kriegman, D. (1997). Eigenfaces vs. Fisherfaces: Recognition using class specific linear projection. *IEEE Transactions PAMI*, *19*(7), 711–720. doi:10.1109/34.598228

Ben-Yacoub, S., Abdeljaoued, Y., & Mayoraz, E. (1999). Fusion of face and speech data for person identity verification. *IEEE Transactions on Neural Networks*, *10*, 1065–1074. doi:10.1109/72.788647

Bishop, C. M. (1995). *Neural networks for pattern recognition*. New York: Oxford University Press.

Bolle, R. (2004). *Guide to biometrics*. New York: Springer.

Brand, M., Oliver, N., & Pentland, A. (1997). Coupled hidden Markov models for complex action recognition. *IEEE Computer Society Conference on Computer Vision and Pattern Recognition* (p. 994). Puerto Rico: IEEE.

Brunelli, R., & Falavigna, D. (1995). Person identification using multiple cues. *IEEE Transactions on Pattern Analysis and Machine Intelligence, 10*, 955–965. doi:10.1109/34.464560

Campbell, J. J. (1997). Speaker Recognition: a tutorial. *Proceedings of the IEEE, 85*(9), 1437–1462. doi:10.1109/5.628714

Ch'ng, S. I., Seng, K. P., & Ang, L.-M. (2010). Scalable Face Recognition System using Split-Train Structure. *Proceedings of the International Conference on Embedded Systems and Intelligent Technology (ICESIT2010)*, CD-ROM: Paper 11.

Chaudhari, U., Navrratil, J., Ramaswamy, G., & Maes, S. (2001). Very large population text-independent speaker identification using transformation enhanced multi-grained models. [IEEE.]. *ICASSP, 01*, 461–464.

Chen, S., Cowan, C., & Grant, P. (1991). Orthogonal Least Squares Learning Algorithm for Radial Basis Function Networks. *IEEE Transactions on Neural Networks, 2*(2), 302–309. doi:10.1109/72.80341

Chibelushi, C., Deravi, F., & Mason, J. (2002). A review of speech-based bimodal recognition. *Multimedia. IEEE Transactions on, 4*(1), 23–37.

Chibelushi, C., Deravi, F., & Mason, J. S. (1993). Voice and facial image integration for speaker recognition. *Proc. IEEE Int. Symp. Multimedia Technologies Future Appl.* Southampton, U.K.: IEEE.

D., A. (2004). *The technology of video and audio streaming.* Oxford Focal Press 2nd ed.

Dean, D., & Sridharan, S. (2010, April). Dynamic visual features for audio visual speaker verification. *Computer Speech & Language, 24*(2), 136–149. doi:10.1016/j.csl.2009.03.007

Dieckmann, U., Plankensteiner, P., & Wagner, T. (1997). SESAM: A biometric person identification system using sensor fusion. *Pattern Recognition Letters, 18*, 827–833. doi:10.1016/S0167-8655(97)00063-9

Enqing, D., Guizhong, L., Yatong, Z., & Yu, C. (2002). *Voice Activity Detection Based on Short-time Energy and Noise Spectrum Adaptation. ICSP.* IEEE.

Fox, N., & Reilly, R. (2003). *Audio visual Speaker Identification Based on Use of Dynamic Audio and Visual Features* (pp. 743–751). Springer-Verlag Berlin Heidelberg.

Fox, N. A., O'Mullane, B. A., & Reilly, R. B. (2005). Audio visual Speaker Identification via Adaptive Fusion Using Reliability Estimates of Both Modalities. In *Lecture notes in Computer Science Audio- and Video-Based Biometric Person Authentication* (pp. 787–796). Berlin, Heidelberg: Springer. doi:10.1007/11527923_82

Gales, M., & Young, S. (2008). *The Application of Hidden Markov Models in Speech Recognition.* Now Publishers Inc.

Ganchev, T., Fakotakis, N., & Kokkinakis, G. (2005). Comparative evaluation of various MFCC implementations on the speaker verification task. *Proc. of the SPECOM-2005, Vol. 1*, (pp. 191-194).

Guo, G.-D., Zhang, H.-J., & Li, S. (2001). Pairwise face recognition. *Computer Vision, 2001. ICCV 2001. Proceedings. Eighth IEEE International Conference on, 2(7)* (pp. 282-287). IEEE.

Hong, L., Jain, A., & Pankanti, S. (October 1999). Can Multibiometrics Improve Performance? *Proc. AutoID, Summit,*, (pp. 59–64). NJ.

Jain, A. K., Ross, A., & Pankanti, S. (2006). Biometrics: A Tool of Information Security. *IEEE Transactions on Information Forensics and Security, 1*(2), 125–143. doi:10.1109/TIFS.2006.873653

Jensen, F. V., & Nielsen, T. D. (2007). *Bayesian networks and decision graphics.* New York: Springer.

Jourlin, P., Luettin, J., Genoud, D., & Wassner, H. (1997). Integrating acoustic and labial information for speaker identification and verification. *Proc. 5th Eur. Conf. Speech Communication Technology*, (pp. 1603–1606). Rhodes, Greece.

Kar, B., Bhatia, S., & Dutta, P. (2007). Audio -Visual Biometric Based Speaker Identification. *Internation Conference on Computational Intelligence and Multimedia Applications, 4* (pp. 94-98). IEEE.

Lathi, B. (2009). *Signal Processing and Linear Systems*. Oxford, UK: Oxford Univ Press.

Liu, H.-C., Su, C.-H., Chiang, Y.-H., & Hung, Y.-P. (2004). Personalized Face Verification System Using Owner-Specific Cluster-Dependent LDA-Subspace. *17th International Conference on Pattern Recognition (ICPR'04)*, (pp. 344-347).

Lu, J., & Plataniotis, K. N. (2002). Boosting face recognition on a large-scale database. *Proceedings of ICIP*, (pp. 109-112).

Lu, J., Yuan, X., & Yahagi, T. (2006). A method of face recognition based on fuzzy clustering and parallel neural networks. *Signal Processing, Volume 86, Issue 8, Special Section: Advances in Signal Processing-assisted Cross-layer Designs*, 2026-2039.

Lüttin, J. (1999). M2VTS Database. In *IDIAP-RR 99-02, IDIAP*. Speaker Verification Experiments on the X.

Messer, K., Matas, J., Kittler, J., Luettin, J., & Maitre, G. (1999). XM2VTSDB: The Extended M2VTS Database. *In Second International Conference on Audio and Video-based Biometric Person Authentication*.

Mika, S., Ratsch, G., Weston, J., Scholkopf, B., & Mullers, K. (1999). Fisher discriminant analysis with kernels. *Neural Networks for Signal Processing IX, 1999. Proceedings of the 1999 IEEE Signal Processing Society Worksho* (pp. 41-48). IEEE.

Nefian, A., & Hayes, M. I. (1999). *An embedded HMM-based approach for face detection and recognition. ICASSP '99. Proceedings* (pp. 3553–3556). IEEE.

Nefian, A. V., Liang, L. H., Fu, T., & Liu, X. X. (2003). A Bayesian Approach to Audio visual Speaker Identification. In *Audio- and Video-Based Biometric Person Authentication Lecture Notes in Computer Science* (p. 1056). Berlin, Heidelberg: Springer. doi:10.1007/3-540-44887-X_88

Patterson, E. K., Gurbuz, S., Tufekci, Z., & Gowdy, J. N. (2002). CUAVE: A new audio visual database for multimodal human-computer interface research. *In Proc. ICASSP*, (pp. 2017-2020).

Pigeon, S., & Vandendorpe, L. (1997). The M2VTS multimodal face database (release 1.00). In *Audio-and Video-based Biometric Person Authentication* (pp. 403–409). Springer. doi:10.1007/BFb0016021

Potamianos, G., Verma, A., Neti, C., Iyengar, G., & Basu, S. (2000). A cascade image transform for speaker independent automatic speechreading. *IEEE International Conference on Multimedia and Expo, vol.2* (pp. 1097-1100). IEEE.

Reynolds, D. (1995). Large population speaker identification using clean and telephone speech. *Signal Processing Letters, IEEE, 2*(3), 46–48. doi:10.1109/97.372913

Reynolds, D. A. (1994). Experimental evaluation of features for robust speaker identification. *IEEE Transactions on Speech and Audio Processing*, 639–643. doi:10.1109/89.326623

Ross, A., & Jain, A. (2003, September). Information fusion in biometrics. *Pattern Recognition Letters, 24*(Issue 13), 2115–2125. doi:10.1016/S0167-8655(03)00079-5

Ross, A., & Poh, N. (2009). Multibiometric Systems: Overview, Case Studies and Open Issues. In *Handbook of Remote Biometrics Advances in Pattern Recognition* (pp. 273–292). London: Springer. doi:10.1007/978-1-84882-385-3_11

Sigurdsson, S., Petersen, K. B., & Lehn-Schiøler, T. (2006). Mel Frequency Cepstral Coefficients: An Evaluation of Robustness of MP3. *Proceedings of the International Symposium on Music Information Retrieval.*

Slaney, M. (1998). *Auditory Toolbox. Version 2.* Interval Research Corportaion #1998-010.

Tse, S.-H., & Lam, K.-M. (2008). *Efficient face recognition with a large database* (pp. 944–949). ICARCV.

Turk, M., & Pentland, A. (1991). Eigenfaces for recognition. *Journal of Cognitive Neuroscience, 3*(1), 71–86. doi:10.1162/jocn.1991.3.1.71

Watkinson, J. (1999). *MPEG-2.* Focal Press.

Wes, S. (2008). *Video over IP: IPTV, Internet video, H.264, P2P, web TV, and streaming: a complete guide to understanding the technology.* Burlington, Massachusetts: Elsevier 2nd ed.

Wong, Y. W., Ch'ng, S. I., Seng, K. P., Ang, L.-M., Chin, S. W., Chew, W. J., et al. (2010). The Audio visual UNMC-VIER Database. *Proceedings of the International Conference on Embedded Systems and Intelligent Technology (ICESIT2010).*

Wu, D., Hou, Y., Zhu, W., Zhang, Y.-Q., & Peha, J. (2001). Streaming video over the internet: Approaches and directions. *IEEE Transactions on Circuits and Systems for Video Technology, Mar 2001, Volume: 11*, 282-300.

Zhou, Z., Chindaro, S., & Deravi, F. (2009). *A Classification Framework for Large-Scale Face Recognition Systems* (pp. 337–346). Advances in Biometrics.

KEY TERMS AND DEFINITIONS

Biometrics: Method of identification of a person using the person's biological traits.

Fusion Scheme: Method of combining different elements using a different fusion rules to get the final result.

Internet Protocol: Communications protocol used to relay data across two or more computers that are connected through the internet or network.

Large-Scale People: A sizeable amount of user population.

Neural Network: A biologically inspired mathematical model that uses artificial neurons to process data.

Radial Basis Function: A distance-based function.

Training Architecture: The structure of the neural network that was used during the training process.

204

Chapter 8
Firewall

Biwu Yang
East Carolina University, USA

ABSTRACT

Firewall is a critical technology in protecting enterprise network systems and individual hosts. Firewalls can be implemented through a specific software application or as a dedicated appliance. Depending on the security policies in an organization, several firewall implementation architectures are available, each with its advantages and disadvantages. Therefore, a thorough understanding of firewall technology, its features and limitations, and implementation considerations is very important in the design and implementation of effective firewall architecture in an organization. This chapter covers the life cycle of firewall design, selection, and implementation.

INTRODUCTION

The function of a firewall is to provide network access regulations, that is, to determine what traffic is allowed and what traffic is not allowed based on network security policies adopted by an organization. Similar to a router, a firewall device is situated inline of the network traffic path, with one interface to receive incoming data packets and another interface to forward the data packets. However, different from a router, a firewall does not need to make a decision for a best path

to forward the data packets. It either allows the packets to go through or drop them.

The decision to allow data packets to go through or not is made by examining various characters of the incoming packets. Depending on the feature and capacity of a firewall, the characters that can be used to make the decision include the source and destination IP addresses, the destination TCP and/or UDP ports specified in a packet, the application layer protocol used, the time of a day, etc.

Firewall filtering criteria is implemented by "firewall rules". Firewall rules are defined based on security policies developed and adopted by an organization. An organization defines its informa-

DOI: 10.4018/978-1-61350-507-6.ch008

tion technology policies to meet their business goals and need. Security policies are part of the general information technology policies. Some security policies are simple to implement and some are difficult. Yet, not all security policies can be implemented through firewall technology. For example, a user access policy may require that network administrators must change their administration password every 30 days; this policy will not be implemented effectively through a firewall device. On the other hand, a security policy to specify that data packets initiated from outside network is not allowed into the internal network unless it is a response to a request initiated by a host in the internal network can be effectively implemented on the firewall at the perimeter network of the organization.

Depending on the security needs and policies, firewall can be implemented as a dedicated device, sometime called firewall appliance, or software solution, which is implemented on a regular computer. Also there are several designs in firewall architectures. For example, a perimeter firewall is typically situated between the outside network (untrusted side) of an organization and the internal network (trusted side). In addition, firewall devices are also used to protect critical network services, such as a server farm, where the key servers are located. In the design of a firewall architecture, several factors must be considered, including the location and selection of firewall devices, the impact of network traffic and throughput, the firewall device management, etc.

TYPE OF FIREWALLS

Firewalls can be classified as software solution and dedicated hardware solution. In the early days, firewalls were software solutions.

As a software solution, a firewall is designed as an application to be installed on a regular computer. The computer would have at least two network interface cards (NIC) installed, one connects to

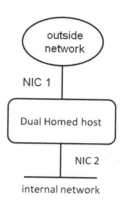

Figure 1. Dual Homed Host in a Network

the "outside" network and the other connects to the "internal" network, as illustrated in Figure 1. The computer is termed "dual homed host". More NICs can be used if the firewall is designed to connect to multiple internal networks.

A hardware solution, also termed as "dedicated firewall" or "firewall appliance", is a device specifically designed to perform the function of monitoring and filtering network traffic. In most cases, this is a "single purpose" computer with a stripped down operating system that is specially designed to perform firewall related functions.

Packet Filtering Firewall

The first generation of firewall uses packet filtering technology (Whitman & Mattord, 2004). Such a firewall would inspect incoming packets based solely on the network layer and transport layer information contained in an IP packet to determine whether the packet should be allowed or dropped.

Some protocol comparison between the OSI model and TCP/IP suite is shown in Table 1. In the TCP/IP suite, the IP header in the network layer indicates the type of protocol, such as ICMP, TCP, UDP, etc., in addition to the source and destination IP addresses. The transport datagram header in the transport layer indicates the TCP and UDP ports. Since most applications use "well known" TCP and/or UDP ports, the firewall administrator can

Table 1. OSI Model and TCP/IP Protocol Suite

OSI Model	TCP/IP Protocol Suite
Application	Application (DHCP, DNS, FTP, HTTP, SMTP, TFTP, …)
Presentation	
Session	
Transport	Transport (TCP, UDP, …)
Network	Network (ARP, IP, ICMP, …)
Data link	Data link
Physical	Physical

set up rules to watch for the protocol types and the ports used, in conjunction with the source and destination IP address to filter incoming packets according to security policies.

Figure 2 shows that a router performs packet filtering. The router may use a filtering table as shown in Table 2, to filter incoming packets.

In this example, incoming packets can come from the external network (from the Serial 0 interface) or from the internal network (from the Ethernet 0 interface). These filtering rules are specified and incoming packets are filtered based on these rules:

1. An external host with IP of 134.25.2.8 is allowed to access an internal web server at 198.31.7.12
2. Any external hosts are not allowed to access the device with the IP of 198.31.7.1 using Telnet
3. External hosts are not allowed to access the internal device with the IP of 198.31.7.254
4. Internal hosts are allowed to access an external web server at 126.34.12.7
5. Internal hosts are not allowed to connect to an external host with the IP of 173.25.41.2
6. An internal host with IP of 198.31.7.5 can connect to the device with the IP of 198.31.7.1 using SSH

A packet filtering firewall treats each passing packet individually, that is, it does not consider whether a packet is a part of an already established communication.

Application Firewall

Application firewall is considered as second generation firewall (Whitman & Mattord, 2004). While the packet filtering firewall uses the information at network layer and transport layer headers, it does not inspect the application layer content of incoming packets. However, sometime the information in the upper layer needs to be

Figure 2. The Router Performs Packet Filtering for Incoming Packets

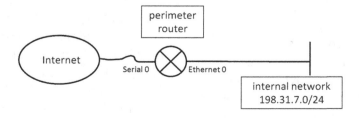

Table 2. Sample Filtering Table

Interface	Source IP	Source Port	Destination IP	Destination Port	Action
Serial 0	134.25.2.8	any	198.31.7.12	80	allow
Serial 0	any	any	198.31.7.1	23	drop
Serial 0	any	any	198.31.7.254	any	drop
Ethernet 0	any	any	126.34.12.7	80	allow
Ethernet 0	any	any	173.25.41.2	any	drop
Ethernet 0	198.31.7.5	any	198.31.7.1	22	allow

inspected to verify the legitimacy of a packet. For example, a company may restrict the employee to use web browser to visit approved web sites only, such as their partner web sites. In this case, merely inspect a packet with TCP port 80 is insufficient, application layer information, the URL, must be also checked. This can be accomplished by using an application firewall.

Application firewall is termed in several other names, including application-level firewall, application gateway firewall, and proxy firewall. It is typically a dedicated computer with specific filtering software installed. Application firewall works on layers 3, 4, 5, and 7 of the OSI model. Upon receiving a packet, the application firewall strips off headers and trailers until the message itself (i.e., the application layer data). It can recognize the characteristics of certain applications protocols, such as FTP, HTTP, SSH, Telnet, etc. It can monitor the traffic with known characteristics so it will recognize the type of traffic even if both ends of an application use non-standard transport layer ports. The application gateway firewall can detect abnormal application behaviors so that it may stop the communication by an application.

The application gateway firewall is also called proxy firewall or proxy server, in that it sits between the clients and remote applications, such that it hides the internal hosts from outside networks.

A proxy server typically works with another firewall device because it is so specifically designed to just handle filtering a few particular applications. As shown in Figure 3, internal hosts are configured on their web browsers to use the proxy server in order to access remote web sites. The router is configured with a rule that it will drop all web traffic initiated from the internal hosts, except those from the proxy server. When the proxy server receives packets from internal hosts, it examines the destination URL in the message, if it is a valid request, it will repackage the packet using its own IP and MAC address and send it forward to the router. In other words, it sends the request on behalf of the internal host. Since the router is configured to accept web traffic initiated from the proxy server, it will forward the web request. When a web response returns, the router forward the packet to the proxy server, the proxy server examines the message (application layer information) and verify it is indeed a response to the request, it will then repackage it and sends to the internal host, again using its IP and MAC address.

A proxy server can also be used to protect internal network resources while allowing requests from external networks. As shown in Figure 4, the domain name of the web service provided by the web server is configured on the proxy server, thus the web requests from external hosts are sent to the proxy server. The proxy server checks the content of the message and forwards it to the web server if the request is valid. The return message is sent from the web server to the proxy server and then it is forwarded to the external client.

The proxy server protects the web server by shielding it from direct access from external

Figure 3. Proxy Firewall

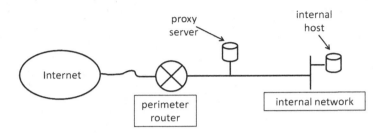

network. In addition, a proxy server can store the recent served content in its memory cache. When it receives a request from a client, it checks the cache first. If the requested information is in the cache, it will send it to the client immediately. Thus proxy server enhances the performance of web service.

Proxy firewalls provide functions that a regular firewall would not cover, such as user-based access control and port forwarding. If a proxy server is used for internal network hosts to access remote servers, with user-based access control, it can grant or deny a connection based on user authentication mechanism. On the other hand, if a proxy server is used for teleworkers to access corporate servers, the port forwarding feature can be used to further protect the servers by allowing connection from an irregular port (not a well-known port). Thus only clients who know the particular port can access the servers. For example, if a randomly selected TCP port 1567 is configured to connect

to a web server, a user must specify this port in the URL when connect to the proxy server; it will then forward the request to the internal web server with port 80.

The major limitation of proxy firewall is that they are specially designed to filter a particular application layer protocol. When another application layer protocol is to be filtered, the proxy server needs a major reconfiguration effort. Also, when a server faces large amount of requests, if the proxy server cannot provide sufficient performance, it might become the bottleneck.

In modern network security design, these servers that provide important information and need to be accessed from the Internet, such as web server and DNS server, are located in a demilitarized zone (DMZ). The DMZ network is isolated from the internal network and therefore its access can be separately controlled. An HTTP proxy server, if necessary, should also be located in DMZ.

Figure 4. Proxy Server to Protect the Internal Web Server

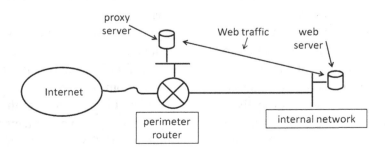

Stateful Inspection Firewall

Statefull inspection firewall is considered as third generation firewall (Whitman & Mattord, 2004). Stateful firewall gets its name because this type of firewall performs stateful packet inspection (SPI). SPI firewall works on layers 3, 4, and 5 of the OSI model. It keeps a state table about the packets transmitted. Unlike packet filtering firewall which treats incoming packets individually, a stateful firewall keeps track of packets passing by and checks if incoming packets belongs to an already established connection. It uses the information to determine the state of connection. The state information includes IP addresses, the transportation protocol (TCP or UDP), TCP header (for example, SYN, RST, ACK, and FIN), etc. It adds the efficiency of packets inspection, once a connection is established, subsequent incoming packets that belong to the same connection will be allowed to pass without further inspection against firewall rules.

Most communications have a state, a state of either "open" or "closed". If an application uses TCP as the transport layer protocol, the TCP uses 3-way handshake to establish a connection before data is transmitted (Forouzan, Behrouz A. 2010). It also has a proper mechanism to close the connection. After the TCP connection is established, the state during the data communication is "open" until it is closed. For applications using UDP as the transport layer, there is no connection state, since it is connectionless protocol, in this case, the firewall will keep a record of transmission to be used for SPI. Figure 5 shows the connection establishment and termination of a TCP session.

Before an application in the client can start sending data using TCP protocol, TCP protocol will first establish the connection. This is done through a 3-way handshaking process.

1. The client sends a SYN segment to the server.
2. The server sends back a SYN+ACK segment. This SYN+ACK segment has dual purposes.

The SYN part is to open a connection in the opposite direction, from the server to the client. The ACK part is to acknowledge the SYN segment sent by the client.
3. The client sends an ACK segment in response to the SYN+ACK segment sent by the server.

At this point, the connection between the client and the server is established and data can be transmitted among them. The state is "established".

When data transmission is completed, another 3-way handshaking process for connection termination takes place.

1. The client sends a FIN segment to the server.
2. The server sends back a FIN+ACK segment. The FIN part is to initiate the closing of the connection in the opposite direction, from the server to the client. The ACK part is to acknowledge the FIN segment sent by the client.
3. The client sends an ACK segment in response to the FIN+ACK segment sent by the server.

At this point, the connection between the client and the server is closed. The state is "closed".

A SPI firewall keeps track of the communication status by a state table. The state table will track the source and destination IP addresses, TCP ports, and the status. Figure 6 shows an example of state table in a SPI firewall during a connection for a client in the internal network to access an external web server.

In this example, the rule in the firewall blocks incoming traffic from external network unless it is in response to a request initiated from a host in the internal network.

The internal client initiates the 3-way handshaking by sending a SYN segment to the external web server. In the packet, it contains the destination IP address of 143.24.35.7 and destination port of 80, as well as the source IP address of 198.33.7.8 and source port of 53034, a randomly selected port number.

Figure 5. TCP Connection Establishment and Termination Process

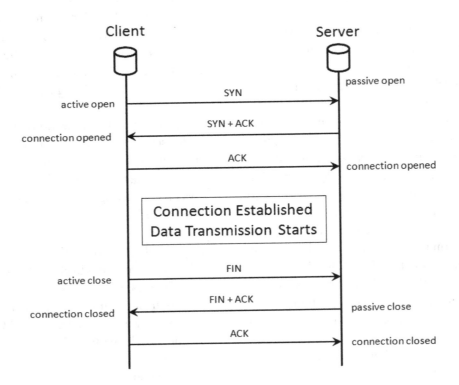

Figure 6. State Table in a SPI Firewall

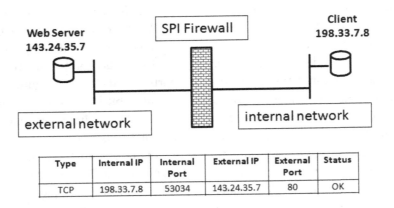

Type	Internal IP	Internal Port	External IP	External Port	Status
TCP	198.33.7.8	53034	143.24.35.7	80	OK

The SPI firewall examines the packet and record these four pieces of information in the state table, and mark the status as "OK". When a SYN+ACK segment (from the web server) arrives as an IP packet, the firewall will compare these four pieces of information contained in the packet with its state table. If it matches, it will let the packet enter the internal network.

Once the connection is "established", a SPI firewall will allow traffics to pass from the internal hosts to external network. However incoming packets from external network will be compared with the state table, if it is part of an existing connection (matching the four pieces of information), it will let it pass. Otherwise, the packet is dropped.

An attacker may send a SYN+ACK segment to the internal host trying to get a TCP RST segment. In a situation without the firewall, the internal host will send a TCP RST segment to indicate it is not a valid SYN+ACK segment. However, the packet that carries a TCP RST segment includes its IP address and port number, thus the attacker will gather the information of internal hosts. Also, an attack might send multiple SYN+ACK packets in a very short period. If the host is busy to respond with TCP RST segment, the attacker might achieve the Denial of Service attack, especially if the target internal host is a server. With SPI firewall, since the incoming SYN+ACK segment does not match with the state table, the packet is simply dropped.

For connectionless protocols, such as UDP, a SPI firewall handles the traffic in a similar way in that it keeps a track of a UDP session in the state table. When an internal host initiates a UDP based request, the state table will keep the connection information of type of protocol (UDP in this case), source and destination IP addresses, and source and destination UDP ports. Incoming packets will be compared with the information in the state table. If it matches, then it is considered a part of the UDP connection and is allowed to enter, otherwise, it will be dropped.

Advanced SPI implementation can handle applications that require port-switching and multiple ports opening, such as FTP, streaming video, videoconferencing (H.323), etc.

In FTP communication, the protocol uses TCP port 21 as a control channel and uses another TCP port, usually dynamically assigned, to transfer data. Figure 7 shows an FTP connection process.

The client and the server first establish a connection with the server.

1. The client sends an "open" request to the server, with a randomly chosen TCP port P (54033 in the example) as source port and port 21 as destination port, which is the control port that the FTP server listens for requests.

2. The FTP server sends back a response and the connection is open.

At this point, the state table in SPI firewall will record the information, as shown in the first row in Figure 7.

After the client and the FTP server establish a connection the data transfer can take place.

1. The client issues a PSV command, which asks the server to select a port for data transfer.

2. The server responds with a random chosen port (45001 in the example) for data transfer.

3. The client can now issue data command, with the source port of P+1 (54034) and destination port 45001.

At this point, the SPI firewall notices the connection initiated by the internal host and save the information in the state table. The returning data packets from the server will be allowed to pass because they match the information in the state table.

FTP can operate in two modes, active and passive. This example shows the FTP session in passive mode. In passive FTP mode, the client asks the FTP server to select a port for data transfer, and then issue a command from the client to the server. Since this communication is initiated from the internal network, the firewall will allow the packets go out and the returning packets in since they belong to an established connection.

However, in active FTP, the process is a little different:

1. The client issues PORT command to let the server know which port the client will use for the data transfer. The source port could

Figure 7. Passive FTP Data Transfer

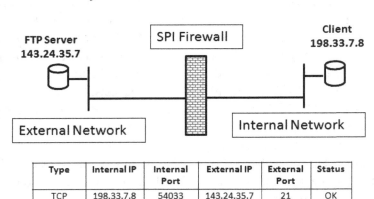

Type	Internal IP	Internal Port	External IP	External Port	Status
TCP	198.33.7.8	54033	143.24.35.7	21	OK
TCP	198.33.7.8	54034	143.24.35.7	45001	OK

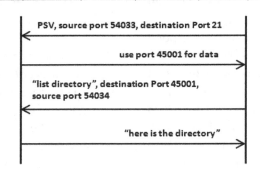

be port P+1 (54034 in the example) and the destination port is port 21.

2. The server will send a response (code 150) to the client to indicate that the server is ready for data transfer. The source port is TCP port 20 (a well known data port for FTP) and the destination port is the port specified at step 1. To the firewall, this is a new connection initiated from the external network, it will block this packet.

Passive FTP mode is considered safe, especially to the firewall at the client side.

Most multimedia serves uses these dual connection model, one for the control channel and another for data transfer. Some applications may even use multiple data channels, such as H.323 videoconferencing. By understanding the operation features of various applications, SPI firewalls can support those applications with complex communication type.

Network Address Translation

Network address translation (NAT) technology was developed to slow down the exhaustion of IPv4 address space. With the exponential growth of World Wide Web sites and more and more services being offered through the World Wide Web, the requests for unique IP addresses have been increasingly demanding. In fact, the IPv4 address space was exhausted on February 1, 2011 (IPv4 Address Report. n.d.). However, the Internet still operates normally thanks to the NAT technology.

This technology involves modifying the IP address information in the IP datagram header before transmitting the data across a router. In particular, organizations take advantage of "private IP address" blocks to hide their internal network

Table 3. IP Blocks for Private Network

Block	Number of addresses
10.0.0.0/8	16,777,216
172.16.0.0/12	1,048,576
192.168.0.0/16	65,536
169.254.0.0/16	65,536

behind a router. Table 3 lists the IP address blocks reserved to be used for private networks.

As shown in Figure 8, an organization uses the NAT technology to translate the IP addresses assigned to the internal network, the private IP address block 192.168.1.0/24 in the figure, to global IP addresses so that the packets can be forwarded to the Internet. From the internal network, all outgoing packets go through the router, where the source IP address in the IP header is replaced with a global (also called public) IP address. For the returning traffic, the router replaces the destination IP address with its original private IP address. The router keeps a translation table so that it knows which address pair has been assigned during the transmission.

There are three address translation schemes supported by NAT:

1. **Static NAT** – There is one-to-one association of the internal private and external global addresses. In other words, the router always uses the same global IP address for the translation for a particular internal host. This is useful when there are Internet based servers on the internal private network, such as web server, FTP server, etc.

2. **Dynamic NAT** – The organization is assigned a small pool of global IP addresses. The router uses a part of the pool for address translation. A global IP address is assigned to an internal host as needed. For example, if the routers uses three global IP addresses for address translation, then three internal hosts can connect to the same external web server, because each of them are independently translated with different global IP address. The term "dynamic NAT" indicates that the association of internal private IP addresses and external global IP addresses are not predetermined; rather it is based on the need. The limitation is the size of the global IP address pool to be used for this purpose. In the above example, only three internal hosts can communicate with external resources at a time.

3. **Dynamic NAT with Port Address** – It is called network address and port translation (NAPT) or port address translation (PAT). This technology is developed to address the limitation of the global IP address pool issue in the Dynamic NAT. This technique allows one global IP address to be shared by

Figure 8. NAT is used between the Internal and External Networks

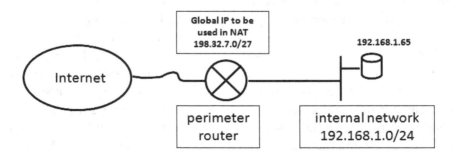

Table 4. NAPT translation table

Private Address	Private Port	Global Address	External Port	Transport Protocol
192.168.1.56	49200	198.32.7.8	80	TCP
192.168.1.67	49201	198.32.7.8	80	TCP
192.168.1.78	49202	198.32.7.8	80	TCP

many internal hosts for address translation by adding another parameter, the transport layer port number. By assigning different port numbers, the router will be able to distinguish which internal host requested external services. Table 4 shows an example of NAPT. In this example, the router keeps a translation table, as shown in Table 4, which has five columns. When three hosts, with IP addresses of 192.168.1.56, 192.168.1.67, 192.168.1.78, wants to connect to the same web server, the router modifies source IP address in the IP header and the source port address in the TCP datagram. In this example, all three internal hosts shared the same global IP address but with different source TCP port. When responses from the web server are received by the router, it will check the TCP destination port address contained in a response packet and determine which internal host should receive the packet by consulting the translation table.

Therefore, although it is not designed as a firewall technology, network address translation technology, especially the NAPT implementation, hides the internal network hosts and IP addressing schemes and thus shields the internal network from potential attacks such as network probing.

Host-Based Firewall

So far, the firewalls discussed are designed to protect the network perimeter; they are located at the boundary of the internal network or at the boundary of an important subset of the internal network, such as DMZ and server farm. Host-based firewall is a firewall application that is installed on a personal computer or a server computer. It provides another layer of security to protect hosts. In a traditional firewall only network security design, the focus was placed on the network perimeters with the goal to shield the internal network from external networks. However, once a packet gets into the internal network, it was considered safe, which may not be true. In addition, network threats can be initiated inside the internal network. Thus host-based firewall is necessary to protect end devices.

Host-based firewall is typically an application layer firewall that can filter traffic based on characteristics of various applications. For server computers, host-based firewall application sits between the operating system and the application services that the server is providing. The host-based firewall should perform packet filtering based on the services it provides, with the information of source and destination IP address, TCP or UDP port, and even application layer data. The following lists some considerations.

- Allow incoming requests for the services it provides. For example, if it is a web server, HTTP and HTTPS requests should be allowed. This can be achieved by checking TCP ports 80 and 443.
- Block incoming requests for the services it do not provide. For example, if the server does not provide FTP service, all FTP requests should be dropped.
- Filter incoming requests for those services that are available for certain network only. For example, if a FTP server is setup for

internal user access only, then the FTP requests from the hosts on the internal network are allowed while the FTP requests initiated from external network are blocked. An FTP may require username and password to get in. However, if those requests can be filtered upon reaching the server, it will reduce the risk of external attackers trying to crack the username and password to the FTP server. This can be achieved by checking the source IP address and TCP port 21 for FTP service.

- Watch for outgoing traffic, stop or disable services that send information out without permission. If a service cannot be stopped, then block the outgoing traffic.

There are many products of host-based firewall available on market for client computers. By default, most of them allows for packets to leave the computer and examines incoming packets. If an incoming packet is in response to a request initiated by the computer, it will allow it to pass; otherwise, it will prompt the user either to allow or deny it. These behaviors can be configured to meet desired needs.

The host-based firewall products for personal computers (also called personal firewalls) are now available with bundled of other features such as antivirus, antispyware, anti-spam, identity protection, etc. Customers who purchase one product can get protection from several aspects of security concerns.

Security Policies and Firewall

Whitman & Mattord (2003, p. 192) pointed out "Management from all communities of interest, including general staff, information technology, and information security, must consider policies as the basis for all information security planning, design, and implement." An organization should develop information security policies to ensure the information technology infrastructure,

network resources, and corporate data as well as employee data are well protected. A policy is not a detail "how to" manual, rather it should provide framework that identifies the important asset and provides instruction on how to protect it. Policies support the mission, vision, and strategic planning of an organization. The realization and execution of policies are further defined by standards and procedures, and implemented with proper technologies. Security policy is typically an integrated component of the broader Information Technology Policy that should include other components, such as acceptable use policy, change policy, management policy, etc.

Security policies specify what defines security and what should be done about the security at a high and broad level. For example, a major content in a security policy is access control, which defines who can access a particular network resource, when the access is granted, what access permission should be given, etc. Simply state, if an attacker cannot access a network resource, it cannot be harmed. The security policy should provide guidelines for proper and valid network access, how policies are enforced, incidence reporting, and procedures to mitigate network threats, etc.

A comprehensive set of security policies is important and critical for developing standards and procedures. Standards are statements in more detail to describe what action should be taken to comply with policies. The procedures and guidelines are detailed steps implemented to comply with the policies. For example, if the password policy (a sub policy of the general security policy) specifies that access to network device for device management must be authenticated. The standards may contain following statements:

- Network engineers and administrators must use individual credentials to authenticate in order to access network devices. Username and password should not be shared.

- To reduce the burden of configuration on network devices, authentication should be processed through a centralized entity.
- Password should be at least 8 characters long and contains certain level of complexity.
- Password must be changed every 30 days and new password cannot be the same as any of 3 previously used password.

The procedure and guideline may provide the detail steps:

- Each individual who has the privilege and the need of accessing network devices for management purpose must register and create a strong password.
- A strong password contains a combination of 4 groups of alphanumeric. The four groups are capital letter, lower case letter, number, and special characters, such as %$#=+(), etc. The password should be at least 8 characters long and contains at least one element from each of the 4 groups.
- The authentication is processed through a central RADIUS server. Network devices are configured to redirect the authentication request to the RADIUS server.
- Password must be changed every 30 days. A password change reminder will be sent via email when a password reaches 25 days old. This reminder will be sent every day afterwards until day 30. The account will be suspended if the password reaches 30 days without change. A password reset procedure must follow to reactivate a suspended account.
- Password history of 3 is kept so a user cannot use any of the previous 3 passwords in order to renew a password.

Example: Development of a Security Policy for Access Control

Access control policy defines limitation of access to systems and data (Panko, 2004). The development of an access control may start with identifying assets in the organization, towards the policies to guide the standards and procedures.

1. List each resource that needs access control
2. Recognize and identify the sensitivity of these resources, for example, which database contains employee personal information.
3. Prioritize the importance of these resources, which one is critical, which one is important
4. Determine who should have access to each resource. The decision should be based on the principle of "least privilege". Level of access can be setup by individual or by "roles".
5. Determine what access permission (authorization) individual (or each role) should have once they access a resource. Authorization level might be "read-only", "read/write", "change", "execute", "admin", etc. Each resource needs a specific authorization list.
6. Decide how access control is implemented. Each resource should have a separate plan of access control implementation. Firewall can be used to implement some access control issues, but not every access control issue can be covered by firewall devices.
7. Documentation. Each group or individual resource should have a specific access and protection policy. Plan for security audit and testing is defined. Guidelines for standards and procedures are developed.

Effective Implementation of Security Policies by Firewalls

Security policies drive the development of standards and procedures, the selection of security solutions, the implementation, and the testing (auditing) of implementation. In the process of selecting security solutions, the goals and objectives of the policy need to be carefully evaluated since different technologies and products may perform identical or similar functions with possible tweak by the vendors.

Not all security policies can or should be implemented by firewalls. Some policies are best implemented with firewalls; others must be implemented through different security technologies. The following list contains some examples of security concerns that can be well covered by firewall technology:

- **Packets should be filtered at the perimeter of the corporate network**–Firewall devices can be used to form a boundary around the corporate network. A perimeter firewall serves as a door between the internal and external networks. Both incoming and outgoing packets can be examined. The filtering criteria could include source and destination IP addresses, transport layer ports, and even application layer characteristics.

- **Servers that provide services to public community in the Internet should be protected yet are available to the Internet**– With firewall device, a Demilitarized Zone (DMZ) could be created which is separate from the internal network. Requests to these servers can be filtered when they enter the DMZ. The filtering criteria can be specifically managed for DMZ.

- **Critical network resources need special protection**–In the network design, those critical network resources, such as database server and mission critical service servers can be located in an area called server farm. Firewalls can be used to protect the server farm by filtering incoming packets and allowing only those requests that meet the security criteria to pass. The server farm design could effectively protect the critical network resources from potential attacks from external networks as well as internal networks.

- **Outgoing traffic needs filtering for potential attacks**–An organization, in addition to protecting its own network resources, should also make efforts to protect the general Internet community. One attack that has potential to cripple many servers is Distributed Denial of Service (DDoS) attack. The attackers first use computer warm or virus to infect hundreds and thousands computers that are in different networks around the world. The attackers then launch spoofed IP packets (use invalid source IP address) from these infected computers to target a server. Since these source IP addresses are invalid, the targeted server will open sessions for these requests and will not close these sessions in a reasonable amount of time because it will not receive valid ACK messages. With sessions open, the internal resource (CPU and memory) in the server computer is occupied. When the resource is exhausted, due to huge amount of requests within a very short period of time, the server will no longer be able to provide its service; the denial of server attack is achieved. To help fight the DDoS, the firewall should filter the outgoing packets and drop any packets with source IP address not belong to the organization, as shown in Figure 9.

On the other hand, some policy may not be suitable for enforcement through firewall devices. For example, if an access control policy specifies that a computer must have antivirus software installed with latest virus definition updates before it can access to the internal network cannot be implemented through the firewall technology. Another example might be that an access control policy specifies that account password of

Figure 9. Filtering Outgoing Traffic to Drop Spoofed Packets

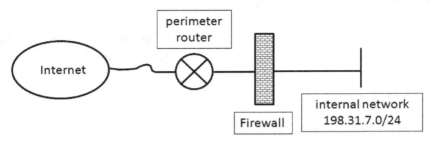

Firewall rule: outgoing packets with the source IP address other
than 198.31.7.0/24 should be dropped.

network administrators must be changed every 30 days.

Therefore the network security personnel should review and analyze security policies to determine which policies should be implemented on firewalls.

FIREWALL ARCHITECTURE

Firewall Devices

As discussed above, firewall function can be implemented as an application or in a dedicated device. Several factors determine the selection and implementation of a firewall technology.

- **Performance**–Probably the most important factor is the performance. Because a firewall is considered as an "inline" device in that it sits in the path of network traffic, if the performance cannot accommodate the amount of traffic flow, the firewall becomes the bottleneck. The performance of a single firewall depends on the capacity of hardware components, such as CPU and memory, as well as the efficiency of the filtering algorithm. Multiple firewalls can be clustered to provide not only fault tolerance but also redundancy features.

- **Cost**–While the cost may not be a determining factor, it is always a sensitive issue. Software solution tends to be less expensive compared with dedicated firewall devices; however, the application software has to work with the host operating system. Its performance largely depends on the performance of the host.

- **Features**–The modern firewall products offer several security functions in the bundle. In addition to regular firewall function, more and more products offer VPN and Intrusion Detection (IDS) or Intrusion Prevention (IPS) functions in the product. With these features bundled together, a dedicated device can provide multiple aspects of protections for an organization. However, the needs of network security protection must be carefully evaluated as what features are required, what features are nice to have, and whether a bundled product provides efficient and effective protection versus multiple single function devices.

Selection of firewall devices has to be coordinated in the firewall architecture to be deployed. Firewall architecture defines the function, the location, and the numbers needed for firewall devices. Network engineers examine the security policies

Figure 10. Single Firewall Architecture

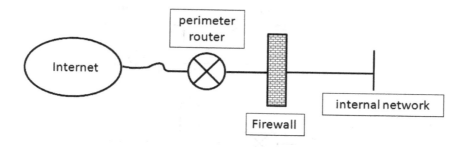

and develop a firewall architecture that will meet the goals and objectives of the components in the security policy that can be accomplished by firewall devices. The following section describes some consideration for firewall architecture.

Single Firewall Architecture

The simplest firewall deployment is to place a firewall device between the perimeter router and the internal network, as shown in Figure 10.

The firewall has two interfaces, one towards the perimeter router and is designated as "outside" network and the other towards the internal network and is designated as "internal" network. The firewall filters incoming packets against the firewall rules. Incoming packets from both directions can be filtered. The advantage is the configuration and management for the single firewall is relatively easy. It can effectively protect the internal network when statefull packet inspection is used. For example, a security policy of "Incoming packets from the Internet will not be allowed to pass until they are in response to requests initiated from hosts in the internal network" can be implemented with this architecture. The limitation of this architecture is that once packets pass the firewall, there is no filtering to them anymore. This architecture cannot effectively protect critical internal network resources such as a server farm because it does not filter packets in the internal network unless a packet passes through the

firewall. This architecture is suitable for a small office/home office (SOHO) which contains a small number of workstations in the internal network.

Single Firewall with More Than Two Interfaces

A more complex single firewall deployment requires three or more interfaces on the firewall device. In addition to the outside network and internal network interfaces, additional interfaces can be used to connect to separate networks that possess unique characteristics. One example is the use of DMZ network, as shown in Figure 11.

The term DMZ comes from the military term Demilitarized Zone. In network design, a DMZ is a network where network resources are provided for public access. Such network resources might include web servers that provide information for public access and a DNS server to resolve domain names of hosts inside the organization. Access to a DNS server by the Internet hosts is necessary if the organization hosts it is own domain space. Since these servers need to be accessed from outside network, the security rules must be set differently compared with access requests toward the internal network. With a separate physical network, it will be easier to set the appropriate rules just for DMZ. An example firewall rule set might include:

Figure 11. One Firewall with Three Interfaces (DMZ network)

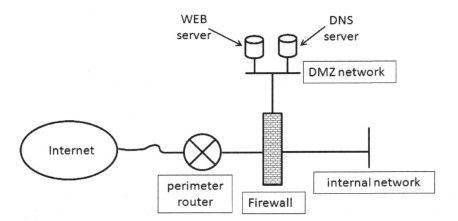

- HTTP and HTTPS traffic with specific destination address for the web server is allowed into DMZ.
- DNS traffic (both UDP and TCP) with specific destination address for the DNS server is allowed into DMZ.
- Returning HTTP/HTTPS/DNS traffic is allowed to leave DMZ.
- DNS traffic initiated from the DNS server is allowed to leave DMZ.
- Network traffic from network administrators workstations (could be defined by individual IP addresses of those workstations or by a subnet) is allowed to get in and out of DMZ, for the purpose of management.
- No other traffic is allowed in and out of DMZ.

With focused targets, this rule set clearly defines what traffic can get in and leave DMZ. When the DMZ servers are equipped with host-based firewall they are well protected.

Another example of a separate physical network could be the extranet services, as shown in Figure 12. Extranet can be defined as "A public-private website or portal, secured or password-protected, specifically designed for selected workers in an organization and selected external partners to conduct internal business." (Extranet 2008). A company may need to provide extranet services for its business partners, such as web based applications for inventory checking and ordering. The access is not from public, nor from its employees, rather is from selected business partners. Thus, the firewall rule set should be different from those from the Internet traffic. With a separate physical network, it will be easier to set the appropriate rule set. An example firewall rule set for the extranet might include:

- HTTP and HTTPS traffic with specific source and destination IP addresses are allowed into the extranet network. The source IP address should be the network of selected business partner network.
- Returning HTTP and HTTPS traffic is allowed to leave the extranet network.
- Network traffic from network administrators workstations (could be defined by individual IP addresses of those workstations or by a subnet) is allowed to get into and out of the extranet network, for the purpose of management.
- No other traffic is allowed in and out of the extranet network.

Figure 12. Single Firewall with DMZ and Extranet Service Network

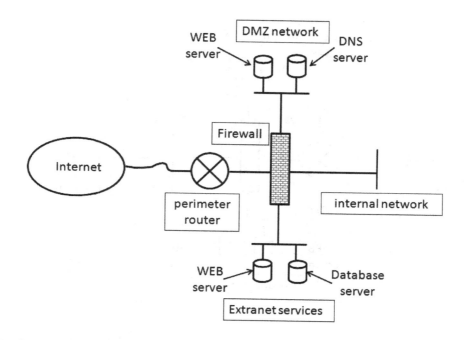

This rule set is very close to the one for DMZ, except that the source IP addresses in the incoming packets can be filtered. Incoming network traffic not from the known partner networks will be dropped.

Double Firewall Architecture

While it seems a single firewall can accommodate the needs for separate physical networks, however, if the network infrastructure is complex and consists of internal network, DMZ network, and extranet network, the firewall could become the bottleneck for the network traffic flow.

Double firewall architecture will help divide the traffic monitoring and filtering process. With double firewall architecture, each firewall can focus on protecting certain part of the enterprise network. For example, as shown in Figure 13, the Firewall A can focus on monitoring and filtering network traffic towards DMZ and Extranet service networks; it can just let traffic towards the internal network go through without filtering. The Firewall

B can focus on monitoring and filtering network traffic towards the internal network. Hence the incoming traffic monitoring and filtering load are distributed between the Firewall A and the Firewall B.

Other Firewall Locations

Firewalls can be used to protect certain important portion of the internal network. One example is to protect the server farm. A server farm is defined as "a group of networked servers housed in one location" (Server Farm. n.d.). With a focused network area, special provisions required to support multiple servers can be easily implemented, such as power line condition, climate control, restrict access, etc. Although the server farm is in the internal network, it is still subject to attacks by hosts from both internal and external networks since it contains critical information of the organization. Statistics also shows that security attacks initiated from the internal network are rising (Waxer, Cindy, 2007). Thus the server farm may warrant

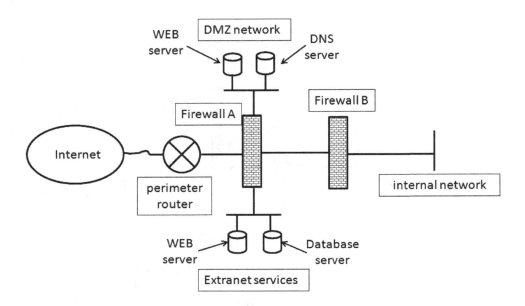

Figure 13. Double Firewall Architecture

additional protection through a separate firewall, Firewall C, as shown in Figure 14. The rule set might include:

- Traffic with specific source addresses and destination IP address with transport layer ports is allowed into the server farm. The source IP address should be the network of the internal network. The transport layer ports identify the application services provided by the servers.
- Network traffic from network administrators workstations (could be defined by individual IP addresses of those workstations or by a subnet) is allowed to get in and out of the server farm, for the purpose of management.
- No other traffic is allowed into the server farm.

With this rule set, only internal network hosts can access to the server farm for the services provided by the server farm. Requests from external networks are blocked since their needs are covered by the services either in DMZ or Extranet networks.

FIREWALL IMPLEMENTATION CONSIDERATIONS

Effective firewall implementation consists of iteration of several phases including security needs analysis, design and selection, implementation, testing, and maintenance.

Security Needs Analysis

An organization should perform periodical assessment of security weakness and vulnerability. The areas to be considered include:

- access control, user authentication and authorization mechanism
- data path to network resources
- access to the outside network
- access control for the data requests from outside network
- employee remote access needs

Figure 14. Firewall to Protect Server Farm

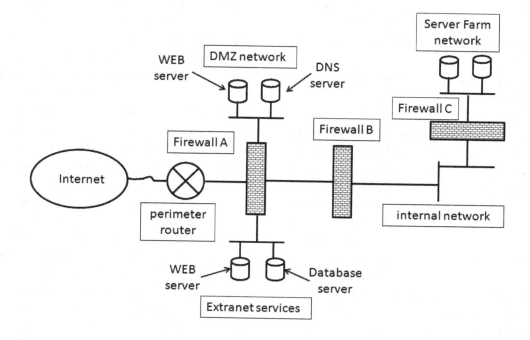

While the focuses are on the security, other aspects related to the information infrastructure should also be considered, including:

- bottlenecks in the infrastructure
- performance, such as load balancing
- resilience of key network infrastructure and network services, such as fault tolerance, backup and disaster recovery plan

Design and Selection

Once the weakness, the vulnerability, and the needs are identified, the IT personnel should recommend effective solutions. Some of the solutions are not related to technology, such as the formation of acceptable network use policy and guidelines of best practices. Technology solutions include design, product evaluation and selection, and implementation of firewall solution.

In identifying effective security technologies, the information technology personnel, especially network security personnel, should realize that firewall is a primary security device and it cannot be used to filter all security threats. For example, while stateful packet inspection firewall is commonly used to protect the internal network, it does expose the internal network IP addresses to the outside. For this reason, other solutions such as proxy and network address translation could be used together with the firewall. In addition to the function of monitoring and filtering packets, intrusion detection system and intrusion prevention system can provide protection from another security aspect. The intrusion detection system and intrusion prevention system can be incorporated into the firewall appliance as modern firewall products typically bundle them together. However, the advantage of incorporating into one device versus the disadvantage of putting extra load on the firewall appliance must be carefully evaluated before a decision is made.

In designing effective firewall architecture, several factors should be considered, including:

- strategic location of firewall devices
- type of firewall, software solution versus firewall appliance, packet filtering versus stateful inspection, network based firewall, host based firewall, etc.
- performance consideration, load balancing
- fault tolerance

Since a firewall situates in the data pathway, it could become a bottleneck if its performance cannot accommodate the traffic flow. To assess the network performance and identify potential bottleneck, a network performance baseline should be established. The baseline should indicate the performance data of firewall devices in a normal network load condition. The baseline can be used to compare with the current operation of network to identify possible bottleneck. The baseline should also be refreshed whenever the network operation characteristics change, for example, adding significant number of computer workstations or new server services are deployed.

In addition to selecting a firewall device with sufficient performance capacity, other measures might help solve the performance issue. For example, double firewall architecture will distribute the packets monitoring and filtering between two firewall devices. Another example is the use of a separate VPN server.

To secure remote access for their employees, many organizations deploy virtual private network (VPN) technology. With VPN solution, legitimate users can establish secure tunnels with the internal network of the organization since the communication is authenticated and encrypted. The modern design of firewall appliance includes several other functions, such as VPN server, Intrusion Detection System, and Intrusion Prevention System. With these bundled features, an organization can deploy a firewall appliance after the perimeter router and provide multiple security related services. An example could be that a firewall appliance serves as a firewall and a VPN server. This approach makes the design of firewall architecture to be simple. Teleworkers can establish a secure VPN connection to the organization network through the same firewall appliance. However, the extra function as a VPN server may impact the firewall performance if the demand of VPN connection increases. In this case, a separate VPN server device can be deployed to relieve the VPN role of the firewall appliance. As shown in Figure 15, a VPN server is placed parallel to the firewall device. When a teleworker initiates a VPN connection request, the VPN server will handle the connection request. Once the VPN connection is authenticated and negotiated, the VPN connection is established and traffic through the established VPN tunnel is allowed to enter the internal network bypass the firewall device.

Figure 15. VPN Server Deployment

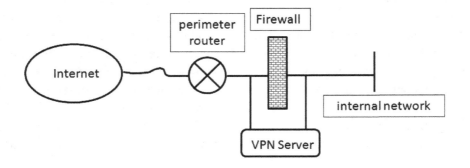

Firewall Design Implementation

The information technology personnel should develop an implementation plan once a firewall architecture design is verified through simulation or prototype test. The implementation plan should include:

- scope of the project
- expectation of the project
- timeline of the project
- phases of the project
- impact of the project
- roll back plan if the project fails to reach the expectation
- responsible parties to carry out the project

In general, unless it is a small scale project, an implementation should be carried out in phases. Clear objectives and expectations should be developed for each phase. Check points should be established to monitor the implementation process. Results should be verified at each phase before continuing on to the next phase.

Testing

Testing of the firewall architecture is to make sure the design and implementation meet the network security requirements. A testing plan should be developed to cover all aspects of objectives and expectations. It may also include some extreme conditions to verify the firewall architecture can sustain the extra load and demand under a severe condition. For example, some penetration tests can be conducted to see when under a severe Denial of Service attack, if the firewall devices can perform normally, if not, what would be the state of the firewall device, open to all traffic or close to all traffic, etc.

Maintenance

Firewall device monitoring and maintenance is a critical aspect of firewall operation. It may take some time for the network to be stabilized after a new firewall architecture design is implemented. Once the network is stabilized, a baseline of network traffic and firewall device performance should be established. Some maintenance measures should be considered, including:

- firewall logging to a central device, for example, a Syslog server.
- firewall log analysis
- firewall audit
- firewall performance monitoring

Network condition can change over times after a firewall architecture is deployed. Such changes include more computer servers and workstations are added to the network; more server services are added; some server services may no longer be needed, etc. Therefore, testing should also be conducted periodically after the firewall architecture is deployed. This is usually termed as auditing. With the same purpose, auditing is trying to find out if the firewall architecture is still performing as it is designed. Auditing can include checking the loggings of firewall device and performing actual testing. Audits should be performed periodically so that the status of the firewall architecture can be verified in a normal interval and problems can be identified and corrected in a timely fashion.

Like any other information systems in an organization, firewall solution is a continuous process from planning, needs analysis, design and selection, implementation, testing, and maintenance. An organization should recognize the nature of the system and make the security a major component of the strategic information technology plan.

CONCLUSION

Firewall is a critical security component in protecting the network infrastructure and network resources in an organization. Well designed firewall architecture can effectively monitor and filter network traffics so that only legitimate packets are allowed into and out of the corporate internal network. In designing a firewall architecture, information technology personnel need to assess and evaluate the network access needs, the weakness and vulnerability of current network access control policy, and impacts to the network; then design and select firewall solution that can address the needs, weakness, and vulnerability appropriately. Once the design is verified, implementation plan should be developed to make sure the implementation can be carried out smoothly and successfully. Once the implementation is in place, ongoing monitoring and maintenance is critical to make sure the firewall design meets the organization's information security goals and expectations.

REFERENCES

Clemmer, L. (May 5, 2010). *The Top Five Firewall Security Tips*. In Bright Hub, retrieved from http://www.brighthub.com/computing/smb-security/articles/40618.aspx

Convery, S. (2004). *Network Security Architectures*. Indianapolis, IN: Cisco Press.

Extranet (November 21, 2008). In *How-to.gov*. Retrieved from http://www.usa.gov/webcontent/resources/glossary.shtml#E

Farm, S. (n.d.). In *Pennsylvania Office of Administration*. Retrieved from http://www.portal.state.pa.us/portal/server.pt/community/glossary/922.

Forouzan, B. A. (2010). *TCP/IP Protocol Suite* (4th ed.). New York, NY: McGraw-Hill.

Frahim, J., & Santos, O. (2010). *Cisco ASA: All-in-One Firewall, IPS, Anti-X, and VPN Adaptive Security Appliance* (2nd ed.). Indianapolis, IN: Cisco Press.

Holden, G. (2003). *Guide to Network Defense and Countermeasures*. Boston, MA: Course Technology.

Hucaby, D. (2005). *Cisco ASA and PIX Firewall Handbook*. Indianapolis, IN: Cisco Press.

IPv4 Address Report. (n.d.). In *IPv4 Address Report*. Retrieved from http://www.potaroo.net/tools/ipv4/.

Kurose, J. F., & Ross, K. W. (2001). *Computer Networking, A Tpo-Down Approach Featuring the Internet*. Boston, MA: Addison Wesley Longman.

Lin, Yang-Dar, Hwang, Ren-Hung, & Baker, F. (2012). *Computer Networks: An Open Source Approach*. New York, NY: McGraw-Hill

Maiwald, E. (2004). *Fundamentals of Network Security*. Burr Ridge, IL: McGraw-Hill Technology Education.

Northcutt, S., Zeltser, L., Winters, S., Kent, K., & Ritchey, R. W. (2005). *Inside Network Perimeter Security* (2nd ed.). Indianapolis, IN: Sams Publishing.

Oppenheimer, P. (2010). *Developing Network Security Strategies*. Indianapolis, IN: Cisco Press.

Panko, R. R. (2004). *Corporate Computer and Network Security*. Upper Saddle River, NJ: Prentice Hall.

Pfleeger, C. P., & Pfleeger, S. L. (2003). *Security in Computing* (3rd ed.). Upper Saddle River, NJ: Prentice Hall.

Santos, O. (2007). *End-to-End Network Security: Defense-in-Depth*. Indianapolis, IN: Cisco Press.

Stallings, W. (2003). *Cryptography and Network Security – Principles and Practices* (3rd ed.). Upper Saddle River, NJ: Prentice Hall.

Tett, M. (June 29, 2009). *The best firewall is....* In ZDNET, retrieved from http://www.zdnet.com.au/the-best-firewall-is-339296782.htm?omnRef=http%3A%2F%2Fwww.all-internet-security.com%2Ftop_10_firewall_software.html

Waxer, C. (April 12, 2007). *The Top 5 Internal Security Threats*. In ITSECURITY. Retrieved from http://www.itsecurity.com/features/the-top-5-internal-security-threats-041207/.

Whitman, M. E., & Mattord, H. J. (2003). *Principles of Information Security*. Boston, MA: Course Technology.

Whitman, M. E., & Mattord, H. J. (2004). *Management of Information Security. Boston, MA: Course Technology. Further Readings Ciampa, M. (2009). Security+ Guide to Network Security Fundamentals* (3rd ed.). Boston, MA: Course Technology.

Whitman, M. E., Mattord, H. J., Austin, R., & Holden, G. (2008). *Guide to Firewalls and Network Security*. Boston, MA: Course Technology.

KEY TERMS AND DEFINITIONS

Demilitarized Zone (DMZ): A separate network from the enterprise internal network to host servers that provide resources to general Internet community, typically web server and DNS server.

Firewall: software application or dedicated hardware device to filter network traffic.

Network Address Translation: Technique to convert outgoing IP packets from the internal private IP address to external public IP address.

Packet Filtering: Also called stateless packet filtering, a packet filtering technique by inspecting incoming packets individually.

Proxy Server: a server forwarding the requests from clients to another host on behalf of the clients.

Server Farm: A network area inside a corporate network where enterprise servers are centrally located.

Stateful Packet Inspection (SPI): Packet inspection technology that keeps state of network connection with information at the transport layer, incoming packets are examined to see if they belong to an existing connection.

Virtual Private Network (VPN): A secure network between two private networks by establishing an encrypted tunnel through the public Internet.

Section 3
Risk Assessment and Management

Chapter 9
Risk Assessment and Real Time Vulnerability Identification in IT Environments

Laerte Peotta de Melo
University of Brasilia, Brazil

Paulo Roberto Lira Gondim
University of Brasilia, Brazil

ABSTRACT

Contrary to static models of risk analysis, the authors propose a pro-active framework for identifying vulnerabilities and assessing risk in real-time. Instead of searching for vulnerabilities from an external point of view, where the information is obtained by simply exploring a digital asset (computational system composed of hardware and software), the authors propose that software agents (sensors) capable of providing application, configuration and location information be incorporated into assets. Any observed changes, such as physical location, software update or installation, hardware modifications, changes in security policy and others, will be immediately reported by the agent, in a pro-active manner, to a central repository. It is possible to assess risk in a certain environment comparing databases of rules and known vulnerabilities with information about each asset, collected by the sensors and stored in the central repository.

INTRODUCTION

Risk analysis may be extremely complex and is directly dependent on the proper planning and prior knowledge of the technological environment in which the analysis will be made, and as such, it is

defined as a process that aims to identify, analyze, reduce or transfer risk. The technological risk analysis tools currently available in the market are highly dependent on proprietary operational systems that tie the "solution" to a single platform. Additionally, these tools base their assessment on collected information regarding past events

DOI: 10.4018/978-1-61350-507-6.ch009

and, consequently, are unable to provide a true real time solution. There is a currently growing preoccupation with information security, resulting in the growth of a new field - technology risk analysis. The role of a technological risk analyst is to identify vulnerabilities, calculate a vulnerability score and verify whether or not the identified vulnerability can potentially affect the company business. If so, he or she must correct the problem in the shortest time possible. At first glance the task seems simple, with few steps to follow; however, the number of vulnerabilities has been increasing exponentially to the point that it has become impossible to identify vulnerabilities in a manual or even semi-automatic manner.

Another point to note in risk analysis is the increasing need for transparency demanded by the market and by regulatory bodies that require corporations to follow strict information security management norms, such as Sarbanes- Oxley (SOX) (Lahti & Lanza, R. P., 2005), Basel Accords I and II, ISO 27001 (IEC/ISO, 2005), ISO 27002 (ISO/IEC, 2005) and BS-7799 (BS, 2001).

The need to adhere to international norms may result in extra costs and, in some cases, loss of competitiveness, albeit typically only in the short term. Medium and long-term effects resulting from the implementation of such norms are clearly beneficial and demonstrate a certain business "maturity" and preparedness that may even attract new investments and increase the trust of stockholders.

Information is the most valuable asset to any organization, be it for-profit or not. A successful attack targeting an organization's digital information assets can not only cause immediate financial losses but can also damage its brand image, having long term effects on its business valuation.

Information security aims at protecting digital information assets and data, guaranteeing the following basic principles:

- **Confidentiality:** ensure that information is only accessed by people or systems who have the proper authorization;
- **Integrity:** ensure that information has not been accidentally or intentionally modified, promptly detecting any unexpected alterations;
- **Authenticity:** ensure that information is genuine, *i.e.* that the party responsible for its generation is really who it claims it is;
- **Availability:** ensure that information is accessible when it is needed;
- **Privacy:** even though it is a complex concept in may be defined, in the realm of information security, as ensuring that each person to whom information is concerned has his or her individuality preserved, given that privacy requirements are usually defined by law;
- **Non-repudiation:** ensuring that a party who generates certain information cannot deny its authenticity.

RELATED WORKS

With regards to the development of this work, we did not identify any previous work that proposed to conduct a risk analysis of information assets in real time, that is to say, at the moment that vulnerability was identified and reported. In this context, we describe below the publications that contributed to meeting our original objective. The information necessary to define risk and security was established in a recent study by Perera and Holsomback. The study further suggested a matrix for risk analysis following the framework. It also provided broad definitions and discussions of the topic and incorporated views of others (literature review) into the discussion to support, refute or demonstrate its position on the topic.

The authors also proposed a risk management system based on IRMA. However, this system is limited in that risk input must always be done manually; consequently, there is always the need for a risk analyst to input information.

A study by Fussell and Field identified and described methods for risk analysis management. However, similar to that noted by Perera and Holsomback, the described method was limited in that there was no systematic automation for collection of the system data to be used in risk management. The OCTAVE method (Operationally Critical Threat, Asset, and Vulnerability Evaluation) was described in. In this method a team known as "analysis team" manages the process and analyzes information, taking direct action when called for, depending on the situation.

The difficulty in implementing this method is related to the need for a team of people to work exclusively in the analysis of information and risk, so that decisions can be made.

MAIN FOCUS OF THE CHAPTER

As a means of providing information security (as embodied by the principles above) organizations employ a process called *risk management*. It basically consists in determining vulnerabilities and threats to the information resources which a company relies on and identifying the appropriate countermeasures to be taken in order to reduce risk to acceptable levels, depending on the value of the information assets analyzed. Risk analysis and risk assessment are fundamental building blocks for an efficient risk management policy, as they are necessary to obtain a clear and accurate picture of the risk to which the organization's information assets are subject. An efficient risk assessment methodology should be able to detect dynamic changes in risk as the organization's information technology infrastructure evolves during the several stages of information lifecycle. However, due to the extremely volatile nature of certain information assets, it is infeasible for current methods to properly detect rapidly changing vulnerabilities and threats. In order to solve this

problem, we introduce a method for automatic real time risk assessment which is capable of providing accurate and up-to-date information about risk through the use of sensors that will collect local information and store the data in a central repository. Comparisons between the information provided by the sensors and vulnerability information available in databases will permit the identification of vulnerabilities in real-time, facilitating the initiation of correction processes. Moreover, this method eliminates the need for manual inspection, lowering the costs of the risk assessment process and eliminating human errors.

RISK STRUCTURES, ATTACKS AND VULNERABILITIES

Risk may be defined differently depending on the specific situation where risk exists. It can be generally defined as the likelihood that a physical situation which can potentially cause damage happens due to the existence of a vulnerability during a period of time.

Risk is considered an uncertain event which happens at an uncertain date independently of the involved person's will, being a random element which may affect regular activities.

Risk management is described by ISO 27001 standard published in 2005, which introduces basic principles and guidelines for the implementation and operation of information security risk management processes regarding global business risks.

The ISO 27001 standard also defines the basic strategy for risk assessment at an organization, which consists in:

- Identifying a risk assessment method which is adequate to the Information Security Management System (ISMS) and the business and legal requirements for information security;
- Develop criteria for accepting risk and identifying acceptable levels of risk;

- Apply the selected risk assessment method ensuring that the risk assessment process outputs results which can be reproduced and compared;

It is also recommended in the ISO 27001 standard that the following information is determined:

- The information assets in the context of the ISMS and their owners;
- The threats to these assets;
- The vulnerabilities which may be exploited by the threats;
- The impacts on confidentiality, integrity and availability;

After obtaining information regarding the assets it is necessary to analyze and evaluate risk from the point of view of impact on business, considering the following aspects:

- Evaluate the impact that a security breach would have on the organization's business, considering the loss of integrity, reliability or availability of assets;
- Determine the likelihood of a security breach happening, considering the existing threats and vulnerabilities, the impact on assets and the security measures and controls already implemented;
- Estimate the risk levels;
- Determine whether the risk is acceptable or if it needs to be addressed according to the risk acceptance criteria defined before.

The ultimate goal in risk management is eliminating risks. However, it is not always possible to completely eliminate risks because of several factors such as: lack of adequate corrections for vulnerabilities and threats, impact on business and production processes (making them inefficient), negative impacts on business and others. When it is not possible to eliminate a given risk,

it should be addressed employing the following countermeasures:

- Apply adequate risk controls;
- Identify and accept risk, clearly specifying and following risk acceptance criteria and complying to the organization's information security policies;
- Avoid risk;
- Transfer risks inherent to business to third parties, such as service providers and insurance companies.

In order to provide accurate information on the overall risk faced by an organization's digital assets, the guidelines presented in the ISO 27001 standard propose periodic risk assessment procedures, providing up to date information about risk. Such periodic risk assessments should be conducted at planned and regular intervals considering changes in the following infrastructure components:

- Organization;
- Technology;
- Business processes and goals;
- Threats;
- Efficiency of deployed risk controls;
- External events, such as changes in law, contracts or social aspects.

Risk Matrix

As risk represents and uncertain random event, there are actions that can be taken in order to reduce the impact of such an event on the continuity of business and production. Such actions take into consideration the information gathered about risk, represented as random variables or fixed values. The main variables that represent risk are, as represented in Figure 1: probability, severity and relevance. Risk can be measured by multiplying probability, severity and relevance variables according to Table 1.

Figure 1. Risk Estimation

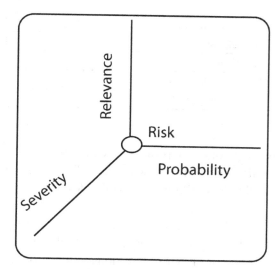

Risk may be represented by a relation between the frequency with which it happens and the consequences generated. Therefore, in order to estimate risk it is also necessary to define variables representing frequency and the consequences generated by each vulnerability. Risk is then given a subjective classification referred to as a *score*.

There is not a clear and objective definition of frequency and consequence of risk, since it is related to an uncertain event. However, a subjective evaluation of risk may mitigate it or even completely eliminate it. Risk has uncertain probabilities of happening, which may be classified according to the criteria proposed in Table 2.

Due to the subjective nature of risk assessment, a risk assessment conducted in one organization may yield values drastically different from the values determined in another organization with similar vulnerabilities and threats but different business process and goals. In other words, a situation involving the same vulnerabilities, threats and digital assets may have a high risk score in one organization, while it is given a low risk score when considering the context of a different organization.

Table 3 shows the categories of risk severity and their detailed description. A given risk may have different severities depending on the organization. This severity may be negligible

Table 1. Risk Matrix

Item	Severity	Probability	Relevance
1	Unavailable	Unavailable	Unavailable
2	Negligible	Negligible	Negligible
3	Marginal	Remote	Small
4	Critical	Improbable	Moderate
5	Catastrophic	Probable	Serious

Table 2. Risk Probability

Item	Category	Description
1	Extremely Remote	It is possible to happen, but very unlikely
2	Remote	Hardly happens
3	Improbable	Has a small probability of happening
4	Probable	Expected to happen
5	Frequent	Expected to happen several times

Table 3. Risk Severity

Item	Category	Description
1	Negligible	Without losses or with negligible losses
2	Marginal	Controllable or low cost losses
3	Critical	High losses, should be corrected immediately
4	Catastrophic	Permanent losses, corrections are inefficient

or low, varying up to catastrophic, which represents a situation where the actual happening of an event may severely affect the business and production processes.

It is important to clearly define the concept of risk and its several characteristics in order to understand how it may affect an organization. The risk is as high as the probability of a breach happening, while its impact depends on the breach. Considering these factors, which determine how risk should be addressed, several actions are taken in order to mitigate or even eliminate risk. Clearly it is impossible, inefficient or simply too expensive to completely eliminate some kinds of risk. In such cases risk countermeasures are taken and controls are put in places in order to restrict or reduce the impact of a given risk on the organization's business.

Logical Vulnerabilities

Vulnerabilities are weakness or points of failure that can be exploited in a information system, considering that such systems are composed both by digital assets and, specially, people, which may be the source of most vulnerabilities. Vulnerability analysis is the first step of risk analysis and management, aiming to identify the weaknesses and problems of an organization's digital assets.

Logical vulnerabilities mainly comprise software glitches and failures that may be exploited in several ways (either locally or remotely) in order to compromise information security. Logical vulnerabilities that may be exploited remotely represent a greater risk, since anyone may take

advantage of them, posing a greater threat to the organization. Some of the methods for exploring logical vulnerabilities are listed below:

- **Exploits:** Automatic computer programs whose goal is to obtain any higher privileges or unexpected actions in the system;
- **DNS Poisoning:** Consists of altering domain name system tables, forcing a given name to be resolved to an arbitrary IP address and redirecting traffic to arbitrary hosts;
- **Buffer Overflow:** Basically consists in abusing the lack of buffer bounds checking in poorly programmed application forcing the execution of arbitrary code, possibly with higher privileges than a user would normally have;
- **Privileges Escalation**: Obtaining higher privileges through illegitimate means for a common system user;
- **Denial of Service (DoS):** DoS attacks work by overloading system resources causing it to be malfunction or disrupting regular operation. Such attacks may be conducted locally or remotely by sending several service requests to a given system.

Physical Vulnerabilities

Physical security is as important as logical security, since there is hardly any logical security mechanisms which will hold if physical security is breached. If an attacker is able to compromise physical security obtaining full physical access to

Figure 2. Vulnerability Lifecycle

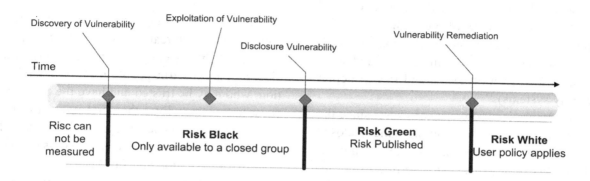

digital assets, he may easily compromise logical security using the appropriate tools (*e.g.* an attacker with physical access to a Unix computer may reboot it with a live CD and alter its /etc/passwd file).

Monitors and other devices irradiate electromagnetic fields which may be captured and interpreted remotely in attacks known as Tempest or van Eck phreaking. Installing metal shields that function as a Faraday Cage, stopping electromagnetic fields from escaping the perimeter, may easily eliminate such vulnerability. On the other hand, someone looking over an operator's shoulders or eavesdropping on conversations can easily obtain information.

Cleaning teams may cause as much problems as hackers, since cleaning personnel has legitimate access to the whole building, being able to enter even the server rooms. Even if they do not attempt any attack or malicious action, they may accidentally disrupt services by accidentally turning off servers or even cutting power.

It is important to bear in mind that the protection level required depends on what needs to be protected and its value to the organization. It is also necessary to observe the sophistication of a potential attacker and the kind of information he would be willing to obtain.

Vulnerability Lifecycle

Every vulnerability has a well-defined finite lifecycle where every phase affects directly the risk associated to it. Figure 2 depicts five distinct points in a timeline which characterize vulnerability lifecycle: discovery, public disclosure, proof of concept, exploitation and correction.

It is difficult to estimate the time before a vulnerability is discovered since it is influenced by several factors such as: motivation, software or hardware quality and software utilization, since the probability of discovering a vulnerability in a highly used software is higher.

The time of discovery and public disclosure of a vulnerability is considered as the time for the creation of an exploit, when a closed group experiments with the vulnerability and develops ways to exploit it. During this time a proof of concept (POC) is usually created. During this phase the vulnerability is not known to users or vendors, thus being assigned an unknown risk. This phase is called a dark risk phase.

The period of time between public disclosure of a vulnerability and the issue of a correction by vendors is called a green risk phase. However, large vendors often have teams testing their products and looking for such vulnerabilities before they are publicly disclosed or even procure information on vulnerabilities from specific vulnerability analysis teams. Such actions eliminate the green risk phase and lower the risk associated with products.

Public disclosure of vulnerabilities and proofs of concept is generally done through public security forums, communities and web-sites, such as Securityfocus[1] and ISS[2] (Internet security systems).

Disclosure is a very critical phase, since the number of attack attempts aiming at the disclosed vulnerability will grow significantly. Both malicious users with a clear purpose of stealing information or disrupting services and people who want to test the new vulnerability are prone to conduct attacks to the systems it affects. During this phase information about the vulnerability becomes publicly available through independent communication channels, being analyzed by security experts and information security professionals.

The period after a correction to a vulnerability is made available by vendors or third-parties is called a mild risk phase. In other words, the organization may be using a product that is affected by a vulnerability already corrected, but it may not know that it is vulnerable. In order to eliminate the risk of being attacked through such vulnerability, the organization should check whether its systems are affected by it and apply the correction.

Threats

A threat is any circumstance or event that can potentially cause an impact on the confidentiality, integrity or availability of information systems used by an organization.

Threats are constantly present in any organization's operations. Any business process, digital information assets and systems are always subject to threats, i.e. there is always an event that can negatively affect them. Threats may be malicious when there is a clear intention of causing losses to the organization or they may be accidental when some kind of human mistake or uncontrolled event causes losses.

Types of Threats

Threats are basically classified in two categories, namely: internal threats and external threats.

Internal threats are the most dangerous type, since they are posed by people inside the organization, who may be trusted and have the power to cause more losses. Even though it may not seems intuitive, people inside an organization have full knowledge of critical assets, have access to confidential information and full knowledge of the organization's internal structure and processes. Hence, using previous information, they have a greater potential for causing losses and succeeding in malicious activities.

External threats may represent the main risk for organizations whose information systems are directly connected to the Internet or any external third-party networks. People for outside the organization remotely conducting malicious actions and attacks are more constrained than insiders, which limits the types of attacks and the possibility of success. External people who may pose a threat to an organization's systems are mainly classified in the following categories:

- **Hackers:** Information security professionals who have a deep knowledge of networking protocols, programming and network operating systems. They may spend a long time studying their target when motivated by curiosity. Hackers will carefully analyze each information system in an organization, determining which vulnerabilities are present and how to exploit them, possibly developing new tools and exploits in order to achieve their goals.
- **Crackers:** May have the same knowledge of hackers, but are motivated by financial profits and not by mere curiosity or personal satisfaction. Crackers act criminally, disrupting regular operations or stealing information that is then put for sale. They will use any available information and method

to gain access to a network. Those individuals are employed by organized crime in order to obtain information that would be impossible to be obtained otherwise.

- **Script Kiddies:** People without advanced knowledge who basically use automated penetration tools, which they do not create. This type of attacker may cause great damage as they do not aim at an specific target, trying to hit the biggest number of systems instead. They seek recognition as hackers, thus being motivated to cause as much damage as possible.
- **Terrorists:** Being an active part of cyber war, digital terrorist aim at governmental systems or at important organizations. Their attacks can be highly sophisticated and may have ideological or political motivations, representing a new form of rioting.

There are several kinds of threats that may compromise a network or system:

- **Physical threats:** disasters, bombs, fire, power outage, flooding, etc;
- **Human threats:** penetration, stealing, bribery, espionage or accidents;
- **Software threats:** Virus, worms, and Trojan horses.

It is necessary to create models for determining which kind of threats has greater probability of affecting an organization.

Threat analysis procedures should be continuously and periodically executed, not being restricted to specific situations. It is hard to identify all threats in only one analysis, since threats are constantly changing and evolving.

An organization's infrastructure is dynamic, undergoing constant alterations. Such alterations may be the deployment of new equipment or systems and also the decommissioning and changing of such digital assets. Greater changes occur

Figure 3. Threat Analysis Cycle

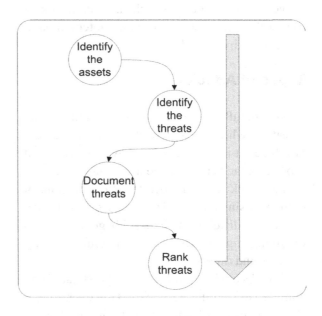

when business processes and internal structure are altered.

Figure 3 depicts the main steps necessary to create a threat analysis process. Assets identification is the first step in an efficient threat analysis, since it is necessary to thoroughly know the environment in order to manage it. The next step is identifying the threats and factors that may compromise the organization's infrastructure and security.

It is necessary to keep detailed documentation of every threat identified in this process. This documentation may consist of reports that define the critical point to be taken into consideration in a centralized manner, which makes it easier to search and access this information.

The most important aspect of threat analysis is the correct classification of the information concerning threats. Threats must be classified in order to prioritize the most critical ones, which represent a greater risk to the organization.

The threat classification process must consider the impact that a given threat may have on the organization's infrastructure. In case that a threat doesn't cause significant losses to an organization it, may not be viable to take actions in order to prevent it, since the cost of the actions would be higher than the cost of correcting potential damage caused by such threat.

Types of Attacks

In order to fully understand the vulnerabilities and threats to which an organization's infrastructure is subject, it is necessary to analyse the different types of attacks that can be used against it.

An attack is any deliberate action that aims at compromising an organization's security. It may consist of different actions with goals such as obtaining higher privileges, bypassing security policies and others.

Attacks are becoming more sophisticated and complex during the past years. However, due to the availability of automated tools and frameworks, the attackers are not required to have all the knowledge necessary to perform such attacks. This also leads to the automated execution of mass attacks, focusing several networks or systems at once without requiring human intervention.

The growth in the number of attacks happened not only because of automation but also because of the sheer growth of the Internet itself. With more systems connected to the Internet, attackers have more targets and while more critical services become connected to it, attackers may profit from successful attacks.

Any organization may be attacked at any time through equipment's connected both to the internet and to its local network. Any network system may be used as a gateway to attack the whole organization, compromising systems that wouldn't normally be vulnerable.

Passive Attacks

This type of attack mainly consists of espionage and communications monitoring, aiming at capturing network traffic and communications in general. Eavesdropping attacks may capture emails, file transfers and other data, which may leak confidential information. For this reason, it is important to take actions and countermeasures in order to preserve the confidentiality of data being exchanged in a network, be it local or the internet. Even if the captured data are encrypted, the collected information may be used to determine IP addressing and hosts access patterns.

Eavesdropping and monitoring attacks are extremely subtle, since they do not generate traffic pattern or cause anomalous behavior in the network. Simply capturing network traffic and storing it for further posterior analysis, these attacks do not noticeably disrupt regular network operations. This makes eavesdropping and monitoring attacks difficult to detect, reducing the countermeasures that could be used against them. Bearing this in mind, it is clear that the best defense against such attacks is prevention and correction.

Active Attacks

Active attacks are based on proactive modification and/or injection of data into a network. These attacks can be classified in mainly four categories, namely: impersonation, replay, altering and denial of service.

Impersonation involves an entity who forges another entity's identity in order to obtain unauthorized access to resources. In such an attack, a malicious user can try to forge an authentication procedure or any credentials that would allow him to obtain higher privileges or to perform unauthorized actions.

In a replay attack, the attacker captures certain network packets and then replays them in the network in order to obtain access to certain resources or to perform unauthorized actions. This type of attack may be used as a building block for more complex attacks. Proper countermeasures should be taken to mitigate these attacks, guaranteeing the authenticity of data transmitted or received in the network.

Altering attacks aim at modifying arbitrary messages or certain parts of messages in order to retard or reorder communication.

Denial of service attacks aim at disrupting regular service operation, making a given service unavailable. Usually, these attacks are based on overloading a server with excessive service requests rendering it unable to respond to legitimate requests, which makes the service unavailable. This attack can also be used as a building block for more sophisticated attacks.

Secure Environments

Security is directly related to the protection of information and assets considered to be valuable to an organization and its business. Such information and assets comprise both material, human, intellectual resources that are important to an organization's business.

Anything that may compromise a system or cause anomalous behavior resulting in losses should be considered a threat. The exact definition of losses and security breaches depends on the system that is being protected and it's important to the organization. Due to the large number of different systems, vulnerabilities and threats that may be present in an information technology environment, it is extremely difficult to guarantee its security.

Making a system secure normally implies in certain trade-offs in terms of usability and performance. The complexity of information security mechanism and countermeasures causes an increase in system loads and the learning curves for secure systems. It is necessary to consider the relations between security and efficiency, given system characteristics such as access media, user interface, communication complexity and computational requirements.

The first phase in designing secure information technology infrastructures comprises not only budget and logical security plans including potential countermeasures but also an assessment of the infrastructure in order to identify the assets and their value. Such an assessment must be conducted considering the organization's business and the importance of each digital asset in its business processes. The following topics should be considered:

- Identify the most important assets related to business;
- Classify the importance of each asset in relation to the business processes;
- Identify the threats to which the assets are subject;
- Identify the vulnerabilities that affect the assets.

Each security control implemented in the assets aims at reducing their inherent risk of being affected by the identified threats through their vulnerabilities. The adopted countermeasures should consider the following topics:

- Identify what needs to be protected;
- Evaluate the main risks to which the asset is subject;
- Develop efficient processes and countermeasures to eliminate the risks.

Security is clearly an important problem for all organizations that rely on digital information assets to do business. As attacks grow more complex (but yet require a low level of expertise from attackers who use automated tools) the number of attacks performed grows each year, threatening the security of most organizations, which are constantly increasing their reliance on networked systems. Therefore, security has become a source of constant preoccupation to information technology professionals and great majority of organizations in the world, which are constantly seeking better and more efficient security solutions and countermeasures. However, it will never be possible to obtain 100% secure systems without compromising usability efficiency, requiring careful analysis of the necessary trade-offs in designing secure environments.

RISK ANALYSIS METHODS AND FRAMEWORKS

Several risk analysis methods and frameworks were developed in order to efficiently and accurately assess the risk related to specific environments and propose proper countermeasures and controls to reduce the impact of threats. This section discusses the main risk analysis methods and frameworks proposed in current literature.

OCTAVE: The Operationally Critical Threat, Asset, and Vulnerability Evaluation

The OCTAVE (Operationally Critical Threat, Asset, and Vulnerability Evaluation) risk analysis framework was developed based on the guidelines of the ISO 27002 standard. It was developed in 2003 by the SEI (Software Engineering Institute) of Carnegie Mellon University under a grant by the American Department of Defense with the goal of mitigating risk in digital business environments.

The main principle is the creation of a risk analysis team, which is responsible for managing risk related to all the information assets in an organization. This team takes direct actions in order to reduce risk, making decisions suited to every specific situation. The method is based on the implementing the necessary countermeasures according to the information obtained in the risk analysis process.

The actual deployment of the OCTAVE framework relies heavily on the risk analysis, specially on its coordinators. Among the responsibilities of the team are the following main topics:

- Identify the important information assets that should be monitored;

- Focus on the analysis of the assets that are most important for the organization's business;
- Identify the vulnerabilities to which the most critical assets are subject according to the main threats identified;
- Determine the impact of each threat on the most critical assets, quantifying the losses on business that may happen in case the security of these assets is compromised;
- Develop security policy and strategies aiming at reducing risk and mitigating possible attacks.

This framework is composed of three different subsequent phases, namely: Organizational View, Technological View and Strategy. Each phase provides information for the execution of the posterior phase, forming a risk analysis process that must be completed in order to properly address the threats and risks in an organization's infrastructure.

Organizational View

All of the OCTAVE deployment phases are of great importance to the correct utilization of this framework and should be executed focusing on the specific characteristics of an organization. In this phase, which is the initial phase, it is expected to obtain information on the information assets of the organization and the vulnerabilities and threats to which they are subject. The risk analysis team should be created in order to determine the most important and critical assets related to the organization's business. Finally, the team should create a report for each asset, containing information about vulnerabilities, threats and risk. This report is called an asset profile, and every asset should have its own profile. The reports and information obtained in this phase are used as input for the second phase. Hence, it is important to obtain accurate information in this phase, since it will be used as a diagnosis of the organization's infrastructure, which is crucial to define the countermeasures and risk control mechanisms to be implemented.

Technological View

In this phase, the information gathered in the first phase and the asset profile are processed in order to identify the vulnerabilities and threats to which the assets are subject. It mainly consists in two steps:

1. Identify the assets which are critical for the organization's business and that would cause the highest impact in case of a security breach. This should be conducted according to criteria defined and agreed the risk analysis team.
2. Evaluate critical assets using methods and tools to verify which vulnerabilities are present in them. The results of this step must be contained in the asset profile and reports generated at this phase.

Strategy

This phase mainly consists in analyzing the risks to which the critical assets are subject and propose strategies and plans to mitigate this risk or eliminate it. The team should propose countermeasures and controls that help reducing the risk of security breach affecting these assets and present a full security strategy. This phase mainly consists of the following steps:

- **Risk analysis:** determine the risk associated to each critical asset in the infrastructure according to the vulnerabilities and threats identified in previous phases.
- **Security Strategy:** Develop security policies and plans aiming at reducing risk and mitigating attacks based on best practices and standards such as the ISO 27002 and ISO 27001.

According to OCATVE's technical manual, the method may be divided into three main topics:

- Development of a threat profile detailing the organization's infrastructure and the threats associated to them;
- Vulnerability Identification: evaluating the infrastructure and determining the critical assets and the vulnerabilities that affect them;
- Development of a security strategy and plans: This is considered the most important part, since it involves the definition of countermeasures, security policies and actions to be taken in order to reduce risk and deal with security issues.

The OCTAVE framework nicely embodies the guidelines proposed in the ISO 27001 standard, focusing on managerial aspects of information security (Figure 4). It considers assets identification, vulnerabilities assessment and the proposal of strategies and countermeasures as a continuous process and not only an effort executed once. This fits nicely into the purposes of information security, since dynamically changing infrastructure, business process and related security requirements need to be continuously evaluated and analyzed in order to efficiently provide information security.

One characteristic that makes this framework impractical is the necessity of a dedicated team to conduct the risk analysis process and take decisions concerning strategy and countermeasures.

CORAS—Risk Assessment of Security Critical Systems

Project CORAS (Risk Assessment of Security Critical Systems) started in January 2001 and was finished in September 2003 by a group of several European corporations. The technical group in charge of the coordination of this project is the SINTEF (The Foundation for Scientific and

Figure 4. OCTAVE and information security processes

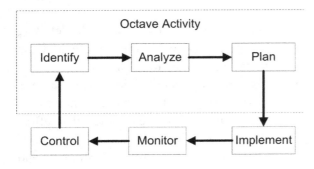

Industrial Research) of the Norwegian Institute of Technology, while Telenor is responsible for administrative management. A The CORAS framework comprises the following components:

- A state of the art risk analysis methods that integrates different risk modeling and assessment techniques;
- Risk analysis based on UML models;
- An application that supports the risk analysis method and provides two repositories: an analysis repository and a refactoring repository, which can be used for reusing experience and information acquired in previous analysis;
- XML based file formats for risk analysis;
- Report generation for consolidating vulnerability information.

The CORAS framework structure is divided in four parts:

1. **Terminology:** Defines important concepts and words to be used in the contexts of security, risk analysis and system documentation;
2. **Library:** It is divided in entities, storage structures and classification systems;
3. **Methods:** Consists in risk analysis techniques, comprising processes and languages used in risk analysis procedures;

4. **Tool:** Applications that implement the risk analysis methods automating and accelerating the risk analysis processes.

AGRIS System

The AGRIS (a Portuguese acronym for Analysis and Management of Security Risks) project was developed by the computer science center of the Federal University of Rio de Janeiro, Brazil. The goal of this project is creating a software tool to support information security management, including threat assessment, vulnerabilities analysis and business impact of threats. The tool generates technical and managerial reports, offering resources for the information security team and managers. This tool has the following main features:

- **Assets visualization:** It is possible to individually visualize information about an specific asset, allowing the analyst to focus on specific vulnerabilities and characteristics;
- **Asset value definition:** Since an asset's value or importance to an organization's business may vary according to different contexts, it is possible to define an asset's value dynamically and individually;
- **Definition of security policy per asset:** The tool allows analyst to define a security policy for each asset being analyzed;
- **Templates:** The system includes many templates that accelerate work by modeling common situations;
- **Benchmarks and adherence:** The tool allows the analysts to make comparisons between an organization's scenario and other scenarios through benchmarks. It also supports tests to determine the adherence to certain standards or pre-established models;
- **Report Generation:** generation of technical and managerial reports that support decision making of both information tech-

nology professionals and business managers. Technical reports include information on the assets, threats, vulnerabilities and risk, while business management reports provide information on the cost of information security solutions;

- **Vulnerability control and correction:** AGRIS may operate by importing data from vulnerability analysis tools, allowing analysts to verify the vulnerabilities and security controls present in the environment. The tool uses this information to provide risk estimation and suggestions of security countermeasures that would correct the vulnerability or reduce risk (based on vulnerability alerts and common knowledge bases). It also allows analysts to add new countermeasures and security controls to its database in case no document related to the vulnerability being analysed is found. All the information concerning vulnerabilities is kept in a central server, which is synchronized with the client application. The tool also provides an investment estimation for the countermeasures proposed, relating each cost to the risk reduced.

The AGRIS tool is composed of three main modules, namely: initialization, processing and management.

1. The initialization module is responsible for user authentication, controlling permissions to execute the tool and modify asset information. It also verifies the integrity of the databases and the information previously stored within the system;

2. The processing module is used to assess the environment, verifying the vulnerabilities and security controls currently present. It is also responsible for loading the vulnerability databases, estimating risk and generating plots. It allows analysts to verify compliance with certain standards and models, running

benchmarks and generating managerial and technical reports;

3. The management module is responsible for the system administration tasks of the tool, such as managing configurations, vulnerability databases, users and permissions.

The method implemented in AGRIS is based on the CRAMM (Government's Risk Analysis and Management Method) which is a framework developed by CCTA (Central Computer and Telecommunications Agency). This method was originally developed in England during the eighties and remains a popular method in the UK.

This method is based on risk mitigation by focusing on identifying assets, their value to the organization's business and suggesting possible solutions or countermeasures that eliminate or reduce risk. However, this method requires tools users (risk analysts) to have previous training or experience with the tool, which may be undesired. This method estimates risk based on vulnerability, threat and exploitation probability, taking into consideration these variables to obtain a risk score.

It latest available version is 5.1, and was launched in 2005. In this version, the guidelines proposed in the standard BS 7799 were incorporated to the tool.

It is crucial to provide application and tools that implement a given risk analysis framework, since manually implementing or executing most frameworks is too complex.

Due to the diversity and complexity of most information technology systems and environments in different organizations, a framework must be dynamically adaptable to the subtleties of each environment without the need to modify application code.

The risk estimation method is of great importance in the risk analysis process, since it must allow the analysts to obtain a clear classification and quantification of the risk associated with different assets, which are subject to different vulnerabilities and threats.

Figure 5. CVSS

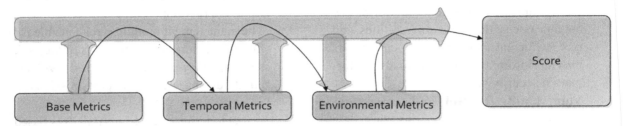

Given the extremely dynamical nature of systems development and security, new vulnerabilities are constantly being discovered, affecting several products, even if they have been exhaustively tested. Hence, it is important that risk analysis tools offer the capability of updating vulnerability information and consequently risk assessment data according to the evolution of vulnerabilities.

Common Vulnerability Scoring System and Common Vulnerabilities and Exposures

Various information security departments such as the NIST (National Institute of Standards and Technology), FIRST (Forum of Incident Response and Security Teams) and CERT (Computer Emergency Response Team), among others, have created a standard to measure and quantify software vulnerabilities, known as Common Vulnerability Scoring System (CVSS). Historically, the industry has used various scoring methods to determine software vulnerability. However, the criteria or processes used were not detailed, which has caused serious management problems to users.

The Common Vulnerabilities and Exposures (CVE) database is the result of collaborative efforts between various entities working with information security, such as the Sans Institute, Cancert, CERT, among others. Massachusetts Institute of Technology's Digital Computer Laboratory (MITRE) is the main keeper of CVE. Given that this is a collaborative project, no pre-specified

contributions are expected. However, financial contributions as well as assistance in disseminating information are permitted.

CVSS utilizes the following three basic metrics to calculate the score of a given vulnerability (Figure 5):

1. **Base metrics:** Contain the attributes that are intrinsic to all vulnerabilities;
2. **Temporal metrics:** Contain the vulnerabilities that evolve with time and are dependent their lifecycle;
3. **Environmental metrics:** Represent those characteristics that are unique to the corporate environment in which they are being considered.

Base Metrics

The basic metrics capture the vulnerability characteristics that remain constant with time and over different environments. The Access Vector, Access Complexity, and Authentication metrics are used to determine how the vulnerability accessed and whether or any special conditions are required to exploit it. The three impact metrics determine the impact of a vulnerability and how it affects an information technology asset or resource. The impact metrics are divided into confidentiality, integrity and availability. For example, a successfully exploited vulnerability may cause a confidentiality breach but no compromise of availability.

The product vendor usually supplies some of the base metrics. Six base metrics are used together with temporal and environmental metrics in order to obtain the final risk estimation:

- **Access Complexity:** measures the complexity of the attacks required to exploit a vulnerability in a certain asset;
- **Access Vector:** indicates whether a vulnerability can be exploited locally or remotely;
- **Authentication:** determines whether an attacker would have to authenticate (and the quantity of times it would have to authenticate) in order to exploit a vulnerability;
- **Confidentiality Impact:** measures the impact on information confidentiality;
- **Integrity Impact:** measures the impact on information integrity;
- **Availability Impact:** measures the impact on information availability.

Temporal Metrics

Threats caused by vulnerabilities may dynamically change as new information becomes available over time. CVSS considers three factors, namely: confirmation of the technical details of a vulnerability, the available corrections for the vulnerability and the availability of exploit code or attack techniques. Temporal metrics do not influence the score value since they are optional. The following temporal metrics are considered:

- **Exploitability:** whether or not it is possible to exploit the vulnerability in real world situations;
- **Remediation Level:** indicates the availability of a corrections or patch;
- **Report Confidence:** represents the confidence on the information obtained about the vulnerability.

Environmental Metrics

Environmental metrics are of great importance in this risk scoring system, since they take into con-

sideration the influence that different contexts and business processes have on the risk assessed for different infrastructures and information systems.

The environmental metrics are used to model the importance of each digital information asset to the organization's business process. Since risk and threats classification may vary for different business and processes, it is important to consider the subtleties of the organization's business in the risk analysis and estimation process. The accurate utilization of these metrics is of great importance to risk analysis, being crucial to the correct estimation of risk scores.

MANAGEMENT OF RESOURCES

According to the ISO 27001 normative of 2005, all informational resources of a company must be identified and managed, based on determined controls that must be previously established. Ideally, informational resources should be documented and categorized according to importance level. The importance of the resource, in case it is compromised, must also be considered. An effective risk analysis starts from the premise that all technological infrastructures have been identified.

Risk management is a continuous process that must always be reevaluated to identify inconsistencies. The process of risk analysis itself can be divided into six parts (Figure 6).

It is reasonable to assume that it would be viable to implement the above-mentioned points in a small to medium size network (of up to 1000 machines). Unfortunately, as soon as the data collection process has been finished and risk scoring initiated, the analysis would already be outdated- that is, the assessment would already represent a past situation. Every passing minute makes risk analysis less efficient. As such, risk analysis may provide a false sense of security. The proposed framework addresses this issue by allowing a real time analysis of the known vulnerabilities and the latest inventory changes.

Figure 6. Risk management processes

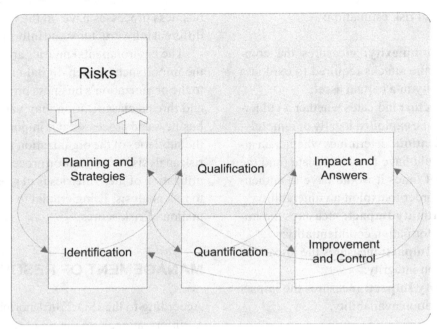

Inventory Procedures

The speed, at which information can be collected and updated, as a result of constant changes, is the key to successful risk analysis. Ideally, inventory tools used should meet the following requirements:

- Client/server architecture support;
- Store all the information in a centralized database;
- Include support for multiple platforms;
- Provide access to information at any time;
- Consume the minimum amount necessary of resources to maintain the proper functioning of the client;
- Have the capacity to inform, even if, for whatever reason, the client is disabled;
- Have the ability to be reconfigured at any moment, in a global user independent manner.

Apart from these initial requirements, the tool must also have the capacity to collect diverse information for the inventory; all the information should be sent to the central database. Essential information includes:

- Version of the current operating system;
- Any corrections made and the respective version of each;
- Information of registered and former users;
- List of installed software and respective versions;
- Verification of installed antivirus systems and updates;
- Information regarding partitions;
- Information regarding the physical location of hardware (information provided by the user);
- List of hardware, such as memory, processor, hard drive, and video card specifications.

Following data collection to obtain the basic characteristics of the IT infrastructure, qualification of each component must then be done, based on the following categories of importance (Table 4).

Once all inventory information has been obtained, it is necessary to qualify each component regarding its importance. This qualification can be obtained by means of a questionnaire that should be responded by managers. In this manner, the company will obtain information regarding the machines/servers that have the greatest impact in case they are compromised, in terms of physical or logical problems. The flow diagram in Figure 7 summarizes the necessary steps for risk analysis data collection from this point forward.

The framework described will be applicable for the following uses:

- Correctly identify all assets and determine their value as well as how critical they are for the company;
- Estimate the probability of the occurrence of a threat and calculate the costs it would entail;
- Identify vulnerable points and establish decisions to minimize or mitigate the risk;
- Create of a strategy to minimize risks.

Framework Proposal

Information from the previously mentioned CVSS and CVE (Common Vulnerabilities and Exposures) databases will be used to populate the internal database (Figure 8), creating a base of vulnerabilities referred to here as central repository.

This information will be cross-checked with the software and hardware data obtained regarding the internal system, creating the basic contents,

Table 4. Important Categories

1	Irrelevant
2	Relevant
3	Important
4	Critical
5	Vital

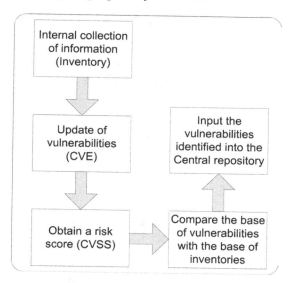

Figure 7. Procedures for Risk Analysis in the context of the proposed framework

which include the IP address of networked machines, installed software's versions, information regarding registered users, type of operating system, hardware specifications (memory, processor, hard drive). The database created from the collected internal information will be referred to as inventory.

The Figure 9 demonstrates the correlation/link between the different information obtained, with CVSS and CVE being maintained by external organizations. The base Inventory and Central Repository is maintained by the company. For this system to be efficient, all of the machines within the domain should have the inventory software sensor installed so as to continuously feed the internal database.

The company should have an established IT policy; if none exists, the company should at minimum draw up "resources usage norms that should followed" by all users within the company. Normatives should contain information regarding:

- Installation and downloading of software, prohibiting users to install any software

Figure 8. CVE/CVSS interaction sensor station

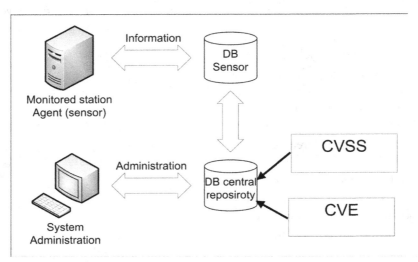

that is not company approved. This will also avoid the installation of unlicensed software;

- Terms of responsibility regarding the use of company technological resources, explaining that it must be work-related;

Figure 9. Risk infrastructure model

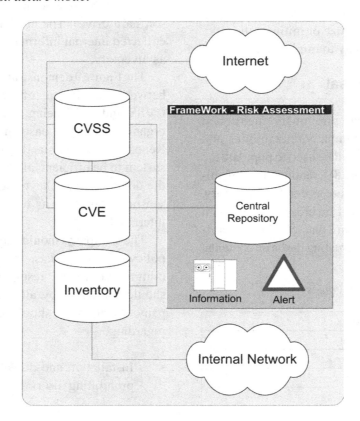

- Definition of mobile resources usage limits(laptops, PDAs, etc.), prohibiting the use of non-company equipment;
- Installation of new technologic resources such that any new equipment must contain the required software and must be inventoried;
- Creation of a login procedure for network users, so that only technological resources that have been inventoried will have access to the local network;
- The development of a dissemination policy so that all employees will be aware of company policies.

Framework Demonstration

The proposed tool was developed in JAVA programming language, with client/server support, where the server permits the visualization through a web browser HTTP protocol. Initial tests used approximately 20 computers, with installed sensor information sent to a central repository.

The information obtained should be displayed or available in a consolidated manner, facilitating the identification of an actual risk resulting from vulnerability, or permitting the visualization of the entire situation.

The various vulnerabilities that have been identified should be assigned to a specific team, initially responsible only for a specific product.

Each team may be responsible for more than one inventoried product. Figure 10 shows a view of the system as seen by the manager. This comprehensive view is only seen by framework managers - framework users have a similar view limited to the products they support (Figure 11).

The system is monitored from the point of view of vulnerabilities (the number of vulnerabilities and the number of products affected).

The framework provides managers with a high level view of products with vulnerabilities and teams that need more attention. Detailed information about teams and/or products can be obtained by managers by selecting the desired team/product (see Figures 10 and 11).

Risk is measured based on the CVSS score and graphically illustrated in the pie charts by the colors red, yellow and green.

Figure 10. Framework manager's perspective of the system

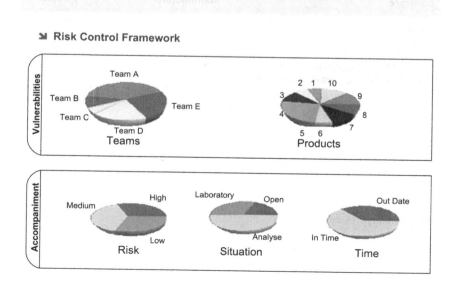

At the moment a framework manager or user takes an action, this action is and must be registered as part of the history of actions taken to resolve the problem.

This facilitates future work as it establishes a minimum knowledge base of procedures already attempted, making it easier to assign and distribute tasks, making the process user independent and auditable.

The history record keeps the dates, actions taken and the name of the person executing the actions. This makes it possible to alter or adjust the vulnerability, through analysis or through laboratory work. It is also important to note the various statuses of the vulnerability situation can be "open", "in the laboratory" or "under analysis". Once the vulnerability is addressed in production,

it is removed from the view. It has been previously demonstrated that even in empirical situations, the mere use of an available correction may result in even greater problems. For this reason, it is recommended that any changes or alterations be tested first in a laboratory situation and only then implemented in a production environment.

Specific Frameworks user´s access to information and system view is limited to the view of his or her team. That is to say, a framework user does not have access to the information of another team (Figure 12) For this reason, the vulnerabilities pie graph is continuous, as the user is associated only to his/her own team. On the other hand, the Products graph is associated with all products that may require intervention and that have had their vulnerabilities inventoried.

Figure 11. Record of an action

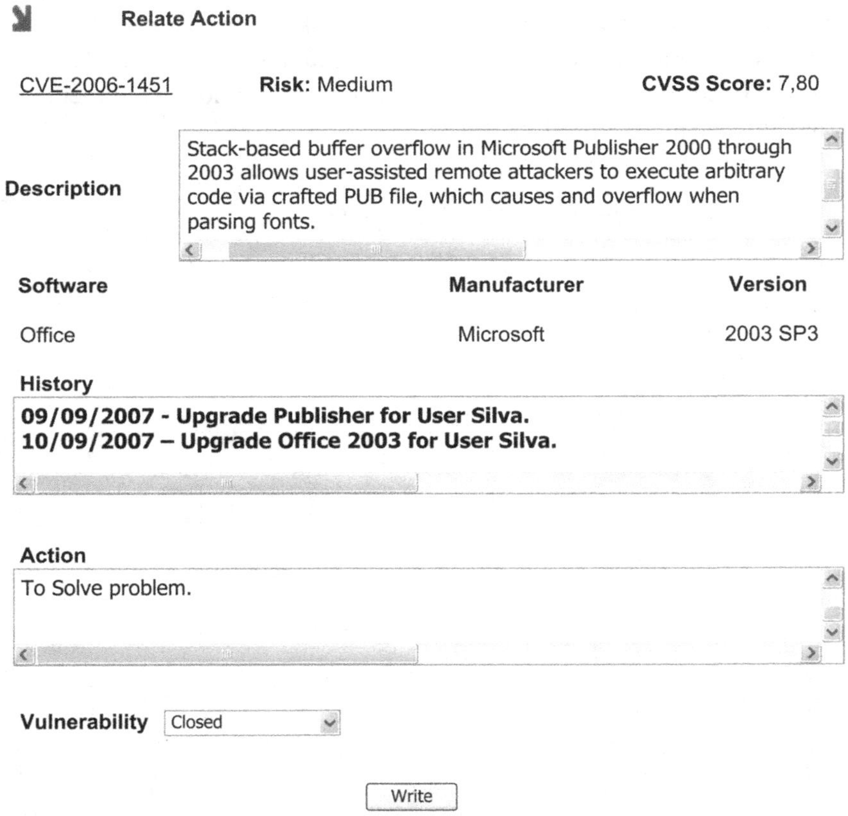

Relate Action

CVE-2006-1451   **Risk:** Medium   **CVSS Score:** 7,80

Description   Stack-based buffer overflow in Microsoft Publisher 2000 through 2003 allows user-assisted remote attackers to execute arbitrary code via crafted PUB file, which causes and overflow when parsing fonts.

Software	Manufacturer	Version
Office	Microsoft	2003 SP3

History

09/09/2007 - Upgrade Publisher for User Silva.
10/09/2007 – Upgrade Office 2003 for User Silva.

Action

To Solve problem.

Vulnerability   Closed

Write

Figure 12. General view of the system as seen by the user

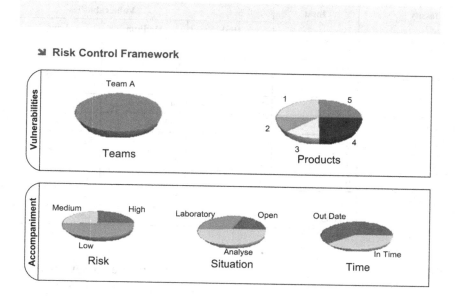

Case Study

For this case study, we analyzed a total inventory of 10,803 different software's, and total of 7,006 registered computers. The predominant operating system in the environmental analysis is Windows 2000, as shown in Table 5.

Using the base CVSS, with a total of 37.212 registered vulnerabilities and classification (low, medium and high), it was a very difficult environment, with a total of 24.33% vulnerable systems, as show in Table 6.

However, the high-risk vulnerabilities represent a small part, totaling 14.83% of all vulnerabilities, the medium risk 27,92% and low-risk total 57,25%.

This is important to clarify that a vulnerability classified as high risk, calculated by CVSS, may not represent the real risk that a computer is subject, to this is due to factors such as location, network components, and security solutions that already exist, therefore, in these cases, you should seek to analyze and understand the vulnerability so that the calculation can be repeated. So the system was efficient in detecting vulnerabilities in real time.

FUTURE RESEARCH DIRECTIONS

Future work includes the hardening of the tools developed and the full scale deployment in the corporate environment. The authors are also investigating how far automation could go on testing and deploying patches and updates as an alternative to reduce the dependency on human testing. Consideration on how sensors could be used to identify suspicious behavior of end users, based on patterns of configuration changes, is also in the scope of future research.

Table 5. Operation System

SO	Total
Win 2000	6.030
Win XP	968
Others	8
Total	**7.006**

Table 6. Vulnerabilities Analysis

ID	Classify	Total	Vulnerabilities			
			High	Medium	Low	Total
0	Software not Classify	12	0	0	0	0
1	Patches	959	6	8	33	47
2	Internal Software	279	0	0	0	0
3	Free Software	1.143	31	74	131	236
4	Software License	1.947	93	164	358	615
5	Suspect Software	850	21	39	52	112
6	Trash Software	4.210	236	413	782	1.431
7	Games	971	0	20	56	76
8	Approved Software	432	3	16	93	112
9	**Total**	**10.803**	**390**	**734**	**1.505**	**2.629**

CONCLUSION

In recent years, much has been invested in the purchase of security equipment, with the use of systems that detect intrusions, antivirus software, firewalls, and anti-spam, among many others. But in reality, is it possible to evaluate if these investments were worthwhile? Much of the generated information is ignored or not seriously considered in the process of information management. It is regarding this issue that risk management may be of help, consolidating all available information and, most importantly, making this information useful.

The fact is, it is impossible to efficiently manage risk if it has not been initially identified as risk. In other words, risk is based on uncertainty—in the absence of uncertainty, risk does not exist. It is in this context that the present work has been developed, with an aim to reduce the variables associated with uncertainty and consequently reduce risk. In this context we propose a framework to control technological risks based on distributed sensors and a centralized vulnerability repository. As new vulnerabilities are published at the CVSS or any configuration change is communicated in real time by sensors throughout the corporate environment, the framework automatically correlates the changes so as to identify new risks. Once identified, the framework assigns the vulnerability to the team responsible for the related product, allowing corporations to take immediate actions to eliminate or mitigate the associated risks. As far as it is known to the authors, a framework based on real time analysis of configuration changes and known vulnerabilities has not been published before.

REFERENCES

Alberts, C., & Dorofee, A. (2001). *An Introduction to the OCTAVE Method*. Pittsburgh, PA - USA: Carnigie Mellon University - Software Engineering Institute. BS. (2001). *7799:2001 - Information Security Management - Specification With Guidance for Use*.

Chew, E., Clay, A., Hash, J., Bartol, N., & Brow, A. (2006). *Guide for developing performance metrics for information security recommendations of the national institute of standards and technology*.

Frei, S., May, M., Fiedler, U., & Plattner, B. (2006). Large-scale vulnerability analysis. *LSAD '06: Proceedings of the 2006 SIGCOMM workshop on Large-scale attack defense* (pp. 131-138). NewYork, NY, USA: ACM Press.

Fussell, L., & Field, S. (2005). The role of the risk management database in the risk management process. 364-369.

IEC/ISO. (2005). 27001:2005 - Information Security Management-Specification With Guidance for Use.

ISO/IEC. (2005). *Information technology—Security techniques—Code of practice for information security management.* ISO.

Lahti, C., & Lanza, R. P. S. (2005). *Sarbanes-Oxley IT Compliance Using COBIT and Open Source Tools.* Syngress. Alberts, C., & Dorofee, A. (2001). *An introduction to the octave method.* USA: Octave.

Mell, P., Scarfone, K., & Romanosky, S. (2006). *Common vulnerability scoring system* (pp. 85–89). IEEE Security and Privacy.

Perera, J., & Holsomback, J. (2005). An integrated risk management tool and process. *Aerospace 2005.* Big Sky, MT: IEEE Conference.

Saidenberg, M., & Schuermann, T. (2003). *The new basel capital accord and Questions for research.* Report.

Scarfone, K., Mell, P., & Romanosky, S. (2007). *A complete guide to the common vulnerability scoring system version 2.0.* USA: NIST.

Schiffman, M. (2005). *A complete guide to the common vulnerability scoring system (cvss).* USA: FIRST.

Scudere, L. (2006). *Risco Digital.* Rio de Janeiro, Brazil: Elsivier.

Stoneburner, G., Goguen, A., & Feringa, A. (2002). *Risk management guide for information technology systems - recommendations of the national institute of standards and technology.* USA: NIST.

Wright, D. A., Romanosky, S., Schiman, M., & Eschelbeck, G. (2004). *CVSS: A common vulnerability scoring system.* USA: National Infrastructure Advisory Council (NIAC).

KEY TERMS AND DEFINITIONS

Exposures: The fact or condition of being exposed.

Methodology: A set or system of methods, principles.

Policy: A plan of action security adopted or pursued by an individual, government, party, business, etc.

Risk: Vulnerable; likely to be lost or damaged.

Score: An evaluative, usually numerical.

Security: The protection of data to ensure that only authorized personnel have access to computer files.

Vulnerability: Susceptible to attack.

ENDNOTES

[1]   http://www.securityfocus.com/
[2]   http://www.iss.net/

Chapter 10
Challenges to Managing Privacy Impact Assessment of Personally Identifiable Data

Cyril Onwubiko
Research Series Limited, UK

ABSTRACT

The challenges organisations face in managing privacy risks are numerous, and inherently diverse. Traditionally, organisations focused on addressing business and security requirements of a project, but most recently, privacy impact assessment has become an essential part of the risk management regime for most projects. Significant efforts are now directed toward providing appropriate guidance on how to conduct privacy impact assessments. Appropriate assessments of privacy invasive technologies, justification for project, collection and handling of personally identifiable data and compliance to privacy legislations possess enormous challenges to carrying out appropriate privacy impact assessments. In this chapter, guidance on how to assess privacy risks of both new and in-service projects is provided. Further, lessons learned from managing privacy risks of new and in-service projects resulting from aggregation, collection, sharing, handling and transportation of personally identifiable information are discussed.

INTRODUCTION

Today's information and communication systems are complex. They span across enterprise boundaries, and use technologies that traverse geographic boundaries, for example, cloud computing. These networks also use a plethora of technologies and software to implement complex business logics, some of which are inherently privacy-invasive, such as location-based technologies, smart cards, radio frequency identification (RFID) tags, and

DOI: 10.4018/978-1-61350-507-6.ch010

biometrics. While these technologies are exciting to use, they pose significant privacy risks.

Traditionally, risk assessments of projects are carried out primarily on the basis of business and security requirements. Most recently, privacy impact assessment (PIA) has been recommended as an essential project initiation process (UK Information Commissioner's Office, 2009) to assess privacy risks associated with new and existing projects. Privacy impact assessment is used to assess privacy risks that may be associated with a project and to ensure that privacy legislations are not breached, and sensitive personal identifiable data (PID) are not compromised too. Privacy risk assessment is an assessment of risks associated with—failing to comply with state or federal privacy legislation—protecting personal information data of individuals, and satisfying privacy requirements of information systems, that may need to be redesigned or retro-fitted at considerable expense (Educause, 2010). This means that privacy risk assessment should be carried out on all projects to ensure that:

1. they comply with privacy legislations or regulations;
2. they provide adequate safeguards to manage, handle, share, store or transport sensitive personal data or personally identifiable information (PII), and
3. finally, they comply with project-specific information systems' privacy requirements.

Managing privacy risks can be challenging, not because of the numerous issues of concern, but also because each project is unique and utilizes fundamentally different technologies and mechanisms to deliver its own service. While the steps involved in carrying out privacy impact assessment are the same for any project, but each assessment of privacy for any project is different.

A project in this chapter refers to a system, programme or scheme. A project may involve a collection of systems that are used to deliver ser-

vice for a specific purpose. For example, a census programme is a project whose aim is to count the number of lawful citizens, by checking and verifying their name, age, address and social or religious inclination, of a particular nation. This project may require the use of information communications technology (ICT) systems, people, electronic and manual processes. Another example, EINSTEIN 2 (EINSTEIN 2, 2009) is a United States project for intrusion detection system that monitors the network gateways of government departments and agencies in the United States for unauthorized traffic. This project involves the use of ICT systems, people and both electronic and manual processes to monitor and collect traffic information. An in-service (existing) project is a programme of work that is already been delivered and in operational use. A new project is a programme of work that is in the initiation stage of the project lifecycle.

There are a good number of sources that provide guidelines for conducting privacy impact assessments as demonstrated by (UK Information Commissioner's Office, 2009; Educause, 2010; Radack S., 2010; Gruteser M., and Grunwald D., 2004; Peirce T., 2009; Abu-Nimeh S. and Mead N. R., 2001); unfortunately, organizations still face difficulty assessing privacy risks associated to new and existing projects. Some of the most common challenges faced by organization are as follows:

1. How to assess appropriately privacy invasive technologies;
2. Justification for project;
3. Difficulty finding privacy experts within own organization;
4. Lack of prescriptive guideline on how to assess privacy risks associated to a project, and how to determine the level of privacy assessments required for a particular project.

In addition, how to appropriately gather and handle personal information data and compliance to privacy regulations and legislations are other challenges associated to conducting privacy impact assessments.

In this chapter, guidance on how to assess privacy risks of both new and in-service projects is provided. Further, lessons learned from managing privacy risks for new and existing projects resulting from collection, aggregation, sharing, handling and transportation of sensitive personal information are discussed.

PRIVACY IMPACT ASSESSMENT

Privacy impact assessment is an assessment of privacy related risks comprising of four distinct assessments:

1. Assessment of the project's characteristics or features such as technologies or mechanisms deployed or intended of use. This assessment is to check if the technologies or mechanisms would be privacy invasive.
2. Assessment of the project's compliance with privacy regulations, state, federal, national, bilateral or multilateral privacy legislations. This relates to compliance with privacy regulations and legislations, especially those that operate where the project is located or situated. For example, the Data Protection Act 1998 in the UK or the 'the Privacy Act' in the US, or other privacy related pieces of legislations in other parts of the world, such as Canada, Australia and Germany.
3. Assessment of personal information data being processed, or to be processed by the project. For example, is personal information data collected identifiable or not; are they sensitive personal data; are they 'obsolete' personal identifiable data etc.
4. Finally, it is an assessment of the collection, sharing, distribution, storage and transportation of personal information data, and whether the processing of personal information is in line with privacy legislations.

It is important to mention that PIA is not only applied to a project, but also applied to a workstream, programme, task, policy, procedure, platform or ICT System.

According to NIST's ITL Security Bulletin 2010 (Radack S., 2010), Personally Identifiable Information (PII) or Personal Identifiable Data (PID) is any information about an individual that is maintained by an agency, including information that can be used to distinguish or trace an individual's identity, such as name, social security number, date and place of birth, mother's maiden name, or biometric records; and any other information that is linked or linkable to an individual, such as medical, educational, financial, and employment information (based on General Accountability Office and Office of Management and Budget definitions). A list of personally identifiable information is provided in Table 1.

It is pertinent to mention that compliance with privacy legislation is dependent on where the project that is being assessed is located. For example, a project in the UK would have to comply with the UK privacy legislations and the wider European Union privacy legislations, and may comply with other privacy legislations of other countries if the organisation wishes to do so.

There are also bilateral and multilateral privacy legislations, such as the Safe Harbor Act (Directive 95/46/EC, 1995), which regulates the processing of personal data within the European Union in addition to Directive 2002/58/EC that protects privacy of electronic communications (Directive 2002/58/EC, 2002). Directive 95/46/EC is also available not only to EU member state (nations), but also, available to other countries outside the EU, which the United States (US) signed up to. Organization operating within bilateral or multilateral privacy legislation should comply with those pieces of privacy legislations. This means that a privacy impact assessment of a project operating in bilateral or multilateral privacy legislation must be equally assessed within the confinements

Table 1. Personal Identifiers

S/N	Personal Identifiers	S/N	Personal Identifiers
1	Names (firstname, surname or lastname)	12	Biometric identifiers such as fingerprints, voice prints etc
2	Addresses (home, business or both)	13	Bank, Financial or Credit card details
3	Post code or Zip code	14	Mother's maiden name
4	Email address	15	Tax, Benefit or Pension records or Record numbers
5	Telephone numbers (Fax numbers)	16	Employment records
6	Driving license number	17	School attendance or records
7	Date of birth	18	Vehicle identifiers and serial numbers including license plate numbers
8	Social insurance number / National insurance number	19	Web universal resource locators (URLs)
9	Medical record numbers / Health records	20	Internet protocol (IP) address numbers
10	DNA data	21	Full face photographic images and any comparable images
11	Any other materials relating to social services including child protection and housing	22	Any other unique identifying number, characteristic, or code.

Personal identifiers (shown in Table 1) comprise of both personal information that are in the public domain and sensitive personal data that when released is likely to cause harm or distress to the individual. These identifiers are derived from a couple of standards – HIPAA (HIPAA (2006) and HMG IA Standard No. 6 (HMG IA Standard No. 6, 2009).

of those bilateral or multilateral privacy agreements, and other specific privacy legislation of its own country. For example, privacy legislation compliance for a privacy impact assessment of a project in the UK would involve assessment of the project's compliance to both UK-specific privacy legislations and EU related privacy legislations.

Privacy impact assessment may seem onerous at times due to the numerous steps involved when carrying out PIA. Depending on the nature of the project, extensive privacy impact assessment maybe required. The UK Information Commissioner's Office (ICO) through its Privacy Impact Assessment Handbook (UK Information Commissioner's Office, 2009) provides useful guidelines. The handbook offers a general purpose framework for carrying out privacy impact assessment.

Our contribution in this chapter is rather unique and much more focused on providing a practical approach to conducting privacy impact assessment that is general-purpose and prescriptive. The usefulness of our contribution can be seen in both the guidelines provided with respect to our Privacy Impact Suitability Assessment (PISA)

Framework (see Figure 1) and Privacy Screening Framework (see Table 4).

In the private sector, for example, privacy impact assessments of projects are not as mandated as it is in the public or government sector. While, PIA may be conducted for certain projects based on best endeavours in the private sector, it is mandatory for all government and public sector projects as an essential risk management activity.

For example, the Department of Homeland Security, National Cyber Security Division of the United States conducted privacy impact assessment of its EINSTEIN 2 Program in 2008 to examine its privacy implications with collecting, analyzing and sharing of Computer Security Information across the Federal Civilian Government (US-CERT, 2008). According to the United States Computer Emergency Readiness Team (US-CERT), the Department of Homeland Security (DHS) must provide this publicly available PIA prior to initiating a new collection of information that uses information technology to collect, maintain or disseminate information that is in an identifiable form or collects identifiable informa-

Figure 1. PISA Framework – Privacy Impact Suitability Assessment Framework

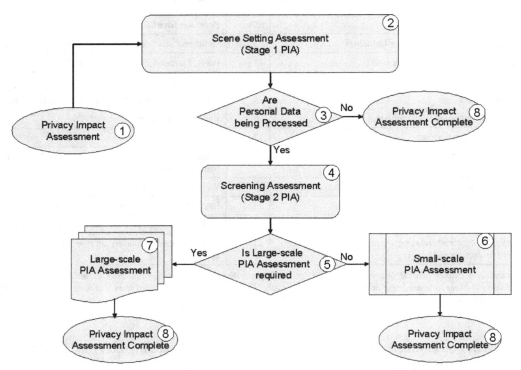

tion through the use of information technology as mandated by the US, E-Government Act of 2002 (Public Law 107-347, 44 U.S.C. § 3501, note), Section 208. Similarly, in the UK, the Information Commissioners Office (ICO), Cabinet Office has recommended privacy impact assessment for all projects, new and existing, whose functionality may require the collection, sharing or use of personal information. This was driven from the UK Data Handling Review of 2008 (Cabinet Office, 2008).

PRIVACY IMPACT SUITABILITY ASSESSMENT (PISA) FRAMEWORK

The privacy impact suitability assessment framework is our proposed framework for assessing a project's suitability for PIA assessment (see Figure 1).

The PISA framework is an eight (8) step privacy assessment model, which aims to evaluate if a project is required to undergo PIA or not; and to determine the level of PIA required, where applicable. The first step (indicated by the small circle on each object) is the start of the PIA assessment. The second step is the scene setting assessment (a.k.a. stage 1 PIA). At this stage, the project is initially assessed as to whether personal information data will be processed by the project. For existing projects, the scene setting assessment will check if information being processed by the project involves personal information data. The third step is when a decision is reached whether the project should or should not undergo a stage 2 PIA assessment. If the outcome shows that personal information data is not being or will not be processed, then PIA is completed (step 8) and that concludes privacy impact assessment for that project. If otherwise, then the fourth step begins. The fourth step is the stage 2 PIA.

Table 2. Privacy Impact Assessment Questions

S/N	Questions
1	Would the workstream, project or ICT system consume, process, transport or store personal information data?
2	What personal information will be processed (collect, share, transport or store) by the project?
3	Why is personal information being collected by the project?
4	What is the intended use of personal information being collected?
5	How would these information be processed, this includes sharing, transporting, exchanging, storing and disposing of personal information?
6	Who are the intended recipient (information controllers), and with whom will personal information be shared, or/and exchanged?
7	How would the project seek to obtain consent from their service consumers (users of the system) with regards to collection of their personal information data?
8	How would service consumer be informed of the justification of the project?
9	How would the information collected be secured?
10	What privacy regulation and legislation apply or required?

The second stage PIA (Stage 2 PIA) starts with the screening exercise when privacy risks of the project are assessed in much more detail than stage 1. This involves assessing the project's characteristics, such as technologies or mechanisms that will be deployed in the project, for example, checking if such technologies are privacy invasive. It also assesses the type of personal data that will be collected, and to ensure the people providing these data are aware and willing. In addition, it assesses if there is good justification for the project. The fifth step is when a decision is reached as to whether small-scale PIA or large-scale PIA is pertinent for the project. The sixth step involves carrying out large-scale or small-scale PIA, and finally, the seventh step completes the assessment. Since every project should be assessed of privacy risk, we thought the framework is a foundational contribution, which assist privacy experts and organization conduct, in a practical way, a privacy assessment of their projects.

Scene Setting Assessment (Stage 1 PIA)

The scene setting assessment (SSA) is the first stage PIA of a project. It is aimed to ascertain if the project will process personal information data, or already processes personal information data. This is applicable to existing project (see Figure 1). To conduct a scene setting PIA assessment of a project, we have designed ten (10) fundamental scene setting questions to help with the assessment in order to deduce the suitability or appropriateness of privacy impact assessment of the project, as shown in Table 2.

Based on the outcome of this assessment (answers to questions on Table 2), a decision should be made, either to proceed, or stop further privacy impact assessment. If it is believed that the project will be used to process personal information data, then further PIA assessments are recommended, otherwise this concludes PIA assessment of the project. Suppose the outcome of the scene setting assessment turns out that the project is handling personal information data. This implies that a second stage PIA (screening assessment), which is a much more thorough assessment than the scene setting assessment, will be required. It is pertinent to mention that, the first stage PIA is mandatory for all projects.

Screening Assessment (Stage 2 PIA)

The second stage PIA is referred to as the screening assessment, during which project stakeholders are interviewed to determine the level of personal data the project intends to process, or has been processing, this is applicable to existing projects (see Figure 1). The aim of the screening assessment is to determine whether a small-scale or large-scale PIA is deemed necessary for the project. A small-scale privacy impact assessment is an abridged privacy risks assessment of a project. It is recommended when a small percentage of the project characteristics underline some privacy concerns. For example, if one or two features of the project characteristics imply privacy concern, then it is justifiable to recommend a small-scale PIA assessment. If more than three aspects of the project characteristics underline privacy concerns, then a large-scale PIA is justifiable. Having said that, there are cases when a small-scale PIA is recommended even a number of a project features seems to underline privacy concerns. For example, if it is perceived that personal data being processed are either none sensitive or the processing is infrequent. None sensitive personal data refers to personal data of a living individual that can only identify an individual when linked or combined with other personal data of that individual. For example, an email server project that collects only two sets of personal data during user registration such as name and email address of the user would justify a small-scale PIA, even though it aggregate significant volumes of personal information data. A large-scale PIA assessment is an extensive, thorough, and detailed privacy risks assessment. A large-scale PIA assessment is recommended when a good percentage of the project characteristics evaluated during a screening exercise underlines serious privacy concerns. For example, a data consolidation project of a health service that links data controllers or sources warrants large-scale privacy risks assessment. Both small-scale and large-scale privacy impact assessments require

project stakeholders to be interviewed in order to determine the areas of the project that involve processing of personal information data, and the level of analysis or manipulation (source linkages) of personal data that are intended.

There is no empirical method of deciding which projects should undergo large-scale or small-scale privacy impact assessment. One approach that has been recommended to determining the level of assessment required for a project is the use of screening questions (Information Commissioner's Office 2009) developed by the ICO. The ICO's proposed screening process is extremely helpful; unfortunately, the screening process does not guarantee that the same project when assessed by two separate organisations would lead to the same level of PIA recommendations. For this reason, proposed the Privacy Screening Framework (see Table 4), in addition, we designed a general purpose legal and privacy assessment questions (see Table 3) to assist organizations assess legal and privacy compliance of projects during PIA assessments.

Table 3 consists of ten (10) questions comprising legal, regulatory and legislative assessment of personal data handling, processing and sharing. The idea behind the provision of the legal and privacy compliance check is to ensure that PIA assessments are consistently evaluated by each organization by following the same prescriptive guideline. After carrying out legal and privacy compliance checks of a project, the next activity in the PIA assessment is the privacy screening assessment.

PRIVACY SCREENING FRAMEWORK (PSF)

The privacy screening framework is our proposed framework that provides the required prescriptive guidance for carrying out large-scale PIA assessments. The PSF framework is flexible, adaptable and self-directing. It is flexible because the PIA

Table 3. Legal & Privacy Compliance Check

	Legal & Privacy Compliance Check	
	Project Name:	
	Project Reference:	
	Organisation:	
	Asset Owner:	
	Name of PIA Assessor:	
	Names of Project Stakeholders:	
	Date Completed:	
No	**Question**	**Response**
1	Will the processing of personal data comply with all relevant and applicable privacy regulations/legislations? For example, Data Protection Act 1998, Data Protection Principles (1-8), The Privacy Act, Human Rights Act 1998, Freedom of Information Act 2000 etc?	
2	Are the business processes to be used (or been utilized) compliant with all relevant and applicable regulations/legislations?	
3	Are there standards and law that this project must comply to? For example, the Federal Information Security Management Act (FISMA), E-Government Act, Tort of Negligence, Tort of Passing off, Public Health requirements, etc?	
4	Are there other privacy related (statutory) compliance arising from privacy policy statement of the organization? For example Code of Connection, Information Governance Statement of Compliance (IGSoC), Caldicott Principles, Fair Credit Reporting Act?	
5	Are there privacy related mandates from the public that this project must satisfy? For example, Public Disclosure of Privacy Practices, and Security Breaches Disclosure Act.	
6	Will the project comply with the Privacy and Electronic Communications Regulations 2003, Fair Credit Reporting Act, Disclosure of Personal Information, etc?	
7	Will the data collected by the project be shared or transport outside the Province of Data Origin but used within the Country of Data Origin?	
8	Will the data collected by the project be shared or transport outside the Country of Origin?	
9	Will the data collected by the project be accessible, or processed, remotely from outside the Country of Data Origin?	
10	Will the data collected by the project be processed by individuals with certain personnel security clearances?	

assessor can choose to add or remove any non-applicable sections of the framework without influencing the end result of the assessment. PSF is adaptable and self-directing because the PIA assessor is required to carry out the assessment, and can modify any sections of the framework that is deemed not applicable to the project's locality or operating environment (see Table 4). For example, when conducting a PIA assessment of a project in the UK, it may not be relevant to evaluate the project based on US-specific privacy legislations except where bilateral mandates are

applicable. Similarly, privacy risk assessment of US-based projects should be evaluated against US-specific privacy legislations and applicable industry regulations, plus bilateral or multilateral privacy understandings, where applicable. Thus, it is equally the case with privacy risk assessment of project hosted in other EU countries such as Belgium, Germany or France.

The privacy screening framework is composed of eight (8) sections. Section 0 is about the project details, comprising project name, reference, organization, asset owner and name of PIA assessor. Section 1 is technology assessment, which focuses primarily on privacy risk assessment of three main areas – privacy-invasive technologies, event and information monitoring technologies, and data capturing and screening technologies. Section 2 is project justification assessment. It is aimed to ensure that the purpose and justification of the project are made known to the public or the users of the system. It has two subcategories – justification for data handling and justification for new data acquisition. Section 3 is identity assessment, which focuses on privacy risks associated to the use, combination and linkage of personal identifiers, such as username, date of birth, national insurance number etc (see Table 1). Section 4 is data assessment. This assesses the quantity and significance of personal data being processed (used, stored or transported). Section 5 is data handling assessment, which focuses on privacy risks associated with data collection policies, procedures and quality assurance. Section 6 is awareness assessment. It deals with privacy risks associated with the security of the information system processing personal information data for the project; in addition, it deals with secure disposal and destruction of the information system holding personal information data, when no longer in use. Finally, section 7 is miscellaneous, which affords the risk assessor the opportunity to profile other pertinent privacy risks particular to systems utilized for the project. For example, privacy concerns with legacy systems, bespoke design and customized solutions etc.

Privacy Impact Assessment of an In-Service Project

A project is said to be in-service when it is already being used to delivery a type of service or another. In every aspect, it means the project has gone live. There are five phases to any project lifecycle: initiation phase, development phase, test phase, in-service phase, and decommission phase. Privacy impact assessment of an in-service

project is the retrospective privacy risk assessment of a project that is already being used to deliver a service. This means that risk assessment of the project was previously completed only on the basis of business and security requirements, without prior assessment of privacy risks associated with the project.

Privacy impact assessment of an existing project is the retrospective assessment of privacy risks associated to that project. First, privacy assessment suitability of the project should be established as shown in Figure 1. Second, privacy risks relating to technologies or mechanisms deployed in the project, data collection and handling procedures applied (see Privacy Screening Framework - Table 4), and compliance to privacy legislations and regulations (see Table 3) should be evaluated. Finally, specific project privacy requirements should be addressed.

Assessing privacy risks of an existing (in-service) project can be challenging, while the outcome is often astonishing and expensive, because of the following:

1. Asset owners and senior information risk owners do not have a clue how damaging results from such assessments may turn up.
2. Outcome could imply privacy violation or breach.
3. Outcome could show that certain technologies are privacy intrusive or that the data collection and handling procedures contravene privacy regulations or legislations. This may lead to such technologies being decommissioned from the project, consequently resulting to significant financial losses to the organization.
4. Outcome could be costly because the result may mean that certain assets in the project may have to be decommissioned, withdrawn or destroyed. It could also result in significant financial penalties such as fines due to breach of privacy. For example, in August 2010, the UK Government's Financial Services

Table 4. Privacy Screening Framework (PSF)

Section	Privacy Screening Framework	
0	**Project Details**	
	Project Name:	
	Project Reference:	
	Organisation:	
	Asset Owner:	
	Names of Assessors: **Date of Assessment:**	
1	**Technology Assessment**	
a	**Privacy-invasive technologies**	**Response**
1a1	Does the project involve new or inherently privacy-invasive technologies? E.g. The use of technologies such as smart cards, RFID, biometrics, locator monitoring technologies, visual surveillance, digital image and video recording, profiling, data mining, and logging of electronic traffic, security events and information management etc?	
1a2	Are all technologies applied to the project well-understood by the organisation?	
1a3	Are there demonstrable concerns that the technologies used in the project may impact privacy?	
1a4	Are privacy impacts (from the project) well-understood by the organisation, and by the service consumers	
1a5	Are there measures applied to avoid or mitigate negative privacy impacts, or at least reduce them to satisfactory levels of those whose privacy is affected?	
b	**Event and information monitoring technologies**	**Response**
1b1	Does the project involve the use of event and information monitoring technologies such as Security Event and Information Management (SEIM), Security Event Management (SEM) or Security Information Management (SIM) systems such that user traffic, user (service consumer) actions and user locations can be monitored?	
1b2	Are organization and service consumers aware that their traffic is being monitored?	
1b3	Is the use of the SEIM/SEM/SIM due to regulatory or security compliance, if yes, please specify?	
1b4	If service consumer data are collected, are these subjected to reprocessing that could lead to the identification of an individual?	
c	**Data capturing and screening technologies**	**Response**
1c1	Does the project involve the use of data capturing, admission and screening technologies such as Biometrics, RFID, Blood sampling toolkit, Lab equipment, X-ray and digital imagery, Data monitors such that user identifiable attributes, characteristics or features are monitored, captured or/and stored?	
	Is the use of the data capturing and screening tool due to regulatory or security compliance, if yes, please specify?	
1c2	Are the organisation and service consumers aware that their traffic are being monitored	
2	**Justification Assessment**	
a	**Justification for data handling**	**Response**
2a1	Are there justifications to why personal data is being handled, and are these being communicated to the service consumers?	
2a2	Do service consumers understand the benefits of the project to them?	
b	**Justification for new data acquisition**	**Response**
2b1	Is the acquisition of pieces of new personal data required, such as user registration details – username, date of birth, national insurance number or social insurance number etc?	
2b2	Will pieces of new additional data collected combined with existing personal information data?	

continued on following page

Table 4. continued

Section	Privacy Screening Framework	
2b3	Do service consumers understand the benefits of the additional data supplied in the overall evaluation of the project?	
3	**Identity Assessment**	
a	**Does the project involve an additional use of existing identifier**	**Response**
3a1	Will the project make use of a combination of existing identifiers (example, username, date of birth, enrolment date, address etc) in its processing or analysis?	
3a2	If yes to **3a1**, how many identifiers will be combined?	
3a3	And which identifiers from **3a2**?	
b	**Does the project involve use of new identifiers for multiple purposes**	**Response**
3b1	Will the project require a new identifier (such as, username, date of birth, enrolment date, address, national insurance number etc) and would this new identifier be combined with existing identifiers?	
3b2	If identifiers are combined, which are those?	
3b3	Will an identifier be used for multiple purposes such as those used for registration/enrolment, authentication and identification or service improvement contact?	
c	**Does the project involve new or substantially changed identity authentication requirements that may be intrusive or onerous**	**Response**
3c1	Will the registration process of the service requires three or more personal identifiable information such as (name, address, national insurance number, date of birth, email address, mother's maiden name etc)?	
3c2	Will the authentication process of the service requires the use of new identifiers, such as post code, pass phrase or PIN (personal identifiable number)?	
3c3	Will the project cache or store personally identifiable information of users (service consumer) during registration?	
3c4	Does the registration process require two or more processes, that is, enrollment and verification (for example, collection of basic personal details and onerous PII details)?	
4	**Data Assessment**	
a	**Will the project result in the handling of a significant amount of new data about people, or significant change in existing data-holdings**	**Response**
4a1	Will the project result in the handling of a significant amount of new data about citizens or users such as name, address, date of birth, national insurance number, mother's maiden name etc. Example national criminal database?	
4a2	Will the project result in the handling of a significant change in existing data-holdings?	
4a3	Will the project combine both new and existing pieces of personal information data?	
b	**Will the project result in the handling of new data about a significant number of people, or a significant change in the population coverage**	**Response**
4b1	Will the project result in the handling of new data about a significant number of service consumers, public or citizens?	
4b2	What is the estimated number of service consumers, public or citizens required to use this service?	
4b3	What category of service consumers, public or citizens is expected to use the service?	
c	**Does the project involve new linkage of personal data with other data sources, or significant change in data linkages**	**Response**
4c1	How many data linkages or data sources (transfer, consolidation or storage) of personal data are in use?	
4c2	Will data collected for other purposes used in this project?	
4c3	Will the project use or combine personal data collected for other purposes with those collected during service consumer registration/enrolment?	

continued on following page

Table 4. continued

Section	Privacy Screening Framework	
4c4	Will the project involve significant change in data linkages / data sources	
5	**Data Handling Assessment**	
a	**Does the project involve new or changed data collection policies or practices that may be unclear or intrusive**	**Response**
5a1	Will the project use new data collection policies that may be unclear or intrusive to service consumers?	
5a2	Will the project require the modification of existing data collection policies that may be unclear or intrusive to service consumers?	
5a3	Will the project involve new data collection practices or procedures that maybe unclear or intrusive to service consumers?	
5a4	Will the project require the modification of existing data collection processes or procedures that may be unclear or intrusive to service consumers?	
b	**Does the project involve new or changed data quality assurance processes and standards that may be unclear or unsatisfactory**	**Response**
5b1	Will the project use new data quality processes or procedures that may be unclear or intrusive to service consumers?	
5b2	Will the project use changed data quality processes or procedures that may be unclear or intrusive to service consumers?	
c	**Does the project involve new or changed data security arrangements that may be unclear or unsatisfactory**	**Response**
5c1	Will the project require new data security arrangements or mechanisms that may be unclear or intrusive to service consumers?	
5c2	Will the project use changed data security arrangement processes or procedures that may be unclear or intrusive to service consumers?	
d	**Does the project involve new or changed data access or disclosure arrangements that may be unclear or unsatisfactory**	**Response**
5d1	Will the project use new data access or disclosure arrangements that may be unclear or intrusive to service consumers?	
5d2	Will the project use changed data access or disclosure arrangements that may be unclear or intrusive to service consumers?	
e	**Does the project involve new or changed data retention arrangements that may be unclear or permissive**	**Response**
5e1	Will the project use new data retention arrangements that may be unclear or intrusive to service consumers?	
5e2	Will the project use changed data retention arrangements that may be unclear or intrusive to service consumers?	
f	**Does the project involve changing the medium of disclosure for publicly available information in such a way that the data becomes more readily accessible than before**	**Response**
5f1	Will the project make publicly available piece of personal information data readily accessible. For example, use of public Internet website that organize and aggregate personal information data, such as data mining?	
6	**Awareness Assessment**	
a	**System / project security**	**Response**
6a1	Will the system/project be known to the general public?	
6a2	Will the system/project be known to competition?	
6a3	Does the system have known or publicly known vulnerabilities?	
6a4	Will the system be used in a vulnerable environment?	

continued on following page

Table 4. Continued

Section	Privacy Screening Framework	
6a5	Will the system be deployed in a restricted test environment?	
6a6	Will the system be deployed in restricted live environment?	
b	**System secure sanitization and destruction**	**Response**
6b1	Has any component of the systems used for the project been decommissioned, re-used or destroyed?	
6b2	If yes to 6b1, were these systems securely sanitized before re-use, or securely destroyed such that personal data they hold cannot be reconstructed from an adversary?	
7	**Miscellaneous**	
7a	Please provide any comments you think may assist with the risk assessment of the system/network or platform being evaluated.	

Authority (FSA) fined Zurich Insurance record data loss fine of £2.3M due to a breach on privacy (Shane D., 2010). There are a number of cases of huge financial penalties being hit on organisations due to privacy breaches, and such breaches are now starting to be publicly disclosed as Government takes new stances to ensure organisations take privacy seriously.

To conduct privacy impact assessment of an existing project we recommend a quick assessment using our privacy impact assessment questionnaire (see Table 2). This assessment is meant to show if PIA is indeed relevant to the project or not. Based on the outcome of this assessment, further privacy assessments of the project will be decided. It is pertinent to mention that privacy impact assessment of in-service projects follow the same methodology as new projects (see Figure 1). This means that, first, privacy suitability assessment of the project (Stage 1 PIA). Second, based on the outcome of the Stage 1 PIA assessment, Stage 2 PIA will commence; otherwise the assessment is concluded. Following the second stage PIA, two sets of assessment is envisaged, either a small-scale or a large scale PIA assessment.

It is pertinent to re-iterate that the outcome of privacy impact assessment of an existing project can be insightful and expensive. We recommended organisations to consider conducting PIA as early

as possible in the project lifecycle to minimize the consequences associated with in-service PIA. For example, PIA of an existing project could reveal that an organisation is in breach of privacy because of the use of technologies that are intrusive in the processing of personal information data. In another case, it may reveal that an organization does not comply with certain privacy regulations or legislations. Either case, the impact it will have on the organization is huge. For instance, it could lead to significant financial penalties, withdrawn accreditation, or/and subsequent termination of the project. In a normal circumstance, breach of privacy attracts a fine and requires fresh risk assessment of the project, which costs both time and money. In an extreme case, it will lead to significant financial penalty (as a result of breach of customer service agreement and resultant fine from the government), affects the organisation brand (negative media publicity), and especially in situations where disclosure of security or privacy breaches are required due to regional or provincial legislation. Finally, it may lead to termination of the project.

Privacy Impact Assessment of a New Project

With new projects it is recommended that privacy requirements are assessed from the outset and consideration to these requirements are made

Table 5. A Comparison of Privacy Impact Assessment of Existing and New Projects

Specific Issues to New and Existing Projects		
S/N	New Project	Existing Project
1	At the early stages of the project initiation phase, functional requirements of the different components of the project may not be known and well understood, hence privacy impact assessment of the project at this stage may be inconclusive.	Functional requirements are known, but the realisation that the project maybe combining multiple personal information identifiers may not have been considered.
2	Often, all the technologies, or mechanisms to be used in the project may not be properly identified, hence privacy assessment relating to technology or mechanism, or even the design cannot be properly evaluated.	Because the project is already in-service, even when privacy risks are identified, addressing all the identified risks may impact service, hence business needs often override privacy requirements.
3	Ownership of risk may become an issue, especially when information security roles and responsibilities have not been defined and agreed on.	Ownership of risk is also an issue with existing projects, especially when prior privacy risks have not been conducted.
4	Expertise in conducting privacy impact assessment for new projects within a single organisation (for example, small to medium-size organisation) is a challenge.	Expertise in conducting privacy impact assessment is also a challenge for existing projects, because: a) Skills to do so may not exist within one organisation, and, b) Expertise to assess existing projects, and manage relationships and interfaces that exist with in-service project can be onerous.
5	The scope or extent to which personal information to be collected will be processed (shared, stored, combined, exchanged) may not be known and well understood.	Where privacy impact assessment may reveal a high likelihood of privacy violation, business needs may override privacy requirements, especially if addressing privacy issues may result to service impacting consequences or significant financial expense.
6	The extent to which different personal information identifiers may be combined, processed or analysed may not be fully determined.	There may be a bias to suppress privacy risk in relation to business needs since privacy impact assessment was carried out retrospectively.
7	The justification of the project to service consumers (users of the systems, public or citizen) may not have been discussed or communicated to the public or wider service consumers.	The justification for existing projects are known, but the use of additional personal identifiers may have not been justified for existing projects, and when there is a scope change to existing project, this is not often communicated to the service consumers.

prior to implementation. This does not mean that privacy impact assessment of new projects is a panacea to all privacy concerns. As shown in Table 5, the difficulty to carrying out privacy impact assessment of new projects are that at the early stages of a project, very little is known of the various components of the project. For example, the entire design of the project may not have been fully developed. Stakeholders may not fully understand all the requirements of the project and detailed functional features of all the technological mechanisms to be deployed in the project may not have been known. Hence, privacy assessment of all the various components of the project, at this stage, is not feasible.

New projects afford an organization the opportunity to consider privacy requirements from the outset. As set out by local, national and international privacy agencies, privacy impact assessment is one way of ensuring that privacy concerns are addressed from the start of project initiation to the entire lifecycle risk management of the project. The fact that a project is new does not make privacy impact assessment of that project any easier compared to PIA assessment of an in-service project. As shown in Figure 1, the same framework is utilized to assess both new and existing projects.

A major concern observed with most privacy impact assessments is that organisations do not often have the right mix of privacy skilled experts to carry out privacy impact assessments. Often, people with limited privacy expertise from varying but related disciplines such as information assurance, information security or information technology are asked to carryout privacy impact assessments. Our recommendation for organisations is to enlist the service of privacy experts to assist with PIA exercise, especially when large-scale PIA is recommended. A lesson learned from carrying out privacy impact assessments is that interpretation of privacy requirements does so often differ among stakeholders.

Table 5 provides some comparisons between PIA of new and existing projects. It is evident that there are issues that are common to both new and existing projects, such as compliance to privacy legislations and regulations. Nevertheless, there are issues that fall under one category but not the other. For example, privacy impact assessment of existing projects may require retrofitting of privacy, or risk acceptance of privacy non-compliant practices; whereas, for new projects, privacy considerations are recommended from the outset, hence retrofitting of privacy requirements are not applicable.

Risk Relating to Aggregation of Personal Identifiable Data

Personally identifiable information (PII) requires special handling/processing procedures in accordance to the Data Protection Act (DPA) Principles 1-8, the Privacy Act and other national and international privacy legislations. This is because the impact of privacy breaches to an individual, which could vary from prolonged personal distress to significant personal financial losses. Unfortunately, privacy breach of a project collecting PII data of citizens will impact a larger population of individuals, resulting to prolong distress to a population of individuals. The cumulative and interdependent risks resulting from the collection of significant number of aligned sensitive personal information data require proportionate

risk mitigation procedures, and additional controls may seem plausible to address risk resulting from aggregation of these PII data. When carrying privacy impact assessment of a project, it is worth taking into consideration (at stage 2 of the PIA assessment) whether personal data from numerous data collectors or sources will be aggregated. That is when a significant number of personally identifiable information is collected or combined proportionate privacy-assurance controls should be required. For example, additional storage, processing and handling requirements may be needed.

Personally identifiable information requires special handling, sharing, storage and retention procedures. While these procedures are essential to protecting PIIs, additional handling and sharing procedures may be required if a significant amount of personal data is required. Further, if these information would be handled in new ways or ways that involved new linkages of personal data, additional controls should be used to address risks resulting from this new practice.

Solutions and Recommendations

In this chapter guidance to conducting privacy impact assessment of both new and in-service projects are provided. Fundamentally, the Privacy Impact Suitability Assessment (PISA) framework is provided to enable organisations successfully carry out privacy impact assessment, knowing that every project should be assessed for privacy risks. The PISA framework is useful and straightforward to use and apply to any project with respect to privacy risks assessments.

To ensure PIA assessments are consistent and straightforward, we proposed the Privacy Screening Framework, which assists privacy assessors to assess projects prescriptively against all the seven categories of privacy risks. The PSF framework is flexible, adaptive and self-directing; which means that the person undertaking the assessment (assessor) can choose to adapt the framework to suit the needs of a particular project. The framework can be utilized and applied by any person. The framework is straightforward and derived based on lessons learned in carrying out PIA assessments for a number of organisations on a number of projects. Further to the frameworks provided, we provided the legal and privacy compliance check (see Table 3) to ensure consistency when assessing privacy regulations and directives compliance.

With the understanding that the earlier privacy assessment is planned in the project initiation programme the better the organization will be in addressing privacy requirements, issues or concerns. We recommend that privacy impact assessment should become an essential part of the risk management process of every project. We hope that this will help organisations plan PIA from the outset of the project, knowing that retrofitting of privacy assessment can be costly as we have seen with PIA assessment of in-service projects.

When planning privacy impact assessment, considerations should be made of risks resulting due to the sheer volume of personally identifiable information the project would process. And when data from different sources will be used, the impact of aggregation of these data should be considered. This should serve as an indicator as to when additional privacy controls may be required due to aggregation effect. Finally, we recommend that privacy impact assessment should be carried out by privacy experts within an organization, and where people with the right skills cannot be found, the services of external privacy agencies should be enlisted.

There is a new privacy legislation in the UK that empowers the UK Information Commissioner's Office to exact financial penalty to any organization in breach of privacy. This will, and has ushered a reawakening of privacy consciousness in organizations, especially, governmental organizations and agencies.

FUTURE RESEARCH DIRECTIONS

We plan to automate the PIA frameworks proposed in this chapter into a toolkit that will assist organizations when carrying out privacy risk assessments. The proposed toolkit will be available for download, or used from www.research-series.com. The provision of automated toolkits to assist with conducting PIA can be helpful, but the challenge will be on the coverage of relevant privacy legislations. This is because local or provincial privacy legislations are different among countries; hence, it will be challenging to cover all applicable privacy legislations in the toolkit.

CONCLUSION

In this chapter, we discussed challenges to managing privacy impact assessment of personally identifiable information. The different issues relating to privacy impact assessment of new and in-service projects are demonstrated and discussed. It was found that in-service projects were challenging to be privacy assessed, and the outcome of privacy impact assessment to an in-service project could be insightful and expensive; and consequently could result to significant financial losses to the organization when found in breach of privacy. Privacy impact assessment frameworks were proposed, discussed and utilized to demonstrate their usefulness when conducting PIA assessments. Each framework was described such as the privacy impact suitability framework, legal and privacy compliance check and privacy screening framework. Finally, issues surrounding aggregation of personally identifiable information were discussed with the view to highlighting associated risks while recommending essential privacy controls to addressing these risks.

REFERENCES

Cabinet Office. (2008), *The Data Handling Procedure in Government: Final Report.* June 2008. Retrieved October 6, 2010 from http://www.cesg.gov.uk/products_services/iatp/documents/data_handling_review.pdf

Directive 95/46/EC, 1995, *Directive 95/46/EC of the European Parliament and of the Council of 24 October 1995 on the protection of individuals with regard to the processing of personal data and on the free movement of such data.* Retrieved April 2, 2011, from http://eur-lex.europa.eu/LexUriServ/LexUriServ.do?uri=CELEX:31995L0046:en:

Directive, H. T. M. L. 2002/58/EC, (2002). *Protection of Privacy to Electronic Communications.* Retrieved November 20, 2010, from http://eur-lex.europa.eu/LexUriServ/LexUriServ.do?uri=CELEX:32002L0058:EN:HTML

Educause, (2010). *Privacy Risks Assessment.* Retrieved October 6, 2010 from http://www.educause.edu/node/645/tid/30444?time=1281348515

EINSTEIN 2, (2009). *US-CERT.* Retrieved March 11, 2011 from http://en.wikipedia.org/wiki/Einstein_(US-CERT_program)

Gruteser M. & Grunwald D. (2004). *A Methodological Assessment of Location Privacy Risks in Wireless Hotspot Networks in Security in Pervasive Computing.* Lecture Notes in Computer Science, 2004, Volume 2802/2004, 113-142, DOI: 10.1007/978-3-540-39881-3_5.

HIPAA. (2006). *Saint Louis University Institutional Review Board HIPPA TIP Sheet*, 31st March 2006. Retrieved November 21, 2010 from www.slu.edu/Documents/provost/irb/hipaa_tip_sheet.doc

HMG IA Standard No. 6 (2009). *Protecting Personal Data and Managing Information Risk.* Cabinet Office, CESG National Technical Authority for Information Assurance, Issue 1.2, March 2009.

Information Commissioner's Office (ICO). (2009). *Privacy Impact Assessment Handbook Version 2.0. Appendix 1 – PIA Screening Process.* Retrieved October 29, 2010, from http://www.ico.gov.uk/upload/documents/pia_handbook_html_v2/html/3-app1.html

Information Commissioner's Office (ICO) Cabinet Office. UK (2009). *Privacy Impact Assessment Handbook Version 2.0.* Retrieved October 6, 2010, from http://www.ico.gov.uk/upload/documents/pia_handbook_html_v2/index.html

Peirce, T. (2009). *RFID Privacy & Security.* IEEE International Conference on Communications, ICC 2009, Dresden, Germany, June 2009 Abu-Nimeh S., & Mead N. R., (2009). *Privacy Risk Assessment in Privacy Requirements Engineering.* 2nd International Workshop on Requirements Engineering and Law, Georgia, USA, 2009

Radack, S. (2010). *Guide To Protecting Personally Identifiable Information (PII).* NIST ITL Security Bulletin for April 2010. Retrieved November 6, 2010 from http://csrc.nist.gov/publications/nistbul/april-2010_guide-protecting-pii.pdf

Shane, D. (2010). *Zurich Insurance hit with Record Data Loss Fine.* August 2010. Retrieved October 22, 2010 from http://www.information-age.com/channels/security-and-continuity/news/1277718/zurich-insurance-hit-with-record-data-loss-fine.thtml

US-CERT. (2008). *Privacy Impact Assessment EINSTEIN Program.* Department of Homeland Security, National Cyber Security Division, United States, May 19, 2008. Retrieved October 8, 2010 from http://www.dhs.gov/xlibrary/assets/privacy/privacy_pia_einstein2.pdf

ADDITIONAL READING

Asif Tufal. (2010). *The Torts of Negligence.* Retrieved November 6, 2010 from http://a-level-law.com/tort/Negligence/Flowchart.pdf.

Charlesworth, A. (2007), *Privacy Impact Assessments: International Study of their Application and Effects*. Law School, Bristol University, October 2007. Retrieved October 2010 from http://www.ico.gov.uk/upload/documents/library/corporate/research_and_reports/lbrouni_piastudy_apph_eur_2910071.pdf

Information Commissioner's Office. (2010). *An overview of the Data Protection Act 1998*. Retrieved October 2010 from http://www.ico.gov.uk/upload/documents/library/Data_Protection/Introductory/DATA_PROTECTION_ACT_OVERVIEW.PPT

Kenneally, E. E., & Claffy, K. (2010). Dialing Privacy and Utility. *IEEE Security & Privacy*, *8*(4), 16–17.

Ministry of Justice. (2010). *Undertaking Privacy Impact Assessments: The Data Protection Act 1998*, 13 August 2010. Retrieved October 2010 from www.justice.gov.uk/guidance/docs/pia-guidance-08-10.pdf

NIST. (2010). *The Federal Information Processing Standard (FIPS) 199, Standards for Security Categorisation of Federal Information and Information Systems*. Retrieved November 6, 2010 from http://csrc.nist.gov/publications/fips/fips199/FIPS-PUB-199-final.pdf.

Onwubiko, C. (2008). *Security Framework for Attack Detection in Computer Networks*. Germany: VDM Publishing.

Robert Gellman (2009). Privacy in the Clouds: Risks to Privacy and Confidentiality from Cloud Computing. *World Privacy Forum*. February 23, 2009

Rodney, J. Petersen (2003). *Security, Privacy, and the Protection of Personally Identifiable Information. EDUCAUSE/Internet2 Computer and Network Security Task Force*. Retrieved November 6, 2010 from http://net.educause.edu/ir/library/powerpoint/SEC0315.pps.

Stolfo, S. J., & Tsidik, G. (2010). Privacy-Preserving Sharing of Sensitive Information. *IEEE Security & Privacy*, *8*(4), 16–17. doi:10.1109/MSP.2010.135

The National Archives. (2010). *Data Protection Act 1998*. Retrieved October 2010 from http://www.legislation.gov.uk/ukpga/1998/29/contents.

Whitehouse (2006). *Office of Management and Budget (OMB) Memorandum M-06-15. Safeguarding Personally Identifiable Information*. Retrieved November 6, 2010 from http://www.whitehouse.gov/sites/default/files/omb/memoranda/fy2006/m-06-15.pdf.

Wikipedia (2010). *Data Protection Act 1998*. Retrieved October 2010 from http://en.wikipedia.org/wiki/Data_Protection_Act_1998.

KEY TERMS AND DEFINITIONS

Data Protection Act (DPA): This is a piece of legislation that governs how personal information of living individuals are processed. Processing of personal information means, how personal information are obtained, shared, recorded or stored (held). This piece of legislation was enacted in 1998 in the United Kingdom (UK).

Personal Data: Personal data is data that relates to a living person who can be identified by those data, or from those data plus other information which is in the possession of, or is likely to come into the possession of, the data controller. For example, first name, last name or/and date of birth of a living person.

Personal Identifiable Data (PID): These are sensitive and personal data that can be used to identify an individual. Personal identifiable data is the same as Personally Identifiable Information (PII), while the former is associated to Europe; the latter is associated with America. Examples of PII include a combination of one or more personal identifiers such as full face photographic images and any comparable images plus name, or date of birth plus address and health records. A full list of personal identifiers is shown in Table 1.

Sensitive Personal Data: These are identifiable personal data whose release would put those persons at significant risk of harm or distress, unless otherwise disclosed by the persons. For example, a person's medical records, bank details, social insurance number (national insurance) or tax records etc.

Chapter 11
Combining Security and Privacy in Requirements Engineering

Saeed Abu-Nimeh
Damballa Inc., USA

Nancy R. Mead
Carnegie Mellon University, USA

ABSTRACT

Security requirements engineering identifies security risks in software in the early stages of the development cycle. In this chapter, the authors present a security requirements approach dubbed SQUARE. They integrate privacy requirements into SQUARE to identify privacy risks in addition to security risks. They present a privacy elicitation technique and then combine security risk assessment techniques with privacy risk assessment techniques.

INTRODUCTION

There have been several initiatives to standardize the processes of software lifecycle. Yet, ISO 12207 is considered the standard of software lifecycle processes (Singh, 1998). The standard divides software lifecycle processes into 5 high level phases: acquisition, supply, development, operation, and maintenance. The acquisition phase concentrates on initiating the project. The supply phase concentrates on developing a project management plan. In the development phase, the software product is designed, created, and tested. In the operation phase, users start utilizing the product, and in the maintenance phase the product is maintained to stay operational.

Software requirements are addressed and discussed at an early stage in the software development phase. Requirements engineering concentrates on the real-world goals for, functions of, and constraints on software systems. In addition, it is concerned with the relationship of these factors to precise specifications of software behavior, and to their evolution over time and across software families (Zave, 1997).

DOI: 10.4018/978-1-61350-507-6.ch011

Requirements elicitation in software development concentrates on functional and nonfunctional requirements. Functional or end user requirements are the tasks that the system under development is expected to perform. However, nonfunctional requirements are the qualities that the system is to adhere to. Functional requirements are not as difficult to tackle, as it is easier to test their implementation in the system under development. Security and privacy requirements are considered nonfunctional requirements, although in many instances they do have functionality (Abu-Nimeh, Miyazaki, & Mead, 2009). The Security Quality Requirements Engineering (SQUARE) method is used to identify software security issues in the early stages of the development lifecycle. Next, we present SQUARE in detail. Then, the integration of privacy requirements into SQUARE is discussed in the following section.

To identify the security and privacy issues in software a risk assessment is needed. Risk assessment is a step in a risk management process. A risk management process involves the identification, assessment, and prioritization of risks related to a situation. Risk assessment is determining in a quantitative or qualitative way the value of these risks. Security risk assessment identifies the threats to systems, while privacy risk assessment identifies data sensitivities in systems. SQUARE relies on security risk assessment techniques to assess the levels of security risk in systems. However, these security risk assessment techniques are not adequate to addressing privacy risks. Therefore, we combine the security risk assessment techniques in SQUARE with privacy risk assessment techniques.

BACKGROUND

Security requirements engineering (Mead, Hough, & Stehney, 2005) aims to identify software security risks in early stages of the design process. Privacy requirements engineering (Chiasera, Casati, Daniel, & Velegrakis, 2008) serves to identify privacy risks early in the design process. Recent research studies (Peeger & Peeger, 2009) have shown that privacy requirements engineering is less mature than security engineering and that underlying engineering principles give little attention to privacy requirements. In addition, (Adams & Sasse, 2001) claim that most of the privacy disclosures happen due to defects in the design, and are not the result of an intentional attack. Therefore, although security and privacy risks overlap, relying merely on protecting the security of users does not necessarily imply the protection of their privacy. For instance, health records can be secured from various types of intrusions; however, the security of such assets does not guarantee that the privacy of patients is secure. The security of such records does not protect against improper authorized access or disclosure of records. SQUARE generates categorized and prioritized security requirements following these nine steps (Mead et al., 2005):

1. Technical definitions are agreed upon by the requirements engineering team and project stakeholders.
2. Assets, business, and security goals are identified.
3. In order to facilitate full understanding of the studied system, artifacts and documentation are created.
4. A security risk assessment is applied to determine the likelihood and impact of possible threats to the system.
5. The best method for eliciting security requirements is determined by the requirements engineering team and the stakeholders.
6. Security requirements are elicited.
7. Security requirements are categorized.
8. Security requirements are prioritized.
9. The security requirements are inspected to ensure consistency and accuracy.

The modified steps to address privacy issues in software and to perform a privacy risk assessment follow in this chapter.

SQUARE FOR PRIVACY

The modified nine steps in SQUARE to adapt the whole process for privacy requirements engineering are (Bijwe & Mead, 2010):

1. **Agreeing on Definitions:** The engineering team and the stakeholders create a comprehensive list of terms that will aid effective communication and reduce ambiguity. A list of terms that are applicable to privacy is provided. For example, this list can include terms like, access, anonymity, authentication, pseudonymity, etc. Then, suggested definitions for the proposed terms with their sources are provided to help the stakeholders understand the basic scope of each term and select one of its definitions.

2. **Identifying Assets and Privacy Goals:** In this step a discussion is initiated among the stakeholders regarding their assets and overall privacy goals for the project. Privacy goals include; (a) ensure that personal data is collected with the users' permission, (b) ensure that the data collected for a specific purpose is not used for other purposes without appropriate authorization, and (c) ensure that the user is aware of the purpose for which personal data is collected.

3. **Collecting Artifacts:** Artifacts that are relevant to privacy include system architecture diagrams, use-case scenarios and diagrams, misuse case scenarios and diagrams, attack trees, and user-role hierarchies. System architecture diagrams provide an overview of the system as it exists, and show how data shows among the different components. Privacy use cases will mostly be related to how the system handles user data and how the system components interact with each other. Misuse cases identify the vulnerabilities of the system and the risks that the system is prone to. Misuse cases can be used to make the system more resistant to such attacks. Attack trees model threats to the system by focusing on the attackers and the ways they may attack the system. User-role hierarchies can determine the access control requirements based on the user role.

4. **Risk Assessment:** The security risk assessment techniques in SQUARE are combined with privacy risk assessment techniques to address privacy risks. Section 4 discusses the process in detail.

5. **Selecting Elicitation Technique:** The privacy requirements elicitation technique (PRET) can be used in this step to select a suitable elicitation technique for privacy. Section 5 discusses PRET in detail.

6. **Eliciting Privacy Requirements:** To elicit privacy requirements, PRET can be used in this step as well.

7. **Categorizing Requirements:** Privacy requirements can have legal implications; therefore, a categorization that suits privacy requirements is needed. (Massey, Otto, & Anton., 2009) use three categories to prioritize legal requirements; (a) nonlegal requirements,(b) legal requirements needing further refinement, and (c) and implementation-ready legal requirements.

8. **Prioritizing Requirements:** The list of requirements provided by the risk assessment (step 4) and the categorization (step 7) are prioritized in this step. (Karlsson, 1996) proposed the pair-wise comparison method to prioritize requirements. The method is based on the analytical hierarchy process (AHP) and derives the relative importance of one requirement over another. Given a set of n requirements, the method requires $n*(n - 1)/2$ comparisons. Using the values given for each comparison, mathematical formulas

can be used to derive the prioritization for the *n* requirements. (Massey et al., 2009) proposed a method to prioritize requirements using two steps. In the first step of finding legal implications, we use the required legal text as input. The main goal of this step is to map the requirements to the subsections in the legal text with the help of legal-domain experts. The second step is calculating a prioritization score for every requirement. This step uses the mapping from the first step to calculate a prioritization score based on a predefined formula.

9. **Inspecting Requirements:** Inspections remove defects and clarify ambiguities in the requirements. There exist a number of methods to carry out inspections, ranging from ad-hoc to use of checklists and even Fagan reviews and scenario-based inspections. Research has shown that scenario-based inspection methods provide a better defect detection rate than checklist or ad-hoc inspections (Porter, Votta, & Basili, 1995). The outcome of this process is a final privacy requirements document that has been agreed upon and verified by all the stakeholders and the requirements engineering team. In the following section, we discuss the modifications to steps 4, 5, and 6 in further detail.

COMBINING SECURITY AND PRIVACY RISK ASSESSMENT TECHNIQUES

Security and privacy risk assessment techniques overlap, yet they address different problems. Generally, security protects systems' resources, including software, storage, networks, and users. However, privacy concentrates on data protection, which includes the application of various policies and procedures to collect and protect data (Abu-Nimeh & Mead, 2010).

The goals of a security risk assessment include the implementation of authentication and authorization systems; however, the goals of a privacy risk assessment relate to privacy policies and procedures. The different procedures in privacy impact assessment and security risk assessment are (Mitrano, Kirby, & Maltz, 2005):

1. **Security risk assessment**
   a. threat identification
   b. vulnerability identification
   c. control analysis
   d. likelihood determination
   e. impact analysis
   f. risk determination
2. **Privacy impact assessment**
   a. data description
   b. data sources
   c. data collection process, data accuracy, data completeness, and data current-ness
   d. data comprehensiveness and documentation
   e. data access description, access procedures, access controls, and access responsibilities
   f. access levels and restrictions
   g. authorized access misuse
   h. shared data restrictions and controls
   i. data relevancy and necessity
   j. possibility of data derivation and aggregation
   k. protection and control of consolidated data
   l. data retrieval
   m. equitable treatment of users
   n. data retention and disposal
   o. user monitoring and protection against unauthorized monitoring

SQUARE relies on two risk assessment techniques in step 4: the Risk Management Guide for Information Technology Systems (NIST SP 800-30) (National Institute of Standards and Technology, 2002) and Yacov Haimes's Risk Filtering, Ranking, and Management Framework (RFRM) (Haimes, 2004). The RFRM approach contains eight phases, some of which were found to be out of scope. Only two relevant phases of RFRM are included in SQUARE: phase III, bicriteria filtering and ranking, and phase IV, multicriteria filtering and ranking.

NIST's model for risk assessment is broken into nine steps, each with an output that serves as the input to the next step. SQUARE excludes steps 1, 8, and 9 in NIST, as they are irrelevant or redundant. Therefore, the steps from NIST's model included in SQUARE are threat identification, vulnerability identification, control analysis, likelihood determination, impact analysis, and risk determination. Clearly, the risk assessment in SQUARE corresponds to the system under analysis. Most importantly, the risk assessment should categorize the likelihood and impact of the major threats to the system (Mead et al., 2005).

Several laws and regulations provide a set of guidelines that can be used to assess privacy risks. For example, the Health Insurance Portability and Accountability Act (HIPAA) addresses privacy concerns of health information systems by enforcing data exchange standards. In addition, Privacy Impact Assessment (PIA) (Flaherty, 2000) is a comprehensive process for determining the privacy, confidentiality, and security risks associated with the collection, use, and disclosure of personal information.

In the following sections, we discuss the combination of PIA and HIPAA with security risk assessment techniques that are used in the Security Quality Requirements Engineering (SQUARE) methodology. Initially, we discuss a classification of PIA and HIPAA following the methodology in (Campbell & Stamp, 2004), after which we explain the addition of privacy impact and risk assessment techniques to the current SQUARE model.

Privacy Impact Assessment

According to (Statistics Canada, 2008), the PIA process is used to determine the privacy, confidentiality, and security risks associated with the collection, use, and disclosure of personal information. In addition, it defines how to mitigate and eliminate the identified risks. The PIA process should be considered in any new program or service delivery initiative, and should communicate to the public the privacy and confidentiality of their information.

According to US-CERT (United States Computer Emergency Readiness Team, 2008), the following should be addressed when conducting a PIA on systems.

1. Characterization of the information: what information is collected and maintained in the system.
2. Uses of the information: use of information and tools to analyze data.
3. Information retention: how long is information retained?
4. Internal sharing and disclosure: which internal organizations share the information?
5. External sharing and disclosure: which external organizations share the information?
6. Notice of collection of information: notifying individuals prior to collection of information.
7. Individual access, redress, and correction: how can individuals access their information?
8. Technical access and security: who can access the information or the system?
9. Technology: what development process was used to develop the system?

Previous research (Heckle & Holden, 2006) proved that PIA works well in combination with other risk assessment techniques. PIA helped to identify the data sensitivities of vote verification systems, while other risk assessments were used to identify the full spectrum of threats to these systems. In the following section we discuss the integration of HIPAA as a privacy risk assessment technique.

HIPAA Privacy Risk Assessment

HIPAA addresses privacy concerns of health information systems by enforcing data exchange standards. The act also provides a guideline to analyze risks. The overall objective of a HIPAA risk analysis is to document the potential risks and vulnerabilities of confidentiality, integrity, or availability of electronic protected health information (ePHI) and to determine the appropriate safeguards to bring the degree of risk to an acceptable and manageable level. Risks found by the analysis fall into three categories: access, storage, and transmission.

The entities of interest in HIPAA are called the Covered Entities (CEs) that must comply with the HIPAA Security Rule. These are health plans (HMOs, group health plans, etc.), health care clearinghouses (billing and repricing companies, etc.), and health care providers (doctors, dentists, hospitals, etc.) who transmit any ePHI. There are seven steps in an HIPAA risk assessment.

1. Inventory and classify assets.
2. Document likely threats to each asset.
3. Conduct a vulnerability assessment.
4. Evaluate current safeguards (administrative, physical, or technical).
5. Document risks.
6. Recommend appropriate safeguards.
7. Create report of results.

Classification of Risk Assessment Techniques

In order to make sure that both the existing security and the proposed privacy risk assessment techniques follow the same methodology and require the same expertise, we apply the classification scheme presented in (Campbell & Stamp, 2004). The proposed privacy risk assessment techniques must conform to the methodology used by the risk assessment techniques in SQUARE; however, they need to address privacy rather than security. In (Campbell & Stamp, 2004), the authors propose a classification scheme for risk assessment methods based on the level of detail of the assessment method and the approach used in that assessment method. They summarize the strengths and weaknesses of assessment methods in a nine-cell matrix as shown in Table 1. This comparative matrix helps the user to understand the following information: what to expect from an assessment method, what the relationship is among different assessment methods, and what the best way is to use an assessment method. Note that this classification scheme does not help us determine which methods are appropriate for addressing security risks and which are appropriate for addressing privacy risks, yet it helps us analyze the methods suitable for privacy and those suitable for security relative to their detail and the assessment approach they follow.

As shown in Table 2, an assessment method can be one of three levels: abstract, midlevel, and concrete. An *abstract* method requires an expert to drive the method. A *concrete* method requires

Table 1. Classification Matrix

Level		Approach		
		Temporal	**Functional**	**Comparative**
Abstract	Expert	Engagement (1)	Sequence (4)	Principles (7)
Mid-Level	Collaborative	Exercise (2)	Assistant (5)	Best Practice (8)
Concrete	Owner	Compliance Testing (3)	Matrix (6)	Audit (9)

Table 2. Approach Level

Level	Abstract	Mid-Level	Concrete
	High Level (3)	Mid-Level (2)	Low Level (1)
Expertise	Requires expert's knowledge	Requires both experts' and owner's knowledge	Requires user's knowledge
Description	How an expert performs an assessment	How both (an expert and owner) perform an assessment	How a system owner performs an assessment
Application	Broad	Middle	Narrow
Driver	Expert	Collaborative (both expert and owner)	Owner

someone who knows the details of the system to drive the method - that is, the owner of the system. A *mid-level* method requires a collaborative effort between an expert and the owner of the system to drive the method.

Table 3 shows the three different approaches that can be followed by risk assessment methods. An assessment method can be temporal, which is a method that stress-tests a system in real-time, functional, which performs threat analysis on the system without testing, or comparative, which compares the system against an explicit standard.

The nine numbered cells in Table 1 (i.e., engagement (1) through audit (9)) show what needs to be done by the driver of the method. They can be summarized as follows:

1. **Engagement:** Experts try to compromise a system without the owner's help.
2. **Exercise:** Owner collaborates with experts to compromise a system.
3. **Compliance Testing:** Similar to door rattling performed by the owner of the system.
4. **Sequence:** Series of questions the user answers, or flow chart.
5. **Assistance:** Similar to an assistant, a track of the system details is kept.
6. **Matrix:** The user looks up a table.

Table 3. Approach Classification

	Temporal	Functional	Comparative
Procedure	Stresses a system and actual tests are applied in real time	It is a blend of the other two approaches. It performs threat analysis, which focuses on how a system functions without testing	A comparison against an explicit standard. The system model and the threat lists are only implicitly present in a generic form
Outcome	The performance of the system as a consequence of the application of those tests	Threat analysis	Comparing the system with an explicit standard
Advantages	Testing the system clears misconceptions	Considers specific threats, vulnerabilities, assets and countermeasures	Simple and focused
Disadvantages	Impractical to test the system, so a model of the system is tested. Similarly, cannot perform all attacks on the system and a subset of attacks is performed	No testing involved	No testing or examination of function and no explicit system model involved

7. **Principles:** This is a list of all comparative types. The user applies principles to the system.
8. **Best Practice:** There is a more specific list than the principle's list.
9. **Audit:** This list is based on an explicit standard, but is more specific than the best practices list.

Refer to (Campbell & Stamp, 2004) for further details on these methods.

Classification of Security Risk Assessment Methods in SQUARE

As we mentioned earlier, SQUARE relies on two risk assessment techniques in step 4: NIST SP 800-30 and RFRM. According to (Campbell & Stamp, 2004), NIST SP 800-30 is considered among the assistant methods. This risk assessment approach is performed by an expert and is a functional approach (see Table 3). However,

RFRM is not listed as one of the risk assessment methods in (Campbell & Stamp, 2004). NIST and RFRM are both concerned with hardware failure or destruction; however, they rank the importance differently. Also, the outputs of both methods concentrate on different aspects. In NIST, the output concentrates on what the attacker can do once inside the system, e.g., destroying data or disclosing information.

In RFRM, the output concentrates on the attacker's ability to break the frontline of a defense system (Mead et al., 2005). Due to the similarity of the NIST model and RFRM, we consider RFRM an assistant method as well.

Classification of Privacy Risk Assessment Methods

PIA and HIPAA are driven by experts. The methods require someone other than the owner of the system to perform the risk assessment. Further, the methods perform threat analysis on the system

Figure 1. Integration of PRET into SQUARE

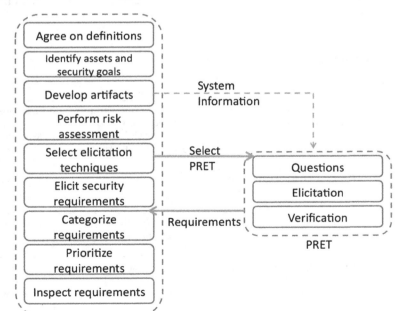

Table 4. Questions included in questionnaire

Question	Response
1. Does the service provider process personal information?	Yes / No
2. In which country or area is the service provided?	
3. What type of service provider? 3.1. If Industrial, does the service provider belong to any of these fields? 3.2. If Governmental, does the service provider belong to any of these fields? 3.3. Is the purpose of the service related to journalism, literary work, academic studies, religious activities, or political activities?	Industrial / Governmental / Academic / Other Medicine / Communication / Education Military branch / Non-military branch / Research Body Yes / No
4. What kind of personal information does the service provider process?	Point of Contact / Social Identification / Personal Identity Data / Demographic Information / Age, Education / Health Information / Financial Information / Personal Information of Children / Other Sensitive Personal Data
5. How does the service provider obtain personal information?	Provided by users / Provided by third parties / Collected automatically from users / Collected automatically from third parties
6. Where does the service provider store personal information?	Client Side / Server Side / The Third Party Client Side / The Third Party Server Side
7. How long does the service provider store personal information?	Does Not Store / One Transaction / Certain Period of Time / Forever
8. Does the service provider use personal information for another purpose?	Yes / No
9. Does the service provider share personal information with others?	Yes / No
10. What privacy protection level does the service provider set?	High / Mid / Low

without testing it. Actually, they consist of a series of questions that are answered by the users of the system as shown in the previous subsections.

Both techniques require the same level of expertise, i.e., expert, used in NIST SP 800- 30 and RFRM. In addition, both methods follow the same methodology, i.e., functional, used in NIST SP 800-30 and RFRM. Consequently, PIA and HIPAA are regarded as assistant methods.

The following goals were met by integrating the PIA and HIPAA risk assessment methods:

1. Introduce risk assessment techniques that address privacy in addition to security;
2. Follow the same assessment methodology;
3. And require the same level of expertise used by the security risk assessment techniques in SQUARE.

Table 5. Auto insurance service questionnaire

Question	Answer
1	Yes
2	USA
3 3.1 3.2 3.3	Industrial - - No
4	Point, Social, Demographic, Age
5	Provided by users, Provided by third parties
6	Server side
7	Forever
8	No
9	No
10	Mid

Based on the previous discussion, our goal is met. We introduced risk assessment techniques that address privacy rather than security, follow the same assessment methodology, and require the same level of expertise used by the security risk assessment techniques in SQUARE (Abu-Nimeh & Mead, 2009).

PRIVACY REQUIREMENTS ELICITATION TECHNIQUES

The privacy requirements elicitation technique (PRET) (Miyazaki, Mead, & Zhan, 2008) is based on SQUARE. The tool helps software engineers and stakeholders elicit privacy requirements using

Table 6. Auto insurance service results

Privacy requirements	Derivation	Explanation	Priority Level
The service architecture shall describe privacy policy statements and enable a user to access them.	W3C- AR020.1, 20.3	Personal data usage (Q1, Q2)	Mid
Before collecting personal data, the data controller shall specify the purpose.	OECD-PP-P9	Personal data usage (Q1)	Mid
The service provider shall limit the collection of personal data and obtain such data by lawful and fair means.	OECD-PP-P7	Personal data collection (Q6)	Mid
The system network communications must be protected from unauthorized information gathering and/or eavesdropping.	Misuse-case-1	Personal data collection (Q6)	Mid
The system should have functional audit logs and usage reports without disclosing identity information.	Misuse-case-2	Personal data collection (Q6)	Mid
The system shall have strong authentication measures in place at all system gateways and entrance points.	Misuse-case-3	Personal data storage (Q7)	Mid
Personal data should be protected by reasonable security safeguards against such risks as loss, unauthorized access, destruction, use, modification or disclosure of data.	OECD-PP-P11	Personal data storage (Q7)	Mid
Personal data shall be accurate, complete and kept up-to-date, if it is possible.	OECD-PP-P8	Personal data storage (Q7)	Mid
The system shall provide a mechanism by which users can verify their data.	OECD-PP-P13	Personal data storage (Q7)	Mid
The system shall provide a data backup mechanism.	Misuse-case-4	Personal data storage (Q7)	Mid
The system shall have a verification process to check whether there is a disclosure agreement between the third party and the person.	Misuse-case-5	Personal data collection from the third party (Q5)	Mid
The service provider shall report to all the customers if the privacy information is breached.	CA-SB-1386	Breach report in JP, USA (Q1, Q2, Q3)	High

a computer-aided approach. PRET uses a questionnaire to elicit information that the requirements engineers and stakeholders complete. The tool contains a database of privacy requirements that is searched to utilize the input from the questionnaire and provides results. Figure 1 depicts the integration of PRET into SQUARE. The first four steps in SQUARE remain the same. In the fifth step, when elicitation techniques are chosen, PRET can be selected to elicit privacy requirements. Here the PRET process starts; the questionnaire is answered and the privacy requirements are elicited. Finally, the privacy requirements are verified and fed back to SQUARE. In SQUARE, the privacy requirements are categorized, prioritized, and inspected in the seventh, eighth, and ninth steps respectively. In the following subsections, we describe the questionnaire design, discuss the various sources used to identify privacy requirements, and illustrate the process involved in requirements elicitation.

Questionnaire Design

Privacy Seal Programs (Markert, 2002) and the OECD Privacy Statement Generator (OECD & Microsoft Corp., 2000) are used to prepare the questionnaire. The OECD generator is a tool that provides users with useful input in the development of a privacy policy and statement. Using the generator and other privacy seal policies, such as TRUSTe and PrivacyMark, 10 questions are included in the questionnaire as shown in Table 4.

Identification of Privacy Requirements

Privacy requirements are collected from multiple sources, which are generally various publicly available privacy laws and principles. In addition, we apply misuse cases to identify privacy requirements. The following sections outline each of these approaches.

Privacy laws and principles. To identify privacy requirements, six privacy principles and laws are studied, from which a subset of privacy requirements are selected. The laws and principles are as follows:

1. OECD Guidelines on the Protection of Privacy
2. The European Commission's Directive on Data Protection
3. Japan's Personal Information Protection Act
4. Privacy laws in the US
   ◦ Privacy Protection Act
   ◦ Video Privacy Protection Act
   ◦ CA-SB-1386 (California)
   ◦ Family Educational Rights and Privacy Act
   ◦ Health Insurance Portability and Accountability Act
   ◦ Children's Online Privacy Protection Act
5. Common Criteria
6. W3C Web Services Architecture Requirements

Table 7. Health care ring questionnaire

Question	Answer
1	Yes
2	Japan
3 3.1 3.2 3.3	Industrial Medicine - No
4	Point, Demographic, Age, Health
5	Provided by users
6	Server side
7	Certain Period of Time
8	No
9	Yes
10	High

Misuse Cases. Misuse cases are used to elicit requirements. The idea behind them is to document and decide how software should act proactively to prevent malicious activities. First, a normal use case is assumed. Then, malicious parties and activities are added to the use case. Afterwards, the relationships among the use cases and the misuse cases are linked. This whole process has proven to be useful in mitigating future attacks.

Decision Process. A decision tree of requirements is built to traverse multiple combinations of question paths. The introduction of subsequent questions is based on the answers to the current question. While the user goes through different nodes in the decision tree, a different set of questions is introduced. Several constraints are checked to ensure that privacy requirements dedicated to certain areas, (e.g., in the US or the EU), are met. In addition, each one of the requirements is assigned a priority based on its source. For instance, requirements derived from laws have higher priority than requirements derived from principles and misuse cases.

Evaluation Case Studies

We evaluate our model using two pseudo-software development projects: an auto insurance service and a health care ring. In Table 5, we show the answers to the questionnaire for the auto insurance service. Then, we show the corresponding privacy requirements elicited by PRET in Table 6. The health care ring's answers to the questionnaire are shown in Table 7 and the elicited privacy requirements are shown in Table 8.

Table 8. Health care ring results

Privacy Requirements	Derivation	Explanation	Priority Level
The service provider shall describe privacy policy statements and enable a user to access them.	W3C-AR020.1, 20.3	Personal data usage (Q1, Q2)	Mid
Before collecting personal data, the service provider shall specify the purpose.	OECD-PP-P9	Personal data usage (Q1)	Mid
The service provider shall obtain prior consent of the person, except for following cases; (1) handling of personal information is based on laws; (2) handling of personal information is based on necessity for the protection of the life, body, or property of an individual; (3) handling of personal information is based on necessity for improving public hygiene or promoting the growth of children; (4) handling of personal information is based on necessity for cooperating with a state institution, a local public body, or an individual or entity entrusted by one in executing the operations prescribed by laws.	PIPA-Article-16	Personal data usage in JP (Q1, Q2, Q3)	High
The service provider shall handle personal information within the scope for the purpose of usage.	PIPA-Article-16	Personal data usage in JP (Q1, Q2, Q3)	High

continued on following page

Table 8. Continued

Privacy Requirements	Derivation	Explanation	Priority Level
The service provider shall limit the collection of personal data and obtain such data by lawful and fair means.	OECD-PP-P7	Personal data collection (Q6)	Mid
The system network communications must be protected from unauthorized information gathering and/or eavesdropping.	Misuse-case-1	Personal data collection (Q6)	Mid
The system should have functional audit logs and usage reports without disclosing identity information.	Misuse-case-2	Personal data collection (Q6)	Mid
The system shall have strong authentication measures in place at all system gateways and entrance points.	Misuse-case-3	Personal data storage (Q7)	Mid
Personal data shall be accurate, complete and kept up-to-date, if it is possible.	OECD-PP-P8	Personal data storage (Q7)	Mid
The system shall provide a mechanism by which users can verify their data.	OECD-PP-P13	Personal data storage (Q7)	Mid
The system shall provide a data backup mechanism.	Misuse-case-4	Personal data storage (Q7)	Mid
The service provider must take necessary and proper measures for the prevention of leakage, loss, or damage, and for other control of security of personal data.	PIPA-Article-20	Personal data storage in JP (Q2, Q7)	High
The service provider shall disclose personal data only with the consent of data subject or by the authority of law.	OECD-PP-P10	Personal data sharing (Q9)	Mid
The service provider shall enable delegation and propagation of privacy policy to the third parties.	W3C-AR020.5	Personal data sharing (Q9)	Mid
The service provider shall gain consensus from users what data they are sharing.	PIPA-Article-23	Personal data sharing in JP (Q2, Q3, Q9)	High
The service provider shall report to all the customers if the privacy information is breached.	CA-SB-1386	Breach report in JP, USA (Q1, Q2, Q3)	High
The system should provide anonymity. Anonymity means other users or subjects are unable to determine the identity of a user bound to a subject or operation.	CC-FPR-ANO	Privacy enhancing technology usage (Q10)	Low
The system should provide pseudonymity. Pseudonymity means a set of users and/or subjects are unable to determine the identity of a user bound to a subject or operation, but that this user is still accountable for its actions.	CC-FPR-PSE	Privacy enhancing technology usage (Q10)	Low

continued on following page

Table 8. continued

Privacy Requirements	Derivation	Explanation	Priority Level
The system should provide unlink-ability. Unlinkability means users and/or subjects are unable to determine whether the same user caused certain specific operations.	CC-FPR-UNL	Privacy enhancing technology usage (Q10)	Low
The system should provide unobserv-ability. Unobservability means users and/or subjects cannot determine whether an operation is being performed	CC-FPR-UNO	Privacy enhancing technology usage (Q10)	Low
The system should provide unobserv-ability, which requires that users and/or subjects cannot determine whether an operation is being performed.	CC-FPR-UNO	Privacy enhancing technology usage (Q10)	Low

CONCLUSION AND FUTURE RESEARCH DIRECTIONS

In this chapter, we discussed a security requirements engineering approach, SQUARE. SQUARE is a structured methodology to address software security issues in early stages of the development lifecycle. Then we discussed the integration of privacy requirements into SQUARE.

First, we introduced PRET, a technique that is designed to elicit privacy requirements in software. PRET relies on SQUARE in some of the steps, but introduces extra steps to be applicable to privacy issues. We evaluated our PRET using the pseudo-software projects of an auto insurance service and a health care ring.

We showed that security risk assessment methods in SQUARE cannot be used as an alternative to privacy risk assessment ones. We presented the addition of privacy risk and impact assessment techniques (HIPAA and PIA) to SQUARE. To make sure that both the existing security and the privacy risk assessment techniques follow the same methodology and require the same expertise, a classification scheme of risk assessment methods was applied. Then, we combined the existing security risk assessment methods in SQUARE,

namely NIST SP 800-30 and RFRM, with PIA and HIPAA. Our extensions to SQUARE took us further down the path of privacy requirements engineering.

Future work will explore building a privacy requirements engineering tool called SQUARE for Privacy (P-SQUARE) that covers all the nine steps of SQUARE. Thus SQUARE will target both privacy and security risks in software. In addition, we will conduct additional case studies and pilot projects for P-SQUARE.

NOTE

The Carnegie Mellon University and Software Engineering Institute Material contained herein is furnished on an "as-is" basis. Carnegie Mellon University makes no warranties of any kind, either expressed or implied, as to any matter including, but not limited to, warranty of fitness for purpose or merchantability, exclusivity, or results obtained from use of the material. Carnegie Mellon University does not make any warranty of any kind with respect to freedom from patent, trademark, or copyright infringement.

REFERENCES

Abu-Nimeh, S., & Mead, N. R. (2009). *Privacy risk assessment in privacy requirements engineering.* In RELAW: The second international workshop on requirements engineering and law.

Abu-Nimeh, S., & Mead, N. R. (2010). *Combining privacy and security risk assessment in security quality requirements engineering.* In 2010 AAAI spring symposium series, intelligent information privacy management.

Abu-Nimeh, S., Miyazaki, S., & Mead, N. R. (2009). *Integrating privacy requirements into security requirements engineering. In* Proceedings of the 21st international conference on software and knowledge engineering (pp. 542--547).

Adams, A., & Sasse, M. A. (2001). *Privacy in multimedia communications: Protecting users, not just data.* In Proceedings of IMH HCI'01 (pp. 49--64). New York: Springer.

Bijwe, A., & Mead, N. R. (2010). *Adapting the square process for privacy requirements engineering* (Tech. Rep. Nos. CMU/SEI-2010-TN-022). Pittsburgh, PA: Carnegie Mellon University.

Campbell, P. L., & Stamp, J. E. (2004). *A classification scheme for risk assessment methods (Tech. Rep. No. SAND2004-4233).* Sandia National Laboratories.

Chiasera, A., Casati, F., Daniel, F., & Velegrakis, Y. (2008). *Engineering privacy requirements in business intelligence applications.* In SDM '08: Proceedings of the 5th VLDB workshop on secure data management (pp. 219--228). Berlin, Heidelberg: Springer-Verlag.

Flaherty, D. H. (2000). Privacy impact assessments: an essential tool for data protection. *In 22nd annual meeting of privacy and data protection officials.*

Haimes, Y. Y. (2004). *Risk modeling, assessment, and management* (2nd edition ed.). New York: Wiley-Interscience.

Heckle, R. R., & Holden, S. H. (2006). *Analytical tools for privacy risks: Assessing efficacy on vote verification technologies.* In Symposium on usable privacy and security. (poster)

Karlsson, J. (1996). *Software requirements prioritizing.* In Proceedings of the international conference on requirements engineering (ICRE '96) (pp. 110--116).

Markert, B. K. (2002). *Comparison of three online privacy seal programs (Tech. Rep.).* SANS Institute.

Massey, A. K., Otto, P. N., & Anton, A. I. (2009). *Prioritizing legal requirements.* In Second international workshop on requirements engineering and law (RELAW '09) (pp. 27--32).

Mead, N. R., Hough, E., & Stehney, T. (2005). *Security quality requirements engineering (SQUARE) methodology (CMU/SEI-2005-TR-009).* Software Engineering Institute, Carnegie Mellon University.

Mitrano, T., Kirby, D. R., & Maltz, L. (2005). *What does privacy have to do with it?* Privacy risk assessment. In Security professionals conference. (presentation)

Miyazaki, S., Mead, N., & Zhan, J. (2008). Computer-aided privacy requirements elicitation technique. *Asia-Pacific Conference on Services Computing, 0,* 367-372.

National Institute of Standards and Technology. (2002). *Risk management guide for information technology systems.* (http://csrc.nist.gov/publications/nistpubs/800-30/sp800-30.pdf)

OECD, & Microsoft Corp. (2000). *OECD privacy statement generator.* Retrieved 25 April 2009, from http://www2.oecd.org/pwv3/

Peeger, S. L., & Peeger, C. P. (2009). Harmonizing privacy with security principles and practices. *IBM Journal of Research and Development, 53*(2).

Porter, A., Votta, L., & Basili, V. (1995). Comparing detection methods for software requirements inspections: A replicated experiment. *IEEE Transactions on Software Engineering, 21*(6), 563–575. doi:10.1109/32.391380

Singh, R. (1998). *International standard ISO/IEC 12207 software life cycle processes. (Tech. Rep.).* Federal Aviation Administration.

Statistics Canada. (2008). *Privacy impact assessment.* (http://www.statcan.gc.ca/about-apercu/pia-efrvp/gloss-eng.htm)

United States Computer Emergency Readiness Team. (2008). *Privacy impact assessment for EINSTEIN 2 (Tech. Rep.).* Department of Homeland Security.

Zave, P. (1997). Classification of research efforts in requirements engineering. *ACM Computing Surveys, 29*(4), 315–321. doi:10.1145/267580.267581

ADDITIONAL READING

Anton, A. (1996). *Goal-Based Requirements Analysis.* IEEE Int. Conf. on Requirements Engineering (ICRE 96), (pp. 136-144). Colorado Springs CO.

Blakley, B., & Heath, C. (2004). *Security Design Patterns.* Technical Guide. The Open Group.

Chung, L. (1993). *Dealing with Security Requirements during the Development of Information System.* Int. Conference on Advanced Information System Engineering (CAiSE 93), Paris (France).

Dennis, J. C. (2001). *Leading the HIPAA privacy risk assessment.* AHIMA Convention Proceedings.

Heckle, R. R., & Holden, S. H. (2006). *Analytical tools for privacy risks: Assessing efficacy on vote verification technologies.* Symposium on Usable Privacy and Security.

Kalloniatis, C., Kavakli, E., & Gritzalis, S. (2007). *Using privacy process patterns for incorporating privacy requirements into the system design process.* ARES 07: Proceedings of the Second International Conference on Availability, Reliability and Security (pp. 1009-1017).

Kalloniatis, C., Kavakli, E., & Gritzalis, S. (2008). Addressing privacy requirements in system design: the PriS method. *Requirements Engineering, 13*(3), 241–255. doi:10.1007/s00766-008-0067-3

Kavakli, E., Kalloniatis, C., Loucopoulos, P., & Gritzalis, S. (2006). *Incorporating Privacy Requirements into the System Design Process.* The PRIS Conceptual Framework. *Internet Research, 16*, 978–1005. doi:10.1108/10662240610656483

Lamsweerde, A. V., & Letier, Handling, E. (2000). Obstacles in Goal-Oriented Requirement Engineering. *IEEE Transactions on Software Engineering, 26*, 978–1005. doi:10.1109/32.879820

Liu, L., Yu, E. S. K., & Mylopoulos, J. (2003). *Security and privacy requirements analysis within social setting.* 11th IEEE International Requirements Engineering Conference (RE'03).

Madsen, M. (2008). *EHR privacy risk assessment using qualitative methods.* HIC 2008 Conference: Australias Health Informatics Conference.

Mead, N. R. (2006). Experiences in Eliciting Security Requirements. *CrossTalk, 19*(12), 14–19.

Mead, N. R. (2010). Benefits and Challenges in the Use of Case Studies for Security Requirements Engineering Methods. *International Journal of Software and Security Engineering (IJSSE), 1*(1).

Mead, N. R., & Hough, E. D. (2006). Security requirements engineering for software systems: case studies in support of software engineering education. *CSEE&T, 2006*, 149–158.

Mead, N. R., & Shoemaker, D. (2008). Novel Methods of Incorporating Security Requirements Engineering into Software Engineering Courses and Curricula. In Ellis,Demurjian, & Naveda (Ed.) *Software Engineering: Effective Teaching and Learning Approaches and Practices* (pp. 98--113). Hershey, PA: IGI Global.

Mead, N. R., Viswanathan, V., & Zhan, J. (2008). *Incorporating Security Requirements Engineering into the Rational Unified Process*. Proceedings of the 2008 International Conference on Information Security and Assurance (ISA). Busan, Korea (pp. 537--542).

Mellado, D., Blanco, C., Sanchez, L. E., & Fernandez-Medina, E. (2010). A systematic review of security requirements engineering. *Computer Standards & Interfaces, 32*, 153–165. doi:10.1016/j.csi.2010.01.006

Mellado, D., Fernandez-Medina, E., & Piattini, M. (2007). A common criteria based security requirements engineering process for the development of secure information systems. *Computer Standards & Interfaces, 29*, 244–253. doi:10.1016/j.csi.2006.04.002

Mellado, D., Fernandez-Medina, E., & Piattini, M. (2008). *Security requirements variability for software product lines*. Symposium on Requirements Engineering for Information Security (SREIS 2008) co-located with ARES 2008 (pp. 1413--1420).

Mellado, D., Fernandez-Medina, E., & Piattini, M. (2008). Towards security requirements management for software product lines: a security domain requirements engineering process. *Computer Standards & Interfaces, 30*, 361–371. doi:10.1016/j.csi.2008.03.004

Mylopolulos, J., Chung, L., & Nixon, B. (1992). Representing and Using non Functional Requirements: a Process Oriented Approach. *IEEE Transactions on Software Engineering, 18*, 483–497. doi:10.1109/32.142871

Nuseibeh, B., & Easterbrook, S. (2000). *Requirements engineering: a roadmap*. ICSE 00: Proceedings of the Conference on The Future of Software Engineering (pp. 35--46). New York, NY: ACM.

Opdahl, A. L., & Sindre, G. (2009). Experimental comparison of attack trees and misuse cases for security threat identification. *Information and Software Technology, 51*, 916–932. doi:10.1016/j.infsof.2008.05.013

Schumacher, M., Fernandez-Buglioni, E., Hybertson, D., Buschmann, F., & Sommerlad, P. (2006). *Security Patterns: Integrating Security and Systems Engineering*. New York: John Wiley & Sons.

Sindre, G., & Opdahl, A. L. (2005). Eliciting security requirements with misuse cases. *Requirements Engineering, 10*, 34–44. doi:10.1007/s00766-004-0194-4

KEY TERMS AND DEFINITIONS

HIPAA: The Health Insurance Portability and Accountability Act is a law in the United States to protect the medical records of patients.

PIA: Privacy Impact Assessment is a process that analyzes the requirements of handling, the risks of the collection, maintenance and dissemination, and the protection mechanisms of private information.

PRET: Privacy Requirements Elicitation Technique, is a tool that helps software engineers and stakeholders elicit privacy requirements early in the software design process using a computer-aided approach.

Requirements Elicitation: The definition of the system as the client understands it.

Requirements Engineering: Capturing user requirements, structuring and representing them in the system to be built.

Risk Assessment: Using standards to identify, evaluate, and estimate the risk levels of a situation.

SQUARE: Security Quality Requirements Engineering is a nine-step process to help organizations build security into the early stages of the production life cycle.

Section 4
Strategic Planning of Information Security

Chapter 12
Regulatory and Policy Compliance with Regard to Identity Theft Prevention, Detection, and Response

Guillermo A. Francia III
Jacksonville State University, USA

Frances Shannon Hutchinson
Jacksonville State University, USA

ABSTRACT

The proliferation of the Internet has intensified the identity theft crisis. Recent surveys indicate staggering losses amounting to almost $50 billion incurred due to almost 9 million cases of identity theft losses. These startling and apparently persistent statistics have prompted the United States and other foreign governments to initiate strategic plans and to enact several regulations in order to curb the crisis. This chapter surveys national and international laws pertaining to identity theft. Further, it discusses regulatory and policy compliance in the field of information security as it relates to identity theft prevention, detection, and response policies or procedures. In order to comply with recently enacted security-focused legislations and to protect the private information of customers or other third-party members, it is important that institutions of all types establish appropriate policies and procedures for dealing with sensitive information.

INTRODUCTION

This chapter discusses regulatory and policy compliance in the field of information security as it relates to identity theft prevention, detection, and response policies or procedures. In order to comply with recently enacted security-focused legislations and to protect the private information of customers or other third-party members, it is important that institutions of all types establish appropriate policies and procedures for dealing with sensitive information. Listed here are certain laws which must be considered when developing identity theft related policies; guidelines for creating, implementing, and enforcing such policies are also cited.

DOI: 10.4018/978-1-61350-507-6.ch012

Figure 1. Annual ID Theft Incidents

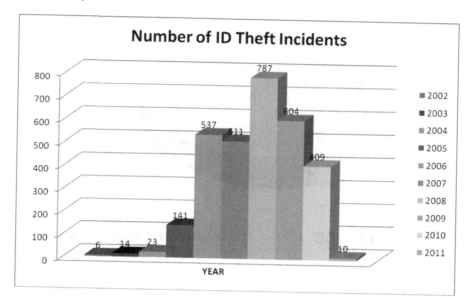

BACKGROUND

Identity theft is a threat that has confounded society since the biblical times. The ubiquity of the Internet and the convenience of electronic transactions have exacerbated the threat and made it even much easier to execute. Recent surveys indicate staggering losses amounting to almost $50 billion incurred due to almost 9 million cases of identity theft losses. A snapshot of several alarming statistics, which are gathered from the Open Security Foundation's DataLossDB (DataLossDB, 2011), pertinent to identity theft is shown in Figures 1 and 2. Figure 1 depicts the frequency of ID theft occurrences each year. As of February, 2011, there are already 10 incidents that involved ID theft.

Figure 2 shows the Personal Identifiable Information (PII) data loss categorized by data type in 2010. The data types are Date of Birth (DOB), Credit Card Number (CCN), Medical/Health information (MED), Social Security Number (SSN), Name and Address (NAA), and other miscellaneous information (MISC).

These startling statistics and their perceived persistent nature have prompted the federal gov-

ernment to initiate a strategic plan and several regulations to curb the crisis. We begin with the definition of important concepts pertaining to regulatory compliance and identity theft.

Definitions

Regulatory Compliance: A goal set by an organization in its attempt to comply with all laws or regulations relevant to that organization.

Policy Compliance: A goal set by an organization in its attempt to encourage and achieve compliance by its members/employees with regard to the organization's policies

Personally Identifiable Information: Any personal information by which an individual may be identified (SSN, bank account number, username/password combination, etc.).

Identity Theft: The co-option of another person's personal information without that person's knowledge and the fraudulent use of such knowledge (Princeton University, 2010)

Figure 2. Personal Identifiable Information Data Loss by Type in 2010

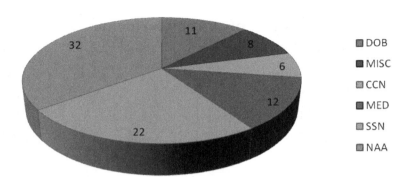

REGULATORY COMPLIANCE

The Necessity of Good Policies and Regulations

As the influences of data collection and data sharing technologies on daily life have continued to increase, so too has the need to protect that data against those who would abuse it. It should come as no surprise that identity theft (or any other fraudulent activity that exploits a person's private information) can be a lucrative practice; for example, many people have grown so accustomed to utilizing online transactions for banking, retail, or subscription fees that they are no longer entirely aware of what companies or websites they have supplied sensitive information to. There are consumers with weak passwords, consumers who bite the bait of phishing scams, and consumers who throw their old credit cards in the garbage without cutting them up first; and, every day, consumers like these are hired to perform tasks that may involve dealing with the sensitive information of hundreds or even thousands of other people. It can be a frightening thought, both for the victims whose information becomes compromised and for the businesses that must deal with legal, monetary, and trust-related ramifications should a security breach occur.

To ensure that the information entrusted to them remains as secure as possible, institutions require appropriate policies and procedures. For example, one policy might state that all employees should be made aware of the dangers of phishing scams, and an accompanying procedure might require that newly-hired employees attend a mandatory security lecture in which phishing scams are mentioned. Such a policy/procedure combination might prevent a new hire from unintentionally providing a fraudulent third party with access information that could then be used to obtain even more confidential data.

So, what policies should be implemented to secure information privacy? Unfortunately, there can be no simple explanation as best practices are largely dependent on the needs of individual businesses, and new policies must be constantly formed in response to successful attacks. The identity theft prevention policies of any institution, however, should at least comply with the regulations and rules of laws which apply to that institution. Figure 3 depicts a support infrastructure for personal data privacy and protection. The two main support columns represent regulations and policies. Although policies may have spawned because of regulations, they may not be totally dependent to them. Some policies regarding data privacy and protection may have been developed to address issues that are endemic to the organization's culture and needs. Compliance, prevention, detection, and recovery provide the base support for the two columns. Compliance ensures that regulations and policies are enforced. Prevention provides the mechanism to proactively prevent breaches. Since no amount of prevention can guarantee protection, a detection mechanism must be in place to discover any problem. Finally, the recovery support ensures the robustness and the resiliency of the system to recover from an unforeseen violation.

This section explores several laws that pertain to information security and identity theft prevention or response; the following section, Policies for Preventing Identity Theft, examines guidelines and methods for developing sound policies in order to comply with such laws.

Gramm-Leach-Bliley Act (GLBA)

The Gramm-Leach-Bliley Act, also known as the Financial Services Modernization Act, was enacted in late 1999 primarily to allow mergers amongst banks, insurance companies, and brokerage firms (Herrmann, 2007). In the field of information security, however, the act is far more famous for its attention to privacy and security requirements in financial institutions. The GLBA opens its security-related sections with a privacy obligation policy, which reads:

"It is the policy of the Congress that each financial institution has an affirmative and continuing obligation to respect the privacy of its customers and to protect the security and confidentiality of those customers' nonpublic personal information." (Gramm-Leach-Bliley Act, 1999)

In other words, the Act helps shift information security away from the low budget of a helpful suggestion and into the spotlight of mandatory federal law. The GLBA places restrictions on the sharing of nonpublic personal information via its Opt-out and Disclosure rules, which together reinforce security by requiring a paper trail of notifications whenever a financial institution wishes to disclose a customer's private information to a

Figure 3. The Personal Data Privacy and Protection Infrastructure

third party; customers will have to be informed of the exchange and, in some cases, must be given the option to reject the transfer of personal information before it takes place (Gramm-Leach-Bliley Act, 1999). Furthermore, the act operates on a level that treats the nonpublic personal information of each and every customer as a valuable asset, the aim of which is that security should be so high that not even one customer will suffer harm due to leaked personally identifiable information (Herrmann, 2007). The most important contribution of the GLBA in terms of identity theft prevention policies, though, is the Safeguards Rule, found in section 501(b) of the Act.

The Safeguards Rule required "every agency or authority" covered by the Gramm-Leach-Bliley Act to establish a set of standards for its corresponding financial institutions to follow. The goals of these standards are threefold:

"(1) to insure the security and confidentiality of customer records and information;

(2) to protect against any anticipated threats or hazards to the security or integrity of such records; and

(3) to protect against unauthorized access to or use of such records or information which could result in substantial harm or inconvenience to any customer." (Gramm-Leach-Bliley Act, 1999)

Fair examples of some standards that were selected to support this rule are those established by the Federal Trade Commission, or FTC. The FTC requires any financial institution under its jurisdiction to "develop, implement, and maintain a comprehensive information security program" (Federal Trade Commission, 2002) that meets all objectives of the Safeguards Rule and spans administrative, technical, and physical layers of safeguards. The standards require that a minimum of one person be delegated the task of coordinating the program and lists areas of business that must be considered during risk assessment (employee training/management, information systems, and detection, prevention, or response to systems failures such as an attack or intrusion) (Federal Trade Commission, 2002). Once the risks have been ascertained, the covered financial institution is required to design and implement safeguards to control those risks and must regularly monitor those safeguards' effectiveness, evaluating and updating the information security program as necessary. Lastly, the financial institution must look outside the scope of its own security practices by requiring, in contract, that any third-party service providers used by the institution implement and maintain appropriate information security safeguards of their own (Federal Trade Commission, 2002). Those who are unfamiliar with terms such as "risk assessment" may find such standards off-putting at first, but the FTC's list closely follows the same steps used for solving

any issue. Perhaps a simpler way to summarize them would be as follows:

1. Select a person (or team of persons) who will be responsible for solving the problem(s)
2. State the problem(s), researching additional information as needed (i.e., perform a risk assessment)
3. Attempt to solve the problem(s) (put security measures in place) and monitor the effects of the solution(s)
4. If the problem(s) still exists, or new problems arise, repeat steps 2 and 3 until adequate solutions are found (evaluation and adjustment of the information security program)
5. Prevent third parties from adding additional problems to the system (select service providers that can be required by contract to implement appropriate information security safeguards)

Any financial institution which handles customer data can expect, at the least, to be required to comply with the GLBA and standards similar to those listed in the FTC Safeguards Rule when developing policies focused on the prevention of identity theft. In certain circumstances, however, additional laws may apply.

Disposal Rule

Most people will agree that files and paperwork which contain confidential information are best kept under lock and key (or the electronic equivalent), inaccessible to all but those who need to see their contents in order to conduct some form of useful work. Information, however, does not stay useful forever; eventually files are deleted and carefully-guarded paperwork becomes garbage. It is at this stage of the confidential data's existence that it is most easily stolen; sadly enough, many cases of identity theft can be contributed to trash that has not been shredded or recycled hard drives that still retain easily recovered "deleted" information. After all, why would a potential identity thief go through the trouble of hacking past a security system or breaking into a filing cabinet when the information he or she seeks is left unguarded and unwanted in a trash bin, or even handed over willingly for spare change at a yard sale?

The Disposal Rule addresses such problems by requiring that "any business or individual who uses a consumer report for a business purpose… is required to take appropriate measures to dispose of sensitive information derived from consumer reports", although it is highly recommended that any personal or financial consumer data be disposed of with similar security standards (Federal Trade Commission, 2005). The "proper" disposal of information might vary according to the information's form (printed document, electronic file, etc.) and the means of the organization that owns it (a small company might shred files individually as they are no longer needed whereas a large corporation may enlist the aid of a third party to destroy its garbage in bulk), but no matter the form of the data or the size of the institution, the goal remains the same: to destroy the personally identifiable information so completely that it cannot be read or reconstructed (Federal Trade Commission, 2005).

Other Laws Concerning Identity Theft Prevention

One of the earliest laws passed by Congress concerning ID Theft is the Counterfeit Access Device and Computer Fraud and Abuse Act of 1984 (18 U.S.C. § 1030). The statute has been amended by several legislative actions such as the USA Patriot Act of 2001.

ID Theft protection is a subject of a variety of additional security-focused legislation. For example, health care providers and their affiliates are subject to the Health Insurance Portability and Accountability Act of 1996 (HIPAA), which specifically protects the rights and information of patients and health care plan participants (Salo-

mon, Cassat, & Thibeau, 2003). Educators must contend with the Family Education Rights and Privacy Act, or FERPA, which strives to protect the information of students (Salomon et al., 2003). In fact, some educational institutions may find themselves covered by both FERPA and HIPAA if that institution is affiliated with a health care provider; the institution's information security program, including those policies which seek to prevent identity theft, must comply with both Acts as well as any other federal law the institution may be affected by.

Fair Credit Reporting Act (FCRA)

Prevention isn't the only area in which the law requires action against identity theft; financial institutions must also make an effort to detect and report incidents in which their systems become compromised. An example of this can be seen in the Fair Credit Reporting Act, which defines the responsibilities of financial institutions and the rights of victims in cases of identity theft (Federal Trade Commission, 2006).

The FCRA requires that "a business that has provided credit, goods, or services to, accepted payment from, or otherwise entered into a transaction with someone who is believed to have fraudulently used another person's identification" (Federal Trade Commission, 2006) must respond to written requests by the victim for transactions records pertaining to the identity theft. The requested documents must be provided by the business; the GLBA (mentioned earlier in this section) does not protect companies from having to disclose relevant records (although state laws or other federal laws may). Only upon determination of one or more of the following circumstances may a business refuse to provide the requested documents:

- "you cannot verify the true identity of the person asking for the information;
- the request for the information is based on a misrepresentation; or

- the information requested is Internet navigational data or similar information about a person's visit to a website or online service." (Federal Trade Commission, 2006)

This section of the FCRA is necessary in order to give identity theft victims and law enforcement a chance at apprehending, or at least assessing the damage done by, an identity thief. Along with other laws, it must finely balance the need for victims to access relevant information while still protecting the privacy of businesses and other consumers' confidential information.

Red Flags Rules

The Red Flags Rules were designed as guidelines to help implement certain requirements of the Fair and Accurate Credit Transactions Act (FACT Act) with regard to identity theft prevention, detection, and mitigation (Department of the Treasury, Federal Deposit Insurance Corporation, Federal Reserve System, Federal Trade Commission, National Credit Union Administration, 2007). However, these guidelines focus primarily on detection via the recognition of "red flags", or events that are commonly associated with identity theft. Those entities which are covered by this legislation must develop a program of policies and procedures that can achieve the following four goals:

- "Identify relevant Red Flags for covered accounts and incorporate those Red Flags into the Program;
- Detect Red Flags that have been incorporated into the Program;
- Respond appropriately to any Red Flags that are detected to prevent and mitigate identity theft; and
- Ensure the Program is updated periodically, to reflect changes in risks to customers or to the safety and soundness of the financial institution or creditor from iden-

tity theft." (Department of the Treasury et al., 2007)

Early detection of an identity theft attempt or of a successful attack is critical both to mitigating the damage caused by the theft and to discovering how to prevent future identity theft attempts. For this reason, it is important that an institution take into account red flags that are particular to that institution in addition to the list of common red flags that is provided in the legislation itself. A red flag may fall under any of the following five categories:

"(1) Alerts, Notifications or Warnings from a Consumer Reporting Agency

(2) Suspicious Documents

(3) Suspicious Personal Identifying Information

(4) Unusual Use of, or Suspicious Activity Related to, the Covered Account

(5) Notice from Customers, Victims of Identity Theft, Law Enforcement Authorities, or Other Persons Regarding Possible Identity Theft in Connection With Covered Accounts Held by the Financial Institution or Creditor" (Department of the Treasury et al., 2007).

For example, if a document that has been provided for identification appears to be altered or forged, then it is a red flag under the suspicious documents category (Department of the Treasury et al., 2007). If a credit account suddenly makes a series of very large purchases (especially if those purchases are from a location that the account owner does not usually purchase from), then that string of purchases should be considered as a red flag of suspicious activity. For each red flag identified in an institution's policy, an accompanying procedure should illustrate the steps that will be taken in response. In the case of the first example, the institution might deny its services until some other form of identifying document can be presented or, depending on the situation, may notify authorities of a possible identity theft attempt. When addressing the second red flag example, many credit companies will freeze the account until contact is established with the account owner to verify whether or not the suspicious purchases were valid. An institution covered by the Red Flags Rules should consider any events or patterns that have alerted it to identity theft in the past and should periodically review its list of red flags to ensure that the list has not become outdated due to changing business practices or new trends in identity theft techniques (Department of the Treasury et al., 2007). The more complete and reliable the red flags list is, the better the chances are that an identity theft attempt will be detected.

On December 18, 2010, President Barack Obama signed S. 3987 into Public Law No: 111-319, also known as the "Red Flag Program Clarification Act of 2010." The law limits the definition of creditor to entities that regularly and in the ordinary course of business: (a) obtain or use consumer credit reports; (b) furnish information to consumer reporting agencies; or (c) advance funds to or on behalf of a person. It excludes creditors that "advance funds on behalf of a person for expenses incidental to a service provided by the creditor to that person." (U.S. Senate 3987, 2010)

State Laws

Although regulatory compliance with federal legislation is important, it is not the only type of law that must be taken into account when forming good policies; state laws, too, have their own standards for what must be done to prevent, detect, and report identity theft. Depending on a financial institution's state jurisdiction, it may be required to adhere to a different set of standards than if it had been located elsewhere. For instance, most states now employ legislation that requires

financial institutions to report security breaches to the victims whose information may have been compromised, but such laws are not uniform throughout every state (Bingisser, 2008). Below are a few examples of the differences amongst various state laws that deal with the notification of affected parties following a security breach (Bingisser, 2008):

- An institution under California jurisdiction must notify affected parties after any security breach that may have exposed personally identifiable information whereas an institution covered by Connecticut law can skip such notification if the breach is unlikely to result in actual harm, such as when a "grey hat" hacker bypasses security without the intention of actually exploiting the data he or she discovers.
- A government agency would be required to report on security breaches if the agency were based in Illinois, but would be excluded from the requirement if it instead fell under the legislation of Georgia or Maine.
- If the compromised data was encrypted, but the encryption key itself was not compromised, then only institutions covered by North Carolina state law will have to report the breach.
- Institutions covered by Maine legislation may not deliver the required reports to victims via electronic notification.

International Laws

Iceland has been actively amending its *Data Protection Act*, which is also known as "*Act on the Protection of Privacy as Regards to the Processing of Personal Data*." The law has been amended four times: *Act No. 90/2001, Act No. 30/2002, Act No. 81/2002* and *Act No. 46/2003*. Its basic provision is "to promote the practice of personal data processing in accordance with fundamental principles and rules regarding data protection and privacy, and to ensure the reliability and integrity of such data and their free flow within the internal market of the European Economic Area." (Personuvernd, 2008).

During the last decade other countries have vigorously pursued and enacted legislation on privacy rights protection. Among these countries are Malta (*Personal Data and Protection of Privacy Regulation (SL 399.25))*, Romania (*Processing of Personal Data and the Protection of Privacy in the Electronic Communications Sector; Law no. 506 (2004))*, and Singapore (*Banking Act, the Statistics Act, the Official Secrets Act, and the Statutory Bodies and Government Companies (Protection of Secrecy) Act)*. (Francia and Ciganek, 2010).

Before developing an identity theft prevention or identity theft response policy, it is important to determine what state legislation applies to the institution in question and how that legisla-

tion interacts with federal or even international regulations of a similar nature. A summary of a sampling of laws and regulations pertaining to identity theft is shown in Table 1.

POLICIES FOR PREVENTING IDENTITY THEFT

The previous section mentioned various forms of legislation that can impact regulatory compliance when developing new policies (or amending old ones) for the prevention of or response to identity theft. This section provides guidelines and advice for the development of sound identity theft prevention policies that will comply with such regulations. Information pertaining to the development of identity theft response policies will be covered in the section "Policies for Responding to Identity Theft."

Table 1. A Sampling of Federal and State Regulations Pertaining to Identity Theft

Regulation	Type	Section/Codification
Alabama Identity Theft Law	State	Ala Code 13A-8-190, et seq.
California Breach Notification Law	State	California Civil Code 1798.82
Canada's Privacy Act	Foreign	1980-81-82-83,c.111,Sch.II
Colorado Identity Theft Statutes	State	Colorado CRS 18-5
Credit Card Fraud	Federal	18 U.S.C. 1029
Delaware Clean Credit and Identity Theft Prevention Act	State	75 Del. Laws c. 328 1
Department of Veterans Affairs Information Security Act (2006)	Federal	38 U.S.C. 5721-28
Drivers Privacy Protection Act (1994) (DPPA)	Federal	18 U.S.C. 2721-2725
Fair and Accurate Credit Transactions Act 2003 (FACTA)	Federal	Red Flags Rule Pub. L. No. 108-159 Stat 1952, Sect 114 and 315
Fair Credit Reporting Act (FCRA)	Federal	15 U.S.C. 1681s
Family Educational Rights and Privacy Act (FERPA)	Federal	20 U.S.C. 1231g; C.F.R. Part 99
Federal Trade Commission Act (FTC Act)	Federal	15 U.S.C. 45(a)
Federal Trade Commission for Safeguarding Customer Information	Federal	Safeguarding Rule 16 C.F.R. Part 314
Florida Identity Theft Law	State	Florida Code 817.568, .569
Georgia Identity Theft Law	State	Ga. Code Ann. 16-9-120 (1998) et seq.
Gramm-Leach-Bliley Act (GLBA)	Federal	Title V 12 C.F.R. 225.28, 225.86
Health Insurance Portability and Accountability Act (1996) (HIPAA)	Federal	45 U.S.C. Part 160 and 164

continued on following page

Table 1. Continued

Regulation	Type	Section/Codification
Iceland's Data Protection Act	Foreign	Act No. 90/2001; Act No. 30/2002; Act No.46/2003
Identity Theft	Federal	18 U.S.C. 1028(a)(7)
Illinois Identity Theft Law	State	720 Ill. Comp State. 5/16G-1 (West 1999) et seq.
Intelligence Reform and Terrorism Prevention Act (2004) (IRTPA)	Federal	Pub. L. 108-458
Mail Theft	Federal	18 U.S.C. 1708
Malta's Personal Data and Protection of Privacy Regulation	Foreign	SL 399.25
Massachusetts Protection of Personal Information	State	Massachusetts 201 CMR 17.00
New South Wales' Privacy and Personal Information Protection Act of 1998	Foreign	Act 133 of 1998
North Carolina Identity Theft Law	State	NC Gen Stat 14-113.20 (2000) et seq.; 1-539.2C
Real ID Act (2005)	Federal	Pub. L. 109-13
Red Flag Clarification Act of 2010	Federal	Pub. L. 111-319
Romania's Processing of Personal data and Protection of Privacy in the Electronic Communications Sector	Foreign	Law 506 (2004)
Sarbanes-Oxley Act (2002)	Federal	Pub. L. 107-204 116 Stat. 745
Securities and Exchange Commission Regulation S-P	Federal	17 C.F.R. Part 248
South Carolina Consumer Identity Theft Protection	State	Section 37-20 (110-200)
USA Patriot Act (2001)-Customer Identification Program Rules	Federal	Section 326 31 U.S.C. 5318(I)
Wisconsin's Unauthorized Use of an Individual's Personal Identifying Information or Documents	State	Wisconsin a. 943.201

Risk Assessment

Risk assessment forms the foundation of any effective security policy. If an entity is unaware of the risks posed to its assets, how can it expect to adequately protect those assets against an attack? Whether the entity is a business, university, government agency or other institution, it must take steps to identify what personally identifiable information it has, how that information is stored, transferred, or processed, and what types of attacks the information may be vulnerable to.

COBIT, or "Control Objectives for Information and related Technology", is a document that provides business guidelines pertaining to risk assessment and other information security needs. Although other such documents are available, COBIT is easy to access and is provided online free of charge, so it is used to illustrate the key points of risk assessment for this section. When beginning the tasks of identifying and defending against potential risks to a system, an institution may find it effective to follow similar guidelines so that important steps are not accidentally overlooked.

According to COBIT, the first step in risk assessment is to establish "risk context". The institution should ask itself, among other things, what its goals are in assessing potential risks and how it will evaluate the risks that are found (here, we assume that the goal is the prevention and detection of identity theft) (IT Governance Institute, 2007). If everyone who participates in the risk assessment can agree on the goals, evaluation measurements, and terminology that will be used, then the assessment process can proceed more smoothly. For example, the risk assessment team will need to decide how revealed risks should be ranked in case the institution does not have the ability to protect itself fully against all vulnerabilities. It could be that the institution wishes to rank the importance of a risk based on how much harm can be done if that risk is exploited, but it should also take into consideration how high the probability is that the risk actually will be exploited; the institution might have to decide, for instance, whether to first protect itself against a small-damage risk that is almost guaranteed to be exploited or a high-damage risk that is somewhat unlikely to ever be exploited.

The second step in risk assessment is "event identification". Simply put, this step involves exploring any identifiable events for potential risks (IT Governance Institute, 2007). Such events could involve anything from the way in which customer registration is handled to the potential consequences of a hardware failure or virus, or even examining events in which personally identifiable information is transferred or stored during the course of an average work day. By examining such events, an organization can also identify many of the risks to which it is exposed.

In the third step, the actual risk assessment itself occurs. Risks that have been exposed must be carefully examined for likelihood and potential impact, and should be given a ranking of importance based on criteria set down by the organization during the establishment of risk context (IT Governance Institute, 2007). It is at this stage that the organization will decide which risks pose the most threat; correspondingly, higher-ranking risks will likely receive more attention, quicker responses, and a greater portion of the institution's security budget compared to lesser risks, especially if there is neither time nor resources to quickly and effectively implement defenses against all revealed risks.

The fourth step in the process is known as "risk response". This is the point at which the institution develops and implements policies and procedures to deal with the risks that were identified and assessed during the previous steps. Generally, the organization must choose to apply one of four "risk strategies" to each risk it encounters: it may seek to prevent a negative event from occurring (avoidance), reduce the damage that a negative event could cause should an attack succeed (reduction), enlist the aid of a third party to either mitigate potential damage or lift responsibility for the risk from the institution (sharing), or do nothing to defend against the risk and prepare itself as best it can for a scenario in which that risk is exploited (acceptance) (IT Governance Institute, 2007). Although the acceptance option might seem odd to some, certain circumstances may prevent the organization from being able to apply any other strategy to a particular risk at a certain time (i.e., budget constraints, lack of in-house expertise, etc.).

The final, and perhaps most important, step of risk assessment is "maintenance and monitoring" of any plans that were implemented during the fourth step (IT Governance Institute, 2007). By examining the results of its new policies and procedures, an institution can determine whether or not it has adequately defended against a particular risk. Additionally, new risks may be discovered (perhaps due to a successful attack) that were not perceived during the first risk assessment. For these reasons, risk assessment should be repeated periodically in order for an organization to continue to improve its information security policies.

In summary, risk assessment is essentially a learning process in which an institution discovers its vulnerabilities so that it can make accurate and informed decisions about how best to compensate for those vulnerabilities and protect its assets. In the case of identity theft, the institution must locate points at which personally identifiable information can be discovered by parties that are not entitled to that information and must think of ways to protect that information against those who would exploit it. Since policies and processes, regulations and requirements differ from one institution to another, it is usually impossible to directly apply the risk assessment work done by one institution to a different institution. Fortunately, resources such as COBIT are available to aid in the process. Certain institutions might also find the Federal Trade Commission website (http://business.ftc.gov/documents/bus58-security-check-reducing-risks-your-computer-systemshandy) useful as it gives quick tips for developing a reliable information security system and also contains references to the site www.sans.org, which composes lists of top security vulnerabilities (Federal Trade Commission, 2003).

Security Best Practices

Certain information security practices have become standard across multiple institutions and may be applied by individual consumers as well as larger organizations. These 'best practices' were not all put into place solely to prevent identity theft, but they can still help a person or institution to protect his, her, or its personally identifiable information.

The first and most obvious practice is also the most simple: consumers and institutions alike must become aware of what personally identifiable information they possess and must then actively protect that information. Many scams, such as email phishing, owe their success to a basic lack of attention. Scammers try to pass themselves off as some entity that is entitled to the personally identifiable information they seek—perhaps by posing as a bank, as an important member of a company to which the victim belongs, or any other such entity. The scam is more likely to fail if the intended victim is wary of those who would seek to steal personally identifiable information. Institutions should examine their collected personally identifiable information to better understand what they have, where it came from, how they acquired

it, where or how it is stored, and how or to whom it is passed on to (for example, in some cases the information might be left in the hands of a third party, or there may be a scenario in which all or part of the information is repeated back to the consumer from whence it came for verification purposes) (Federal Trade Commission). Simply by understanding how the process works, the institution can be more alert for scammers—it will be better able to guess what information a scam is most likely after, where in the process it is likely to occur, and how to tell scams apart from legitimate business correspondence or transactions.

The second practice closely follows the first: one should always be aware of whom they are dealing with (OnGuard Online). If phishing scams are similar to a fisherman casting bait to hook his meal, then so certain other scams are akin to spiders spinning webs to ensnare their victims. Recently, it has become popular for scammers to create fake versions of real websites using commonly misspelled versions of the site's namespace. For instance, instead of "youtube.com", the scammer might create a new website and name it "youube.com" (misspelled by one letter), a fake site that displays the Youtube logo but which is not actually affiliated with the true website at all. (Caution: this particular 'fake Youtube' name actually exists. Do not navigate to it.) This site might then inform an unwitting victim that he or she has won some sort of prize that requires him or her to enter personally identifiable information before the prize can be claimed (similar to phishing scams). Alternatively, the site might try to replicate the original's login or registration page designs in order to fool would-be Youtube users into giving away access information. Such a site can be much more dangerous than the average phishing scam, however, because it can hide an additional threat that can catch even a wary user: hiding malware or spyware on the site in such a way that it is downloaded to the victim's computer within a second or so, thus doing harm even before there is time for the person to realize his or her mistake and navigate away. Adding on to the danger is the fact that many consumers are encouraged *not* to follow external links to important websites (like banks or businesses), but rather to type out the site's address (OnGuard Online). This may be an excellent practice, but even the most cautionary typist may make an error; if consumers or employees are cautioned to type out business or bank addresses, then they should also be cautioned to double-check their spelling prior to actually navigating to the site. Even after the site has been reached, it is a good idea to verify its authenticity by closely examining the Uniform Resource Locator (URL) for unexpected differences or, in the case of a site that requires personally identifiable information from the user, to check for signs that the site truly is secure (for instance, that the URL begins with "https" rather than "http") (OnGuard Online) even after it has been confirmed as a legitimate business site.

A third best practice is to "scale down" the personally identifiable information that is kept as much as possible (Federal Trade Commission). For consumers, this might mean anything from emptying out an inbox full of emails that could contain such information to simply resisting the urge to write down hard-to-remember personally identifiable information and store it in an unsafe place (similar, for instance, to cases in which users with bad memories might write their usernames and passwords for particular sites on a sticky note and attach it to the computer). Institutions, however, can be composed of many people and tend to deal with information on a much larger scale; they may also be reluctant to destroy information that might somehow prove useful in the future. For the sake of losing as little information as can be helped in the event of a security breach, however, it is important for businesses not to keep any unnecessary information; therefore, the business must distinguish necessary information from unnecessary information and commit fully to discarding all information that is not needed. As an example, let us take the popular online game

World of Warcraft. This business makes almost all of its revenue via the subscription fees its players pay for the privilege of keeping a game account active. When a user creates an account, that account is tied specifically to that user and is not meant to be used by or transferred to anyone else; also, everything that the user earns or accomplishes in-game is tied to the account on which that user plays. The problem that World of Warcraft faces is this: when its users become too busy to play or become bored of the game, those users tend to cancel their subscriptions. However, when the company expands the game or when a user's life reverts to a less demanding pace, those users tend to come back to the game–expecting, of course, to retain all of the in-game rewards that were earned when last they played. The game must retain certain information in order to verify the identity of the user should he or she ever return to reactivate an old account. However, it must also consider the possibility that the user will never reactivate, and so should dispose of as much information as possible (especially payment information) the moment the user deactivates an account. A clean line must be drawn between the information which is truly necessary and that which is not before an institution can best defend against identity theft.

A fourth best practice is to keep all security software up-to-date, preferably through automatic updates (OnGuard Online). Since attackers are always finding new vulnerabilities to exploit, it is vital that anti-spyware and anti-virus programs be kept as up-to-date as possible in order to properly combat the newly-discovered vulnerabilities. Spyware, for instance, might easily lead to identity theft, either by monitoring a user's activity to discover his or her habits (for instance, revealing what banks a particular person or institution might be affiliated with) or by key logging to discover personally identifiable information that a user types (or, similarly, a username/password combination that may lead to the acquisition of such information) (OnGuard Online). Of course, one side effect of constant change is that updatable programs may occasionally create risks of their own, but such issues are generally rare and quickly patched.

Along with keeping anti-virus and anti-spyware software updated, an individual or institution should think carefully about which operating system and browser to use and should understand the security issues involved with each; this is the fifth practice (OnGuard Online). As an example, the Internet Explorer browser is often looked upon as having the weakest security because it is the browser whose vulnerabilities are most often exploited. The weakness of this browser's security might actually be a bit of an exaggeration; since Internet Explorer comes pre-installed on every computer with a Windows operating system, it is the most widely-owned of all the browsers and therefore makes a more tempting target for attackers, so it is likely that more effort has been put into attacking Internet Explorer than any other browser. Regardless, an institution wishing to protect its assets from attack might want to choose a browser that feels more secure (or, at least, is attacked less often), such as Mozilla Firefox or Google Chrome. The browser and operating system should work together to meet the institution's needs and to perform useful work, but they can also create vulnerabilities that an attacker might exploit in order to access protected information. As with the aforementioned anti-virus and anti-spyware software, operating systems and web browsers should both be updated to defend against newly-discovered vulnerabilities.

The sixth practice is fairly straightforward: lock the personally identifiable information that is kept so that it will be more difficult for an intruder to access (Federal Trade Commission). In the case of hard-copy printouts or handwritten information, locked filing cabinets and locked doors can be used, with keys provided only to those who require them in order to perform useful work (such keys should also be removed from any person or persons who no longer need them). Papers containing personally identifiable information

should not be left lying around on desks, where the information might be seen or taken by an unintended individual; if a file is not in use, then it should be locked up (Federal Trade Commission). When information is stored electronically, similar precautions should be taken; for instance, usernames and passwords should be required in order to access the information. When possible, sensitive information should be encrypted (especially if it is going to be transferred). Also, sensitive information should not be stored on any computer that has access to the Internet unless it is absolutely necessary for the institution to function; neither should it be stored on laptops, which can be easily stolen (Federal Trade Commission). A variety of practices exist for keeping information under lock and key; before creating an identity theft prevention policy, an institution should examine the way in which personally identifiable information is currently stored and used and should improve upon the information's protection where possible. Once the policy has been written, employees should be informed of all the procedures to which they are expected to adhere and why those procedures are important for the security of the information they must handle. Special attention should be paid to the manner in which employees treat sensitive documents from day to day; another matter of concern is the password, which the average user creates to be too weak to serve its purpose. An ideal password, for instance, should be no fewer than eight characters long (preferably not all alphanumeric), should not be made up of common words, personal information, or easy-to-guess keystroke patterns (such as "qwertyuiop" or "0987"), should not be identical to a password used on a separate account, and should be changed at least once every 90 days (OnGuard Online).

The final best practice is to discard information properly (Federal Trade Commission). As stated previously, personally identifiable information is easiest to obtain when it is sitting at the bottom of a garbage can or in a reused computer's recycle bin.

Just because the information is no longer needed by a particular institution, it does not mean that the institution loses responsibility for the copies of that information that it possesses; electronic or hard-copy trash that could be used to commit identity theft should be disposed of completely and irrevocably. Whether the institution's copies exist only in the work environment or are retained by work-at-home employees, paper records should be shredded, burned, or pulverized (Federal Trade Commission, 2005) while electronic records should be completely wiped via procedures such as reformatting or using wipe utility programs to ensure that no personally identifiable information can be recovered (Federal Trade Commission).

Additional Measures

While practices that have been generalized and proven to be effective across multiple institutions are certainly useful, it is important to remember that certain institutions may have particular methods or security requirements that can have an impact when developing and complying with an effective identity theft prevention policy.

One business, for example, might have a large number of telecommuting employees. Such an employee may be required to handle personally identifiable information. Now the organization must ask itself questions that generic best practices might not cover: how should the telecommuting employees receive the needed information? Can that information be kept safe during transit (encrypting emails, for example)? Will the employee handle, transmit, and destroy that information in compliance with the business's policies? The last question is, perhaps, the most important. If an employee is physically present at an office every morning, then that office can control what operating systems and web browsers the employee has available to him or her, ensure that all security software is updated on time, hold mandatory meetings or training sessions about information security, or display signs and posters that remind the employee of the institution's security policies and encourage compliance with them; a telecommuting employee can only receive emails, text messages, electronic files, or telephone calls. For example, if a telecommuting employee lives too far away to make mandatory security meetings practical, the business will have to decide what to do about it. Would the institution feel comfortable enough to host some or all of those meetings via online discussion groups, or will the employee be excused from such meetings due to his or her status as a telecommuter? If the employee is excused from those security-themed meetings, then how can the institution ensure that he or she still learns about business's policies and follows required procedures? In such a situation, the institution might have to analyze decisions specific to telecommuters, such as how information should be kept and accessed at the employee's home and what security software should be installed on the employee's work computer (Federal Trade Commission, 2006). These decisions should be written into a policy to which the telecommuting employee must adhere. For example, the telecommuters might be required to complete a company-sponsored online security course in order to compensate for being unable to attend security meetings, or the company might provide copies of its anti-virus or anti-spyware software to the employee and require that those programs be kept installed, updated, and running on any computer that the employee uses to perform work or to store personally identifiable information.

On the alternate end of the security spectrum, not all best practices apply to every organization. Particularly small or old-fashioned institutions may still have non-networked computers; such a machine would not require nearly as much security as a networked computer because physical access would be required in order to retrieve information from it. Likewise, in a business that does not collect hard copies of sensitive information, there would be no filing cabinets to lock.

An identity theft prevention policy should be tailored for the institution that is to abide by it; the policy should not overlook potentially risky events simply because other types of institutions might not possess those events, nor should it include any unnecessary rules that will only serve to inflate the document, making the policy less appealing to read and increasing the potential for confusion. A policy that is direct, concise, complete, and easy to understand is more likely to achieve policy compliance than a roundabout, overly-lengthy or incomplete policy would.

POLICIES FOR RESPONDING TO IDENTITY THEFT

Once a policy has been developed regarding the prevention of identity theft, an institution must come to terms with the fact that a security breach could still occur despite its best efforts to prevent such an event. In order to ensure that certain legal requirements are met as well as to avoid confusion during or after an identity theft incident, policies should be developed that specify how a potential case of identity theft can be detected and what the affected institution should do in response to such a case.

Developing a Response Plan

Before an institution can respond to a security breach, it must first be made aware that the breach occurred. Information can be stolen more subtly than any physical item because the thief does not have to actually take anything from its expected place; a copy of the information, either written to a new file by a program, attached in an email, or memorized and copied out by hand, will suffice just as well as the original source. If protected information is not carefully monitored, then there is a possibility that no one will realize that the information is being stolen until it is too late.

The following tips for detection of potential identity theft are cited by the FTC in regard to the Safeguards Rule (Federal Trade Commission, 2006):

1. Keep logs of activity on your network and monitor them for signs of unauthorized access to customer information.
2. Use an up-to-date intrusion detection system to alert you of attacks.
3. Monitor both in- and out-bound transfers of information for indications of a compromise, such as unexpectedly large amounts of data being transmitted from your system to an unknown user.
4. Insert a dummy account into each of your customer lists and monitor the account to detect any unauthorized changes.

Preferably, one or more of these systems should be written into a policy so that an intrusion which compromises personally identifiable information will be detected. Additionally, employees should be made aware of signs that could indicate a potential intrusion or intrusion attempt (for example, an company computer that refuses to shut down or restart, displays pop-up ads when the employee is not surfing the web, or inexplicably slows in performance may be affected by spyware) (On-Guard Online).

Once an intrusion has been detected, the institution must determine how to respond to it. In a large institution, the policy might first need to define how information about the security breach should spread within the institution itself; for instance, an employee who suspects a security breach might first be required to speak with his or her supervisor. Depending on the supervisor's position in the company, he or she might need to report the potential breach to someone else or attempt to handle the problem directly. If action against the intrusion can be taken quickly, an attacked institution might be able to mitigate the potential damage, so there should be as direct a line as is reasonable from every employee to the person or persons who will have the knowledge and authority to deal with an information security problem. Furthermore, an individual or small team of individuals should be held directly responsible for deciding what to do in the event of a security breach so that the institution can take controlled, coordinated steps toward ending the intrusion and securing its information.

The first step in a response policy should be to give instructions for, or at least put someone in charge of, securing the compromised information against further intrusion, as well as taking any measures that might be necessary to secure uncompromised information that could be vulnerable to the same type of attack (OnGuard Online). The second step should be for the institution to determine how the breach occurred so that measures can be taken to protect against it in the future; depending on the means of the institution and the appropriateness of the situation, third-party security professionals might also be called in to provide additional opinions and assistance (OnGuard Online).

Assessing and putting a stop to security intrusions is not enough, however; depending on the nature of the compromised information, an institution may be required to notify law enforcement officials, affected customers, or even certain third-party organizations about the breach. An institution's response policy should be designed with clear reference to applicable laws so that informed decisions can be made about whom the institution must contact and what information should be shared. Whenever the compromised information poses a risk to identity theft, law enforcement officials should be advised so that they will be aware of the potential for damage and can mitigate it as much as possible (Federal Trade Commission, 2004). In some cases, it is sufficient to notify local police; if, however, local police are inexperienced with handling cases of identity theft, then a local FBI office can be contacted instead (Federal Trade Commission, 2004). When the

compromised information affects a third-party organization (for example, if a customer's credit information is stolen from an organization other than that credit card company), that organization should also be notified so that it may immediately begin monitoring the compromised data for signs of fraud and identity theft (Federal Trade Commission, 2004). Slightly more difficult is the scenario in which the institution must inform its own customers that their data has been compromised; not only would many institutions prefer never to complete the informing process as it could cost them customers and trust, but the laws that require institutions to do so can vary greatly depending on the institution's location (see section 2.6 for more information). The response policy should clearly state the demands of applicable regulations so that the affected institution will be able to abide by them even through the confusion that might follow a successful attack.

Regardless of location, many businesses are subject to the FCRA, which states that identity theft victims have the right to demand transaction records that could relate to the theft. A victim may choose to involve law enforcement when seeking to obtain the requested information, which must be delivered free of charge within 30 days of receiving a written request for it (Federal Trade Commission, 2006). A policy that is written for an institution under this act should provide clear and detailed compliance instructions; if the policy is too confusing, then an employee might (a) resist giving out the required transaction records for fear that he or she is being tricked into giving away more information than necessary, and hence could be fired or (b) give away unnecessary information or give the information to someone who is not truly entitled to it by not following proper procedures.

Finally, the most important step in responding to a case (or potential case) of identity theft is to reevaluate the institution's vulnerabilities via another risk assessment. If possible, security measures should be added or amended so that a similar security breach will not happen again. If amendments are called for, then the institution's identity theft prevention policy should be updated (or even rewritten) to reflect necessary changes. Once the panic from the incident has died down, the institution should also evaluate the effectiveness of its response policy; if things were handled smoothly, quickly, and without causing further incident, then the identity theft response policy has served its purpose. If not, then the response policy may require revision and should be changed to correct or compensate for failures experienced during the incident.

POLICY COMPLIANCE

Defining identity theft prevention and identity theft response policies that recognize and adhere to government regulations is certainly important, but it is only half the battle. Even the most well-written and carefully planned policies can serve little purpose if they are not followed; policy compliance is critical in order to achieve the policy's goals.

There are two general areas of focus when attempting to ensure policy compliance: technical and nontechnical. The technical area covers ways in which compliance can be automated via the use of software or hardware modifications (a simple example of this would be adjusting a website's registration page so that it is impossible for a user to register with a weak password.) Nontechnical methods tend to center around people and are generally focused on encouraging individuals to comply with a policy, usually by attempting to increase understanding of the policy. Both technical and nontechnical compliance techniques can impact a policy's success just as technical and nontechnical threats can compromise security, so for any policy to be truly effective, both areas must be addressed.

Nontechnical Compliance

The person-oriented side of compliance, sometimes known as "behavioral compliance", (Greene, 2006) can prove a daunting task for any information security specialist. The institution's vulnerabilities have been documented, preventative measures have been found to counteract possible attacks, and procedures have been established to ensure that any crisis that does emerge can be dealt with swiftly and appropriately–but how does one convince dozens, hundreds, or even thousands of individuals to put forth the effort required to make policies and procedures successful, especially when said individuals perceive no foreseeable benefit from compliance? In order to better understand how to achieve this goal, one must examine each step of policy compliance from the point of view of those who must comply with it. These steps include introduction, reinforcement, adaptation, and enforcement.

The introduction step of policy compliance refers to the manner in which the policy is first presented to those who must abide by it. Introduction is an important step because it will set the tone for compliance (or lack thereof); if the policy is introduced in a poor fashion, then it is likely to meet some form of resistance, whereas a well-done introduction may inspire an audience to achieve full policy compliance quickly. So, what separates a weak introduction from a strong one? To illustrate, let us examine two policy introduction scenarios: one, a company-wide email explaining the new policy, and two, a mandatory-attendance training program.

First, we will examine the email. The email contains a copy of the new policy and a brief but well-written introduction explaining that the policy must be followed by all employees. Some of the employees do not check their emails regularly and so remain unaware of the new policy for several days. Others open the email, but upon reading the words "information security", decide that the policy must be full of "technical mumbo-jumbo" and will not apply to them. Of the employees that read the email and recognize that it might apply to them, many fail to understand how following the policy could possibly benefit anyone and decide to treat it as a suggestion rather than a rule that can have real consequences. Very few employees speak of the email to one another and the policy is quickly forgotten by most of the staff. As far as compliance is concerned, this policy is off to a very bad start. This is not to say that sending an email about a new policy is a terrible idea, but in this scenario, the email is not reinforced by additional measures or materials; alone, it cannot make a strong enough impression to ensure that the policy is taken seriously.

Next, we examine the training program. The program is held in a presentation-like setting that includes audience participation via certain hands-on training tools and a question and answer session. Before explaining the policy itself, the speaker first describes the vulnerabilities that the policy was written to correct and demonstrates how such vulnerabilities can threaten security. When the policy is explained, some demonstrations are provided that help to prove it will be effective if followed. The employees leave the meeting with an understanding of what the new policy is, why it is important, and how it applies to each member of the institution.

The examples above are extreme cases, but they can help show the impact that a good introduction can have on behavioral policy compliance. Now it is important to examine the differences between the two approaches to determine why one succeeded when the other failed. The first difference is scope; each individual must feel that he or she is partially responsible for adhering to the policy so that security is not compromised. Organization-wide emails often have individuals to whom the contents of the mail do not apply, so those individuals learn to ignore "important" messages if given the slightest inkling that the message was intended for a group to which that individual does not belong; being invited to at-

tend a training session in which that individual might be expected to respond to a question or participate in a demonstration, however, helps to send the message that *everyone* is expected to comply with the policy. The second difference is that the training session was able to explain the vulnerabilities threatening the system in a way that email could not: by demonstrating the system's weaknesses first-hand. If an individual cannot understand the vulnerability that a policy is written to correct, then that individual is not likely to comply with the policy (Siponen, Mahmood, & Pahnila, 2009). By demonstrating the ill effects of noncompliance (for example, by proving that a weak password is easy to hack), one can help to ensure that individuals more fully understand the risks vulnerabilities present (Greene, 2006). Lastly, by presenting the information in a group environment, the training session could help to mitigate the anxiety and defensive nature that people often adapt when feeling uninformed about a topic (Greene, 2006). A mindset in which an individual can feel that they are learning along with everyone else can help to ease resistance against the policy and turn the experience of change into a more positive one. For a policy introduction to be effective, those affected by it must not only have a clear understanding of what the policy entails, but must also believe that it is possible to comply with the policy and that compliance will achieve real results (Siponen et al., 2009).

However, there was one issue that neither the email nor the training approach addressed. Neither approach takes any type of individual into account besides employees! What if the institution implementing the policy were a university? Students would not receive an email or attend a training session that was meant for employees, yet students would still require access to the university's computer labs and would be expected to adhere to certain university policies. When taking policy education into account, it is vital to completely identify and educate all stakeholders who must abide by the policy (Madigan, Petrulich, & Motuk, 2004).

Introduction may have a significant influence, but alone, it is not enough; the introduction must be reinforced if individuals are to continue to comply with the policy. Some of the methods for reinforcement are simple; reminders of the policy (or specific procedures relating to it) can be posted in or around areas that the policy applies to (Greene, 2006). For example, a screensaver might remind employees to never leave their machines logged in and unattended while a poster placed near the trash receptacle could remind individuals to abide by the rules of proper disposal of sensitive information. Reminders that are placed in key locations can help to avert accidents or laziness by reminding people of what the policy requires for a particular task. Positive reinforcement may also help to ensure compliance; for instance, if a security incident occurs elsewhere due to a vulnerability type that the institution's new policy is supposed to avert, then telling individuals about it may boost their perception of how well the policy works and can remind them of why that policy is important (Siponen et al., 2009).

More important than written or verbal reminders, however, is the perception of compliance from other stakeholders. For example, take a scenario in which three desk clerks admit patients into a health care facility. The system is slowly being computerized, but many patients' files are still kept in a filing cabinet. One rule of a new policy is that no documents containing personally identifiable information will be left outside of the filing cabinet unless said documents are in use. However, one of the three workers is resistant to the policy and has a tendency to leave patient files lying around long after they are no longer needed because the worker does not like the hassle of repeatedly locking and unlocking the filing cabinet, although the worker does agree that the filing cabinet ought to be locked at all times. This worker is not new to the center and has seniority over the other two. Over time, the other two workers become frustrated at

complying with the center's policy because they have perceived no ill effects from the first worker's lack of compliance. Eventually, they might cease to comply with the policy themselves.

Peer pressure can be a powerful motivator either for better or for worse, and leaders can exert more of that pressure than anyone else (Greene, 2006). After all, if the person who is supposed to be enforcing the new policy does not abide by it, then why should anyone else? A policy can either be reinforced or its initial efforts negated completely depending on whether or not people perceive the policy as being followed by others. For this reason, it is important that individuals in managerial positions adhere strictly to information security policies themselves so as to set an example for others.

Adaptation is achieved when the policy continues to evolve based on changes in the institution that created it. This means more than revising the policy to reflect necessary changes due to security violations; each statement of the policy must remain applicable to the current state of things. For instance, if an institution were to move entirely from paper files to digital (so much so that there was no longer any need for filing cabinets), then policy statements concerning the locking of filing cabinets would no longer be applicable. Stakeholders who read the policy after the conversion would view the policy as being outdated and would view the unnecessary information as having wasted their time. For this reason, it is important that policies be kept as current as possible so that they will reflect actual practices (Greene, 2006). This can help both to maintain the impression that the policy is useful and to avoid potential confusion.

Lastly, a policy cannot be of use if it cannot be enforced. While many security trends can now be monitored by an automated process, others cannot. For example, in a university's computer science facility, the doors to the labs are constantly locked and password-protected; however, certain students have taken to propping the lab doors open with trash cans, a practice that negates the effectiveness of the lock-and-password procedure. As is the case with this scenario, sometimes the working environment must be monitored by people in order to ensure behavioral policy compliance.

Once a violation of policy is found, there comes the unpleasant task of dealing with the violation and enforcing the policy. Sometimes individuals who have violated the policy meet with a punishment. For instance, a student caught propping open the lab door might be temporarily banned from using the university's computer labs. While punishing someone for a violation is never pleasant, it is important that such punishments be consistent and clearly explained. If the punishment is only threatened and never applied, then the policy will appear to be less important and will be more difficult to enforce in the future, while if the punishment is only given to certain people or by certain managers, questions of fairness (and possible legal involvement) may arise (Greene, 2006).

Technical Compliance

The emphasis of technical compliance is very different from that of nontechnical compliance. Rather than focusing on how to encourage people to follow a policy, many forms of this compliance type are designed to make it impossible for people *not* to follow policies. Usually, this means implementing some form of automatic policy compliance, such as the password example given earlier (in which the system rejects passwords that are too weak).

Technical compliance methods cannot be as easily generalized as nontechnical compliance methods because separate institutions have different technologies available to them and varying requirements to meet; a bank's requirements will differ from those of a hospital, which will differ from those of a university, which will differ from those of a small business, and so on. Even so, there are a few automation techniques of technical compliance that are applicable to most, if not all,

institutions. A few examples of useful automations are given below:

1. **Enforcement of strong usernames or passwords:** As mentioned earlier, programs and websites can be configured not to accept passwords (or usernames) that do not meet certain criteria. This method can ensure compliance with policies that require strong passwords.

2. **Automatic patching:** Computers used to perform work for the institution should look for browser, operating system, anti-virus, and anti-malware patches at startup. Since many users have a tendency to put off such updates until a later date, the user should not be able to easily postpone the patch or cancel the reboot that follows it (if applicable). This method can ensure compliance with policies that require the operating system, browser, anti-virus and/or anti-malware software to remain updated.

3. **Restricted access:** In addition to the usual username/password combination, some scenarios may require that additional security be put in place to ensure that only individuals who need to access a particular file can obtain it. For instance, if there are several agents working at an insurance firm and each agent is only allowed to access the information of his or her own clients, then security should be put into place so that each time a logged-in agent tries to obtain a file from the database, the system first verifies that the file actually belongs to a client of that agent. This method can ensure compliance with policies that require personally identifiable information to be viewed strictly on a need-to-know basis.

4. **Disallowing change:** In some cases, it may be possible to prevent users from accidentally or intentionally making any change to a computer. A good example of this method would be a university computer lab that wishes to

prevent students from introducing malware and viruses to the computer, as well as to stop said students from installing software that has not been approved by the university (such as a video game). In this example, an image is made of a "clean" partition (that is, the state of the computer with the operating system and approved software installed, but no other files or programs). The computers and university network are then configured in such a way that each computer simply reloads the original image every time it is turned on, so any changes a student might make (creating new files, installing new software, etc.) are erased upon reboot. This method can ensure compliance with policies that require publicly-used machines to contain only approved software; it can also save a great deal of time and effort that would otherwise be spent painstakingly checking each computer for the offending software or documents.

Automation of policies can ensure compliance and, in many cases, can greatly ease the workload of security professionals or those in management positions. Even so, it is important that both the policy and all of the procedures that can be associated with a particular event be fully understood before automating policy compliance, lest unintentional harm be done. Take, for instance, the insurance agency example used to illustrate the concept of restricted access. Preventing unwarranted access to clients' personally identifiable information is certainly in line with general identity theft prevention policies, but what if one of the agents leaves unexpectedly? How will the agency transfer that person's clients to a new agent? The automated security systems must take such scenarios into account and must sometimes allow for a bypass of the usual security features so that business can continue without overly inconveniencing the client.

One study proposes that the violation of a security requirement "…is acceptable when the security policy specifies additional requirements that apply in case of violation of other security requirements" (Brunel, Cuppens, Cuppens, Sans, & Bodeveix, 2007). In other words, certain real-life demands may require that a security violation be allowed to occur under specific conditions, but policy compliance can still be met so long as those conditions are predefined and additional compliance strategies exist to handle them. The need for such exceptions will likely occur infrequently when seeking compliance with identity theft prevention or identity theft response policies, but they must still be taken into account.

Password Management

Various scenarios throughout this document have used password-related security threats as examples. The reason for this is that passwords have become an extremely common form of security; anyone who owns a computer is likely to have at least one password in order to protect that computer from unauthorized use. When email, online banking, online shopping, database access and website subscriptions are taken into account, it becomes apparent that a given user could be tied to many different password systems. Even in instances where tokens, biometrics, or other such authentication measures are implemented, passwords are usually used to complement the system and increase its security (Hitachi ID Systems, Inc., 2010). Because passwords are so common, most institutions will need to include a password management section as part of their information security policy; for this reason, password management is presented here as a demonstration of technical and nontechnical compliance techniques for a given policy.

Several best practices for creating a strong password were listed in the "Best Practices" section of this paper. However, even a password that adheres to all the do's and don'ts of strong password creation may be compromised in other ways. If the password is stored on a workstation, server, or backup media in plaintext or transmitted over a network in plaintext, or if it is stored or transmitted in a form that can be easily converted to plaintext, then the password may become compromised (Hitachi ID Systems, Inc., 2010). Also, if a user creates a strong password but writes the password down or shares it with someone else, the password will no longer be secret and may become compromised (Hitachi ID Systems, Inc., 2010). A password that is never changed could also become compromised, perhaps without the account owner's knowledge. Let us say that a particular institution chooses to address these issues by including the following items in its policy:

- Passwords must be at least 8 characters long and must contain at least 1 non-alphanumeric character, one lowercase letter, one uppercase letter, and one digit. The password should not contain the user's login ID, a dictionary word over 3 letters long, or the user's personal information (name, date of birth, etc.)
- Passwords must be changed at least once every 90 days
- Passwords should neither be written down, saved to a desktop, nor shared with others
- Password files must be encrypted during both storage and transfer utilizing an encryption method that cannot readily be broken
- When a user is no longer affiliated with the institution, all passwords that have been shared with that user must be changed

First, the institution examines ways in which it can automate the enforcement of its policy, beginning with the creation of a new password. When a user creates a new password for a particular system, the system automatically checks to ensure that the password adheres to the policy's specifications. In this particular system, however, the database does not retain most of the user's personal information (name, date of birth, etc.), so the system cannot be automated to check against the inclusion of such information in the password. The exclusion of personal information in a password is instead enforced by a nontechnical compliance strategy in which users are educated about the ease of guessing a password that contains personal information and are warned not to create such passwords.

The second item on the policy list can be automated as well. If 90 or more days have elapsed since the user last changed his or her password, the system will not allow that user full access until the password has been changed (in other words, the user can only access those features which are necessary in order to change the password). A password history is kept in the system and checks the new password against old ones to ensure that users do not try to keep their old passwords (Hitachi ID Systems, Inc., 2010). In order to stop users from sidestepping this system by changing their password multiple times until the old password is dropped from system's history and becomes usable again, an additional limit is placed that prevents users from changing their passwords more than a few times in a given day (Hitachi ID Systems, Inc., 2010).

The third item is more difficult to automate; there is nothing the system can do outright to prevent users from disclosing their passwords to others or from writing the passwords down. However, browsers through which the users perform login activities can be configured not to save passwords or to clear out saved passwords at the end of a session. This technical compliance technique is important in case a machine's physical security becomes compromised. Whenever a written-down password is located, the institution confronts the responsible user and sends out a memo to remind other users that writing down a password is against the institution's policy. Unfortunately, many users in this institution continue to write down their passwords or constantly approach the IT department for help, claiming that the security scheme has made the passwords too difficult to remember. The institution now has a choice: it can either revise its policy so that some of the password requirements are removed (thereby making the passwords somewhat less secure but also making them easier to remember), implement password synchronization (in a case where two or more systems require passwords, synchronization technology is used so that only one password must be remembered and maintained for both systems) (Hitachi ID Systems, Inc., 2010), implement single sign-on (a technique in which independent systems' logins are consolidated into a single authentication process, again reducing the number of passwords that must be remembered) (Hitachi ID Systems, Inc., 2010), or change the means by which users authenticate themselves to the system (for example, using a token/password combination to maintain a similar level of security to the current one given a slightly weaker password). In addition to these technical adjustments, the institution plans to reconsider the way in which it informs its users about the threat of a written password being compromised.

The policy's approach to password sharing can also be reinforced with nontechnical compliance techniques, specifically awareness training sessions. Users are not only cautioned against applicable social engineering techniques, but also against sharing common passwords with their coworkers. Many users will not see any harm in sharing a password if they believe the person they are sharing it with may also be entitled to it. For instance, if a password is required in order to access a particular room and one user forgets the password, it is likely that user will be able to convince someone else to share the room's password. Even users that are not actually entitled to enter the room may be able to gain access by asking friendly coworkers for help; since the users all work for the same institution, many will not see the harm in sharing the password with them. Former users that are no longer affiliated with the institution but retain contacts there may also be able to gain access to restricted areas this way. The institution informs users that even this type of password sharing can pose a severe security risk; in addition, it ensures that security personnel who are able to validate the identities and access rights of users are always on hand to assist with the retrieval of forgotten passwords so that the users are not forced to resort to pressuring other users for them. To help combat social engineering, the institution uses the nontechnical compliance technique of warning its users, perhaps on an institution-owned email page or login, that the user will never be asked for his or her passwords through email, phone, or by technical staff.

Item four is addressed primarily with technical compliance techniques. The institution is careful to encrypt any passwords that are stored in its database and keeps the machines on which such passwords are stored disconnected from the Internet whenever possible. The institution is also aware of events in which passwords are transported and takes care to ensure that transported passwords are encrypted at all times. Client devices or applications that use cached passwords are accounted for and the cached passwords are also encrypted (Hitachi ID Systems, Inc., 2010). The requirement for password encryption is also listed as a topic that must be addressed whenever the institution wishes to develop an application or purchase software that will make use of passwords.

For the fifth item, the applied compliance techniques will depend largely on the setup of the institution. As in the example for item three, restricted areas may be protected by a password; if a user leaves the institution but the password remains unchanged, then that user would retain access to that area. The institution may be able to use a technical compliance technique that will automatically change certain passwords when a user that had access rights to them is marked as having those rights revoked (either because the user is leaving or because the user has been assigned to a new position that no longer requires access to certain items or areas). The new (random) password is then sent to administrators or managers to be distributed to the rest of the users. If such a system is not feasible, the institution must have someone check the user's access rights personally and invent new common passwords. Another possible nontechnical compliance procedure would be to inform relevant stakeholders of the user's departure or change of position so that they will not reveal the changed password to that user.

In addition to addressing the five policy items listed above, the institution might employ other procedures that can prevent a password from being compromised. A technical example would be to implement a lockout system that prevents anyone from successfully logging into an account if a specified sequence of failed logins occurs within a given time frame on that account; for instance, if a user, intruder, or device attempts to log in 10 times within 5 minutes and enters an incorrect password for all ten attempts, then that account might be made inaccessible until the lockdown is removed (perhaps after a set period of time has elapsed) (Hitachi ID Systems, Inc., 2010). This can help to prevent an attack by guessing, but it also gives attackers a means by which to execute a denial-of-service attack (in which the attacker repeatedly enters incorrect passwords to keep the account in lockdown mode) (Hitachi ID Systems, Inc., 2010). A nontechnical example of an additional password-related security procedure would be to conduct thorough IT support training in which the IT staff is trained to conduct authentication prior to every password reset and in which they are warned about trends in security threats, such as those posed by social engineering.

AUDITING

Even after every measure has been taken to research, design, implement, and comply with a policy, there is still one reoccurring test that the institution must pass, and that is the audit. Any institution can claim regulatory and policy compliance, but after so many information security scandals, people want more than claims; they want proof. Consumers want proof that their personally identifiable information has not been compromised. Employers and information security professionals want proof that the policies they so carefully designed and employed are being followed and are proving effective. Employees want proof that the effort they have spent in adhering to the policies has not been wasted (or else want to hide the proof that they have not been adhering to policy at all). By examining an institution's current and past states, an audit can help to provide that proof.

Auditing, whether performed internally or by a third party, can help an institution to determine whether policy compliance has actually been achieved and may help to expose vulnerabilities that have come about since the policy was implemented. The audit can be conducted using a variety of methods; just as policy compliance can be split into nontechnical and technical procedures, so too can the auditing process. An auditor may gather evidence about nontechnical compliance by collecting statements from various stakeholders or by observing individuals as they work (Cannon, Bergmann, & Pamplin, 2006), while strong evidence about technical compliance can be gathered quickly and efficiently via the use of auditing tools. One such tool is Microsoft's SQL Services Best Practices Analyzer, which checks SQL servers for compliance with certain best practices (Natan, 2005). Similar tools exist to automatically check for particular features of policy compliance within a specific environment; for instance, one such tool might analyze each employee's computer to search for unauthorized software or peer-to-peer files (Greene, 2006) while another might focus on detecting passwords that somehow violate company policy (Natan, 2005). Yet another tool might trace each business process from beginning to end (Cannon et al., 2006) to ensure that they comply with policies both individually and as a working system. Auditing tools like these can pinpoint small-scale noncompliance issues or security vulnerabilities quickly and may also detect large-scale issues that would have otherwise gone unnoticed (for instance, if many passwords or usernames in a system are too similar) (Natan, 2005). Such tools do not always come without a price, however; some of them can be expensive and may require specialized training if the tools are to be used properly (Cannon et al., 2006). Depending on the auditing tool and the information that it collects, questions of privacy and the security of the tool's collected data may also come into question (Cannon et al., 2006).

Perhaps more important than the auditing methods themselves is determining how the audit will be staffed; this holds especially true for an internal audit in which many participants will know one another and may be reluctant to bring forth evidence that illustrates a particular group or person in a poor light. The auditing process should never be left to a single individual or group (Natan, 2005) because personal expectations and bias can affect the outcome of the audit; the work should be split as evenly and thoroughly as possible so that each layer of the institution's infrastructure has a chance to affect the outcome (and hopefully compensate for individual biases). Even an external auditor may require internal assistance; when selecting staff members to assist in the auditing process, such an auditor should search for the following criteria (Cannon et al., 2006):

- The provider of the work should be independent and objective.
- He or she must have an acceptable level of professional competence, experience, and qualification to perform the given task
- The auditor and the prospective helper must agree on the scope of the work to be done and the approach that will be used to accomplish it
- The auditor must determine the level of review and supervision that will be required

Basically, the auditor must be certain that the work done will be unbiased and of "sufficient quality, quantity, and relevance" (Cannon et al., 2006). To help ensure that an audit's results remain as accurate and useful as possible, institutions that choose to implement internal auditing should adhere to similarly strict standards.

Lastly, an audit is unlikely to be successful unless there are procedures in place to facilitate the auditing process. A simple explanation of this is that no one can audit what isn't there; if there are few automated compliance procedures, then certain auditing tools will be of little use. Likewise, if little to no data is kept that helps to trace policy-relevant information (such as who has received a copy of a particular individual's personally identifiable information), then the audit will be unable to conclusively determine whether or not a breach in policy compliance has occurred. Since audits are generally performed on an annual basis at best, the auditing process must analyze the past as well as the present, but it cannot do this if no records of the past have been kept.

An appropriate procedure model for ensuring policy compliance should include several key elements, including the following: monitoring of the work environment to facilitate data gathering and report creation; analysis of the work environment, generated reports, future trends, and violations; and proper documentation of all policy violation incidents and the methods employed to detect and respond to said incidents (Madigan et al., 2004). One proposed procedure model that attempts to facilitate policy compliance (and, by its nature, the auditing system) is the Governance and Compliance Maturity Model, or GOCOMM (Gheorghe, Massacci, Neuhaus, & Pretschner, 2009). The goal of this procedure model is continual assessment and automation of business processes, which it measures based on the four requirements of control, correlation, automation, and measurements (Gheorghe et al., 2009). Basically, an institution can raise its GOCOMM maturity level by implementing controls over business processes, recognizing the correlations between those controls and the corresponding policies or regulations, automating evidence collection, and evaluating the effectiveness of the controls using valid measurements (Gheorghe et al., 2009). The five levels of the process are defined as follows (Gheorghe et al., 2009):

"Level 0: Chaos. No adequately documented level of control over business processes. A traditional audit is likely to fail.

Level 1: Control. The business has controls in place, but they are inadequately correlated with objectives. When objectives change, there is no process in place that could say which controls need to change because of the changed objective.

We suspect that most organizations are at level 1.

Level 2: Correlation. The controls are correlated with objectives, but they do not (all) operate automatically.

Level 3: Automation. Controls operate automatically, but no indicator judges the performance of processes and controls.

Level 4: Measurement. There are automatically and consistently computed indicators in place that allow continuous assessment of governance and compliance."

The higher an institution climbs in such a procedure model, the more useful an audit of that institution is likely to be. The procedures required to implement this model can provide valuable documentation and quickly-assessed automated processes that will provide auditors with evidence to prove or disprove policy compliance so that the institution can better determine whether or not it is truly secure and, if not, what areas require improvement.

DISCUSSIONS & FUTURE RESEARCH DIRECTIONS

In theory, defending against identity theft sounds simple; just perform the risk assessment, create the policy and procedures, then audit and revise as necessary. Unfortunately, it is often much more complex in practice.

The main impairment when attempting to protect one's assets against identity theft is that it can be very, very difficult to coordinate the thoughts and actions of people. Some individuals are lazy (or just very busy) and will attempt to bypass any compliance measures that cause them to spend 'too much' time or go out of their way. Other individuals are more trusting than most and may be especially prone to social engineering, even when repeatedly warned against it. If a company makes a passionate but fact-deprived effort to inform its employees about the need for a new policy, then still other individuals may decide that the policy's demands are extreme or paranoid and might ignore them for that reason. Discovering the actual thoughts and actions of those that handle confidential information can be a tricky process, and changing a person's nature, beliefs or daily habits can prove nearly impossible. Thus, a study on the repercussions of the general attitude and perception towards privacy protection is a logical extension to this research.

Users whose confidential information the system keeps sometimes unwittingly contribute to the difficulty, especially when those users have false expectations of the system or are not well-informed as to whom they should contact and what information they will need to have on hand in order to process a request. As an example, many users will often call a company with only their name, address, and date-of-birth on hand since it is bothersome to remember account numbers. If the user is able to obtain some service using only this information, then the user is often happy; if not, then the user is often frustrated or even furious. Thanks to Internet sites such as Facebook and

MySpace, it is usually easy to obtain a person's full name and address or full name and date of birth without even needing to know the person, so a good company policy would be to deny service until an account number or other verification were provided. However, thanks to the attitudes of the end users, workers who must answer the phones will only see negative results from adhering to the policy and positive results from bypassing it. This sort of feedback may be especially damaging for hospitals or similar locations where the front-desk worker is constantly bombarded with emotional relatives and friends who are desperate for news of their loved ones, since empathy with the caller may increase the likelihood that the worker will not abide by the policy. Clearly, a study on the mitigation of the risk involved in social engineering would provide a most welcome relief to this dilemma.

Problems can propagate from management and administration as well. Oftentimes, the person who controls a company or organization's budget is not well-informed about information security issues. That person (or group of people) may deny funding or time for training sessions, new software, or other items that would be needed to implement a secure identity theft prevention policy. Others in administrative positions may take a minimalist approach to security in which they attempt to do as little as possible to comply with federal regulations, or attempt to shift the blame for successful attacks away from the company and onto the consumer or some other entity without ever addressing the vulnerabilities that allowed the attack to succeed.

Issues can arise even with the legislation itself. Currently, there is a large need for individuals who are knowledgeable about both law and information security—two separate fields that can be very expensive, time-consuming, and difficult to pursue. As a result of this unfilled gap, laws pertaining to identity theft and other issues that may involve digital information are more likely to be written by individuals that have very little experience related to the topic. Even when knowledgeable individuals are found, there is still the issue of time; technology moves very quickly and constantly replaces older methods with new ones, whereas legislation moves very slowly and is unlikely to be revised again soon once accepted. Laws pertaining to issues such as identity theft must be specific enough to be enforced, yet they must also be flexible enough to remain applicable to any new technologies that may be invented in the years to come. In short, although there is a definite and recognized need for legislation that pertains to the field of information security, the means by which such legislation is formed must be further refined lest the produced laws prove inapplicable or even harmful to society.

The obstacles currently faced may be best overcome by carefully identifying, not only where vulnerabilities exist, but why they have come to exist there. It is especially important to examine, not only the processes by which confidential information is obtained and used, but the people that must daily adhere to those processes. If a procedure does not seem to work, then a company may ask itself: what is the procedure meant to do? Is the procedure's meaning clear to others? Is the procedure too complex or does it interfere with day-to-day business? Is there some hidden detail about the nature of the business that could make a simple procedure difficult to follow? Questions such as these may help to reveal the root of vulnerability or an alternative method of defending against it.

CONCLUSION

In order to prevent identity theft or respond to an incident of it, institutions should create identity theft prevention and identity theft response policies. These policies can be used to help the institution comply with government regulations in addition to protecting valuable assets. Those who develop such policies should take into account the individual requirements of and laws applicable to the institution for which the policy is written. Measures should be taken to encourage or ensure policy compliance and annual audits should be performed to assess the effectiveness of those measures. If the developed policy is clear, concise, and complete, it is more likely to be effective.

Additional resources, including many of those referenced throughout this document, can be found at business.ftc.gov. Additionally, the full-text version of the COBIT document (mentioned in the "Risk Assessment" section under "Policies for Preventing Identity Theft") can be found in PDF format at http://www.isaca.org/Knowledge-Center/cobit/Documents/CobiT_4.1.pdf. (Note: This website may require users to register before granting access to the document).

REFERENCES

Bergmann, T. S., Cannon, D. L., & Pamplin, B. (2006). *CISA Certified Information Systems Auditor Study Guide*. Indianapolis: Wiley Publishing, Inc.

Bingisser, G. M. (2008, February 25). *Data Privacy and Breach Reporting: Compliance with Varying State Laws*. Retrieved September 22, 2010, from http://www.lctjournal.washington.edu/Vol4/a09Bingisser.html

Brunel, J., Cuppens, F., Cuppens, N., Sans, T., & Bodeveix, J.-P. (2007). *Security Policy Compliance with Violation Management*. Workshop on Formal Methods in Security Engineering (pp. 31-40). Virginia: ACM.

DataLossDB, Open Security Foundation. (2011). *Data Loss Statistics*. Retrieved February 10, 2011: http://datalossdb.org/statistics.

Department of the Treasury, Federal Deposit Insurance Corporation, Federal Reserve System, Federal Trade Commission, National Credit Union Administration. (2007, November 9*). Identity Theft Red Flags and Address Discrepancies Under the Fair and accurate Credit Transactions Act of 2003; Final Rule*. Retrieved October 27, 2010, from http://ftc.gov/os/fedreg/2007/november/071109redflags.pdf

Federal Trade Commission. (2002, May 23). *Standards for Safeguarding Customer Information; Final Rule*. Retrieved September 22, 2010, from http://www.ftc.gov/os/2002/05/67fr36585.pdf

Federal Trade Commission. (2003, June). *Security Check: Reducing Risks to Your Computer Systems*. Retrieved October 2, 2010, from http://business.ftc.gov/documents/bus58-security-check-reducing-risks-your-computer-systems

Federal Trade Commission. (2004, June). *Information Compromise and the Risk of Identity Theft: Guidance for Your Business*. Retrieved October 1, 2010, from http://business.ftc.gov/documents/bus59-information-compromise-and-risk-id-theft-guidance-your-business

Federal Trade Commission. (2005, June). *Disposing of Consumer Report Information? New Rule Tells How*. Retrieved September 23, 2010, from http://business.ftc.gov/documents/alt152-disposing-consumer-report-information-new-rule-tells-how

Federal Trade Commission. (2006, May). *Businesses Must Provide Victims and Law Enforcement with Transaction Records Relating to Identity Theft*. Retrieved September 29, 2010, from http://business.ftc.gov/documents/bus66-businesses-must-provide-victims-and-law-enforcement-transaction-records-relating-identity

Federal Trade Commission. (2006, April). *Financial Institutions and Customer Information: Complying with the Safeguards Rule.* Retrieved October 2, 2010, from http://business.ftc.gov/documents/bus54-financial-institutions-and-customer-information-complying-safeguards-rule

Federal Trade Commission. (n.d.). *Protecting Personal Information: A Guide for Business.* Retrieved September 29, 2010, from http://www.ftc.gov/bcp/edu/pubs/business/idtheft/bus69.pdf

Francia, G. A., & Ciganek, A. (2010). Global Information Security Regulations, Case Studies and Cultural Issues. In M. E. Whitman & H. J. Mattord (Eds.), *Readings and Cases in the Management of Information Security, Volume II: Legal and Ethical Issues in Information Security Management*: Course Technology.

Gheorghe, G., Massacci, F., Neuhaus, S., & Pretschner, A. (2009). *GoCoMM: A governance and Compliance Maturity Model.* Conference on Computer and Communications Security (pp. 33-38). Chicago: ACM.

Gramm-Leach-Bliley Act. (1999, November 12). Retrieved September 22, 2010, from http://www.ftc.gov/privacy/glbact/glbsub1.htm

Greene, S. S. (2006). *Security Policies and Procedures: Principles and Practices.* Upper Saddle River: Pearson Education, Inc.

Herrmann, D. S. (2007). *Complete Guide to Security and Privacy Metrics: Measuring Regulatory Compliance, Operational Resilience, and ROI.* Auerbach Publications. doi:10.1201/9781420013283

Hitachi, I. D. (2010). *Systems, Inc.* Password Management Best Practices.

IT Governance Institute. (2007). *COBIT 4.1.* Retrieved September 20, 2010, from http://www.isaca.org/Knowledge-Center/cobit/Documents/CobiT_4.1.pdf

Madigan, E. M., Petrulich, C., & Motuk, K. (2004). The Cost of Non-Compliance: When Policies Fail. *User Services Conference* (pp. 47-51). Baltimore: ACM.

Natan, R. B. (2005). *Implementing Database Security and Auditing.* Elsevier, Inc.

OnGuard Online. (n.d.). *7 Practices for Computer Security.* Retrieved September 25, 2010, from http://www.onguardonline.gov/topics/computer-security.aspx

Personuvernd (2008). *The Data Protection Act. Iceland.* Retrieved February 21, 2011 from http://www.personuvernd.is/information-in-english/greinar//nr/438

Princeton University. (2010, September 20). *WordNet.* Retrieved September 23, 2010, from http://wordnetweb.princeton.edu/perl/webwn

Salomon, K. D., Cassat, P. C., & Thibeau, B. E. (2003, March 20). *IT Security for Higher Education: A Legal Perspective.* Retrieved September 22, 2010, from http://net.educause.edu/ir/library/pdf/CSD2746.pdf

Siponen, M., Mahmood, M. A., & Pahnila, S. (2009, December). Technical Opinion: Are Employees Putting Your Company at Risk by Not Following Information Security Policies? *Communications of the ACM, 145*–147. doi:10.1145/1610252.1610289

U.S.Senate Bill S.3987. (2010). *An Act to Amend the Fair Credit Reporting Act With Respect to the Applicability of Identity Theft Guidelines to Creditors.* Retrieved February 7, 2011 from http://www.gpo.gov/fdsys/pkg/BILLS-111s3987enr/pdf/BILLS-111s3987enr.pdf.

KEY TERMS AND DEFINITIONS

Identity Theft: The fraudulent use of another person's personal information.

Personally Identifiable Information: Any personal information by which an individual may be identified (SSN, bank account number, username/password combination, etc.).

Policy Compliance: An organization-specific and established goal set as an attempt to encourage and achieve policy compliance by its members/employees.

Red Flag Rules: Guidelines to help implement certain requirements of the Fair and Accurate Credit Transactions Act with regard to identity theft prevention, detection, and mitigation.

Regulatory Compliance: An organization-specific and established goal set as an attempt to comply with relevant laws or regulations.

Risk Assessment: The evaluation of the value of risk associated with a recognized threat.

Security Best Practices: Techniques or processes that have been proven to uphold information security standards that apply to large institutions as well as individuals.

Compilation of References

Aboba, B., Blunk, L., Vollbrecht, J., Carlson, J., & Levkowetz, H. (Eds.). (2004). *Extensible Authentication Protocol (EAP)*. RFC 3748, 2004.

Abrams, M. D. & Joyce M. V. (1995). *Trusted System Concepts. Computers & Security, 14*(1). Elsevier Advanced Technology.

Abu-Nimeh, S., & Mead, N. R. (2009). *Privacy risk assessment in privacy requirements engineering.* In RELAW: The second international workshop on requirements engineering and law.

Abu-Nimeh, S., & Mead, N. R. (2010). *Combining privacy and security risk assessment in security quality requirements engineering.* In 2010 AAAI spring symposium series, intelligent information privacy management.

Abu-Nimeh, S., Miyazaki, S., & Mead, N. R. (2009). *Integrating privacy requirements into security requirements engineering. In* Proceedings of the 21st international conference on software and knowledge engineering (pp. 542--547).

Adams, A., & Sasse, M. A. (2001). *Privacy in multimedia communications: Protecting users, not just data.* In Proceedings of IMH HCI'01 (pp. 49--64). New York: Springer.

Aiello, M., Chiarella, D., & Papaleo, G. (2009). Statistical anomaly detection on real e-mail traffic. [JIAS]. *Journal of Information Assurance and Security, 6*(4), 604–609.

Aiello, M., Avanzini, D., Chiarella, D., & Papaleo, G. (2006). *A Tool for Complete Log Mail Analysis: LMA.* Paper presented at the Terena Networking Conference 2006 (TNC2006), Security on the Backbone: Detecting and Responding to Attacks, Catania, Italy.

Aiello, M., Avanzini, D., Chiarella, D., & Papaleo, G. (2006b). *Worm Detection Using E-mail Data Mining. Paper* presented at the Primo Workshop Italiano su PRIvacy e Security (PRISE2006), Roma, Italy.

Aiello, M., Avanzini, D., Chiarella, D., & Papaleo, G. (2007). *SMTP sniffing for intrusion detection purposes.* In Proceedings of Secondo Workshop Italiano su PRIvacy e Security (PRISE2007), Roma, Italy, (pp. 53 – 58).

Aiello, M., Chiarella, D., & Papaleo, G. (2008). *Statistical anomaly detection on real e-mail traffic.* In Proceedings of the International Workshop on Computational Intelligence in Security for Information Systems (CISIS2008), Genova, Italy, (pp. 170 – 175).

Albuquerque, S. L., Gondim, P. R. L., & Monteiro, C. C. (2010). *Aspectos de Segurança na Interconexão de Redes Celulares e WLANs.* Paper presented at 10th Brazilian Security Symposium (SBSeg2010).

Alireza Pourshahid, A., & Tran, T. (2007). *Modeling Trust in E-Commerce: An Approach Based on User Requirements.* Paper presented at IEEE International Conference on Electronic E-commerce (ICEC 2007).

Almeida, M. (2007)., *Microsoft.com defaced.* Retrieved July, 14, 2010 from www.bit-shield.com/Link200705MS_Defaced.html.

Al-Riyami, S. S., & Paterson, K. (2003). Certificateless Public Key Cryptography. In C.-S. Laih (Ed.), *ASIACRYPT 2003: Vol. 2894. Lecture Notes in Computer Science* (pp. 452-473). Springer, Heidelberg.

Al-Riyami, S. S., & Paterson, K. (2005). CBE from CL-PKE: A generic construction and efficient schemes. In S. Vaudenay (Ed.) *PKC 2005: Vol. 3386. Lecture Notes in Computer Science* (pp. 398-415). Springer, Heidelberg.

Al-Zarouni, M. (2006). *Mobile Handset Forensic Evidence: a challenge for Law Enforcement.* Proceedings of the 4th Australian Digital Forensics Conference, Edith.

Al-Zarouni, M. (2007). *Introduction to Mobile Phone Flasher Devices and Considerations for their Use in Mobile Phone Forensics.* Proceedings of the 5th Australian Digital Forensics Conference.

Anand, R., Bajpai, G., Bhaskar, V. (2010). *3D Signature for Efficient Authentication in Multimodal Biometric Security Systems.* IACSIT International Journal of Engineering and Technology, 2 (2)

Andrews, J. H. (1998). *Testing Using Logfile Analysis: Tools, Methods and Issues.* In Proceedings of the 13th International Conference on Automated Software Engineering (ASE 98), (pp. 157 – 166).

Andrews, J. H., & Zhang, Y. (2000). *Broad Spectrum Studies of log File Analysis.* In Proceedings of the 22nd International Conference on Software Engineering, Limerick, Ireland, (pp. 105 – 114).

Apup Ramabhardran, Forensic investigation process model for windows mobile devices, Security Group, TaTa ELxi

Arkko, J., & Haverinen, H. (2006). Extensible Authentication Protocol Method for 3rd Generation Authentication and Key Agreement (EAP-AKA). *RFC, 4187,* 2006.

Aronowitz, H., Burshtein, D., & Amir, A. (2004). Text independent speaker recognition using speaker dependent word spotting. *Proc. ICSLP,* (pp. 1789-1792).

Ashcroft, J. (2001). *Technical Working Group for Electronic Crime Scene Investigation.* US Dpt of Justice, 2001. Retrieved from ww.ncjrs.gov/pdffiles1/nij/187736.pdf

Attorney, U. S. (2007). *Former Navy contractor sentenced for damaging Navy computer system.* Retrieved February, 20, 2011, from www.usdoj.gov/criminal/cybercrime/sylvestreSent.pdf.

Attorney, U. S. (2008a). *News release.* Retrieved February, 20, 2011, from www.usdoj.gov/criminal/cybercrime/dierkingCharge.pdf.

Attorney, U. S. (2008b). *Computer tech pleads guilty to identify theft of Calpine corporation executive.* Retrieved February, 20, 2011, from www.usdoj.gov/criminal/cybercrime/smithPlea.pdf.

Au, M. H., Mu, Y., Chen, J., Wong, D. S., Liu, J. K., & Yang, G. (2007). Malicious KGC attacks in certificateless cryptography. In R. Deng & P. Samarati (Eds.), *Proceedings of the 2nd ACM Symposium on information, Computer and Communications Security* (pp. 302-311). Singapore, ASIACCS '07. New York, NY: ACM, Avizienis, A., Laprie, J. -C., Randell, B., & Landwehr, C. (2004). Basic Concepts and Taxonomy of Dependable and Secure Computing. *IEEE Transactions on Dependable and Secure Computing, 1*(1), 11-33.

Axelsson, S. (1998). *Intrusion detection systems: A survey and taxonomy.* Technical Report 99 - 15, Chalmers University of Technology, Goteborg, Sweden Department of Computer Engineering.

Ayers, R., Jansen, W., Moenner, L., & Delaitre, A. (2007). *Cell phone forensic tools: An overview and analysis update.* Retrieved from http://csrc.nist.gov/publications/nistir/nistir-7387.pdf

Azzini, A., Marrara, S., Sassi, R., & Scotti, F. (2008). A fuzzy approach to multimodal biometric continuous authentication. *Fuzzy Optimization and Decision Making, 7*(3). doi:10.1007/s10700-008-9034-1

Baek, J., Newmarch, J., Safavi-Naini, R., & Susilo, W. (2004). A Survey of Identity-Based Cryptography. In *Proceedings of the 10th Annual Conference for Australian Unix User's Group, (AUUG '04)* (pp. 95-102). Springer-Verlag.

Baek, J., Susilo, W., & Zhou, J. (2007) New Constructions of Fuzzy Identity-Based Encryption. In R. Deng and P. Samarati (Eds.), *Proceedings of the 2nd ACM symposium on Information, computer and communications security, ASIACCS '07 (Singapore, March 20 - 22, 2007)* (pp. 368-370). New York, NY: ACM.

Baker, W. H., & Hylender, C. D. Valentine (2008). *Data Breach Investigations Report.* Retrieved February, 20, 2011, from www.verizonbusiness.com.

Barken, L. (2004). *How Secure is your Wireless Network? Safeguarding Your Wi-Fi LAN.* New York: Prentice Hall.

Belhumeur, P., Hespanha, J., & Kriegman, D. (1997). Eigenfaces vs. Fisherfaces: Recognition using class specific linear projection. *IEEE Transactions PAMI, 19*(7), 711–720. doi:10.1109/34.598228

Ben-Yacoub, S., Abdeljaoued, Y., & Mayoraz, E. (1999). Fusion of face and speech data for person identity verification. *IEEE Transactions on Neural Networks, 10,* 1065–1074. doi:10.1109/72.788647

Bergmann, T. S., Cannon, D. L., & Pamplin, B. (2006). *CISA Certified Information Systems Auditor Study Guide.* Indianapolis: Wiley Publishing, Inc.

Bicakci, K., & Tavli, B. (2009). Denial-of-Service attacks and countermeasures in IEEE 802.11 wireless networks. *Computer Standards & Interfaces,* 931–941. doi:10.1016/j.csi.2008.09.038

Bijwe, A., & Mead, N. R. (2010). *Adapting the square process for privacy requirements engineering* (Tech. Rep. Nos. CMU/SEI-2010-TN-022). Pittsburgh, PA: Carnegie Mellon University.

Bingisser, G. M. (2008, February 25). *Data Privacy and Breach Reporting: Compliance with Varying State Laws.* Retrieved September 22, 2010, from http://www.lctjournal.washington.edu/Vol4/a09Bingisser.html

Bishop, C. M. (1995). *Neural networks for pattern recognition.* New York: Oxford University Press.

Bittau, A., Handley, M., & Lackey, J. (2006). The final nail in WEP's coffin. *IEEE Symposium on Security and Privacy, SP '06.*

Bluden, B. (2009). *Anti forensics: the rootkit connections.* Black Hat USA, 2009

Bolle, R. (2004). *Guide to biometrics.* New York: Springer.

Boneh, D., & Franklin, M. (2001). Identity-Based Encryption from the Weil Pairing. In J. Kilian (Ed.), *CRYPTO 2001: Vol. 2139. Lecture Notes In Computer Science* (pp. 213-229). Springer, Heidelberg.

Boneh, D., Di Crescenzo, G., Ostrovsky, R., & Persiano, G. (2004). Public key encryption with keyword search. In *Advances in Cryptology, Eurocrypt'04: Vol. 3027. Lecture Notes In Computer Science* (pp. 506-522). Springer-Verlag.

Borisov, N., Goldberg, I., & Wagner, D. (2001). Intercepting Mobile Communications: The Insecurity of 802.11. *Proceedings Seventh Annual International Conference on Mobile Computing And Networking,* 180-189.

Brand, M., Oliver, N., & Pentland, A. (1997). Coupled hidden Markov models for complex action recognition. *IEEE Computer Society Conference on Computer Vision and Pattern Recognition* (p. 994). Puerto Rico: IEEE.

Breeuwsma, M., de Jongh, M., Klaver, C., Van Der Knijff, R., & Roeloffs, M., (2007) Forensic Data Recovery from Flash Memory. *Small Scale Digital Device Forensics Journal, 1*(1), June 2007

Brent. (2010). *Android Rooted: What is Nandroid Backup?* march 2010, http://www.simplemobilereview.com/android-rooted-what-is-nandroid-backup/

Brian, D., (2009). Digital forensics works. *IEEE security and Privacy, march/April 2009, 7*(2).

Brodkin, J. (2008). *Mobile phones to be primary Internet device by 2020, experts predict.* Network World, Retrieved from http://www.networkworld.com/news/2008/121508-pew-report.html

Bron, C., & Kerbosch, J. (1973). Finding all Cliques of an Undirected Graph. *Communications of the ACM, 16*(9), 575–577. doi:10.1145/362342.362367

Brosso, M. I. L. (2006). *Autenticação Contínua de Usuários em Redes de Computadores. Unpublished doctoral theses.* Brazil: University of São Paulo.

Brunel, J., Cuppens, F., Cuppens, N., Sans, T., & Bodeveix, J.-P. (2007). *Security Policy Compliance with Violation Management.* Workshop on Formal Methods in Security Engineering (pp. 31-40). Virginia: ACM.

Brunelli, R., & Falavigna, D. (1995). Person identification using multiple cues. *IEEE Transactions on Pattern Analysis and Machine Intelligence, 10,* 955–965. doi:10.1109/34.464560

BSI Bundesamt für Sicherheit in der Informationstechnik (Ed.). (2009). *Die Lage der IT-Sicherheit in Deutschland.* Bonn: BSI.

Bundeswirtschaftsministerium (2009). *Bundeswirtschaftsministerium unterstützt Unternehmen beim Schutz gegen Computerkriminalität.* Retrieved February, 20, 2011, from www.bmwi.de/BMWi/Navigation/Presse/pressemitteilungen,did=286748.html.

Bursch, D. (2005). *IT-Security im Unternehmen - Grundlagen, Strategien.* Berlin: VDM.

Cabinet Office. (2008), *The Data Handling Procedure in Government: Final Report.* June 2008. Retrieved October 6, 2010 from http://www.cesg.gov.uk/products_services/iatp/documents/data_handling_review.pdf

Cache, J., Wright, J., & Lu, V. (2010). *Hacking Exposed: Wireless Security Secrets and Solutions* (2nd ed.). New York: McGraw-Hill/Osborne.

Calderon, T. G., Chandra, A., & Cheh, J. J. (2006). Modeling an intelligent continuous authentication system to protect financial information resources. *International Journal of Accounting Information Systems, 7.*

Calixto, M. (2008). Quantum computation and cryptography: an overview. *Natural Computing, 8*(4), 663–679. doi:10.1007/s11047-008-9094-8

Campbell, J. J. (1997). Speaker Recognition: a tutorial. *Proceedings of the IEEE, 85*(9), 1437–1462. doi:10.1109/5.628714

Campbell, P. L., & Stamp, J. E. (2004). *A classification scheme for risk assessment methods (Tech. Rep. No. SAND2004-4233).* Sandia National Laboratories.

Canetti, R., Halevi, S., & Katz, J. (2003). A Forward-Secure Public-Key Encryption Scheme. In *Proceedings of the 22nd international Conference on theory and Applications of Cryptographic Techniques - EUROCRYPT 2003: Vol. 2656. Lecture Notes in Computer Science* (pp. 255-271). Springer-Verlag, Berlin, Heidelberg.

Casey, E. (2004). *Digital Evidence and Computer Crime: Forensic Science, Computers and the Internet* (2nd ed.). London: Elsevier.

Casey, E. (2007, June). What does "forensically sound" really mean? *Digital Investigation, 4*(2), 49–50. doi:10.1016/j.diin.2007.05.001

Casey, E. (2010). Introduction to Windows Mobile Forensics. *Digital Investigation, 6*(3-4), 136–146. doi:10.1016/j.diin.2010.01.004

Caviglione, L. (2009). Understanding and Exploiting the Reverse Patterns of Peer-to-Peer File-Sharing Applications. *Network Security, 1*(7), 8–12. doi:10.1016/S1353-4858(09)70087-X

Caviglione, L., & Cervellera, C. (2008). A Peer-to-Peer System for Optimized Content Replication. *European Journal of Operational Research, 196*(2), 423–433.

Caviglione, L., Aiello, M., & Papaleo, G. (2010). *A Scalable and Cost-Effective Framework for Traffic Monitoring in Virtual LANs.* Paper presented at the 21st International Tyrrhenian Workshop on Digital Communications (IT-WDC): Trustworthy Internet, Isola di Ponza, Italy.

Chaudhari, U., Navrratil, J., Ramaswamy, G., & Maes, S. (2001). Very large population text-independent speaker identification using transformation enhanced multi-grained models. [IEEE.]. *ICASSP, 01,* 461–464.

Chen, S., Cowan, C., & Grant, P. (1991). Orthogonal Least Squares Learning Algorithm for Radial Basis Function Networks. *IEEE Transactions on Neural Networks, 2*(2), 302–309. doi:10.1109/72.80341

Chen, L. (2007). An Interpretation of Identity-Based Cryptography. In A. Aldini and R. Gorrieri (Eds.), *Foundations of Security Analysis and Design IV: Vol. 4677. Lecture Notes in Computer Science* (pp. 183-208). Springer-Verlag, Berlin, Heidelberg.

Cheney, J. S. (2010*). Heartland Payment Systems: Lessons Learned from a Data Breach.* Retrieved February, 18, 2011, from www.philadelphiafed.org/payment-cards-center/publications/discussion-papers/2010/D-2010-January-Heartland-Payment-Systems.pdf.

Chevonne, T. D. & Dampier, D. A., (2010). A platform Independent Process Model for

Chiarella, D. (2010). Worm *detection: a monitoring behavior based system for Anomaly Detection.* Ph.D. Thesis INF/01 DISI-TH-2010-1, DISI - University of Genoa.

Chiasera, A., Casati, F., Daniel, F., & Velegrakis, Y. (2008). *Engineering privacy requirements in business intelligence applications.* In SDM '08: Proceedings of the 5th VLDB workshop on secure data management (pp. 219--228). Berlin, Heidelberg: Springer-Verlag.

Chibelushi, C., Deravi, F., & Mason, J. (2002). A review of speech-based bimodal recognition. *Multimedia. IEEE Transactions on, 4*(1), 23–37.

Chibelushi, C., Deravi, F., & Mason, J. S. (1993). Voice and facial image integration for speaker recognition. *Proc. IEEE Int. Symp. Multimedia Technologies Future Appl.* Southampton, U.K.: IEEE.

Ch'ng, S. I., Seng, K. P., & Ang, L.-M. (2010). Scalable Face Recognition System using Split-Train Structure. *Proceedings of the International Conference on Embedded Systems and Intelligent Technology (ICESIT2010),* CD-ROM: Paper 11.

Christian, S. J. Peron &. Michael Legary. (2006) Digital Anti-Forensics: Emerging trends in data transformation techniques. Seccuris Labs. Retrieved from www.seccuris.com/documents/papers/Seccuris-Antiforensics.pdf, Cowan University, Perth Western Australia, December 4th 2006

Chuvakin, A. (2009). *Five Mistakes of Security Log Analysis.* netForensics Inc., Retrieved March 2011, http://www.computerworld.com/s/article/print/96587/Five_mistakes_of_log_analysis

Claburn, T. (2019). *Hacker Accused of Video Extortion.* Retrieved February, 20, 2011, from www.informationweek.com/news/windows/security/showArticle.jhtml?articleID=225701396&cid=RSSfeed_TechWeb.

Clancy, T. C., & Goergen, N. (2008). Security in Cognitive Radio Networks: Threats and Mitigation. In *3rd International Conference on Cognitive Radio Oriented Wireless Networks and Communications. CrownCom 2008* (pp. 1-8). Singapore.

Clarke, N., & Furnell, S. (2007). Advanced user authentication for mobile devices. *Computers & Security, 26.*

Clarke, N., Furnell, S., Rodwell, P., & Reynolds, P. (2002a). Acceptance of Subscriber Authentication for Mobile Telephony Devices. *Computers & Security, 21*(3). doi:10.1016/S0167-4048(02)00304-8

Clarke, N., Furnell, S., Rodwell, P., & Reynolds, P. (2002b). *Biometric Authentication for Mobile Devices.* Paper present at 3rd Australian Information Warfare and Security Conference 2002.

Clemmer, L. (May 5, 2010). *The Top Five Firewall Security Tips.* In Bright Hub, retrieved from http://www.brighthub.com/computing/smb-security/articles/40618.aspx

Cocks, C. (2001). An Identity-Based Encryption Scheme Based on Quadratic Residues. In *Proceedings of IMA 2001: Vol. 2260. Lecture Notes in Computer Science* (pp. 360-363). Springer- Verlag.

Conrad, E. (2007). *Types of Cryptographic Attacks.* GIAC Research in the Common Body of Knowledge.

Convery, S. (2004). *Network Security Architectures.* Indianapolis, IN: Cisco Press.

Cooper, D., Santesson, S., Farrell, S., Boeyen, S., Housley, R., Polk, W. (2008). *Internet X.509 Public Key Infrastructure Certificate and Certificate Revocation List (CRL) Profile.* RFC 5280.

Coppersmith, D. (2010). Cryptography. *IBM Journal of Research and Development, 31*(2), 244–248. doi:10.1147/JRD.1987.5390134

Cross, M. (2008). *Scene of the Cybercrime* (2nd ed.). Burlington: Elsevier.

D., A. (2004). *The technology of video and audio streaming.* Oxford Focal Press 2nd ed.

Da Silva, E., Nogueira, M., dos Santos, A., & Albini, L. (2008). Identity-Based Key Management in Mobile Ad Hoc Networks. *IEEE Wireless Communications Magazine, Techniques and Applications, Special issue on ". Dependability Issues with Ubiquitous Wireless Access, 15*(5), 46–52.

Dagon, D., Qin, X., Gu, G., Lee, W., Grizzard, J., Levine, J., & Owen, H. (2004). *HoneyStat: Local Worm Detection Using Honeypots.* In Proceedings of the 7th International Symposium on Recent Advances in Intrusion Detection (RAID), Sophia Antipolis, France.

Dai-Yon, C., Hyun Jung, K., & Hyoung-Yong, L. (2007) *Analysis of Trust in Internet and Mobile Commerce Adoption, System Sciences, 2007.* HICSS 2007. 40th Annual Hawaii International Conference on Jan. 2007 Page(s):50 – 50.

Damle, P. (2002). *Social Engineering: A Tip of the Iceberg.* In ISACA Journal, No. 2. Retrieved February, 18, 2011, from www.isaca.org/Journal/Past-Issues/2002/Volume-2/Pages/Social-Engineering-A-Tip-of-the-Iceberg.aspx.

Damousis, I. G., Tzovaras, D., Bekiaris, E. (2008). *Unobtrusive Multimodal Biometric Authentication: The HUMABIO Project Concept*. EURASIP Journal on Advances in Signal Processing archive, 2008.

Dannecker, G. (1996). Neuer Entwicklungen im Bereich der Computerkriminalität. *Betriebsberater, 25*, 1285–1293.

D'Arcy, J., & Hovav, A. (2007). Deterring Internal Information Systems Misuse. *Communications of the ACM, 50*(10), 113–117. doi:10.1145/1290958.1290971

DataLossDB, Open Security Foundation. (2011). *Data Loss Statistics*. Retrieved February 10, 2011: http://datalossdb.org/statistics.

Datta, A., & Hauswirth, M. (2003). *Beyond "web of trust": Enabling P2P E-commerce*. Paper presented at IEEE International Conference on Electronic E-commerce (ICEC 2003).

Dean, D., & Sridharan, S. (2010, April). Dynamic visual features for audio visual speaker verification. *Computer Speech & Language, 24*(2), 136–149. doi:10.1016/j.csl.2009.03.007

Deng, H., Mukherjee, A., & Agrawal, D. P. (2004). Threshold and Identity-based Key Management and Authentication for Wireless Ad Hoc Networks. In *Proceedings of the international Conference on information Technology: Coding and Computing (Itcc'04): Vol. 2. ITCC. IEEE Computer Society*. Washington, DC.

Denning, P. J., & Denning, D. E. (2010). The Profession of IT - Discussing Cyber Attack. *Communications of the ACM, 53*(9), 29–31. doi:10.1145/1810891.1810904

Denning, D. E. (1987). An intrusion detection model. *IEEE Transactions on Software Engineering, 3*(2), 222–232. doi:10.1109/TSE.1987.232894

Dent, A. W. (2008). A survey of certificateless encryption schemes and security models. *International Journal of Information Security, 7*(5), 349–377. doi:10.1007/s10207-008-0055-0

Department of the Treasury, Federal Deposit Insurance Corporation, Federal Reserve System, Federal Trade Commission, National Credit Union Administration. (2007, November 9). *Identity Theft Red Flags and Address Discrepancies Under the Fair and accurate Credit Transactions Act of 2003; Final Rule*. Retrieved October 27, 2010, from http://ftc.gov/os/fedreg/2007/november/071109redflags.pdf

Deri, L. (2010). *The nTop Project Homepage*. Retrieved March 2011, http://www.ntop.org/

Deri, L., Carbone, R., & Suin, S. (2001). *Monitoring Networks Using Ntop*. In proceedings of 2001 IEEE/IFIP International Symposium on Integrated Network Management, Seattle, WA, USA, (pp. 199 – 212).

Dieckmann, U., Plankensteiner, P., & Wagner, T. (1997). SESAM: A biometric person identification system using sensor fusion. *Pattern Recognition Letters, 18*, 827–833. doi:10.1016/S0167-8655(97)00063-9

Dierks, T., & Rescorla, E. (2008). The Transport Layer Security (TLS) Protocol Version 1.2. *RFC, 5246*, 2008.

Directive 95/46/EC, 1995, *Directive 95/46/EC of the European Parliament and of the Council of 24 October 1995 on the protection of individuals with regard to the processing of personal data and on the free movement of such data*. Retrieved April 2, 2011, from http://eur-lex.europa.eu/LexUriServ/LexUriServ.do?uri=CELEX:31995L0046:en:

Directive, H. T. M. L. 2002/58/EC, (2002). *Protection of Privacy to Electronic Communications*. Retrieved November 20, 2010, from http://eur-lex.europa.eu/LexUriServ/LexUriServ.do?uri=CELEX:32002L0058:EN:HTML

Distefano, A., Gianluigi, M., & Francesco, P. (2010). Android ant-forensic through a local paradigm. *Digital Investigation, 7*, 2010. doi:10.1016/j.diin.2010.05.011

Disterer, G., Alles, A., & Hervatin, A. (2007). Denial-of-Service (DoS) Attacks: Prevention, Intrusion Detection, and Mitigation. In Janczewski, J. & Colarik, A. M. (Eds.), *Cyber Warfare and Cyber Terrorism*, 262-272. Hershey Idea Group.

Du, Y., Wang, W.-Q., & Pang, Y.-G. (2004). *An intrusion detection method using average hamming distance*. In Proceedings of the Third International Conference on Machine Learning and Cybernetics, Shanghai, (pp. 2914 – 2918).

Eckert, C. (2001). *IT-Sicherheit: Konzepte - Verfahren – Produkte*. München: Oldenbourg.

Edney, J., & Arbaugh, W. (2004). *Real 802.11 Security: Wi-Fi Protected Access and 802.11i*. Reading, MA: Addison-Wesley.

Educause, (2010). *Privacy Risks Assessment*. Retrieved October 6, 2010 from http://www.educause.edu/node/645/tid/30444?time=1281348515

EINSTEIN 2, (2009). *US-CERT*. Retrieved March 11, 2011 from http://en.wikipedia.org/wiki/Einstein_(US-CERT_program)

Emmanuel, S. (2010). P., (2010), Network forensic frameworks: survey and research challenges. *Digital Investigation*, 7.

Enqing, D., Guizhong, L., Yatong, Z., & Yu, C. (2002). *Voice Activity Detection Based on Short-time Energy and Noise Spectrum Adaptation. ICSP*. IEEE.

Eschweiler, J., & Psille, D. E. A. (2006). *Security@Work - Pragmatische Konzeption und Implementierung von IT-Sicherheit*. Berlin: Springer.

Estvez-Tapiador, J. M., Garcia-Teodoro, P., & Diaz-Verdejo, J. E. (2004). Anomaly detection methods in wired networks: A survey and taxonomy. *Computer Communications*, 27(16), 1569–1584. doi:10.1016/S0140-3664(04)00238-5

ETSI TS 133 234 (2010). Universal Mobile Telecommunications System (UMTS); LTE; 3G security; *Wireless Local Area Network (WLAN) interworking security, 9*.2.0, Release 9.

Expert: 'Flasher' technology digs deeper for digital evidence. (n.d.). Retrieved from http://www.physorg.com/news95611284.html

Extranet (November 21, 2008). In *How-to.gov*. Retrieved from http://www.usa.gov/webcontent/resources/glossary.shtml#E

Farm, S. (n.d.). In *Pennsylvania Office of Administration*. Retrieved from http://www.portal.state.pa.us/portal/server.pt/community/glossary/922.

Federal Trade Commission. (2002, May 23). *Standards for Safeguarding Customer Information; Final Rule*. Retrieved September 22, 2010, from http://www.ftc.gov/os/2002/05/67fr36585.pdf

Federal Trade Commission. (2003, June). *Security Check: Reducing Risks to Your Computer Systems*. Retrieved October 2, 2010, from http://business.ftc.gov/documents/bus58-security-check-reducing-risks-your-computer-systems

Federal Trade Commission. (2004, June). *Information Compromise and the Risk of Identity Theft: Guidance for Your Business*. Retrieved October 1, 2010, from http://business.ftc.gov/documents/bus59-information-compromise-and-risk-id-theft-guidance-your-business

Federal Trade Commission. (2005, June). *Disposing of Consumer Report Information? New Rule Tells How*. Retrieved September 23, 2010, from http://business.ftc.gov/documents/alt152-disposing-consumer-report-information-new-rule-tells-how

Federal Trade Commission. (2006, May). *Businesses Must Provide Victims and Law Enforcement with Transaction Records Relating to Identity Theft*. Retrieved September 29, 2010, from http://business.ftc.gov/documents/bus66-businesses-must-provide-victims-and-law-enforcement-transaction-records-relating-identity

Federal Trade Commission. (2006, April). *Financial Institutions and Customer Information: Complying with the Safeguards Rule*. Retrieved October 2, 2010, from http://business.ftc.gov/documents/bus54-financial-institutions-and-customer-information-complying-safeguards-rule

Federal Trade Commission. (n.d.). *Protecting Personal Information: A Guide for Business*. Retrieved September 29, 2010, from http://www.ftc.gov/bcp/edu/pubs/business/idtheft/bus69.pdf

Flaherty, D. H. (2000). Privacy impact assessments: an essential tool for data protection. *In 22nd annual meeting of privacy and data protection officials*.

Forouzan, B. (2007). *Data communications and Networking*. New York: McGraw-Hill.

Forouzan, B. A. (2010). *TCP/IP Protocol Suite* (4th ed.). New York, NY: McGraw-Hill.

Fox, N., & Reilly, R. (2003). *Audio visual Speaker Identification Based on Use of Dynamic Audio and Visual Features* (pp. 743–751). Springer-Verlag Berlin Heidelberg.

Fox, N. A., O'Mullane, B. A., & Reilly, R. B. (2005). Audio visual Speaker Identification via Adaptive Fusion Using Reliability Estimates of Both Modalities. In *Lecture notes in Computer Science Audio- and Video-Based Biometric Person Authentication* (pp. 787–796). Berlin, Heidelberg: Springer. doi:10.1007/11527923_82

Frahim, J., & Santos, O. (2010). *Cisco ASA: All-in-One Firewall, IPS, Anti-X, and VPN Adaptive Security Appliance* (2nd ed.). Indianapolis, IN: Cisco Press.

Francia, G. A., & Ciganek, A. (2010). Global Information Security Regulations, Case Studies and Cultural Issues. In M. E. Whitman & H. J. Mattord (Eds.), *Readings and Cases in the Management of Information Security, Volume II: Legal and Ethical Issues in Information Security Management*: Course Technology.

Frankel, S., Eydt, B., Owens, L., & Scarfone, K. (2007). *Establishing Wireless Robust Security Networks: A Guide to IEEE 802.11i.* NIST SP 800-97.

Frei, S., May, M., Fiedler, U., & Plattner, B. (2006). Large-scale vulnerability analysis. *LSAD '06: Proceedings of the 2006 SIGCOMM workshop on Large-scale attack defense* (pp. 131-138). New York, NY, USA: ACM Press.

FTS4BT: Bluetooth Protocol Analyzer and Packet Sniffer. (n.d.). Retrieved from http://www.fte.com

Funk, P., & Blake-Wilson, S. (2008). Extensible Authentication Protocol Tunneled Transport Layer Security Authenticated Protocol Version 0 (EAP-TTLSv0). *RFC, 5281*, 2008.

Furnell, S. M., Clarke, N., & Karatzouni, S. (2008). Beyond the PIN: Enhancing user authentication for mobile devices. *Computer Fraud & Security, 2008*(8). doi:10.1016/S1361-3723(08)70127-1

Furnell, S. M., Dowland, P. S., Illingworth, H. M., & Reynolds, P. L. (2000). Authentication and Supervision: A Survey of User Attitudes. *Computers & Security, 19*.

Fussell, L., & Field, S. (2005). The role of the risk management database in the risk management process. 364-369.

Gagné, M. (2003). Identity-Based Encryption: a Survey. [RSA Laboratories]. *CryptoBytes, 6*(1), 10–19.

Gales, M., & Young, S. (2008). *The Application of Hidden Markov Models in Speech Recognition*. Now Publishers Inc.

Galindo, D., Morillo, P., & Rafols, C. (2008). Improved certificate-based encryption in the standard model. *Journal of Systems and Software, 81*(7), 1218–1226. doi:10.1016/j.jss.2007.09.009

Ganchev, T., Fakotakis, N., & Kokkinakis, G. (2005). Comparative evaluation of various MFCC implementations on the speaker verification task. *Proc. of the SPECOM-2005, Vol. 1*, (pp. 191-194).

Gangishetti, R., Gorantla, M. C., Lal Das, M., & Saxena, A. (2007). Threshold key issuing in identity-based cryptosystems. *Computer Standards & Interfaces, 29*(2), 260–264. doi:10.1016/j.csi.2006.05.001

Garca-Teodoro, P., Daz-Verdejo, J., Maci-Fernandez, G., & Vazquez, E. (2009). Anomaly-based network intrusion detection: Techniques, systems and challenges. *Computers & Security, 28*(1), 18–28. doi:10.1016/j.cose.2008.08.003

Gassner, S. (2009). *Computerkriminalität bedroht den deutschen Mittelstand*. Retrieved February, 18, 2011, from www.silicon.de/sicherheit/management/0,39039020,39171050,00/computerkriminalitaet+bedroht+den+deutschen+mittelstand.htm.

Gaudin, S. (2003). *August was Worst Month Ever for Viruses, Worms*. Technet News.

Gehrmann, C., Persson, J., & Smeets, B. (2004). *Bluetooth Security*. Artech House.

General characteristics of the subscriber identity module file system. (n.d.). Retrieved from http://mobileforensics.files.wordpress.com/2007/02/sim-file-system.pdf

Gentry, C. (2003). Certificate-based encryption and the certificate-revocation problem. In *Proceedings of the 22nd international Conference on theory and Applications of Cryptographic Techniques EUROCRYPT 2003: Vol. 2656. Lecture Notes in Computer Science* (pp. 272-291). Springer-Verlag, Berlin, Heidelberg.

Gentry, C., & Silverberg, A. (2002). Hierarchical ID-Based Cryptography, In Y. Zheng (Ed.), *Proceedings of the 8th international Conference on the theory and Application of Cryptology and information Security: Advances in Cryptology, Asiacrypt '02: Vol. 2501. Lecture Notes In Computer Science* (pp.548-566). Springer-Verlag.

George, M. (2005). *Technical Challenges and Directions for Digital Forensics*. SADFE'05 Proceedings of the first international workshop on systematic approaches to digital; forensic engineering, 2005.

Geschonneck, A. (2004). *Computer-Forensik*. Heidelberg: DPunkt.

Gheorghe, G., Massacci, F., Neuhaus, S., & Pretschner, A. (2009). *GoCoMM: A governance and Compliance Maturity Model*. Conference on Computer and Communications Security (pp. 33-38). Chicago: ACM.

Gold, S. (2009). *First arrests in Heartland Payment Systems data breach*. Retrieved March, 19, 2009, from www.infosecurity-magazine.com/news /090216_HeartlandArrests.html.

Goodin, D. (2010). *PC consultant pleads not guilty to malware "sextortion" plot*. Retrieved February, 18, 2011, from www.theregister.co.uk/2010/07/21/mijangos_not_guilty_plea/.

Gorantla, M., Gangishetti, R., & Saxena, A. (2005). A Survey on ID-Based Cryptographic Primitives, *Cryptology ePrint Archive*, Report2005/094. Retrieved from http://eprint.iacr.org/2005/094.

Gorman, L. O. (2003). Comparing Passwords, Tokens, and Biometrics for User Authentication. Contributed paper. *Proceedings of the IEEE, 91*(12).

Gorman, S., & Perez, E. (2009). *Hackers indicated in Widespread ATM Heist*. Retrieved February, 20, 2011, from online.wsj.com/article/SB125786711092441245.html.

Gorman, S., Cole, A., & Dreazen, Y. (2009). *Computer Spies Breach Fighter-Jet Project*. Retrieved February, 20, 2011, from online.wsj.com/article/SB124027491029837401.html.

Goudelis, G., Tefas, A., & Pitas, I. (2005). *On Emerging Biometric Technologies*. Paper presented at 3rd COST 275 Workshop - Biometrics on the Internet.

GPP07 Specification of the Subscriber Identity Module - Mobile Equipment (SIM - ME) interface, 3rd Generation Partnership Project, TS 11.11 V8.14.0 (Release 1999). *Technical Specification,* June 2007.<URL: http://www.3gpp.org/ftp/Specs/archive/11_series/11.11/1111-8e0.zip>.

Grafinkel, S. L. (2010). Digital Forensic research: the next 10 years. *Digital Investigation, 7,* 2010.

Gramm-Leach-Bliley Act. (1999, November 12). Retrieved September 22, 2010, from http://www.ftc.gov/privacy/glbact/glbsub1.htm

Greene, S. S. (2006). *Security Policies and Procedures: Principles and Practices*. Upper Saddle River: Pearson Education, Inc.

Gruteser M. & Grunwald D. (2004). *A Methodological Assessment of Location Privacy Risks in Wireless Hotspot Networks in Security in Pervasive Computing*. Lecture Notes in Computer Science, 2004, Volume 2802/2004, 113-142, DOI: 10.1007/978-3-540-39881-3_5.

GSM-1. (2011). *Global GSM and 3GSM Mobile Connections*. GSM world. Retrieved from www.gsmworld.com (accessed March 11th, 2011).

GSM-11-11 (n.d.). *Digital cellular telecommunications system (Phase 2+); Specification of the Subscriber Identity Module - Mobile Equipment (SIM - ME) interface (GSM 11.11)*. ETSI, European Telecommunications Standards Institute, http://www.ttfn.net/techno/smartcards/gsm11-11.pdf

GSM-2. (n.d.). Retrieved from http://gsmworld.com/newsroom/press-releases/2070.htm#nav-6

Guo, G.-D., Zhang, H.-J., & Li, S. (2001). Pairwise face recognition. *Computer Vision, 2001. ICCV 2001. Proceedings. Eighth IEEE International Conference on, 2(7)* (pp. 282-287). IEEE.

Haataja, K., & Hypponen, K. (2008). Man-in-the-Middle Attacks on Bluetooth: A comprehensive Analysis, a Novel Attack, and Countermeasures. *Proc. 3rd Int'l Symposium, Communications, Control, and Signal Processing,* 1096-1102, IEEE Press. Hager, S., & Midkiff, C. (2203). Demonstrating Vulnerabilities in Bluetooth Security. *Proc. IEEE Global Telecommunication Conferecne,* (3), 1420-1424. Washington, D.C: IEEE Press.

Hachman, M. (2010). Gartner: Android, Symbian will win Mobile OS wars. Retrieved from http://www.pcmag.com/article2/0,2817,2368992,00.asp

Haimes, Y. Y. (2004). *Risk modeling, assessment, and management* (2nd edition ed.). New York: Wiley-Interscience.

Harrington, M. (2007). *Hex Dumping Primer Part 1*. Retrieved from.

Harris, R. (2006). Arriving at an anti-forensic consensus: Examining how to define and control the anti-forensic problem. *Digital Investigation, 3S,* 2006.

Harris, E. (2010). *The Next Step in the Spam Control War: Greylisting.* Retrieved March 2011, http://projects.puremagic.com/greylisting/

Haverinen, H., Ed., & J. Salowey, Ed.(2006). *Extensible Authentication Protocol Method for Global System for Mobile Communications (GSM) Subscriber Identity Modules (EAP-SIM).* RFC 4186, 2006.

Heckle, R. R., & Holden, S. H. (2006). *Analytical tools for privacy risks: Assessing efficacy on vote verification technologies.* In Symposium on usable privacy and security. (poster)

Herrmann, D. S. (2007). *Complete Guide to Security and Privacy Metrics: Measuring Regulatory Compliance, Operational Resilience, and ROI.* Auerbach Publications. doi:10.1201/9781420013283

Higginbotham, S. (2010). Ericsson CEO Predicts 50 Billion Internet Connected Devices by 2020. Retrieved from http://gigaom.com/2010/04/14/ericsson-sees-the-internet-of-things-by-2020

Hilley, S. (2007). Anti-forensics with a small army of exploits. *Digital Investigation,* 4.

HIPAA. (2006). *Saint Louis University Institutional Review Board HIPPA TIP Sheet,* 31st March 2006. Retrieved November 21, 2010 from www.slu.edu/Documents/provost/irb/hipaa_tip_sheet.doc

Hitachi, I. D. (2010). *Systems, Inc.* Password Management Best Practices.

HMG IA Standard No. 6 (2009). *Protecting Personal Data and Managing Information Risk.* Cabinet Office, CESG National Technical Authority for Information Assurance, Issue 1.2, March 2009.

Holden, G. (2003). *Guide to Network Defense and Countermeasures.* Boston, MA: Course Technology.

Hong, L., Jain, A., & Pankanti, S. (October 1999). Can Multibiometrics Improve Performance? *Proc. AutoID, Summit,,* (pp. 59–64). NJ.

Hoog, A., & Strzempka, K. (2010). *iPhone Forensics White Paper, Independent Research and Reviews of iPhone Forensic Tools.* Retrieved from http://www.viaforensics.com/education/white-papers/iphone-forensics.

Horwitz, J., & Lynn, B. (2002). Toward Hierarchical Identity-Based Encryption. In L. R. Knudsen (Ed.), In *Proceedings of the international Conference on the theory and Applications of Cryptographic Techniques: Advances in Cryptology, Eurocrypt '02: Vol. 2332. Lecture Notes In Computer Science* (pp. 466-481). Springer-Verlag.

How 802.11 Wireless Works. (2003). Retrieved from Microsoft Technet website http://technet.microsoft.com/en-us/library/cc757419(WS.10).asp

http://digitalforensicsmagazine.com/blogs/wp-content/uploads/2010/07/Cell-Phone-Evidence-Extraction-Process-Development-1.8.pdf

http://www.mobileforensicscentral.com/mfc/include/Hex_Primer_Pt_1.pdf

Hucaby, D. (2005). *Cisco ASA and PIX Firewall Handbook.* Indianapolis, IN: Cisco Press.

IEC/ISO. (2005). 27001:2005 - Information Security Management-Specification With Guidance for Use.

IHCFC Workshop - Guide to Forensic Computing Training Courses. (n.d.). http://www.ioce.org/core.php?ID=17

Ikehara, C. S., & Crosby, M. E. (2010). *Physiological Measures Used for Identification of Cognitive States and Continuous Authentication.* Paper presented at 28th ACM Conference on Human Factors in Computing Systems (CHI2010).

Ilgun, K., Kemmerer, R. A., & Porras, P. A. (1995). State transition analysis: A rule-based intrusion detection approach. *IEEE Transactions on Software Engineering,* 21(3), 181–199. doi:10.1109/32.372146

Information Commissioner's Office (ICO). (2009). *Privacy Impact Assessment Handbook Version 2.0. Appendix 1 – PIA Screening Process.* Retrieved October 29, 2010, from http://www.ico.gov.uk/upload/documents/pia_handbook_html_v2/html/3-app1.html

IOCE-1999. Retrieved from http://www.ioce.org/fileadmin/user_upload/1999/1999%20training%20workshop.doc

IOCE-2002. Retrieved from http://www.ioce.org/fileadmin/user_upload/2002/G8%20Proposed%20principles%20for%20forensic%20evidence.pdf

IPv4 Address Report. (n.d.). In *IPv4 Address Report*. Retrieved from http://www.potaroo.net/tools/ipv4/.

ISO/IEC. (2005). *Information technology — Security techniques — Code of practice for information security management*. ISO.

IT Governance Institute. (2007). *COBIT 4.1*. Retrieved September 20, 2010, from http://www.isaca.org/Knowledge-Center/cobit/Documents/CobiT_4.1.pdf

Jain, A. K., Ross, A., & Prabhakar, S. (2004). An Introduction to Biometric Recognition. *IEEE Transactions on Circuits and Systems for Video Technology, 14*(1). doi:10.1109/TCSVT.2003.818349

Jain, A. K., Ross, A., & Pankanti, S. (2006). Biometrics: A Tool of Information Security. *IEEE Transactions on Information Forensics and Security, 1*(2), 125–143. doi:10.1109/TIFS.2006.873653

Jao, D. (2008). *Public Key Cryptography. Contents 2007*. ON, Canada: University of Waterloo.

Jensen, F. V., & Nielsen, T. D. (2007). *Bayesian networks and decision graphics*. New York: Springer.

Josang, A., Ismail, R., Boyd, C. (2007). A survey of trust and reputation systems for online service provision. *Decision Support Systems, 43* (2). Elsevier Science Publishers B. V.

Jourlin, P., Luettin, J., Genoud, D., & Wassner, H. (1997). Integrating acoustic and labial information for speaker identification and verification. *Proc. 5th Eur. Conf. Speech Communication Technology*, (pp. 1603–1606). Rhodes, Greece.

Kar, B., Bhatia, S., & Dutta, P. (2007). Audio -Visual Biometric Based Speaker Identification. *Internation Conference on Computational Intelligence and Multimedia Applications, 4* (pp. 94-98). IEEE.

Karlsson, J. (1996). *Software requirements prioritizing*. In Proceedings of the international conference on requirements engineering (ICRE '96) (pp. 110--116).

Kempf, D. (2009). *ITK-Branche im Würgegriff der Hacker-Industrie?* Retrieved February, 20, 2011, from www.bitkom.org/files/documents/keynote_prof__kempf_industrialisierung_der_computerkriminalitaet.pdf

Keonwoo, K., Dowon, H., & Jea-Cheol, R. (2008). Forensic Data Acquisition from Cell Phones using JTAG Interface. *Security and Management, 2008*, 410–414.

Kessler, G. (2010). *Cell Phone Analysis: Technology, Tools, and Processes. Mobile Forensics World*. Chicago: Purdue University.

Kevin, J. (2010, May). The forensic use of mobile phones boxes. *Digital Investigation, 6*(3-4), 168–178. doi:10.1016/j.diin.2010.01.006

Klaver, C. (2010). Windows Mobile advanced forensics. *Investigation, 6*(1-2), 147–16.

Klosterman, A. J., & Ganger, G. R. (2000). *Secure Continuous Biometric-Enhanced Authentication*. CMU SCS Technical Report CMU-CS-00-134, 2000.

Koch, T., Ard, A., & Golub, K. (2004). *Log Analysis of User Behavior in the Renardus Web Service*. In Proceedings of the 2004 Joint ACM/IEEE Conference on Digital Libraries, Tuscon, AZ, USA, (pp. 378 – 382).

Koien, G. M., & Haslestad, T. (2003). Security Aspects of 3G-WLAN Interworking. *IEEE Communications Magazine, 41*(11). doi:10.1109/MCOM.2003.1244927

Krebs, B. (2009a). *Payment Processor Breach May Be Largest Ever*. Retrieved February, 20, 2011, from voices.washingtonpost.com/securityfix/2009/01/payment_processor_breach_may_b.html?hpid= topnews.

Krebs, B. (2009b). *Hackers Break Into Virginia Health Professions Database*. Retrieved February, 20, 2011, from voices.washingtonpost.com/securityfix/2009/05/hackers_break_into_virginia_he.html.

Kreibich, C., & Crowcroft, J. (2003). *Honeycomb: Creating Intrusion Detection Signatures Using Honeypots*. In Proceedings of the Second Workshop on Hot Topics in Networks (HotNetsII).

Kremp, M. (2009). *Last Browser Standing*. Retrieved from February, 20, 2011, from www.spiegel.de/netzwelt/tech/0,1518,614979,00.html.

Kumar, K. P., Shailaja, G., & Saxena, A. (2006). Secure and Efficient Threshold Key Issuing Protocol for ID-Based Cryptosystems. *Cryptology ePrint Archive*, Report 2006/245. Retrieved from http://eprint.iacr.org/2006/245.pdf.

Kumar, S., & Spafford, E. H. (1995). *A software architecture to support misuse intrusion detection.* In Proceedings of the 18th National Information Security Conference, Baltimore, USA, (pp. 194 – 204).

Kurose, J. F., & Ross, K. W. (2001). *Computer Networking, A Tpo-Down Approach Featuring the Internet.* Boston, MA: Addison Wesley Longman.

Kwon, S., & Lee, S. (2006). Identity-based key issuing without secure channel in a broad area. In *Proceedings of the 7th international conference on Information security applications: Part I: Vol. 4298. Lecture Notes In Computer Science* (pp. 30-44). Jeju Island, Korea, Springer-Verlag, Berlin, Heidelberg.

L.M.S.C of the IEEE Computer Society.(2007). *Wireless LAN Medium access control (MAC) and physical layer (PHY) specifications,* technical report, IEEE Standard 802.11, 2007 revision.

Lahti, C., & Lanza, R. P. S. (2005). *Sarbanes-Oxley IT Compliance Using COBIT and Open Source Tools.* Syngress. Alberts, C., & Dorofee, A. (2001). *An introduction to the octave method.* USA: Octave.

Landeskriminalamt Nordrhein-Westfalen, L. K. A. (Ed.). (2008). *Computerkriminalität - Lagebild 2008.* Düsseldorf: LKA.

Lathi, B. (2009). *Signal Processing and Linear Systems.* Oxford, UK: Oxford Univ Press.

Lauf, A. P., Peters, R. A., & Robinson, W. H. (2010). A distributed intrusion detection system for resource-constrained devices in ad-hoc networks. *Ad Hoc Networks, 8*(3), 253–266. doi:10.1016/j.adhoc.2009.08.002

Laurie, A., Holtmann, M., & Herfurt, M. (2004). Hacking Bluetooth enabled mobile phones and beyond - Full Disclosure. *21st Chaos Communication Congress,* Germany. *LeCroy—Protocol Solutions Group.* (n.d.). Retrieved from http://www.lecroy.com

Lee, B., Boyd, C., Dawson, E., Kim, K., Yang, J., & Yoo, S. (2004). Secure key issuing in ID-based cryptography. In *Proceedings of the Second Workshop on Australasian information security, Data Mining and Web intelligence, and Software internationalisation – Vol. 32* (pp. 69 -74). Dunedin, New Zealand, ACM International Conference Proceeding Series, vol. 54. Australian Computer Society, Darlinghurst, Australia.

Lee, H., Kim, D., Kim, S., & Oh, H. (2005). Identity-Based Key Agreement Protocols in a Multiple PKG Environment. In *Computational Science and its applications - ICCSA 2005: Vol. 3483. Lecture Notes in Computer Science* (pp. 877-886).

Lei, P., & Lynn, M. B. (2005). *Reproducibility of Digital Evidence in Forensic Investigations.* DFRWS, Digital Forensic research Workshop, 2005, New Orleans, LA, USA

Lessard J., & Kessler G.C. (2010), Android Forensics: Simplifying Cell Phone Examinations. Small Scale Digital Forensics Journal, 4(1), September 2010,

Li, H., Dai, Y., Tian, L., & Yang, H. (2009). Identity-Based Authentication for Cloud Computing. In M. G. Jaatun, G. Zhao, and C. Rong (Eds.), *Proceedings of the 1st international Conference on Cloud Computing: Vol. 5931. Lecture Notes in Computer Science* (pp. 157-166). Beijing, China, Springer-Verlag, Berlin, Heidelberg.

Li, W.-J., Hershkop, S., & Stolfo, S. J. (2004). *Email Archive Analysis Through Graphical Visualization.* In Proceedings of the 2004 ACM Workshop on Visualization and data Mining for Computer Security, Washington, USA, (pp. 4 – 9).

Lin, Yang-Dar, Hwang, Ren-Hung, & Baker, F. (2012). *Computer Networks: An Open Source Approach.* New York, NY: McGraw-Hill

Liu, H.-C., Su, C.-H., Chiang, Y.-H., & Hung, Y.-P. (2004). Personalized Face Verification System Using Owner-Specific Cluster-Dependent LDA-Subspace. *17th International Conference on Pattern Recognition (ICPR'04),* (pp. 344-347).

Loo, A. (2009). Security Threats of Smart Phones and Bluetooth. *Communications of the ACM, 52*(3), 150–152. doi:10.1145/1467247.1467282

Lu, J., & Plataniotis, K. N. (2002). Boosting face recognition on a large-scale database. *Proceedings of ICIP,* (pp. 109-112).

Lu, J., Yuan, X., & Yahagi, T. (2006). A method of face recognition based on fuzzy clustering and parallel neural networks. *Signal Processing, Volume 86, Issue 8, Special Section: Advances in Signal Processing-assisted Cross-layer Designs,* 2026-2039.

Lu, Y., Li, J., & Xiao, J. (2008). Generic Construction of Certificate-Based Encryption. In *Proceedings of 2008 The 9th International Conference for Young Computer Scientists* (pp. 1589-1594).

Lüttin, J. (1999). M2VTS Database. In *IDIAP-RR 99-02, IDIAP*. Speaker Verification Experiments on the X.

Lynn, B. (2002). Authenticated ID-based Encryption. *Cryptology ePrint Archive*, Report 2002/072. Retrieved from http://eprint.iacr.org/2002/072.

Madigan, E. M., Petrulich, C., & Motuk, K. (2004). The Cost of Non-Compliance: When Policies Fail. *User Services Conference* (pp. 47-51). Baltimore: ACM.

Maiwald, E. (2004). *Fundamentals of Network Security*. Burr Ridge, IL: McGraw-Hill Technology Education.

Marcus Rogers Anti-Forensics. (2005). *Lockheed martin*. Retrieved from www.cyberforensics.purdue.edu

Marcus, K. R. (2005). *Lockheed presentation, Anti-forensics*. Retrieved from www.cyberforensics.purdue.edu

Markert, B. K. (2002). *Comparison of three online privacy seal programs (Tech. Rep.)*. SANS Institute.

Massey, A. K., Otto, P. N., & Anton, A. I. (2009). *Prioritizing legal requirements*. In Second international workshop on requirements engineering and law (RELAW '09) (pp. 27--32).

Mead, N. R., Hough, E., & Stehney, T. (2005). *Security quality requirements engineering (SQUARE) methodology (CMU/SEI-2005-TR-009)*. Software Engineering Institute, Carnegie Mellon University.

Mell, P., Scarfone, K., & Romanosky, S. (2006). *Common vulnerability scoring system* (pp. 85–89). IEEE Security and Privacy.

Menezes, A., Van Oorschot, P., & Vanstone, S. (1996). *Handbook of Applied Cryptography*. United States, December 16, CRC Press.

Messaging Anti-Abuse Working Group MAAWG. (2008). *Email Metrics Program #9*. Retrieved February, 20, 2011, from http://www.maawg.org/about/MAAWG_2008-Q2_Metrics_Report9.pdf.

Messer, K., Matas, J., Kittler, J., Luettin, J., & Maitre, G. (1999). XM2VTSDB: The Extended M2VTS Database. *In Second International Conference on Audio and Video-based Biometric Person Authentication.*

Mika, S., Ratsch, G., Weston, J., Scholkopf, B., & Mullers, K. (1999). Fisher discriminant analysis with kernels. *Neural Networks for Signal Processing IX, 1999. Proceedings of the 1999 IEEE Signal Processing Society Worksho* (pp. 41-48). IEEE.

Mislan, R. (2010a). The growing need for on-scene triage of mobile devices. *Digital Investigation, 6*, 112–124. doi:10.1016/j.diin.2010.03.001

Mislan, R. (2010). *Creating laboratories for Undergraduate Courses in Mobile Forensics.*

Mitrano, T., Kirby, D. R., & Maltz, L. (2005). *What does privacy have to do with it?* Privacy risk assessment. In Security professionals conference. (presentation)

Miyazaki, S., Mead, N., & Zhan, J. (2008). Computer-aided privacy requirements elicitation technique. *Asia-Pacific Conference on Services Computing, 0*, 367-372.

Mohay, G., Anderson, A., Collie, B., Vel, O. d., & McKemmish, R. (2003). *Computer and Intrusion Forensics*. Norwood: Artech.

Moore, D., Paxson, V., Savage, S., Shannon, C., Staniford, S., & Weaver, N. (2003). *Inside the slammer worm* (pp. 33–39). IEEE Magazine of Security and Privacy.

Morrow, R. (2002). *Bluetooth Implementation and Use*. New York: McGraw-Hill Professional.

Mullins, K. J. (2007). The Mobilr Phone Network (GSM) Turns Twenty. Digital Journal, Retrieved March 11, 2001, http://www.digitaljournal.com/article/225547

Murphy, C. (2010). *Celullar Phone Evidence Data Extraction and Documentation*. Digital Forensics Magazine, 2010.

Murphy, C. (2010). The fraternal clone method for CDMA cell phones. *Small Scale Digital Forensics Journal, 3*(1), June 2009.

Nance, K., & Armstrong, H. (2010). *Digital Forensics: Defining an Education Agenda*. Proceedings of the 43rd Hawaii International Conference on System Sciences – 2010.

Narayanan, V., & Dondeti, L. (2008). EAP Extensions for EAP Re-authentication Protocol (ERP). *RFC, 5296*, 2008.

Natan, R. B. (2005). *Implementing Database Security and Auditing*. Elsevier, Inc.

National Institute of Standards and Technology. (2002). *Risk management guide for information technology systems*. (http://csrc.nist.gov/publications/nistpubs/800-30/sp800-30.pdf)

Nefian, A., & Hayes, M. I. (1999). *An embedded HMM-based approach for face detection and recognition*. ICASSP '99. Proceedings (pp. 3553–3556). IEEE.

Nefian, A. V., Liang, L. H., Fu, T., & Liu, X. X. (2003). A Bayesian Approach to Audio visual Speaker Identification. In *Audio- and Video-Based Biometric Person Authentication Lecture Notes in Computer Science* (p. 1056). Berlin, Heidelberg: Springer. doi:10.1007/3-540-44887-X_88

Nitschmann, J., & Leyendecker, H. (2008). *Steuerskandal*. Retrieved February, 20, 2011, from www.sueddeutsche.de/finanzen/287/301284/text.

NN. (1983). *Anschlag auf südhessisches Rechenzentrum zeigt Schwächen bei der Security-Planung auf*. Retrieved February, 20, 2011, from www.computerwoche.de/1180467.

NN. (2007). *Chinesische Trojaner auf PCs im Kanzleramt*. Retrieved February, 20, 2011, from www.spiegel.de/netzwelt/tech/0,1518,501954,00.html.

NN. (2008). *Spionage-Angriffe auf belgische Computer*. Retrieved from February, 20, 2011, from www.heise.de/newsticker/Spionage-Angriffe-auf-belgische-Computer--/meldung/107340.

NN. (2009). *Chinesen verstärken Cyber-Attacken auf deutsche Regierung*. Retrieved February, 20, 2011, from www.spiegel.de/netzwelt/web/0,1518,617374,00.html.

Northcutt, S., Zeltser, L., Winters, S., Kent, K., & Ritchey, R. W. (2005). *Inside Network Perimeter Security* (2nd ed.). Indianapolis, IN: Sams Publishing.

O'Connor, T. P., (2009). Provider Side Cell Phone Forensics. *Small Scale Digital Device Forensics Journal, 3*(1), June 2009.

OECD, & Microsoft Corp. (2000). *OECD privacy statement generator*. Retrieved 25 April 2009, from http://www2.oecd.org/pwv3/

Oh, J., Lee, K., & Moon, S. (2005). Lecture Notes. In *Computer Science* (*Vol. 3803*, pp. 290–303). How to Solve Key Escrow and Identity Revocation in Identity-Based Encryption Schemes, In *Information Systems Security-* Berlin, Heidelberg: Springer-Verlag.

OnGuard Online. (n.d.). *7 Practices for Computer Security*. Retrieved September 25, 2010, from http://www.onguardonline.gov/topics/computer-security.aspx

Oppenheimer, P. (2010). *Developing Network Security Strategies*. Indianapolis, IN: Cisco Press.

Owen, P., Thomas, P., et al. (2010). *An Analysis of the Digital Forensic Examination of Mobile Phones*. 2010 fourth International conference on Next Generation mobile applications, services, and technologies.

Owens, W. A., Dam, K. W., & Lin, H. S. (2009). *Technology, Policy, Law, and Ethics Regarding U.S. Acquisition and Use of Cyberattack Capabilities*. National Research Council. Washington: National Academic Press.

Panko, R. R. (2004). *Corporate Computer and Network Security*. Upper Saddle River, NJ: Prentice Hall.

Paterson, K. G., & Price, G. (2003, July 9). A comparison between traditional public key infrastructures and identity-based cryptography [Elsevier.]. *Information Security Technical Report, 8*(3), 57–72. doi:10.1016/S1363-4127(03)00308-X

Patterson, E. K., Gurbuz, S., Tufekci, Z., & Gowdy, J. N. (2002). CUAVE: A new audio visual database for multimodal human-computer interface research. *In Proc. ICASSP*, (pp. 2017-2020).

Peeger, S. L., & Peeger, C. P. (2009). Harmonizing privacy with security principles and practices. *IBM Journal of Research and Development, 53*(2).

Peirce, T. (2009). *RFID Privacy & Security*. IEEE International Conference on Communications, ICC 2009, Dresden, Germany, June 2009 Abu-Nimeh S., & Mead N. R., (2009). *Privacy Risk Assessment in Privacy Requirements Engineering*. 2nd International Workshop on Requirements Engineering and Law, Georgia, USA, 2009

Penev, T. (2005). *Identity Based Public Key Infrastructures, Darmstadt University of Technology*, Department of Informatics, Bachelor Thesis.

Perera, J., & Holsomback, J. (2005). An integrated risk management tool and process. *Aerospace 2005.* Big Sky, MT: IEEE Conference.

Perry, M., O'hara, K., Sellen, A., Brown, B., & Harper, R. (2001). Dealing with Mobility: Understanding Access Anytime, Anywhere. *ACM Transactions on Computer-Human Interaction, 8*(4), 323–347. doi:10.1145/504704.504707

Personuvernd (2008). *The Data Protection Act. Iceland.* Retrieved February 21, 2011 from http://www.personuvernd.is/information-in-english/greinar//nr/438

Pfleeger, C. P., & Pfleeger, S. L. (2003). *Security in Computing* (3rd ed.). Upper Saddle River, NJ: Prentice Hall.

Pigeon, S., & Vandendorpe, L. (1997). The M2VTS multimodal face database (release 1.00). In *Audio- and Video-based Biometric Person Authentication* (pp. 403–409). Springer. doi:10.1007/BFb0016021

Pooters, I. (2010). Full user data acquisition from Symbian smart phones. *Digital Investigation 6*(3-4), 125-135 (2010). Proceeding SIGITE'10, ACM Conference on Information Technology Education.

Porter, A., Votta, L., & Basili, V. (1995). Comparing detection methods for software requirements inspections: A replicated experiment. *IEEE Transactions on Software Engineering, 21*(6), 563–575. doi:10.1109/32.391380

Potamianos, G., Verma, A., Neti, C., Iyengar, G., & Basu, S. (2000). A cascade image transform for speaker independent automatic speechreading. *IEEE International Conference on Multimedia and Expo, vol.2* (pp. 1097-1100). IEEE.

Potter, B. (2003). Wireless Security Future. *IEEE Security and Privacy, 1*(4), 68–72. doi:10.1109/MSECP.2003.1219074

Potter, B., & Fleck, B. (2003). *802.11 Securit.* O'Reilly.

Princeton University. (2010, September 20). *WordNet.* Retrieved September 23, 2010, from http://wordnetweb.princeton.edu/perl/webwn

Punja, S., & Mislan, R. (2008). Mobile device analysis. *Small Scale Digital Device Forensics Journal, 2*(1), 2008.

Pusara, M., & Brodley, C. E. (2004). *User ReAuthentication via Mouse Movements.* Paper present at 2004 ACM workshop on Visualization and data mining for computer security.

PWC. (2007). *Wirtschaftskriminalität 2007 - Sicherheitslage der deutschen Wirtschaft.* Retrieved February, 20, 2011, from www.eulerhermes.de/de/dokumente/veruntreuung-wirtschaftskriminalitaet-2007.pdf/veruntreuung-wirtschaftskriminalitaet-2007.pdf.

Qualcomm CDMA technologies. (n.d.). R-UIM: QUALCOMM'S System Solutions to Support Removable User Identity Module Smart Cards. Retrieved from www.laneros.com/attachment.php?attachmentid=17476&d=1117732896

Radack, S. (2010). *Guide To Protecting Personally Identifiable Information (PII).* NIST ITL Security Bulletin for April 2010. Retrieved November 6, 2010 from http://csrc.nist.gov/publications/nistbul/april-2010_guide-protecting-pii.pdf

Rahal, S. M., Aboalsamah, H. A., & Muteb, K. N. (2006). Multimodal Biometric Authentication System – MBAS. Paper presented at 2nd Information and Communication Technologies (ICTTA '06).

Ramelsberger, A. (2008). *Steueraffäre.* Retrieved February, 20, 2011, from www.sueddeutsche.de/politik/416/434164/text.

Reith, M., C. Carr & G. Gunsch. (2002). An examination of Digital Forensics Models. *International Journal of Digital Evidence, 1*(3), Fall 2002.

Rekhis, S., & Boudriga, N. (2010). *Formal Investigation of Anti-forensic Attacks.* 2010 International Workshop on Systematic Approaches to Digital Forensic Engineering.

Rescorla, E. (2000). HTTP Over TLS. *RFC, 2818*, 2000.

Reynolds, D. (1995). Large population speaker identification using clean and telephone speech. *Signal Processing Letters, IEEE, 2*(3), 46–48. doi:10.1109/97.372913

Reynolds, D. A. (1994). Experimental evaluation of features for robust speaker identification. *IEEE Transactions on Speech and Audio Processing,* 639–643. doi:10.1109/89.326623

Richter, N. (2008). *Geschäfte in der Telefonzelle*. Retrieved February, 16, 2009, from www.sueddeutsche.de/finanzen/266/448759/text.

Riera, A., Soriafrisch, A., Caparrini, M., Cester, I., & Ruffini, G. (2009). Multimodal Physiological Biometrics Authentication. In *Biometrics. Theory, Methods, and Applications*. IEEE. doi:10.1002/9780470522356.ch18

Ritzer, U. (2008a). *Steuersünder wollen Bank verklagen*. Retrieved February, 20, 2011, from www.sueddeutsche.de/finanzen/908/302904/text.

Ritzer, U. (2008b). *Tippgeber in Todesangst*. Retrieved February, 20, 2011, from www.sueddeutsche.de/finanzen/288/301285/text.

Roberts, P. (2004). *Mydoom Sets Speed Records*. IDG News, January 2004, Retrieved March 2011, http://www.pcworld.com/article/id,114461-page,1/article.html

Ross, A., & Jain, A. (2003, September). Information fusion in biometrics. *Pattern Recognition Letters*, *24*(Issue 13), 2115–2125. doi:10.1016/S0167-8655(03)00079-5

Ross, A., & Poh, N. (2009). Multibiometric Systems: Overview, Case Studies and Open Issues. In *Handbook of Remote Biometrics Advances in Pattern Recognition* (pp. 273–292). London: Springer. doi:10.1007/978-1-84882-385-3_11

Sahai, A., & Waters, B. (2005). Fuzzy Identity-Based Encryption. In *Advances in Cryptology, Eurocrypt'05: Vol. 3494. Lecture Notes In Computer Science* (pp. 457-473), Springer-Verlag.

Saidenberg, M., & Schuermann, T. (2003). *The new basel capital accord and Questions for research*. Report.

Salomon, K. D., Cassat, P. C., & Thibeau, B. E. (2003, March 20). *IT Security for Higher Education: A Legal Perspective*. Retrieved September 22, 2010, from http://net.educause.edu/ir/library/pdf/CSD2746.pdf

Santos, O. (2007). *End-to-End Network Security: Defense-in-Depth*. Indianapolis, IN: Cisco Press.

Sauver, J. S. (2009). *Passwords*. Paper presented at Northwest Academic Computing Consortium (NWACC) Security Meeting.

Savold, i A. & Gubian, P., (2008). *Symbian Forensics: an overview*. International Conference on Intelligent Information Hiding and Multimedia Signal Processing., 2008.

Savoldi, A., & Gubian, P. (2007). *SIM and USIM File system: a forensic perspective*. ACM Symposium on applied Computing 07.

Savoldi, A., & Gubian, P. (2007a). *Data Hiding in SIM/USIM Cards: A Steganographic Approach*. Second International Workshop on Systematic Approaches to Digital Forensic Engineering (SADFE'07).

Savoldi, A., & Gubian, P. (2009). *A comparison between windows mobile and symbian s60 embedded forensics*. Fifth International Conference on International Conference on Intelligent Information Hiding and Multimedia Signal Processing., 2009

Scarfone, K., Mell, P., & Romanosky, S. (2007). *A complete guide to the common vulnerability scoring system version 2.0*. USA: NIST.

Scarfone, K., & Padgette, J. (2008). *Guide to Bluetooth Security*. NIST SP 800-121.

Scarfone, K., Dicoi, D., Sexton, M., & Tibbs, C. (2008). *Guide to Securing Legacy IEEE 802.11 Wireless Networks* (revision 1). NIST SP 800-48.

Scheiner, B. (2003). *Practical Cryptography*. New York: John Wiley.

Schiffman, M. (2005). *A complete guide to the common vulnerability scoring system (cvss)*. USA: FIRST.

Schneier, B. (1996). *Applied Cryptography: Protocols, Algorithms, and Source Code in C* (2nd ed.). John Wiley & Sons.

Schridde, C., Smith, M., & Freisleben, B. (2008). An Identity-Based Key Agreement Protocol for the Network Layer. In *Proceedings of the 6th international conference on Security and Cryptography for Networks, Amalfi, Italy. Lecture Notes in Computer Science*. (pp. 409–422) Springer, Heidelberg.

Scudere, L. (2006). *Risco Digital*. Rio de Janeiro, Brazil: Elsivier.

SevDev Group. (2009). *Information Warfare Monitor*. Retrieved March, 31, 2009, from www.infowar-monitor.net/ghostnet.

Shaked, Y., & Wool, A. (2005). Cracking the Bluetooth Pin. *Proc. 3ʳᵈ Int'l Conf. Mobile Systems, Applications, and Services*, 39-50. New York: ACM Press.

Shamir, A. (1985). Identity-based cryptosystems and signature schemes. In G. R. Blakley and D. Chaum (Eds.), *Proceedings of CRYPTO 84 on Advances in Cryptology, Santa Barbara, California, United States* (pp. 47-53). Springer-Verlag New York, New York.

Shane, D. (2010). *Zurich Insurance hit with Record Data Loss Fine*. August 2010. Retrieved October 22, 2010 from http://www.information-age.com/channels/security-and-continuity/news/1277718/zurich-insurance-hit-with-record-data-loss-fine.tthml

Shaoyen, C. (2009). *Research on mobile forensic software system based on windows mobile*. 2009 international conference on wireless networks and information systems.

Sharma, L. K., et al. (2010). Taxonomy of cell planning. *International Journal of Reviews in Computing, 3*, June 2010, http://www.ijric.org/volumes/Vol3/9Vol3.pdf

Shivankar, R., & Ashish, K. S. (2009), *Mobile Forensics: guidelines and challenges in data preservation and acquisition, 2009*. IEEE Student Conference on Research and Development, SCOReD 2009.

Shoniregun, C. A., Tindale, I., Logvynovskiy, A., & Fanning, T. (2005). Securing mobile product ecology for mobile commerce (mC). *Services Computing, 2005 IEEE International Conference on, 2*, 11-15 July 2005, 211 – 216.

Sigurdsson, S., Petersen, K. B., & Lehn-Schiøler, T. (2006). Mel Frequency Cepstral Coefficients: An Evaluation of Robustness of MP3. *Proceedings of the International Symposium on Music Information Retrieval.*

Simon, D., Aboba, B., & Hurst, R. (2008). The EAP-TLS Authentication Protocol. *RFC, 5216*, 2008.

Singh, R. (1998). *International standard ISO/IEC 12207 software life cycle processes. (Tech. Rep.)*. Federal Aviation Administration.

Siponen, M., Mahmood, M. A., & Pahnila, S. (2009, December). Technical Opinion: Are Employees Putting Your Company at Risk by Not Following Information Security Policies? *Communications of the ACM*, 145–147. doi:10.1145/1610252.1610289

Slaney, M. (1998). *Auditory Toolbox. Version 2.* Interval Research Corportaion #1998-010.

Smartphones Based on Invariants, Fifth International Workshop on Systematic Approaches to Digital Forensic Engineering.

Sobieraj, S., & Mislan, R. (2007). *Mobile phones: Digital photo metadata*. Retrieved from http://www.cerias.purdue.edu/symposium/2007/materials/pdfs/E26-CF9.pdf

Sood, A. K., & Enbody, R. (2011). Chain Exploitation - Social Networks Malware. *ISACA Journal, 1*, 31–36.

Stallings, W. (2003). *Cryptography and Network Security – Principles and Practices* (3rd ed.). Upper Saddle River, NJ: Prentice Hall.

Statistics Canada. (2008). *Privacy impact assessment.* (http://www.statcan.gc.ca/about-apercu/pia-efrvp/gloss-eng.htm)

Stearley, J. (2004). *Towards Informatics Analysis of Syslogs*. In Proceedings of the 2004 IEEE International Conference on Cluster Computing, San Diego, USA, (pp 309 – 318).

Stillich, S. (2004). *Der Wurm von der Wümme*. Retrieved March, 27, March, 2009, from www.stern.de/computer-technik/internet/:Sasser-Programmierer-Der-Wurm-W%FCmme/25454.html?id=525454&eid=501069&pr=1.

Stoneburner, G., Goguen, A., & Feringa, A. (2002). *Risk management guide for information technology systems - recommendations of the national institute of standards and technology*. USA: NIST.

Suzanne, C. (2010). Smart phone growth explodes, dumb phones not so much. http://technolog.msnbc.msn.com/_news/2011/02/07/6005519-smart-phone-growth-explodes-dumb-phones-not-so-much

Takada, T., & Koide, H. (2002). *Tudumi: Information Visualization System for Monitoring and Auditing Computer logs*. In Proceedings of the Sixth International Conference on Information Visualization, London, UK, (pp. 570–576).

Tett, M. (June 29, 2009). *The best firewall is….* In ZDNET, retrieved from http://www.zdnet.com.au/the-best-firewall-is-339296782.htm?omnRef=http%3A%2F%2Fwww.all-internet-security.com%2Ftop_10_firewall_software.html

Tews, E., & Beck, M. (2009). Practical attacks against WEP and WPA. *Proceedings of the Second ACM Conference on Wireless Network Security*, 79-86.

Tews, E., Weinmann, R., & Pyshkin, A. (2007). Breaking 104 bit wep in less than 60 seconds. *WISA*, (4867) 188-202. New York: Springer.

The Bluetooth Special Interest Group (SIG). Retrieved from http://www.bluetooth.org

The trifinite group (2007). Retrieved from http://www.trifinite.org.

The Wi-Fi Alliance. (n.d.). Retrieved from http://www.wi-fi.org.

Thompson, M. R., Olson, D., Cowles, R., Mullen, S., & Helm, M. (2002). *CA-based Trust Model for Grid Authentication and Identity Delegation*. Memo published by Grid Certificate Policy WG. Retrived July 17, 2010, from http://www.gridcp.es.net/Documents/GGF6/TrustModel-final.pdf.

Tongshen, H., Qingzhang, X. C., & Kezhen, Y. (2004). *Design and Implementation of Firewall-log-based Online Attack Detection System*. In Proceedings of the 3rd International Conference on Information Security, Shanghai, China, (pp. 146 – 149).

Tse, S.-H., & Lam, K.-M. (2008). *Efficient face recognition with a large database* (pp. 944–949). ICARCV.

Turk, M., & Pentland, A. (1991). Eigenfaces for recognition. *Journal of Cognitive Neuroscience*, *3*(1), 71–86. doi:10.1162/jocn.1991.3.1.71

U.S. Senate Bill S.3987. (2010). *An Act to Amend the Fair Credit Reporting Act With Respect to the Applicability of Identity Theft Guidelines to Creditors*. Retrieved February 7, 2011 from http://www.gpo.gov/fdsys/pkg/BILLS-111s3987enr/pdf/BILLS-111s3987enr.pdf.

Underwood, S. (2010). Visions of the future. *Communications of the ACM*, *53*(7), 25–25. doi:10.1145/1785414.1785426

United States Computer Emergency Readiness Team. (2008). *Privacy impact assessment for EIN-STEIN 2 (Tech. Rep.)*. Department of Homeland Security.

US Department of Justice. (2003). *Local FBI Employee Indicted for Public Corruption*. Retrieved February, 20, 2011, from www.usdoj.gov/criminal/cybercrime/fudgeIndict.htm.

US Department of Justice. (2005). *New York Teen Pleads Guilty*. Retrieved February, 20, 2011, from www.usdoj.gov/criminal/cybercrime/grecoPlea.htm.

US Department of Justice. (2006a). *Michigan Man Gets 30 Months for Conspiracy to Order Destructive Computer Attacks*. Retrieved February, 20, 2011, from www.usdoj.gov/criminal/cybercrime/araboSent.htm.

US Department of Justice. (2006b). *Former technology manager sentenced to a year in prison for computer hacking offense*. Retrieved February, 20, 2011, from www.usdoj.gov/criminal/cybercrime/sheaSent.htm.

US Department of Justice. (2007a). *Hackers from India Indicted for Online Brokerage Intrusion Scheme*. Retrieved February, 20, 2011, from www.usdoj.gov/criminal/cybercrime/marimuthuIndict.htm.

US Department of Justice. (2007b). *Former computer contractor pleads guilty to hacking Daimler Chrysler*. Retrieved February, 20, 2011, from www.usdoj.gov/criminal/cybercrime/johnsPlea.pdf.

US Department of Justice. (2008a). *San Jose Woman charged with fraud*. Retrieved February, 20, 2011, from www.usdoj.gov/criminal/cybercrime/leotiotaIndict.pdf.

US Department of Justice. (2008b). *Former assistant bank branch manager pleads guilty*. Retrieved February, 20, 2011, from www.usdoj.gov/criminal/cybercrime/covelliPlea.pdf.

US-CERT. (2008). *Privacy Impact Assessment EINSTEIN Program*. Department of Homeland Security, National Cyber Security Division, United States, May 19, 2008. Retrieved October 8, 2010 from http://www.dhs.gov/xlibrary/assets/privacy/privacy_pia_einstein2.pdf

Vacca, J. (2006). *Guide to Wireless Network Security* (1st ed.). New York: Springer.

Van Tilborg, H. C. A. (1999). *Fundamentals of Cryptology: A Professional Reference and Interactive Tutorial* (1st ed.). Norwell, MA, USA: Kluwer Academic Publishers.

Véras, A. L. M., & Ruggiero, W. V. (2005). *Autenticação Contínua de Usuários em Aplicações Seguras na Web.* Paper present at V Brazilian Symposium on Information and Computer Systems Security.

Verwoerd, T., & Hunt, R. (2002). Intrusion detection techniques and approaches. *Computer Communications, 25*(15), 1356–1365. doi:10.1016/S0140-3664(02)00037-3

Wang, C., & Liu, J. (2008). A Practical Key Issuing Scheme in Identity-Based Cryptosystem. In *Proceedings of the 2008 ISECS International Colloquium on Computing, Communication, Control, and Management - Volume 01* (pp. 454-457). CCCM. IEEE Computer Society, Washington, DC.

Wang, Y., & Abdel-Wahab, H. (2006). *A Multilayer Approach of Anomaly Detection for Email Systems.* In Proceedings of the 11th IEEE Symposium on Computers and Communications (ISCC2006), Cagliari, Italy, (pp 48-53).

Wang, Y., & Vassileva, J. (2007). *A Review on Trust and Reputation for Web Service Selection.* Paper presented at 27th International Conference on Distributed Computing Systems Workshops (ICDCSW'07).

Watkinson, J. (1999). *MPEG-2.* Focal Press.

Waxer, C. (April 12, 2007). *The Top 5 Internal Security Threats.* In ITSECURITY. Retrieved from http://www.itsecurity.com/features/the-top-5-internal-security-threats-041207/.

Wayne, J. & Aurelian, D. (2009). *Mobile Forensic Reference Materials.* A methodology and reification, NIST IR-7617, National Institute of standards.

Wayne, J. & Aurelian, D. (2010). *Guide to Simfill use and development.* NIST IR-7658, National Institute of standards.

Wayne, J. & Ayers, R. (2006). *Guidelines on Cell Phone forensics: Recommendations of the National Institute of Standards and Technology.* Draft, Special publication 800-101.

Wayne, J. & Ayers, R. (2006), *Guidelines on PDA forensics.* NIST Special publication 800-72.

Wayne, J., & Aurelian, D. (2008). *Overcoming Impediments to Cell Phone Forensics.* HICSS '08 Proceedings of the Proceedings of the 41st Annual Hawaii.

Wayne, J., & Scarfone, K. (2008). *Guidelines on cell phones and PDA security.* NIST Special Publication 800-124

Welch, D., & Lathrop, S. (2003). Wireless Security Threat Taxonomy. *Proceedings of the 2003 IEEE workshop on information assurance,* 76-83.

Wes, S. (2008). *Video over IP: IPTV, Internet video, H.264, P2P, web TV, and streaming: a complete guide to understanding the technology.* Burlington, Massachusetts: Elsevier 2nd ed.

Whitman, M. E., & Mattord, H. J. (2003). *Principles of Information Security.* Boston, MA: Course Technology.

Whitman, M. E., & Mattord, H. J. (2004). *Management of Information Security.* Boston, MA: Course Technology. *Further Readings Ciampa, M. (2009). Security+ Guide to Network Security Fundamentals* (3rd ed.). Boston, MA: Course Technology.

Whitman, M. E., Mattord, H. J., Austin, R., & Holden, G. (2008). *Guide to Firewalls and Network Security.* Boston, MA: Course Technology.

William, S. (2002). *Wireless communications and networking.* New York: Prentice hall.

Wong, Y. W., Ch'ng, S. I., Seng, K. P., Ang, L.-M., Chin, S. W., Chew, W. J., et al. (2010). The Audio visual UNMC-VIER Database. *Proceedings of the International Conference on Embedded Systems and Intelligent Technology (ICESIT2010).*

WPA-PSK Rainbow tables. (n.d.). Retrieved from http://www.renderlab.net/projects/WPA-tables/.

Wright, D. A., Romanosky, S., Schiman, M., & Eschelbeck, G. (2004). *CVSS: A common vulnerability scoring system.* USA: National Infrastructure Advisory Council (NIAC).

Wu, D., Hou, Y., Zhu, W., Zhang, Y.-Q., & Peha, J. (2001). Streaming video over the internet: Approaches and directions. *IEEE Transactions on Circuits and Systems for Video Technology, Mar 2001, Volume: 11,* 282-300.

Yinghua, G., & Slay, J. (2010). *A function oriented methodology to validate and verify forensic copy function of digital forensic tools.* 2010 International conference on availability, reliability and security.

Zareen, A. (2010). *Mobile phone forensics: Challenges, analysis, and tool classifications.* Fifth International workshop on systematic approaches to digital forensic engineering, SADFE '10.

Zave, P. (1997). Classification of research efforts in requirements engineering. *ACM Computing Surveys, 29*(4), 315–321. doi:10.1145/267580.267581

Zhang, X., & Li, C. (2009). The security in cognitive radio networks: a survey. In *Proceedings of the 2009 international Conference on Wireless Communications and Mobile Computing: Connecting the World Wirelessly* (pp. 309-313). IWCMC '09. ACM, New York, NY.

Zhihong, L., & Minxia, L. (2008). Research on Influencing Factors of Consumer Initial Trust Based on Mobile Commerce. *Electronic Commerce and Security, 2008 International Symposium on,* 3-5 Aug. 2008 pp. 263–267.

Zhou, Z., Chindaro, S., & Deravi, F. (2009). *A Classification Framework for Large-Scale Face Recognition Systems* (pp. 337–346). Advances in Biometrics.

Zou, C. C., Gao, L., Gong, W., & Towsley, D. (2003). *Monitoring and Early Warning for Internet Worms.* In Proceedings of the 10th ACM Symposium on Computer and Communication Security, Washington DC, USA, (pp. 39 – 58).

About the Contributors

Te-Shun Chou received his Bachelor degree in Electronics Engineering from Feng Chia University, Taiwan, R.O.C. in 1989, and the Master's degree and Doctoral degree both in Electrical Engineering from Florida International University, Miami, Florida in 1992 and 2007, respectively. In 2008, he joined East Carolina University, Greenville, North Carolina, where he is currently an Assistant Professor with the Department of Technology Systems. His research interests include soft computing, wireless sensor network, and network security, especially intrusion detection and incident response.

* * *

Saeed Abu-Nimeh is a senior researcher at Damballa Inc. His research areas include web security, phishing and spam detection, and machine learning. He received his MS and PhD in computer science from Southern Methodist University.

Maurizio Aiello graduated in Physics at the University of Genoa in 1994. He started working as a Unix sysadmin and network manager both for academic institutions and enterprises. He is responsible for the network infrastructure of National Research Council (CNR), Liguria Region. He is responsible for the research commitment "Network Security", and is involved in different Scientific Councils. Consultant designated by CNR for themes related to National Security inside governative Institutions. He teaches at the university of Genoa and he is involved in a start-up enterprise (Cleis Security). His main research interest are in protocol characterization, modeling and intrusion detection by anomaly detection.

Silas Leite Albuquerque is Bachelor in Military Sciences at Military Academy of Agulhas Negras (AMAN - 1992), Computer Engineer at Military Engineering Institute (IME - 1998), Master of Science in Computer Science at University of Brasilia (UnB - 2003) and PhD student in Electrical Engineering also at University of Brasilia, where he is working with subjects like security aspects of heterogeneous networks interconnection and continuous authentication. He is currently member of Digital TV Laboratory at UnB and professor at Institute of Higher Education of Brasilia (IESB). He has experience in Engineering and Computer Science, with emphasis on Information Security and Software Engineering, mainly focusing issues relating to development of information security systems, combat simulation, psychometrics and psychological evaluation.

Li-Minn Ang completed his Bachelor of Engineering and PhD at Edith Cowan University in Perth, Australia in 1996 and 2001 respectively. He then taught at Monash University before joining The University of Nottingham Malaysia Campus in 2004. His research interests are in the fields of signal, image, vision processing and reconfigurable computing.

Sue Inn Ch'ng obtained her MEng (Electronic) in 2009 from Nottingham University Malaysia Campus (UNMC). She is currently a PhD student in the Department of Electrical and Electronic Engineering in UNMC. Her research interest is in image processing and pattern recognition.

Georg W. Disterer is Professor of Information Management at undergraduate and graduate level at the University of Applied Sciences and Arts Hannover (Germany). He holds degrees in mathematics and business administration and is certified public expert for information technology. Before joining the university he worked as a consultant with international consulting firms and as an administrative director for a professional service firm. His major research interests are in information management, IT governance, and knowledge management.

Davide Chiarella is a fellow researcher of National Research Council, one of the most active research public organizations of Italy. He received a PhD degree in Information Technology and MCS degree from the University of Genoa in 2010 and in 2005, respectively. His research interests include network intrusion detection, virus and worm detection, data mining, computational linguistics and natural language processing.

Luca Caviglione has a PhD in Electronic and Computer Engineering from the University of Genova. He participates in many Research Projects funded by the European Union (EU), and by the Italian Ministry of Research (MIUR). He is author or coauthor of more than sixty academic publications (conferences, journals and book chapters) about TCP/IP networking, P2P systems, QoS architectures and wireless networks. In 2006 he was with the Genoa Research Unit of the Italian National Consortium for Telecommunications. Since 2007, he works at the Genoa Branch of the Istituto di Studi sui Sistemi Intelligenti per l'Automazione of the Italian National Research Council. He is a Work Group Leader of the Italian IPv6 Task Force and he has filed, as a coauthor, several patents in the field of p2p. He is also a Professional Engineer.

Guillermo A. Francia, III received his BS in Mechanical Engineering degree from Mapua Tech in 1978. His Ph.D. in Computer Science is from New Mexico Tech. Before joining Jacksonville State University (JSU), he was the chairman of the Computer Science department at Kansas Wesleyan University. Dr. Francia is a recipient of numerous grants. His projects have been funded by prestigious institutions such as the National Science Foundation, Eisenhower Foundation, Department of Education, Department of Defense, and Microsoft Corporation. In 1996, Dr. Francia received one of the five national awards for Innovators in Higher Education from Microsoft Corporation. Dr. Francia served as a Fulbright scholar to Malta in 2007. He has published articles and book chapters on numerous subjects such as Computer Security, Digital Forensics, Regulatory Compliance, Educational Technology, Expert Systems, Computer Networking, Software Testing, and Parallel Processing. Currently, Dr. Francia is the Director of the Center for Information Security and Assurance at JSU.

Paulo Roberto de Lira Gondim is Computer Engineer at Military Engineering Institute (1987), Master of Science in Compution and Systems by the same Institute (1992) and PhD in Electrical Engineering from Pontificia Universidade Catolica of Rio de Janeiro (1998). He has experience in computer science, with emphasis on Communication Networks and Digital Television, acting on the following topics: digital television, wireless technologies, information security and mobility management. He is currently assistant professor at Electrical Engineering Department of the University of Brasilia and Scholar Productivity in Innovative Technology Development and Extension of the National Council for Scientific and Technological Development - Level 2.

Frances Shannon Hutchinson graduated magna cum laude from Jacksonville State University with a bachelor's degree in computer science and is currently studying to obtain a master's degree in computer systems and software design. She is a member of the Upsilon Pi Epsilon (UPE) honor society and is certified as an Information Systems Security (INFOSEC) professional and a Systems Administrator, CNSSI 4013 entry level. Frances is actively involved in the design and implementation of the "Red Flag Rules" policy and compliance tools for Jacksonville State University. Her research interests include identity theft protection, game design, web development, information assurance, and information security policy design.

Faisal Kaleem received his MS degree in Electrical Engineering from Florida International University in 1999 and currently finishing up his PhD degree in Electrical Engineering. He joined Florida International University in 1998 and served in the capacity of lecturer in various departments. Currently, he is serving as an instructor in the department of Electrical and Computer Engineering. He has received numerous awards including the university wide Faculty Award for Excellence in Teaching. He is also a Certified Trainer with strong skills in Computer Networking, Programming, Database Design, and Information Security. He currently holds various certifications in the above areas, including the Certified Information Systems Security Professional (CISSP).His research interests include Network Security, Wired and Wireless Networks, and Fuzzy Logic based Systems.

Halim M. Khelalfa received his PhD from the *Illinois Institute of Technology, Chicago (1985). He is currently an associate* professor in the Faculty of Computer Science and Engineering at the University of Wollongong in Dubai. From 1988 to 2002, he directed the Basic Software Laboratory at the Centre of Research on Scientific and Technical Information (CERIST), Algeria. Prior to this, as a Member of Technical Staff at AT&T Bells Laboratories, he was one of the three founders of the Computer Performance and Analysis Group of the Software Development Systems in Naperville, Illinois, USA. His current research interests include performance evaluation of servers and networks, digital forensics, malicious software, obfuscation, and intrusion prevention.

Nancy R. Mead is a senior member of the technical staff in the Networked Systems Survivability Program at the Software Engineering Institute (SEI). Mead is also a faculty member in the Master of Software Engineering and Master of Information Systems Management programs at Carnegie Mellon University. She is currently involved in the study of software security engineering and the development of professional infrastructure for software engineers. Her research interests are in the areas of software security, software requirements engineering, and software architectures. She is a Fellow of the Institute of

Electrical and Electronic Engineers, Inc. (IEEE) and the IEEE Computer Society and is a Distinguished Member of the Association for Computing Machinery (ACM). Mead is a member of numerous advisory boards and committees. Dr. Mead received her PhD in mathematics from the Polytechnic Institute of New York, and received a BA and an MS in mathematics from New York University.

Laerte Peotta de Melo holds a degree in electrical, electronic Modality by University Mackenzie-SP (1996), specialization in computer networks security by Catholic University of Brasilia (2004) and pursuing a Master Degree in Electrical Engineering at the University of Brasilia. Currently is Senior Security Analyst in information technology - Bank of Brazil - working in the area if information security and computer forensic. Professor and researcher at Catholic University of Brasilia, post-graduation in computer networks security. Experience in electrical engineering area, with emphasis in telecommunications systems, acting mainly in the following subjects: Information security, Risk assessment, computer networks security, combat to digital crime, Information technology governance, compliance and free software.

Michele Nogueira is PhD in Computer Science by the University of Pierre et Marie Curie, LIP6, France, and professor at the Department of Informatics of Federal University of Paraná, Brazil. Michele received her M.Sc in Computer Science at Federal University of Minas Gerais, Brazil, 2004. She has worked on security area for many years; her research interests are security, wireless networks and dependability. She is member of the IEEE Communication Society (ComSoc) and the Association for Computing Machinery (ACM).

Fong Tien Ong graduated his BEng (Hons) in Electrical and Electronics Engineering from The University of Nottingham Malaysia Campus year 2010. Currently, he pursues his PhD in the research interest of Audio Visual Authentication and Recognition with Encryption over Internet Protocol.

Cyril Onwubiko is a reputable information security consultant with over 12 years hands-on experience in managing information security, information assurance and national cyber security projects. He has authored several books, and published over 30 academic articles at reputable conferences and journals. He is a member of the IEEE, Institute of Information Security Professionals (IISP), and CESG Listed Advisor Scheme (CLAS). Currently, he is the chair of the Intelligence and Security Assurance, E-Security Group at Research Series Limited. You can reach him at www.research-series.com or www.research-series.com/cyril

Guy Pujolle received the PhD in Computer Science from the University of Paris IX in 1975. He is currently Professor at the University Pierre et Marie Curie and member of the Scientific Advisory Board of the France Telecom Group. Pujolle is chairman of IFIP Working Group on "Network and Internetwork Architectures". His research interests include wireless networks, security, protocols, high performance networking and intelligence in networking.

Kah Phooi Seng received her PhD and Bachelor degree (first class honours) from University of Tasmania, Australia in 2001 and 1997 respectively. Currently, she is a member of the School of Electrical & Electronic Engineering at The University of Nottingham Malaysia Campus. Her research interests are in the fields of intelligent visual processing, biometrics and multi-biometrics, artificial intelligence and signal processing.

Jenny Torres is a PhD student in Computer Science at the University of Pierre et Marie Curie, LIP6, France. She received her MSc in Computer Science at University Paris 12 Val de Marne, France, in 2009 and her MSc in Telecommunications and Network Management at the Escuela Politécnica del Ejército, Ecuador, in 2008. She has network administration and configuration experience and her research interests are security, network management, wireless networks, Future Internet and identity management.

Gianluca Papaleo was born in Sarno (SA) on 1980. He graduated with honours in 2005 in Computer Science at the Computer Science Department of the University of Genoa with the thesis: *"e-mail flow Analysis for Intrusion Detection Purposes"*. From year 2006 he is a research fellow at Consiglio Nazionale delle Ricerche Area di Genova, where he is part of the network administrator's team. His research interests are about network security, intrusion detection and worm detection.

Biwu Yang is a professor in the Department of Technology Systems, East Carolina University. He joined the Department since 1995 and he teaches in the area of computer data networking and information security. During the academic year of 2004-2005, he led the effort in the department to attain the status of Centers of Academic Excellence in Information Assurance Education sponsored by National Security Agency. Currently, Dr. Yang's duty has been reassigned to be coordinator of platform research and development, Emerging Academic Initiatives, East Carolina University. His current duty includes research, evaluation, development, and deployment of new technologies to support teaching, learning, and research. He also serves as the technology coordinator for the Global Partners in Education with more than 30 partner universities from more than 20 countries. He coordinates and collaborates with technical support personnel from the partner universities around the world.

Kang Yen received the BS degree in geophysics from National Central University in 1974 and the MS degree in electrical engineering from University of Virginia in 1979. He received the PhD degree in electrical engineering from Vanderbilt University in 1985. He joined the Department of Electrical & Computer Engineering at Florida International University in 1985. Currently, he is Professor & Chairperson of the department. His research interest is System Theory, Digital Signal Processing in Communications, and Network Security.

Index

proof of concept (POC) 235
Proxy Firewall 207-208
Proxy Server 28-29, 207-208, 227
Pseudo Random Generation Algorithm (PRGA) 27
pseudo-random number generator (PRNG) 23
Public Key Infrastructure (PKI) 144, 159, 165-168, 170-171, 175-176, 178-179
public land mobile networks (PLMN) 104
Public switched telecommunication network (PSTN) 75-76

Q

Quality of Service (QoS) 20, 49, 178
Quantum computers 178
Quantum cryptography 178

R

radial basis function (RBF) 190, 194, 196, 200-201, 203
Radio Frequencies (RF) 18-19, 31, 33, 76
Radio Frequency Communication (RFCOMM) 34-35, 39
radio frequency identification (RFID) 156, 254, 270
Rainbow Tables 28, 44
Read-after-Read (RAR) 92
Read-after-Write (RAW) 38, 55, 86, 92, 188, 197
real-time transport protocol (RTP) 198
Red Flags Rules 298-299
Registration Authority (RA) 166
Replay Attack 25, 239
Requirements Elicitation 274-275, 282-283, 287, 289
Requirements Engineering 270, 273-277, 286-290
RFIDs 18, 156, 254, 270
Risk Assessment 229, 231-233, 242, 244, 255, 261-262, 266, 270, 273-282, 286-288, 290, 296, 301-303, 308, 318, 320, 322
Risk Filtering, Ranking, and Management Framework (RFRM) 277, 280-281, 286
Robust Security Network (RSN) 23
Rogue APs 26, 28, 32

S

sabotage 5, 10-11
Safeguards Rule 295-296, 307, 321
Sarbanes- Oxley (SOX) 230
Satellite TV 18
Script Kiddies 237
Secure Shell (SSH) 21, 28, 206-207

Secure Simple Pairing (SSP) 37
Secure Socket Layer (SSL) 29-30, 169
Security Best Practices 303, 322
Security Quality Requirements Engineering (SQUARE) 170, 273-278, 280-283, 286-287, 290
Sensitive Personal Data 255-257, 260, 272
server farm 205, 214, 217, 219, 221-223, 227
Service Discovery Protocol (SDP) 34
Service Set Identifiers (SSIDs) 26, 28, 30-31
signal-to-noise ratio (SNR) 187, 196
Simple Mail Transfer Protocol (SMTP) 52-56, 58, 64, 68, 70
Simple Network Management Protocol (SNMP) 31
Skype 17
small office/home office (SOHO) 30, 219
small scale digital devices (SSD or SSDD) 80, 126
smart-phone 134, 147
Social Security Number (SSN) 168, 256, 293, 322
Source Address (SA) 176
SPAM 2, 48, 52, 58, 69
Special Interest Group (SIG) 34, 44
Stateful Packet Inspection (SPI) 209-212, 223, 227
statistical methods 52
Structured Query Language (SQL) 56, 316
Subscriber identification module (SIM) Card 76-77, 86, 92, 97, 100, 105, 111, 123, 133
Substitution cipher 164
Support Vector Machines (SVM) 187
Synchronization SouRCe (SSRC) 198

T

t-commerce 135, 161
TCP/IP protocol 12, 206, 226
Telecommunications Industry Association (TIA) 76
Telephony Control Protocol (TCS) 35
Temporal Key Integrity Protocol (TKIP) 24
The Proposed Standards for the Exchange of Digital Evidence 79
Time Division Multiple Access (TDMA) 73, 75
Traffic Flow Analysis 25
Training Architecture 183, 185, 192, 200, 203
transport stream (TS) 129, 138, 159, 197-198, 313
trojan horses 3, 237
trusted computing base (TCB) 118
trusted party 136-138, 161
Trusted Third Parties (TTP) 144, 162, 166, 168, 175
trustee 137-138
trustor 137-138
Trust Systems 161